THIS BUSINESS OF

Television

Revised and Updated Second Edition

Howard J. Blumenthal
and Oliver R. Goodenough

BILLBOARD BOOKS
AN IMPRINT OF WATSON-GUPTILL PUBLICATIONS/NEW YORK

*To our wives, Sherri Blumenthal and Alison Clarkson,
for their patience and support.*

Senior Editor: Bob Nirkind
Editor: Margaret Sobel
Production Manager: Hector Campbell
Design and Composition: Areta Buk
Jacket Design: Areta Buk

Revised and updated 2nd edition published in 1998 by Billboard Books,
an imprint of Watson-Guptill Publications, a division of VNU Business Media, Inc.,
770 Broadway, New York, NY 10003
www.watsonguptill.com

Library of Congress Cataloging-in-Publication Data

Blumenthal, Howard J.
    This business of television / by Howard J. Blumenthal and Oliver R.
Goodenough.—Rev. and updated 2nd ed.
      p.   cm.
    Includes bibliographical references and index.
    ISBN 0-8230-7704-7
    1. Television broadcasting—United States. 2. Television—Law and
legislation—United States. I. Goodenough, Oliver R. II. Title.
HE8700.8.B58   1998
384.55'0973—dc21   98-4860
                                                                      CIP

Manufactured in the United States of America

First printing, 1998

5 6 7 8 / 04 03

Acknowledgments

The authors wish to thank the following people and organizations for their assistance in preparing this book:

Alfredo Alessandrelli, Radio Televisione Italia
Bruce Apar, Video Business
Norm Blumenthal
Ave Butensky, TVB
Brian Byrne, Byrne Enterprises
Dana Calderwood
Mary Collins, BBC Worldwide Television
Willem-Jan Doff, NOS, Netherlands
Tim Duncan
Michael Fields, WNET
Ron Giles
Ron Goldberg
Arthur Greenwald
Wolfgang Homering, ZDF, Germany
Philip M. Jones, CTE (Carlton) Limited, UK
Stu Kantor, PBS
Gene Kapp
James H. Kaye, WGA
Lynn Kestin
Rebecca Kramer, Viewer's Choice Pay-Per-View
Peter Krasilovsky, Arlen Communications
Cinden Lester, Dept. of Communication and the Arts, Australia
Colin Leventhal, Channel Four Television, UK
Alan Levy, Primestar
Jack Loftus, Nielsen Media Research
Michael Montagne, Telefilm Canada
Jay Rayvid
Denise Seomin, FOX Sports
Ives Swennen, RTBF, Belgium
Karin Schintgen, CLT, Luxembourg
Brigid Sullivan, WGBH
Craig Tanner, ATSC
Kate Taylor, WGBH
The Staff of Ultimate TV (www.ultimatetv.com)
Rick Ungaro
Eytan Urbas, Guthy-Renker
Olivier-René Veillon, La Sept ARTE

Lane Venardos, CBS News
John Wolf, AAAA
Jim Warren

Thanks to the many people at local stations and cable networks who answered our questions. Margaret Sobel and Bob Nirkind at Billboard Books deserve a very special "thank you."

The authors also thank Pam Dein, Michael Formica, and David-Eric Dayton at the Vermont Law School for their research. And a very special thanks to Laura Gillen, also of the Vermont Law School, for her help in coordinating this project.

Preface to the Second Edition

This Business of Television has several purposes.

First, the book is intended as a desktop reference work covering all facets of the television and video businesses. A producer who needs to learn about the workings of PBS will find a useful section here. A writer who is considering membership in WGA will find a summary of Writer's Guild activities, including jurisdiction, an explanation of key agreements and their terms, and membership information. An advertising sales executive making the move from traditional broadcast to a regional sports network will learn the basic structure of that business. Showing how video stores and direct-mail clubs work, outlining the basic terms of a studio rental deal, explaining how to hire an agent—*This Business of Television* should be the definitive source of basic information about the television and video industries.

The book's second purpose is to provide a legal overview of the television business. Lengthy sections on personal rights, the protection of creative properties, financing, and regulation should function as indispensable reference material. While a book like this cannot possibly detail all the nuances of, for example, copyright law, it does discuss in plain language the legal underpinnings of television. In the appendixes we also provide excerpts from some of the most important legal sources. The inclusion of some of the appendixes on an enclosed disk is an innovation of which we are proud.

Third, *This Business of Television* includes a considerable number of useful forms and form agreements in the appendixes and on the enclosed floppy diskette. We have provided concise "boilerplate" contracts for the most common business transactions in television, such as hiring production personnel or optioning rights to creative properties.

In this second edition, we have sought to bring all of the discussions up to date. We have added chapters on some of the emerging areas of television: religious television, home shopping, satellite TV, and the ever more important international marketplace. The changes brought about by the 1996 Telecommunications Act have also required extensive treatment.

We sincerely hope that you find *This Business of Television* to be a useful work.

Howard J. Blumenthal and Oliver R. Goodenough
May 1998

Before Using the Information in This Book

We have sought to keep this book current through spring 1998. Please note, however, that certain union figures based on variable contract years may reflect an earlier date, and that the legal appendixes have specified dates for including amendments.

The information and forms provided in *This Business of Television* are intended for background only. This book should *not* serve as a substitute for the expertise that can be provided only by an experienced specialist, such as an attorney or accountant. It is not our intention to transform an untrained individual into an "instant expert." Instead, our goal is to create an informed television or video professional. The reader is encouraged to hire a lawyer to review the final versions of forms and contracts, to secure an accountant for tax and accounting matters, and to retain the services of an expert financial advisor.

This book was originally written in 1990 and revised through 1998. We have attempted to keep our facts and figures accurate to early 1998. We encourage readers to continue their research by consulting industry trade magazines and other professionals working in the business for updated information.

Contents

Disc Contents

The enclosed Disc is formatted in Microsoft Word Version 6.0 for Windows 95, but can be used by most word-processing programs. It includes the following material in two files entitled Appendix A and Appendix B:

APPENDIX A   **LEGAL DOCUMENTS AND FORMS**

User's Guide
A1   Communications Act of 1934: Excerpts
A2   Code of Federal Regulations
A3   The Copyright Law of 1976: Excerpts

APPENDIX B   **CONTRACTS**

User's Guide to the Contract Forms

RIGHTS ACQUISITION
B1   Issue Checklist
B2   Submission Release Letter

Introduction

The business of television is fast-paced and poised for rapid growth in the twenty-first century. Change has been the rule in the television industry since its inception, and the business will continue to evolve with global expansion and technological innovation. Still, traditional approaches and deeply-rooted customs—some dating from the time when radio ruled the airwaves—continue to dominate some parts of the industry. Others, such as digital television and convergence with the Internet, are making new rules.

EARLY HISTORY OF BROADCASTING

The roots of the invention called television extend back to 1876, when Alexander Graham Bell first demonstrated his telephone to an astonished public. Bell's invention prompted the public to consider a future based in electronic communication media. Speculating wildly on things to come, magazines published illustrations showing wall-sized screens—the visual complement to Bell's audio-only telephone. Other inventors supplied pieces of the puzzle that eventually became television. Marconi discovered how to propagate radio waves; Fessenden, how to send radio signals on modulating wave forms; and DeForest, how to amplify and generate waves. Other inventors became fascinated with the idea of wireless transmission of visual images. In time, the inventions were consolidated in various ways. No one person invented television.

On the business side, American Telephone and Telegraph (AT&T) was formed to exploit Bell's patents and the other patents needed to provide commercial telephone service. Rather than building a single nationwide system, AT&T licensed the technology to local franchises, and then connected them to supply national service. (AT&T licensed the technology to its franchises for stock rather than cash, so it owned majority positions in most of its franchises before the turn of the century.) AT&T's purchase of Western Electric as its manufacturing division completed the picture: now a single company provided all aspects of telephone communication service.

Although the telephone was successful by 1900, and wireless communication was possible before World War I (inventor Reginald Fessenden successfully broadcast both voice and music as early as 1906), little consideration was given to possible public applications of the technology. Legend has it that young David Sarnoff—then a middle-level manager at American Marconi, a telegraph company with interests in wireless technology—wrote a memo in 1914 describing a radio music box that could be sold to individual households. The commercial potential of radio broadcasting became clear almost immediately after World War I. Amateurs who had learned about wireless technology during the war created their own stations in garages and attics. Officially the Navy controlled wireless broadcasting—it was seen mainly as a form of maritime communication—but two important electric companies, Westinghouse and General Electric, along with AT&T, were anxious to see the technology made available in the commercial marketplace. The Navy, realizing that it would not be able to retain control over broadcasting, removed the one foreign force in U.S. broadcasting by pressuring British Marconi to sell all the stock of its U.S. operation, American Marconi, to a new company owned by General Electric. That company was named the Radio Corporation of America, or RCA.

Westinghouse and GE started manufacturing radio receivers by 1918. In 1920, Westinghouse opened its first radio station, KDKA in Pittsburgh, and in 1921, the company started WJZ in New York City. In the same period, GE's WGY in Schenectady, New York (its hometown), went on the air. AT&T's first station, WEAF, went on the air in 1922. By 1925, most major cities were served by multiple radio stations, frequently affiliated with an emerging network.

The growth of radio stations did not proceed according to AT&T's plans. True to its origins, AT&T saw the entire notion of broadcasting as an outgrowth of telephone service. In one instance, AT&T denied competitive networks access to its long-distance phone lines. The conflict between common carrier and broadcaster became increasingly clear; under pressure from the government, AT&T eventually sold its stations and technology to RCA, reserving only the right to provide the "long lines" service that connected one radio station to another. GE and Westinghouse also invested in RCA, became partners, and contributed their stations. By 1927, there was sufficient belief in the potential of network broadcasting to form an RCA subsidiary called the National Broadcasting Company, or NBC.

COMMERCIAL RADIO AND THE GROWTH OF THE NETWORKS

AT&T originated the idea of paid commercial advertising on radio with a real-estate commercial that aired on WEAF in 1922. Within just two more years, AT&T became a leading producer of programs for the stations on its temporary network linkups. AT&T married sponsors to programs: *The Ipana Troubadours, The A&P Gypsies,* and *The Eveready Hour* were among the more popular offerings. Westinghouse's WJZ presented programs sponsored by Rheingold Beer, Schrafft's Restaurants, and Wanamaker, a department store. Other companies followed, but AT&T objected on the grounds that it was the only company permitted to charge for commercial use of electronic media. The ensuing battle resulted in AT&T's withdrawal from RCA.

As early as 1927, under the executive leadership of David Sarnoff, NBC was operating two networks: the Red Network, fed by WEAF (later, WNBC), and the Blue Network, fed by WJZ (later, WABC). (The networks' names came from the identifying colors on the switching panel.) NBC was not the only network at that time, but it was the only one with stations in most of the largest cities. A year later, William Paley bought a struggling network called United Independent Broadcasters, renamed it the Columbia Broadcasting System (CBS), and began aggressively seeking affiliates in major cities.

ABC came much later, in 1943, when radio's golden age was already drawing to a close. NBC's dominance had long been a cause for concern at the Federal Communications Commission (FCC), and in 1941, the Commission finally required NBC to divest itself of one of its two networks. NBC sold the Blue network in 1943 to Life Savers tycoon Edward J. Noble, who established the American Broadcasting Company. By 1951, Noble had sold out to United Paramount Theaters and the third of network television's pioneers: Leonard Goldenson.

THE TRANSITION FROM RADIO TO TELEVISION

The concept of transmitting pictures as well as sound dates back to the late 1800s. The technology needed to capture an image from real life via a camera's pickup tube and then transmit the image back to a television screen took about 50 years to develop. In 1930, engineers at RCA were able to display 60 lines of resolution, resulting in a crude television image. Nine years later, that number had increased to 441. In 1941, the National Television Standards Committee (NTSC), representing 15 leading electronic manufacturers, approved the 525-1ine system that is still in use today in the U.S. and in many other countries. The new high-definition standards double the resolution.

World War II delayed the start-up of large-scale television broadcasting. By 1943, however, NBC was broadcasting occasional boxing matches; by 1944, Gillette had agreed to sponsor three nights a week of NBC boxing and wrestling coverage. At about the same time, CBS debuted its first regularly scheduled entry: a game show called *Missus Goes A 'Shopping* (it had been a popular program on CBS radio). ABC, then called ABC-Blue, also started with a game show, *Ladies Be Seated*. A fourth network, DuMont, began with low-budget programs: cooking shows and travelogues. At the outset, much of the programming was experimental, and the scheduling somewhat informal. As more television sets were sold and more viewers became available, the system became more organized.

By 1948, television broadcasting had changed dramatically. ABC, CBS, and NBC were programming for nearly four hours each night, typically from 7:00 P.M. until 11:00 P.M., with occasional lapses for local programming. DuMont operated only on weekdays, with one notable exception on Saturday nights: the *Original Amateur Hour*. Many of the network programs were low-priced filler or sports coverage, which was inexpensive to produce because the event did not have to be staged. There was also an abundance of public affairs, talk, and other low-cost formats—plus the beginnings of the hit shows that would soon drive the business. *Texaco Star Theater* (NBC), featuring Milton Berle, became the top show, followed by *Toast of the Town* (CBS), later renamed *The Ed Sullivan Show*. Both debuted during the summer of 1948, prior to the introduction of the first full-fledged fall season. An early version of Sid Caesar's *Your Show of Shows* (NBC) also debuted in 1948.

By 1950, the pattern was set, and it would not change in any substantive way for the next three decades. Each of the networks—reduced to three with the demise of DuMont in 1956—worked closely with advertisers and advertising agencies to develop programs that would reach the largest possible audience. In the 1980s, new networks, such as FOX, took shape, and by the 1990s, with cable, home video and satellite distribution into the home, the patterns had dramatically changed, with ABC, CBS, and NBC reaching only half of their former viewership numbers.

THE EVOLUTION OF NETWORK PROGRAMMING

In the 1950s, situation comedies tended to feature young urban couples *(The Honeymooners, I Love Lucy);* those adapted from radio frequently retained an ethnic twist *(The Goldbergs, Mama, Amos 'n' Andy).* In the 1960s, the young suburban families on sitcoms like *The Dick Van Dyke Show, Bewitched, My Three Sons, The Partridge Family,* and *The Brady Bunch* reflected changes in the American lifestyle. CBS had a long run with sitcoms that had a strong rural appeal: *Petticoat Junction, The Beverly Hillbillies, Green Acres, The Andy Griffith Show.* By the 1970s, though, the old formulas were no longer working. ABC introduced shows intended for younger viewers *(Laverne & Shirley, Happy Days, Three's Company);* CBS depended heavily upon Norman Lear for progressive sitcoms that featured social topics *(All in the Family, Maude, One Day at a Time);* and MTM produced sitcoms about independent women *(The Mary Tyler Moore Show, Rhoda).* In the 1990s, the most popular sitcoms featured single people living among friends in the city *(Seinfeld, Friends)* or decidedly unorthodox suburban families *(Third Rock from the Sun,* with its alien characters, and *The Simpsons,* with an animated suburban family).

Programs based on certain themes have remained popular throughout the history of television. Sitcoms with military themes, for example—*Sergeant Bilko, McHale's Navy, M*A*S*H**—have been consistently popular. Shows whose families feature outspoken children have also been successful year after year, though some have been of higher quality than others; the best include *Leave It to Beaver, Make Room for Daddy, Family Ties, The Cosby Show, Roseanne,* and *The Simpsons.*

Dramatic programs based on cops, lawyers, detectives, spies, medical, and military themes have been consistent performers, though some years find more of one type of program than another (the range of jobs that seem to lend themselves to television is remarkably limited). In the 1990s, dramas about lawyers, cops, and doctors have been especially durable. In the 1950s and into the 1960s, westerns like *Gunsmoke, Have Gun Will Travel, Wagon Train, Peter Gunn,* and *Bat Masterson* were very popular, but since then, only a small number have succeeded (notably, in recent times, *Dr. Quinn, Medicine Woman*). Anthology shows (*The Twilight Zone, Alfred Hitchcock Presents*) did well in the 1950s and 1960s, especially those that featured live drama (*Playhouse 90, Armstrong Circle Theater, Philco Television Playhouse*), but these formats have disappeared. Shows about reporters (*Lou Grant, The Reporters*) have occasionally succeeded, and the reporter show is one of the few "occupational" genres outside of those listed above that seem worth a programmer's—or producer's—risk. *Frasier* and *The Bob Newhart Show* are among the few successful sitcoms starring psychologists or psychiatrists. Family soap operas (*The Big Valley, The Waltons, Family*) have been successful, particularly if there is a big-money business at the heart of the family (*Falcon Crest, Dallas*).

Other types of programs besides comedy and drama have come and gone in prime time as well. In the fall of 1958, there were 12 game shows on the network prime-time schedules; by 1962, there were four; by 1967, the format was relegated to daytime, and in 1998, there was only one daytime network game show, *The Price Is Right*. Game shows have since found their place in daytime and fringe periods, mainly as cable and syndicated programs. Variety shows featuring big stars were among the most popular shows in the 1950s and 1960s; in 1963, for example, the fall schedule included regularly scheduled programs featuring Mitch Miller, Red Skelton, Jack Benny, Garry Moore, Andy Williams, Danny Kaye, Sid Caesar, Perry Como, Edie Adams, Bob Hope, Jack Paar, Lawrence Welk, Jerry Lewis, Jackie Gleason, Ed Sullivan, and Judy Garland. Ten years later, only Sonny & Cher, Flip Wilson, Dean Martin, and Carol Burnett were on the air with variety shows (Bob Hope also appeared regularly, but less often than before). A year after that, only Sonny (without Cher) and Carol Burnett remained.

Daytime schedules have also been dominated by a limited number of formats. Soap operas began as 15-minute programs in the 1950s (many were exported from popular radio serials), and by the 1980s, many were an hour long. Roughly half of the daytime schedule has been occupied by soaps since the 1950s (in the 1990s, soaps dominated network daytime to the exclusion of games and other formerly popular formats). The other half has been filled mainly with game shows, plus occasional talk and variety shows (*The Tennessee Ernie Ford Show, Art Linkletter's House Party, Dinah's Place,* and, more recently, *The Oprah Winfrey Show* and *The Rosie O'Donnell Show*). Syndication now supplies the most popular daytime talk shows.

For a complete year-by-year analysis of network prime-time programming through 1980, see the woefully out-of-print *Watching TV: Four Decades of American Television,* by Harry Castleman and Walter J. Podrazik. The same authors have prepared *The TV Schedule Book,* which includes detailed daytime and weekend schedules through 1982. *The Encyclopedia of Daytime Television* by Wesley Hyatt is another good source.

OTHER TELEVISION BROADCASTERS

From the 1940s until the late 1960s, the term "television" described the activities of the three networks, plus an assortment of independent stations—located mostly in the larger cities—that were unaffiliated with any network. The independent stations showed plenty of movies and sports coverage as well as inexpensive syndicated cartoon programs and other low-cost fare.

EDUCATIONAL AND PUBLIC TELEVISION

In some cities, educational television stations were on the air in the early 1950s in some cities, but the present-day system of public television broadcasting did not take shape until the late 1960s. Attempts at networks, co-productions between stations, and group program-buying were only occasionally successful. (National Educational Television, or NET, started as one of several organizations that sent tapes by mail from one station to another). Community groups, school boards, municipal organizations, and other local entities provided the stations with small budgets and limited funds. In 1967, the Carnegie Commission on Educational Television recommended that Congress establish a corporation for public television, as an expansion on earlier educational efforts. Later that year, Congress established the Corporation for Public Broadcasting (CPB) as both a funding source for public television stations as well as a buffer organization between Congress and a new public television network.

What began as a non-commercial network financed by the government and foundation grants has since become a confederation of independently owned and operated, non-profit stations that have become indispensable to certain audience segments. Public television is especially popular with preschoolers (because of programs like *Sesame Street* and *Barney and Friends),* and with viewers who enjoy documentaries, opera, classical music, ballet, nature shows, drama, and British comedy.

NON-BROADCAST TELEVISION

Television has long been considered to be a mass medium, but television has served a significant variety of non-broadcast functions since the 1970s, made possible by the invention of affordable video recorders and players. Sony's "3/4-inch" U-Matic format, the first to house videotape in a viable cassette format, was introduced in 1975. Colleges have videotaped classwork since that time (and earlier, for those who operated television studios). Some high schools have a long non-broadcast history as well. Closed-circuit television services have also been a part of the business since the 1950s—for surveillance and, later, for the distribution of training and information programming throughout large organizations, such as corporations.

Still, non-broadcast television, now almost universally called "video," did not blossom until the late 1970s, when a combination of more affordable equipment and the VHS cassette standard encouraged corporate managers to invest in small-scale video set ups. Many of these operations have grown considerably, and most corporations now use video as a primary communications tool. Some companies have experimented with annual reports on video; others use it regularly for employee communication and training, merchandising, public relations (in the form of electronic news releases), presenting sales literature in a dynamic way, demonstrating products, and other applications. Closed-circuit services continue to grow as well, supplying hospitals and hotels with movie channels, for example. With the coming convergence of video and computer technology, multimedia applications will further increase the variety of non-broadcast activities.

THE 1970S AND THE REINVENTION OF THE TELEVISION INDUSTRY

From the early 1950s until the mid-1970s, television was a closed business, of limited interest to outside entrepreneurs. Television stations changed hands, but not often. Since the demise of DuMont in 1956, talk of a fourth commercial network was initiated by many companies, but nearly every plan faltered for the same reason: limited channel capacity. After a brief freeze on commercial television licensing, the FCC had devised a plan in 1952 that would allow only the very largest markets to have five or six VHF stations; most large markets, in fact, were limited to four or five. Other stations were licensed to operate on the UHF band—channels 14 to 83—but this was a "no man's land" because many sets could not receive the signals, and even viewers who owned VHF/UHF sets rarely watched the UHF band. Stations on the VHF band were almost always affiliated with either ABC, CBS, NBC, or public television. In order to build a successful new network, most of the stations would have to be on the VHF band—and there simply weren't enough unaffiliated major-market VHF stations to support a fourth commercial network. Some independent stations grew, and some even affiliated in ad-hoc networks, such as Operation Prime Time, but limited channel capacity was the single greatest impediment to further growth of the television industry.

By the mid-1970s, three developments had conspired to change not only this situation, but the entire definition of television.

First, the FCC lifted several restrictions which had limited the growth of cable television. Until the early 1970s, the FCC routinely passed rules that limited the ability of cable operators to pursue business in the top 100 markets, taking the view that broadcast interests were to be protected, and that cable operators were attempting to make money unfairly with the broadcaster's product. By 1972, the FCC had changed its stance, and within five years, cable operators were fighting over the valuable franchises for communities of every size. In 1972, 6.5 million households were subscribers to cable; in 1982, the number had jumped to 29 million; in 1998, the projected subscriber count exceeds 65 million, or just over two-thirds of the current 97 million U.S. television households.

The second development that has changed the nature of television follows from the first. With a system of distribution and a growing universe of potential viewers, corporations with interests in the television and/or entertainment industries created cable television networks. Time, Inc. developed HBO and, later, Cinemax and The Comedy Channel (which became Comedy Central when it was merged with HA!). Syndication leader Viacom launched Showtime, and later purchased several networks developed by Warner (later Warner-Amex): The Movie Channel, Nickelodeon, and other services. Smaller companies also succeeded: Georgia entrepreneur Ted Turner, who was already familiar with the cable business because of the success of his superstation, WTCG (later renamed WTBS), developed cable's first 24-hour news channel, CNN. Turner followed with a second news service and, after the purchase of the MGM film library, with Turner Network Television (TNT). Special-interest networks such as The Weather Channel and ESPN have also flourished. The broadcast networks were generally slow to start, but Disney ABC is now a major cable network owner (ESPN, parts of Lifetime and A&E), and NBC is active worldwide with CNBC and the newer MSNBC. More cable channels are constantly in development, and new ventures are often started with the support of large cable system operators (MSOs).

The third development is the videocassette recorder. The VCR is now a part of television viewing in over 90 percent of U.S. households. After a slow start, growth of the installed base of VCRs was brisk: 2.3 million by late 1981, 25 million by 1985, 65 million by 1990, and 85 million in 1998.

CHANGES IN THE 1980S AND 1990S

The 1970s presented only a glimpse of the more fundamental shifts that were destined to alter the entire television industry through the turn of the century.

First, individual television stations began to change hands more often. Prior to the 1980s, ownership of a television station was not only a serious commitment to the community's well-being, it was also a business venture that was rarely put on the market. With changes in the laws regarding the transfer (sale) of broadcast stations, and the start of Wall Street interest in media properties, a market developed for buying and selling television stations (and newspapers, magazines, radio stations and movie studios). In New York City, for example, WOR, long an RKO General station, was sold to MCA Universal; WNEW, the flagship station for the old Metromedia station group, was sold to Rupert Murdoch as a key station in the new FOX group (it is now called WNYW). In Los Angeles, RKO's KHJ was sold to Disney, and became KCAL. Stations were sold for high cash values; new companies, such as Act III Broadcasting, began to buy and operate independent stations and convert them into FOX affiliates. By the mid-1990s, many long time network affiliates in the largest markets had been sold, traded, or persuaded to dispose of relationships with roots tracing back more than 50 years. In Philadelphia, for example, WCAU (one of the first CBS broadcast stations) became an NBC affiliate, and KYW, a Westinghouse station long affiliated with NBC, became the fourth largest market's CBS station. This move was part of a larger change, as Westinghouse purchased CBS (then, in 1997, Westinghouse changed its company name to CBS).

As a result of Wall Street maneuvering, each of the networks changed hands in the 1980s. Previously, the buying or selling of a network seemed impossible because of tradition and government barriers. This changed when Capital Cities successfully merged with ABC. GE then purchased RCA, and with it, NBC. The change at CBS was engineered in the boardroom, as stockholder Laurence Tisch took over, supposedly with the blessing of patriarch William Paley. In the 1990s, Disney bought ABC and Westinghouse bought CBS.

The second fundamental change in broadcast television has been the development and success of new broadcast networks. The FOX network has succeeded by focusing its appeal on the younger demographic that advertisers seek. The story began with relatively low-cost programming available to affiliates for a modest number of nights per week. Through the 1990s, FOX has become a formidable competitor, in part because of shrewd business practices, but mostly because some of the network's shows have become hits: *Married . . . with Children, The Simpsons,* and *The X-Files* are three of many high-profile examples. The success of FOX encouraged the development of a second studio-based network, WBTV, and an alliance of several station groups with Paramount in UPN. As these networks have grown, they have eliminated the old concept of an independent television station. Apart from local news, most local stations have virtually no commitment to the local community they serve. In today's world, a local television station is, by and large, a retransmitter for network signals (and as a result, apart from local news and the rare public-affairs program, no longer relevant to activities in the community it serves).

The third major change in television has been the establishment of home entertainment alternatives. From the start of television until the late 1970s, a handful of stations represented the entire range of electronic home entertainment (apart from radio and records). The networks and some independent stations completely owned the idea of television. Videogames were the one non-traditional signal to appear on a TV set, but in time, VCRs, dozens of cable networks, and satellites with dozens of pay-per-view movie channels changed people's leisure-time habits. The networks have lost half of their audience, compared with the percentage of television viewers they served in the 1970s. The Internet is not only providing yet another alternative, it is moving toward a role as a television distribution medium.

PART 1

Distribution Systems

U.S. Commercial Network Television

Domestic television programming is delivered in four principal ways: land-based broadcast, cablecast, satellite-based broadcast, and as prerecorded product.

The first chapter in this distribution section deals with commercial network television, a U.S. television network that supplies a schedule of programming to television stations that it owns, and to stations affiliated with the network. In today's global marketplace, a network's programming may also be seen outside the U.S. and in special markets, such as on airline screens. Chapters 1 through 10 discuss the organization and structure of each of these distribution systems.

OVERVIEW

From a viewer's perspective, the differences between the operations of the three largest television networks—NBC, CBS, and ABC—are barely noticeable. Each supplies its owned stations and affiliates with a regular schedule of prime-time, daytime, morning, late-night, news, and sports programming. With few exceptions, each network's full program schedule can be seen in every U.S. metropolitan area. Each is a giant company with a single goal—to supply the largest possible number of desirable viewers to the advertisers who provide the networks with revenues and thus fund the programs.

Three newer networks, FOX, UPN, and WB, were built by accumulating unaffiliated independent stations. While FOX is farthest along, none of these networks yet offers the full range of programs offered by NBC, CBS, and ABC.

PBS, the only non-commercial national broadcast network in the U.S., is discussed in chapter 4.

NBC

When the television business began in the mid-1940s, NBC was in the best position to exploit the new medium. It was owned by RCA, the electronics manufacturer that pioneered the development of television studio equipment and led the new industry in its manufacture of transmitters and home receivers. NBC made its first experimental television broadcast in 1931, and its first regularly scheduled broadcasts in 1943.

Because it possessed the technology plus the stars who could bring their popularity from radio to television, NBC was able to build an affiliate network of local television stations faster than CBS or ABC. Its programs immediately reached a larger audience; this led to higher advertising rates, which in turn permitted innovation and expansion. NBC was the first network with a regularly scheduled morning program *(Today)* and a late-night program *(Broadway Open House* and, later, *The Steve Allen Show;* the latter established the now-familiar *Tonight Show* format). NBC was also an early leader in news and sports coverage. Largely as a result of the RCA connection, NBC's firsts include *Wide Wide World,* an early globe-trotting magazine series; first television coverage of the Oscar and Emmy awards; first color coverage of the World Series (September 28, 1955); and many other special programs. More recently, NBC was the first network with stereo broadcasting. NBC's most successful and/or notable series have included *Concentration, Jeopardy!, The Dean Martin Show, Kraft Music Hall, Cheers, The Cosby Show, Hill Street Blues, Little House on the Prairie, Rowan & Martin's Laugh-In, Dragnet, Bonanza, Star Trek, Seinfeld, ER,* and *Saturday Night Live.* NBC News and NBC Sports, described later in this book, have been significant industry contributors since the start of television.

OWNERSHIP

NBC operated as a unit of RCA until 1985, when RCA was sold to General Electric. GE sold NBC's radio stations, but maintains ownership of NBC (officially "The National Broadcasting Company"— a somewhat inappropriate name for global commerce).

OWNED AND OPERATED STATIONS

NBC's owned and operated ("O&O") stations are WNBC (New York), KNBC (Los Angeles), WMAQ (Chicago), WCAU (Philadelphia), WRC (Washington, DC), WVJ (Miami), KNSD (San Diego), WNCN (Raleigh-Durham, NC), WCMH (Columbus, OH), WJAR (Providence, RI), and WVTM (Birmingham, AL).

NEW MEDIA AND INTERNATIONAL

NBC has been aggressive in cable, international television, and new media. It operates two cable television ventures: CNBC, a business talk and information network seen in the U.S., Europe and Asia; and MSNBC, a joint venture with Microsoft which includes a cable news network and a Web site. NBC is also very active internationally. NBC Europe launched as SuperChannel in Europe in 1993; a similar operation was launched in Asia in 1994. In 1993, NBC launched a 24-hour Spanish news service called Canal de Noticias NBC (but closed it down in 1997 due to increased competition). With CNBC and MSNBC, cable operators can now work with two NBC news services in Latin America. In addition to the MSNBC venture, NBC Interactive Media is involved with several technology-based businesses, such as NBC Desktop Video.

CBS

CBS Radio went on the air in 1927 as the Columbia Phonograph Broadcasting System, but in less than two years, William S. Paley, whose father's cigar company had been advertising on the network, bought it. At the time, it was a fledgling organization, but Paley, Frank Stanton, and a team of talented executives built CBS into a strong competitor to NBC.

Heading into the television age, CBS had two big problems. First, because it had concentrated on the development of a color TV system, CBS had not applied for television licenses; as late as 1951, CBS owned just one TV station. Second, it lacked the star power of NBC. In a remarkable series of tactical maneuvers (CBS lawyers came up with a capital gains–tax loophole as part of an inducement for stars to sign with the network), Paley lured many successful shows and performers from NBC radio, notably *Amos 'n' Andy,* Jack Benny, Red Skelton, and *Burns & Allen.*

CBS became television's "Tiffany network": consistently profitable, well-managed, and classy. CBS nurtured its reputation as the network where the biggest stars could be seen (Lucille Ball, Jackie Gleason, Danny Kaye, Arthur Godfrey, Carol Burnett). It was also the network of Edward R. Murrow, Walter Cronkite, and a powerful group of CBS News correspondents—and of *Captain Kangaroo,* for years the most popular personality in children's television.

CBS News is responsible for several daily news programs, including *The CBS Evening News with Dan Rather* and *CBS Morning News,* plus cut-ins *(CBS Newsbreak,* short newscasts seen between programs). The division also programs several prime-time series

(60 Minutes, 48 Hours) and provides special-event coverage (elections, crisis coverage).

CBS Sports produces sports coverage and sports information programs on weekends.

TECHNOLOGY

In its long history, CBS has rarely been fortunate with television or video technology. The company's early attempts at developing a color television standard were costly and, despite its technical superiority over competing systems, the CBS color standard was not adopted. CBS also developed some early home video recorders and other devices that appeared promising but did not result in profitable products. (The technical strength of CBS was in audio; CBS engineers developed the long-playing record album, a standard for more than two decades.)

OWNERSHIP AND CORPORATE INFORMATION

In 1986 stockholder Laurence Tisch took control of the company, and sold off assets unrelated to broadcasting. CBS Records was sold to Sony in 1988; the magazine group was sold to the division's president. Other non-broadcasting ventures have been sold or scrapped. CBS, Inc. (the company changed its name from the Columbia Broadcasting System in 1974) was acquired by Westinghouse in 1996. The company, now called CBS Corporation, includes CBS Television (news, entertainment, sports divisions), CBS Station Group, and CBS Cable. The former Westinghouse has sold off its non-broadcast assets to focus exclusively on electronic media.

OWNED AND OPERATED STATIONS

CBS owns and operates fourteen television stations: WCBS (New York), KCBS (Los Angeles), WBBM (Chicago), KYW (Philadelphia), KPIX (San Francisco), WBZ (Boston), WWJ (Detroit), WCCO (Minneapolis), WFOR (Miami), KCNC (Denver), KDKA (Pittsburgh), WJZ (Baltimore), KUTV (Salt Lake City), and WFRV (Green Bay, WI). Some of these stations, notably KYW, KPIX, and WBZ, were Westinghouse stations prior to the merger.

CABLE AND INTERNATIONAL

CBS tried and failed to enter the cable business in the 1980s with a much-publicized arts venture called, appropriately, CBS Cable. Reluctant to fail again, and in the midst of future ownership questions, CBS was relatively quiet until the mid-1990s. In 1996, CBS purchased TeleNoticias, in part to fill the gap created by NBC's exit from the Latin news marketplace, and in a $1.5 billion stock swap, acquired The Nashville Network and Country Music Television. The company also started work on a new cable network called Eye on People. In 1997, CBS entered the Internet business with a large investment in Sportsline, a leading Web sports information service.

ABC

ABC was formed as a result of a Justice Department ruling that required NBC to divest itself of one of its two radio networks—NBC Red or NBC Blue. Since NBC Blue was the weaker network, it was sold in 1943. The buyer was Life Savers magnate Edward J. Noble, who came into broadcasting at a time when his competitors were diverting radio profits to build expensive television stations. Lacking stars, programs, and cash, Noble carefully managed his resources and focused on building television stations in five major markets: New York City, Los Angeles, Chicago, San Francisco, and Detroit.

Building the stations was financially draining, and building an entire network was beyond Noble's capability. In 1951, after being romanced by CBS (which wanted ABC's stations but planned to disband the network), Noble sold ABC to United Paramount Theatres—the theater chain resulting from an antitrust divestiture by Paramount Pictures. Leonard Goldenson, a Paramount executive, took charge.

Through its first two decades, until the early 1970s, ABC struggled. The network had fewer affiliates than CBS or NBC, so it reached a smaller audience, and received a smaller share of advertising revenues. This difficult condition forced ABC to innovate, resulting in a proud tradition of notable firsts. ABC was the first network to look to Hollywood, mostly for programming produced on film (at the time, a radical idea)—specifically, to Warner Brothers for *77 Sunset Strip, Maverick,* and *Cheyenne,* and to Disney for *The Mickey Mouse Club* and *Disneyland* (the latter, which shifted to NBC in 1961, was later known as both *Walt Disney's Wonderful World of Color* and *The Wonderful World of Disney*). ABC's move prompted NBC's long relationship with Universal; CBS started working with all of the film studios. ABC also leaned heavily on gimmicky exploitation shows *(Batman* and, later, *Charlie's Angels);* low-cost sports coverage *(Wide World of Sports);* late-night rock concerts *(In Concert);* and new forms, like the miniseries *(Roots).* By the mid-1970s, ABC had developed a schedule strong enough to woo a number of affiliates and finally gain parity with CBS and NBC. Since then, ABC has built its once cash-poor sports and news divisions into industry leaders.

OWNERSHIP AND CORPORATE INFORMATION

Historically, ABC's corporate vision has encompassed magazine publishing, and some involvement in the record industry (Impulse!, a jazz label, started at ABC). With its 1985 merger, ABC joined with Capital Cities Communications (in part to assure a successor for ABC founder and visionary Leonard Goldenson), and some TV and radio stations were sold to comply with FCC rules. Capital Cities and ABC's publishing groups were also transformed.

But things changed again in 1996, as Capital Cities/ABC became part of Disney in a $19 billion merger. The new organization is a worldwide entertainment and publishing giant. Its broadcast holdings include the ABC television and radio networks and stations, and its cable holdings include significant ownership in ESPN, The Disney Channel, E! Entertainment Television, and joint ownership of Lifetime (with Hearst) and A&E (with Hearst and NBC). Other Disney holdings include the theme parks and movie company, sports teams including 25 percent of the California Angels, and the NHL's Mighty Ducks. (In 1998, Disney sold the Dodgers to FOX.)

NEW MEDIA AND OTHER ENTERPRISES

Disney has been active in new media with its own successful children's CD-ROM products (generally based on motion picture licenses) and several versions of a Disney online service (on the Web, for example). Disney is, of course, a major international brand and licensor, but in addition, the organization owns cable operations in Germany, Japan, and Scandinavia. ABC Video Enterprises manages special-interest home video projects, as well as ABC's participation in Lifetime (33 percent ownership), A&E (38 percent), and ESPN (80 percent). There are also investments in European production companies (Germany's Tele-Munchen, for example), and in other new media ventures.

OWNED AND OPERATED STATIONS

With the exception of Philadelphia's WPVI on channel 6, the rest of ABC's top five O&Os broadcast on Channel 7 (a marketing idea left over from the 1950s): WABC (New York), KABC (Los Angeles), WLS (Chicago), and KGO (San Francisco). The other ABC O&Os are KTRK (Houston, TX), WTVD (Raleigh-Durham, NC), KFSN (Fresno, CA), WJRT (Flint, MI), and WTVG (Toledo, OH).

FOX

In the 1950s, there were four networks: CBS, NBC, ABC, and DuMont. In retrospect, it is clear that only two or three could survive, due mostly to the limited availability of VHF stations in major markets. DuMont lasted until 1955 because of the success of several major market stations, including New York Channel 5 (then WNBD). After its network folded, DuMont's station group was purchased in 1959 by John Kluge, who renamed the group Metromedia (flagship WNBD became WNEW, again the most important station in the group, still Channel 5). In 1985, the Metromedia stations were sold to Rupert Murdoch, and became the FOX station group (WNEW became WNYW). This group reached approximately 20 percent of television households, and became the basis for the new FOX network.

FOX went on the air October 9, 1986, with *The Late Show Starring Joan Rivers*. The show was aggressively marketed, but it failed. Other low-cost programs followed as the network found its way. Seeking to attract young-adult viewers, the network had hits with *Married...With Children,* a cynical family sitcom, and *America's Most Wanted,* a reality show that encouraged viewers to help catch criminals. FOX's first signature series was *The Simpsons,* and FOX built on its success with younger viewers with *Beverly Hills 90210* and *The X-Files.* In its first five years, FOX moved from a block of Sunday night programs to five nights of programming, plus a children's block on weekday afternoons. By 1996–97, FOX was programming two hours every night, and three hours on Sundays, plus a mid-morning show, *FOX After Breakfast,* and children's programs on weekday afternoons and Saturday mornings. A year later, the strategy changed (FOX moves quickly!), moving the company out of daytime, out of the children's broadcast business (and onto a new cable business), and heavily into sports. Indeed, FOX Sports is becoming a contender—it carried the 1996 World Series, and has carried NHL and NFL games, including the 1997 Super Bowl XXXI. Future contracts include World Series and All-Star games in alternating years. And FOX News is beginning to emerge, with the 1996 premiere of the one-hour *FOX News Sunday,* and a planned cable news channel.

OWNERSHIP AND CORPORATE INFORMATION

FOX, or more correctly, the Fox Broadcasting Company, is part of Fox Television, which is a division of Rupert Murdoch's international media conglomerate, News Corp. FBC does not own anything besides the network itself; sister companies operate the station group

(Fox Television Stations); the movie studio (Twentieth Century-Fox); the television production operation (Twentieth Television); and other ventures (a home video label, Deluxe Laboratories).

There are over 200 FOX affiliates covering nearly 99 percent of U.S. households. As a result of a deal with New World, FOX now has VHF affiliates in many major markets.

OWNED AND OPERATED STATIONS

There are 22 FOX owned and operated stations, including one in each of the following markets: WNYW (New York), KTTV (Los Angeles), WFLD (Chicago), WTXF (Philadelphia), WFXT (Bostson), WTTG (Washington, DC), KDFW (Dallas), WJBK (Detroit), and WAGA (Atlanta). Only the stations in Chicago, Philadelphia and Boston are UHFs.

UPN

UPN, the United-Paramount Network, debuted on January 16, 1995, with a two-hour episode of *Star Trek: Voyager*. The network took shape about a year before, as United Television (a station group), and Chris-Craft Industries (another station group) joined forces with Paramount, a leading studio. UPN affiliates cover just over 90 percent of the U.S.

As of the 1996–97 season, UPN programmed three nights a week, for two hours a night. *Star Trek: Voyager*, its most popular series, generally comes in at around number 50 on the ratings list of 100 prime-time broadcast network series. Other UPN series, such as *Moesha,* are typically in positions in the 80s and 90s. In 1998, Disney disbanded its syndicated "Disney Afternoon" lineup in favor of a two-hour afternoon program block on UPN stations. Overall, UPN scores between a third and a half of ABC, CBS, or NBC's audience shares and ratings. In the 1996–97 season, Paramount produced about half of UPN's nighttime programs.

THE WB NETWORK

The Warner Bros. Television Network is owned, of course, by Warner Brothers. The network is growing slowly, but several high-profile successes have contributed to the leap from three nights per week in 1997 to four nights in 1998 (*Buffy the Vampire Slayer*, for example). In prime-time, programs are generally low-rated, again in the bottom 20 of the 100 prime-time programs. But this network has an advantage—a successful children's programming block that consists of *Tiny Toons Adventures,* and *Animaniacs.*

Warner Brothers Television produces about half of the network's prime-time progamming, and its animation group produces just about the entire children's schedule.

Most of the network's larger affiliates belong to the Tribune station group: WPIX in New York; KTLA in Los Angeles; WGN in Chicago; WPHL in Philadelphia; WVI in Boston; and WBDN in Washington, DC (which is managed, but not owned, by Tribune). With few exceptions (notably in New York, Los Angeles, and Chicago), all of the WB Network's affiliates are UHF stations. Still, the network has affiliates in all major markets, and in most (but not all) medium-sized markets.

Many broadcast markets often support only four television stations. Because WB arrived late, it has found itself without affiliates in some markets. The solution is WeB—effectively establishing a cable-only affiliate in markets where a broadcast affiliate is unavailable.

PAXNET

As a result of some very complicated deal-making, Paxson Communications' 73 television stations became a network in 1998. It's a small network focused on family programming, such as movies and, at least at the start, off-network programming from ABC, CBS, and NBC. The new network's target is female viewers, and the first batch of program acquisitions reflects that strategy: *Touched by an Angel; Dr. Quinn, Medicine Woman; I'll Fly Away;* and *Sisters.* The business model is based on a $73 million investment in programming, which results in total ownership of the time slots. The network sells 40 percent of the program time, and local affiliates sell 60 percent. They're looking for a 1 rating in prime-time and an 80 sale of commercial time to generate $400 million in revenue (local plus network revenues combined). (See Chapter 41 for explanation of ratings.) Some home shopping and religious programming will fill the weekend hours. It's a fledgling story, but one that just might work and one that is certainly representative of the entrepreneurial trends in the contemporary television business. It might pick up the few remaining independent stations by offering a real opportunity to make money. Also, the network will add to its base with cable operators.

NETWORK STRUCTURE

ABC, CBS, and NBC are organized along similar lines, though specific policies, procedures, and reporting structures vary from one company to the next. Power has historically been shared between Los Angeles, where the entertainment programs are produced, and New York City, where the advertising agencies, news and sports departments, and corporate headquarters are located. New York City has lost considerable ground in the past two decades, and will probably continue to do so. Eventually, the networks will probably be headquartered in Los Angeles, with sales offices in New York.

The three major broadcast networks each have an entertainment division, responsible for all programming other than news and sports. There are separate news divisions and sports divisions, typically organized as separate companies with their own presidents. The NBC Television Network is the company responsible for advertising sales and affiliate relations; CBS divides these functions into CBS Marketing, which sells advertising and promotes the network, and CBS Affiliate Relations. There is a television stations group, which owns and manages the owned and operated ("O&O") stations. In addition, there are backroom departments as well, such as Operations, Technical Services, Administration, Personnel and Labor Relations and Corporate Communications. There may be international, cable, new business development, and new ventures groups as well. Each of the networks may place these under different corporate departments, but the functions are nearly identical.

The entertainment division supervises the development and production of original programs, acquires completed films, and schedules the programming. Departments include children's programming, comedy, drama, late-night, motion pictures for television, miniseries, and specials. A vice president oversees each area; he or she supervises a staff that includes one or more directors and managers who develop new programming and supervise current productions. The entertainment division operates as a self-contained organization, and includes a business-affairs group for negotiating agreements with producers, performers, and other key creative people. Casting and scheduling completes the department's list of responsibilities.

FOX, because it came along decades after NBC, CBS, and ABC were organized, is organized like a cross between a broadcast network and a cable network, with a senior executive in charge of each aspect of the operation: programming, finance and administration, publicity and corporate creative services, on-air promotion, research, business affairs, and affiliate relations. Operations at WBTV and UPN are similar, but smaller in scale.

THE NETWORK PROGRAM SCHEDULE

The networks provide programming only for certain parts of the day. Early-morning and sports programs are generally developed and produced by the networks (some sports programs are exceptions). News and most news magazines are developed and produced internally.

Until recently, daytime, prime-time, and children's programs were more often produced by studios (such as Universal and Paramount) and independent production companies (such as Carsey-Werner and Spelling) than by the networks themselves. (For instance, the 1996–97 ABC schedule was produced entirely by ABC and Disney's own production companies, such as JUMBO Pictures, which was responsible for two animated series in the network's Saturday morning schedule. (This was prompted, in part, by FCC rules [now repealed, see page 12] and the pattern is still changing.) A small number of established companies typically supply the network programmers in charge of each of these areas. The networks are also actively involved in daytime production; ABC, for example, produces all four of its daytime dramas *(All My Children, One Life to Live, General Hospital,* and *Loving),* but P&G Productions (corporate kin to TV's largest advertiser, Procter & Gamble) produces the CBS daytime dramas, *As the World Turns* and *Guiding Light.* (P&G also produces NBC's *Another World.)*

CHANGES IN NETWORK TELEVISION

From the late 1940s until the late 1970s, the three networks were essentially "the only game in town." Network programming dominated viewership, with public television and, in the largest markets only, one or two independent stations occasionally popular among specific audience segments.

The real product of the networks is not programs, but people: the networks earn money by delivering the largest possible audience of desirable viewers to advertisers. The greater the number of desirable viewers, the higher the advertising rate can be. For a prime-time series in 1996 (according to *Advertising Age,* an industry trade magazine), the average cost of a single network 30-second spot was $188,000 on ABC, $187,000 on NBC, $132,000 on CBS (as a result of poor ratings performance), and $131,000 on FOX. (As a rule, commercial spots are not sold singly; see Chapter 42 for a complete explanation of advertising on network television.) The most popular series charge as much as $1 million per minute (NBC's hit series *ER* and *Seinfeld* are in this elite group).

One half-hour program is likely to include at least 12 30-second spots, costing an average of about $500,000 each (the actual price depends on the program's rating within a desired demographic segment). The daytime commercial load is even heavier (more commercials per hour—with lower production costs).

Sitcoms cost about $500,000 to license ($800,000 or more to produce). Prime-time hours are licensed at about half as much (they actually cost an average of $1.2 million, with the studios earning back the deficit and profits from secondary markets and syndication), but the network typically buys two runs, allowing roughly 75 percent gross profit per hour, on average. Even after the deduction of network overhead and other expenses, selling advertising time on network television should be very profitable.

Network license fees are likely to increase. NBC's deal to keep *ER* on the network costs $284 million per year ($13 million per episode). This figure is outrageously high; in 1997, CBS's decision to pay more than $1 million per episode of *Cosby* was big news.

As cable viewership increases, the audience for broadcast network programming becomes smaller. Total network share of national television advertising spending has been dropping steadily since 1980. In 1979, the networks received roughly 60 percent of national advertising revenues; by 1987, the percentage had dropped to about 50 percent, and for the 1996–97 season, given a total TV ad volume of $42.5 billion, network advertising accounted for just over $13 billion, or about 30 percent. (Roughly 20–25 percent of total U.S. advertising dollars are spent on television). At the same time, the networks' combined prime-time audience share has steadily dropped from 93 percent in 1977 to 89 percent in 1980 to 74 percent in 1985 to 65 percent in 1990 to 61 percent in 1996. (Some sources quote 67 percent, but the pattern remains.) Cable controls about 22 percent and the remaining 10 percent or so belongs to syndicated programs. On a 24-hour basis, according to *Electronic Media* (Feb. 2, 1998), total viewership on ABC, CBS, and NBC stations has dropped from a total share of 82 in 1975 to a 61 in 1985 to a 46 in 1995, and is expected to drop to 28 in 2005. This has been marginally offset by a modest annual increase in the number of U.S. TV households.

In households that receive television through a cable system, viewers watch ABC, CBS, and NBC for roughly 26 hours per week; viewers who watch these networks via broadcast devote an average of nearly 32 hours per week. To put this another way, cable has taken about one of every five hours away from network viewing. Most successful cable networks are now global operations with big-time programming resources. The broadcast networks operate, by and large, as they have for decades, dealing with local affiliate relations, big-time producers, a rigid program philosophy, and a pronounced difficulty in moving as quickly as newer media operations. But the networks are beginning to rework their ways of doing business. The traditional network-and-affiliate model may change, perhaps offering affiliates an opportunity to share both the risks and rewards of the programming business, which would ultimately give affiliates a louder voice in network decisions. ABC and FOX have gotten money from affiliates to defray the costs of sports rights. Higher advertising rates on top network programs, and staff cuts to reduce the enormous size of network operations are constantly under discussion. Home video, video games, and, in the 1990s, Internet and computer use are also taking time away from network television viewing. Fewer viewers now choose from more television channels—and other entertainment options. What will happen as viewers routinely choose from 110-plus channels via cable or satellite services? And how will viewership patterns change as computers and television continue to converge, confusing the difference between Web sites and television channels?

Network shares are unlikely to increase. Cutbacks and more efficient operation will reduce operating costs only so far. Clearly, the networks will need to modify their business model at some point in the early years of the next century—and continue to do so as the environment continues to change. Networks are expanding their visions to include international operations and high-risk new media ventures. But the days of local television stations, the heart of domestic network operations, may be numbered.

2

Local Television

The traditional system for the delivery of broadcast television signals to U.S. households is the local TV station. Licensed by the FCC to operate on assigned frequencies, as of 1997, 681 stations operated on the VHF band (channels 2–13) and 874 on the UHF band (channels 14–83). Of the 681 VHF stations, 557 are commercial; of the 874 UHF stations, 241 are commercial. The others are educational. The number of VHF licenses issued has been relatively stable over the years: since 1960, only 100 have been added, mostly in outlying areas. In the same period, the number of commercial UHF stations has increased tenfold.

LPTV (low-power TV) licenses add to the total: 1,945 LPTV stations were licensed as of spring 1997: 1,402 on VHF and 543 on UHF. Approximately one-third of these licenses were actively broadcasting. With the changeover to advanced television, these numbers will change—and licenses will change hands at an accelerated rate.

THE TOP MARKETS

In television, and in some other industries, a top-10 market indicates markets 1–10, and a top-20 market refers, depending upon usage, to either markets 1–20, or 11–20.

Markets are ranked by the total number of households with television sets that can generally receive broadcasts from a particular city's principal broadcasters. There are nuances (see page 410 for details).

According to Nielsen, New York City is the largest television market. The 19 million people, or 6.8 million television households in New York City and its suburbs account for roughly 7 percent of all U.S. television households. Los Angeles is second with about 5 million television households, or 5 percent of the U.S. total. Next comes Chicago with just over 3 million households, or about 3.25 percent, followed by Philadelphia's 2.6 million and 2.75 percent. San Francisco introduces a more complicated concept: a market that encompasses several old-style cities (San Francisco, Oakland, and San Jose), plus newer business centers (notably, the Silicon Valley and places like Palo Alto, located between San Francisco and San Jose). The total San Francisco market ranks number five, with roughly the same numbers as Philadelphia (here, the issue of which counties are and are not counted becomes complicated; cable carriage of nearby signals makes the concept even messier). In total, the top-five markets account for approximately one-fifth of all television households. Add the next five markets—Boston, Washington, DC, Dallas-Fort Worth, Detroit, and Atlanta, and the number of total households is 29 million, nearly one-third of U.S. households. Each of the markets in the 11–25 range has between 1 and 1.5 million households, and accounts for between 1 and 1.5 percent of viewership. Nielsen measures 211 U.S. television markets.

STATION OWNERSHIP AND AFFILIATION

The most valuable asset of a local television station is its operating license. The primary responsibility of each station's general manager is to protect and preserve that license, keeping it free from legal entanglements and challenges from the public that the station serves.

When television began, there were experimental television stations operating in most large cities, and in many smaller ones. The FCC began actively licensing television stations in 1947, but by 1948, the number of new applications was overwhelming. From October 1948 until July 1952, the FGC did not approve any new licenses, using the period to develop a plan for "fair, efficient and equitable" allotments. Most VHF stations were licensed in the ten years following 1952. The majority were started by local businesspeople, or by companies that already had interests in other local media. Many VHF television stations were outgrowths of local radio stations, completing local media empires—the *Chicago Tribune,* for example, started WGN ("World's Greatest Newspaper") radio and, later, WGN television. Other stations were intended, from the start, as building blocks for national networks: WNBC in New York, WRC in Washington DC, WMAQ in Chicago, WKYC in Cleveland, and KNBC in Los Angeles have been owned and operated by NBC since the start of its television network. Some companies, such as Westinghouse, owned and operated radio stations in various cities; when television came along, they duplicated the pattern wherever competition for licenses allowed.

The vast majority of television stations are now owned by station groups. Local ownership has diminished greatly. Stations were bought and sold in the 1980s with a regularity that would have seemed impossible 15 or 20 years earlier. Television stations are glamorous media properties, and they appeared to avoid the risk inherent in other entertainment industry ventures, such as motion-picture production. The FCC also eased its rules on license transfers—specifically, the amount of time an owner must hold a property prior to sale. In the past, the minimum ownership period was three years, but that rule has been eliminated.

The rules regarding media ownership have changed several times since the 1940s, and recent decisions, related to the 1996 Communications Act, strongly favor group ownership. The current rules set no limit on the number of stations that can be owned by a single entity. However, a single company cannot own two stations within a single market (to put this in official terms, no two stations whose "grade B contours"—the outer extent of their transmission areas—overlap). The only significant limitation in the current rules is the overall reach of the station group—no more than 35 percent of the U.S. population.

There are nuances, however. A UHF station is assessed at half the value of VHF stations for the percentage limit, so a single company could theoretically own UHF stations reaching 50 percent of the U.S., and still comply with the rules. Rules are also relaxed for companies that are more than half-owned by minority groups.

STATION GROUPS

Group ownership has become the dominant form of station ownership in the U.S.—and most stations are owned by companies with holdings in other media.

Viacom, for example, owns Simon & Schuster (arguably the largest book publisher), Paramount, radio stations, MTV, Nickelodeon, Blockbuster Video, and a variety of other cable networks. Its Paramount station group, the nation's seventh largest group, covers 19 percent of the U.S. and ten of the top-20 markets. It includes KTXA, Dallas-Fort Worth; KTXH, Houston; WBFS, Miami; WDCA, Washington, DC; WKBD, Detroit; WPSG, Philadelphia; WSBK, Boston; WTOG, Tampa; WUPA-TV, Atlanta; WVIT, Hartford, CT; and KMOV, St. Louis. Most are UPN affiliates; the final two are NBC and CBS affiliates, respectively.

The Hearst Corporation owns newspapers, major magazines (*Cosmopolitan, Esquire, Good Housekeeping* and many others), significant interests in the Lifetime and A&E cable networks, and a group of television stations operated under the Hearst Broadcasting company. They are WBAL-TV, Baltimore; WCVB-TV, Boston; WISN-TV, Milwaukee; WTAE-TV, Pittsburgh; WDTN-TV, Dayton; KMBC-TV, Kansas City; and WWWB-TV, Tampa. Most are ABC affiliates. WBAL-TV is an NBC affiliate, while WWWB-TV is a WB Network affiliate.

Westinghouse, long a powerful station group, merged its station group with the CBS owned and operated stations in 1996, and bought all of CBS later the same year. The combined total—now called the CBS Station Group—covers 32 percent of the U.S. with 14 television stations. The largest station group without direct network ownership is Tribune, whose ten stations cover 21.5 percent of the U.S., and are, for the most part, affiliated with WBTV (see Chapter 1).

The broadcast networks also own stations, assuring clearances for network programs in critical markets in all time slots.

Station groups vary in the control and direction of their individual stations. For example, some central offices negotiate with syndicators on a group-wide basis; others encourage individual station management to make decisions based on local market conditions. In theory, general managers in station groups are encouraged to work together, sharing information about programming and personnel; in practice, this happens only on occasion.

NETWORK AFFILIATION

The affiliate relationship between the networks and local television stations is based upon compatible needs. The networks' program schedule must reach as many households as possible, which is best accomplished with a network of affiliated stations in every television market (and this is virtually assured if the network happens to own the station). The local stations need programming to fill their schedules, which the networks supply without a requirement for direct cash payment.

The *quid pro quo* between the network and its affiliate works as follows. The network provides a schedule of programs, with national or regional commercials included, as well as financial compensation for the airtime. The programs are offered to the affiliate, but if the affiliate chooses not to clear the time to run every program, then another station in the market may secure a clearance for that program (the transaction is often instigated by a competitive station; the network is obligated to do business with the station requesting the program). Affiliates may choose to schedule programs as they deem appropriate, though the network's affiliate-relations department usually encourages stations to run programs in accordance with the network schedule.

The networks theoretically buy airtime from their affiliates, but the formulas used to determine the rates are arcane, and sometimes blatantly unfair. In larger markets, what the network pays is only a fraction of an affiliate's overall revenues, while in smaller markets, network compensation contributes as much as 25–30 percent of revenues. In general, the smaller the market, the greater percentage of its revenues is network compensation (or "netcomp"). For ABC, CBS, and NBC, a typical netcomp formula takes the following factors into account: the number of commercial minutes in the hour, and the ratio of those sold nationally versus those sold locally; the "daypart" (programming time of day), which takes into account the size and demographic profile of the audience; the size of the market; the relative strength of the station, versus that of others in the market; and the amount of time that the program occupies. In the ten largest television markets, the total annual netcomp to each affiliate is likely to be less than $2 million. In smaller markets, the figure will be several hundreds of thousands of dollars a year, or even less. NBC and CBS each pay approximately $200 million per year in netcomp; ABC pays approximately $170 million.

Affiliates of ABC, CBS, and NBC depend upon their networks for a national news feed, or national material used in local newscasts (see page 214) Typically, the network feed is now one of several sources, such as CONUS and other news-feed services, and the networks also share coverage on an ad-hoc basis.

The relationship between affiliates and the network is subject to FCC regulations (see page 135). Networks may not control the rates, nor may they represent their affiliates, for the sale of non-network time; of course, this provision excludes network O&O's.

Network affiliation dictates an overall programming strategy for local stations. News is a large part of just about every network affiliate operation.

Besides news, most network affiliates program only a limited number of local hours per day: a few hours on weekday mornings, several more in the late afternoons. These are typically filled by syndicated programs. Once a mainstay, locally produced programs are now almost non-existent on U.S. television.

Most network television affiliations were established in the 1950s and early 1960s, frequently as an extension of a radio affiliation. Stations only occasionally changed affiliations. In the dynamic business climate of the 1980s, however, more affiliates changed allegiance than ever before. Most of the action was, however, in isolated situations. Several Miami stations changed affiliations, for example, but this kind of activity was still relatively uncommon.

By the mid-1990s, the situation had profoundly changed. Foundation alliances were broken: KYW, a longtime NBC affiliate, and WCAU, which figured prominently in CBS corporate history, switched networks. This was the result of the Westinghouse-CBS station group merger. This followed a 1994 maneuver by FOX, in which the New World station group was paid $500 million to switch to FOX (most stations had previously been affiliated with CBS, some with NBC). FOX continues on its quest for fewer UHF and more VHF affiliates, thereby increasing its viewership and visibility, and distancing itself from UPN and WBTV.

Besides the cash, there were two other incentives. FOX had just outbid CBS for NFL rights, and because FOX programs fewer hours per week than CBS, stations were given roughly 40 percent more time to sell on their own. CBS responded by increasing the term of its affiliation agreements: previously two years on average, the more common term became five to ten years. To encourage stations to sign, up to $10 million per year was guaranteed. Along the way, stations were discouraged from pre-empting network prime-time shows. In some cases, stations help to pay for programming; NBC not only asks that affiliates waive compensation for the Olympics (whose rights they own through 2008), the network also receives cash to help foot the bill.

Protection from cable television has also become an issue in the network-affiliate relationship. NBC, for example, regularly used programming produced by affiliates to feed its CNBC and MSNBC cable services. CBS affiliates extracted a promise from the network for protection. NBC has not yet made such an agreement.

ABC, CBS, and NBC maintain approximately 200 affiliated stations. FOX is still building up; in 1997, there were 176 FOX affiliates (covering 96 percent of U.S. households).

FOX, UPN, WBTV, AND INDEPENDENT STATIONS

Strictly speaking, FOX is not (yet) a network. FOX does not program enough prime-time hours per week to be subject to FCC rules regarding networks, and independent television stations affiliated with FOX are similarly unaffected by the rules that affect affiliates of ABC, CBS, and NBC.

FOX does not, for example, compensate its affiliates. Instead, stations pay FOX when programs exceed ratings expectations. WBTV uses a similar plan. UPN was designed as a program source by and for station groups. It's run by the station groups, and for the three nights of programming per week, no network compensation concept exists.

Independently programmed, unaffiliated VHF and UHF stations are relatively rare. In most markets, the few remaining "indies" have become affiliated with either UPN or WB, or HSN (Home Shopping Network, see page 281), or a religious or Spanish-language broadcast network.

One example of an independent station is Philadelphia's WGTW, operating on UHF channel 48. Paid and religious programming fills some of the schedule, and the remainder is devoted to movies and syndicated programs, typically series whose age has lessened their value. In 1997, for example, these series included the once-popular *Mama's Family, Hawaii Five-0, The Rockford Files,* and *Gilligan's Island.*

From the 1950s until the 1980s, "indies" were a viable alternative to network programming. Local sports, syndicated movie, cartoon, and off-network comedy and drama packages were their mainstay. Some local programs, such as news, sports, or hosted children's cartoon shows, were very popular. Today, the best indies are FOX affiliates, so their prime-time schedules are filled with network programming. Movies have moved to cable networks. Local sports has moved to FOX Sports. Children no longer watch Officer Joe Bolton's wraparounds of old *Three Stooges* episodes; they tune to WBTV afternoon programming, or to Nickelodeon or the Cartoon Network instead.

Still, many independent stations continue to operate as a hybrid of a network affiliate and their former selves. Many hours are still filled with off-network programs and movies bought from syndicators. They do not command the advertising rates charged by affiliates of the larger networks, but they operate with a much smaller staff, and typically, an indie's pay scale is lower than the scale at network affiliates. As a result, an indie can often make a profit even with low advertising revenues. Many do not produce any original programming; news on an indie or FOX affiliate must be profitable—or it will be replaced by a syndicated series.

SPANISH-LANGUAGE STATIONS

Spanish-language stations are generally affiliated with a Spanish-language network. There are two U.S. Spanish-language broadcast networks: Univision, and Telemundo. Most large Hispanic markets support at least one Spanish-language broadcast station. In general, advertising rates are low in comparison with general U.S. audience shares. Within the next five years, the Hispanic market is likely to mature, attracting considerably more advertising dollars and adding a great deal of value to these networks and their affiliated stations. (If current population trends continue, approximately 20 percent of U.S. citizens will be Hispanic early in the next century.) Largely due to the efforts of Univision, Nielsen now collects and publishes ratings information on Hispanic viewing. According to Nielsen, there are approximately 7.5 million U.S. Hispanic households. Of the top 20 shows, at least 15 are typically on Univision.

Univision, the largest network, reaches 92 percent of U.S. Hispanic households through 39 broadcast stations and approximately 740 cable affiliates. Among Hispanics, Univision is the most-watched U.S. network. Univision's power is in the stations it owns in markets with large Hispanic populations: WXTV, New York; KMEX, Los Angeles; WLTV, Miami; WGBO, Chicago; KXLN, Houston; KUVN, Garland, TX (outside Dallas); KDTV, San Francisco; KWEX, San Antonio; and KTVW, Phoenix. (There are several other O&Os in smaller markets.) In addition, Univision's affiliates operate UHF stations in Boston, Denver, San Diego, Tampa-St. Petersburg, Washington, DC, and some smaller markets.

Univision broadcasts 24 hours of programming each day from a Miami production center. Approximately half of this programming is original, mostly produced in Miami; the other half is acquired from Televisa (see page 526), Venevision (see page 530), and other Spanish producers and broadcasters. Popular programs originating from Miami include *Sábado Gigante* (an audience participation and variety series seen on Saturday nights), *Cristina* (a daytime talk show following the tried-and-true format of a roaming host, an active audience, and a few interesting people in chairs on a platform), and *Primer Impacto*. There are news programs, magazines shows, sitcoms, dramas, novelas (very popular Spanish-language soap operas produced mostly in Venezuela; see page 530), specials, a Spanish-language version of *Sesame Street* called *Plaza Sesame*. Sports coverage includes major-league soccer every Sunday afternoon. Local stations also produce their own programming. This is not a provincial imitation, but a full-scale television network with a giant audience and extremely popular programming. Local stations produce their own news and other programming.

In 1996, Univision became the U.S.'s first billion-dollar Spanish-language media company. Ad revenues for 1996 totaled more than $300 million.

Telemundo, the second largest Spanish-language network, runs a distant second to Univision, the result of high expansion costs, poor programming decisions, and simply being outpaced by a very effective competitor. By the end of 1997, Telemundo's audience share had eroded to just 15 percent. Still, Telemundo owns stations in the seven largest Hispanic markets: WNJU, New Jersey (just outside New York City); KVEA, Los Angeles; WSNS, Chicago; WSCV, Fort Lauderdale (reaching Miami); KVDA, San Antonio; KSTS, San Jose (reaching San Francisco); and KTMD, Galveston (reaching Houston). Telemundo also owns and operates WKAQ, Puerto Rico. Telemundo reaches approximately 85 percent of Hispanic households in the U.S.

Telemundo broadcasts 24 hours a day, seven days a week; its current priority is to create, produce and air programs that people want to see (misjudgment of audience interests was a contributing factor to the network's very serious financial problems). Programs are acquired, created as original productions (a major deal with one of Mexico's largest television companies, Television Azteca, did not produce ratings), and produced at the network's facilities in Hollywood, and in Hialeah, FL. In late 1997, Telemundo was purchased for $700 million by Sony Pictures Entertainment, Liberty Media, and other investors (Apollo Management and Bastion Capital). A complete overhaul of the network's management, programming, advertising strategies and marketing is in the works. Sony will manage the network.

HOME SHOPPING CHANNELS

Several companies now supply round-the-clock shopping to affiliates. Typically, these affiliates are UHF and LPTV stations. The Home Shopping Network (HSN) offers independent stations part-time and full-time affiliation, and pays a netcomp fee for the use of airtime. (For a detailed explanation of home shopping via television, see Chapter 30.)

RELIGIOUS BROADCASTING

In most cities, there is at least one station, typically a UHF or LPTV station, that broadcasts religious programming. These stations are typically owned by religious organizations, and most often affiliated with Trinity Broadcasting Network, a huge international operation that reaches its masses through cable television, satellites, and other media. The religious stations are self-supporting via contributions to a national service; effectively, they are direct-marketing tools for national or regional organizations. (For more on religious broadcasting, see Chapter 27).

LPTV

The FCC has licensed approximately 2,000 low-power television (LPTV) stations; the number has almost doubled since 1991. An LPTV station serves a very narrow geographic area, typically 20–40 miles. By definition, these operations are small in scale, with start-up costs around $250,000, and annual operating costs of $500,000–$750,000 with a half-dozen people on staff. Most LPTV stations feed low-cost satellite networks to subscribers; programming consists mostly of religious shows, home shopping, music, and Spanish-language services. Local programs, if offered at all, are on the order of cable's public-access channels.

STATION OPERATIONS

Most television stations are organized along similar lines.

The *general manager,* frequently a vice president of the company that owns the station, usually oversees day-to-day operations. The most important aspects of the job are guarding the station's valuable license and growing revenues. The former requires positive relations with community institutions and civic groups, and a judicious supervision of the station's news and other local programming. (Network programming is rarely inflammatory, whereas syndicated programs, notably talk shows, may demand more attention.) The latter responsibility requires an understanding of the syndication marketplace as well as the ability to pick the right shows and schedule them in the proper time periods; many of these decisions are now made at the group, not station, level, though scheduling is more often a local decision. The GM also works closely with the sales department (many GMs were former salespeople) to set rates for the commercials and the time periods.

The *sales department* manages the station's commercial inventory, sells local spots, and works with the station's rep firm (see page 28) to sell national spots.

The sales department is often responsible for the *traffic department,* which prepares the commercial log; the log indicates to master control which commercials and programs to play and when to play them, and tells the billing department how to invoice advertisers. Research (audience measurement) and special events are often part of the sales department as well.

The *creative services* department is responsible for shaping and promoting the station as a consumer brand. This group handles on-air promotion, advertisements for the station's programming in other media, public relations, and special promotional tie-ins. At some stations, these functions are segregated into on-air and off-air departments.

At most local stations, the *programming department* is no longer a powerful force. The big deals are typically negotiated at the group level (individual stations no longer buy important shows on their own). Few stations produce their own programming (outside of news and, perhaps, public affairs), so the program department's functions are largely related to scheduling, some selection of syndicated programs to fill time slots, and the occasional special, such as a parade. (One notable exception is Boston's WCVB, an ABC affiliate owned by Hearst. WCVB has been airing *Chronicle,* a daily magazine series, since 1982, The show has a staff of 22 people, and because the show's ratings are as high as their syndicated competition, it's profitable, even with a staff of 22 people.)

The *engineering* or *operations department* supervises the station's technical and maintenance staff; runs the studios, control rooms, master control (the control room responsible for assembling the air feed), and transmission facilities; and acquires new equipment. With the transition to digital television, this group has gained importance.

The *public affairs* or *community affairs department* encourages interaction between station personnel and the community; this may take the form of locally produced talk or magazine programs, and/or public appearances by the stations' on-air news personnel and some executives. The *production department*—which is sometimes part of the programming department—may employ producers and directors, produce commercials for local advertisers, and schedule the non-news use of studio and editing facilities.

The *business* or *finance department* is responsible not only for traditional accounting functions, but for the overall financial operation of the station.

Each of these departments has its own manager, director, or vice president—titles are determined by the policies of the station group, or by local tradition.

BUDGET OVERVIEW

The following describes, in general terms, typical network affiliate expenditures.

News is the biggest cost item, but also the largest revenue producer. In many of the top 50 markets, the average cost of news is approximately 23 percent of the total operating budget. In "news hungry" cities such as New York and Washington, the figure approaches 30 percent; in smaller markets, the percentage is more likely to be about 15 percent.

Upgrading technical equipment is an ongoing issue. New equipment becomes available every year, but most stations delay new purchases until they are essential. In larger markets, stations upgrade their facilities to compete effectively against other stations. The network affiliate also needs non-technical equipment: cars for the sales staff, copiers, and computers. At a well-run station, capital costs run approximately 5 percent of the annual budget; these costs may be higher in the short run if the physical plant is old or neglected. With the upgrade to digital television, these costs are likely to double or even triple, at least for the next few years.

Sales commissions and salaries cost a mature station about 18 percent of operating expenses.

As with the share of the budget that goes toward news, programming costs for network affiliates shrinks with market size. In the top 50 markets, the average is about 20 to 25 percent of operating expenses; in smaller markets, the average is in the teens. Programming costs cover payments for syndicated programs purchased for cash as well as original non-news programming, though some stations include news costs in the budget category of programming.

The G&A (general and administrative) budget pays the mortgage or rental of the physical plant; health and other insurance; salaries for the general manager and the business department staff; and other miscellaneous items. These outlays average 35 percent of total operating expenses.

The allocations differ for independent stations, mainly because the program hours are filled not with network programming (which is essentially provided at no charge), but with syndicated programs that must be acquired, either with cash or in exchange for commercial airtime. Although as much as half of an independent station's programming might be acquired by barter deals requiring little or no cash outlay (see Chapter 3), the typical balance is more like one-third barter, two-thirds cash acquisitions. The cash requirements for this type of operation are substantial: 55 to 60 percent of the total budget goes to program expense.

ADVERTISING SALES BY LOCAL STATIONS

The station's principal source of income is the sale of commercial time—its advertising "inventory." The object of the game is, simply, to maximize the value of this inventory, to collect as much in total sales as possible.

The cost of commercial spots is tied, in a general way, to ratings. The most popular shows generally command the highest rates, but this is not always the case. Sales managers exercise considerable flexibility over their inventory. They can price each spot according to market conditions, and they routinely change their prices. It's a game: to sell the inventory at the highest possible price before it expires. And it's a game that must be played carefully. If prices are reduced at the last minute, because a sales manager needs to close a month with additional revenues, then advertisers will wait until the end of the month before they buy the time. There are many such examples, and a skillful sales manager can maneuver through most of them.

The business of local television sales involves packaging large numbers of commercials in many time slots to allow sponsors to reach specific demographic groups—and/or to associate advertisers with specific types of programming. The objective is not simply to sell the current inventory, but to develop long-term client relationships with advertisers whose sales improve as a result of television exposure.

ABC, CBS, and NBC affiliates have less time available for sale locally than affiliates to UPN or WB (FOX is somewhere in between). Affiliates can sell as little as a minute per hour during dayparts programmed by the networks. As a result, most of the affiliates' avails are in news or syndicated programs. A network affiliate's weekday inventory of 30-second spots totals about 200 units (the figure is slightly higher during political campaigns).

A station's inventory is further reduced by barter transactions. In essence, a syndicator provides a program at no charge to the station, but trades for, or "holds back," some ad slots—say, $4^{1}/_{2}$ of perhaps 6 or $6^{1}/_{2}$ minutes of commercial time (the actual ratio may vary depending upon the program, and the deal). Many game shows and talk shows are offered by syndicators on a barter basis (see Chapter 3 for an explanation of barter syndication). Approximately 30 percent of FOX, WBTV or UPN stations' commercial revenues typically pay for barter programming; for network affiliates, the number is lower, usually about 20 percent. It is common for a station to trade airtime for goods; if, for example, a station needs cars, it might trade $50,000 of airtime for a like amount in automobiles from a local dealer. The practice is also common for office furniture, and in deals with restaurants and hotels. And the practice is not limited to trades within the station's local area. Complicated barter transactions involving multiple stations have become common; some stations like them, others don't. Of course, all stations generally prefer cash for their commercial time.

The local sales manager takes charge of sales to local clients. Much of this activity is reactive: order-taking from established customers, presenting new packages based on well-known advertiser needs. Increasingly, stations are seeking out new business from customers who do not presently advertise on television at all. Local sales of commercial time accounts for 30 to 40 percent of a station's revenues, depending upon market size.

NATIONAL SALES THROUGH REP FIRMS

Regional or national advertisers who want to buy time in a local market work with a particular station's national sales representative, or "rep firm," to negotiate prices and time slots. Formerly independent rep firms have been consolidated in the 1990s. Petry owns Blair; both are managed separately under the PMC corporate umbrella, and they generate $2 billion annually—roughly one-fourth of the spot TV marketplace. Cox Broadcasting owns MMT Sales, Telerep, and Harrington, Righter and Persons. Katz owns Seltel. Reps work exclusively for one station in each market, and operate—in theory, at least—as extensions of the station's sales staff. The station's rep firm receives a call from an advertising agency whose client needs to buy time on a certain station. The rep firm then meets with the station's national sales manager to assemble a competitive package based on the dates, cost of the target audience, and dayparts that the agency wants to buy on its client's behalf. The agency and the rep firm negotiate, and the station receives an order.

In the past decade, rep firms have become aggressive in seeking spot sales (as opposed to just taking orders). In a large market like Washington, DC, roughly 30 to 50 percent of a station's sales of remaining inventory comes directly from national rep firms.

The rep firms typically charge a commission of 6 to 10 percent on each transaction; the advertising agency takes its cut of 15 percent from its client as well. The station receives its net after these deductions. Rep firms do more than sell advertising time. They also advise their clients as to which syndicated programs are the most promising.

Many station groups are now selling their own local spots, effectively replacing the work done by a rep firm by doing the work in-house. This situation has allowed rep firms to work with more than one station in each market—a clear break with a long-standing tradition.

RATES FOR COMMERCIAL SPOTS

Even within a single market, there is considerable variation in the cost of commercial spots. As a starting point, the cost is based on the number of people who see the show—or, more accurately, on a ratings service's estimate of viewership. In Washington, DC (a top-10 market), during slower times of the year, a spot on a daytime show may have cost less than $150. In Philadelphia (a top-5 market), a 30-second spot on a morning program might cost $500 (but could cost as little as $300 or as much as $700, depending upon the season, the show's popularity, and many other factors). Back in DC, the cost of a spot on a Washington Redskins game aired in prime-time might be as high as $20,000. The price also depends upon the available inventory (and how anxious the sales manager is to sell off the time); the prices charged by the competition; the size of the overall package and its component parts; the anticipated ratings; and the skill of the sales staff.

The prices for commercial spots are based upon each program's ratings. When an advertising media planner determines how best to market a product, he or she orders the purchase of a certain number of gross rating points in a particular market. The media buyer then purchases programs whose ratings equate to the gross rating point formula (see page 424), and generally spreads the buy so that it favors stations whose programs suit the demographic requirements of the media plan. A product seeking a younger audience, for example, might be best served by purchasing time on FOX.

Stations vary in their annual gross sales of commercial time, from year to year and from market to market. In a top-10 market like Washington, DC, a network affiliate might gross about $100 million. In a top-50 market, a network affiliate might gross $40 million, and in a top-100 market, perhaps $15 million. These figures are only the roughest estimates; the actual situation varies from market to market, and among stations within a market.

3

Syndication

On average, the larger commercial networks supply 20–25 half hours per day of programming to their affiliates. This includes morning shows; daytime talk, soaps, and game shows; evening news; prime-time; late night; plus some overnight news programming. On weekends, the feed differs, usually with some news and public affairs; children's programming; and sports.

ABC, CBS and NBC affiliates program about two to three hours of news per day. The remainder of the schedule—about 12–14 half hours—must be filled with other programming. Most is typically filled with programs acquired from syndicators. (In addition, particularly on affiliates of smaller networks, some program time is sold for infomercials and religious programming.)

FOX affiliates receive about half as much network programming, and usually produce less local news; about 20 half-hour slots per day are filled with syndicated programs. That number is higher for UPN and WB affiliates, and higher still for the few remaining unaffiliated local television stations, who may fill their entire schedules with syndicated programs.

HISTORY AND EVOLUTION OF THE SYNDICATION BUSINESS

The basic structure of broadcast syndication was established in the 1930s as salespeople called on local radio program directors, who purchased programming on a market-exclusive basis.

One of the more successful radio program syndicators was Ziv, a Cincinnati firm that marketed dozens of radio series. Ziv started purchasing movie footage for television syndication in the 1940s, negotiating for television and radio rights to properties such as *The Cisco Kid*. Ziv-TV became an active supplier in the 1950s by concentrating on two time periods not yet fully exploited by the networks: 7:30 P.M. and 10:30 P.M. Programs produced on film *(Sea Hunt, Whirlybirds, Highway Patrol)* and the first color film series *(Cisco Kid)* were at first considered risky by the networks, who soon followed Ziv's lead into these formats. Ziv also produced programming (1957's *Tombstone Territory)* for ABC. In the 1950s, most other syndicators distributed movie product repackaged for television *(Little Rascals, Laurel and Hardy)*.

By 1963, Group W Productions (part of Westinghouse Broadcasting) was in production with *The Mike Douglas Show*, a daytime program produced at the station group's Cleveland facility. *The Mike Douglas Show* stayed on the air until the early 1970s (in the interim, the show moved from Cleveland to Philadelphia). The talk/variety format was successful for Group W, which subsequently distributed *The Merv Griffin Show, The David Frost Show*, and other programs. With *Douglas*, Group W successfully experimented with a new form of financing called barter syndication (see page 36). *Hee-Haw, Wild Kingdom*, and *The Lawrence Welk Show* are examples of another phenomenon—former network shows that continued production, but changed their form of distribution to syndication.

The present-day syndication business began to take shape in the early 1970s, when the FCC required the divestiture of the networks' syndication businesses. Viacom, the CBS spin-off, was immediately successful, mining a library that included *I Love Lucy, The Andy Griffith Show, The Honeymooners, The Twilight Zone, The Dick Van Dyke Show, The Beverly Hillbillies, Hawaii Five-O, Perry Mason, Hogan's Heroes, Gunsmoke, My Three Sons*, and other classics. ABC's spinoff, Worldvision, worked from a library that included *The Streets of San Francisco, The Fugitive* and, in the main, other properties from Quinn Martin Productions. NBC's spin-off company, MTA Syndication, ceased operations in the early 1980s. Many off-network programs have been extremely successful over a remarkably long term, especially Viacom properties such as *I Love Lucy, The Andy Griffith Show*, and *The Honeymooners*. (Some have formed the foundation for Viacom's Nick at Nite and TV Land cable ventures.)

The market for first-run syndicated product was established largely as a result of another FCC action, known as the Prime Time Access Rule (see page 35), as networks were effectively required to allow affiliates to program the 7:00 P.M.–8:00 P.M. hour. The FCC action created an opportunity for light entertainment programs, particularly game shows, as well as entertainment magazine programs. In the 1970s, game shows dominated, with small distributors financing new versions of classic shows *(Name That Tune)*, or creating new evening versions of current network programs that were already on the network schedule *($10,000 Pyramid* [which became *$25,000 Pyramid,* then *$100,000 Pyramid,* in syndication], *Family Feud, The Price Is Right).*

KingWorld, best known from the 1950s until the 1970s as the distributor of *The Little Rascals,* became the most aggressive supplier of programming for this time slot. Realizing that the 7:00 P.M.–8:00 P.M. slot could deliver a large audience to national advertisers, KingWorld executives identified *Wheel of Fortune* as the type of game show that could succeed; it debuted in syndication in 1983. The business concept eventually extended beyond simply distributing a game show, to developing a package strong enough to anchor the evening schedule. With *Wheel* sold to well over 100 stations (a higher "clearance," or rate of sale, than most game shows achieve), KingWorld started work on a second half-hour, and sold *Jeopardy!*—which debuted in the 1984–85 season— as a companion to *Wheel.* Then KingWorld started working on early-fringe (late afternoon), and placed *The Oprah Winfrey Show* (formerly a local talk show on Chicago's WLS) on many of the *Wheel of Fortune/Jeopardy!* stations. Further ventures into daytime talk did not fare as well.

Programs that anchor schedules are called *franchise shows,* and they are the most valuable syndicated properties. Through the mid-1990s, the most successful franchise shows included *The Oprah Winfrey Show, Wheel of Fortune,* and *Jeopardy!*—all from KingWorld (which perfected the concept of franchise shows). Paramount's *Entertainment Tonight* has been another successful franchise.

CURRENT PROGRAMMING

Among more recent programs, talk shows, game shows, off-network sitcoms and dramas distributed from the larger firms have dominated. The most popular syndicated series in the 1996–97 season were: *Home Improvement* (off-network sitcom; Buena Vista), *Seinfeld* (off-network sitcom; Columbia), *Entertainment Tonight* (entertainment news; Paramount), *Mad About You* (off-network sitcom; Columbia Tri-Star), *Wheel of Fortune* (game show produced for syndication; KingWorld), *The Simpsons* (off-network animated sitcom; Twentieth), *Jeopardy!* (game show produced for syndication; KingWorld), *Star Trek: Deep Space Nine* (drama produced for syndication; Paramount), *Access Hollywood* (entertainment news; Warner Brothers and NBC), and *The Oprah Winfrey Show* (talk show produced for syndication; KingWorld).

NEW SYNDICATED PROGRAMMING

The marketplace tends to look at new syndicated programs in one of seven categories: half-hour strips (five 30-minute episodes per week), hour strips, half-hour weeklies, hour weeklies, off-network half hours, off-network hours, and series for children.

The odds against any television program moving from concept to pilot to production to anything resembling a hit show are extremely high. In syndication, many new series are discussed and promoted, but only a small percentage actually make it to the fall schedules.

For any new syndication property, the process typically begins during the summer or winter some two years before the series reaches the air (say, for example, summer 1999). The better part of a year is typically spent acquiring rights, negotiating, developing the creative concept, and preparing the pitch. The concept begins to take shape as a business proposition the following spring (2000), with pilots produced in the summer so that deal-making can begin in the fall. The official launch of new programs is often held, with great fanfare, at the NATPE convention, held each January, but in reality, most significant deals are made prior to the convention. Syndicators continue to sell through the winter and early spring (2001), making the decision to go with a series for fall (2001), or cancel (and lose their investment and opportunity to place the series) by springtime. Then, the new series begins production for a fall debut. (This is a typical cycle, though many series, notably children's animation and dramatic series involving special effects, require much longer lead times for production.)

Original programs for syndication are especially difficult to launch because they lack the established audience enjoyed by off-network series.

TALK SHOWS

In the early 1990s, many syndicators launched new talk shows, hoping to capitalize on the success of Oprah Winfrey, Phil Donahue, and Sally Jessy Raphael. Most failed, but some, including Montel Williams, Ricki Lake, Maury Povich, and Jenny Jones, succeeded. And just when syndicators felt the market for new talk shows was fading, *The Rosie O'Donnell Show* became an instant hit. In syndication, there are essentially two types of talk shows. One involves a host sitting at a desk, interviewing celebrities and introducing acts (the Merv Griffin, Johnny Carson, Jay Leno tradition). *(LIVE with Regis and Kathie Lee* places hosts and guests on stools.) The other involves a roving host who facilitates audience questions addressed to onstage guests (the Phil Donahue, Sally Jessy Raphael, Oprah Winfrey tradition). These are the only formats that seem to "work" in syndication. The critical ingredient is the host, but the backstage producing talent also plays a significant role in the series' success.

ENTERTAINMENT AND NEWSMAGAZINES

There are two types of magazine shows as well. One is the entertainment newsmagazine *(Entertainment Tonight,* for example). The other is a hosted series of investigative reports, often presented with sizzle *(Hard Copy, Inside Edition).* These ventures are large productions involving a full-scale news operation, and are most often produced by big studios with deep pockets. The critical ingredient here seems to be the producers' story instinct, though familiar anchors and reporters ease comfort levels with new series.

GAME SHOWS

Game shows' popularity seem to be cyclical. They were very popular in the mid-1980s *(Family Feud* and *The Price Is Right,* for example), but most game show time slots were taken by talk shows, and by the mid-1990s, only two game shows remained— *Wheel of Fortune* and *Jeopardy!.* Late night, sex and relationship games worked for a season, but faded. Attempts to bring back classics placed *The Dating Game* and *The Newlywed Game* on the air for the 1996–97 season, but with far less success than they enjoyed during their "Golden Age." New game shows, such as *BZZZ!,* have found the market tough. As of this writing, in early 1998, the only new game show planned for the 1998–99 season with much promise is a renovated *Hollywood Squares,* and it is being positioned as a comedy/game format.

Bringing back old shows is generally perceived as a safer bet than introducing a new series, but this approach can also fail (the best example: the combination of mega-star Bill Cosby and the old Groucho Marx vehicle, *You Bet Your Life!*). The hybrid game/reality series, *The People's Court,* was brought back by Warner Brothers for the 1997 season (hosted by former New York City mayor Ed Koch). In recent memory, no new game show has succeeded in syndication.

CHILDREN'S PROGRAMS

Most of the market for syndicated children's programming has matured to a point where it no longer exists. Independent stations that once filled their after-school hours with cartoons continue to do so—but they are no longer independent stations. Instead, these stations became FOX and WBTV affiliates. They filled their afternoon schedules with FOX Kids' Network and Warner Brothers animated series. UPN affiliates continue to buy syndicated programming for their afternoon children's schedule. Some morning time slots on FOX, WBTV, and UPN stations are filled with syndicated cartoons.

Nearly all children's programs shown in syndication are animated. From time to time, a live action hybrid succeeds; *Mighty Morphin Power Rangers* and *Beakman's World* are among this short list of exceptions.

OTHER TYPES OF PROGRAMS

For many years, syndication was a great place for entrepreneurs and unusual ideas. The long list of examples includes *Lifestyles of the Rich and Famous* and *Star Search; Siskel & Ebert* (lifted from a successful PBS series); wrestling programs from World Wrestling Foundation; *Benny Hill;* and *Tales from the Darkside.*

With higher stakes, and fewer time slots, syndication is no longer the place for innovative series, particularly five-day strips. But on weekends, some syndicated series have found audiences and made money with once-a-week airings. Some examples are *Martha Stewart Living, Hercules, XENA, Babylon 5, America's Dumbest Criminals, Viper,* and *It's Showtime at the Apollo.* As a result of pressures in today's syndication marketplace, notably limited time slots and high failure rates, most special-interest programs have migrated to cable networks.

THE PRIME-TIME ACCESS RULE

The Prime-Time Access Rule (PTAR), enacted by the FCC in 1971, limited network affiliates in the top 50 markets to three hours of network prime-time programming from Monday through Saturday night—thus creating the 8:00–11:00 P.M. block known as primetime. A new daypart called *prime access* (7:00–8:00 P.M. in the East and West, 6:00–7:00 P.M. Central and Mountain Time) also came into being. The FCC intended to limit the networks' grip on the best viewing hours, to introduce diversity of program forms and content in a time period with enough viewers, and to encourage new producers and distributors to enter the television business.

With the possible exception of KingWorld's growth from a small-time syndicator to a big one, the goals have not been met. Indeed the rule was officially rescinded in 1995, effective 1996. Its legacy, however, continues. In Philadelphia, in the 1996–97 season, WPVI (ABC) schedules a pair of KingWorld game shows *(Wheel of Fortune* and *Jeopardy!); KYW (CBS) airs two magazines shows, both from major studios *(Entertainment Tonight* and *Hard Copy); WCAU (NBC) runs two Warner Brothers magazines *(EXTRA* and *Access Hollywood).* In the same slot, the FOX, UPN and WB stations run off-network sitcoms (with the exception of *Real TV,* a magazine from Paramount, on the FOX station). The continuing missing component—and the one long-term failing of the PTAR when in effect—is locally produced programming during prime access. For most of the 1980s, Group W's *Evening Magazine* and *PM Magazine* combined a syndicated package with some local production, but nationally syndicated programs dominate the time slots (and this is likely to be true for as long as the rule survives).

CASH AND BARTER SYNDICATION

"Straight cash" or "cash syndication" is an old-style financing format for syndication. It is fairly straightforward: the syndicator wants to license the program in each market for the highest possible cash price. Since about 1993, straight cash syndication has not been common practice (except for the purchase of older syndicated series for relatively low prices).

In today's marketplace, the deal typically involves a cash payment from the station (or more often, station group) to the syndicator. However, in addition to this cash payment, the syndicator gets the right to sell commercial spots in the program. The station is essentially trading, or bartering, the value of its air time instead of paying cash. This approach limits the stations' cash outlay, and increases the potential upside for the syndicator.

Cash-plus-barter is the format most often used for popular game, news/magazine, and talk-show strips. It is now used for sitcoms as well. The price, and the number of spots that the syndicator holds back, is determined by the program's popularity. According to *Electronic Media* (January 19, 1998), a 30-second barter ad unit (that is, one commercial) cost $105,000 on the most expensive cash-plus-barter series, *Home Improvement;* the same spot on *Seinfeld,* another successful series, cost $81,000. These off-network series demand high prices because there is little risk; they will attract precisely the size and demographic profile needed by the media buyer to satisfy the advertiser's strategy. By comparison, prices on *Entertainment Tonight* averaged $72,000, the *The Oprah Winfrey Show* averaged $52,000 per 30-second unit, and on *The Rosie O'Donnell Show,* they were $37,000. Mid-range performers included *Hard Copy* ($16,000), *LIVE with Regis and Kathie Lee* ($13,000) and *Sally Jessy Raphael* ($13,000). At the lower end was *The People's Court,* whose spots cost just $6,000.

The syndicator and program producer receive only a percentage of barter revenues. The most successful off-network series also demand a significant cash payment from individual stations (or from the station groups who buy such programs for multiple stations). *Friends,* distributed by Warner Brothers, earned $250,000 per episode in New York and LA, $200,000 in Chicago, and less as market size decreased. This deal also allowed the syndicator to hold back three 30-second spots per episode.

Barter syndication is the preferred format for once-a-week shows, children's shows, and some daily strips (a *strip* is a group of five shows per week, usually airing Monday through Friday in the same time slot)—also late fringe. A barter program is generally targeted to break even or better with a clearance of above 75 percent of U.S. households, and an average rating for the time period. With a higher clearance, or a higher rating, a barter program can be a very significant money-maker. On the other hand, if the clearance or rating falls below expectations, the program can cost the syndicator money (see page 41).

CASH-PLUS-BARTER SYNDICATION, STEP-BY-STEP

The following section moves through the process of cash-plus-barter syndication, tracing the way in which the syndicator licenses a program in each market for as much money as possible.

1. The syndicator negotiates with a producer, studio, or network for the right to syndicate a series. (These days, the syndicator and the network—or cable network—are often owned by the same large media company.)

   The syndicator's estimated life-of-series revenues (appropriately discounted for the time value of money) is frequently the starting point for negotiations. If the series is an original production, or additional episodes for an existing series, then the syndicator's payment will be used to pay a portion of production costs. A co-financing arrangement with another distributor, sometimes involving the sale of international rights, for example, may also cover some production costs.

2. Based on the cost of the property, and the costs of marketing and selling the program (see below), the syndicator targets the amounts to be extracted from each market. The value of a program in New York or Los Angeles, for example, will be much higher than in Baltimore or San Diego; the price in smaller markets will be still lower.

3. The syndicator provides its sales force with marketing materials consistent with a unified sales strategy (suggested time slots, anticipated viewership demographics). The sales staff is also presented with the budget targets, and the numbers that it must meet in order to succeed.

4. The company's senior executives visit several important station groups to muster support for the series. As a result of changes in FCC rules regarding station ownership, a small number of station groups control very large audiences; without the support of these groups, the series does not get on the air.

    Armed with commitments from (at best) a few of these station groups, the syndicator's sales force then visits other groups. If the property is especially desirable, groups and stations bid against one another, and can drive the price up higher than the syndicator's original estimate. (There's a certain amount of playing one group against another to raise the price and close the deal.) More often, the program will suit the needs of only one or two stations in the market (most stations have only limited time slots to fill). The salesperson will negotiate with a head of programming for a group, or with the station's general manager or program director. To break even, the syndicator must clear (sell to stations in) considerably more than half of the country, and must get its asking price in the majority of the larger markets.

5. Marketing generally begins in the fall, and by January's NATPE (National Association of Television Program Executives) convention, the syndicator's plans become clear. Marketing continues through the spring and early summer. A very successful syndicated series will clear just about every market—over 200 stations—and coverage of more than 97 percent of the country is typical of the most successful syndicated series.

6. When a station makes a commitment to a syndicator's program, the fee takes the form of a limited license, with payments due annually over the course of the agreement. The station's advertising sales force sells commercial time in the program, hoping to make a profit on the program purchase; and although a time

slot is often negotiated, the station often reserves (and acts upon) the right to move the program to a less desirable time slot if it does not perform well. In cash-plus-barter syndication, the syndicator's advertising sales force does the same.

7. The syndicator deducts a sales commission, typically 35 percent of gross revenues. The syndicator usually collects an additional 10–15 percent to cover the cost of marketing and distributing the program, including advertising and promotion, convention expenses, editing, videotape and film transfer costs, satellite costs, and a percentage of the company's overhead. In addition, the syndicator earns advertising revenues from the spots it has "held back" in the barter portion of the deal.

8. The program's producer or studio receives revenues after the syndicator recoups the advance plus marketing and some overhead. These dollars may be used to cover a production deficit, or for other company projects, or be taken as profits. These net revenues result only from this one distribution of the program; there may be subsequent or ongoing syndication deals (or cable sales) in addition.

   Here's how the numbers might work for an offering of a reasonably well-known off-network half-hour sitcom with 60+ episodes (three seasons' worth, generally considered the minimum number of episodes for purposes of national syndication):

Gross cumulative package selling price (all U.S. markets):	$40,000,000
Syndicator's expenses (15%):	($ 6,000,000)
Syndicator's sales commission (35%):	($14,000,000)
Return to producer/studio on this distribution:	$20,000,000

Prices paid for newer off-network sitcoms have broken previous records: *Home Improvement* and *Roseanne* are among an increasing number of popular series earning more than $1 million per episode, and *Friends* has earned nearly $2 million.

The barter industry has created a new type of advertising sales company, one that sells available time in syndicated programs to advertisers. These companies are typically owned by one or more syndicators, and handle sales for their owners, and sometimes for one or more other syndication companies. Camelot Entertainment Sales, for example, is the barter advertising arm of KingWorld, and Premier is Paramount's barter ad sales group. Every major syndicator now owns a barter advertising sales company.

DEVELOPING AN ORIGINAL SYNDICATED SERIES

Well over a hundred original syndicated series are currently on the air in the U.S. For producers and syndicators, the process is challenging (though perhaps no more so than getting a network series on the air). The process begins as the syndicator reviews proposals for original productions, joint ventures, and acquisitions. Most proposals are turned down on the spot because they are inappropriate for the syndication marketplace (stations are unlikely to put the program on the air because of content or time slot issues); because they will not compete effectively (an original game show, for example, is less likely to succeed than one with an established name); or because they require further development. For those projects that seem viable, the syndicator estimates income potential.

This estimate of income potential is based on two figures: the number of markets that the program is expected to clear, and the anticipated rating (a national average of local ratings, generally keyed to a specific and desirable demographic group, such as women 18–34). These two figures allow the syndicator to determine the price that national advertisers are likely to pay for each barter spot. The number of spots held back by the syndicator is then multiplied by the price per spot to determine the total estimated revenues for the program. The CPM, or cost per one thousand viewers, also plays an important role, and this is a negotiable figure based on the series' strength. *The Rosie O'Donnell Show,* for example, is a powerful communicator with women, and earns a $16 CPM, but *Martha Stewart Living* is slightly less powerful, and earns just over $12. Lesser series typically cost (very roughly) $5 to $10.

If the numbers look promising, and the program has a serious chance of succeeding in a marketplace where severe competition is the rule, the syndicator commissions a demonstration tape ("demo"), or, in some cases, a full-scale pilot. A demonstration tape usually costs roughly $50,000–$100,000; a pilot costs between $150,000 and $350,000, sometimes more. The syndicator generally pays the production costs for the entire pilot or demo. In recent years, launching a new syndicated strip series (five days per week) has become especially difficult, because successful shows occupy the time slots with the largest potential audience. Massive sums of marketing and promotion dollars must be spent to tell viewers about a new show—and with so many options available via cable, viewers tend not to support new programs (regardless of whether they're syndicated, on cable, or on a broadcast network). Because syndication launches have become risky ventures, alliances have developed between syndicators and producers, station groups, sponsors, and foreign television companies to help cushion the risk and strengthen the property.

Two selling operations occur simultaneously. The barter advertising sales force presents the pilot or demo tape to advertising agencies, who can commit their client's advertising dollars to the venture. The program sales force presents the program to station groups. Stations are encouraged not only to clear the series, but to schedule it in a time slot with a high HUT level (Households Using Television, a measure of the number of households viewing television at a particular time).

The selling period begins in the fall, continues through the NATPE convention in January, and goes on through the winter and spring. The process has become stressful for syndicators because many stations tentatively commit to several shows, not making final decisions until plans are announced by the other stations in the market. The situation is especially sensitive with regard to clearances in New York, Los Angeles, and Chicago; it is difficult, if not impossible, to succeed in barter syndication without clearances and good time slots in all three markets. By summer, the fog clears—the marketplace has determined which programs will be a "go" for fall, and production commences.

Advertisers sometimes pay for the commercial time in advance, but the syndicator often serves as the bank, providing the money upfront for production and marketing. The program goes on the air, presumably in a flurry of on-air promotion and supported by some print and radio advertising. If the cumulative national rating is equal to the syndicator's estimate, no further action is required. If the national rating falls below the estimate, the syndicator must repay the difference in cost between the higher estimated rating and the lower actual one. If the rating is higher, then the syndicator did not properly estimate its level of risk, and the company must wait until the following year to negotiate a better price with its clients (presuming, of course, that the program's ratings remain at the same level, or get better!). A risky arrangement indeed.

Since the risk belongs to the syndicator, so does much of the reward. Prior to the distribution of any payments to producers, or other third parties (such as those with profit participation in the property), the syndicator deducts a fee, typically 35 percent of gross, plus about 10 to 15 percent in expenses. In addition, the barter advertising company—which typically belongs to the syndicator—receives 10 to 15 percent of the revenues. The advertising agencies also take a deduction; their traditional fee for any media buy is 15 percent of the cost of the advertising time (payable by the advertiser). The syndicator will recoup the costs of the production, typically with overhead deductions and interest added. After all of these costs are deducted, the net is shared among the syndicator, who typically receives the largest share, and any third-party participants.

If the deal is cash-plus-barter, then the syndicator also collects a cash license fee from stations who clear the show. The cash received is then subject to some of the syndicator-related expenses described above (but not those costs associated with advertising, which is relevant only to the barter aspect of the deal).

SAMPLE BUSINESS MODEL: ORIGINAL SYNDICATED PROGRAM

Although the actual numbers are certain to vary, the following model—the launch of a first-run hour-long talk show (195 episodes, or 39 weeks) that has succeeded in syndication before—illustrates how the cash-plus-barter system generates profits. In this example, the syndicator's strategy emphasizes clearances in daytime and early-fringe time slots. In order to get a high CPM (cost per thousand viewers) from advertisers, the syndicator has guaranteed a high percentage of viewers in the women 18–49 group. The syndicator will sell two minutes, or four 30-second spots in each half hour; for five shows a week, the syndicator would thus hold back twenty 30-second spots. In addition, stations pay a cash license fee to the syndicator.

First, the net annual income is calculated by making certain assumptions about the marketplace, and the program's performance.

Estimated national clearance: 70%

Estimated average household national rating[1]: 2 (or 2,000,000 households, based on a universe of 98,000,000 U.S. television households

VPS (Viewers Per Set) in the target demographic: 40% (since advertising is sold based on a specific demographic group, the rates are based only on that group)

Estimated average national household rating × total TV households × VPS: $0.02 \times 0.4 \times 98$ million = 784,000 Women 18–49

---

1 Based on assumption of about half the clearances in daytime with an average of 1.5–2, and half in early fringe, with 2.5.

Estimated CPM for Women 18–49: $6.00

Price per 30-second spot (total women 18–49 divided by $1,000^2 \times$ CPM: $784 \times \$6.00 = \$4,700$

Minus ad agency's 15% commission = $3,995

Net revenue from 200 30-second spots, per week: $79,000

Cash license fees (paid by stations) per week: $\$2,000^3 \times 50^4$ markets = $100,000

Total syndicator net income: $179,000 × 52 weeks = $9,308,000

Next, the syndicator's first-year costs are calculated.

Pilot production costs:	$300,000
First-year (39 weeks) production costs:	$4,000,000
Total rights and production costs:	$4,300,000

Finally, the syndicator must consider its costs of marketing and sales.

Marketing (first-class launch, including trade advertising, convention expenses, local radio and print advertising, plus satellite distribution): $1,500,000

Distribution fee (35% of net income, above): $9,308,000 × 0.35 = $3,257,800

Total first year marketing and sales costs: $4,757,800

The net profit for the first year is calculated as follows:

Net income:	$9,308,000
Production costs:	($4,300,000)
Marketing/sales costs:	($4,757,800)
Net profit (loss):	$250,200

The picture appears less risky in subsequent years, when the $300,000 pilot cost and the high cost of launch marketing disappear (in fact, there would be a considerably smaller marketing budget to encourage the long-term success of the series).

---

2   The figure is divided by 1,000 because the basis is cost-per-thousand.
3   Which means that New York City pays about $10,000 and Flint/Saginaw pays about $500.
4   The top 50 markets accounts for roughly 70 percent of the country, which is roughly the percentage that the syndicator needs to break even.

Still, there is considerable risk, if the stations or advertisers pay less than anticipated by the syndicator, or worse, if the series does not perform as promised.

ANOTHER BUSINESS MODEL

The formula for a lower-budget, once-a-week show, such as a non-fiction home improvement show, is less complicated. In the following model, production costs are low, the show has been on the air for several years, and the series receives revenues from a foreign version. The key to the formula, however, is a relatively high CPM because the series attracts almost exclusively men 18–49 with an interest in the sponsor's products. This allows the distributor to sell national spots to advertisers who are willing to pay a premium to reach potential customers.

National clearance:	65%
Rating:1 (assume 1% of 98,000,000 homes, or 980,000 men 18–49)	
CPM:	$10.00
Price per 30-second spot (980 × $10):	$9,800
Gross advertising revenues for six 30-second spots (before deduction of ad agency's 15% commission):	$58,800
Deduct 15% ad agency commission:	($8,820)
Net advertising revenues after commission:	$49,980
Weekly income from British version:	$5,000
Net weekly revenues:	$54,980
Production costs/week:	($30,000)
Average marketing costs/week:	($5,000)
Distribution costs/week (33% of net weekly revenues):	($16,490)
Net weekly profit:	$3,490

Note that there is no cash license fee. The commercial time is split 50/50 between the distributor and the station so that each has seven 30-second spots to sell per week.

SYNDICATION OF OFF-NETWORK SERIES

Off-network series get the biggest ratings in the syndication marketplace, but for syndicators, they may not be as profitable as a series in which a greater number of barter spots can be sold. In fact, because the marketplace is so competitive, some off-network series are not syndicated at all; instead, they are sold to cable networks (this process is far simpler: it typically involves only a cash license fee). A top-rated off-network series, like *ER,* fetched more than $1 million per episode from TNT. USA paid over $700,00 for *Walker: Texas Ranger* and Lifetime paid $600,000 for *Ellen,* two good examples of proven properties likely to match the current demographic profile of these two cable networks. The number of runs per episode on a commercial network is typically two; on a cable network, it may be more like ten. Currently, three-year deals are common, but as prices soar for the best properties, cable networks may also demand longer terms. As the cable business continues to evolve, cash-plus-barter deals are likely to become common as well.

With cable networks often owned by large media companies, there is a tendency to try to keep a successful series "in the family." FOX, for example, kept both *The X-Files* and *NYPD Blue* inside as the fX network outbid rival cable networks for the exclusive off-network rights to these top-rated series. Both of these series are also sold by Twentieth Television (another FOX entity-owned operation) into broadcast syndication.

Public Television

Non-commercial broadcasting dates back to the 1920s, when some colleges started radio stations. Later realizing the value of their right to broadcast on government-assigned frequencies, or licenses, many colleges sold their properties to commercial ventures. In 1927, 98 non-commercial radio stations were on the air; in 1945, there were just 25. Relying on contributions and grants alone, most stations could barely support themselves—and in most instances, no other means of support was available.

As television took shape, there were grand plans for programs that would teach children, and educate the general public. And when the FCC lifted its freeze on new television station licenses in 1952 (see page 42), the FCC licensed 80 VHF and 162 UHF non-commercial educational television stations. Later, the number was increased to a total of 600 allotments.

Non-commercial television began in 1953 when KUHT went on the air in Houston, Texas. For the next 15 years, non-commercial stations started up in most of the nation's largest markets. Programming was predominantly educational, with some children's, cultural, and arts programming as well. Financial support was elusive. There was no uniform system for financing non-commercial broadcasting, so individual stations devised their own schemes for raising money.

Through the early 1960s, the idea of a viable alternative to commercial television became a political agenda item. Different factions favored a new network whose programs would be cultural, educational, local, national, politically involved, politically uninvolved, and so on—depending upon the organization behind the plan.

A series of events in 1967 changed everything. First, the Carnegie Commission on Educational Television (CCET) completed a two-year study recommending that Congress establish a non-commercial television system with a broader view than the old educational concept—a service that would be renamed public television. The new service would not be educational (the word "educational" was deemed somber and static in the report). The new public television would include an improved form of instructional or classroom television during the day, and high-quality general interest programs in the evening. CCET also recommended that existing non-commercial stations be joined in a network that would be supported by federal funds.

Many of the commission's suggestions were made a part of the Public Broadcasting Act of 1967, which structured ongoing federal support for the new public broadcasting system.

CORPORATION FOR PUBLIC BROADCASTING (CPB)

The Corporation for Public Broadcasting was created by an act of Congress, The Public Broadcasting Act of 1967. CPB, in turn, created the Public Broadcasting Service (PBS) in 1969 and National Public Radio (NPR) in 1970. Proposed by CCET, the new CPB was supposed to serve as a buffer between the government and the new PBS (see below). It has served that purpose, although the original CCET concept of a board of directors composed of government appointees and private citizens was changed to a board composed entirely of government appointees. The result has been a closer relationship between the federal government and public television than was originally intended. CPB's principal role is the distribution of an annual congressional appropriation to public television stations and producers. In addition, according to the Public Broadcasting Act of 1967, CPB has the following responsibilities: encouraging the development of a wide range of program suppliers; maintaining high-quality program standards; assuring balanced reporting on controversial topics; interconnecting stations in a network that allows stations to program and schedule in accordance with local desires; nurturing new station development; conducting research and training; and operating a program archive. In its day-to-day operations, CPB's principal activities are the funding of new programs that air on PBS, funding for station activities, and funding NPR. CPB is the largest single source of funding for public television programming, generally in three broad subject areas: news and public affairs, cultural and children's, and drama and arts.

CPB works closely with PBS to determine which programs are to be funded, and how much money will be apportioned for each project. CPB's total annual budget is a congressional appropriation; in fiscal year 1996, it totaled $275 million.

CPB is the largest single source of funding for the development of public television programs. In 1996, CPB provided partial funding for numerous children's and educational programs including the daily children's series *The Charlie Horse Music Pizza* ($67,000); the three-hour mini-series *Children in America's Schools* ($300,000); the third season (20 episodes) of the hard-issue teen journalism series *In the Mix* ($365,000); the one-shot *Lamb Chop's Special Passover* ($115,000; the second season (20 episodes) of *The Puzzle Place;* and the first season (65 episodes) of *Where in Time Is Carmen Sandiego?* In the same year, contributions to cultural, art and drama series included *American Visions* mini-series (8 episodes; $500,000); *The Face of Russia* (a three-part mini-series; $15,000); a documentary called *Family Name,* about slavery in America ($75,000); the *National Memorial Day and Capitol Fourth Concerts at the U.S. Capitol* (a pair of specials; $300,000 total); and many other series (a complete list of all CPB contributions appears on its Web site: http://www.cpb.org). Monies were also paid for various news and public-affairs programs.

CPB also funds other initiatives. *Ready to Learn,* for example, helps preschool children in preparation for elementary school through a variety of media including television, workshops, books, educational materials, and workshops for teachers and families.

In 1981, Walter Annenberg (who made his fortune by publishing *TV Guide*) funded the Annenberg/CPB Project. Based on the success-ful Open University model in the U.K. (http://www.open.ac.uk), the new venture's goal was to extend the educational reach of public television by supporting college-level education. This was accomplished by distance learning (courses via television, for example), and by open access to the course work (no admission requirements). The project also promotes the use of technology in education. In 1991, the Annenberg/CPB Math and Science Project was added to help schools and communities improve their elementary and secondary math and science programs. The result-ing programming includes documentaries, televised college courses, panel discussions and other formats. Some Annenberg/CPB programs have been quite popular (such as *Race to Save the Planet, The Brain,* and *The Constitution: That Delicate Balance*). Some lesser-knowns *(French In Action,* for example) have also been extremely effective.

PUBLIC BROADCASTING SERVICE (PBS)

The Public Broadcasting Service, or PBS, is the network that the Public Broadcasting Act required CPB to create. PBS debuted in 1970, with 12 hours of programming per week provided by National Educational Television (NET).

The network concept did not last long. The Nixon administration, dismayed by a perceived liberal bias in news and information programs on public television, stymied the network's growth by vetoing a significant funding measure. To further limit the power of a potentially unfriendly network, the administration forced PBS to reorganize in 1973, decentralizing the power center and strengthening individual stations. PBS became a membership organization, funded largely by dues paid by member stations. Under the 1973 Partnership Agreement, CPB was required to allocate a specific portion of its budget—roughly 50 percent—to local stations.

Although the ways in which money travels between CPB, PBS, and PBS member stations is somewhat convoluted, member stations ultimately finance PBS by providing more than 85 percent of PBS's annual operating budget. The remaining 15 percent comes from ancillary revenues—including the sale, rental, and licensing of PBS programs to institutions such as schools and hospitals—and from a satellite-based data delivery system. Less than 2 percent of PBS's annual budget comes directly from CPB.

PBS is the foremost distributor of programming to public television stations (but not the only one; see below). The PBS National Program Service acquires the programs distributed by PBS and broadcast on PBS member stations. PBS does not produce its own programming; instead, it provides partial funding to producers. Programs are produced by member stations, other domestic and international broadcasters, and independent producers.

PBS program operations are divided into three groups: Children's & Cultural, News & Public Affairs, and Acquisitions (which acquires only completed programs). Each group works closely with program suppliers in the development and financing of acquisitions and new productions. There is a difference in approach between a program executive at PBS and one at a commercial network, however. Unlike their network counterparts, PBS program executives provide guidance of a general nature but are not deeply involved in creative or production decisions.

Most viewers perceive PBS to be a television network, and an increasing number of decisions regarding program pick-up and renewal are made at the national level. As A&E, The History

Channel, The Discovery Channel, HGTV, The Learning Channel, Food Network, Nickelodeon, Nick Jr., and other cable networks nibble off pieces of PBS's distinctive programming profile, centralized network-style decision-making is a reasonable strategy.

PBS ORGANIZATION

PBS is organized in three divisions. Programming Services operates the national program service, the Ready to Learn Service, and coordinates fund-raising activities. Strategic and Systems Services handles the physical and technical aspects of program distribution, station relations, program promotion, and technical R&D. Learning Ventures operates an adult learning service (ALS; see below), PBS Teacher Resources, PBS Online, and PBS Learning Media (which includes PBS Home Video). In short, the first two groups handle typical network functions (although few networks would cluster program promotion and technical services in a single unit). PBS also operates a for-profit subsidiary called PBS Enterprises.

Adult Learning Service (ALS) provides adult learners with education via television. Courses are shown on public television stations, and anyone may watch for their own enjoyment. Approximately 370,000 students pay tuition to colleges and universities each year to participate in this coordinated effort between PBS, member stations, and area colleges. Going the Distance is another ALS venture, in which public television helps adult learners to earn college degrees through distance learning and televised course work. It's a partnership between PBS, local public television stations, and colleges and universities.

K-12 Learning Services acquires and distributes programming on public television stations for classroom use. Most stations supply schools with support materials provided by program producers and community organizations. Many stations also transmit classroom programming after midnight so that schools can record the programs and replay them when needed.

PBS Enterprises develops goods and services, mainly related to new technologies. Its National Datacast, Inc., subsidiary uses an invisible portion of the broadcast signal to transmit data. PBS Engineering is an R&D group that works on behalf of the system; its accomplishments include the nation's first satellite distribution system, and the development of closed captioning.

PBS is also part of a joint venture devoted to business training and professional development. It's called The Business Channel, and it's a joint venture with Williams Communications (a high-tech company). The company is preparing for on-demand desktop video.

OTHER PUBLIC TELEVISION PROGRAM DISTRIBUTORS

PBS is not the only distributor of programs to public television stations. In fact, distribution of programs to public television stations is somewhat convoluted.

There are four types of programming seen on public television stations. One is "commissioned" programming. Individual stations pool programming funds, then hire a commissioning agent, such as PBS, to fund a particular type of production. Since the producer must arrange for additional funding, the producer must have access to corporate and foundation funds, and, often, to sources of ancillary revenue, such as international program sales, home video, or merchandising. WGBH, Boston and WNET, New York have been very successful public television producers because the organizations can put together the deals necessary to finance and produce public television programming. The task requires a skill set not found in most commercial production companies.

The "acquisition" path is akin to syndication. A producer works with a distributor to arrange for carriage of the program on public television stations. Although deals vary, the distributor takes about one-third of the monies paid by the stations as a commission. The producer retains all other monies and the rights to the program. This format has proven ideal for the distribution of completed programs, such as situation comedies from the U.K.

The "royalty free" approach essentially provides stations with free programming. With a sufficiently large audience, however, a clever producer can convince a commercial concern to become involved as a production underwriter. The commercial concern, let's say Cuisinart, gains considerable publicity for its product among the upscale, affluent, ready-to-buy public television viewers of a cooking program. In addition, the producer earns money by selling a cookbook at the end of each episode (the FCC's Second Report and Order permits the sale of program-related products of nominal cost).

A fourth approach is not often used. It's called "access," and the concept is related to a congressional regulation that provides access to the satellites used by public television by any reasonable third party. From time to time, a program will be distributed through the access system, but it's not typically carried by many stations.

PBS is involved, at least to some degree, in each of the four above businesses. APS, the American Program Service (based in Boston; it's the former EEN, or Eastern Educational Network), distributes a large number of the programs seen on public television, including movie packages, series once seen on the commercial networks, and Britcoms, the popular British situation comedies. SECA, the Southern Educational Communications Association (based in Columbia, South Carolina, and now including the former Pacific Mountain Network), and CEN, Central Education Network (based in Des Plaines, Illinois), are the other two major distributors. Independent producers, unaffiliated with stations, sometimes choose to distribute their programs through these companies. Generally, producers start with PBS, then go to APS, then to SECA and CEN. Available funds are the reason why.

PUBLIC TELEVISION STATIONS

In 1996, 173 non-commercial, educational licensees operated 345 PBS member stations. These stations are owned by approximately 190 entities. Some of these entities own a single station, like WXXI in Rochester, New York; some own a large station and a smaller one, like WQED and its sister WQEX, both in Pittsburgh; and some are regional networks that operate multiple stations of various sizes throughout a geographic area, such as a state (Kentucky Educational Television, New Hampshire Public Television, Maine Public Broadcasting Network, and Nebraska Educational Telecommunications Commission). Of the 173 licensees, 88 are community organizations (non-profit community groups, including local arts, cultural, educational, and civic organizations), 56 are colleges or universities, 21 are state authorities, and 8 are local educational or municipal authorities.

Each licensee operates as a stand-alone non-profit company. Most do not consider themselves to be PBS affiliates in anything like the commercial sense of the term, nor do they consider themselves to be PBS stations. This attitude reflects the grassroots individualism that developed during the Nixon years, and the fact that each station or group is responsible for its own financing and program decisions.

OVERALL FUNDING FOR PUBLIC TELEVISION

According to a 1994 funding analysis by CPB, public television's total income equals approximately $1.4 billion. The largest contributors of this income, each in the range of $200–300 million, were: CPB (whose money comes from the federal government), individual subscribers, state governments, and businesses. These four groups accounted for about 60 percent of public television income. State colleges contributed a total of just under $95 million, and foundations contributed just under $80 million. The remainder, from local governments, other public colleges, and private colleges added about $85 million more. Auctions contributed $20 million, and other sources completed the picture with an additional $85 million.

PBS is funded, in large part, by assessing member stations for programming and number of members. In 1996, this assessment totaled $108.6 million of the $167 million PBS budget. Another $20 million came from ALS, K-12 Learning Service, and PBS Video (home video) customers, and another $22 million came from CPB.

FUNDING FOR LOCAL STATIONS

Program funding comes from several sources. Although each station differs in its approach, the following is a reasonably representative model. Approximately 40 to 50 percent of station revenues comes directly from "Viewers Like You," people who watch and support public television. Federal and state government allocations add approximately 15 percent. Contributions from corporations and foundations, and from state organizations (such as a state council on the arts), add another 15 percent. Funding for specific program projects—from underwriters, PBS, CPB, the National Endowment for the Arts, the National Endowment for the Humanities, the National Science Foundation, and other sources—accounts for between 10 and 25 percent, depending upon specific project budgets. The remainder comes from auctions, special fund-raising events, subscription and advertising income from a monthly program guide, facilities leasing (renting television studios or editing rooms to outside producers), special funding grants for capital projects, local grant programs, and other miscellaneous sources.

Where does the money go? The biggest chunk—roughly 35 to 45 percent—pays for the acquisition and production of programming (many programs are jointly produced by multiple public television stations and other entities, including domestic and international producers and broadcasters). Another 20 to 25 percent pays for marketing, including advertising, public relations, the preparation of program listings, and special events to promote the station and its programs. Between 15 and 20 percent goes to the station's day-to-day operations: salaries, office expenses, and the maintenance of the physical plant. The remaining 10 to 30 percent goes to capital additions, debt retirement, cash reserves, and miscellaneous items. (There is considerable flexibility, and not much accountability, related to at least half of a station's budget; coincidentally, roughly half of the station's revenues are contributed by individual viewers).

Each public television station builds its own program schedule. At many stations, the prime-time schedule is taken intact from PBS, with few local variations. Some stations, including several in major markets, build their own schedules, placing at least some PBS programs wherever they please. This creates a tough situation for PBS, its producers and its underwriters. The general feeling is that a larger audience might be reached with consistent national program schedules, but this conflicts with the essentially local philosophy of most local public television stations (who, in contrast with their commercial counterparts, are deeply involved with community interests).

PRODUCTION AND FUNDING OF PROGRAMS FOR PUBLIC TELEVISION

In commercial television, most entertainment programs are produced in Los Angeles; most news and talk shows are produced in New York; and some news programs are produced in Washington, DC In public television, programs of all kinds are produced all over the country. Several stations are big contributors. At WGBH, Boston, success is measured in decades for *NOVA, The Victory Garden,* and *Evening at Pops;* other long-running series include *This Old House* (a co-production with Morash Associates), *Mystery!, The New Yankee Workshop, FRONTLINE, Masterpiece Theater,* and *The American Experience.* WGBH's children productions have included *ZOOM, Where in the World Is Carmen Sandiego?* (co-produced with WQED, Pittsburgh), and the animated series, *Arthur* (produced with Canada's CINAR animation production). The other large producing station is WNET, New York City, home of *Great Performances, American Masters, Nature,* and other popular series and specials. *The Charlie Rose Show* is not produced by WNET, but by Rose Communications; still, WNET presents the show to the system. Lots of other stations contribute regular series: for sixteen seasons, Maryland Public Television has produced *Motorweek;* WPBT, Miami produces the *Nightly Business Report.* WTTW, Chicago has been a consistent contributor, and so has South Carolina Public Television, among a great many others.

Each of these stations operates as a kind of production company. Some projects are created in-house by full-time personnel or free-lance producers; other programs are developed in association with outside producers or production companies. Stations that are active in national programming maintain a full-time staff to develop and nurture properties, and to arrange funding. Station executives pitch the project to CPB, PBS, corporate underwriters, foundations, and other sources. If the project is worthy (and fortunate), further development or production begins.

The project budget is likely to include more than the physical cost of production, however. Other costs include closed captioning, outreach marketing to schools or community groups, and promotional marketing. Because PBS is not quite a network, PBS has no significant network promotion budget, so each program must pay for its own advertising, public relations, and promotion. In order to fund its national program activities, the producing station takes a markup (usually called station overhead) of approximately 20 percent of the overall project cost. When added together, these additional costs can add as much as one-third to the program's cost.

PRODUCTION COMPANIES

Many programs seen on public television are produced by the stations, but some, notably *Sesame Street* from Children's Television Workshop (CTW), are produced by production companies. (CTW is now in a new network joint venture called Noggin with Nickelodeon.) Other production companies active in public television include MacNeil-Lehrer Productions *(The NewsHour with Jim Lehrer)*, Lancit Media *(Puzzle Place* and *Reading Rainbow)*, Big Feats! Entertainment *(Wishbone)*, Ken Burns Films *(The Civil War, Baseball)*, Family Communications *(Mister Rogers Neighborhood)* and Globalvision (various *Frontline* episodes). As public television continues to evolve, an increasing number of production companies historically associated with commercial television are becoming suppliers to PBS.

Independent producers may work directly with PBS, CPB, or member stations in the development and production of new projects. The advantage of working with a station is clout: maneuvering through the sometimes byzantine process of garnering support among other member stations is nearly impossible for most producers to do without a station partner.

AUDIENCE MEASUREMENT AND PROGRAM SUCCESS

Public television is non-commercial, so ratings do not guide programming decisions. Still, public television enjoys the most impact when large numbers of interested viewers tune in. The most popular public television programs are typically seen by 10–15 million households. The most popular PBS programs have been *Carreras Domingo Pavarotti (The Three Tenors in Concert)*, various episodes of *The Civil War,* some National Geographic specials, and some presidential election coverage.

A strong special, such as *Les Miserables in Concert,* one of the Three Tenors performances, or *Yanni in Concert: Live at the Acropolis,* can be important for another reason: it can draw a larger-than-average audience during a fund drive. Highly-regarded self-help speakers, such as Deepak Chopra and John Bradshaw, also draw large numbers of viewers. Public television stations depend upon viewer contributions for about half of their annual revenues.

FUNDING FOR NATIONAL PRODUCTIONS

Finding money to produce and promote public television projects is a major challenge for all concerned. The process frequently involves piecing together financing from a variety of sources to make up the total, with one or more entities carrying a deficit—a deficit that may not be easily recouped. Funding sources for a typical national program break down as follows (with varying ratios depending upon the particular program): corporate grants, 15 percent of the annual production budget; PBS, 40 percent; CPB, 30 percent; the Challenge Fund, government grants, and endowments, 10 percent; and foundation grants, 5 percent.

Programs with commercial value in other channels of distribution may be partially financed by motion picture companies—many *American Playhouse* productions have been financed this way. The upfront sale of home video rights may also contribute to the production budget. And as the international marketplace continues to grow, an increasing number of public television projects are being produced with international partners providing co-production financing.

Although the majority of productions funded by grants are initiated by the producer, some projects begin with a foundation or endowment seeking, for example, to establish a national forum (dance, arts for children, and so on).

FUNDING FROM OTHER GOVERNMENT AGENCIES

Some federal agencies contribute to specific public television projects. The National Endowment for the Arts (NEA), for example, provides partial funding for *Great Performances, American Playhouse,* and *Live from Lincoln Center,* and for limited series such as *American Visions* (the Robert Hughes series about American art). The National Endowment for the Humanities (NEH) grants production dollars for *The American Experience;* and more recently, for Ken Burns' *The West.* The National Science Foundation (NSF) provided funding for the popular children's series, *The Magic School Bus.* Sometimes, these foundations will work together with other organizations, as the NSF did with National Institutes of Health (NIH) on *The Brain.* Some of these grants must be matched by monies from other sources, frequently dollar for dollar.

FUNDING FROM PRIVATE CHARITIES AND FOUNDATIONS

Private foundations and trusts contribute a relatively small percentage of the overall public television production budget, but their contributions have been essential to financing such public television staples as *Sesame Street, The American Experience,* and special series like *The Civil War.* Charities and foundations often support local public television stations, or local plays of national programs, as well as other initiatives.

CORPORATE FUNDING

In this era of corporate downsizing and careful attention to stock prices, the funding of public television programs is not a priority for many companies. Fuel and transportation companies, for many years the most significant funders of arts programming, have cut back their involvement. Mobil continues to fund *Masterpiece Theater* and *Mystery!,* but Exxon, Texaco, and Gulf are no longer in the mix. Ford funds *Washington Week in Review,* and GM money is often behind specials (Ken Burns' *Thomas Jefferson,* for example). For several years, Toyota and Delta Air Lines funded *Where in the World Is Carmen Sandiego?,* but the sole funder in the startup season of *Where in Time Is Carmen Sandiego?* was Delta Air Lines. Some smaller companies have become active: *This Old House,* for example, is funded by ACE Hardware, State Farm Insurance, and the Glidden Company. *Evening at Pops* receives funds from Fidelity Investments and an unusual source: the Massachusetts Office of Travel and Tourism. Some series continue to appeal to large corporations. *NOVA,* for example, is funded by Merck and Prudential. But names like these are seen less frequently on PBS than in the past. And the size of their contributions rarely cover even half the production budget.

Rules (see below) regarding the connection between content and corporate sponsorship are no longer as strict. *The New Yankee*

Workshop is partially supported by funding from several companies in the home improvement business: the Thompson Miniwax Company; Delta Machinery Corporation, manufacturers of quality woodworking machinery and accessories; and Porter-Cable, manufacturers of professional, portable electric power tools.

Local corporations also support local public television stations, and airings of particular series and programs.

PBS FUNDING OF INDIVIDUAL PROGRAMS

Under a funding system begun in 1990, the head of programming for the entire PBS system decides which programs will be funded by PBS. The 1995 National Program Service fund was $310.5 million. This paid for approximately 1,600 hours of original programming. Some statistics: 50 percent of those 1,600 hours were public-affairs shows; 17 percent were cultural and arts programs; 18 percent were children's programs; 7 percent were how-to programs; 5 percent were science and nature programs; and 0.1 percent were college courses. Just shy of 33 percent of the money went to public television stations working with independent producers, 29 percent went directly to independent producers, 28 percent was paid to producing stations, 7 percent was paid to foreign producers, and the other 2 percent or so was paid to various combinations of stations, producers and production companies who did not fit tidily into the other categories.

PBS RULES REGARDING PROGRAM FINANCING

PBS strictly limits the ways in which production financing can be arranged, and the ways that the financing sources may be credited. This may be an issue for any funding source, but it is especially important for corporate funders. The philosophy behind these rules encourages public television to maintain its non-commercial image in the minds of viewers (and legislators), and to ensure that editorial control of the program cannot be surrendered in exchange for financing. In other words, airtime cannot be traded for any form of sponsorship or financing.

A comprehensive document, *PBS National Program Funding Standards and Practices,* is available from PBS. The following paraphrases many of its important rules:

- There can be no perception of a commercial relationship between the funder and the content of the program. This can be a judgment call, depending in part on the sensitivity of the issues involved. A major camera company can fund a photography how-to series, provided that its products are not prominently featured—but a major oil company funding a series on environmental conservation might not be acceptable.

- The funder may not affect the producer's decisions about script or topic selection, casting, or the choice of staff members—nor may the funder or its representatives attend editing sessions.

- The funder may not hold the copyright to the program. Furthermore, the funder cannot claim any future distribution rights, since a funder's plans for future exploitation of these rights might affect the content of the PBS program.

- Funding cannot be provided by the manufacturers or marketers of cigarettes or distilled spirits.

- On-air underwriting credits are subject to the overall test of whether the credit is consistent with the non-commercial nature of public television, [and] consistent with the individual guidelines in credit elements.

The appropriate form for underwriters is outlined in some detail in the standards and practices document:

- The name of the funder must be preceded only by a generic and non-promotional phrase. Something akin to "the people of [Company]" is acceptable, but "the experts at [Company]" is not.

- A credit can include a brief audio or video clip, but only if it is not blatantly commercial. Well-known people (such as a company spokesperson) cannot be incorporated into credits, but general employee shots are allowed. A corporate mascot or logo like the Merrill Lynch bull is acceptable, but not mascots or logos associated with specific brands or products (Tony the Tiger for Kellogg's Frosted Flakes). One brand-name product can be shown and identified by audio, but it cannot be demonstrated or shown in operation. Up to three target markets can be mentioned (a company can say it makes computers for home, office, and education).

- Funding credits may appear at the beginning of a program, *must* appear at the end, and should generally run 10 to 15 seconds long for each underwriter. A total of no more than 30 seconds can be allotted to underwriter credits.

- Credits given in exchange for services—transportation provided by American Airlines—may be incorporated into the normal production credits, and are not subject to the 30-second limitation.

Producers are encouraged to minimize clutter and to keep these credits brief.

• A program producer or distributor's credit may appear in the traditional end-of-show position (Children's Television Workshop).

There are many nuances, and some inconsistencies, so public television program producers are always wise to check with PBS Program Business Affairs before making commitments for under-writing credits. There are special rules regarding programs that will be seen by children—that is, programs shown during daytime hours—as well as rules regarding the print advertising and promotion of programs shown on PBS.

LICENSING REVENUES FROM CHILDREN'S PROGRAMS

Sesame Street is one of the world's most valuable merchandise licenses. Over 5,000 different *Sesame Street* products worldwide generate over $800 million per year in retail sales; perhaps $100 million of those dollars return to CTW, the company behind *Sesame Street*. The license that caught journalists' notice, and caused PBS to be more careful about management of licensing revenues, was Barney. In 1994, Forbes called Barney one of the three wealthiest U.S. entertainers, second only to Oprah Winfrey and Steven Spielberg. Barney's two-year retail merchandise gross in 1994–95 was estimated at $500 million. By comparison, Thomas the Tank Engine grossed about $250 million annually. *Arthur,* in its first year with a significant number of licensed products in the marketplace, should gross up to $100 million. Assuming a 50 percent wholesale price on these items, and a 10 percent (of wholesale) return to the licensee, $100 million in retail sales should return $5 million to the licensee. In the case of public television, this would likely be shared among the original license holder (the creator, author, etc.), and the producer (or producing station), with a commission paid to the licensing agent (several firms specialize in connecting buyers and sellers). In the real world, where most licenses don't earn Barney-style revenues, licensing revenues are used to subsidize production. According to a *New York Times* report (September 24, 1997), WGBH was $2 million short of its $12 million budget for the first 30 half-hour episodes of *Arthur,* and was hoping that merchandise license royalties would make up the deficit. A bona fide hit series changes everything, of course.

5

Cable Systems

Cable television began as community antenna TV (CATV). In the early 1950s, some towns found that their reception was limited because of mountains and other obstructions that blocked incoming television broadcast signals. Local entrepreneurs constructed mountaintop antennas and charged a monthly subscription fee for access to the improved signals. Since these cable systems were not subject to the same technical limitations as broadcast television, every channel could be filled.[1] CATV operators began filling their empty channels. A system in San Diego, for example, imported stations from nearby Los Angeles; some channels showed local productions (called "local origination" or "local O").

From the early 1950s until the mid-1970s, cable television grew slowly. In most parts of the country, viewers were satisfied with their reception; the appeal of an independent station imported from a nearby city was limited because syndication was still in its early days, and program choices were generally undistinguished. In short, there was no real product for cable operators to sell beyond improved reception. The FCC limited cable's growth as well. In 1965—with 1,325 cable systems and 1.2 million subscribers in place—the FCC issued its First Report and Order, saying any significant risk from CATV competition that could destroy or seriously degrade the service offered by a television broadcaster would be prevented by the FCC.

The report included a Notice of Inquiry and Notice of Proposed Rule-Making. Restrictive rules were soon adopted which effectively

---

1 On broadcast television, most adjacent channels are not permitted because of possible interference. This is why, for example, channels 2 and 4 are used in New York, and channel 3—but neither 2 nor 4—is used in nearby Philadelphia.

prevented operators in the top 100 markets from importing signals from other markets. In addition, the FCC required that any microwave facility bringing a distant signal into a market with four or more channels had to present "a clear and substantial showing that in the particular case a grant would not pose a substantial threat to UHF service in the area."

Cable operators and broadcasters were in and out of the courts through the 1960s and early 1970s, challenging these rules, their copyright implications, and the FCC's jurisdiction. The FCC modified and amended its regulations several times, gradually moving from a stance that favored broadcasters to one that encouraged the growth of cable. (See Chapter 13 for a further discussion of the development of cable regulation.)

The mid-1970s brought a complete turnaround. With changes in FCC rules, cable systems were built in some large and medium-sized cities, and the number of national cable households began to grow. In the same period, RCA and Western Union launched satellites that could be used to distribute programming to cable television systems. Cable operators had an abundance of channel capacity, and as more systems were built, large companies and intrepid smaller ones began renting satellite time to beam programming from cable networks to local systems equipped with receiving dishes.

Home Box Office (a made-for-cable service) and WTCG (an independent television station in Atlanta, since renamed WTBS) were among the first cable services to be distributed nationally, in 1976, via RCA's Satcom I. Five years later, more than a dozen satellite networks were available to cable operators and viewers, including CNN, Showtime, The Movie Channel, CBN, C-SPAN, Cinemax, ESPN, Nickelodeon, and many smaller part-time networks. By the mid-1980s, enough new networks had been added—MTV, VH1, The Disney Channel, The Weather Channel— that new services were fighting for what became a limited number of channels on most cable systems (most early cable systems supported only a dozen channels). Today, the trend is toward building or rebuilding systems with capacity for 100 channels or more, but problems with channel capacity continue to limit the development and short-term success of new networks.

GROWTH OF CABLE SUBSCRIBERS

Although industry estimates vary, approximately 63 million households now subscribe to cable television; this cable penetration is approximately equal to 66 percent of U.S. television households. Subscribers are served by 11,220 cable systems nationwide. On average, 2 million households have been added every year since 1980. For most of this period, cable has grown without competition. Direct-to-home satellites (see Chapter 14) may eventually affect cable's growth, but this trend is not yet evident.

CABLE FRANCHISES

The technology of cable television requires a hard-wired connection between the transmitting facility ("head end") and each household. Cables must run through varied terrain, and through various rights of way. For this reason, as well as the desire of local municipalities to assure their constituents the best possible cable service, the municipal government controls and regulates local cable television operation. One or more cable companies apply for the right to provide service to each community. Each submits a proposal which includes an explanation of the technical capabilities of the system, the channels that will be offered, the channel capacity of the system (at start-up and with future expansion), the rate schedule, the construction schedule, and background on the company and the individuals involved.

After a period of study (and lobbying by the cable operators), a franchise is awarded to one company, typically to provide service for a 15-year period. The franchise is a form of contract. If the cable company does not comply with the terms of the contract—does not, for example, lay cables in poorer areas, or offer the number of channels promised—the franchise may be challenged or, in rare instances, revoked. Cable franchises are generally awarded on a non-exclusive basis, but because of the expense involved, nearly all municipalities are served by cable companies that operate as monopolies. (See Chapter 13 for more details on cable franchises.)

ORGANIZATION OF A LOCAL CABLE OPERATION

Most cable systems are owned by multiple system owners, or MSOs (see page 66), and operated locally by a general manager. System size varies widely: the largest, in New York City, serves just over 1 million subscribers, and most city systems serve 100,000–200,000 subscribers. It's not unusual to find a city segmented so that, for instance, the north side is served by one cable system and the south side by another.

Decisions about which channels the system should carry are usually made by a national programming director, though the unique requirements of certain markets (a higher-than-average number of Hispanics, for example) could alter those national decisions. Independently owned cable systems are also run by a general manager, and make their own program decisions; all departments report to the GM.

The largest department is usually marketing or sales/marketing. The local cable business requires an ongoing marketing relationship with each individual subscriber. The initial sell is done by direct marketing, either by mail, or by phone, or in scattered circumstances, in person. Maintaining current subscribers, and encouraging them to add pay services, cable boxes on second and third sets, remote controls and other features, and to purchase pay-per-view programs, are the objectives of most marketing departments. Their media includes monthly bill stuffers, telemarketing, advertising on local media, a monthly cable guide, as well as advertisements on local cable channels.

Local systems do not edit or publish their own cable guides; the task of assembling program information from each channel is too costly. *The Cable Guide* is one of several monthly publications that cable companies can purchase at bulk rate, adding a line on the cover to associate what is essentially a national magazine with their own local system. Guides are mailed by the publisher.

The quality of customer service also affects the percentage of subscribers who leave the system (as in any subscription business, this is called the "churn rate"). Customer service representatives respond to questions about programming, service, and billing.

The operation of the cable system's physical plant involves maintenance and upgrading of satellite and terrestrial equipment. A cable company's head end is a master control facility where incoming satellite signals are received, then automatically assigned to channels on the system. The head end may also include a videotape playback facility where local commercials play from racks of tape machines, and where locally originated program sources are fed from tape machines or computers. Such sources may include an on-air program guide (again, this is most often purchased from a national packager who customizes for each market), or a classified ad channel. The installation and maintenance of the cable system itself—running cables to new locations, repairing line problems, and connecting individual households to the system—is usually a separate department in larger operations.

Two more departments are now commonplace, even among the smallest cable systems. The advertising sales department sells commercial spots to local merchants, and frequently produces commercials for its clients. Rates are set locally, based on what the market will bear. A production department may employ several producers, directors, and studio crews to produce original programming, such as coverage of local sporting events.

Public access is also a part of some systems, frequently as a result of a promise made in the franchise proposal to dedicate one or more channels for this purpose. Typically, a local producer or entrepreneur purchases a block of time on a public access channel, sells time to commercial sponsors, and uses some or all of the proceeds to cover the cost of production. Additional money can be made by selling products to viewers. If the program is unsponsored (many public access programs are non-commercial), production resources are generally supplied by a school, by the cable system (as part of the franchise agreement), or by an organization whose marketing interests are served by supporting specific types of public-access programs. Public-access programs and the financial practices associated with them are essentially unregulated, and there has been some controversy about the use of public-access channels for programs that feature nudity and break other taboos. Most cable systems self-regulate their public-access channels. Some claim freedom of speech as a defense for programs that may be offensive; local community groups or municipal government officials may take action in these situations and seek to influence the cable operation's program policies.

With channel capacity so precious, many local access channels have been eliminated in favor of national program services.

HOW A CABLE SYSTEM MAKES MONEY

The financial basis of a local cable franchise is essentially a wholesale/retail relationship. The operator of a cable system pays each cable network a monthly fee in the range of 5 to 40 cents per subscriber per month. The operator bundles together approximately two dozen networks, adds the local broadcast stations (sometimes with improved reception), and sells the package to subscribers as "basic cable" for about $20–25, taking a markup of 100 percent or more (the wholesale price would be about half that amount). The cost of basic service may be considerably higher or lower, of course, depending on local company policy, with some federal constraints (see page 143). Many cable networks offer channels to the operator in a barter arrangement that exchanges the program schedule for an increased number of viewers—viewers who will subsequently be sold to advertisers by the network. Pay services are even more profitable to the system operator: the wholesale price per subscriber per month is about $4–$5, and the retail price to subscribers is usually $8–$9.

Given a small system with 10,000 subscribers, with a pay channel like HBO in 25 percent of households, the monthly revenues for a cable system after paying the per-subscriber charges to the basic networks, would be 10,000 × $10 for the basic service (assuming a $10 wholesale price), or $100,000. HBO service, after deducting the HBO charge, would yield 10,000 × .25 × $4, or an additional $10,000, for a total of $110,000. From this amount, the cable system would cover operating costs and capital recovery. With a second and third pay channel (such as Cinemax and Showtime) in 15 percent of the households, the monthly revenues would increase by roughly 3,000 households × $8, yielding an additional $24,000.

Between one-third and one-half of a cable system's income goes to programming costs; up to one-third goes to payroll costs (including marketing and distribution); and up to the final third, to marketing, administration, operations, and profit.

MULTIPLE SYSTEM OPERATORS (MSOS)

Some cable systems are still locally owned and operated, but most are owned by larger companies that control dozens or even hundreds of systems. The top 20 Multiple System Operators (MSOs) serve about 55 million households, or 83 percent of all cable households.

As of late 1996, the leading MSOs were TCI (Tele-Communications Inc.) with 15 million subscribers; Time Warner with 12 million; Continental Cablevision with 4.2 million; Comcast Corporation with 3.4 million; Cox Communications with 3.2 million; and Cablevision Systems with 2.8 million. Adelphia Cable Communications, Jones Intercable, Marcus Cable, Century Communications, Viacom Cable, The Lenfest Group, and Falcon Cable TV each serve over 1 million subscribers.

As the larger MSOs have grown, they have exerted increasing control over the development of the programming services. At first, MSOs encouraged the growth of promising new services by making channels available even before the services were up and running. In time, MSOs also became investors in new services, often using access to their subscriber bases as a negotiating point.

TCI, the country's largest MSO, has spun off Liberty Media Corporation to manage its part ownership of cable networks, including all of the Time Warner channels (TNT, TBS, HBO, CNN,

Cartoon Network, CNN Headline News, Cinemax, Turner Classic Movies), plus Court TV, The Discovery Channel, E! Entertainment Television, and others. Time Warner also owns one of the largest MSOs. Cablevision Systems owns the nation's largest cable operation (in Nassau and Suffolk counties outside New York City), and several others in large urban areas on the East Coast. The company also owns 75 percent of American Movie Classics, plus large stakes in some smaller networks, regional SportsChannel operations (now affiliated with FOX Sports), MSG Network (the second largest regional sports network, also a FOX Sports affiliate), Madison Square Garden, the New York Knicks, and the New York Rangers. It also operates Radio City Music Hall, and owns a consumer electronics chain called Nobody Beats the Wiz.

Historically, legislators, regulators, and the courts have not permitted distributors of radio, television, or motion picture product to own the companies which provide their "software." Two examples: the Supreme Court ordered the motion picture studios to sell their theaters in 1948, and the television networks were required to sell off their syndication operations in 1970. (Today, Sony is again in the production and exhibition business.) The current government and business climate has permitted large companies, such as Time Warner and TCI, to own not only the programming but the distribution system. Whether this signals a change in government policy, or a temporary situation that will eventually result in mandatory divestiture, remains to be seen.

THE GROWING STRENGTH OF LOCAL CABLE SYSTEMS

Many cable systems sell advertising time to local sponsors—in local breaks in the MTV, Weather Channel, ESPN, and CNN schedules, for example. Since no reliable rating system exists to determine viewership of individual cable channels on individual cable systems (see Chapter 41), rates are largely negotiable, and the market is limited. When rating information becomes available, cable will probably become a competitive local advertising medium, taking business away from newspapers, billboards, and local radio and television stations.

Cable also presents an unusual opportunity to advertise to a very specific geographic area at a relatively low cost. In a suburban town of 10,000 subscribers, a commercial on the cable system can be an extremely effective way to reach new customers for a car dealership, supermarket, or ice cream parlor. Some cable systems have linked up to provide advertisers with tens and even hundreds of thousands of subscribers within a geographic region.

In Rochester, New York, Time Warner created the cable equivalent of a local television station, WGRC. This station buys programming, produces a news program, and sells advertising as if it was a broadcaster. In other cities and towns, cable operators have petitioned the broadcast networks for status as affiliates in areas where there are not enough broadcast station allocations to support ABC, CBS, NBC, PBS, and a FOX affiliate. Warner Brothers Network's WeB TV turns the concept around, encouraging affiliation with cable operators where no broadcast station is available (see page 18).

DIGITAL CABLE

One of the constant problems plaguing the growth of cable television has been the lack of channel capacity. Cable operators increase revenues mostly as a result of offering new channels—but technology has limited this option. Digital systems, now being tested, will eventually allow cable operators to send as many as 14 digital channels through the same "pipes"—the same coaxial cables with the same available bandwidth—and through compression (and some reduction in picture quality), they'll be able to offer many more channels.

For the viewer, this is likely to cause an increase in cable bills (which is the whole idea, from the cable operator's perspective), and, of course, more viewing options. From an advertiser's perspective, the situation could cause even more fragmentation of the television audience—an advantage for reaching specific audience segments. It's difficult to predict the result of 100-plus cable channels in every household, but within the next five to ten years, this situation is likely to be commonplace.

An increasing number of cable operators are selling fast Internet service through "cable modems," too.

6

Basic Cable Networks

In today's media universe, some cable networks have overwhelmed their competition on broadcast networks (Nickelodeon), become the video equivalent of household appliances (The Weather Channel), and developed significant worldwide brands (Nickelodeon, CNN, The Discovery Channel). In short, cable networks have not only matured, they have reinvented television throughout the world. (See Chapter 40 about television brand development and marketing.)

Most cable networks are owned by large media/entertainment companies. Viacom owns MTV, Nickelodeon, VH1, Showtime, and The Movie Channel. Time Warner owns TNT, TBS, HBO, CNN, CNN Headline News, Cartoon Network, Cinemax, and Turner Classic Movies, and owns part of Comedy Central, Court TV, and BET. CBS owns The Nashville Network and Country Music TV. Disney/ABC owns The Disney Channel, but also owns most of ESPN and ESPN2, half of Lifetime, and just over a third of A&E and The History Channel. Big-company ownership of significant media properties is not new; many of these networks were started by large companies in hopes of a rich cable future. Some companies remain entrepreneurial, but are now large companies: Discovery Communications, for example, owns not only The Discovery Channel, but also The Learning Channel, Animal Planet, and various interactive ventures. Only a small number of players remain specialized: Landmark Communications, owner of The Weather Channel, is one of a now-small number of examples.

BASIC CABLE NETWORKS

There are two types of cable networks: basic and pay. Basic cable networks are generally provided to subscribers as part of a lower-priced monthly package, and generally include commercials. Pay cable networks are generally made available on premium-priced tiers, or sold à la carte, and do not generally interrupt programming with commercials (the exceptions are the pay sports networks, which are premium services that do show commercials).

Although there are some variations, a basic cable network is a 24-hour advertiser-supported program service. The most successful cable networks reach about two-thirds of U.S. television households. Some cable networks, such as superstations, offer general-interest programming, with dayparts appealing to children, sports fans, and so on. Most cable networks are more targeted; they program only children's programs, or news, or sports, or weather.

As of late 1996, there were over 150 cable networks in the U.S., with many more in development. Only a few dozen are well-known. Fewer than 20 percent of U.S. cable households can receive more than 50 channels on their cable system. This total includes local broadcast signals (figure one each for NBC, CBS, ABC, FOX, UPN and WB, plus two PBS stations), so the number of channels available is likely to be no more than 40; as many as one-third of a cable system's channels must be used for retransmitting local broadcast channels, for municipal use, or for leased access (often, to home shopping services).

Major MSOs, who essentially control the cable business, dole out channels with considerable business savvy. Established channels assess a monthly per-subscriber license fee from MSOs, and this, in combination with commercial advertising, accounts for the bulk of their domestic revenues. As TBS changed from superstation to basic cable network in 1998, the network charged MSOs 25 cents per subscriber per month; by comparison, USA Network charges 33 cents, and TNT charges about 50 cents, while Lifetime costs less than 25 cents. New networks are more likely to pay the MSOs; one current MSO deal (circa 1997) required several new networks to pay between $5 and $8 per subscriber as an upfront payment, and waive per-subscriber license fees for the first three years of operation. To launch Animal Planet, a new service, the network's owner, Discovery Communications reportedly paid TCI $50 million. Animal Planet's subscriber count was jump-started with 10 million TCI subs.

ORGANIZATION OF A CABLE NETWORK

A cable network is typically headed by a president, who is charged with daily operation and with growth (specifically, increasing the number of subscribers). He or she reports to a board of directors, typically senior executives from the large media company or companies that own the network. Several executives responsible for programming, advertising sales, marketing, operations, and legal affairs, report directly to the president. While the actual structure varies depending upon the network's needs and the people involved, every network includes these functions, typically at the vice president level.

The programming department is responsible for the development and production of original programs, and for the acquisition of completed programs. This responsibility may be divided by program type or by daypart.

The marketing department typically handles public relations, promotion, licensing, and advertising.

The cable network's marketing department may also include affiliate relations and advertising sales. The affiliate relations group manages MSO relationships, and works closely with the marketing department to develop and implement local promotions.

The sales department sells commercial time on a CPM basis. Prices are based on ratings information available from Nielsen (see page 402).

The network's operations functions may be organized into one or several departments. Engineering supervises the technical aspects of production, the master control facility, and the satellite transmissions. If the network does a lot of production with its own facilities, a full-scale engineering department may be required (this is the case at CNN, for example). At other networks, where technical requirements are not as complicated (a movie channel, for example), the operations group may include financial and accounting departments, personnel, and general administrative functions.

NETWORKS AS PROGRAM PROVIDERS

The real power of cable television—and the reason why cable networks have been so successful in drawing audiences away from broadcast networks—is each individual channel's ability to serve a particular segment of the audience.

NETWORKS WITH GENERAL-INTEREST PROGRAMMING

The name of the game here is viewers—as many as possible. TBS, USA Network, TNT, and Lifetime all fill their schedules with high-profile off-network programming. Each of these networks reaches over 66 million households, more than two-thirds of all U.S. TV households. Each cultivates a slightly different image.

Lifetime's skew is women, evidenced mostly by its on-air look and style of program promos, and by the network's choice of subjects for made-for-TV movies, some talk/service shows, and specials *(Carly Simon Live at Grand Central Station, Weddings of a Lifetime)* and its choice of off-network fare: *Sisters, Designing Women.* But a high percentage of its program schedule demonstrates an interest in all viewers: a game show called *Debt, L.A. Law, The Commish,* and *Unsolved Mysteries.* Lifetime is owned by Hearst and Disney/ABC.

TBS and TNT, both begun with Turner Broadcasting and now owned by Time Warner, are seen in just about all—70 million— cable households (TBS has about a million more subscribers than TNT). TBS programs about 30 movies a week, mostly from its own library of more than 8,000 films (built by acquiring the MGM, RKO, and pre-1950s WB catalogs). TBS also programs a surprising number of documentaries (and wins many awards for this programming); notables include the weekly *National Geographic EXPLORER,* regular specials from Cousteau and the Audubon Society, and many documentaries about sports *(Hank Aaron: Chasing the Dream),* music *(America's Music: The Roots of Country),* history and social consciousness *(Cold War: A Television History)* and the movies *(Hollywood's Amazing Animal Actors).* Both program children's cartoons in the morning, off-network sitcoms and dramas in the afternoon, and movies or sports at night. Sports are also important, particularly in prime-time and on weekends. In addition to local Atlanta teams, TBS also has rights to PGA, auto racing, and other sports, and the Goodwill Games.

TNT, the youngest of the top ten cable networks, debuted in October 1988. It places much more emphasis on original motion pictures *(Gettysburg),* mini-series, movies from the Turner library, and sports.

Both TBS and TNT fill many hours with children's cartoons (Turner owns Hanna-Barbera and many Warner Brothers cartoons), and with off-network sitcoms.

USA Network is the highest-rated cable network in prime-time, and has been so for most of the 1990s. Considerable emphasis is placed on original made-for-TV movies, always with mass market appeal and often with well-known performers. USA also produces more original prime-time series than any other cable network *(The Big Easy, La Femme Nikita, Pacific Blue, Duckman).* Daytime, once filled with game shows, is now occupied by a three-hour live talk and entertainment block. Sports coverage and children's cartoons complete the schedule. In 1997, USA Network was combined with Universal Television, Home Shopping Network, and the Silver King station group under new ownership (led by Barry Diller). The new company, called USA Networks follows an increasingly common formula: a single company not only produces, but owns its distribution system.

A&E, which began with the merger of The Entertainment Channel and ARTS (Alpha Repertory Television Service), is a general-interest network as well. There are some movies, but the network's biggest draw is a documentary series, *Biography,* one of cable's highest-rated series. A&E also emphasizes mysteries— both mystery movies, and stories of unexplained phenomena told through documentaries. Many of A&E's programs are off-network: *McMillan and Wife, The Equalizer, Quincy, M.E., Law and Order.* Other documentary series, such as *America's Castles* (about the mansions and wealthy lifestyles of families from the past), have also been popular. There are some music specials, and some investigative journalism series as well. Most of A&E's historical programming has moved to a new network owned by A&E: The History Channel.

Cable networks have become a significant market for off-network product from ABC, CBS, and NBC. In 1997, the right to play a hit series like *ER* cost TNT $800,000 per episode; *Walker, Texas Ranger* drew $725,000 from USA. Deals typically run for a limited number of plays per week over a period of several years.

SUPERSTATIONS

A superstation is a broadcast station licensed to operate in a single market, whose signal is distributed nationally via satellite. The station itself is officially uninvolved in the national distribution, which is done by a *common carrier,* or a company that owns or leases time on a microwave and/or satellite. In the early days of cable, superstations made great sense—cable operators had channels to fill, and these television stations were filled with programming that people wanted to see. In today's world, where most cable systems struggle with channel-capacity issues, and few local stations are unaffiliated with broadcast networks, where most sporting events are licensed to local pay cable services, where off-network syndicated reruns often spend time on cable before landing on local stations, the superstation concept is no longer as interesting to viewers or cable operators. Still, a successful superstation can attract national advertisers, and thus charge ad rates based on a national, not local, audience.

A new concept called a "free market superstation" has emerged. This concept involves ownership of program distribution rights, locking up local sports rights for national distribution, and ownership of the common carrier. Previously, TBS was distributed via Southern Satellite; as of 1998, TBS effectively owns its common carrier. From a local cable operator's perspective, the free-market superstation concept allows sale of local spots in a very popular network.

TBS Superstation continues to exist as a local station in Atlanta as WTBS. The local feed includes local advertising. The national feed includes only national spots. TBS is the largest cable network with 73 million subscribers (this figure includes a few million who receive the signal via home satellite and other means).

The traditional superstation format is still in use by several stations. The largest distributor is UVTV, whose "product" includes WGN, Chicago; WPIX, New York; and KTLA, Los Angeles. WWOR, distributed by Advanced Entertainment Corp., is a factor mainly in the Northeast.

Superstations are a good deal for almost all concerned. The cable system buys the service for a few cents per subscriber per month and bundles it as part of basic service. The one major cost to the cable system is a copyright-licensing fee for carriage of a distant signal. With the free-market concept, TBS is no longer involved in this aspect of superstation operations.

An FCC rule called "syndex" requires common carriers to block out or replace a program in any market where a local broadcaster owns exclusive rights to program. TBS owns its national rights, so syndex is no longer an issue for that network.

SPECIAL-INTEREST NETWORKS

Several special interests have emerged as sufficiently broad in scale to support large networks. Many other special interests appeal to a comparatively small number of households. With a limited number of slots available on most cable systems, niche networks find growth challenging.

The most successful networks offer a perfect balance between programming and advertising. Programming attracts a large number of viewers within a particular demographic segment (or several), and advertisers pay to reach that segment. ESPN is an excellent example: on cable, there is no better way to reach large numbers of men 18–49. Similarly, Nickelodeon's programming attracts large numbers of children (the specific age demographic depends upon the daypart).

NEWS

In 1980, when Ted Turner launched CNN, many industry observers wondered whether television could support a channel that showed nothing but news. CNN becomes a ratings champ as a major news story unfolds, but CNN's ratings are sluggish without major ongoing news stories. Half-hour programs, such as *Larry King Live,* encourage prime-time viewership. And during periods with good-sized scandals, wars, or other such events, CNN's ratings become sluggish. CNN operates several networks: CNNI (international), CNNfn (financial news), and Headline News.

While there have been rumblings of competitive news networks through the 1980s and 1990s, no network has emerged as a significant competitor to CNN.

Business news, shown during daytime hours on CNBC, and throughout the day on Bloomberg Information Television (which shows weather, news, sports, and other information on its multimedia screen), are niche news services.

C-SPAN is a non-commercial network that mainly shows live coverage of government proceedings. Court TV provides coverage and analysis of court cases.

Chapter 20 covers news programming and production.

SPORTS

In the pre-cable era, most local sports programming was seen on local television stations. In order to establish themselves, local and regional sports networks increased the amount of money paid to local sports teams in exchange for rights. And as these networks gained clout, they bought more of the games. Eventually, only a small number of games were broadcast live on local television stations.

On the national level, the major broadcast networks own most of the rights to most important national sporting events, but ESPN is a very significant player as is FOX Sports (regional sports networks). in second-level sports coverage. ESPN2 is more of a niche network, with daytime programming focused on fitness, and coverage of sporting events with younger appeal.

Sports news services are just beginning to grow; as of this writing, CNN/SI (a joint venture between CNN and Sports Illustrated—two Time Warner brands) and ESPNews are making deals to encourage distribution in significant numbers. (For more on CNN's ventures, see page 217.)

Chapter 22 covers sports programming, deals, sports marketing, and production.

THE WEATHER CHANNEL

There's only one, and it has become a utility, a kind of video appliance. Like CNN, The Weather Channel becomes wildly popular when there's a big story, or in this case, a big storm. Since weather is a local phenomenon, The Weather Channel makes use of regional reporting and forecasting computers. These computers display local data, including weather statistics, local radar, and forecasts. The local segments are often sponsored by local companies.

The Weather Channel makes money in two ways: through per-subscriber license fees, and by selling advertising. Many regular and special segments, such as weather maps, are sponsored by major national brands. (See also page 219.)

MUSIC

Music networks offer the clearest example of market segmentation. MTV's appeal begins in the young teenage years, and drops off before age 30. VH1's appeal begins in the mid-20s and goes up through the 30s and early 40s. Niche music networks have, by and large, found little acceptance from MSOs. The exception is country music; The Nashville Network and CMT are two mainstream music services with broad-based appeal—and not only in rural areas. Country music is now as much of a city phenomenon as rock or other mainstream pop. Attempts at other types of music networks (jazz, for example, and classical music) have not captured the interest of MSOs.

CHILDREN'S NETWORKS

Nickelodeon completely dominates children's television. Its programs fill the lists of top cable series, and its cumulative ratings are considerably larger, on a per-episode basis, than that of programs distributed by networks or syndicators.

Cartoon Network, which shows mostly off-network and off-syndication cartoons, is the second choice of most young viewers. Many of the cartoons come from Hanna-Barbera and Warner Bros., which is owned by Time Warner.

The Disney Channel is currently being reshaped by executives who built Nickelodeon.

Chapter 23, covering the development, production, and distribution of children's programming, begins on page 238.

MOVIE CHANNELS

There are two types of movie channels: pay, or premium, channels like HBO and Cinemax, which show mostly new movies, and some other types of programming, and basic channels, like Turner Classic Movies and American Movie Classics, which show old films.

Premiered in 1984, American Movie Classics (AMC) follows an old cable tradition: presenting movies without commercial interruption. In fact, AMC is one of the only basic cable services that does not accept advertising. Movies are acquired from studios and syndicators; most of the films have been seen on television many times, so they can be purchased for a relatively low price. Key selling points are uninterrupted, uncut, and never, ever colorized movies. Marquee value is minimal, but the channel is an important cornerstone in the sales pitch to older cable subscribers. AMC reaches 61 million subscribers. AMC's original programs include *Remember WENN*, a comedy/drama series that recalls life in a 1930s/1940s radio station; *Gotta Dance*, featuring ballroom dancing; and *Reflections on the Silver Screen with Professor Richard Brown*, an interview series whose guests have included Katharine Hepburn, Gene Kelly, Tony Curtis, Jimmy Stewart, Jack Lemmon, and many other stars. AMC specials have included *Blacklist: Hollywood on Trial*, and *America's Movie Place Memories*.

Turner Classic Movies (TCM) benefits from Turner and Time Warner's ownership of many older film libraries. It's a newer network (April 1994 debut), and it features more stars and more well-known films. But AMC "got there first," and most cable operators are reluctant to eliminate the popular AMC from their lineup. So TCM waits, as many channels do, for more open slots. As of late 1996, TCM had about 11 million subscribers.

DISCOVERY NETWORKS

The Discovery Channel is one of cable television's great success stories. It's also an entrepreneurial story—one of the few new network organizations begun and subsequently managed by a true visionary, John Hendricks. Nowadays, Discovery Communications employs more than 2,000 people and includes subsidiaries such as Discovery Networks U.S. It's owned by Hendricks, Liberty Media (part of TCI), Cox Communications, and Advance/Newhouse Communications.

The Discovery Channel is much more than one of the U.S.'s largest cable networks. Launched in June 1985, The Discovery Channel is part of Discovery Networks U.S., which now includes seven domestic networks, a powerful presence on satellite and cable services outside the U.S., consumer products, and other ventures. The flagship network is The Discovery Channel, which serves 69 million households with a prime-time schedule filled with non-fiction programs that emphasize nature, science, and technology, as well as history and adventure, and, during the daytime hours, plenty of lifestyle programming *(HouseSmart, Home Matters, Interior Motives)*. The variety in The Discovery Channel's schedule is the basis for four new channels, delivered digitally via satellite: Discovery Civilization (a history network), Discovery Kids, Discovery Science, and Discovery Travel & Living (the company owns The Travel Channel).

Discovery Networks also owns and operates The Learning Channel, which debuted in 1980 and was acquired by Discovery in 1991. With 48 million subscribers, TLC is poised for growth. Discovery invested more than $70 million for 773 hours of new TLC programming in the 1996–97 season. Series include *Myth America* (how U.S. history has evolved into legend), *SeaTek* (underwater magazine), *Medical Detectives, Popular Science* (in association with the magazine), *Paleoworld, Great Books, Wonders of Weather,* etc. Mornings are filled, from 6:00 A.M. until noon, with *READY, SET, LEARN!*—pre-school programming hosted by Rory, a popular children's singer.

Animal Planet, which debuted in June 1996, is also a Discovery Network. It is filled with documentaries, talk, game and other shows of interest to animal lovers.

NICHE ENTERTAINMENT NETWORKS

Comedy has always been a television staple, so Comedy Central makes sense. After a more broad-based approach (and a merger between two competing comedy networks for a relatively small niche), Comedy Central adopted a cutting-edge approach for adults 25–34. This is reflected in programs like *Dream On* (an off-HBO sitcom), *Dr. Katz* (an animated series), *Politically Incorrect* (which moved to ABC as a late-night series), and *The Daily Show* (daily commentary). Comedy Central has also succeed with *Ab Fab,* more formally known as *Absolutely Fabulous,* a BBC series set in London's fashion industry. Just over half of Comedy Central's programming is original; the rest of the schedule is filled with *Saturday Night Live* reruns, movies, and some off-network and off-HBO product.

The fast-growing Sci-Fi Channel mines another niche based on a genre of television programming that has been popular since the 1950s. Owned by USA Networks, the Sci-Fi Channel was launched in September 1992, and by mid-1996, the network boasted over 30 million subscribers. Many of its programs are off-network and syndication chestnuts *(The Twilight Zone, Lost in Space, Dark Shadows)*, and two hours per week are devoted to c/net's television series (theoretically as a launch pad for a full-scale network about computing to accompany c/net's successful Web site). The Sci-Fi Channel's resources are limited, but the network does produce some original programming: a pop-culture magazine series called *The Anti-Gravity Room;* a news magazine about space exploration called *Inside Space;* and a biography series about science fiction authors. No original science fiction series or movies yet, but they're planned for the future.

Food and cooking shows also have a long history on television. The category has a second advantage: production costs are generally low. There are few celebrities, studio productions occur in small spaces with one or two performers, and location productions require little more than a single camera. The Food Network updates the tradition of televised how-to-cook shows, adds some sizzle with restaurant reviews, and serves a reliable audience with a full schedule of special-interest programming. Nearly all of the programs are original (and nearly all of its programs are produced in one of television's busiest studios—a single midtown Manhattan studio which produced over 3,000 programs in 1997). The Food Network's primary owners are the *Providence Journal,* Tribune Broadcasting, and Continental Cablevision. Home & Garden TV (HGTV), owned by E.W. Scripps, fills a comparable niche.

Launched in June 1990, E! Entertainment Television targets adults 18–49 and serves 40 million subscribers with off-network sitcoms, such as *WKRP in Cincinnati,* and *Alice.* But several original E! productions have given the network considerable visibility, making the potential of this network clear. Series like *The Gossip Show,* and *Talk Soup* suggest a large market for programs about the entertainment business, while Howard Stern's televised radio show was a shrewd way to interest new viewers in a young-looking network. E! is owned by Time Warner and five leading MSOs: Comcast, Continental, Cox, NewChannels, and TCI.

NETWORKS FOR SMALLER NICHE AUDIENCES

The Golf Channel, The Game Show Network, The Outdoor Life Network, The Jewish Television Network, and about fifty others may sound as if they haven't got a chance in the competitive television marketplace. But this is not entirely true.

The entrepreneurial Golf Channel is building a presence both on television and the Web. It's jointly owned by FOX and six of the largest MSOs (Comcast, Continental, Cablevision, etc.). The channel runs nothing but golf, 24 hours a day—golf movies, live call-in golf talk shows, tours of the world's greatest courses, golf lessons, even a nightly golf news show. The concept was born in 1991, when an Alabama entrepreneur proved, via market research, the viability of a channel devoted exclusively to golf. Almost $10 million was raised as start-up money. By 1994, six MSOs were in the game, and the channel launched in 1995. Like American Movie Classics, which has become a cornerstone in the reasons why a family will initially subscribe to cable television, the Golf Channel has become a must-have for some upscale households. The buying power of these audience members helps to explain the channel's potential appeal to advertisers.

The Outdoor Life Network was formed by several former executives from ESPN. Programming includes alpine and winter sports (programs about skiing, mountain biking, rock climbing), ocean and water sports (diving, cruising, jet skiing, sailing, surfing), field sports (fishing, hunting, rafting, gathering edible wild mushrooms), nature and conservation (birding, National Parks), and adventure and exploration (extreme sports, white-water rafting). The sales pitch to the business community: outdoor enthusiasts spend more than $44 billion a year; interest is 52 percent male and 48 percent female; among 18 emerging cable networks, Outdoor Life was rated number one among men 18–34, and number two among all adults 18–49; The network is owned, in part, by three large MSOs, whose involvement makes carriage on their systems more likely. At the end of 1996, the network had 6 million subscribers.

As channel capacity increases—and it will increase to over 100 channels in the next few years—The Outdoor Life Network is likely to "own" its market segment. The same will be said for its sister service, Speedvision Network, which concentrates on fast-moving vehicles (cars, planes, etc.). The Golf Channel has already established its position.

Not every new network will succeed. Most, in fact, will fail, losing millions of dollars for their investors. In order to succeed, a network must possess the right combination of senior executives, whose experience with other cable networks, solid business judgment, and willingness to take risks are keys to the success of the new enterprise. This team provides the credibility that major investors, such as MSOs, need to see before they will provide channel allocations and/or funding. Underlying all of this, of course, is a concept that will result in programming that viewers really want to see, programming that can be produced or acquired, at a reasonable price, so that it can fill a 24-hour, seven-day schedule. These viewers must be quantifiable, typically from another medium (such as a magazine), and reaching them must be a priority for a significant number of advertisers whose budgets are large enough to support the production of commercials as well as the purchase of commercial time.

EXPANSION OF SINGLE CABLE NETWORKS INTO MULTI-CHANNEL DIGITAL BRANDS

When DBS debuted in the U.S., HBO and Showtime offered a unique approach to their existing product. They expanded their program schedules to fill multiple channels. The concept, similar in spirit to a movie multiplex theater, became known as multi-plexing. Movies (and other programming) were offered at staggered start times; in fact, by simply offering its east and west coast feeds, HBO essentially created a second channel.

MTV struggled with M2, a second music channel, and in 1998, debuted a suite of digital channels. MTV Rocks offers heavier rock sounds, like heavy metal. MTV Indie focuses on techno and rap, mostly from independent record labels. MTV Ritmo is a Spanish-language service whose music is Cuban, dance-pop, and Tejano. MTV's sister company, VH1, is also part of the digital suite with VH1 Soul, VH1 Country, and VH1 Smooth (new age, soft jazz, and adult contemporary). M2 is the final channel in the suite.

Nickelodeon's Nick at Nite was expanded to create the TV Land network. ESPN has launched a news channel, and CNN has expanded into several news channels.

At present, these channels can be seen mostly via satellite (and, in some cases, on the occasional cable system). As cable channel capacity increases, these digital suites will become full-scale channels—if the owners are willing to wait for a return on their investments. Approximately five million cable households should be able to receive a digital tier of cable channels by the year 2000 (probably at an additional cost of approximately $10 per month, though deals will vary). Digital channels are not, contrary to the connotation of the term digital, channels with enhanced audio or video quality. Instead, digital channels are compressed signals—as many as twelve digital channels can be squeezed through the bandwidth used for a single analog channel.

Pay Television and Pay-Per-View

A ccording to Walter Troy Spencer, "The concept of pay TV is almost as old as the practical technology of television itself. As early as 1938, viewers in England could watch prize fights telecast in theaters."[1]

Through the 1950s and 1960s, several entrepreneurs tried to build an over-the-air pay TV business. The best known was Subscription Television, Inc., headed by Pat Weaver, the NBC executive who started *The Today Show* and *The Tonight Show*. Weaver's plan was to bring pay television to Los Angeles and San Francisco, but the company failed mainly because of pressure from theater owners and local broadcasters. Other ventures, mostly experimental, enjoyed varying degrees of success, but none could truly be called the start of a new industry. Each venture was based on a similar principle: a schedule of programs is broadcast (or cablecast), but its signal is scrambled. Viewers pay a subscription fee, and either buy a device in order to see the programming or rent the device as part of the subscription fee.

The FCC approved pay television service in December 1968; an unsuccessful Supreme Court appeal by the National Association of Theater Owners and the Joint Committee Against Toll TV delayed any forward motion until September 1969. In 1972, the FCC authorized several over-the-air pay TV stations on UHF. By 1983, 18 full-power UHF stations were broadcasting as pay television outlets—commonly called over-the-air subscription TV, subscription TV, or simply STV— serving nearly 1 million households. As cable, with its multiple

---

1 Walter Troy Spencer, "Pay TV: An Alternative," *The Ultimate Television Book,* ed. Judy Fireman (New York: Workman, 1977)

pay services, became available and increased its penetration, the business eroded quickly. By the late 1980s, most STV stations had switched to over-the-air shopping channels (see Chapter 30).

During its brief heyday, STV offered HBO-style service on a UHF station in approximately a dozen major metropolitan areas that were not yet served by cable. ON TV, owned by Oak Media Development, was the industry leader. Subscribers paid a monthly fee, received a monthly program guide, and—via a descrambler— were able to see recent motion pictures, sporting events, Broadway productions like *Ain't Misbehavin'*, rock concerts featuring the Rolling Stones, and other special programs.

PAY CABLE

Pay cable began on November 8, 1972, with a Time-Life experiment. A new service called Home Box Office was cablecast to 365 Service Electric Cable TV subscribers in Wilkes-Barre, Pennsylvania. The first night's offering was an NHL game live from Madison Square Garden, followed by a recent film called *Sometimes a Great Notion*. In January 1973, HBO transmitted its first championship boxing match: Foreman vs. Frazier, from Kingston, Jamaica. In March, HBO showed its first pay TV special, coverage of the Pennsylvania Folk Festival. HBO remained a regional service until September 30, 1975; on that date, HBO became the first cable service delivered via satellite.

Cable television and pay television are ideal partners. Once a household becomes comfortable with the idea of paying a monthly bill for television service, the incremental addition of a pay service—or several pay services—is not a hard sell. Since cable households by and large require a "cable box" (more accurately, a "converter"), the installation of an enhanced model containing a pay TV descrambler is not a difficult barrier.

Pay cable penetration has always lagged behind basic cable penetration: at the end of 1980, there were 17.6 million cable households, but only 9.1 million subscribed to a pay service. At the end of 1989, the absolute numbers were higher and the ratio had narrowed: 52.6 million basic cable subs, and 40.5 million pay subs. For the past few years, approximately 75 percent of all cable subs have generally been taking at least one pay service.

PAY CABLE NETWORKS

HBO is the largest pay cable network, with about 22 million subs. It is followed by The Disney Channel, with 16 million, Showtime with 15 million, The Movie Channel, also with 15 million, and Cinemax, with 9 million. These figures tell only part of the story since each of these channels serves additional subscribers via satellite subscription services (see Chapter 14). The total number of HBO subscribers, then, includes not only HBO's pay cable households, but also subscribers to five or six HBO channels available via satellite.

HBO and Cinemax are owned by Time Warner. Showtime, which debuted nationally in March 1978, is operated and half-owned by Viacom's Showtime Networks group. Through the years, Viacom has had several partners; the latest is TCI. The Movie Channel began as The Star Channel in 1973, by "bicycling" (physically shipping) tapes of motion pictures from one local Warner Cable system to another. When American Express joined Warner Cable in a new venture called Warner Amex Satellite Entertainment Company (WASEC) in 1979, the service was renamed The Movie Channel. After a period in which Viacom effectively replaced American Express as the partner, Viacom bought the channel.

PROGRAMMING

HBO has been the leading service from the start—the player whose muscular negotiations with Hollywood at one time helped Showtime to grow, largely as a result of studio resentment. For years, HBO has featured big-name boxing matches (now also a Showtime specialty) and coverage of the best Wimbledon matches. It also had sufficient foresight and clout to develop and produce its own motion pictures, thus assuring product flow, and HBO has dominated the CableACE Awards with high-impact, high-visibility motion pictures and television programs. (HBO also consistently wins the Best Made-for-TV Emmy award.) HBO's original films often appeal to large audiences and impress critics, whose print reviews tend to increase awareness of the network. Among its many success stories: *Truman, And the Band Played On, The Josephine Baker Story, If These Walls Could Talk,* and *Gotti.* Family programming has included the Peabody winner *How Do You Spell God?* Numerous award-winning documentaries have added a distinguished veneer to the network's original programming: *5 American Handguns 5 American Kids, Abortion: Desperate Choices,* and *Taxicab Confessions* are representative.

HBO programs roughly four major events (two music, two comedy) per year. In recent years, Whitney Houston and Garth Brooks have headlined, adding to a long list of superstars (Bette

Midler, Paul Simon, Barbra Streisand, and many others) whose specials have brought considerable attention to the network. One of its biggest long-term successes is *Comic Relief*, a fund-raiser starring Robin Williams, Billy Crystal and Whoopi Goldberg. HBO also broke new ground with the first stand-up comedy series. In the early 1990s, HBO moved into situation comedy; hits include *Dream On* and *The Larry Sanders Show*. But this approach has faded in favor of high-impact socially relevant movies,

From the start, HBO established a classy network identity, using expensive animation packages to introduce features and even interstitial programs.

HBO also operates four production companies: HBO Independent Productions, which specializes in product for the broadcast networks *(Roc, Martin, The Ben Stiller Show, Everybody Loves Raymond)*; HBO Downtown Productions, whose focus has been primarily cable *(Dr. Katz, The Chris Rock Show, Politically Incorrect with Bill Maher)*; HBO Animation started in 1996; and HBO-NYC which has been responsible for many of HBO's high-profile movies.

HBO International started with a presence in Hungary and Latin America in 1991, then moved on to Asia in 1992 (as a joint venture with several movie studios), and so on, through Eastern Europe and elsewhere. HBO Ole was the first Spanish-language premium service in Latin America; it was also set up as a joint venture between HBO, several movie studios, and a Venezuelan company. HBO Brazil, which programs in Portuguese, is also part of the box.

Cinemax began as an all-movie service (hence the name), and after years of blending comedy and music specials into the mix, Cinemax is, once again, an all-movie service. Its particular spin is more youthful and more urban and probably more male than HBO's, but only by degrees.

For its first few years, Showtime struggled to differentiate itself from HBO. Broadway shows *(Master Harold and the Boys, Sunday in the Park with George)*, comedy series *(It's Gary Shandling's Show, Super Dave)*, children's programs *(Shelley Duvall's Faerie Tale Theater)*, and a broader variety of music programs have helped to give Showtime a distinctive identity. By 1983, it was clear that the best offensive tool was exclusive-rights deals with large motion picture studios; that year, Showtime signed the first "output deal" for pay TV, with Paramount. This deal guaranteed a supply of Paramount movies that viewers could see at home only by subscribing to Showtime. The result of Showtime's move was that pay cable networks immediately started competing for studio product (HBO currently has rights to films from Warner Brothers,

Paramount, Columbia, and FOX, though rights to Paramount films will belong to Showtime, now a sister company under Viacom, in a few years.)

Through the 1980s, Showtime grew with a series of output deals for pictures from small and large releasing companies. Through the 1990s, Showtime has fallen seriously behind. Its legacy of adult entertainment *(The Red Shoe Diaries)*, genre films (1997's "Sci Friday" science fiction films), boxing, and output deals continue to move the network along, but the network is losing traction. In one example, TCI, the largest MSO, dropped Showtime to start its own pay TV movie network, Starz.

MOVIES ON PAY TV

Pay television services are, for the most part, in the business of exhibiting recent motion pictures. Viewers pay a fee to see the motion pictures about a year after they have appeared in theaters. The period when a motion picture is released for pay TV is called the "pay television window"; it frequently overlaps with windows for airline release and home-video release. Although the sequences of windows varies depending upon the deal, the following is roughly representative for a major studio release.

Theatrical release:	January through April 1998
Airline:	March 1998
Home Video:	April 1998
Pay-per-view:	May 1998
Hotel and related services:	May or June 1998
Pay cable:	Winter 1998–99

Each film studio has a department responsible for the licensing of motion pictures to pay television. Independent production companies sell pay TV exhibition as one of several ancillary rights, and sometimes pre-sell home-video rights as well (though film studios, which have their own video labels, rarely do the latter).

In general, most major studio movies are not sold to television by individual title. Instead, they are grouped as packages that usually contain mid-line, marginal and top titles, frequently in batches of dozens of pictures. Unless there is an exclusive output deal, more than one pay service usually licenses each package. The services schedule the films from the package according to appeal; some of the films are never scheduled. After pay TV, the films are then licensed (or in the case of a studio, transferred internally) to a syndication company, which supplies first basic cable and possibly broadcast network, then local stations.

Some individual pictures, groups of pictures, or even complete packages are sold on an exclusive basis to a single pay TV company, usually for a limited period (one year, for example). The real value in an exclusive license is during the early weeks of the pay TV window, when there is excitement in the marketplace about viewing a hit title at home. This excitement helps to differentiate the service, and improves viewer satisfaction with pay TV as well. But as the hubbub dies down, the value of the exclusivity drops quickly.

A major motion picture release is typically sold by the studio's pay TV division directly to each pay network. The average sale is in the millions of dollars; obviously, the actual negotiated prices vary widely. To an independent company with a film that had a $4 million production budget and a domestic theatrical gross of $5 million, the pay TV licenses will probably be worth $250,000–$500,000.

HBO has been a successful small movie studio, whose best films cost about $8 million to produce. Without the costs associated with theatrical marketing and distribution, recoupment comes more quickly to HBO than it does to a studio. After multiple HBO plays, films are typically sold to broadcasters and cablecasters in other countries, and to video stores and consumers. The $8 million price tag is relatively high for an HBO film; most cost $3–$4 million or so.

THE ECONOMICS OF PAY CABLE

Pay television services are sold at a wholesale price to cable operators and MSOs, who add a markup as they resell the service to subscribers. HBO's wholesale cost per subscriber is about $5. Most cable subscribers pay about $10 per month for the service. These numbers vary by market, and with special promotions.

Growth in subscription revenues can be achieved only by increasing the wholesale cost per subscriber that the network charges the cable operator or by increasing the gross number of subs (which might be done by decreasing the wholesale cost). There is a finite universe of cable subscribers, and a historically-accurate percentage of cable households that will subscribe to pay services. Most pay cable networks grew quickly through the mid-1980s, but by the late 1980s, growth had slowed. The business has been rejuvenated by direct-to-home satellite services (HBO operates a "multiplex" of several channels), and by the growth of the international television marketplace. HBO, for example, operates services in Asia (HBO Asia) and Latin America (HBO Ole).

THE DISNEY CHANNEL

The Disney Channel is a non-commercial basic service for 22 million subscribers; an additional 5 million subscribers see it as a pay service. The network offers cable operators a choice: The Disney Channel can be sold as either a pay service (to directly increase revenues) or a basic service (to enhance the value of the basic tier[s] and generate more new subscriptions, more renewals, and less churn). By emphasizing the basic service approach and de-emphasizing pay, the network moved from 6 million to 30 million subscribers in the mid-1990s. This approach allows a more reasonable competition with Nickelodeon, a network that grew, in part, because Disney did not approach the cable business with the right strategy. In recent years, the Disney Channel has developed a new strategy involving more regularly-scheduled, mass appeal children's programming, and less special events programming. As the network adds more subscribers, it's likely to add advertising.

PAY-PER-VIEW

Pay-per-view (PPV) is a different form of pay television. The concept is simple: special programs and recently released movies are shown on one or more channels used exclusively for PPV ("dedicated channels"). In order to watch the program, the viewer agrees to pay a separate charge—either by calling a special telephone number, or, on newer in-home hardware, by pressing a button on the cable console. PPV is a transaction-based, one-purchase-at-a-time business that depends upon impulse buys, and requires a sophisticated marketing infrastructure. Viewers must be made aware of the PPV offerings in a variety of media, through a dedicated 24-hour "barker" channel (which features nothing but around-the-clock promos for PPV programs), direct mailings, advertisements, and bill stuffers. In addition, viewers must be encouraged to buy at the time when the product is actually available.

A pay-per-view operation requires special hardware at the head end and in each household. At the head end, the cable operator must install a special computer that enables individual households to view each individual program. In each household, the cable converter must include an individual computer address that permits communication with the computer in the head end. In addition, a customer order-processing system is needed. Rudimentary systems simply post a telephone number for ordering; this is not ideal for impulse buys because it requires the customer to do more than press a button on a TV remote control. Newer, more sophisticated systems include such a button—or, more often, the entry of a special ID code—but also require some form of verification to confirm that the person pressing the button will actually pay for the film (four-year-olds are notorious button-pushers). Newer computer systems not only take the order and enable (or activate) the addressable converter in the viewer's home, but take care of record-keeping and billing as well. (An addressable converter is a cable box whose subscription code can be read by a central computer.)

More than half of U.S. cable households are equipped to receive pay-per-view programming; cable operators have been slow to change their customers over to addressable converters. Six million more receive PPV via DBS satellite systems. Compared with basic cable, pay cable, or home video, PPV is a relatively small business. According to a 1997 Veronis, Suhler & Associates report, PPV-equipped households purchased an average of 3.6 movies in 1996, representing approximately 2.5 percent of their total purchases and rentals of video product for the year. DBS subscribers buy more movies than their cable counterparts (an average of 5.7 versus 3.2 movies). Piracy is also a factor; the Video Software Dealers Association estimates approximately 4 million illegal ("pirate") cable boxes equipped for PPV.

According to Showtime Event Television (SET), PPV revenues totaled approximately $1.2 billion in 1997. Roughly $600 million came from movie revenues, $400 million from special events (particularly sports), and $250 million was earned by adult services.

For cable operators, the big challenge has been marketing. Most cable operators don't do much local advertising, and promoting PPV service is a bit more complicated than advertising the availability of a new channel. The obvious benefits are often missed because consumers are either confused or unaware: pay as you go, no tapes to return, hit movies are always in stock, etc. Promotional schemes are often concocted by the PPV network and spoon-fed to the cable operators, who often lack a marketing staff or dedicated PPV manager.

PAY-PER-VIEW PROGRAMMING

Fighting accounts for nearly all PPV special-event revenue. In 1996, here's how the numbers played: boxing (56.7 percent), wrestling (35.2 percent) and combat sports (6.4 percent).

The most successful pay-per-view event to date was the boxing match between Evander Holyfield and Mike Tyson, held in November 1996. Approximately 1.65 million households paid $49.95 to watch the fight, for a gross exceeding $80 million.

Showtime Event Television (SET) charged cable operators $27.50 per subscriber. Boxing has proven to be pay-per-view's most successful format; in fact, according to *Variety* (November 18, 1996), nine of the top ten PPV events involved either Tyson, Holyfield, or both. Most of these events cost subscribers about $40, and most were seen by about a million subs.

The most successful non-boxing PPV event was *Wrestlemania VII,* which earned $24 million at a $29.95 price. Concerts and other special events tend to be less lucrative, with very low buy rates (typically under 5 percent).

For PPV movies, the direct competition is home video: PPV's retail prices for motion pictures are generally competitive with the rental prices charged by neighborhood video stores. For big feature films—and these are the only titles that make sense for PPV—the pay-per-view window opens after the film has been in the video stores for a month or more.

THE ECONOMICS OF PAY-PER-VIEW

An increasing number of systems have found that several PPV channels are preferable to one, provided that channels are available. The first two channels show first-run movies. When programmed properly, a new feature starts at the top of the hour on at least one of the channels. A third channel is used for action/adventure films or special events. Some systems successfully operate a fourth channel with adult material ("hard" R-rated films and special programs but they're usually careful about hard-core "X" material), with virtually no marketing expense.

Movies can be a significant source of income for PPV services. On a successful four-channel PPV system, two major movie channels can account for 40 to 50 percent of revenue. A month with one giant title will generally do better than a month with several name titles but no blockbuster. The cumulative monthly rate for a movie channel averages about 18 percent—that is, the total number of orders for a movie amounts to 18 percent of the number of households that receive the channel. The adult channel is a dependable contributor of up to 20 to 25 percent of monthly PPV income.

Events are less predictable. Ideally, an event should be a big-ticket item with lots of visibility, supported by a major national and local marketing campaign. As much as 40 percent of this market consists of wrestling from WWF and Turner. For Viewer's Choice, boxing generates, on average, just under 60 percent of event revenue, followed by wrestling at 34 percent; other sports and the occasional concert make up the rest. Prices for most of these events are about $30, but some retail prices (for mega boxing matches, etc.) are as high as $50. Buy rates in these categories, nationally, are 5 to 10 percent of the PPV households.

DSS viewers tend to buy many more PPV movies. According to Paul Kagan Associates, PPV revenues from DSS households jumped from $21 million in 1994 to $202 million just two years later. By comparison, cable PPV revenues moved from $157 million to $215 million in the same period. Special events brought in $412 million in 1996 PPV revenues, and adult movies, $210 million.

Customarily, the cable operator and the PPV network equally share PPV revenues, although other deals may be negotiated.

PAY-PER-VIEW NETWORKS

Cable companies buy events and motion pictures from pay-per-view networks. The largest are Viewer's Choice and Hot Choice (formerly Viewer's Choice II), owned by Pay-Per-View Network, Inc. (in turn owned by six cable MSOs and three movie studios). These networks serve 17 million addressable households, respectively, on over 900 cable systems. With DSS, Viewers Choice Home Theater now offers Choice 1 and Choice 2 with a varied schedule of movies, three more channels in a movie-of-the-day schedule, and four more that show a movie-of-the-week (same movie all week along). Hot Choice, which completes the 11-channel Home Theater package, features action, adventure, horror, science fiction and some adult entertainment.

Request Television is a subsidiary of Reiss Media Enterprises, whose majority shareholders include Twentieth Century Fox and TCI. Request offers five analog channels to cable operators; over 1,100 cable operators use the service. The various channels offer a variety of movies and some special events, and also accommodate staggered movie-start times. In late 1996, Request debuted a 27-channel digital PPV service.

Adult services include Playboy at Night (625 systems); and from Spice Networks, Spice (700), and Adam & Eve (100). There are many more smaller adult services.

HOTEL AND INSTITUTIONAL SYSTEMS

The hotel pay-per-view business was built, in large part, by Spectravision, which offered a handful of movies per day (including adult entertainment). On Command, a newer company, acquired Spectravision in 1996. On Command supplies on-demand movie programming to over 3,000 hotels, mostly hotel chains such as

Marriott, Hilton, Doubletree, and other companies. The package is sold on a turnkey basis, from TV sets and cabling to interfaces with the hotel's internal guest billing system (the turnkey package varies, depending upon the individual deal). The hotel gets about 10 percent of transactional revenue, and about 10 percent of hotel rooms tend to buy on any given night. On Command, or one of its competitors, licenses films as the second pay TV window—immediately after theatrical release, but prior to pay-per-view. Between a quarter and a half of transaction revenues go to the movie distributor as royalties (generally, better-known films command higher royalties, but movies are often bought in bundles). On Command gets about half the transactional revenues to cover costs (primarily a field service force). In a 500-room hotel property, the rooms are fed by a stack of perhaps 60 videocassette players with about forty different movies. (This is a rough formula, actual sites certainly vary.) Although this system seems somewhat old-fashioned, the economics of this business, as of 1998, make more sense than satellite delivery. Certainly, this may change to a digital delivery system in the future; the cost of ripping out an existing analog system does not often justify a new digital system.

Average retail price is about $8.95 per movie.

LodgeNet, based in South Dakota, generally serves economy-priced hotels. On Command focuses on hotels for business travelers. Other players are quite small by comparison.

Roughly half of the hotel pay-per-view revenues are adult entertainment.

8

Satellite Distribution

The first communications satellite, Echo I, was launched by NASA in 1960, but it was not until the 1965 launch of Intelsat I (also called Early Bird) that satellite transmission became a part of commercial broadcast technology. In the early years, satellites were used by television networks to transmit live broadcasts from Europe. In 1974, RCA's Satcom I and Satcom II, and Western Union's Westar I and Westar II, made nationwide distribution of cable network programming possible. Through the 1970s and 1980s, several dozen satellites capable of retransmitting television programming were placed in orbit.

With satellite transmission, an uplink sends a television signal to the satellite. One of the satellite's transponders retransmits the signal back to earth, where the signal can be received by any downlink (a satellite receiving dish with related equipment) within a certain geographic region—the satellite's "footprint." Most local television broadcasters—and several million consumers—have a downlink.

Broadcast and cable networks generally transmit signals to their affiliated broadcast stations, or local cable operators, via the C-band (3 to 4.2 Gigahertz). In order to receive a C-band signal (which is relatively low power), the satellite dish must be 8 to 10 feet in diameter. Networks typically lease several transponders— one for an east coast feed, another for a west coast feed, and so on. Commercial network feeds are no longer available for viewing by individuals. However, many cable and digital satellite networks can be received by consumers who own C-band dishes.

Ku-band satellites use the 11.7–12.1 Ghz frequency range; this band is known as FSS (Fixed Satellite Service). There are over three dozen FSS communications satellites currently in orbit over North America, ranging in power from 20 to 45 watts per transponder (these are higher power than the C-band satellites); the FSS satellites require dish diameter of approximately three feet for clear reception. A second Ku-band, from 12.2 to 12.7 Ghz, is known as the BSS (Broadcast Satellite Service) band. This band is for use by higher-powered satellites (with 100 to 200 watts); the required satellite antenna size is about 12 to 18 inches.

DISTRIBUTION VIA C-BAND AND KU-BAND

For the first few years of satellite transmission, signals were intended mainly for retransmission by cable companies. But as more people bought satellite dishes, they could receive HBO for free, and this presented a threat to the pay services. The issue was resolved by scrambling the signal—and charging the subscriber a monthly fee for descrambling. All satellite receivers now include a built-in descrambler that can be enabled, or activated, by paying a monthly fee to one of several companies offering packages of channels. In time, the idea of home satellite subscriptions took hold, and now, there are a variety of consolidators who sell program packages that include both basic and pay cable packages. Pricing is generally comparable to cable television.

More than 8 million households owned satellite dishes by the end of 1997. New technologies have resolved many (but not all) satellite service piracy issues. Still, DBS is beginning to have an impact on both home video and cable revenues. Roughly half of DBS subscribers cancel their cable subscriptions shortly after installing a dish, and most stop renting videocassettes as well (or cut their rentals to a minimum).

DISTRIBUTION VIA DIRECT-TO-HOME SATELLITES

Higher-powered satellites made small, low-cost dishes viable. There are several variations on the home satellite formula, both technically and in terms of the consumer offerings.

One format is DSS. DSS is broadcast via a high-power Ku-band satellite, and requires an 18-inch dish that can be mounted on the roof, patio, or windowsill, and a receiver located inside the home. Dishes are sold by consumer electronics manufacturers through retailers. In the U.S., consumers subscribe to USSB and/or DirecTV.

USSB AND DIRECTV

USSB's principal business is the sale of pay TV multiplexes. For $34.95 per month or $379 per year, USSB sells three different HBO schedules (HBO, HBO2, HBO3) plus HBO's west coast feed (HBO, delayed 3 hours); two Showtime schedules and west coast feed; The Movie Channel (regular and west coast); Cinemax (regular and west coast); and The Sundance Channel. USSB is a public company, controlled by Hubbard Broadcasting.

DirecTV takes a different approach. The company offers just about every basic cable network (including, as of March 1998, MTV, Nickelodeon, and others formerly available on USSB) and sells the basic package, which includes dozens of channels, for $19.95 per month (a package with fewer channels sells for $14.95 per month). The most popular package is Total Choice, which offers more than 70 channels for $29.99 per month. Total Choice Gold, at $39.99, adds about two dozen regional sports channels. DirecTV is also in the pay-per-view business; a popular motion picture might be offered on several channels, with convenient start times at, say, 8:00 P.M., 8:30 P.M., and 9:00 P.M. There are 55 movie channels with popular films starting at staggered half-hours. Other pay-per-view channels are devoted to single movies, and some channels show several movies in a single day. Most films cost about $3 per movie. DirecTV is about choice, so there are many program options, and à la carte services. (The Golf Channel, for example, can be purchased for $6.95 per month.) DirecTV is owned by Hughes Electronics.

Since USSB and DirecTV can be received with the same dish, consumers can subscribe to one, the other, or both services. But neither service offers local broadcast channels. (There are some exceptions to this, mainly in rural areas.)

USSB has been growing at roughly half the rate of DirecTV. The companies now market their services in some cooperative ways; both include links to one another's Web sites, for example.

PRIMESTAR

Originally formed by cable companies to serve viewers outside cable service areas, Primestar is a partnership between cable MSOs: TCI, Time Warner, MediaOne, Cox, Comcast, and GE-American Communications. Primestar does not require the consumer to purchase the dish (it's a 39-inch dish, twice the diameter of the DSS dish; this dish is necessary because the Primestar satellite is medium-powered), but there's a $149 installation fee. This small upfront investment is more than cable customers pay, but less than DSS customers pay. The basic monthly package includes the usual dozens of channels, and costs $32.99 per month. An enhanced package, with multi-channel HBO and Showtime, costs

$59.99. Primestar is also planning a small-dish service for 1998. In its early years, Primestar was sold through cable operators (the service was intended as the answer for customers whose homes were not passed by cable), but increased competition encouraged a relationship with Radio Shack, which takes a percentage of installation and programming revenues.

DISH NETWORK

EchoStar's entrepreneurial DISH Network built its loyal dealer network from retailers who were experienced in selling and installing larger satellite dishes. DISH has positioned itself as the value leader; the basic tier, at $19.99 per month, includes 40 popular cable networks. Premium service, which includes the usual pay network multiplexes, costs $10 more. Pay-per-view movies are $3 each.

None of these systems allows for easy consumer access to local television broadcast stations. Each requires that the consumer either subscribe to cable to receive local stations (the combined cost of service makes cable a much better deal), or install a broadcast antenna (lousy broadcast signals were a leading reason why people subscribed to cable in the first place).

There are a finite number of high-power satellite ("full Conus"—Continental U.S) licenses available. A viable DBS satellite service seeks three such licenses: one for the east coast, one for the west coast, and a third as a backup to guarantee service (satellites fail from time to time).

FCC RULES: COMMON CARRIERS AND SATELLITE TRANSMISSION

The Satellite Home Viewer's Act governs the importation of broadcast network and superstation signals. Individuals receiving satellite signals may not receive any broadcast transmissions unless they are located in a "white area," where no local stations can be received. Individuals whose homes are located outside the reach of their local network affiliates can pay to receive a package of "distant network signals." A variety of stations participate; satellite dish owners may receive, for example, ABC from WJLA in Washington, DC, CBS from WRAL in Raleigh-Durham, NC, or NBC from WNBC in New York—even though they live far from these cities.

For an explanation of the regulation of satellite operations, see Chapter 14.

9

Home Video

For our purposes, the term "television" refers to a signal that is transmitted from one location and received in another. The term "video" refers to physical media that are played in the location where the programming is viewed; video does not involve transmission or reception. Examples of video include home videocassettes, videodiscs and videogames. A non-broadcast production, such as coverage of a family wedding, is also called a "video." As telephones, computers and video converge, the distinction between old-style television and newer forms of video may require a new definition.

HISTORY

The home video business began in the early 1970s with a series of consumer products. First came the videogame in 1972, a home version of a recently introduced arcade pastime. Pong and Odyssey were the first devices that transformed the TV set into something other than a box that received broadcast television transmissions. Sony's Betamax arrived in 1975, followed in 1977 by the first VHS machines from Matsushita's JVC subsidiary. Several other home video formats, such as the Funai system marketed by Technicolor, never gained popularity. In 1978, Magnavox sold its first laser videodisc system, followed in 1981 by RCA's CED videodisc, a system based on a traditional phonograph stylus. JVC announced plans for a third system called VHD that was never released in the U.S. The newest laserdisc format, DVD, is intended to be a cross-platform compact disc that can be used with a personal computer, as a home video player, and as an audio CD player (see page 115).

VIDEOCASSETTES

Introduced by Sony in 1975, the videocassette recorder (VCR) was first marketed as a machine that could record and play back television programs. Sony had the right idea with Betamax; that format was initially superior to VHS, a competitive system devised by JVC and released two years later. Ultimately, VHS became the dominant format; Matsushita (which owned 51 percent of JVC) also aggressively licensed the VHS format to other manufacturers, which resulted in a large installed base of VHS machines and a demand for pre-recorded tapes in the VHS format. Consumer acceptance was also a factor: a slower recording/playback speed and more tape per cassette meant VHS tapes could record more programming than Betamax cassettes. While the concept of "time-shift viewing" was initially the principal reason why consumers purchased VCRs, the ability to play pre-recorded movies quickly became an equally compelling reason to buy a machine.

By 1977, several companies were selling pre-recorded video-cassettes by mail. As more VCRs were sold, an increasing number of film and television companies released product from their libraries on their own newly founded labels, or else licensed films to independent labels—Magnetic Video, for example, licensed films from the Twentieth Century-Fox library. Most labels released films primarily for rental through a new type of retail outlet, the video store. Some companies, notably the entrepreneurial Vestron Video, also created videocassettes specifically for direct sale to consumers: "sell-through product."

With VCR penetration rapidly rising, and a new distribution system to reach the consumers now in place, each of the motion picture studios formed a home video label—first to release material from their libraries, then to aggressively market recent box-office hits.

Ultimately, home video became a distribution system for major motion pictures. Although there are niche markets for original home video product, and many success stories, the vast majority of consumers who rent and buy videos have never rented or purchased anything but a movie.

DISTRIBUTION

The home video business employs a unique distribution system, a hybrid with roots in both record and book distribution. In a simple example, a major motion picture studio such as Warner Bros. produces a film for theatrical release. The film finishes its first theatrical run; then the studio's video division, Warner Home Video, releases the film on cassette (and, in some instances, on laserdisc or DVD). Independently produced films are licensed to the label that makes the best offer.

The videocassette reaches the consumer in one of several different ways. Large retail accounts—record-store chains, drugstores, and mass merchants—are frequently serviced directly by the label via a direct sale (also called direct distribution). The label's sales force takes orders from a buyer at a large chain, and arranges for shipment of a specified number of titles at a price based on volume of units ordered and other factors.

The majority of video retail accounts, however, are serviced with two-step distribution, which operates as follows. A video distributor like Ingram will take orders from video chains and some individual stores. It pre-orders the proper quantities of each title from the label before a "pre-book" or "order cut-off" date. The home video label then ships these tapes to Ingram, who sends them to a central warehouse (in the case of a chain) or to individual stores. The store decides whether to sell or to rent the cassette. Official release dates, called "street dates," are determined by the label.

Since barriers to entry and capital requirements are small, independent producers of special-interest programs release their own home video product. This is an especially viable method for titles that require distribution to a focused group of retail or direct-marketing outlets. For example, the producer of a baby-care tape would work with stores and marketers that specialize in related products. There are many examples of success in niche markets, including exercise, golf, how-to, and travel videos.

VIDEO STORES

The early years of video distribution at the local level were dominated by local "mom and pop" operations, storefronts staffed by members of the owner's family or by people living in the neighborhood. Working with limited inventories—and frequently offering sidelines like VCR repairs, candy, and popcorn—many of these stores were, and still are, successful. Many videos are also rented through supermarkets and smaller retail outlets. There is no accurate count of total video retailers available, but the total number exceeds 20,000 in the U.S. alone. Many are small local video stores whose family-oriented economics and thorough understanding of individual customer preferences allow successful competition against the likes of Blockbuster, the largest domestic chain.

Running a video store can be a complicated business, relying as it does on accurately tracking product that is repeatedly being rented and returned to the store. It also requires a sizeable capital investment to stock at least 3,000 titles for rental. Once, store owners favored membership fees to help them capitalize, and traded long-term discounts to customers for short-term cash. But now, with the proliferation of larger stores that do not charge a membership fee, neighborhood stores have eliminated fees and have dropped their prices to compete. In addition, the store must invest in new titles regularly—and correctly estimate the number of copies of hit titles necessary to satisfy most customers, but not so many that the shelves are still full by 8:00 P.M. on a Saturday night. Stores must also order enough copies of smaller films to satisfy customers, but not so many that their shelves become cluttered with unwanted merchandise.

To a certain extent, the selection of titles and the accurate forecasting of the number of each rental title needed to cover demand, are the keys to a successful business. The formula is not, however, quite so straightforward. Movie companies regularly offer special deals to video stores: lower prices on films that they're currently pushing, for example, and package deals that make individual calculations somewhat difficult. Movie companies also pay "slotting fees," essentially purchasing shelf space in major chains to assure placement for their most important product (this practice is common in supermarkets and drug stores for a wide range of consumer products). The costs associated with slotting fees and other promotional monies paid allow the larger distributors to dominate the product mix—and to keep the smaller players out.

A small neighborhood video store stocks up to 3,000 titles; a medium-sized store, typically located in a strip shopping center, up to 5,000; a large chain store, like Blockbuster, between 7,000 and 10,000. Like most retail operations, the success of a video store depends mostly upon the convenience of the location and the store's ability to stock the most desirable titles in sufficiently large numbers. Customer service plays a very minor role; most people simply rent from the store that's nearest to their home. The business is almost entirely based on new releases; these are the titles that the studios/labels sell, the ones that they advertise, and the ones that consumers want (because almost no promotional dollars are attached to older "library" titles).

Noting that large video chains account for less than one-third of all video retail outlets (including supermarkets, dry cleaners, convenience markets, etc.), and that 95 percent of all video retailers own just one store, the four largest video store chains are Blockbuster (4,000 stores); Movie Gallery (1,500 stores); Hollywood

Entertainment (1,000 stores); and West Coast Entertainment, whose brand is called West Coast Video (600 stores). Blockbuster's stores are roughly 80 percent company-owned; Hollywood Entertainment owns all but a few of its stores. West Coast Video owns just under half of its units; the other half are franchises. The video store can be an ideal format for franchising. Several franchise systems have given the mom-and-pop outlets the benefits of regional advertising, superior signage, group purchasing, and inventory control.

The total cost of opening a single West Coast Video store is up to a half-million dollars (there are many variables, so no single projection can be accurate). In addition to an upfront franchise fee, West Coast charges each operator 7 percent of gross monthly revenues. Like many franchise operations (in many businesses), West Coast is more concerned with operators who can open up a new retail territory and succeed with multiple stores operating as a single business operation. If all goes as planned, the investment is recouped within three years of store opening.

Franchising is subject to legal regulation, generally aimed at preventing fraud and excessive use of the franchise's power to strip away any economic benefits to the franchise's value proposition.

VIDEO STORES: A BUSINESS MODEL BASED ON RENTALS

Video stores typically purchase cassettes for rental (and, to a far lesser extent, for sale as sell-through product). Cassettes are purchased for a wholesale price based on number of units ordered, and resold for a retail price that is suggested by the label. Antitrust laws generally require that the wholesale price offered to one buyer must be offered to all buyers purchasing the same number of units. The store (or chain) determines the number of cassettes that will be offered for rental, and the number that will be offered for sale. With an average price of $29.95 per cassette, and an average rental price of $2.50 for newer titles and $2.00 for older ones, the apparent break-even point is 12 rental transactions. In fact, the number is far higher, because of the cost of wages, rent, and other overhead items. Rental fees only provide 75 to 90 percent of the average store's revenues; the other 10 to 25 percent is made up by sales of cassettes and accessories, as well as other hardware (VCRs and camcorders) and software (videogame cartridges, CDs, and audiocassettes).

Small video stores typically establish a monthly budget for the purchase of new titles, and then work with the individual label's sales representative to put together an order.

Blockbuster is far more sophisticated. When a studio announces plans to release a film, the studio recommends a number of units for purchase. Blockbuster's buyers then attempt to match the rental profile of the new film with an established product whose rental history is meticulously recorded in the company's extensive database. Blockbuster's forecasts for a film such as *Flubber*, starring Robin Williams, would be based on a previous Robin Williams children's comedy. The forecasts are based on similar appeal as rental items, typically to a similar demographic. In fact, demographics play a pivotal role, as each store's individual purchases are based on the makeup of the store's customer base. An upscale area on New York City's Upper East Side, for example, might be very different from a working-class neighborhood in Brooklyn. The Upper East Side store might get multiple copies of a critically acclaimed foreign film, while the Brooklyn store might get none. The computer forecasts are then supplied to the individual store manager for revision (the store manager is on site, knows the customers and their patterns; the computer does not). The store manager then revises the list, sends it back to headquarters within 48 hours, and the computer generates the order list. Still, that's only part of the story. Every title that Blockbuster buys is scrutinized in a post-mortem meeting that analyzes the buying decision. This information is then added to the database, thereby sharpening the next buying decision on similar titles.

When a customer signs up as a Blockbuster member, he or she provides a home address. Customer demographics and buying patterns are carefully matched—so that Blockbuster knows not only the title's success, but the store's success with the title, and the title's performance on any city block within any zip code.

SELL-THROUGH PRODUCT

Once again, video stores are places where consumers *rent* videos. Video stores are not, by and large, places where consumers go to buy much of anything (except, perhaps, some candy for the night's movie, or an extra blank tape). Fitness tapes, for example, are far more likely to succeed in K-Mart or Wal-Mart than at Blockbuster. Music tapes do better in record stores. Documentaries and classic films are sold, quite successfully, at Barnes & Noble, Borders, and other bookstore chains, and at stores that specialize in video product for purchase, such as Suncoast (which is located primarily in shopping malls). Mail-order catalogs also play a significant role; the Signals catalog (which is a public television joint venture), for example, sells a healthy number of Britcom and how-to tapes.

Bookstores order video titles from large wholesalers who supply books and other merchandise to large chains. Smaller bookstore chains order through book wholesalers. Bookstores typically purchase product on a 100 percent returnable basis— any product can be returned to the label or distributor if it does not sell within a specified period of time (usually 60 days). These returned videocassettes are generally good for invoice credit from the distributor, credit that can be used to purchase other product. Bookstores tend to group all their tapes in one video section, which is stocked by a distributor or rack jobber (see below). Movies and children's programs thus appear on the same shelves as cooking shows. In an ideal world, cooking videos would be placed alongside cookbooks, but this is not the way merchandising has evolved. As a result, most special-interest video programs have not sold particularly well in bookstores.

Record stores concentrate on music videos, but most sell movies, too. Chain record stores and most independents buy directly from the labels—or, more accurately, from large distribution systems such as PolyGram and WEA that operate as sister companies to record labels. Smaller stores buy from distributors known as rack jobbers. Rack jobbers also service mass merchandisers via a plan-o-gram system, in which each rack position is filled with a specific title. Plan-o-gram positions are determined by the type of store and customer base, the sales potential of each video title, and the ongoing success of titles already in position.

Specialty stores with video sidelines, such as sporting goods stores, may order from their own distributors, from video distributors, or directly from the labels. Generally, the labels sell in accordance with each retail segment's customs and procedures.

OPERATION OF A HOME VIDEO LABEL

The supply side of the home video business is dominated by labels that operate as sister companies to motion picture studios. Medium-sized companies find it difficult to license enough product to justify substantial overhead, though some independent companies have succeeded via aggressive management. Smaller labels generally require a special type of product profile, or a unique distribution system, in order to survive. Kultur, for example, offers arts programming, such as opera, classical music, and ballet. A&E Home Video has been very successful with cassette versions of its popular *Biography* series, often merchandised in a specially de-signed section in Barnes & Noble retail stores.

A home video label is organized very much like a book or record company. A senior executive, typically a president, oversees all aspects of the operation. A programming department is responsible for the acquisition of new titles and for original productions, if any. If the company is a large one, the programming department may be subdivided into groups for feature film acquisition, for non-movie product, and for original production. The operations department supervises duplication, packaging, warehousing, shipping, and inventory. The marketing department creates the package design, sales literature, and dealer promotions. The sales department sells certain accounts directly, and supervises the work of independent distributors and reps for other accounts. An accounting department takes care of billing and royalties, as well as traditional bookkeeping and reporting functions.

The major home video labels, the ones owned by major motion picture studios, concentrate almost exclusively on new releases for rental. Typically, there are five "windows" during the life cycle of a new motion picture. The first, which lasts just under six months, is theatrical. The second is home video, which begins just as the theatrical run ends, and benefits from the substantial dollars spent in marketing a new movie. The third is pay-per-view, the fourth is pay cable, and the final window is television (basic cable, network, syndication). In the real world, most movies run no more than a month in theaters, leaving home video consumers with a four or five month wait. Home video exclusives may be as brief as 30 or 60 days before the next window, pay-per-view, opens. The system is convoluted, based on traditions established in the 1980s, and does not always recognize the powerful demand within the home video marketplace. Airline and hotel showings are secondary modes of exhibition and do not affect the home video release.

Motion picture studios tend to ignore library, or catalog, product—allotting almost no marketing dollars, and reissuing a remarkably small number of classic films per year. As a result, consumers show little interest in the vast majority of assets owned by each studio, and video stores tend not to stock many older titles. Since there is so much risk involved in new releases, and so little risk in established product, one can't help but wonder why the studios have been so reluctant to aggressively market their libraries.

The economics of the home video label are based on a standard retail model. The following is an example of the costs involved for a title with a $19.95 list price and one-step distribution:

Rights and royalties	$1.50
Cassette and duplication	$2.50
Cover	$1.00
Advertising and promotion	$1.50
Label overhead and profit	$7.50
WHOLESALE PRICE	$14.00
Dealer markup	$5.95
RETAIL PRICE	$19.95

This model is applicable to high-visibility product like major motion picture releases, where sales exceeding 100,000 units are possible. Dealer markup may be lower if the emphasis is on selling a large number of copies to consumers.

Sometimes the mass-consumer market is sacrificed for higher profits from sales to smaller groups, such as the video stores. By pricing a film at $90 ($65 dealer cost), the label is saying that the film is intended not for sell-through, but for the rental pipeline. A true blockbuster title will sell about 400,000 units at this price point. The same title, priced at $24.95, would probably sell between 3 million and 6 million units; at $19.95, it would probably sell over 5 million units, maybe as many as 10 million. Some titles are released in a tiered-pricing scheme, first releasing a title at a higher price to capture purchases for rental, then at a lower price to encourage sell-through to consumers.

A home video label earns money only by selling cassettes (and a comparatively small number of DVD or laser discs). Although a cassette may be rented by dozens of customers, the label does not receive any further payment for these rentals.

Since many non-theatrical products are made for home video, or assembled from existing sources and repackaged for home video, the cost of production must be deducted from the label's net sales. A cooking tape that costs $100,000 to produce would have to sell about 20,000 units in order to break even—assuming that roughly $5 per unit is available to cover the cost of production.

HOME VIDEO AS A CONSUMER GOODS MARKETING MEDIUM

There is now a VCR in more than 80 percent of U.S. television households. This installed base has reached advertiser "critical mass"—that is, there are now enough VCR households to make home video a viable advertising medium.

There is a fundamental problem, however, with home video as an advertising tool. With a fast-forward button on every VCR, it's easy to scan past the commercials. Still, the movie companies have found the first five or even ten minutes of a videocassette to be a productive environment for showing coming attractions—the tradition of watching these movie commercials is well established in movie theaters, and to a great extent, the ritual has been carried to home video.

Some advertisers have successfully used home video as a medium for imaginative forms of promotional marketing. Typically, a large consumer goods company works with a video company on a big title, one that consumers are likely to buy (a top Disney film, for example). The consumer goods company offers a rebate to viewers who purchase the tape. With the right title, all parties come out winners. The consumer goods company increases brand awareness and, perhaps, expands its relationship with an individual customer, who now associates a particular airline or cereal company with an entertainment vehicle. The video company gets some advertising and public relations, and keeps the retail price down. The customer pays less for the tape. A relatively complex system allows the consumer goods company to calculate the effectiveness of each promotional campaign, but often the benefits are qualitative. There are now many types of video promotions; a watchful eye, particularly around the holiday season, will reveal the approaches currently in vogue.

DIRECT MARKETING OF VIDEOCASSETTES

Videocassettes are sold though several direct-marketing formats. The simplest format is the catalog sale, by which a catalog company buys at wholesale price and sells at retail. This system is used by a wide variety of catalog marketers, including L.L. Bean, whose video products are mainly private-label productions; Disney, whose video products are offered along with music boxes, records, clothing, toys, and other items; and specialty firms whose products appeal to viewers with a particular area of interest (such as fishing). Other catalogs offer primarily videocassettes, with hundreds of titles available, frequently at discount prices. The largest catalog operation is PCB (Publisher's Central Bureau), followed by Video Choice, which is owned by Playboy.

Video catalogs thrive on diversity. Big-name motion pictures do well, but so do classics and esoteric films that are not stocked with any consistency in video stores. Catalog companies generally buy from the labels at below-wholesale prices, since they order such large volumes.

Video clubs are now as common as record and book clubs, and follow the same procedures. A consumer signs up, receives one or more tapes for a very low price, and agrees to purchase a specified number of tapes in the future. Some clubs resemble catalog operations, using "positive option" sales—the consumer buys only what he or she wants.

Negative option clubs are more complicated. The club selects a title as its monthly selection; club members who want to buy the title do nothing, but members who do *not* want the title must notify the club within a specified period. The negative-option format has been successful for Columbia House and, more recently, for BMG Video Club and Time-Life Video Club.

Continuity or subscription clubs are used to sell certain product lines. Columbia House, for example, sells a series of *I Love Lucy* tapes; the consumer buys the first one for $4.95, then receives a new one every four to six weeks until he/she decides to cancel, paying $29.95 for each tape. Continuity distribution is best for series programming: examples include *World War II with Walter Cronkite, The World at War, Star Trek,* and James Bond movies. TV series, movies on the same topic, and military histories are among the best-sellers. Once again, the clubs buy at below-wholesale prices.

VIDEODISCS

The consumer videodisc industry began in the 1970s. By the early 1980s, three incompatible systems were competing not only among themselves, but against several videocassette recording systems as well. LaserVision was the only system to survive the competition, and after an extraordinarily sluggish decade in the 1980s, the laserdisc system has found favor among videophiles, who appreciate the high-quality audio and video presentation.

As of this writing, nearly 10,000 laserdisc titles are available, with several hundred additional titles released annually. Household penetration is nearly 2 percent, a number that may slightly increase due to the popularity of home theater. Laserdiscs are sold only in selected video stores, and only the rare retail outlet rents laserdiscs. The business is a small one, so many studios and film distributors release discs through one of two large distributors, Image Entertainment or Pioneer LDC. (Warner, MGM/UA, and MCA home video divisions release their own laserdisc titles.) Most laserdiscs are sold to consumers for $25.95 to $34.95.

The economics of laserdiscs are similar to the videocassette model, but the manufacturing cost is higher and the advertising costs are lower (the disc benefits from the promotional investment for the videocassette). A major laserdisc release will sell 10,000 to 50,000 units; a lesser title, 2,000 to 10,000 units.

The newer DVD format has just begun its product curve. Initial consumer reaction has been positive, but in order for the format to succeed as planned, it must become a ubiquitous replacement for computer CD-ROMs, audio CDs, and videocassettes.

BUSINESS AND PROFESSIONAL VIDEO

Many production companies have built a business by creating, producing, and distributing off-the-shelf products for business—programs that train employees, for example. Typically, these tapes are developed in response to a marketplace need, though in some cases, such as John Cleese's successful series of humorous business how-to's, a market can be created for a desirable product. Budgets are generally kept low, and retail prices kept high—the only model that works in an environment where unit sales are likely to be low, and cost of sales high.

Video is also used as a selling tool. Promotional videos—promoting a resort, for example, sometimes supplement printed brochures. (For more about business and professional video, see page 320.)

10

New Technologies

Through the 1990s, technology has transformed the television business. The three-network system has toppled. Most U.S. households subscribe to cable TV and own at least one VCR. M More than ten million enjoy motion pictures in home theaters with screens exceeding 40 inches (measured diagonally, as always, to make the set seem larger than it really is). The Internet provides an alternative form of on-screen information and entertainment; video is becoming part of the Internet. Change is happening fast, fueled in part by available investment dollars and an impetus toward an improved worldwide communications system involving telephones, television, computers, and interactive work and play devices.

It's impossible to forecast the future, but it is possible to review some key concepts.

BANDWIDTH

The technical concept of bandwidth is the foundation for the future of television, and the convergence of television, telephones, and computers. A television channel occupies approximately 6 MHz of space on the VHF (and UHF) band of the electromagnetic spectrum (this figure includes the picture information, audio signal, guard bands to prevent interference with neighboring channels, and some other applications). This space is sufficient for the delivery of one broadcast television channel. An AM radio station, whose signal is composed mostly of an audio signal, occupies just 10 kHz, or roughly 1/100 of the bandwidth required for a television channel. An FM radio station offers better sound partly because it occupies more bandwidth—so more signal information can be passed from transmitter to receiver. An FM radio station occupies approximately 200 kHz. Although the electromagnetic spectrum is massive, a finite part of the spectrum is available for radio and television transmissions. Broadcasters share this part of the spectrum with aviation, maritime, military, police, armed forces, and other institutions.

Satellites generally use the part of the spectrum from 3,000 MHz to 300 GHz. Once again, this wide range is used not only by television, but also for weather, military, and other applications. There are technical reasons why this part of the spectrum is well-suited to satellite transmission, and why the VHF (and UHF) band is assigned to television. The concept of bandwidth also applies to hard wires, such as television and telephone cables.

COMPRESSION

One way to gain the benefit of additional bandwidth is to make the signal itself more compact—to squeeze more information through the same-sized transmission channel, or, in the lingo, through the same "pipe." Another way to accomplish this task is to eliminate redundant information. A "compression algorithm" (a software design that controls compression) might recognize a blue sky that does not change for several seconds, or longer. Rather than storing all of the sky's data in every frame, the compression algorithm stores only the new data. By eliminating this data, the relative size of a digital file containing, for example, a motion picture, can be smaller. And as those who download files from the Internet know, a smaller file will transfer faster. Certain types of programming lend themselves to compression. A presentation based mainly on talking heads against fixed backgrounds is an ideal candidate for compression. Talk and game shows present few problems. Soap operas and sitcoms present surprisingly few problems as well. Sporting events, with their multiple views and fast-moving images, are not as well-suited. Compression technology is constantly improving, so the current state of the art is not necessarily a reflection of compression's capabilities in, say, five or ten years—when digital television will be commonplace.

Audio is compressed as well. Dolby Digital is, for example, a compression algorithm for six loudspeakers presenting surround sound for home theaters.

Compression technology is used not only in digital transmission of television signals, but also in digital recording and playback media, such as DVD (see page 115).

Compression is also likely to play a key role in the changeover to digital broadcast and cable television. With the bandwidth required for a single analog channel, it is possible to broadcast multiple digital channels. In short, this means that KGO, San Francisco, could broadcast a handful of digital channels, including its original KGO, Channel 7 feed, in a digital era. This would allow, for example, a KGO home shopping channel, a KGO news channel, and a KGO movie channel, all under the same local brand name. KGO could also offer some level of Internet service and transmit data, and perhaps video, audio and telephone, to a new kind of digital receiver. Compression levels the playing field, and, at least in theory, could place local broadcasters in a new relationship with, for example, local telephone companies.

TRANSMISSION SYSTEMS

The cables that make cable television possible are made of copper or other conductive metal. Copper wires have traditionally been used to interconnect households for cable service and for telephone service. During the past decade, telephone companies have rewired most of their long-distance networks and many local systems with fiber-optic cable. This has been done for three principal reasons: fiber-optic cable maintains a high-quality signal; it is more reliable than copper wiring and less likely to deteriorate (so it requires less service, and ultimately saves telephone companies money); and its bandwidth is thousands of times greater than copper wire.

DIGITAL TELEVISION

Although the format is not universally accepted for all forms of television, the U.S. standard for terrestrial digital broadcasting has been accepted by the FCC. The standard was recommended by the ATSC (Advanced Television Systems Committee), the result of well over a decade's development by companies and research firms that ultimately agreed to work together in a "Grand Alliance." (These companies, some of whom worked together prior to the 1993 formation of the Grand Alliance, were AT&T and Zenith; General Instrument Corporation and MIT; Philips, Thomson, and the David Sarnoff Research Center.)

Sadly, no single digital format has gained worldwide acceptance. There is a competing European system (known as Digital Video Broadcasting, or DVB), and there are variations on the basic theme that distinguish the digital systems that will be used by U.S. cable and satellite services. The lack of consensus is chilling; after decades of inconvenience and expense due to incompatibility between NTSC (the system of 525 lines developed by the U.S.), PAL (the 625-line system devised by the British), and SECAM (the French 625-line system), the international television industries have been mired in the same sort of mess. As television continues to grow as a global medium, a single system would seem to be highly desirable.

The key points in the ATSC digital television standard are:

• MPEG2 digital video compression. The algorithm includes the use of B-frames, or bi-directional frames, intended to improve picture quality.

• Dolby Digital audio compression. This format is already popular in home theaters. Six discrete audio signals are sent to the front left, front center, and front right, to the rear left and rear right, and to a sub-woofer (for lower-frequency signals). The effect is somewhat three-dimensional, adding a realistic, theater-like feeling to the home viewing experience. (It's also called 5.1 channel; five channels plus one sub-woofer channel.)

• Vestigial Sideband (VSB) transmission technology that encourages broad coverage, minimizes interference with analog broadcasts and digital signals.

• MPEG transport of digital data packets.

• A matrix of 18 scanning formats made up of various resolution levels (480, 720, or 1080 lines), aspect ratios (4:3, which is the traditional television rectangle, and 16:9, which is more like the shape of a movie screen), and both interlaced and progressive scanning. (Interlaced scanning paints alternate lines on the screen; progressive scanning paints each line in sequence. The first is used in television, the second, in computers.) High-Definition Television (HDTV) is addressed in some of the scanning formats (see below).

FCC GRANT OF SECOND "DIGITAL" CHANNELS

To encourage the development of advanced television in the U.S., every broadcast television station has been granted a second television channel (initially, this was to be a loan, but industry groups are lobbying for a permanent grant). One channel will be used for conventional programming, and the other will be used for unspecified advanced services, or at least, additional services. These may or may not include HDTV, and may include home shopping, movies or religious programming. (In fact, the channels are not required to be used for television broadcasts and might, according to one scenario, be used for business data services.) At the end of a nine-year transition period, ending in 2006, the U.S. will convert to a digital-only system (2010 or later seems more likely). Conventional TV sets would receive digital signals, but only with a special digital-to-analog converter (these are not exotic devices, though the manufacturers are likely to position them as "advanced technology"). After the transition period, channel allocations might be shuffled, and as each broadcaster gives up the second channel, these would be auctioned to reduce the federal deficit (this is the plan; whether it comes to pass is another matter). Those who win the new licenses will be able to build national services, presumably using the same frequency nationwide (so that NBC could, in theory, own Channel 4 across the whole U.S. and perhaps benefit from a marketing advantage). New, not-yet-conceived telecommunications and television convergence services may use this newly available spectrum as well. (It's too far into the future to make any reasonable predictions.)

Using today's technology, it is possible to transmit an analog and a digital signal within the 6-MHz VHF or UHF spectrum allocation for a single analog television channel. And there's enough excess capacity to accommodate stock quotations. Given this reality, there is reason to question why the FCC has allotted additional spectrum to television stations—and did not simply require manufacturers to add a converter for existing and new TV sets. For more specific information, see FCC grant of second "digital" channels in Chapter 12.

The cost of changing an analog station to digital is substantial, probably not less than $3 million for the smallest operations and as much as $10 million for the largest installations. The biggest costs are in equipment replacement: every camera, switcher, tape machine, router, audio console, editing facility, blank tape (or, hard disk in place of some tape recorders), plus a great deal of equipment in the transmission center. The costs are difficult to estimate because the definition of digital TV is still an open issue. HDTV will require a complete changeover in every control room (because the monitors will be the "old" aspect ratio, and so on), and rethinking of many tried-and-true production techniques. (The standard talking head of a news anchor will now be surrounded by approximately one-third more horizontal screen real estate—how will news programs be redesigned?). Digital TV that involves only compressed signals will not be high-definition, and will require an entirely different series of changes. If interactive features are added to the digital signal, then the director of a TV news program may be calling for changes on Web pages at the same time as she calls cameras. (Of course, with a technological changeover, investment in robotic cameras and other automated gear probably makes economic sense as well. This is contrary, however, to the needs and desires of skilled television engineers and technicians, whose talents will continue to be in demand for higher-quality productions.)

The effect of these plans on cable is not yet clear. In theory, cable could lead the way, and most cable networks are currently developing, testing, or trying out digital networks (often as secondary services). In practice, the channel capacity of most contemporary cable systems is limited (so that new cable networks cannot be added unless others are dropped), so few digital networks will reach nationwide cable audiences unless the cable infrastructure is modernized (via fiber optics, for example or digital compression which expands the possible number of channels).

HIGH-DEFINITION TELEVISION (HDTV)

The centerpiece application of digital television may be HDTV (although they are often confused with one another, the two concepts are not the same). As presently conceived, HDTV (short for High-Definition Television) is a wide-screen format (16:9, roughly one-third wider than current TV sets) with four times the clarity of our current system (twice the vertical resolution and twice the horizontal resolution).

Present-day television equipment cannot accommodate the range of technical requirements demanded by HDTV. This means that video cameras, video switchers and other control equipment, videotape recorders and players, television transmitters, and cable television headends would all have to be replaced or substantially revamped in order to produce and broadcast in HDTV. The faux wood-grain painted onto television scenery presumes a relatively low resolution home receiver; with HDTV's clarity, a great deal of television scenery will need to be rebuilt. Ditto for some costumes, and for an embarrassing number of hairpieces, make-up jobs, and so on.

DBS seems a likely candidate for HDTV transmission of digital networks. Bandwidth limitations are less restrictive, and the DBS industry grew from a tradition of compressed video, so they are likely to take a leading position.

DIGITAL PLAYBACK AND RECORDING

Digital video will also change professional and amateur recording and playback equipment. The digital standards currently under development for broadcast and cable television may or may not match the standards currently in use at home: DV (Digital Video), which is used by the latest generation of consumer camcorders; DAT (Digital Audio Tape), an advanced (typically professional) audio recording and playback format; and DVD (Digital Versatile Disc), which is advancing as a video playback medium, and perhaps, as a replacement for CD-ROM and for audio compact discs.

State-of-the-art professional installations are already making use of digital tape formats, such as Digital Beta, which offer flawless dubs, better dropout compensation, and smoother operation in an editing facility. Since the mid-1990s, digital video camcorders have been available to consumers. At the same time, digital cameras have become popular among computer users.

To record and play digital video, consumers will need a new type of VCR, one based on digital technology—and more specifically, upon MPEG-2 video compression.

The videodisc, as a recording and playback medium, has been available in various forms since the early 1980s. Laserdiscs did not find acceptance because they competed against the recordable tape formats. Still, the combination of superior reliability and random access makes some form of disc the likely long-term winner.

DVD (Digital Versatile Discs) could replace tape as the dominant home recording and playback medium in the digital era. The format also could someday replace audio compact discs (CDs) and CD-ROMs used in personal computers as well. As personal computers continue to transform themselves into home entertainment and information centers, watching movies and television shows on the computer screen will become more commonplace. DVD could be a central format for this type of application—and, of course, for computer games.

INTERNET ISSUES

It is possible that the Internet will dramatically change the way that the world receives and perceives television. Full-motion video is currently a reality on the relatively young Internet medium; the picture quality is marginal and the images are jumpy, but the situation is improving rapidly, and with the fast access available via ASDL and cable modems, the new paradigm may evolve quickly. Television (and radio) signals can be transmitted and received, in real time.

As the Internet continues to evolve, its ability to distribute television throughout the world may cause every network to reconsider its business model. HBO might, for example, distribute its pay service(s) to Internet viewers who pay a de-scrambling fee; in this scenario, perhaps HBO Internet viewers would subscribe to a cable Internet service via a cable modem. Would cable systems continue to exist, or would HBO simply distribute its wares directly to subscribers? In 1998, the World Wrestling Federation announced plans for pay-per-view distribution of events via the Internet. In this same world, CBS might become a worldwide service almost overnight. The Canadian Broadcasting Corporation, which has been so careful about protecting its role and Canada's identity, might become the most popular network in Australia. Similarly, Canada might find its borders crossed not only by U.S. broadcast signals, but by Internet channels from every English- and French-speaking nation.

Similarly, the concept of "set-top box" is evolving. This device, already the replacement for the old-fashioned cable converter ("cable box") in thousands of households, may incorporate a cable modem, networked computer, data storage, telephone, and/or audience measurement device. It is likely that this box-in whatever form it takes—will allow cable television viewers access to the Worldwide Web and to e-mail service on their television sets.

Certainly, it's impossible to predict how the Internet will change television. Or how television, in its digital form, might transform or mate with the Internet to devise something entirely new.

PART 2

Regulation of Distribution

11

FCC Basics

The Federal Communications Commission (FCC) is the principal government agency that regulates the television business. Its jurisdiction covers the means of mass television distribution: traditional broadcast, cable and satellite, and most emerging television technologies at the intersection of telephone, computing and digital signals. Only home and business videos which do not use radio, wire, fiber, or other means of instantaneous mass distribution currently escape FCC control. The FCC also regulates interstate telephone service.

ORIGINS OF THE FCC

Television broadcasting involves sending signals on specific frequencies of radio waves. Radio waves are like light: there is a continuous spectrum of different waves, like the colors of the rainbow in the visible spectrum. Each small "color" gradation of the radio waves provides a different frequency, or broadcast channel. The spectrum of useful radio waves is broad, but not limitless. Some portions of the spectrum, like the FM band, travel limited distances, and can be reused in other parts of the country. Other frequencies, like the AM and short-wave bands, can travel great distances—particularly at night, when the reflective effect of the ionosphere is greater. If there are two stations broadcasting on the same frequency within range of each other, the signals will cross and interfere with each other, resulting in poor reception.

The first attempt at broadcast regulation in the U.S. was the Radio Act of 1912, which provided for the licensing of radio broadcasters by the Secretary of Commerce. Basically, this law allowed anyone who applied to get a license. Transmission was largely in Morse code; as long as the airwaves were plentiful and the broadcasters few, there was no need to police who used what band. With the widespread introduction of sound reproduction via radio in the 1920s, however, the commercial potential of radio became clear, and the number of stations skyrocketed.

Faced with the need to bring some order to the use of a now-crowded spectrum, Congress passed the 1927 Radio Act, which set up the Federal Radio Commission. This Commission was empowered to pick and choose among potential broadcasters, assigning specific frequencies to particular licensees. The 1927 Act mandated that the standard for deciding who would qualify for a license was to be one of "public interest, convenience, and necessity." This phrase, the basis for regulating monopolies, had come into use in connection with the licensing of "natural monopolies": public utilities (such as water, gas, phone, and electric companies) and common carriers (such as railroads). When the 1927 Radio Act was drawn up, Congress thought that a "public interest, convenience, and necessity" approach should be used in dividing up the radio spectrum—even though the radio spectrum at that time provided enough diversity to prevent a true monopoly in most locations.

The 1927 Act was in effect until Congress adopted the Communications Act of 1934, which has remained the basis of communications law ever since. Although closely modeled on its 1927 predecessor, the 1934 Act created a new agency, the FCC, which took over the functions of the Radio Commission. The FCC also assumed, from the Interstate Commerce Commission, jurisdiction over interstate telephone and telegraph communications.

The FCC is a quasi-autonomous commission which has elements of each of the legislative, judicial, and executive branches of government. It is one of a group of independent regulatory agencies that provide expert oversight in various areas of commercial activity. Others include the Federal Aviation Agency (FAA), the Federal Trade Commission (FTC) and the Securities and Exchange Commission (SEC). Each agency is established by acts of Congress, which set an overall framework of law and delegate the elaboration and implementation of that law to the agency.

ORGANIZATION OF THE FCC

The FCC consists of five Commissioners (seven before 1983), one of whom serves as "Chairman." These Commissioners are nominated by the President for staggered five-year terms. The President cannot appoint more than three of the five from one political party, and all appointments are subject to Senate approval. The Commissioners oversee a staff of about 2,100. The chairman serves as the executive officer, with his actions subject to the approval of the majority of the Commission. Notwithstanding the President's role in naming the Commissioners, Congress has traditionally held great power to influence the FCC. The 1998 budget for the FCC topped $186 million, of which a target of $162 million was set for the FCC to raise through fees and other generated income.

As of 1998, the FCC includes the Comission itself and 14 major staff units, seven of which are the major operational bureaus: the Office of Legislative Affairs, the Office of Plans and Policy, the Office of the Managing Director, the Office of the Administrative Law Judges, the Office of Public Affairs, the Office of the General Counsel, the Office of Engineering and Technology, the Field Operations Bureau, the Common Carrier Bureau, the Mass Media Bureau, the Cable Services Bureau, the Wireless Telecommunications Bureau, and the Compliance and International Bureau. All of these branches report to the Managing Director. The more independent Office of the Inspector General reports directly to the Commission. The Mass Media Bureau oversees many aspects of broadcast television, as well as radio stations and new mass-media video technologies. The Cable Services Bureau handles many aspects of cable television (such as consumer protection, competition, "must-carry" and rulemaking), and the International Bureau handles some satellite issues. These organizational lines are periodically reviewed and adjusted.

The Commissioners set overall approaches; policy specifics are generally articulated at the staff level, then reviewed by the Commission before being adopted as official actions. The staff handles applications for licensing and renewal, again, with the Commission approving significant actions before they become official.

FUNCTIONING OF THE FCC

In its control of television, the FCC performs several distinct functions: rule-making, licensing and registration, adjudication, enforcement, and informal influence. Contacts with industry and public representatives during some activities must be "on the record" or documented to provide a public record and a fair opportunity for all sides to be heard. Other types of contacts, such as informal lobbying, go undocumented.

Rule-making is just what it sounds like: the process of issuing new rules and regulations, and amending or deleting existing ones. Rule-making is governed by both internal FCC procedures and federal laws, including the Administrative Procedure Act and related regulations. Proposals for change may come from the public or regulated industries—or they may percolate within the FCC itself, often in response to less formal pressures from public and industry representatives, members of Congress, or the Administration. The formal procedure can begin with a notice of inquiry, which designates general interest. Once discussion has moved to the point where a specific change is contemplated, the FCC announces a notice of proposed rule-making and invites comments. If the proposed change is of sufficient importance or controversy, an oral hearing in front of the Commission may be scheduled, though this is unusual. Once all the comments have been reviewed, the staff prepares—and the Commission reviews and issues—a report and order. This document sets out the final rule or regulation, describing the rationale behind it. The final report and order, as with most FCC actions, can be appealed to the U.S. Court of Appeals for the District of Columbia for judicial review.

Licensing is the method by which the broadcast spectrum allocations controlled by the FCC are made and reviewed. It is described in detail on pages 124. Cable systems go through the simpler process of registration (see page 140).

Adjudication refers to the process by which the FCC settles disputes, either between private parties (as in a license challenge or the awarding of a new channel) or between the FCC and a private party (as in a disputed disciplinary action). In a formal adjudication, there will be a hearing, conducted in accordance with the Administrative Procedure Act and the general require-ments of due process. The first hearing is usually before an administrative law judge, a specially designated staff attorney. These hearings are modeled on traditional trials, with sworn testimony, opposing lawyers, and the like. The decisions of the administrative law judges are subject to appeal within the FCC, first to the Review Board, then to the full Commission. As usual, further appeals to the Court of Appeals, and thereafter the Supreme Court, are possible. If all appeals are pursued, adjudication can be time-consuming and expensive.

Enforcement involves action by the FCC to correct what it sees as lapses or wrong doing by entities subject to its jurisdiction. Most commonly, this involves a broadcast licensee violating required practices. The worst penalty that can be imposed is the loss of a license, either through a failure to renew (rare) or an outright revocation (rarer still). This extreme penalty is usually imposed only if the licensee has a history of flagrant mismanagement, deception bordering on fraud, or gross negligence. For less serious transgressions, short-term or conditional renewals may be given, or fines assessed. The announced cause is seldom related to program content, since both the First Amendment and Section 326 of the 1934 Act prohibit censorship. Indecent or obscene programming, however, is an exception to this principle, and is treated differently under both the Constitution and the 1934 Act (see page 193). Changes made under the 1996 Telecommunications Act preventing competitive challenge, make license renewal protests even less likely to be brought.

Informal influence describes the FCC's ability—and willingness—to affect the television world without going through formal action. A concerned telephone call or letter from the FCC, for example, will certainly get the attention of a station manager. Public statements, articles, and congressional testimony by Commission members and senior staff are also followed closely by the industry.

FCC PHILOSOPHY

Since its birth in 1934, the FCC has undergone an unusual number of changes in both its underlying philosophy and its rules and administrative actions. Some of this is inevitable in industries that have evolved as much as television and other communications businesses have over the years. Historically speaking, when faced with a change in the television business, the FCC has reacted in a predictable fashion. First, the agency ignores the change; then it tries to protect the status quo; and finally, with a certain degree of public and congressional prodding, it incorporates the changes into a new status quo.

There is some justification, under the 1934 Act, for the FCC's protective tendency. The 1934 Act called on the FCC to regulate in the public interest, and from the beginning, the FCC has viewed this to mean strong, free broadcast service at the local level. This interpretation has made the health of the local broadcast station of particular concern to the FCC. Much of its conservatism has been motivated by this principle, rather than simply by knee-jerk protection of the establishment.

The FCC gave recognition to the new medium of television in 1941, approving the first attempts at commercial broadcasting. From 1948 to 1952, the licensing of television stations was suspended in order to allow the FCC to study potential interference problems and develop an orderly system of assigning portions of the broadcast spectrum to particular stations. In 1952, when licensing recommenced, the UHF channels were allocated as well. With the promulgation of color standards in 1953, a basic framework for broadcast television was complete.

The history of cable regulation, discussed more fully in Chapter 13, was marked by the FCC, first ignoring the phenomenon of cable television, then trying to suppress it, and finally encouraging it within the FCC's sphere of control. The resulting Cable Communications Policy Act of 1984 clearly put cable operations under FCC authority—and clearly limited that authority in several respects.

The 1980s saw a sizeable deregulation of the communications industry, sparked by the deregulatory spirit which climaxed during the Reagan presidency. But deregulation also gained impetus from a weakening in the argument that had led to the creation of the FCC in the first place. With cable, low-power broadcasting, and home video, many new programming sources became available to most Americans. Expanding satellite and Internet television will continue this trend. The rationale behind the FCC's regulation of broadcasting, in contrast, was that since there were only so many channels in the broadcast spectrum, television had to be treated as a natural monopoly. Since viewers now have a wider range of options, the FCC has returned on many issues to the accepted verities of a free-market, laissez-faire approach.

This trend toward lessening control has continued through the 1990s, with a few notable exceptions, such as cable rate regulation. Congressional action, in the 1992 Cable Act and in the 1996 Telecommunications Act, has spurred some of these changes, as has the march of technological innovation. The FCC itself has become more and more comfortable with competition as a defining ethos. Nonetheless, the government remains a player. High-definition television and the reallocation of the broadcast spectrum are issues of the near future in which Congress is taking a direct lead. The patchwork of FCC control and permissiveness is described in the chapters that follow: Chapter 12 deals with the regulation of broadcast television; Chapter 13, with the regulation of cable; Chapter 14, with satellite delivery and other new technologies.

The FCC and Broadcast Regulation

The FCC regulates broadcast television at both the local and network levels. The local control is the most pervasive—the very existence of local broadcast stations depends upon obtaining and renewing an FCC license. The FCC's intervention at the network level has had a significant effect on shaping the structure of the television industry, but these restrictions have been significantly loosened over the past decade.

LOCAL REGULATION: LICENSING

The FCC decides who can use the broadcast airwaves, and exercises this authority by granting broadcast licenses to individuals and companies. Such a license is required for any significant broadcast activity, including all broadcast television. FCC licenses are quite specific as to the type of service permitted, the assigned frequency, the location of the transmitter, the applicable technical standards, and the signal strength. In television, the licensing process begins with the potential station identifying an available frequency and location. Ever since the early 1950s, the FCC has maintained a list of pre-determined allocations for television channels, and few standard VHF and UHF frequencies are unassigned. (There are some more "low-power" allocations still available; see page 130.) Sometimes, new allocations are approved or are open for assignment; on rare occasions, an existing license may be revoked or abandoned, creating a new opening. Prior to 1996, a would-be entrant into the station business could also try to obtain a license by filing a competing application when an existing license came up for renewal (see page 131). The 1996

Telecommunications Act removed the possibility of such a competitive challenge. Now a "disinterested" challenge must be made. Only after the license is revoked would new applications be entertained.

Presuming that a frequency is available, the first step in seeking a license is filing an application for a construction permit. This permit, when issued, allows a period of time to build the specified broadcasting facilities and to get them running properly. For television stations, this interval is typically 18 to 24 months. Once the facilities are built, the FCC will review the technical and other pertinent data on their performance and, if satisfied, will issue the actual broadcast license to the station. Reflecting changes made by the 1996 Telecommunications Act, television licenses now run for eight years.

In order to obtain a license or, for that matter, a construction permit, the licensee must meet a series of statutory requirements. First, the licensee must be a U.S. citizen, or a company owned principally by U.S. citizens. With corporate licenses, foreign ownership of more than 20 percent is prohibited; when Rupert Murdoch and his News Corporation acquired the stations that would constitute the FOX Network, he changed his citizenship from Australian to American. Second, the applicant must qualify as to character. Stations are supposed to be assigned to promote the public interest, so an owner with a serious criminal record or other major character defects would be undesirable. The third requirement is one of financial resources. This means not only the ability to build the facility, but also the ability to operate without revenues for some months when starting up broadcasting. The fourth requirement is meeting technical standards, such as protecting other stations from interference.

In granting a license, the FCC can consider other qualifications, such as minority involvement or local control. Additional criteria are particularly likely to be used if there are competing applications for the same openings, as is often the case with new applications.

RESTRICTIONS ON LICENSE HOLDING

In order to promote diversity of media ownership on the local level, the FCC adopted rules in 1975 that prohibit ownership of both broadcasting properties and newspapers in the same market. For instance, when a subsidiary of Murdoch's News Corporation acquired Channel 5 in New York City, the parent company had to sell the *New York Post*. Most newspaper/television ownership combinations that existed before the rule went into effect, however, did not require divestiture.

Locally, no entity is permitted to hold more than one license for television service in a given market, absent a highly unusual waiver. The 1996 Telecommunications Act has directed the FCC to examine loosening these restrictions, and revisions to these rules may be forthcoming, although a continued limit on the ownership of VHS stations to one to a market appears likely. Prior to the 1996 changes, there were limitations on combining ownership of radio service with television service in a given market (some pre-1970 combinations including AM, FM, and TV were "grandfathered," or permitted because they existed before the rule took effect). Some exceptions to these rules were possible. Perhaps the most important involved the largest 25 markets, where many competing voices were available. The 1996 changes direct the FCC to expand this approach to the top 50 markets. Other exceptions can be made for "failed" services and for good cause shown on a case-by-case basis.

To ensure diversity at the national level, the FCC for a long time maintained rules limiting the total number of broadcast stations that can be subject to common ownership. The 1996 Telecommunications Act significantly reduced this restriction. First it dropped all limits on the *number* of stations that could be owned. It preserved a limit on the percentage of the total national TV audience which a station group could reach in the aggregate, but increased that percentage to 35 percent. Under the old rules, the percentage could be increased for minority-controlled stations. It is not yet clear whether such a minority benefit will continue under the 1996 Act rules.

EQUAL EMPLOYMENT OPPORTUNITY

The FCC requires any licensee with five or more employees to establish and maintain an equal employment opportunity (EEO) program. The goal is to increase the employment of women and minorities in the broadcast industry. Since few television licensees can operate with fewer than five employees, most stations are subject to EEO rules.

Stations must submit a five-point EEO plan when applying for a new license or assigning/transferring an existing one. Required information includes who in the proposed organization is responsible for implementing the program, the recruitment policies and methods to be employed, and the training available both on the job and from outside technical or professional schools. After obtaining a license to operate, each station is required to file an annual employment report detailing the number and percentage of employees by each job category, sex, and minority group. These reports describe the success or failure of the EEO plan, and must be available for review by the public. If a station is not meeting expected targets—both for the total number of women and minorities employed and for the number in management positions—the plan's failure will be reviewed by the FCC, usually in the context of license renewal.

The EEO targets are based on the availability of women and minorities in the civilian labor pool for the area covered by the broadcaster's license. All broadcasters must have targets for women; however, minority targets are required only if blacks, Hispanics, Asians/Pacific Islanders, and Native American/Alaskan Indians represent 5 percent or more of the area's labor pool.

Using a 50/50 guideline, the FCC keys the target for station employment at 50 percent of the group's ratio to the available labor force. For example, if Hispanics represent 20 percent of the local labor pool, employees of Hispanic origin would have to constitute at least ten percent of the station's full-time staff. Further FCC requirements set targets for hiring, retention, and promotion of women and minorities in the "upper-four job categories" (officials/managers, professionals, technicians, and sales workers). At stations with five to ten full-time employees, women and minorities should be represented in these positions at 25 percent of their availability in the labor force. This proportion jumps to 50 percent for stations with 11 or more full-time employees. Meeting these targets, while important, is not the end of the story; stations must meet additional EEO requirements.

When applying for renewal of a license, a broadcast station must give an even more detailed report on equal employment opportunity. This report indicates the actual number of women and minorities hired and promoted in the previous 12 months as well as any complaints that have been filed with the EEO Commission. The station also supplies figures for the labor-force composition in its operating area, and the sources of that data. While the breakdown of its current employees by race and sex is an undisputed number, the proportion of women and minorities in a local labor force is sometimes debatable. The FCC reporting form allows some flexibility, in that the station can use data other than the census-based Metropolitan Statistical Area (M.S.A.), city percentages, or county percentages—provided that the station can offer the usually skeptical FCC a solid explanation for doing so. There are civil penalties for stations that fail to comply with EEO requirements. Adherence to an EEO plan is commonly scrutinized at license-renewal time.

Cable operators are also required to have an EEO plan and follow similar FCC guidelines for the percentage of women and minorities employed. Unlike broadcasters, however, cable operators do not have to file the EEO plan with the FCC as part of a certification request. Cable operators must file annual reports on their actual employment personnel practices; these reports, as well as the EEO plan, are reviewed both at the time of filing and in the re-certification process. Cable companies have been fined for non-compliance—and in some cases, they have lost their certification to operate (see page 141).

Periodically, the FCC's EEO rules come under attack, with opponents charging that they constitute reverse discrimination, and proponents calling for the requirements to be based on parity, not 50 percent. When the FCC has tried to back off on the issue, however, Congress has made it clear that the rules are here to stay. EEO compliance is the one area of FCC activity in which the deregulatory fever of the 1980s and 1990s has had almost no impact.

HIGH-DEFINITION / DIGITAL TELEVISION

The U.S. was a historical leader in the introduction of television service. There have been drawbacks to this leadership: the U.S. has been stuck using a relatively primitive technical standard. The limited number of "lines" and restricted aspect ratio (the ratio of screen width to height) of the American standard result in poor detail resolution to the broadcast image, and a constricted view. For years, much of the rest of the world enjoyed a somewhat better system (the British PAL system and the French system offer 625 lines, for roughly 20 percent more image clarity than the 525-line NTSC system developed by the U.S.). The new ATSC systems agreed to by government and industry for the U.S., however, requires greater bandwidth than is currently used for broadcasting, which in turn means that the spectrum will have to be re-allocated. The new FCC rule assigns each digital television (DTV) broadcaster a 6 MHz–wide digital channel. Eligibility for a DTV license is limited to analog broadcasters in existence as of April 3, 1997. For every video signal transmitted on its present analog station, the broadcaster must also transmit a video signal on its digital station, although simulcasting is not initially a requirement.

The rule also requires that the four networks (ABC, CBS, NBC, and FOX) begin broadcasting in digital by May 1, 1999, in the top ten television markets. They must broadcast in digital in the top 30 markets by November 1, 1999. All remaining commercial stations must broadcast in digital by May 1, 2002, and noncommercial stations by May 1, 2003. The rules contemplate up to a one-year (possibly longer) extension of the deadlines to accommodate delays in construction of the facilities necessary to broadcast digital signals.

The stations must begin simulcasting by April 1, 2003, and must be completely simulcasting by April 1, 2005. They will be allowed to retain their analog channels until the conversion is complete. Notwithstanding a trend toward auctioning broadcast spectrum allocations, this new channel was to be awarded for free, in part because of the burden of the costs of purchasing new transmission equipment which would fall on each station as a result of the changeover. The FCC has established an analog license give-back goal of 2006, when operational digital broadcasters will surrender their analog licenses. The public stations' give-back goal is 2007.

For a brief while, it looked as though the future of broadcasting was set—digital HDTV would come over the air through a mandated standard via existing stations. The combination of the speed of technological and business change, the gathering consensus for taking the FCC out of the standards business, and a good dose of old-fashioned greed has upset this cozy expectation.

First of all, the growing reliance on market forces, or perhaps the new, strong players left out of the standards battle (including Microsoft) have persuaded the FCC to back off from many of its proposed technical mandates that would have governed the HDTV standard. While many of these new entries into the debate have strongly argued that government standard-setting only serves to lock in obsolete technologies, there is also something to be said for government help in avoiding technology wars in an area of shared national access like television.

The FCC helped take the lead in deciding on the technical standard for U.S. television when it started up and when it switched over to color. The choices made may or may not have been the best available, but at least there *was* a standard. The decision to settle on a single approach led to quick implementation and consumer acceptance. In the deregulatory spirit of the 1980s and 1990s, however, standard-setting has acquired a bad name; far better, it was thought, to allow the marketplace to decide on the best approach. Unfortunately, the one example of this theory as applied on the mass-consumer level has not been a happy one: AM stereo. The determination of a standard for AM stereo broadcasting has been left to the marketplace. The result? The adoption by different AM stations of competing standards, which in turn has led to confusion among radio listeners and very slow acceptance of the new technology. There is no reason to think that a total free-market approach to digital and/or HDTV will fare any better.

While the standards question is being re-opened on one side, the spectrum utilization question is gaining new interest on the other. Digitalization not only allows for the compression of one high definition signal in the allotted new channel, it also allows for multiple programs to be broadcast over that spectrum space at a lower level of definition. This has led to a game of chicken between Congress and parts of the broadcast community over whether the new spectrum allocations would have to go to HDTV or whether some or all of it could go to these expanded broadcast options. Where will this all shake out? At this writing, any firm prediction seems perilous, particularly when further advances in technology, and yet another distribution medium—the World Wide Web—may change the entire calculus yet again before the issues are fully resolved. What is certain is a significant shake-up in the technical world of broadcast television, a world that has otherwise changed relatively little since the 1950s.

LOW-POWER STATIONS

When the original spectrum allocation structure was set up in 1952, the goal was to permit every community in the U.S. to receive at least one television station, and to offer as many communities as possible two channels. To prevent signal interference between broadcasters on the same channel in certain adjacent areas, a patchwork of assignments was made, particularly on the VHF band. This setup left a number of frequency gaps that were too small to be filled by normal full-power stations.

In 1982, as part of the move to broaden viewer options, the FCC made licenses available for a new kind of television station that, because it would operate at considerably reduced power, could be slotted into such a gap. This development created a rush of applications that threatened to overwhelm the Commission's resources. In an unprecedented relaxation of the FCC's oversight responsibility, Congress amended the Communications Act to allow the FCC to hold a lottery among the potential applicants for each low-power opening. This arrangement would take the place of the FCC evaluating each applicant according to the "public interest, convenience, or necessity" standard. Once the lottery produces a winner, the winner's application is still studied by itself to ensure that it meets the necessary standards described on page 125. In the lotteries, the odds are weighted to favor applications showing minority and/or local control; the presence of each of these factors will double the winning chances of the applicant. The lottery system has greatly reduced—but not eliminated—the FCC's administrative burden in licensing low-power television (LPTV) stations.

There is no upper limit on the number of low-power stations that can be owned by a single group. While many low-power stations have been licensed, they have had only limited economic impact, and figure only marginally in the television industry as a whole.

MULTIPOINT DISTRIBUTION SERVICE

Another relatively new class of broadcast service is Multipoint Distribution. This resembles a cross between low-power television and cellular phones. A pair of band segments have been set aside for mid-range and local transmissions on a line-of-sight basis. A special converter receives the signals and feeds them to the television on an otherwise unused normal broadcast channel. Many of these small transmitters (the "multipoints") may be scattered around a service area. Multipoint services have also been licensed through a lottery approach. Because of the need for a converter and other technical limitations, the multipoint systems have been slow to catch on, particularly in areas already wired for cable, although systems offering multiple channels have had some success. This area has attracted some interest from the telephone companies, which have unrestricted access to this technology. When digital compression permits a significant increase in the number of deliverable channels, multipoint distribution may become a more significant player.

LICENSE RENEWALS

The Communications Act sets television licenses to a term of eight years, at which time they come up for review and renewal. Up until 1981, this was a time-consuming ordeal, requiring reams of supporting material on how the station was serving the public interest, convenience, and necessity. As part of deregulation, the renewal application was shortened to "postcard" size, although certain attachments relating to broadcast violence complaints may be necessary. It is due four months before the license expires.

A "public-interest" review is still carried out, but it consists, at least at the FCC level, largely of looking into any complaints from the public or any record of non-compliance with FCC rules and procedures. If the record is clean, renewal is customarily granted at the staff level unless it is contested by some third party. The 1996 Act has created a level of "renewal expectancy" as to the substance of the review. Since the broadcaster must give notice of the upcoming renewal on its own airwaves, this act alone can occasionally spark disgruntled viewers to complain. Any parties who do wish to contest the renewal can search the station's public inspection file (see below) for evidence of lapses and failures. Prior to enactment of the 1996 Telecommunications Act, a competing applicant could mount a combination challenge and replacement application. This direct incentive to bringing a challenge has now been dropped, and a decrease in the already small number of challenges is expected.

If the station has problems with its record, or if there is a contest from a concerned third party, there can be a further FCC review on the matter, sometimes before an administrative law judge. That judge's decision is subject to appeal to the Commission and the courts.

A contested renewal is a rarity, and a successful challenge to a license renewal is even more unusual. Even so, challengers have sometimes prevailed—and because a failure to renew is, in effect, a commercial death sentence, even the slim possibility that renewal might not happen encourages broadcasters to comply with the FCC's requirements.

PUBLIC INSPECTION FILE

Under FCC regulations, every television station has to maintain a public inspection file. This file must contain a wide variety of information, including (1) copies of the license renewal application, Ownership Report Forms, and Annual Employment Forms; (2) information on station ownership, network affiliation, management agreements, political broadcasts, and children's programming; (3) the FCC publication *The Public and Broadcasting—A Procedure Manual;* and (4) letters and other communications from the public and from citizen groups.

Certification that the public information file is complete is a necessary part of the renewal process. While the file must be kept available for public inspection, the public seldom looks at it, though potential challengers to a station's license renewal will.

LICENSE TRANSFERS

The FCC regulates the transfer of station licenses—not only when occasioned by the outright sale of the business or of the company holding the license, but also as part of any material change of ownership. Even the conversion of the owning company from corporate to partnership form, without any change of ultimate control, would have to be cleared with the FCC. As one would expect, minor adjustments in company structure, or in the make-up of minority ownership, can be reported on abbreviated forms and receive little, if any, scrutiny.

The transfer of control of a station, however, is a more serious matter. In theory, a TV broadcast license cannot be sold. Either the company holding the license is sold, or the facilities and goodwill of the station are sold to an entity that asks the FCC to reassign it the license. In either event, the FCC reviews the change to ensure that it is consistent with the public-interest standard. Prior to deregulation, this review process was rigorous, and the possibility of challenge an ever-present threat; more recently, however, this degree of scrutiny has been relaxed. The FCC also eliminated the "anti-trafficking" rules that had previously prevented sales of stations within three years of a prior transfer.

The FCC's relaxations of these rules, its expansion of the maximum number of stations that can be owned by any one group, and the easy availability of mergers-and-acquisitions financing in the 1980s led to a major boom in station sales during the 1980s. The early 1990s, saw less station sale activity. Activity is picking up again in the aftermath of the 1996 Telecommunications Act, with its further relaxation of the multiple ownership rules.

STATION OPERATIONS

In addition to overseeing the birth, life, and death of television stations, the FCC controls many of the operating procedures of a station.

First of all, there are a number of technical and housekeeping rules for television broadcasters. Station identification messages (either visual or aural) must be broadcast at the beginning and end of each broadcast day, and also hourly (as close to on-the-hour as is reasonably possible). Certain logs must be kept, although since deregulation, the number of logs has been greatly reduced, and such logs need cover only certain technical matters. Every station must also maintain the Emergency Broadcast System.

Some FCC rules govern advertising (see page 433). The FCC also requires a station to disclose commercial support of programming, and prohibits a station from receiving undisclosed compensation for the inclusion of material in a broadcast. These restrictions have their origin in the "payola" scandals of popular music on radio in the 1950s, when disc jockeys took bribes to play certain songs. Section 507 of the Communications Act prohibits a station, or any other entity connected with the production or broadcasting of a television program, from accepting or paying "valuable consideration" (which need not be cash) for the broadcast of any matter without disclosing the fact of that payment to the viewers. Section 507 is the reason for the "promotional consideration" announcements familiar to game-show viewers. It is typical for television employment contracts to contain a provision requiring the employee to obey Section 507.

POLITICAL BROADCASTING

Until it was dropped by the FCC in 1987, the "fairness doctrine" required that stations offer a reasonable opportunity for groups or individuals to express opposing points of view on controversial subjects of public importance. This requirement was a corollary to the "natural monopoly" view of television broadcasting; as that philosophy faded in the 1980s, so did support for the fairness doctrine. One related prohibition, the "personal attack rule," continues to provide a right to respond on the air to "personal attacks" broadcast against specific individuals or groups.

There is another vestige of the fairness-doctrine idea in the limited field of political broadcasts. Under Section 315 of the Communications Act, a television broadcaster that gives or sells airtime to one candidate for a particular political office must provide an "equal opportunity" to other legally qualified candidates for the same office. There are exceptions, though, for coverage of a candidate in bona fide newscasts, interviews, and documentaries. Thus, the appearance of a candidate who is legitimately in the news on *Meet the Press* or on local news does not mean that other candidates are entitled to an equal amount of airtime. Since televised debates are generally viewed as part of news coverage, they also fall outside Section 315. On the other hand, if a station does sell television advertising to one candidate, it must be willing to sell it to competitors for the same office on the same terms.

Broadcasters are limited in the rates that they can charge candidates for political ads. At no time may a station charge more for a political ad than for "comparable use." During the 45 days before a primary and 60 days before a general or special election, the charges cannot exceed those offered to the station's most-favored commercial advertisers, including any applicable discounts.

The final aspect of these politically related rules is the "reasonable access" provision. This applies only to candidates for federal elective office: the President, the Vice President, and Congress. In short, broadcasters must sell (or give, a less likely option) candidates for these offices reasonable amounts of advertising time to get their messages across.

In each of these situations, there is a definition of the kind of legally qualified candidate for public office who is entitled to benefit from these rules. In practice, most stations are happy to comply with these rules, as they provide an excuse to charge political candidates full rates for the periodic barrage of candidate ads. With the increasing pressure for campaign finance reform and for getting some public value back from the essentially free spectrum allocation given to broadcasters, the late 1990s has seen proposals for giving free advertising access to federal candidates. The future of these proposals is questionable.

CHILDREN'S BROADCASTING

The FCC's move into regulating broadcasting aimed at children is discussed in Chapter 18.

NETWORK ISSUES

There are four principal areas in which the FCC traditionally governed the operations of network television: (1) affiliation agreements, (2) multiple-station ownership, (3) prime-time access, and (4) the financial interest and syndication ("fin-syn") rules. In the deregulatory atmosphere of the 1990s, all but the first have been repealed or extensively modified.

AFFILIATION AGREEMENTS

The FCC protects the local affiliates in their relationships with the broadcast networks most importantly, by preventing the network from forcing affiliates to take their programming. The affiliates may decline to take any given network offering for a host of reasons. In addition, the affiliation cannot be exclusive: the affiliate is allowed to take programs from any other source with which it can reach agreement, including another network. Other regulations prevent the network from controlling the affiliate's own advertising inventory, either by setting rates or by acting as a national sales representative for the station. The rules now permit affiliation with companies operating two or more networks, unless such combination includes more than one of the current "big four"—ABC, CBS, NBC and FOX—or a combination of one of the big four with WBTV or UPN. The old rule that set a two-year maximum for the length of an affiliation agreement was dropped in 1989.

MULTIPLE-STATION OWNERSHIP

The FCC rules about multiple-station ownership in effect before the 1996 Telecommunication Act had the effect over the years of keeping most network affiliates under separate ownership from the networks themselves. Nonetheless, each of the networks—including FOX—assembled a formidable group of network-owned and -operated stations (O&Os) in most of the key markets. The independent stations in these markets also tend to be owned by major station groups. And since these markets are critical to the success of syndicated program offerings, the networks (through their O&Os) and the major station groups are big players in the syndication scene. To this extent, the FCC's ownership restrictions never achieved their objectives. The 1996 Act removed the total number limits but kept a 35 percent coverage ceiling in effect (see page 126).

PRIME-TIME ACCESS

For many years, the FCC helped independent program suppliers facing a small number of broadcasters in the major markets by imposing the *prime-time access* rules (see page 35). Prime-time access required that network affiliates in the top 50 markets take no more than three hours of network programming in the four-hour prime-time block, including re-runs of a program that was formerly on the networks. Although some lip service was given to the notion that the prime-time access rules should encourage the production of local and public affairs programs, the syndicators of shows like *Wheel of Fortune* (KingWorld) and *Entertainment Tonight* (Paramount)—distributing these programs nationally—were the real beneficiaries. In 1995 the rule was rescinded, effective August 30, 1996.

THE FINANCIAL INTEREST AND SYNDICATION RULES

The most important of the FCC's former network restrictions were the financial interest and syndication (fin-syn) rules. In their classic form, the fin-syn rules, adopted in 1970, completely barred the networks from acquiring any financial interest in the broadcast of outside-produced programs (those not solely produced by the network) other than the right to exhibit the programs on the network.

With the growing power of satellite, cable and other broadcast networks, the potential for network domination was seen to be receding, and the need for additional network resources was seen to be increasing. This perception led first to the significant watering-down of these rules in 1991 and then to their full repeal by the FCC in 1995. The losers in this repeal have been independent producers, who more and more often must give up any significant back-end ownership to the networks—broadcast and cable—who commission their programs.

The FCC and Cable Regulation

C able television is subject to a regulatory structure that works on three levels: federal, state, and local.

FEDERAL CABLE REGULATION

At the federal level, the FCC now has clear authority, granted by the Cable Communications Policy Act of 1984, to regulate the operation of cable systems. This was not always the case. In the 1950s, when cable television was beginning, the FCC took a hands-off position. Cable operations tended to be small, and to the extent that they had any impact on broadcasting, they merely extended the reach of established stations into areas where the stations would not otherwise have been received.

The FCC's hands-off attitude changed in the early 1960s, as more and more cable operators began to "import" signals from beyond the local area. These distant signals were picked up in their local broadcast area, then transmitted (usually by microwave relay) to a distant cable company, which in turn "cablecast" them as supplemental channels. This action provided both the grounds and the means for regulation by the FCC. For the first time, local stations started viewing cable as a competitor to their operations, rather than as merely an extension of those operations. The FCC shared this concern, and sought to protect established broadcasters. The microwave or other telecommunications link that usually brought the distant signal to the cable company was a common carrier or a radio transmission—and those forms were clearly subject to FCC jurisdiction.

In 1966, the FCC issued a series of rules on cable. The first was the "must-carry" rule, which required a cable system to carry the signals of all the local stations. A second rule called for blacking out distant signals when they duplicated programs offered by a local broadcaster. A third rule flatly prohibited the importation of distant signals into the biggest 100 markets, although cable systems could file with the FCC requesting permission and giving justification for why such service was necessary (permission was seldom granted). At about the same time, FCC regulations made it impractical for telephone companies to be involved as cable-service providers—thus barring one of the strongest potential cable operators from the business.

The FCC's right to maintain these and other restrictions was challenged both in the courts and in Congress. In 1968, the Supreme Court affirmed the FCC's jurisdiction over cable, to an extent "reasonably ancillary to the effective performance of the Commission's various responsibilities for the regulation of broadcasting." In 1970, the FCC imposed the "anti-siphoning" rule, which greatly restricted the showing of movies and sports events on cable services. In 1972, a compromise was worked out between the cable industry, the FCC, and the broadcasting interests; this agreement settled the issue of FCC control over cable and relaxed the distant-signal rules, so that wiring the top 100 television markets for cable could continue.

Two further developments spurred cable growth in the mid-1970s—one technical, the other legal. On the technical level, modern communications satellites suddenly made national signal transmission much less expensive. Until then, the major broadcast networks used much more costly cable and microwave networks to distribute their services around the country. In 1975, HBO used a satellite link to become the first cable programming service available nationwide; HBO was followed by Ted Turner's WTCG, an independent station licensed to operate in Atlanta and later renamed WTBS (and subsequently, TBS Superstation). On the legal end, the FCC's anti-siphoning rules were struck down in the courts in 1977 for violating the First Amendment. In addition, in the deregulatory climate of the Reagan years, the FCC further loosened its distant-signal rules. In 1984, Congress adopted the Cable Communications Policy Act (the Cable Act) as an amendment to the Communications Act of 1934.

THE 1984 AND 1992 CABLE ACTS

The 1984 Cable Act (which became Title VI of the Communications Act of 1934) granted the FCC the express power to regulate cable television. In many instances, this power totally pre-empts the authority of state and local governments. Even in those areas where state and local action is permitted, the 1984 Act provides guidelines and parameters. The 1984 Act also makes clear the fact that cable services, like broadcast television, are not common carriers, and therefore do not have to provide general access to all comers. The 1992 Cable Act both added to and subtracted from the regulatory mantle. The 1996 Telecommunications Act has further changed aspects of the picture.

DEFINITION OF A CABLE SYSTEM

The 1984 Cable Act provided a definition of a "cable system" covered by its provisions. If the cables utilize public rights-of-way of any kind, the installation is likely to be a cable system, subject to regulation. Small cable systems with under 1,000 subscribers, however, are exempt from some of the general rules. If the lines stay all within one continuous property, such as common antennae for an apartment complex, the system may not be covered by the FCC jurisdiction.

REGISTRATION

All cable systems which carry any broadcast signals must be registered with the FCC. Registration takes the form of a filing that discloses information about the system—who its owners are, for example, and which services are to be carried on the system. In addition to FCC registration, the 1984 Cable Act requires that all cable systems be franchised by state or local authorities (see page 146).

DISTANT-SIGNAL RULES

It is now permissible for a cable system to import signals broadcast from other communities, subject to the specific black-out provisions discussed below and subject to payment of the mandated copyright fees. Importation is generally done via microwave or satellite, using common carriers. Broadcast stations, by contrast, have no right to rebroadcast material from other stations without consent.

FCC rules still restrict importing material from distant channels that duplicates local transmissions. For instance, the law allows a local station to prevent a cable system carrying network programming from a distant source that duplicates network programming carried by the local station. In addition, there is a blackout provision that can apply to syndicated programming duplicated from a distant station. In order to avail itself of this protection, the local station running the syndicated programming must have an agreement with the syndicator which provides for local exclusivity, and must give notice of the request for this protection to both the FCC and the local cable company.

SPORTS BLACKOUTS
Cable companies cannot import a distant signal in order to circumvent the blackout of a sports event on a local channel. These blackouts are negotiated by teams so that a local broadcast of a game will not undercut fan interest in attending the game itself.

ORIGINAL PROGRAMMING AND TECHNICAL STANDARDS
The FCC does not require that a cable system carry any non-broadcast channels. If, however, the system produces its own programming, many general FCC rules apply. These rules pertain to obscene material (page 192); equal-opportunity advertising for political candidates (page 144); lotteries and gambling-related cablecasting (page 433); and sponsorship identification, sponsor lists, and payola prevention (page 134).

The FCC also has jurisdiction over technical standards for cable television. Under the 1984 Act, most of these requirements were softened to become simply guidelines that help promote standardization within the industry. The 1992 Act introduced some standards, particularly relating to signal noise and color signals. Other technical requirements relate to testing and signal leakage.

EQUAL EMPLOYMENT OPPORTUNITY AND CONSUMER PRIVACY
Cable systems employing six or more people full-time are subject to the equal employment opportunity requirements of the Communications Act and the FCC, which are described in detail in Chapter 14. To reduce paperwork, cable systems are not required to file their EEO plan with the FCC in advance, but annual reports are required. For the most part, the FCC guidelines and policies for broadcasters essentially apply to cable systems, with only minor variation.

CROSS-OWNERSHIP
Prior to 1996, there were a number of cross-ownership restrictions on cable. For instance, cross-ownership between broadcasting stations and cable operations was prohibited; national broadcast networks could not own any cable systems, and local broadcasters could not own cable systems within their broadcast area. It is worth

noting that these restrictions applied to ownership of cable *systems*, and not to program services or networks. The broadcast networks indeed have had financial interests in cable networks for some time (see Chapter 6). The 1996 Act eliminated the broadcast network ownership ban, although it allowed the FCC certain rule-making authority to ensure fair treatment of other, non-affiliated services and stations. Under the old rules, telephone companies were prohibited from owning cable systems within the areas for which they provide local telephone service; these too have been repealed by the 1996 Act, although restrictions continue on the purchase of an existing service by a local phone company. Restrictions on cross-ownership between cable systems and multipoint distribution (see page 131) have largely survived the 1996 Act, although exemptions can now exist where a cable operator faces effective competition from other sources. It also removed the *statutory* prohibition against cross-ownership between local broadcast stations and local cable services, but retained the FCC's authority to maintain a regulatory ban. In 1993 the FCC instituted multiple-system ownership rules, setting a 30 percent cap on any one owner's share of the national cable pie. A 5 percent addition can be made for a minority-controlled system.

LOCAL STATION CARRIAGE

The must-carry rule, requiring cable systems to carry all local broadcast signals has had a checkered history. It survived the enactment of the 1984 Cable Act, but was thrown out in 1985 by court order as violating the First Amendment. A subsequent effort by the FCC to redraft the must-carry rule to meet First Amendment scrutiny also failed. Congress entered the picture in the 1992 Cable Act, with a somewhat different approach. A local station was given the choice between opting for granting a free "retransmission consent" coupled with must-carry on the one hand, or negotiating an arms-length retransmission agreement with the cable provider on the other. As implemented by FCC rules, this version of must-carry divides up the cable universe into three tiers: systems with 12 or fewer channels; systems with 13 to 36 channels; and systems with more than 36 channels. The first group must carry at least three local commercial stations and one "public" station. The second and third groups must carry "all" local commercial stations, at least up to one-third of the total available cable channels, plus all the non-duplicative local "public" stations (at least one and up to three for the second group; at least three for the third).

These rules also give the broadcast channels limited rights to designate channel allocation in the cable system, and require the cable system to maintain minimum signal quality standards. If the broadcast station does not opt for the forced free-consent/must-carry deal, then it can either *forbid* carriage, or seek compensation to permit it. Low-power stations (see page 130), with some exceptions, do not qualify for must-carry status.

These choices were initially made in 1993. They are scheduled to be revisited every three years. As it turned out, the negotiations delivered little cost compensation, although some powerful station owners were able to squeeze out some additional channel space from the cable owners from *other* projects, often set for a six-year deal. The 1996 cycle, for those not under six-year contracts, was relatively non-contentious, with many stations opting for the free-consent/must-carry option. It should be noted that cable systems have generally carried most local broadcast channels, perhaps because subscribers expect it.

THEFT OF SERVICES
The 1984 Cable Act made it expressly illegal to take signals from a cable system without authorization. This sets up punishment for the use of private taps and "black box" decoders, ranging from a relatively small fine and jail sentence for private users to up to $50,000 and two years in jail for first-time offenders engaging in signal theft for profit, and up to $100,000 and five years for repeaters. The affected cable system can also sue for damages.

THE 1992 CABLE ACT AND RATE REGULATION
During the early 1990s, there was growing pressure at both the state and federal levels to increase the regulation of cable television, particularly in the area of rates charged to customers. As cable established itself as a mainstream business, many systems raised their rates faster than general inflation. In the spirit of free enterprise, they sought to charge what the market would bear. There were also complaints about sub-standard service in some areas. Since cable systems were generally not subject to direct competition from competing cable operators, and since satellite, telephone and other competitors were not yet a threat, the old arguments for regulating natural monopolies attracted new adherents. All of this led to the re-enactment of rate regulation in the 1992 Cable Act.

The terms of this measure of re-regulation are complex: the staff of the Cable Services Bureau grew from 6 to 230 employees, in large part to oversee the process. The regulatory structure makes an important distinction between a "basic tier" of services and "cable programming services." The basic-tier consists, at a minimum, of the local must-carry broadcast stations (see page 142) and the PEG access channels (see page 000). The operator can add other satellite signals if it wishes. The basic tier rates were initially rolled back for most systems under a series of FCC orders in 1993 and 1994. Further authority to regulate basic rates was then granted to the local franchising authority; although appeals can be made to the FCC and the FCC itself regulates in some instances. Rate-setting is done on either a relatively simple "benchmark" approach or a complicated "cost of service" basis, both of which are meant to keep a relationship between increases and the more general rate of inflation.

Regulation of the Cable Programming Service tier has stayed with the FCC. Decisions are made on a "reasonableness" standard also involving pre-determined "benchmarks." One by-product of these restrictions has been a slow-down in the addition of channels in existing cable systems. Because of such results, the emergence of new entrants into the multi-channel distribution world and a return by the now-Republican Congress to market enthusiasm, the 1996 Act has repealed all rate-setting for the Cable Programming Service tier effective March 31, 1999.

The entire rate-regulation scheme will not apply to systems facing "effective competition." Under the 1992 approach, "effective competition" was narrowly defined. The 1996 Act has expanded it by adding systems facing essentially any form of multi-channel competition offered by a local telephone company. Should a telephone company jump into this kind of service, whether through owning multipoint broadcast systems (see page 131) or through its own wired network (see page 156), then most rate regulation disappears for the traditional cable company in the same area.

POLITICAL BROADCAST RULES

Some of the rules governing political access which apply to broadcast television (see page 134) have cable equivalents. These apply mainly to cable operators who have "cablecasting" channels over which they have programming control. Public-access channels are not generally included. For instance, the equal-access rule applies: if time is made available to one candidate it must be made available to all for the same office. Personal attack and political editorial rules also apply, requiring notice to the affected party and a reasonable opportunity to respond.

COPYRIGHT ASPECTS OF CABLE TELEVISION

All material carried by cable television—including programs, commercials, and music—must be cleared for copyright permission. In the case of original cable programming, such as that provided by Showtime, MTV, and other basic and pay cable services, the cablecast itself is a public performance and requires a license from the copyright proprietor (see page 166). Under the old 1909 Copyright Act, the retransmission by cable of material broadcast by an over-the-air station was not a new performance or duplication. Therefore, the license obtained by the original broadcaster extended to subsequent cable distribution. This was changed by the 1976 Copyright Act.

The 1976 Copyright Act set up a *compulsory license* structure for cable companies retransmitting broadcast signals. Under this arrangement, the cable system can transmit non-local broadcast signals, provided it pays the broadcaster an appropriate fee (which is collected and administered by the Librarian of Congress; see discussion on page 169). The basis on which these fees are calculated depends on the cable system's level of revenues. Systems with less than $75,000 in annual gross receipts pay a token amount for transmitting an unlimited number of imported signals. Systems with more than $75,000 and up to $292,000 in gross annual receipts pay 0.5 percent of their gross receipts up to $146,000 and 1 percent of gross receipts thereafter—again, with no limit on the number of imported signals. Finally, for systems with more than $292,000 in annual gross receipts, a complicated formula is used that is based on the kind and number of stations the cable system carries, and on whether the system is in a top-100 market or not. These formulas can make the first imported signal, if it is from an independent station, cost a cable system in a top-50 market royalties of almost 1.5 percent of gross receipts, with fees for additional signals trailing off from there. There is also a charge of 3.75 percent of gross receipts for carrying each distant signal in excess of the number that would have been permitted under the FCC's pre-1980 rules. Once received, the royalties are divided by the Tribunal among the copyright owners of the programs carried, who must file claims to share in the pot. Among the major beneficiaries have been the copyright owners of movies and sports programs.

STATE AND LOCAL CABLE REGULATION

At the state and local level, a patchwork of regulatory systems has evolved. Some states have set up quite active statewide regulatory boards for cable; other states leave regulation largely to the local communities. State and local control arises not only from the general legislative power, but also from the ability to govern the access of the cable company to the public rights-of-way. This access is necessary for maintaining and operating a system of any size, since cable can run throughout a community only if it follows the public roads, either above ground on poles or below ground in conduits. Access to these roads is in the hands of the state government or the municipalities.

State and local regulation is restricted, however, to those areas where the FCC has not asserted exclusive jurisdiction. While the states and localities can govern franchising and utility-pole attachments, subject to the requirements of the 1984 Act, they are largely prohibited from otherwise interfering in the operations of cable systems. The major addition to state and local authority under the 1992 Act was the administration of rate regulation for the basic tier.

FRANCHISING

The most important means by which states and local communities control cable is the franchising of cable systems. The power to franchise comes from control of the public rights-of-way. The 1984 Act set only sketchy parameters for franchising, but it also made holding a franchise a requirement for FCC registration. In most states, the franchising power has been delegated to the local level, where it is normally exercised by the city or town council.

The typical franchising process goes as follows. First, the local government may seek knowledgeable advisors to help it through the technical and legal considerations in awarding a cable franchise. The next step is usually a request for proposals, which announces to the cable television industry that the locality would like to award a franchise. Then comes the response from the interested cable companies, which submit proposals (often of great length) suggesting what they will provide and why each is the best candidate to provide the service requested. For better or worse, local political connections and concerns can sometimes influence the process, providing work for well-connected lawyers, lobbyists, and other local consultants with clout. The selection process continues with a review of the competing proposals. This review usually involves an investigation by the local council and its advisors of the applicants and their proposals—an inspection of their finances, operating experience, and the feasibility of the various promises which have been made. In the process of this review, there should be a public hearing on the merits of each proposal, at which community members and other interested parties can air their views.

Once a potential franchise has been chosen, the town council or other franchising authority negotiates an agreement with the company, based on the proposal and setting forth the terms of the franchise. The financial deal is subject to a Cable Act limitation: no more than 5 percent of gross revenues from the franchised service can be taken as the franchise fee. The agreement also includes the franchise term, technical and construction specifications, and requirements for certain levels of service, including the number of channels set aside for community access, local educational use, and other public-interest uses. Most franchises are awarded on a non-exclusive basis; in theory, another company can approach the municipality and propose the wiring of a further system within the service area. As a practical matter, given the high costs of entry, it is relatively rare for another service to come in and bid on a territory that has already been franchised. Franchise agreements are often challenged in court by disappointed claimants, who cite alleged flaws in the way the franchise was awarded.

When a franchise comes up for renewal, the Cable Act provides certain safeguards to protect the interests of the existing franchisee. As modified by the 1992 Act, the process now has two stages: a relatively informal "first stage proceeding" under section 626(a) and a more formal proposal and response under section 626(c). The 626(a) proceeding comes either at the franchisee's request—given within a six-month period starting three years before the renewal date—or at the initiative of the franchising authority. There are two principal themes in the process: (1) the needs of the community and (2) the record of the cable operator. This initial procedure helps to get the various agendas on the table. It is followed by the preparation of a formal proposal for renewal by the operator. Once this is received, the franchising authority must either renew relatively automatically without a hearing based on the proposal or it must hold a formal hearing and review under section 626(c). The hearing evaluates the level of service according to the following criteria, as specified in the Cable Act:

(A) The cable operator has substantially complied with the material terms of the existing franchise and with applicable law;

(B) The quality of the operator's service, including signal quality, response to consumer complaints, and billing practices, but without regard to the mix or the level of cable services or other services provided over the system, has been reasonable in light of community needs;

(C) The operator has the financial, legal, and technical ability to provide the services, facilities, and equipment as set forth in the operator's proposal; and

(D) The operator's proposal is reasonable to meet the future cable-related community needs and interests, taking into account the cost of meeting such needs and interests.

Although the franchising authority can theoretically deny a renewal to the existing operator, it can do so only if the franchisee has a documented record of poor performance or inability to meet one of these four criteria. The franchise authority may not consider a competing offer, except perhaps to help provide background for evaluating these criteria. This process acts to cut down the leverage of the municipality at renewal time, and helps protect the status quo. By now, the most desirable franchises in the country have been awarded, and franchises coming up for renewal are the main arena for competition between cable operators.

UTILITY-POLE ATTACHMENTS

The states are permitted to control the attachment of cable lines to existing telephone and electric utility poles and conduits. In most circumstances, it is more sensible (and cheaper) for a cable company to add its cable lines to these poles and conduits than to set up new poles or dig new underground channels. This puts the cable company at the mercy of the owner of the existing poles and conduits. In order to prevent extortionate requests and to encourage the installation of cable, most states and localities have adopted rules that cap the rates which can be charged for such pole attachments. To the extent that states and localities had not adopted appropriate rules to govern this, the FCC retained jurisdiction, and the 1996 Act further strengthened the rights of cable operators and other telecommunication carriers to have utility pole access

RATE REGULATION

Federal rate control has been a field of hotly contested action, as described on page 143 above. At this writing, state and local governments are involved in regulating the rates charged by cable companies for their basic-tier service in accordance with federal rules.

OTHER RULES AND PRE-EMPTION

The issue of cross-ownership of cable stations and other media outlets has largely been pre-empted by the Cable Act and the FCC, as have all aspects of satellite television. However, states and localities do retain their normal power to enact rules for reasons of public benefit and general safety.

FCC Regulation of Satellite Broadcasting, Telephone, Video and Other "New Technologies"

At the end of the twentieth century, a series of new technologies are threatening to overturn the relatively settled broadcast/cable duality in electronic television distribution. Satellite and multipoint delivery systems are already making significant inroads. Video via phone lines (and phone via cable) is starting to appear. Access to video through the World Wide Web via Internet connections is available in a somewhat rudimentary form, but can be expected to blossom as modem transmission speeds increase and as digital compression and other techniques reduce the data required for computer-generated pictures.

Against this background of change, however, there are familiar themes in the possible regulatory interventions. Notwithstanding the variety of channels on offer on each of these systems, the opportunity to provide the *bundle of channels,* i.e., to be a *system,* remains limited. In cable, the cost of entry is high: stringing wire across poles through the service area. This has tended to produce a monopoly in most areas. Local phone service until recently has been similarly limited to a single provider. Satellite services are limited to a relative handful per country by the international allocation of orbital slots for direct broadcast satellite (DBS) operators. Multipoint services face frequency allocation limits that in turn constrain the possibility for unlimited entry. There may be significant choices within a particular service, but between services there is much less choice.

Furthermore, the economies of these systems are such that regional, national or even international services are favored over local providers. Outside of traditional broadcasters and public-access cable, there isn't much room for local or the offbeat programs. Given this set of dynamics, most of the multi-channel distribution systems have come to look like the video equivalent of competing shopping malls—"competitors" offering nearly identical selections of national-chain retailers with similar, rather bland, product lines. There is little room for the vibrancy and diversity of an urban shopping street. The principle opportunity to avoid the "shopping mall" sameness of pre-packed systems will come from open video systems, i.e., systems offering customer choice on a dial-a-supplier basis, or from Internet delivered Web-page video. The traditional leader in keeping video opportunities varied has, somewhat ironically, been the adult programming industry. The wild card is in some ways the FCC—what kind of competition will its regulatory policies promote?

The FCC's regulation of television has carried over into satellite, telephone, Internet and the other new distribution technologies; the only areas in which the FCC is not somehow involved are home and business video, which do not use any form of mass electronic distribution. The FCC, helped on by the 1996 Act, is promoting competition between these different sources of multi-channel systems, removing the walls to entry that had stood between the providers of what used to be technically different services. At least there now can be a number of "video shopping malls" in the same town. How much FCC regulation preserves the possibility of access to a wide range of specialty services will also be a measure of how much real competition exists.

SATELLITE TELEVISION

From the beginning of the "space age," the FCC has regulated the services of communication satellites under its authority over radio transmissions and common carriers in the communications business. This gives a baseline of U.S. government intervention. On the issues of satellite location and frequency allocation and on most aspects of direct broadcast satellites, the UN-affiliated International Telecommunications Union plays a role as well. The rules governing domestic and international services have grown differently over time, and each needs to be looked at in its historical and technical context.

U.S. NETWORK FEEDS VIA SATELLITE

The launching of satellites for communications use dates back to the 1960s and 1970s (see page 93). At the time, the principle envisioned uses were phone, telex, and other data transmission functions. While the FCC has, from early on, controlled rates and technical aspects for communications satellites, since 1972 it has maintained an "open skies" policy with respect to domestic communication satellite services, allowing almost any technically competent and financially qualified company to launch and operate a domestic communications satellite. The result of the open-skies policy has been an abundance of satellite communications channels that could be used to transmit television programming as well as voice and data. On the reception front, the FCC dropped its regulation of receive-only satellite antennae in 1979, and the Telecommunications Act of 1996 gives the FCC the affirmative power to pre-empt most local regulation in the area. These developments helped make satellite the carrier of choice for the national feeds of broadcast and cable networks alike—replacing the land lines and microwave systems of earlier eras.

Since there were stringent cross-ownership restrictions between common carriers on the one hand and broadcasters/cable systems on the other, the television companies have not owned or leased their own satellite facilities for this kind of use. Instead, they contract with common-carrier satellite companies for carrying the signals. The technical nature of the satellites handling these feeds has required relatively large antennae for their reception. The intention of these transmissions was to deliver broadcast, and later cable, network services to licensed users such as local affiliates and cable lead-ends, where large, industrial-sized receivers would be little impediment.

In the early days of satellite-transmitted television feeds, most signals were open and unscrambled. Consequently, the business of supplying these large receiving dishes to private individuals became viable. While the initial investment was significant, many people, particularly in remote areas with no cable service, installed dishes and settled back to enjoy shows plucked out of the air, ostensibly free of charge. This led to two steps to prevent what the cable services (and especially the pay services) saw as a threat to their revenues: scrambling and legal restrictions.

Scrambling significantly decreases one's ability to intercept a viewable signal, although bootleg "black boxes" to descramble signals do exist. Such unauthorized intercepts were, however, rendered illegal. By a balancing legal mandate, the scrambled channels had to be licensed by their providers in areas where these signals are not otherwise available via cable and/or broadcast stations. A legitimate business in issuing such licenses and their implementing decoders evolved. Since the offerings available without paying for decoders then grew less interesting, the sale of dishes for picking up common-carrier satellite television feeds stagnated and has since been largely replaced by a much more interesting technology, direct broadcast television.

INTERNATIONAL COMMUNICATIONS SATELLITES

While the domestic communications satellite business was growing rapidly in a relatively unregulated environment, international service was initially confined to two authorized vehicles. In 1962 an act of Congress established the Communication Satellite Corporation (COMSAT). It was given broad powers to work internationally to promote and run space-based communications. Another outgrowth of this 1962 legislation was the eventual formation of the International Telecommunications Satellite Organization (INTELSAT), an international body whose powers derived from the interlocking set of agreements between its participating member countries. Together, COMSAT and INTELSAT for some time effectively monopolized trans-border satellite communications, including trans-oceanic feeds of television programming such as international news reports. There are other national and regional satellite unions, such as ARABSAT, the European Space Agency, and INTERSPUTNIK, which serves the former Soviet bloc.

With respect to the U.S., this monopoly started to crack in the 1980s, when legislation permitted competition. The U.S. has authorized progressively wider international penetration of satellite service under FCC control. The sticking point is at the other end of this process: the foreign countries involved. Many still feel bound by the INTELSAT/COMSAT connection. There is some talk of privatizing INTELSAT. Whether or not this occurs, it appears likely that the structure of INTELSAT will change over the upcoming years.

INTERNATIONAL REGULATION OF FREQUENCIES AND ORBITAL POSITIONS

In one sense the room for satellites to orbit the earth is vast. Nonetheless, certain kinds of usable locations are surprisingly limited. This is particularly true of the coveted "geosynchronous" locations, a band around the equator at a very precise altitude (around 23,000 miles out) where the orbiting satellite keeps perfect time with the rotation of the earth, thereby appearing, from the standpoint of a ground observer, to stay dependably in the same spot in the sky. The alternative for continuous service is a sizable fleet of "non-stationary" satellites, which hand communications links off to one another like stations in a cellular phone network. The slots for geosynchronous placement are also constrained by the potential for signal interference from satellites operating with similar frequencies in nearby spots in the sky. Since the frequencies suitable and reserved for satellite transmissions, both up and down, are also limited by technical factors, the potential for chaos in a free-for-all satellite world became apparent early on.

The ITU had long mediated ground-based broadcast frequency overlaps between nations. In 1963 it took on the coordination of satellite frequencies, and in 1973 added the assignment of orbital positions. In the early days, the ITU made its allocations on a "first come, first served" basis. This gave the two major space-exploring nations, the USA and the USSR, a head start in snapping up orbital placement resources. In 1985 the developing countries managed to get the issue of "equitable access" onto the ITU agenda, and a compromise was agreed to that on the one hand reserved enough orbital slots and frequencies to allow each ITU member country to meet its communication needs while letting most other services continue to be assigned "first come, first served." Because the frequencies suitable for DBS service are further limited, and because access for this kind of service is seen as a matter of national security in many countries, specific DBS orbital and frequency assignments were set by the ITU in this process.

DIRECT BROADCAST SATELLITES

The regulation of U.S. DBS service is somewhat schizophrenic: the FCC approach is relatively hands-off against a background of internationally mandated scarcity. The key to a commercially successful DBS service has been the use of medium and high-power satellites (100 to 400 watts per "transponder") which have allowed the use of receiver dish antennas as small as 18 inches. The signals are sent in digital code to increase capacity and prevent piracy. Unauthorized descrambling is against federal law.

Domestically, the FCC regulates every direct broadcast satellite, originally under its general authority over the radio broadcast spectrum. This authority was specifically confirmed by the 1996 Act. The first request for a DBS license came in 1980; by 1982, the FCC had established procedures and rules for granting them. These "interim" rules—still in effect—have some provisions similar to those for broadcast stations. For instance, foreign ownership and control of a DBS service is restricted, and cannot exceed 20 percent direct ownership. Ownership is otherwise unrestricted. There are also equal employment opportunity requirements, including one for filing an EEO plan as part of the application for initiating a DBS service if the operator exercises programming control.

The FCC grants construction permits and DBS licenses—technically, interim licenses—to applicants once a public comment period and a staff review determine that the proposed system is in the public interest. The review is done on a case-by-case basis. Once granted, the normal license term is five years. An unusually long (six-year) construction period is allowed, since the DBS business is still in an early stage. The technical specifications of a DBS service must agree with international standards, and there are ongoing public-service requirements, including some educational content. Licensing under these standards is not the real hurdle for most would-be DBS providers. Getting access to one of the eight internationally designated U.S. DBS orbital slots is the greater challenge. By the mid-1990s, four services had successfully put together the necessary package of programming options and satellite slots: DirecTV, USSB, The DISH Network and Primestar.

In 1995 the FCC canceled outstanding but not-yet-utilized construction permits and reclaimed a significant number of allocated channels. Rather than parse them out among existing licensees, the FCC, with enthusiastic Congressional blessing auctioned the allocation. The 27 channels at the "full-CONUS" slot (full continental U.S. coverage) sold for $682.5 million to MCI; the 24 in a less desirable slot without full U.S. coverage brought in $52.3 million. The money went to the U.S. government. Digital compression currently allows approximately four to eight programming channels per transponder channel.

The last variable in this allocation struggle involves transboundary delivery. The "footprint" of the DBS satellite, i.e., the area on earth where its signal can be received, does not respect national boundaries. Signals for U.S. services overlap into Mexico and Canada, and their satellites will cover some or all of the U.S. There are even small island kingdoms in the Pacific whose service footprint hits portions of the U.S. Looking outward, the FCC has declared information access a human right, and will not limit the spillover of U.S. services abroad. Looking inward, it has been holding up plans of U.S. companies to offer services into the U.S. via Canadian slot locations. Canada, for its part, has implemented rules blocking the reception of U.S. DBS north of the border. How these international conflicts play out will be one of the interesting issues in DBS over the coming years.

TELEPHONES, FIBER OPTICS AND VIDEO ON DEMAND

Optical fiber is viewed by many as the delivery system of the future for the television industry. It has a huge capacity for data transmission, and could carry an unprecedented number of program

options. In addition, it is a fully two-way medium, permitting
instant pay-per-view ordering and other interactive services. With
some exceptions, fiber-optic installation has often been the
province of the telephone companies, which had until recently
been shut out of ownership of broadcasting and of cable facilities
in those areas where they provide phone service. The seemingly
natural combination of audio and video systems under one fiber-
optic network required a change in this basic restriction, and the
1996 Act has dropped the prohibition, with only a few caveats.

IMPACT OF THE 1996 ACT

The 1996 Telecommunications Act lowered most of the barriers
keeping telephone companies out of the television business. In
the area of cable, where the old rules kept phone companies out,
it now lets them in: the 1996 Act specifically repealed the
prohibition of telephone company ownership of cable systems in
geographic areas where it also provides local exchange service
(LEC). As a bow to preserving competition, the local exchange
provider cannot purchase an existing cable system unless there is
significant competition from other sources (see page 142). Nor is
this the only way for LECs to get into the video programming business. They may also provide multipoint services (see page 131),
common-carrier businesses for other providers, and "switched
video," i.e., an interactive "pay-per-view" service giving video on
demand but *without* providing a scheduled service.

Another brand new option is the idea of an "open video system"
(OVS). This is a kind of hybrid between a common-carrier and a
cable service, which in theory will offer a kind of call-up, on-
demand access for scheduled services. OVS operation does require
certification by the FCC. The process sets rules requiring relatively
open access to interested programming service providers on
reasonable and non-discriminatory terms. It also protects providers of sports, network and syndicated programs against
exclusivity and non-duplication. For instance, an OVS cannot
favor its own offerings in operating the system. Certification also
frees up the OVS provider for many—although by no means all—
of the regulations that apply to cable services. Among those that
remain are public, education and governmental access and must-
carry rules on local public and commercial broadcast services.

A wrinkle that remains to be fully worked out is the line-use
charge which the local exchange company will apply to all of these
new, and particularly time consuming, uses of local lines. Indeed,
the ability to deliver high-quality video via existing phone lines,

even in an age of high compression, remains a sources of concern. The coaxial lines of cable companies remain attractive potential vehicles for high-capacity, two-way switched services, i.e., what phones provide, only better. If they face sufficient competition, cable systems can seek OVS certification. And in an interesting turn-about, under the 1996 Act cable systems can now also start to offer local exchange access, i.e., traditional phone service.

The competitive vision of the 1996 Act sees a variety of delivery systems—switched and unswitched, via traditional broadcast, multipoint send and receive broadcast, satellite and interactive satellite, telephone and cable connections using wire and fiber and transmitting scheduled services and pay-per-view, on-demand access—all going head-to-head. The FCC nonetheless is keeping its hand in most of these areas—increasing regulation is always possible. The remaining wild card, yet to come to its full potential and yet to be integrated into the regulatory structure, is the Internet.

VIDEO VIA THE INTERNET

The Internet is already a powerful, if crude, source of video. For users with the right technology (a powerful computer and digital video programming, currently downloadable for free on the Web) literally hundreds of television and radio signals can be accessed in real time from the home-pages of broadcasters around the world. A computer in California can access Brazilian, Mexican, or even Croatian television feeds. The picture has low fidelity, but the sound is decent, and as modem speeds increase and compression gets better, viewing quality will go up. This gives the potential for a truly open video system, where any Web site can become a programming source.

The legal challenges inherent in this will be many and varied, from copyright questions, to access charges, to censorship. These are only starting to play themselves out. On one level, the government has been deeply immersed in the Internet—as operator, standard setter, and regulator of the telecommunications access points. On the other hand, it has yet to involve itself in the video aspects of the Web. The one significant content initiative to date, an anti-indecency law, was declared unconstitutional. Other initiatives are likely to follow. The only certainties are that the regulatory system will change significantly once again over the next few years to meet the challenge of the Net, and that new challenges will loom on the horizon from unforeseen sources before we expect them.

PART 3

Regulation Of Programming

Content Regulation: An Introduction

FREE SPEECH AND THE FIRST AMENDMENT

Early in the history of the United States, the founders of our federal government shared a thorough understanding of the need for governmental power—and a healthy fear of the abuses to which such power is prone. Therefore, between 1789 and 1791, shortly after the adoption of the Constitution, the states ratified the Bill of Rights, a series of ten amendments to the Constitution. The purpose of these amendments was to limit the authority of the newly established central power. The First Amendment established three fundamental aspects of liberty: freedom of speech, freedom of religion, and access to government. It reads as follows:

> Congress shall make no law respecting an establishment of religion, or prohibiting the free exercise thereof, or abridging the freedom of speech, or of the press; or the right of the people peaceably to assemble, and to petition the Government for a redress of grievances.

Television has repeatedly been recognized as a medium that is subject to First Amendment protection.

At first, these limits on governmental power applied only to Congress (that is, the federal government), although some states enacted similar measures in their own constitutions. After the Civil War, a series of additional constitutional amendments were adopted which did apply to the states. Perhaps chief among these was the Fourteenth Amendment:

> No State shall make or enforce any law which shall abridge the privileges or immunities of citizens of the United States; nor shall any State deprive any person of life, liberty, or

property, without due process of law; nor deny to any person within its jurisdiction the equal protection of the law.

No specific reference was made in the Fourteenth Amendment to the Bill of Rights or to the First Amendment. In the first half of the twentieth century, however, a series of judicial decisions confirmed that the Fourteenth Amendment concepts of due process and equal protection "incorporated" most, if not all, of the Bill of Rights' elements and made them applicable to the states. The applicability of the free-speech and free-press aspects of the First Amendment to state laws was recognized by the Supreme Court in decisions between 1925 and 1931.

The language of the First Amendment is extremely broad. Congress and, by incorporation, the states, "shall make no law . . . abridging the freedom of speech, or of the press." If taken literally, this wording would seem to imply that speech, the press, and (by extension) television are to be completely free of governmental regulation. Notwithstanding the plain language of the amendment, however, courts have always recognized exceptions and balanced the government's interest in various content restrictions against the free speech "interest" expressed in the First Amendment. The results of this process are rules that govern the content of television programming.

RULES THAT GOVERN CONTENT

The content of television production is subject to a series of laws and restrictions—most of them imposed by our legal system, some of them imposed by the television industry on itself as a matter of self-regulation. Some of these rules, such as those governing obscenity, are enforced directly by the government with criminal penalties. More prevalent are the laws enabling private individuals and companies to control the use of creative properties, the expression of certain kinds of hurtful falsehoods, or the invasion of rights of privacy and publicity.

These rules and restrictions can be viewed negatively—as handcuffs on the activities of program creator—because they conflict with the freedoms granted by the First Amendment. They can also be viewed positively, as rights that can be asserted to protect the economic and moral interests of individuals, businesses, and the community. However they are considered, these restrictions form the legal structure within which programming is created. Anyone participating in the production process will benefit from a working knowledge of them.

The three chapters that follow deal with these content rules. The level of detail in a general treatment such as this must be, by its very nature, somewhat superficial. Therefore, we have supplied in Appendix C1 a bibliography of books and other reference works for those who wish to research these issues in greater depth.

In addition, many content issues are governed by state law, and there are likely to be variations in the law from state to state, even when the laws recognize the same underlying principles. When we do cite specific state laws, we have paid particular attention to the laws of California and New York, since so much of the television industry is concentrated in these states. In cases for which an exact knowledge of the applicable state or federal law is important, it is advisable to consult a local attorney.

16

Copyright and the Protection of Creative Properties

There is one restriction on television content which itself has a constitutional basis. Article 1, Section 8 of the Constitution reads: "Congress shall have power . . . to promote the progress of science and useful arts by securing for limited times to authors and inventors the exclusive right to their respective writings and discoveries . . . ."

Following this lead, Congress has created a series of copyright laws, starting in 1790. The most recent general revision was enacted in 1976. Works created before January 1, 1978 (when the 1976 Act took effect) were subject to the provisions of the 1909 Copyright Act with respect to events prior to 1978. For events after December 31, 1977, these works are governed by the 1976 Act, modified by certain special provisions. All works created since January 1, 1978, are fully covered by the rules of the 1976 Act, which introduced several innovations discussed more fully below. The major developments in copyright law since 1976 have been the changes made necessary by the U.S. joining the Berne Convention, which became effective March 1, 1989.

SCOPE OF FEDERAL LAW

Under the 1909 Act, most unpublished works were subject to state law protection under theories of "common law copyright." With a few limited exceptions, such as stage plays, federal copyright extended only to *published* works. Under the 1976 Act, federal copyright has been extended to cover all unpublished works as well, and the role of state law has almost completely disappeared.

MATERIAL PROTECTED BY COPYRIGHT LAW

The Copyright Act of 1976 gives protection for "original works of authorship." Section 102 of the law states:

(a) Copyright protection subsists, in accordance with this title, in original works of authorship fixed in any tangible medium of expression, now known or later developed, from which they can be perceived, reproduced, or otherwise communicated, either directly or with the aid of a machine or device. Works of authorship include the following categories:

    (1) literary works;

    (2) musical works, including any accompanying words;

    (3) dramatic works, including any accompanying music;

    (4) pantomimes and choreographic works;

    (5) pictorial, graphic, and sculptural works;

    (6) motion pictures and other audiovisual works;

    (7) sound recordings; and

    (8) architectural works.

(b) In no case does copyright protection for an original work of authorship extend to any idea, procedure, process, system, method of operation, concept, principle, or discovery, regardless of the form in which it is described, explained, illustrated, or embodied in such work.

Television programs receive protection as "motion pictures or other audiovisual works." Scripts are protected as "literary works" or "dramatic works"; designs, as "pictorial, graphic, and sculptural works." Indeed, any creative work which is "fixed in a tangible medium of expression" (and thus satisfies the constitutional requirement of a "writing") can potentially be covered by copyright protection—provided it is not simply an "idea," "concept," or "principle."

Courts have held that the *expression* of an idea is copyrightable, but that the underlying idea itself is not. Infringement occurs only if there is a "substantial similarity" between a protected element in the copyrighted work and some element of the new work. Of course, it is not always easy to tell where a raw idea leaves off and protectable expression begins. The point where an illegal rip-off occurs is a matter for judgment in each case, and a lawyer's advice may be helpful. There is also the "smell test": if the proposed use "stinks" to you, it probably will to a judge.

To prove an infringement of copyright, there must be evidence of copying. Proof of actual copying can be inferred from access, which indicates the opportunity to copy. If the similar work was a truly independent creation, no infringement has taken place.

Although ideas are free from copyright protection, they can be subject to contractual protection (see page 177). Names of charac ters and names of shows, like ideas, are not subject to copyright protection. They can, however, receive protection under theories of unfair competition if the name is so strongly established that there could be public confusion over the new use (see page 436).

"Formats" fall into a gray area. For instance, the idea of a game show that awards prizes for answering questions cannot be copyrighted, nor can such aspects of a game show as a board listing the questions, a pretty female co-star, or a display which indicates the score. A near clone of the total look and overall feel of a particular game show would probably be found to be a copyright violation, but even if one game shares some aspects of play with another, there may be copyright violation. On the other hand, a few clever lines of fiction or a few bars of music can constitute protectable expression.

Like ideas, facts, in and of themselves, are not copyrightable. Still, whether fact or fiction, a particular motion picture or video sequence, as shot and preserved on film or tape, is very likely to have enough expressive content for copyright protection, if only in the choices made in framing the shot. Therefore, one must be particularly careful in copying *verbatim* video clips or recorded audio segments. Courts have implied that video clips as short as seven or eight seconds can contain enough expression to merit protection, notwithstanding the doctrine of fair use (page 170).

RIGHTS PROTECTED BY COPYRIGHT LAW

United States copyright law gives the copyright owner(s) a particular set of exclusive rights in a work in the United States. The general rules are set forth in Section 106 of the 1976 Act:

Subject to sections 107 through 120, the owner of copyright under this title has the exclusive rights to do and to authorize any of the following:

(1) to reproduce the copyrighted work in copies or phono-records;

(2) to prepare derivative works based upon the copyrighted work;

(3) to distribute copies or phonorecords of the copyrighted work to the public by sale or other transfer of owner-ship, or by rental, lease, or lending;

(4) in the case of literary, musical, dramatic, and choreographic works, pantomimes, and motion pictures and other

audiovisual works, to perform the copyrighted work publicly;

(5) in the case of literary, musical, dramatic, and choreographic works, pantomimes, and pictorial, graphic, or sculptural works, including the individual images of a motion picture or other audiovisual work, to display the copyrighted work publicly; and

(6) in the case of sound recordings, to perform the copyrighted work publicly by means of a digital audio transmission.

The copyright owner controls the making and distribution of reproductions of the work, including prints and videocassettes. In most cases, however, once an authorized copy has been sold, further dispositions of that copy are free from control. This is sometimes called the "first sale doctrine." A special exception to this rule, however, prevents the rental of *sound* recordings and computer software. Rentals of authorized video copies are not restricted.

No one can create a derivative work without the owner's authorization. This includes the production and/or distribution of sequels, re-makes, series, spin-offs, dubbed versions, novelizations, and any other work that embodies elements of protected expression from the original work.

The owner controls the public performance or display of a copyrighted work, but its private performance or display is not restricted. For example, a videocassette can legally be shown for free by its rightful owner in the home to family and normal guests. Charge admission, however, or change the venue to a public bar, and the showing probably becomes a public performance, subject to the control of the copyright holder.

AUTHORSHIP AND WORK FOR HIRE

Under the 1976 Copyright Act, the author or authors of the work own the copyright, from the moment of the work's creation. Joint authors share the ownership of their copyrighted work. Unless they agree otherwise, each joint owner can authorize the non-exclusive use of the work, subject to a responsibility to account for the other author's share of any earnings. Exclusive licenses require the consent of all authors.

The "author," however, is not always the living person who creates the product. Under the "work for hire" doctrine of the 1976 Act, an individual or company that employs the actual creator can be deemed the author. Employment generally means just that: showing up for work on a regular basis and having the necessary tax and social security payments drawn from one's paycheck (see page 455). These rules on *actual* employment are relaxed in the case of audiovisual works for film or television, where a consultant's or other independent contractor's work can be "for hire" if there is a signed written agreement expressly confirming this fact. Collective works, translations, compilations, and instructional works can also be considered works for hire on this basis.

COPYRIGHT REGISTRATION

The formal requirements for obtaining copyright protection have been significantly loosened under the 1976 Act, and even further liberalized by the Berne Convention changes. Under the old (1909) act, publication with notice (see below) and registration were both necessary for federal protection, but copyright now attaches automatically at the moment of creation.

Under the 1909 law and, to a lesser degree, under the 1976 law prior to the Berne Convention's amendments, registration at publication was a requirement for protection. Although copyright itself is no longer at stake, some protections of copyright can be lost by the failure to take certain registration steps. For a work of U.S. origin, which cannot claim all the protections of the Berne Convention, registration is a prerequisite for bringing a copyright infringement case against a third party. Registration can be done at almost any time to make a suit possible, but should be done as soon as possible to avoid procedural delays. Early registration (within three months of publication) is also necessary in order to claim the statutory damages provided under the Copyright Act (see page 174) for infringement of a published work. The Berne Convention removes these incentives and penalties with respect to most foreign-source works.

Copyright registration forms as well as information about current fees and procedures, can be obtained by writing to the Copyright Office, Library of Congress, Washington, DC 20540 or through the Copyright Website at http://marvel.loc.gov/copyright/.

COPYRIGHT NOTICE

Until the Berne Convention took effect in the U.S. on March 1, 1989, giving *notice* of copyright in a conspicuous place on the work itself was still required to preserve protection for a published work. This notice combines three elements. The first element is a use of the word "copyright," the abbreviation "Copr.," or the symbol ©. For sound recordings, the symbol © is also used to indicate a copyright notice. The next element is the year of first publication of the work. Certain private circulations of a work do not constitute publication. The third element is the name of the entity—whether a real person or a business—that is claiming copyright ownership. By custom, notices went on or near the title page of a written work, or in the head credits or final credits of a film or television program. Publication of a copyrighted work prior to March 1, 1989, without this type of notice could result in a loss of copyright protection. Provisions for correcting errors in notice are set out in the law.

Since March 1, 1989, the Berne Convention makes notice unnecessary for protection, even for U.S. authors. Notice is still necessary under the Uniform Copyright Convention, which continues in force for the U.S. and adds protection in a few additional countries, most notably the countries of the former U.S.S.R. Notice is also useful in deterring potential infringers, in establishing the chain of title on the work itself, and in negating an "innocent infringement" defense. As a rule of thumb, if displaying or distributing the work makes one think that claiming copyright protection might be necessary, then notice is probably a good idea.

DEPOSIT OF COPYRIGHTED WORKS

In order to help build the collections of the Library of Congress, a prerequisite of registration was always the deposit of two complete copies of the best edition of the work. Even now, with registration voluntary, two copies of the best edition of any work *published* in the U.S. must be deposited with the Library of Congress within three months of publication. For certain classes of works, where deposit of the whole is difficult or impractical, special exceptions can be made. For sculptures or certain motion pictures, for instance, a deposit of photographs or other identifying material may suffice.

SUPPLEMENTS/SUBSTITUTES

In addition to the copyright law procedures, authors sometimes take additional steps to help prove their rights in the material they have written. For instance, the Writer's Guild of America maintains in both its New York and Los Angeles offices a registry for television and film scripts, treatments, and other material. Registration with the Guild does not provide any additional legal protection other than that normally provided by copyright, but it can serve as useful evidence that the author in question created the material. In fact, the registry is primarily used to establish that an idea or written material existed on a certain date. While registered works are rarely withdrawn as evidence for copyright or contractual disputes, written confirmation from the Writers Guild registry that a work was deposited on a given date is frequently requested as evidence. This service cannot be used to establish credit for a given work, however, and registration does not imply credit for authorship. Registration is open to members and non-members of the WGA alike.

As a similar evidentiary matter, authors sometimes mail copies of their work to themselves in a sealed envelope, hoping that the postmark will provide some proof as to the date of creation and the original authorship of the writer. This measure is of dubious value, and of no value whatsoever if the envelope is opened prior to its formal presentation as evidence.

COMPULSORY LICENSES AND OTHER SPECIFIC EXCEPTIONS

There are certain exceptions in the copyright law to the exclusive rights normally enjoyed by a copyright holder. For instance, various compulsory licenses are granted under the Copyright Act. Section 111 gives cable systems a compulsory license to retransmit any material going out over the air on a traditional U.S. television broadcast. For distant signals imported into the area, the cable system must make a required payment to the Copyright Office. The Librarian of Congress then acts as a disbursing agent, distributing payments among the program copyright holders who file claim (see page 145). In the case of a controversy over the distribution, a Copyright Royalty Arbitration Panel is convened to settle the matter. Similar provisions exist under Section 119, setting up a statutory license for certain satellite rebroadcasts of superstations and network stations in otherwise underserved areas. This provision also seeks to encourage the setting of fees by voluntary negotiation.

The Librarian of Congress also has jurisdiction over the licensing rates that public broadcasters pay for certain published non-dramatic musical works and published pictorial, graphic, and sculptural works (see Section 118 of the Copyright Act). Other television-related exceptions to the copyright holder's rights include the right of a transmitting organization, such as a station or cable company, to make "ephemeral" copies of the work for help in duly licensed transmissions (see Section 112 of the Copyright Act).

Section 110 permits the use of copyrighted materials "in the course of face-to-face teaching activities of a nonprofit educational institution, in a classroom or similar place devoted to instruction"— provided, in the case of audiovisual works, that the copy being shown was lawfully made. Under Section 108, libraries and other archival institutions can also do limited copying to keep the items in their collection in good condition.

FAIR USE

The 1976 Copyright Act finally codified what used to be court-made law—that the "fair use" of copyrighted material does not represent an infringement of copyright. Section 107 of the 1976 Act provides that "the fair use of a copyrighted work . . . for purposes such as criticism, comment, news reporting, teaching (including multiple copies for classroom use), scholarship or research, is not an infringement of copyright." The statute goes on to specify four factors which are to be taken into account, non-exclusively, in determining whether fair use has been made:

(1) the purpose and character of the use, including whether such use is of a commercial nature or is for non-profit educational purposes;
(2) the nature of the copyrighted work;
(3) the amount and substantiality of the portion used in relation to the copyrighted work as a whole; and
(4) the effect of the use upon the potential market or value of the copyrighted work.

Fair use does not require the permission of the copyright holder. In the television context, fair use permits the use of short excerpts of films, television programs, and other copyrighted works for purposes such as news, information, reviewing, and teaching. Excerpts of a little over a minute or more from a feature film, however, have been held to be excessive and beyond the scope of fair use, and at least the E&O insurer (explained below) balks at copyrighted excerpts in excess of 30 seconds for "fair use. Fair use is generally not permitted for material that has not been previously broadcast or otherwise published, although this is not in itself a bar to fair use.

THE FIRST AMENDMENT AND NEWS ITEMS

In limited cases, the First Amendment also provides a means, analogous to fair use, for reproducing copyrighted works without permission. This exception to copyright law pertains to cases where the information in the copyrighted work—typically a film clip or still photograph—is so newsworthy in and of itself that, in the words of *Nimmer on Copyright*, "no amount of words describing the idea . . . could substitute for the public insight gained through the photographs." This rationale has been applied to photographs of the My Lai massacre and the Zapruder film of the Kennedy assassination.

TERM OF COPYRIGHT

The 1909 statute provided for an initial copyright term of 28 years from the date of publication, or 28 years from the date of registration in the case of unpublished works. The 1909 Act established a further renewal term, also of 28 years, available for the extension of the copyright. This renewal term was extended until the 1976 Act set it at 47 years, giving a total of 75 years of protection to works that have been properly copyrighted and renewed under the 1909 Act. Thus, any pre-1978 copyright, even if properly renewed, will go into the public domain in the United States 75 years after its copyright date. For instance, in 1998, anything copyrighted in the U.S. prior to 1923 should be in the public domain. It must be noted that the term of foreign copyright protection can vary, with some countries giving shorter protections and others longer.

Post-1978 works have a copyright period of the life of the author plus 50 years. In the case of works with multiple authors, the time runs from the death of the author who is the last to die. Works made for hire, and works published under pseudonyms, have a copyright term of a flat 75 years from the date of initial publication, or 100 years from the date of creation, whichever expires first.

TERMINATION

The copyright law permits authors and (after they are dead) certain specified individuals to terminate the licenses, assignments, and other transfers of copyrights after a relatively long period has passed. These termination windows reflect the intention that certain aspects of the renewal copyright were meant to benefit authors and not assignees. Section 203 of the Copyright Act provides a right of termination for post-1978 transfers of rights. This allows the copyright holder—or, if he or she is dead, designated family member—to terminate grants of copyright by notice to the grantee given within a five-year window that starts 35 years from the date of the grant, or, in the case of grants covering rights to publish the work that starts 40 years from the grant or 35 years from publication, whichever is earlier. This termination will shut off new uses under the grant, but the continued use of derivative works prepared by the licensee prior to the termination is permitted. Thus, a television film made under a valid grant can still be shown after the termination. It may, however, have to face competition from a new version made under the grant of new rights.

There is also a provision allowing the termination of grants made prior to 1978. Under Section 304 of the Copyright Act, an author or the designated family members can terminate prior grants within a five-year window starting either on January 1, 1978, or 56 years from the date the copyright was originally secured, whichever is later. This allows the author or his or her heirs to enjoy the benefits of the extended renewal term given by the new Act. There is also an exception permitting the continued use of previously created or derivative works.

In the case of each of these termination rights, no advance waiver will be effective. It should also be noted that in the case of a work for hire, the employer is actually considered the author, and so the paid creator would not have the benefit or these terminations.

There is one further termination right, which carries over from the 1909 Act. Under Section 304(a), the renewal procedures for pre-1978 copyrights still in their first term are preserved. Grants of the renewal term could be made by the author in advance. This grant, however, was not effective against the authorized family members who could exercise the renewal right if the author died before he or she could exercise the renewal right. This gives an unlimited termination right to the family members in this narrow circumstance, although it can be waived in advance by the family members. The statute holds no exception for derivative works, and a Supreme Court case has established that there is no automatic right to continue to exploit already produced films or television programs based on such a terminated grant. Over time, the works for which this is a problem will naturally make their way through the system.

EXCLUSIVE LICENSES, ASSIGNMENTS, MORTGAGES

The copyright law requires that an *exclusive* assignment or license (including a mortgage or other security interest in the copyrighted work) be in a signed document in order to be effective between the parties. Indeed, in order to be effective against certain third parties, any such exclusive license or assignment should not only be executed as a signed agreement, but also be recorded with the Copyright Office. This gives legal notice to the world in general of the contents of the license or assignment.

COPYRIGHT INFRINGEMENT

A copyright is infringed when someone exercises one of the exclusive rights granted by the Copyright Act without the consent from the copyright holder, without approval from a licensee of the copyright holder, or without the excuse of a compulsory license, fair use, or other exception. In order to win a lawsuit over an infringement, the plaintiff must prove several key elements. It must be shown that there is a valid copyright in the material. The person suing must be either the copyright owner or the holder of an *exclusive* right which is being infringed. The exclusive-rights concept also applies to beneficial rights. For instance, an author who has assigned his or her original rights to someone else while retaining a royalty interest may still be able to sue as a beneficial-rights owner.

It must also be shown that a protected element of the original work has been used in some forbidden way. This involves establishing two points: first, that the infringing item or element is "substantially similar" to the protected work, and second, that the protected work was actually the basis for the infringing item or element. The former is determined by the judge or jury via straightforward comparison, without the testimony of experts. The latter can be proven directly or inferred so long as the plaintiff can prove that the alleged infringer had *access* to the original work. For example, if the original author had kept the original work in a trunk and never showed it to anyone, there could be no infringement because access was impossible.

Generally, an outraged copyright owner can sue not only the original infringer, but also anyone along the chain of publication. Lack of knowledge that a protected work is being infringed is not a defense, although it may reduce damage liability. For instance, if a scriptwriter plagiarizes a protected book in a teleplay and then sells it to a producer as an original piece, the producer, network, and individual stations can all, in theory, be sued as infringers.

E&O INSURANCE

This kind of exposure to liability makes Errors and Omissions (E&O) insurance a key part of any contract for distribution or telecasting. Most such contracts call for the producer to get and maintain E&O coverage for at least the first few years a program is shown; sometimes the required coverage period is linked to the three-year statute of limitations on copyright claims. E&O insurance also covers claims for libel, slander, privacy, and publicity; it does not usually cover contract disputes. Limits on E&O coverage of $3 million for all occurrences and $1 million per single claim are common. Most distribution agreements call for the naming of the distributor as an additional insured on the policy.

E&O insurers generally require that certain clearance procedures be followed, and sometimes they print out a list of steps to take on their application form. In addition to setting out the insurance requirements, this list is also a useful reminder of good production practices.

REMEDIES FOR INFRINGEMENT

The winning plaintiff in an infringement lawsuit has several possible remedies available. The first is an injunction against any further infringing use. The court can also force a recall of copies still in the channels of distribution or forbid further unauthorized showings.

In addition to putting a stop to the infringement, the aggrieved party can also recover damages and profits. The *damages* may be set to reflect actual harm suffered, such as lost sales; recovering *profits* involves compensating the plaintiff with the economic benefits of the infringement. Both approaches are inherently speculative, and may be inadequate to right the wrong. For instance, if a money-losing TV show is based without permission on a copyrighted film that also lost money, an amount of real damages and improper profits may be hard to prove. It is for such a situation that the Copyright Law has established "statutory damages." This is a set amount which a court can levy as damages—an award based simply on the infringement itself, which does not require proof of a particular level of actual harm. For most infringements, the range of these damages is currently $500 to $20,000 for all infringements of a given copyright; for willful infringements, the statutory damages can be up to $100,000.

Awards of legal fees may also be given, which in some cases may exceed actual damages.

CRIMINAL PENALTIES

In addition to the civil remedies discussed above, there are also criminal penalties for infringement done "willfully and for purposes of commercial advantage or private financial gain." For serious commercial piracy of motion pictures (including television programs) involving making or selling more than 65 copies within any six-month period, the penalty is a fee of up to $250,000 and up to five years in jail.

TAPING AND PIRACY

Before the advent of home video, the unauthorized copying of an audiovisual program was expensive and difficult. Infringing uses of such a copy, even if made, were relatively easy to police. Home video machines, however, have changed this, creating both a simple mechanism for creating copies and a widespread and quite private market for their use. "Time shifting," the practice of recording shows off a broadcast station or cable service for later viewing, is probably the most benign (and the hardest to police) of these activities. When VCRs first came into use, the production community brought suit against Sony in an attempt either to stop the sale of VCRs, or to set up an extra charge on the sale of blank cassettes that would be deposited into a group fund. Producers would then collect a share of this fund, much as they do with compulsory cable license fees. This scheme was squashed when the U.S. Supreme Court held that home recording for the purposes of time shifting constituted fair use, not copyright infringement. The Internet is not yet a source of significant piracy, in part because of band-width limitations. As band-width availability and digital compression advance, this may change over time.

Outright piracy—that is, the unauthorized copying of works not publicly disseminated by broadcast or cable, or the unauthorized copying of any program or film for commercial purposes—is punishable by the civil and criminal statutes of the Copyright Law. While at a practical level the practice of copying tapes for friends and family is unlikely to come to anyone's notice, the potential penalties are stiff. Commercial piracy is a major concern of the production and distribution communities; they expend considerable resources in the U.S. and in some other countries on finding and closing down pirates.

INTERNATIONAL IMPLICATIONS OF COPYRIGHT LAW

The scope of the U.S. copyright law is essentially domestic. Although unpublished works by foreign authors are fully protected, that protection will cease on publication unless (1) one or more of the authors is a national, domiciliary, or governmental authority of a country that has a copyright treaty with the U.S. or is a stateless person; (2) the work is first published in the U.S. or in a country which is, at the time of publication, a member of the Universal Copyright Convention; (3) the work is first published by the United Nations or the Organization of American States; (4) the work is a Berne Convention work; or (5) the country of origin is covered by a special presidential proclamation. The law of most foreign countries is similarly limited, and will not protect a U.S.-source work unless there are applicable international agreements in effect.

The U.S. was a relative latecomer in joining the conventions (most notably, the Berne Convention and the Universal Copyright Convention) that offer the major degree of international copyright protection. U.S. copyright law evolved with a variety of idiosyncrasies which did not meet the requirements of the conventions, and which the U.S. was reluctant to give up. Therefore, up until 1955—when the U.S. joined the Universal Copyright Convention (UCC)— protection of a U.S. work abroad depended upon either the existence of an individually negotiated treaty between the U.S. and the foreign country in question, or the simultaneous publication of the work in the U.S. and a country (frequently Canada) that was an adherent to one or more of the conventions. The UCC was, in fact, tailored to permit such elements of the 1909 Act as the notice requirements, which were not permitted under the Berne Convention. The UCC gave protection throughout much of the world, but there were still gaps, some of which could be closed by joining the Berne Convention. With the adoption of the 1976 Copyright Act, many of the inconsistencies were eliminated, and the U.S. began to seriously consider joining Berne as well.

The principal stumbling block to the U.S. joining the Berne Convention was the Convention's requirement that moral rights (see page 187) be protected. With the determination that the U.S. gave enough protection to moral rights to qualify for Berne without changing existing law, Congress ratified the Berne Convention, which came into effect on March 1, 1989. Adherence to Berne did require some changes to U.S. law, particularly in the area of formalities (see page 167). Foreign works coming under Berne get even easier treatment on the registration point— copyright registration is not a prerequisite to bringing a lawsuit.

Under Berne, U.S. works will receive the same protection in another Berne country as applies to works originally copyrighted in that country. In some cases, this can include a copyright term in excess of that granted in the U.S. Whenever a question of foreign copyrights is raised, it is wise to consult with a knowledgeable expert.

International copyright protection has gained additional support in the 1990s through the activities of the World Trade Organization (WTO) and of the World Intellectual Property Organization (WIPO). As part of the most recent revisions of the General Agreement on Tariffs and Trade (GATT), a new side agreement was ratified, called the "Agreement on Trade Related Aspects of Intellectual Property Rights, Including Trade in Counterfeit Goods," or, more usably, "TRIPS." This agreement established certain minimum standards for intellectual property protection as a prerequisite for WTO membership. In large degree, it piggy backs on the Berne rules, but does not require the moral rights protection which clashes with traditional U.S. free-market notions (see page 187). It does require some form of compensation for video rentals in countries where pirating is widespread. The WIPO copyright treaty has taken a similar approach. TRIPS also extends protection to computer programs and sound recordings.

PROTECTION OF IDEAS

Although it is not possible to copyright an idea, that does not mean that an idea is completely unprotectable. In most states, it is possible to obtain at least some protection under contract theories for an idea disclosed to another when the two parties have made a deal requiring compensation for the idea. For instance, a signed contract to pay for disclosing an idea will normally be enforced. A studio or producer may request a well-known author to submit raw ideas for programming, and can agree to pay for the ideas. The most notorious example of such an arrangement was the subject of a lawsuit which found that Art Buchwald had supplied the idea behind the film *Coming to America*. Buchwald had a signed contract with Paramount Pictures promising to pay him for ideas he supplied, with extra payments and net profits due if an idea were actually used as a basis for the film. Buchwald's victory over Paramount was not complete; after years of making money, no net profits have been generated by *Coming to America*.

Where there is a signed contract, the most frequently contested issue is whether or not the idea in question, or enough of it, was actually used. An idea, by its very nature, lacks those expressive elements which would give rise to copyright protection. Therefore, the standard of similarity necessary for an idea case is generally less stringent than that which would be required for a copyright infringement case. Frequently the contract will provide words such as "based on" to indicate the necessary relationship between the idea and the final product. In applying the "based on" concept, courts have used a variety of analyses, including a kind of mental paternity test. If it can be shown that the end product evolved naturally from the original idea, the final product will be held to be based upon the idea, even if many changes have been made and the number of actual elements in common has become relatively sparse. Any defendant in such an action will try to show a different source for the end product.

Even in the absence of a signed, written agreement, courts will sometimes still give protection to the provider of an idea. For instance, if there is a verbal understanding or if it is the accepted expectation in the industry that a payment would be made if the idea was disclosed and used, then an implied contract will sometimes be found.

Other theories for giving implied protection are "unjust en-richment," fraud, and the breach of a fiduciary relationship. For example, if an attorney (who has a fiduciary relationship to his client) uses for his own profit a television program idea disclosed by the client in confidence, it is likely that the client would be able to recover the fair value of the idea from the attorney.

In some states, such as New York, it must be shown that the idea was original and novel before any contract protection, whether express or implied, will be given. In such a state, an idea that was relatively obvious may not be given any legal protection.

UNSOLICITED MATERIAL

The desire of authors to impose implied contracts on producers, on the one hand, and the desire of producers, on the other hand, to avoid them, has led to a variety of strategies in the submission of unsolicited material. Some producers refuse to review any unsolicited material, returning such submissions to the sender either unopened or unread. Other producers will review such material, but will first send a letter to the person submitting the material seeking to counter any implication that a contract exists for its use. (A sample of such a letter appears in Appendix B2.) Some producers find that these actions are too time-consuming— they simply send rejections for material they don't wish to use, and negotiate agreements for material which they do wish to use.

Writers, when submitting unsolicited material, will sometimes seek to set up the implication that payment is to be made, even if non-copyrightable aspects of the material should be used. A writer may enclose with the material a letter which spells out, in some non-threatening manner, that the writer expects to be compensated if the material is used by the producer. While the efficacy of these one-sided letters is open to question, they are probably better than nothing.

In the end, the writer's greatest protection probably comes from the fact that it is usually relatively inexpensive, in the overall scheme of a production, for an established producer to pay a rights fee of some kind to the persons actually supplying ideas for the program. Indeed, such a license with one person can provide, under the paternity-test theory, protection against claims brought by other potential originators of the idea. Before bringing charges of theft for aspects of a project that was casually submitted, the aggrieved writer should consider that similar ideas may have been suggested to active production companies on more than one occasion.

Protection of Personal Rights

LIBEL AND SLANDER

Libel and slander are twin actions frequently linked under the word "defamation." Defamation has been defined as the publication or broadcast of false information, not otherwise privileged, which exposes the person (or other entity) so described to hatred, contempt, or ridicule; which causes the person to be shunned or avoided; or which has the tendency to injure the person in his or her occupation. Liability attaches not only to the individual who writes or speaks the falsehood, but to any other entity "publishing" it as well. Broadcasting by a network, cable network, or local station will generally constitute such publishing. A cable system simply supplying an outside service may be free from challenge on the theory that it is a mere transmitter.

These are difficult and confused areas of the law. Indeed, one of the most respected legal treatises on the subject declares:

> It must be confessed at the beginning that there is a great deal of the law of defamation which makes no sense. It contains anomalies and absurdities for which no legal writer has ever had a kind word, and it is a curious compound of a strict liability imposed upon innocent defendants, as rigid in extremes as anything found in the law, with a blind and almost perverse refusal to compensate the plaintiff for real and very serious harm.[1]

Libel involves written defamation and *slander* involves spoken defamation—the distinction is one of the anomalies mentioned

---

1 *Prosser and Keaton on the Law of Torts,* 5th edition, 1984.

above. In the case of slander, it is frequently necessary to prove actual specific damages, while in the case of libel, such damages can often be presumed from the nature of the defamatory writing. Although it is still open to some dispute in a few states, any form of recorded television production will generally be treated under the laws of libel even though it is not in a written form. Purely live broadcast may constitute slander in some states.

REQUIREMENTS FOR DEFAMATION

The first prerequisite for defamation is that the offensive statement in fact describes the person complaining of the falsehood. The actual name need not be used for the claim to succeed, so long as a reasonable person would think that the person complaining is the one to whom the defamatory statement in fact refers. Defamation claims have been upheld even when not only the name has been changed, but many of the personal characteristics, such as body shape, hair color, and age. If the claimant can show that there was sufficient identifying detail to lead reasonable people to believe that he or she was the one being talked about, then an action for defamation can be sustained. Ironically, the very act of changing names and some character traits can give rise to the kind of falsehood which is actionable. Therefore, if fictionalization of a real character is to take place in a program, the writer, producer, and director are advised to go to great lengths to clearly distance the fictionalized character from its original model. Coy references to a real person, made under a veil of fiction, can be dangerous. Defamation applies only to living persons, though, so the reputation of a dead individual receives no protection from libel and slander.

The second requirement for defamation is that the statement in question be false. Truth is, in and of itself, a complete defense against defamation. There is also a distinction between fact and opinion. The courts have held that an opinion in itself is not subject to being true or false; it merely represents the opinion of the speaker. The difference between opinion and fact, however, is not always possible or easy to discern. The statement that "Joe is a liar" on the one hand constitutes an opinion as to Joe's veracity; on the other hand, it can be taken as a statement of fact that Joe lies about things. Even though "opinions" are not absolutely safe from challenge, in practice, it is still generally helpful to couch controversial conclusions as matters of opinion. The talk-show host who begins every third sentence with "Well, in my opinion" is demonstrating the influence of somebody's legal department.

The third element of defamation is that the false statement must expose the person to some kind of harm to his or her reputation. Thus, the statement "Joe loves his country," even if false, would not generally be judged defamatory. False imputations of dishonesty, adultery, or venereal infections, however, are clearly within the danger zone.

DEFAMATION AND THE FIRST AMENDMENT

Overlying these traditional aspects of defamation are requirements imposed by the First Amendment of the Constitution. In order to encourage robust reporting and a free exercise of the creative arts, the Supreme Court held in 1964—in the famous case of *The New York Times v. Sullivan*—that the First Amendment prevents recovery for defamation against a public figure unless some kind of *fault* is demonstrated. A public official or other public figure who has been harmed must show that the author or publisher of a defamatory statement had "actual malice" in publishing of the falsehood in order to recover damages. Actual malice in this context does not mean hatred; rather, it has the technical meaning of either an actual knowledge that the statement in question was false, or a reckless disregard for the truth or falsehood of the statement. In the case of a private individual, the standard set by the Supreme Court is one of negligence in checking out the information that is published or broadcast, and requires that greater care be taken by the producer or reporter. As a practical matter, a finding of malice for statements made by the media about a public person is rare. The author and publisher of the supposedly libelous material will probably have exercised at least some care in their research. This includes checking sources, seeking confirmation, and asking for a response from the affected person. The negligence standard as applied to non-public figures is somewhat more stringent; therefore, the author and broadcaster of material relating to private people should exert themselves even more than normal to insure a truthful program. The distinction between a public and private person is sometimes a tricky one, and is frequently linked to context. A person who saves the President's life will be a public person within the context of that event, but may still be a private person in the context of his or her home life. In either case, a court will very seldom impose liability on a journalist, writer, or producer who can demonstrate that he or she has acted within normal journalistic standards of professional responsibility.

PRIOR RESTRAINT AND DAMAGES

In enforcing the rules against libel and slander, a court will almost never prevent publication in advance. Such a prevention is called a "prior restraint" and, as an absolute exercise in information control, is repugnant for First Amendment reasons. The more usual remedy for a proven case of defamation is damages. As discussed above, in certain instances it may be necessary for a plaintiff to prove actual damages to reputation. In other cases, damages will be presumed from the statement itself. The chance of a plaintiff winning a suit and obtaining substantial damages is more likely for claims dealing with sexual matters or other general societal taboos than in the context of a political debate, where a certain level of robust charge and counter-charge is expected and tolerated.

BAD BEHAVIOR BY NEWS REPORTERS

The death of Princess Diana in 1997 underscored a somewhat different question—the behavior of those involved in gathering news, as distinct from the information gathered. This was also a factor in the mid-1990s Food Lion case, where ABC News planted workers in the meat department of the supermarket chain. ABC lost in the lower court because of the "fraud" in getting its reporters employed. Courts are not always able to disassociate the bad methods of news collection from the effects of legitimate news so collected. Keeping news gathering behavior within the realm of legality is important.

PRIVACY AND PUBLICITY

The related rights of privacy and publicity are relative newcomers to American law. They have evolved considerably over the last hundred years, and they are still evolving. The *right of privacy* was first discussed in a *Harvard Law Review* article written in 1890 by Samuel Warren and the eventual Supreme Court justice Louis Brandeis. They suggested that a right to be "left alone" existed in the "common law"—that is, as a matter of judicial recognition, without ever having been enacted by a legislature. The first test of right to privacy came in the state of New York in 1902. The case was brought by a young woman whose picture was used, without her permission, in a poster advertising baking flour. The New York Court of Appeals would not accept the common-law basis for the right of privacy, so she lost her case. This decision led to the passage by the New York state legislature of a statute creating a "right of privacy." The successor to this statute, New York Civil Rights Law, Section 50, now reads, in part:

> A person, firm or corporation that uses for advertising purposes, or for the purposes of trade, the name, portrait or picture of any living person without having first obtained the written consent of such person, or if a minor of his or her partner or guardian, is guilty of a misdemeanor.

A companion provision, Section 51, provides a civil damage remedy for violations of this right. Note that the items covered are "name, portrait, picture or voice."

If the New York court was hesitant to create a new right based on a *Harvard Law Review* article, the courts in many other states were not. For instance, in 1905, the Georgia Supreme Court held that the right of privacy did exist even without a statute. California has also recognized a common-law privacy right. Over the years, most states have come down on one side or the other of this choice. Many states which did not recognize the right at common law subsequently adopted statutes, frequently based on the New York model.

Another law review article—this time published in 1960 and written by the famous legal commentator, William Prosser—had a significant impact. Prosser suggested that the law of privacy had four parts: (1) a right against intrusion into a person's life and affairs, including by eavesdropping and spying; (2) a right against the public disclosure of embarrassing private facts; (3) a right against being put in a "false light"; and (4) a right against the appropriation of a person's identity by others, particularly for commercial purposes. The last of these four was an aspect of the right which is covered by the New York statute and its imitators. Although Prosser was writing as a private citizen and not as a judge or legislator, his analysis was adopted as the basis of the law in many states, particularly in those where the right of privacy was held to exist at common law.

The *right of publicity* is similar to New York's statutory privacy right and Prosser's fourth right of privacy. The two major distinctions that have come to be most frequently recognized are (1) that the right of publicity will be strongest in cases where the person in question actually exploits his or her persona, and (2) that the right of publicity can survive the death of the person whose identity is being exploited. The privacy right, as with defamation, was generally viewed to terminate on the death of the person in question. Thus, in 1985, California adopted a statutory publicity-right provision, supplementing its common-law and statutory rights of privacy. The new statute permits the heirs of a deceased celebrity to continue to exploit his or her identity in commercial products for a period of up to 50 years after the celebrity's death.

By 1998, most states had adopted, either by statute or as a matter of common law, some form of the rights of privacy and publicity. Most states, at a minimum, protect living people against commercial appropriation of their names and likenesses. There is, however, tremendous diversity between the laws of the different states, as to which further aspects of the rights they recognize. Given the confusion on these issues, it is important to know which state's rules will apply. In general, courts will apply the law of the domicile of the person seeking privacy or publicity protection. While this rule may help courts in reaching a decision, or a local programmer with only one or two states to worry about, it is less helpful to the producer or distributor of national programming.

Luckily, the free-speech provisions of the First Amendment of the United States Constitution supply an overall national standard, at least with respect to factual statements on matters of general public interest.

The Supreme Court ruled on the problem in 1967, in the case of *Time, Inc. v. Hill*. This case involved a New York privacy law-suit by members of a family who had been the victims of a crime some years before. *Life* magazine, a Time, Inc. publication, had run an article which set scenes from a play that was based loosely on this crime in the family's old house. The article implied inaccurate details about the family and the crime. (Richard Nixon repre-sented the family in its appeal.) The Supreme Court held that privacy and publicity claims by public figures (including the family, in this case) would require a showing of the same element of "malice"—knowing falsehood or reckless disregard for truth—that had to be proved for a defamation claim.

Even without reference to the First Amendment, most privacy statutes and common-law formulations on the state level have been interpreted to hold that truthful biographical, informational, or news uses are "non-commercial" and therefore not a violation. This conclusion would apply even to a program broadcast on commercial television in a for-profit manner.

An extension of this logic allows, without consent, the name and likeness of an individual who appears in the program to be used in advertisements for the program itself—and, provided that the name and likeness are linked to the program in some way, they can even be used in ads for the service that runs the program.

DOCUDRAMAS

The laws—and exceptions—governing the rights of defamation, privacy, and publicity display themselves most vividly in the context of docudramas. This is because the application of the constitutional aspects of libel, slander, privacy, and publicity law to docudramas must overcome an inherent contradiction. There is supposedly no First Amendment protection for a depiction that is knowingly false or deliberately fictionalized—the essence of the malice standard that applies to both defamation and privacy/publicity. Yet a docudrama is, of necessity, a fictionalized presentation of events based in truth. A print biographer can perhaps claim the goal of absolute accuracy, but a docudrama producer never can.

To begin with, the words spoken—unless they come directly from court transcripts or other *verbatim* sources—will always be, at best, reconstructions of past events. The characters will be played by actors, and not by the people themselves. The requirements of production will inevitably cause deletions and compressions of events and characters. Quite conscious fictionalization is a necessary part of the process—and the docudrama is a legally permissible art form.

The leading opinion as to the docudrama's blending of fact and fiction arose from the film *Missing*. In his opinion, the judge, Milton Pollack, stated:

> Self-evidently a docudrama partakes of author's license—it is a creative interpretation of reality—and if alterations of fact in scenes portrayed are not made with serious doubts of truth of the essence of the telescoped composite, such scenes do not ground a charge of actual malice.[2]

The *Missing* case and other docudrama cases suggest this simple guideline: a docudrama producer may use limited fictionalization, creating composite characters, incidents and dialogue, provided that the end result—with respect to any material questions—is representationally true, and provided that such representational truth has been arrived at responsibly.

Docudrama producers should stick to the following procedures in order to help keep their productions within legally permissible bounds:

Select a topic and characters of legitimate public interest. The First Amendment protections will be much less helpful in the examination of private events in the lives of private people.

---

2   *Davis v. Costa-Gavras,* 654 F. Supp 653, 658 (S.D.N.Y. 1987)

Depict dead people. Death wipes out protection against defamation and the right of privacy (although not the right of publicity).

Get releases. If releases can be obtained, they provide the best line of defense. However, it may be better never to ask for a release than to ask and be refused.

Do voluminous research. The backup work for a docudrama should be even more rigorous than the research for a hard news piece. Minor incidents and personality traits should also be noted. A wealth of accurate detail from numerous sources will give the scriptwriter the raw material from which to work, and will provide a higher level of protection. All research must be recorded and catalogued, so that it can be easily referenced as the review process goes forward.

Have a factual basis for every aspect of the script. Even with those scenes or characters that are fictionalized, there must be a factual basis for their "representational truth." Invented dialogue should reflect the opinions of the speaker. Although it is clear that excursions into "representational truth" are permitted, there is a point at which fictionalization goes too far. As a general matter, the more controversial or emotionally charged the item, the more literal the depiction should be; sex and nudity are particularly dicey. The film should also respect chronology, and should try not to use composite characters to portray major figures.

Have a legal review of the script and film. A legal review will act as a useful check on the natural exuberance of producers and writers, and can prove helpful in demonstrating lack of negligence and malice.

Use disclaimers. An appropriate disclaimer, alerting the audience to the presence of fictionalized elements, should be placed in the credits. The greater the prominence of the disclaimer, the greater the protection it offers.

MORAL RIGHTS

The doctrine of moral rights developed in continental Europe. In addition to the "economic rights" Americans traditionally associate with copyright, European authors generally have a second set of "moral rights" in their work. In their classic form, these rights include (1) the right to control publication; (2) the right to withdraw the work; (3) the right to have authorship accurately attributed; and (4) the right to maintain the integrity of the work, by preventing desecration and unauthorized changes. These rights are typically held to be inalienable: they are not subject to a general waiver. In most countries, the rights are transmitted after death to the author's family or to a designated representative; in some countries, such as France, the rights are said to be perpetual.

In the context of audiovisual productions, which are by their nature collaborative works, the European jurisdictions typically recognize at least the scriptwriter and director as the "creators" of the work, with the power to exercise these rights. Some countries add the composer of the musical score and author of any underlying work to this list. The existence of these moral rights can significantly restrict the exploitation of an audiovisual production. For instance, French filmmakers have effectively barred the colorizing of their old black-and-white films for the French market, at least without specific consent. The re-editing of films for use on television, such as cutting for time purposes or inserting ad breaks, may also be restricted. In effect, the original version cannot be tampered with by the producers without the express approval of the designated creators.

In the U.S., there has been a general resistance to expressly recognizing the existence of any moral rights. Ironically, the U.S. copyright law, by giving the author control over publication and the preparation of derivative or otherwise infringing works, actually accords the author the power to control all of the usual moral rights as a matter of contract. Other laws, such as privacy, libel, and unfair competition, cover some of the same territory as moral rights. When the U.S. joined the Berne Convention on copyright, which requires moral rights protection for authors, Congress pointed to these various rules in justifying going forward without changing U.S. law. The big difference between U.S. law and the provisions of most of the signatories to the Berne Convention is that classic moral rights cannot be contracted away on a general basis—the equivalent U.S. copyright protections and other legal rights, by contrast, can be, and usually are. The U.S. approach seems to be acceptable under the Berne Convention.

The American freedom to waive moral rights is both a blessing and a curse. On the one hand, it permits a freer commerce in film and television programming than is possible in Europe. In the case of a commissioned product with high commercial value and low artistic pretense—such as *Frasier* or *Rugrats*—the ability to waive is probably no loss to society. On the other hand, some people consider colorizing the best black-and-white films as deplorable as painting a mustache on the Mona Lisa.

There is, however, a critical difference between television product and a painting such as the Mona Lisa. The painting is a one-of-a-kind object, and a mustache on it would be an irreparable act. A television film or other program, by contrast, is quite freely reproducible, and changes such as colorization or editing can be made without in any way damaging the existing copies of the original work. Congress, in acting on the colorization issue, recognized this by setting up a mechanism for the preservation of certain designated film masterpieces in their original form. It also required that colorized versions of these films disclose prominently that the colorization was done without the participation of the original creative team, if that is the case. As a practical matter, these disclaimers have been broadly adopted for application to most colorized films, whether or not required by law.

In the final analysis, the arguments for an unwaivable moral rights law depend on a view of the creative processes that is at heart a nineteenth-century one. In this view, the author/artist is a special being, with the power to pierce the veil of ordinary existence and bring us all, through art, into contact with the sublime. Under such a view, the artist must retain control over each particular use of his or her work. For most areas of television production, it makes more sense for the producer to be able to obtain general waivers of these rights, particularly when the creative person has been commissioned and well-compensated to exercise his or her craft.

UNFAIR COMPETITION

The laws of unfair competition protect the names and reputations of individuals or companies from being falsely involved in connection with goods or services. (See page 436 for a more detailed discussion of the law of unfair competition.) At the federal level, this law is embodied in the Lanham Act; there are also similar state principles. The laws of unfair competition can protect individuals and organizations against the use of their names or other indicia of identity in such a way as to falsely suggest the origin of a program. Thus, using a well-known title or making some other statement which implies that a program was authorized by-or originated with-someone who had not given his or her consent, would be actionable.

18

Protection of Society

Most of the issues relevant to the content of television programming, such as copyright, privacy, and publicity, are private rights that are exercised or waived by the private entities involved. There are, however, certain restrictions which are imposed and enforced as a matter of criminal and civil law by our government, on the theory that they protect society at large. In keeping with the principles of the First Amendment, these rules are neither very numerous, nor very broad in their applicability. Nonetheless, they can have quite powerful repercussions. The 1990s witnessed a new initiative designed to sidestep First Amendment objections. This partially "voluntary" initiative has combined program content ratings with a device—the V-chip—which can screen out certain programming.

OBSCENITY

Notwithstanding the loosening of constraints over the past 30 years, the taboos against sex in the U.S. are very strong: so strong, indeed, that certain kinds of sexual speech are still held to be simply outside the coverage of the First Amendment. Since material labeled "obscene" is not protected by the First Amendment, it is subject to outright banning and criminal prosecution by the federal and state governments. The key question, therefore, is what constitutes obscene material. The Supreme Court, as the final arbiter on this matter, has wrestled with a definition of obscenity over the years, and has produced a series of pronouncements. Perhaps the most forthright, if the least specific, was the statement by one Supreme Court justice that he knew pornography when he saw it.

The currently applicable test for obscenity was enunciated in the case of *Miller v. California* in 1973. Under this test, for material to be obscene, all three of the following factors must be proven: (1) the average person, applying contemporary community standards, would find that the work, taken as a whole, appeals to prurient interests; (2) the work, as measured by contemporary community standards, depicts or describes-in a patently offensive way—sexual conduct specifically defined by the applicable state law; and (3) the work taken as a whole lacks serious literary, artistic, political, or scientific value.

This standard, when reduced to its bare essence, is not too different from "I know it when I see it." In effect, if the material contains explicit sexual depictions which are likely to arouse and offend (in the opinion of the judge or jury) a sufficiently broad segment of the population, it will be deemed obscene—unless the work has some aspect of general merit that removes it from punishment. Because the strength of the sexual taboo has ebbed somewhat in most communities in the past 30 years, the community-standard aspect of this test has led to the permitting of fairly explicit sexual material, particularly in major urban centers.

The dissemination of overtly sexual material by television is generally limited to such media as home video, satellite delivery, or late-night, local cablecast; in each case, adults have a personal choice as to whether or not to view it. In fact, the Supreme Court has held that the private possession and perusal of obscene material in the home is not punishable. The consenting-adults argument, however, is no defense for transactions in obscene material: a private sale of an explicit videotape from one adult to another could still be illegal. From a practical standpoint, though, few people are likely to complain about truly private transactions unless they involve minors, violence, or some other aggravating factor, and such sales are relatively unlikely to be punished.

Most states have anti-pornography statutes of one kind or another on their books. Some carry very serious criminal penalties. The enforcement of these statutes—or lack of enforcement— reflects the level of community concern. In conservative areas such as Cincinnati, Ohio, prosecutors and other enforcers of these laws may stand to gain more politically by bringing cases against supposedly obscene material than will prosecutors in more permissive places such as New York City and Los Angeles. There are also serious federal criminal laws forbidding the dissemination of obscene material. For instance, there are laws against shipping obscene material, including videos, in the mails or via interstate commerce. In 1996, the Congress adopted the Communication Decency Act. It was a short-lived attempt to regulate indecent material on the Web—widely viewed as an exercise in cynical overreacting by legislators eager to court "family values" credit at the expense of well-established First Amendment jurisprudence. These provisions were overturned by the Supreme Court in 1997.

OBSCENITY AND THE FCC

There are federal laws and FCC regulations governing the appearance of obscene and indecent material on broadcast television, and of obscene matter on cable television. Ironically, in its original formulation in the Communications Act, the prohibition against the use of indecent language via radio communication was paired with a provision forbidding the FCC to exercise any censorship over the content of broadcasts. The prohibition has since been moved out of the Communications Act and into the title on Crimes and Criminal Procedure. It reads, at 18 U.S.C. § 1464:

> Whoever utters any obscene, indecent, or profane language by means of radio communication shall be fined under this title or imprisoned not more than two years, or both.

The distribution of obscene material via cable or subscription television is punishable under both Title 18 and the Cable Act. Title 18, § 1468, provides:

> (a) Whoever knowingly utters any obscene language or distributes any obscene matter by means of cable television or subscription services on television, shall be punished by imprisonment for not more than two years or by fine in accordance with this title, or both.

> (b) As used in this section, the term "distribute" means to send, transmit, retransmit, telecast, broadcast, or cablecast, including by wire, microwave, or satellite, or to produce or provide material for such distribution.

> (c) Nothing in this chapter, or the Cable Communications Policy Act of 1984, or any other provision of Federal law, is intended to interfere with or preempt the power of the States, including political subdivisions thereof, to regulate the uttering of language that is obscene or otherwise unprotected by the Constitution or the distribution of matter that is obscene or otherwise unprotected by the Constitution, of any sort, by means of cable television or subscription services on television.

The Cable Act provides in Section 639 [47 U.S.C. § 559]:

> Whoever transmits over any cable system any matter which is obscene or otherwise unprotected by the Constitution of the United States shall be fined under Title 18 or imprisoned not more than two years, or both.

There have been differences between the FCC's approach to broadcast television and its approach to cable and satellite television.

For some time, the broadcast rules have applied not only to "obscene" material, but also to material that is merely "indecent." Indecency includes the use of offensive words, even in contexts where no graphic sexual description is involved: thus the problem with George Carlin's famous seven words you can't use on the airwaves. Indecency probably also includes non-sexual nudity. While 24-hour bans on broadcast TV indecency have been struck down, Congress in 1992 mandated a late-night "safe harbor" of midnight to 6:00 A.M. FCC rules implementing this were largely upheld in 1995, rolling the starting time back to 10:00 P.M. In the late 1990s, Congress and the FCC initiated a new approach to sexual content in broadcast television: ratings and the V-Chip. This program in discussed below at page 197.

The laws governing cable services, however, provide only for the prohibition of obscene material. There has been a tradition of greater latitude in the cable area. This is partly due to the lesser legal control of cable—and also to the fact that the decision to receive cable is elective, and that in most cases, the more risqué channels can be switched off at the box in the home. Public-access services have been particularly active in showing non-obscene nudity, largely in a late-night time slot. Use of non-obscene sexual images and language is a matter for the programming policies of the cable system and network, exercised largely in light of commercial considerations. Satellite services, with their increased pay-per-view capacity, are also more open to non-obscene sexual content. Hard-core material would still fall afoul of the obscenity standard.

NATIONAL SECURITY

In limited circumstances, the government can censor material that would endanger the national security. This authority has been quite narrowly defined, applying only when an immediate, specific threat from the publication or telecast of the material can be shown. For instance, it has been held that the government could prevent the publication of the sailing dates of transports, or the number and location of troops in time of war—and that the government can suppress a magazine article explaining in full detail how to build a hydrogen bomb. In the *Pentagon Papers* case, by contrast, the Supreme Court allowed the publication of an in-house Department of Defense study critical of the conduct of the Vietnam War. The government had simply not met the heavy burden of justification necessary to stop the information from flowing.

Even if information, once gathered, is hard to suppress on national-security grounds, the government and military can limit the access of reporters, including television newspeople, to sensitive material and locations. Furthermore, as a *quid pro quo* for obtaining access to military areas and missions, reporters will sometimes agree to limit certain aspects of their stories. This self-censorship, encouraged by the government, can be quite effective. Government officials sometimes sign contracts agreeing to keep certain information secret, and these contracts can be enforced.

PRE-TRIAL PUBLICITY

The First Amendment guarantees of free speech sometimes come into conflict with another constitutional guarantee: the right to a fair trial. It is sometimes claimed that pre-trial publicity of a particularly inflammatory nature can so prejudice public opinion about a criminal case that it becomes impossible for the defendant to receive a fair hearing by a jury. As a result, in certain very rare cases, there may be an injunction against publishing or televising a particular piece of information about the case. This remedy is granted only on proof that no other option, including moving the location of the trial to a city or town where the case is less well-known, will protect the rights of the accused.

"SON OF SAM" LAWS

In the 1980s the federal government and many states adopted so-called "Son of Sam" Laws. These laws are aimed at preventing a criminal from being able to profit from selling the rights to the story of his or her crimes to the media. In the late 1970s, New York City was the scene of a series of brutal attacks by a psychopathic killer who sent notes about his crimes signed with the name "Son of Sam." Enraged at the notion that this criminal might profit from a sale of the media rights to his crimes, New York State enacted a statute that confiscates any monies paid to the criminal (or to entities such as agents collecting on his behalf) for books, movies, magazine articles, or television shows in which the crime is reenacted or the criminal's "thoughts, feelings, opinions or emotions" about the crime are expressed. The funds so confiscated are given to a crime victims' compensation board, which then disburses them to victims of the crime. Similar laws were enacted by the federal government and by many states.

In 1991 many of the first round of the "Son of Sam" Laws ran afoul of the Constitution. The U.S. Supreme Court held that they could violate free speech. Since then, states have focused on broader laws permitting victims to attack criminals' assets more broadly. Even these laws may run into constitutional problems.

CHILDREN'S PROGRAMMING

Protecting children from "bad" programming, and ensuring that they have "good" programming available have been popular goals. After many years of false starts, canceled proceedings, and vetoed legislation, Congress finally enacted legislation regulating children's television in 1990. The Children's Television Act of 1990 restricts the amount of advertising that can run in children's programming on both broadcast and cable television to 10.5 minutes per hour on weekends and 12 on weekdays (shorter periods are treated proportionately). The Act also requires the FCC to regulate program-length commercials, and calls on broadcast stations to serve "the educational and information needs of children through the licensee's overall programming, including programming specifically designed to serve such needs." The degree to which a broadcast station has met this standard is considered in connection with license renewal.

The original FCC rules, implementing this mandate were finalized in August 1991. They define children's programming as being aimed at 12 years old and under. "Program-length commercials" are defined as "a program associated with a product, in which commercials for that product are aired." This continues to allow product-driven shows to air, but if direct sales pitches for the product are contained within the program or in adjacent spots, then the entire program counts against the commercial time limits. The FCC did not narrowly define programs that would serve "the educational and informational needs of children" and recognized that this could include fictional programs. These initial rules did not satisfy critics—and small wonder when a show like *The Jetsons* was promoted as educational because it showed children what life would be like in the twenty-first century.

Therefore, in August 1996, the FCC promulgated further rules on educational and informational programming. These made a distinction between programming that furthers the educational and informational needs of children 16 and under and "programming *specifically designed* to serve those educational and informational needs." This specifically designed programming (also called "core programming") must make serving such needs "as a significant purpose"; must air between 7:00 A.M. and 10:00 P.M.; must be regularly scheduled weekly fare; must be at least 30 minutes in length; and must have its educational and informational objective and the target child audience specified in writing in the station's Children's Television Programming Report. Stations which broadcast at least three hours per week of such core programming are conclusively deemed to comply with the public service requirement for this issue. Because the definition of educational and informational needs is left very open and vague in the rules, there is still considerable leeway in the rules. There is also the possibility of showing that other forms of programming can meet the public-service requirement. Nonetheless, most stations are meeting the three-hour safe-harbor rule, and most networks are being more intentional about their offerings. The impact on Saturday morning TV has been noticeable, with ABC's Disney-linked line-up of specifically designed programs being the most prominent success.

VIOLENCE ON TELEVISION

The level of violence on U.S. television often surprises visitors from other developed countries; for whatever reason, violent acts are a staple of U.S. programming. After many failed efforts to mobilize legislative and regulatory controls, the 1996 Telecommunication Act gave the FCC the power to work with the television industry to develop a TV rating system to disclose sexual, violent or in-decent content. This system, discussed more fully below at page 198, is paired with content-based ratings which are keyed both generally and specifically to on-screen violence. As this becomes operational, parental control over what is watched will receive a technological boost. Interestingly, surveys of television violence suggest that even before the V-chip the overall rates of violence on network television has declined in the 1990s, reflecting increased societal concern. Of course, some shows remain quite violent. Until the U.S. public as a whole loses its taste for violence-laced fantasy, violent programming will remain a significant pre-sence on television. Indeed, the availability of V-chip blocking may even lead to an *increased* level of violence in those shows willing to accept a violent rating.

V-CHIPS AND SELF-REGULATION BY THE TELEVISION INDUSTRY

The private side of the television business regulates itself for the protection of society. Industry-wide self-regulation has been held to impinge on the antitrust rules, so industry-wide controls have been hard to maintain without some government sponsorship. For instance, the National Association of Broadcasters code relating to program content was abandoned in 1982 as part of the settlement of an antitrust suit brought by the Justice Department, which saw the code as an example of impermissible coordination between supposedly competing businesses. This necessary government mandate was passed by Congress in 1996 as part of the Telecommunications Act. It provides both for an exemption from antitrust rules for companies coming together to cooperate on a program ratings system and for the FCC to set regulations for coding these standards in a form that can be "read" by a programmable device in a television set (the "V-chip"). The V-chip can be set simply to block out shows with ratings that the parent—or other person controlling the chip's workings—finds objectionable.

TRADITIONAL SELF-REGULATION: "STANDARDS AND PRACTICES"

Even before the ratings and the V-chip, considerable control has been exercised at the individual company level. Each of the networks maintains a standards-and-practices department, which reviews programming and advertisements in the light of company-wide standards. These departments issue and administer guidelines on a variety of issues. Many of their concerns reflect the need to conform with the FCC restrictions described in Chapter 12, the intellectual property rules described in Chapter 16, and the personal rights requirements described in Chapter 17. Other standards-and-practices recommendations reflect the twin goals of serving the good of society and preserving the image of the network (and, by association, of its advertisers). The areas of concern are predictable: alcohol, criminal activities, drugs, human relationships, obscenity, physical infirmities, race, religion, color, age, national origin, sex and sexuality, and violence. The list reads like a program guide for some of the more popular daytime talk shows, or an assignment board for a local news team during sweeps weeks: all of society's hot and tricky topics are there.

The stated requirements of the networks on these issues tend toward the general and platitudinous. One network, for instance, in setting guidelines for programming on "human relationships" declared: "The presentation of marriage, the family, interpersonal relationships, and other material dealing with sexuality shall not be treated exploitatively or irresponsibly, but with sensitivity." This pious injunction to be nice about things is at odds with the fact that nice is usually not as interesting to most of the audience as nasty, or at least mildly nasty. Applying standards that are worded this way is a matter of balancing the prospect of attracting a big audience with the consequences of offending some of its members. Where the balance comes out changes over time. Reflecting increases in societal acceptance of crudity, the word "ass" became acceptable on the broadcast networks in 1997.

Outside of broadcast networks, there is much less institutionalized hand-wringing over program content. Most cable and satellite services, for instance, are aimed at specific target groups; the broadcast networks still seek to reach a broad cross-section of American society. The programming people at a cable or satellite network are generally quite in touch with what their audience wants to see, and if they get a little too aggressive, a memo from the advertising salespeople will usually correct the matter. There are few centralized politeness brigades to keep things within bounds.

Where they exist at networks, cable companies, or local stations, the standards and practices departments and their rules serve to institutionalize, on a private basis, the kind of community-standard approach that underlies the Supreme Court's rulings on obscenity. What is prohibited and what is permitted reflect general societal taboos. As usual, sex comes in for considerable regulation. Violence, which has been until recently subject to much less societal condemnation, is permitted to a far greater extent. Predictably, as the pressure to control some of this violence grows at a societal level, the violence level of television programming is coming under more and more scrutiny by both broadcast and cable companies.

CONTENT RATINGS AND THE V-CHIP

The combination of increasing concern over the content of television programming—particularly on-screen violence—and technological advancement, has led to a new public/private initiative on the control of program content. Here the approach is not prohibition at the front end by banning certain kinds of content. Rather, the idea is to provide the consumer in the home both with sufficient information about the content of programs to make advance decisions and with a device to help enforce those decisions when the consumer's *children* are turning on the set.

The keys to the public side of this are provisions included in the 1996 Telecommunications Act. These mandated the FCC to set disclosure conventions—the compliance with which would be voluntary-and technical standards for the devices—the V-chips—that could interpret the ratings from codes included in the shows themselves and could block shows with offending ratings. Including the V-chips themselves in U.S. television sets is to become mandatory. The Act also confirmed the antitrust exemption for companies in the private sector to cooperate in developing the ratings system. On the private side, after some high-profile arm-twisting by the President, most major television production and distribution companies (with at least the temporary and partial exception of NBC) have come together to assist in developing the ratings code and to agree to put the code listings in programs.

As of 1998, the ratings proposed by the industry alliance are:

TV-Y: appropriate for all children;
TV-Y7: appropriate for children 7 and older;
TV-G: appropriate for a general audience;
TV-PG: parental guidance suggested;
TV-14: parents strongly cautioned—probably not suitable for children under 14; and
TV-MA: mature audiences only.

The phrasing of these ratings reflects the influence of the MPAA ratings system "voluntarily" in effect for theatrical films.

These age-based guidelines went into effect on most broadcast and cable services on January 1, 1997, with ratings labels appearing at the beginning of affected programs. During 1997, an additional tier of ratings—this one warning of specific content concerns—was proposed and implemented. These labels include:

S: sexual content;
V: violence;
L: coarse language; and
D: suggestive dialogue.

NBC in particular has opposed adding these additional labels. It and some other smaller companies have not complied with them, as is their right under the voluntary nature of the ratings. By the beginning of 1998, most disagreements were resolved; the suggested labels were adopted by the FCC, allowing FCC action on the regulations which would provide the standards necessary to permit the construction of V-chips, which would interact with the ratings to block out offending programs.

PUBLIC PRESSURE

In the end, the content of television programming in the U.S. is highly responsive to the desires of the public. Television production is so costly that unless there is a market for the resulting program, it will generally not be made. Furthermore, most programming depends upon commercial support, and few product manufacturers will want to antagonize public opinion by sponsoring programs that significant special-interest groups might protest as offensive. In fact, consumer campaigns can be quite effective in persuading sponsors and other program supporters to leave certain types of content without financial backing. The mass-distribution systems of broadcast television are much more susceptible to this type of boycott than is the essentially personal world of home video; cable and satellite transmission lie somewhere in between. In sum, the content of programming reflects what the audience wants: society protects itself on the issues that truly arouse public opinion, and leaves the rest to find their markets.

PART 4

Programming and Production

19

Program Development: Overview and Prime-Time Fiction

The success of any television or video venture depends, in large part, upon the quality of its programs. There is no single path to follow in the development of a television show or series, but there are traditions common throughout the industry.

DEVELOPMENT OF PROGRAM CONCEPTS

Television programs grow from a fantastic variety of source ideas: news events, social issues, personalities, board games, family relationships, fads and trends, books, toys, a writer's imagination.

In its raw and undeveloped form, an idea or concept has no real value. There are far more ideas than there are programs produced. Program development adds value to an idea. Eventually, after an investment of time (always) and money (frequently), the idea becomes a marketable property, gathering enough momentum to go into production.

Some ideas are created and developed within an organization, often by salaried personnel with no direct financial interest in the success or failure of the project. This is often the situation at local television stations, corporate and institutional facilities, and local cable companies—entities where in-house development and in-house production are common. The situation is different at broadcast and cable networks, and at syndicators, where ideas may be generated by either inside or outside personnel, but development is most often carried through by outside writers, producers, and production companies. A producer or production company may originate and develop an idea independently, or may be asked to develop an idea that originated within a network or syndication company.

DEVELOPMENT FUNDING

The ways in which program development is funded depends upon company tradition. Some companies spend their own money to grow properties; others are cautious, and look for partners before significant dollars are spent. The costs of rights acquisition, writers, attorneys, budget preparation, travel, and other production elements can quickly add up to tens of thousands of dollars, or more. Odds of a program actually being produced are generally increased if a network or studio is funding development. Production companies that fund their own development without an immediate distribution channel often lose their investment.

In the exalted world of prime-time television, the most successful or promising production companies and producers enter into development deals with networks and studios. This "umbrella" arrangement, commits the network or studio to a set amount paid to the production company in exchange for the right to participate in the eventual production, should it occur. Most producers do not enjoy these relationships, and instead must pitch other pro-duction companies, networks and studios in order to sell a concept and receive money to develop it further.

Most often, development is funded by the network or syndicator. The producer, writer, production company, or studio present the partially developed property to the end user at a *pitch meeting*. At this meeting, the creative/production team explains the concept, features and benefits of the property to the syndicator's programmer, often presenting some written material and sometimes some concept sketches as well. (Concept sketches are more common in animation, though they may be used to set the scene for a science fiction series, etc.) The programmer may make suggestions or counterproposals; if the pitch is successful, the end user will commit to funding further work on the project and may repay the development costs incurred to date. If the project is likely to be expensive, because of location shooting or big-name stars or for other reasons, then a rough budget should be part of the pitch; similarly, if the program or series is likely to be inexpensive, this becomes a selling point and should be discussed as well.

Regardless of the arrangement, until the final decision to produce is made, the project can be terminated at any time and the development investment lost—unless another network or syndicator can be sold on the project (see discussion of turnaround, page 208). While a project is in development, the awkward balance between spending money to add value to the idea and the desire to wager as little as possible is a constant source of tension.

ACQUISITION OF RIGHTS

If the idea for a television program or series is based on an existing property, then appropriate rights to that property must be acquired before any significant development work begins. The illustration below represents the most common steps in the acquisition of rights to a published work (in this case a book). Many of the basic concepts in acquiring *any* property are outlined in this section.

Books are often the source material for audiovisual productions. The most lucrative market for published works is in the motion picture business, where audiovisual rights in properties are regularly licensed or purchased for subsequent use in theatrical features, most of which end up on television as well. The occasional blockbuster novel finds its way to an initial television production, most often via a mini-series; otherwise, programmers usually wind up with those properties not already tied up in film deals.

The most aggressive film and television producers compete for titles before the books are published. Studios and major Hollywood production companies maintain sources (called "scouts") in the publishing community (authors, editors, and agents), so advance looks at promising manuscripts are common. *Kirkus Reviews, Publishers Weekly,* and reviews in newspapers and magazines are also sources of information about new titles. Most major production companies hire readers who summarize new books and analyze their potential in the feature and television marketplace.

Once a desirable property has been identified, the production company (typically, through an assistant in the development department) contacts the appropriate publisher's subsidiary-rights department to find out who holds the television rights to the property. In some cases, the publisher will be empowered to negotiate on the author's behalf; often, however, these rights are retained by the author, who generally turns the work of negotiation over to a literary agent or attorney (see page 353).

Although a rights agreement between publisher or author and production company may be lengthy, two key issues guide the negotiation: money, and creative control of the property.

RIGHTS NEGOTIATION—THE MONEY

During the early stages of development, when a project and its potential market are unformed, the producer tries to limit cash expenditures. Rather than buying a property outright, producers usually negotiate the terms of the purchase (including the eventual purchase, or "exercise," price), then pay a fraction of the exercise price—typically 10 percent—for the exclusive option to purchase the property within a set period, such as one year from signing the agreement. This option money is sometimes credited against the exercise price. In many cases, up to two additional option periods, each six months long, may be initiated by the producer, for an additional 5 percent of the purchase price per option period. (These additional monies are often applied against the exercise price.) Sometimes the extensions are tied to the commitment of a particular writer, director, or star to the property, or are linked to some other type of progress in development, such as a development deal with a network or syndicator.

Successful fiction works command the highest prices, with most purchases in the $25,000 to $100,000 range for a TV movie. In general, rates for made-for-TV and made-for-home-video productions are considerably lower than those paid for turning a book into a major motion picture, where hundreds of thousands of dollars—or even millions—is the norm. Mini-series are the one exception: since each segment is considered the equivalent of a movie-of-the-week, the rights fees are high. Television series are not generally based upon books.

The rights to a non-fiction book may also be meaningful or valuable because of a title's special franchise, or because of its authority in a particular field. If a title is especially popular, the rights to a non-fiction book might be as expensive as those to a work of fiction.

More often, however, non-fiction books are purchased as the basis for a non-fiction series on the same subject. The author may be an expert, or the organization or depth of the information presented in the book may be unique or special. In these situations, the prices paid are usually much less than for fiction works: for a series, the up-front fee may run $500 to $5,000, sometimes as high as $10,000 if there is competition for the rights. The author might also receive a small per-episode royalty as a result of strenuous negotiating, or as a "giveback" from a producer who is buying the rights for a relatively low price. This royalty may be as low as 1 or 2 percent of the producer's per-episode budget, though 5 percent is more common. The author might also be paid a fee or salary for a role in the production, either as a performer, writer, producer, executive producer, or consultant.

The life stories of real individuals are sometimes the basis for entertainment programming. It is not always necessary to secure the permission of an individual in order to base a program on his or her life (see Chapter 17). Nonetheless, life-story rights are frequently acquired (and paid for) in order to forestall any legal problems and to obtain the person's cooperation in the process. The option/exercise fee approach is often used here as well. If the producer is acquiring rights from more than one individual for a single program, the total fees typically do not exceed the amounts that would be paid for a work of fiction. In addition, the inevitable surrender of control by the individual over the details of his or her life story can be a painful step.

COMMISSIONS AND OTHER DEDUCTIONS

The author rarely manages to keep all of the proceeds of the rights sale. In fact, the check usually goes first to the author's agent, who deducts a 10 or 15 percent commission and then writes the author a second check. A lawyer's compensation is based on either a flat fee, an hourly fee, or a monthly retainer. Since the lawyer receives the money shortly after the work is done, and gets paid even if the deal does not go through, the lawyer does not benefit directly from a windfall success, as an agent might. Some lawyers do receive a percentage of their clients' income in addition to, or in lieu of, standard fees (this practice is mostly limited to the Los Angeles community). Publishers usually insist on some involvement in television and movie deals: a 50/50 split with the author is typical. (In this case, the agent's commission and/or lawyer's fees is either deducted from the author's 50 percent or taken off the top.) If the author has some clout, or if the publisher lacks confidence in a property's television potential, then a different split is arranged; for example, the author might receive 75 percent and the publisher, 25 percent.

RIGHTS NEGOTIATION—CREATIVE CONTROL

Although many authors press the issue, producers rarely consider an author's request or demand for creative control of a television project. There are several reasons why. First, since the producer usually surrenders this control to the financing source in exchange for the money to produce the series, the right to creative control is not a grant that can be made by a producer. Second, authors are stereotypically regarded as "difficult"; an author's insistence on protecting a personal vision can place the producer in conflict with the network or distributor, and in extreme instances, send a production wildly over-budget. Third, authors come from a different milieu, where a reader slowly works his or her way through a sheaf of printed pages; television's need for faster-moving plotlines, fewer sub-plots, fewer characters, clearer delineation between the good guys and the bad guys, fewer locations, pacing between commercial breaks, and limited overall running time often upset a caring author. Ultimately, only one person can make a final decision. And in television, that person is the producer or program executive, not the author.

Certainly there are exceptions: a top author may insist on writing the screenplay for the television adaptation, or at least the first draft; an author may be an experienced producer; or an author with special expertise may be retained as a technical consultant by the producer.

Playwrights are a different breed; they make their living writing stories told by actors and directors. Their craft is similar to that of the television writer; in fact, many television writers start their careers in the theater. A playwright typically controls the media rights to his or her properties, with no need to involve the play's publisher or producer(s), other than financially. Most successful playwrights are represented by agents or lawyers.

TREATMENTS, SCRIPTS, AND DEALS

As development progresses, the idea—whether derived from an existing work or freshly invented—must be described on paper. A treatment is a brief (two to ten pages) script outline that describes the story by explaining what happens in each of the key scenes and provides insight into the personalities and interactions of the characters; it may also include some sample dialogue to illuminate character. It also offers enough information about the production's key components—performers, locations, sets, special effects, wardrobe, etc.—so a production manager can generate an estimate of the cost of production.

The script is more complete, providing a scene-by-scene breakdown, stage instructions, and all of the dialogue. Treatments and scripts are the currency of writers working in the Los Angeles film and prime-time television community, and are widely used throughout the television industry, not only for production, but for development and as samples of a writer's talent.

The treatment is a selling tool that the producer shows to potential sources of financing. Therefore, when a producer hires a writer to help with development, it may be to the producer's advantage to commit only to the writing of the story. If the property is a strong one—and the producer and writer have solid credentials—the financing source (a network, a studio, or a production company) will agree to go forward, usually through a *step deal*. (All of the "steps" described below are negotiated in advance.)

The step deal usually begins with the commissioning of a more detailed treatment, one that includes sample dialogue and character descriptions, and incorporates the inevitable changes required by the program executive. If the concept is a series, then the treatment may also include a long description of one sample episode (presumably the pilot), along with character sketches and brief outlines of a full season's programs. This stage may involve more than preparing a treatment—it may also require the producer to arrange commitments from key performers or from a director.

If the detailed treatment shows promise, the program executive pays for the second step. For most network, pay, and cable programs, the writer or writing team is paid to produce a full script or teleplay, from first to final drafts. The producer usually owns the script as a work for hire, subject to the rights of the financing source and any retained rights of the author. Under the WGA agreement, when the program is produced, the writer can receive further residuals for reuse as well as royalties. If the writer originated the work, and is entitled to a "separation of rights," then he or she will also have rights (see page 335) for additional programs in the series. If extra rewriting is required, the producer may choose any writer to do the work.

The financing source may decide not to proceed with the next step, and may cancel development at any point—for example, after one of the script drafts has been submitted. In this case, the project can be frozen with the financier, it can revert to the producer with no strings attached, or (most commonly) it can go into *turnaround*. In turnaround, the financier pulls out of the deal, so the producer once again owns the rights to the script and is free to seek an alternative source of financing. If the producer is successful in placing the project with another company, then he or she repays some of the development costs to the original financing party, which also receives some "back end" participation (see page 302), typically 5 to 10 percent of the producer's net revenues, after recoupment of production and other costs.

THE IMPORTANCE OF WRITERS

Writers—and their ideas—drive the network television business. Top writers are given producer's credits, sometimes as perks, more often as entitlements to control and shape the content of a series. A writer who creates a series receives a special credit and a per-episode royalty, and frequently writes at least a few episodes each season—sometimes, many more. In addition, he or she may serve in a staff capacity—often as a story editor, supervising other writers and doing rewrites—and receive additional fees.

DEVELOPMENT DEALS

A studio or large production company may offer an independent producer or successful writer a *development deal.* In such a deal, the talent gets a guaranteed annual sum—hundreds of thousands a year, sometimes up to $1 million or $2 million—while the studio provides offices, a development fund, and other essential services. The dollars spent are deducted from the earnings of the talent from any property created under the arrangement. The studio gets a first look at anything the talent originates, typically on a step-deal basis, complete with turnaround. When a project goes into production, the talent earns fees as writer, director, producer, story editor, or whatever the talent's representative has negotiated and the realities of the guild agreements allow. Royalties and bonuses are also paid, and the talent's production company may be entitled to a significant portion of the project's "back end" revenues.

PACKAGING

The writer/producer team or hybrid may drive the development effort, but a project will not be approved for production until performers and other key participants are added. Many of the writers and producers who develop projects seek additional power to complete the package and this power is supplied by agencies such as the William Morris Agency, ICM, and CAA. Their client lists include many of the top performers, writers, directors, producers, music professionals, and designers in the entertainment business. These agencies cannot produce programming—to do so would be a conflict of interest, since they would be competing against their clients—so they work with producers and supply a full roster of performers and behind-the-scenes personnel in exchange for a hefty share of the producer's gross. This "cut" is often 5 percent of the production budget plus 5 percent from available revenues after recoupment (see page 299 for a discussion of recoupment).

Alternately, these agencies supply the same people to the production à la carte at a far lower commission—10 or 15 percent of the individual agency client's gross salary or fee. Some producers find agency packaging departments to be extremely helpful in selling programs to network buyers; other producers resent the agencies and their growing clout, regarding the packaging agency as an unwelcome co-producer.

PILOTS

Producing a pilot is the most expensive and elaborate phase of development; it is also the last action before either full production is ordered or the project is dropped altogether. A pilot is a special program made as a kind of model or prototype, to demonstrate what an episode in the proposed series will look like. Sometimes the pilot is a truncated version of the show (a "demo"), but in prime-time fiction on the networks, a pilot is most often a full-length program, using actual sets, locations, cast, and other production resources. Since the economies of scale do not apply to a pilot, and because a pilot frequently involves unexpected events (the need to replace a performer, special effects that did not work as planned, the need for replacement scenes when the first ones simply didn't "work"), the cost of the pilot is inevitably higher than the cost of a single episode in a series.

Pilots are necessary because it is nearly impossible to assess the impact of a program without actually making it. Scripts can be read, concepts discussed and embellished, designs reviewed, and casts auditioned and put through the paces in a rehearsal hall—but so much depends upon the chemistry and how the elements work together that producing a sample show is the only way to gauge the program's chances. Therefore, before a broadcast network or other end user commits to ordering multiple episodes of a series, it almost always wants to see (and is usually willing to pay for) a pilot. Sometimes, a network will commit to a small number of episodes in lieu of a pilot, or in lieu of a second or third pilot, thus benefiting from some economies of scale and allowing the new series some time on the air to find an audience. Occasionally, a movie-of-the-week or other special is made as a "back door pilot" but also as a program that stands on its own. Sometimes, in the depths of rerun season, a network will air some pilots, both as a means of measuring audience reaction and as a way to "burn off" the cost of the pilot and recoup some financial value from it.

The pilot is a valuable sales tool for syndication and international sales, where lining up stations and foreign markets before production begins is critical.

MADE-FOR-TV MOVIES

The market for made-for-TV movies includes not only ABC, CBS, and NBC, but also cable networks including HBO, Showtime, TNT, USA, Lifetime, and all of the pay TV networks. Many foreign broadcasters, movie studios, and home video companies are also in the game. Movies that are shown on television in the U.S. are sometimes shown in movie theaters in other countries.

Showtime is the leading market for made-for-TV movies—roughly one a week—but their production budgets are comparatively low at $2 million per picture. HBO produces more than a dozen pictures a year, usually spending between $4 and $8 million for meaningful properties. TNT produces less than a dozen, and spends about half as much per picture.

The broadcast networks typically pay a license fee of about $2.5 million per picture. This covers about two-thirds of the budget. The remainder comes from license fees paid by foreign broadcasters or cable networks. Broadcast networks do not, as a rule, license films that have been shown on basic or pay cable.

International sales often guide development decisions. It is easier, for example, to sell a thriller with a name-brand male star than a comedy with a clever director who is known mainly in English-speaking countries. A browse through the ads in any issue of *Variety* (particularly the issues published for MIP and MIPCOM in the spring and fall) show what's selling: action and science fiction (both are light on dialogue).

News, Magazines and Documentaries

For many viewers, television news programs are the primary source of information about world, national, and regional events, as well as weather and sports. News programming is also the basis for television magazine series, and for several cable networks.

BROADCAST NETWORK NEWS

ABC, CBS, and NBC each operate a news division (FOX has begun its news effort, but it's well behind the others). Each employs approximately a thousand employees in its news division, mostly in New York City; a Washington, DC bureau concentrates on national news, and some other bureaus, in London, for example, contribute regional stories. In the U.S., network affiliates contribute local stories, but major stories are often reported by network reporters on location.

PROGRAMMING

The news divisions at ABC, CBS, and NBC are responsible for a substantial number of program hours per week. ABC, for example, produces 21 hours per week, or more than a quarter of the network's entire weekly feed to its affiliates: *Good Morning America* (5 × 2 hours, plus 1 hour on Sunday), *World News Tonight* (7 × 30 mins.), *Nightline* (5 × 30 mins.), *Prime Time Live* (1 × 1 hour), *20/20* (2 × 1 hour), *This Week* (1 × 1 hour), two overnight shows, *World News Now and World News This Morning* (total of 3 hours, but set up so affiliates can run all or part of each series), plus regularly scheduled reports through the day, breaking news, and special event coverage.

Each network's signature news show is the evening news. Each network's half-hour evening newscast is fed live to affiliates at

6:30 P.M. Eastern Time. The network feeds the evening news again at 7:00 P.M., and at least one more time for West Coast affiliates, either as a videotape of the original production, or, if stories have changed, as a new production. These programs are often seen outside the U.S. as well. The networks' morning shows have also become signature pieces.

Each network news division also controls several hours of prime-time with newsmagazine programs: *60 Minutes, 48 Hours,* and *Public Eye with Bryant Gumbel* on CBS; *Dateline NBC* (several nights a week) on NBC; *Prime Time Live* and *20/20* on ABC. In the mid and late 1990s, this formula proved especially effective, and not as costly as other prime-time programs (and more profitable), so these programs proliferated.

On Sunday mornings, networks compete for a relatively limited but upscale audience with *CBS News Sunday Morning,* NBC's *Sunday Today* and ABC's *Good Morning America Sunday.* Also on Sunday are ABC's *This Week* and NBC's *Meet the Press* (both scoring a 3 share). *Face the Nation,* on CBS, has not attracted as large an audience (average of about 2). The quality of these viewers far outweighs their numbers, however, and so *CBS News Sunday Morning* (for example) is a profitable venture. *FOX News Sunday,* which appeals to somewhat younger viewers, is just beginning to establish itself.

Special events are an important part of network news coverage. Some, like political conventions, are scheduled and planned in advance; others, like the outbreak of war, or the death of a world figure, may pre-empt regularly scheduled programming. News executives have the option to pre-empt programming with breaking stories, but they must operate with considerable discretion. In theory, they consult closely with entertainment (or sports) executives. For shorter reports and updates, pre-empting several minutes of a program is generally preferable to pre-empting commercials.

THE BUSINESS OF NETWORK NEWS

For many years, network news was operated without much regard for budget restrictions, and with no connection to the concept of profitability. News was the only truly serious and responsible aspect of a network organization, whose primary mission was entertainment. This role began to change in the 1980s. Newsmagazines, such as *60 Minutes,* cost less to produce than many prime-time dramas, and earned a higher rating, often attracting upscale, well-educated viewers. These programs are owned by the networks, so there is no packaging fee to be paid to the producer or studio. This tradition continues with *Dateline NBC,* a series that aired in prime-time, three nights a week on NBC in 1997. These programs are driven by story selection, and also by personality: people watch *20/20* because they like Hugh Downs and Barbara Walters, for example. The popularity of many network news programs can also be traced to a particular producer's style (as in the case of Don Hewitt, the longtime genius behind CBS's *60 Minutes*).

For its first three decades, network news was primarily concerned with covering stories, and not with budgetary concerns. This changed in the 1980s as the networks became more conscious of their costs. Over the next few years, producers became keenly aware of the cost of each story, and made decisions accordingly. Also, budgets for individual stories were paid by individual programs; no longer was a producer allowed to research, shoot and edit a piece without a commitment from a specific program to broadcast the piece (remarkably, this had been common practice for decades).

Television news has become a part of the entertainment business. Big stories, especially if they involve a war or a presidential scandal, get big numbers, which means more money. During the sweeps (when advertising rates are set on the basis of ratings), networks and local stations clearly determine which stories will be covered (and promoted) most aggressively on the basis of audience appeal. This desire to reach the largest possible audience is balanced by responsible journalists who work hard to get an accurate, timely, honest, unbiased story to the people. Some programs, such as syndicated "tabloid" newsmagazines, clearly emphasize audience appeal over social or political significance. The networks tend to emphasize social and political significance, but are certainly not beyond self-promotion (taking the television audience "backstage" to one of their most popular series, for example). Certainly, the appeal of individual news anchors has become as important as the stories themselves. A newsmagazine with the "wrong" host (one who is not especially popular with prime-time audiences, for example) will not succeed, regardless of the quality of its journalism.

NETWORK AND LOCAL NEWS FEEDS

Each of the networks produces news reports for use on local stations. CBS stations, for example, distribute specially produced stories via their newspath service. This coverage is funded by affiliated stations, who pay for the cost of correspondents, production personnel, shooting and editing, and satellite time. In recent years, the relationship has become considerably more reciprocal. Local stations have routinely covered local news stories (which is typically presented with a voice-over by a network correspondent). These stories are then fed throughout the network. The networks have all become more responsive to the importance of local news, assigning a small staff of dedicated reporters to coverage of stories specifically for use on affiliates' reports.

NEWS ON PBS

PBS does not maintain a news department. It does feed a nightly newscast, *The NewsHour with Jim Lehrer*, produced by MacNeil-Lehrer Productions. In addition, other member stations produce news and public-service programs. WGBH, for example, produces *Frontline;* Maryland Public Television produces *Wall $treet Week.* Typically, these programs are funded in the same way that other PBS programs are funded. The productions operate as independent units, tied to the network for purposes of partial funding and distribution. To a certain extent they are also linked to PBS by way of program practices permitted by public television's charter.

DEVELOPMENT OF NEWS PROGRAMMING

Most information programs seen on a network—news and magazine shows, talk shows, and documentaries—are produced in-house by the network's news division.

The concept behind a particular information program begins as a theoretical discussion among reporters, producers, and executives. After a few creative sessions, the ideas are written down and presented to a program executive who controls budgets and who can arrange for airtime on the network schedule. The program executive nurtures internal support for the project. A production unit is assembled, frequently with the program's originators in key roles, and one or more shows are produced.

The process is similar at the local station level, although staff, technical, and financial resources are likely to be more limited.

SYNDICATED NEWS PROGRAMS

News and newsmagazine programs distributed to cable and local stations via syndication are frequently the work of a large production entity—Paramount, in the case of *Entertainment Tonight*, and FOX, for *REAL TV.* One or more producers and writers are hired to develop an idea that was created internally or licensed from a creator, who generally receives a weekly royalty payment if the show goes into production. Royalties are paid even if the creator is not directly involved in ongoing production. The program is typically developed up to the point of a short-form pilot (about 15 minutes is common). The pilot is then shown to local stations and cable networks as a selling tool, and presented to advertising agencies and advertisers for the sale of barter time (see Chapter 3). If a sufficient number of clearances and a sufficient percentage of viewing households can be reached, the program begins production.

Because news and magazine shows can require large staffs and a web of correspondents throughout the country or the world, production units for these types of programs are usually set up under the aegis of a big company.

DOCUMENTARIES

Aside from some specialized series, such as the highly successful *Biography* series on A&E, and various Ken Burns projects for PBS (notably *The Civil War*), documentaries do not typically attract significant numbers of viewers. Still, high profile documentary series can attract large numbers of viewers and considerable prestige. CNN's production of *The Cold War* is budgeted at $12 million for 24 hours of programming. The series has been sold to the BBC, to Germany's ARD, and to other countries—all essential to make up costs not recouped by CNN's advertising.

With the growth of cable, the number of documentary markets has grown to include: The Discovery Channel, Animal Planet, The Learning Channel, A&E, The History Channel, HBO, TBS, American Movie Classics, and more. According to *Variety* (September 23, 1996), "Nearly 2,000 documentaries were made for cable last year, and . . . that figure can't help but increase." Typically, budgets for these programs are between $100,000 and $200,000—and costs are often kept low because the networks have invested in large libraries of film footage for use in multiple programs. Series, like A&E's *Biography,* are often manufactured in bulk, in accordance with a prescribed format and efficient production methods.

The broadcast networks rarely program documentaries because they do not, as a rule, generate a large enough audience. On occasion, a major network anchor will become involved in a particular issue, resulting in a prime-time documentary (which is often more like a single-topic newsmagazine), but again, these are exceptions. On the major commercial networks, news magazine programs have largely replaced documentaries. Some public television stations produce their own documentaries about local history and social issues.

PROGRAM DEVELOPMENT

Program development for documentary production more or less follows these steps. First, the producer develops the creative concept based on his or her personal interest, or on a programmer's interest in one or more shows about a particular subject (the environment, for example). Other idea sources include popular books whose rights are available, or the work of an individual or institution that has attracted public notice. The producer then works out a budget; writes a proposal describing the project; and pitches it to programmers and other sources of financing (foundations, sponsors, endowment organizations, foreign broadcasters, and so on). Although some documentaries are funded quickly, these are the exceptions; one to three years is usually needed to gather production funds. Production is typically small-scale—single-camera with plenty of editing—and the staff is minimal. The schedule, though, can run almost a year.

THE DOCUMENTARY BUSINESS

A distinguished, high-quality, hour-long documentary special costs $500,000–$750,000 to produce. Domestic cable ad revenues are not likely to total more than $200,000 (hence, the budget for a cable documentary in the $100,000-plus range). This leaves two markets to be mined: international, and home video. Assume a home-video retail price of $19.95, and a return to the label of about $10 per unit. About $3 can be earmarked for recoupment of production costs, and in today's market, 50,000 unit sales is a reasonable domestic estimate for a title with name value, so that adds $150,000 to the pot. The gamble: at least $150,000 in international sales to cable, broadcast, and home video.

Not every documentary costs a half-million dollars. Most documentary series episodes cost less than $200,000. This budget is possible on a series whose production systems encourage real savings. A&E's *Biography* is the best example of this approach.

Since documentaries are not widely regarded as big moneymakers, a producer can usually raise the necessary funds without selling off either ownership interests or creative control.

CABLE NEWS NETWORKS

CNN offers a level of production quality and journalistic prowess that is competitive with commercial network news. There are several principal differences between CNN and network news operations. First, CNN is a truly international organization with over

3,500 employees worldwide. Where the broadcast networks have cut their international newsgathering activities, CNN has expanded. CNN is a ubiquitous news source, available not only in the U.S. but throughout much of the world, on a 24-hour basis. CNN also produces hundreds of hours of weekly news programming, compared with perhaps two dozen hours a week by NBC, ABC, or CBS. While most CNN programming is standard newscasts, the network's ability to provide full-scale coverage of a major event is now unparalleled in the television industry. However, it is interesting to note that CNN's viewership is relatively modest—except during big news stories, when its round-the-clock coverage can become enormously popular.

Headline News debuted in January 1982, less than two years after the launch of CNN. The emphasis: quick, concise, and up-to-the-minute. CNNI (CNN International) launched in September 1985, first serving American visitors to hotels abroad; now it is distributed to more than 100 million households outside the U.S. and operates 24 hours a day. There are four CNNI signals distributed to Asia, Europe, Latin America, and the U.S., accommodating differences in time zones. CNNI is also distributed in multiple languages, and dubbed in many countries (in addition CNN Español operates as a stand-alone service). CNN Financial Network debuted in December 1995, with a somewhat lighter approach to business news and an emphasis on personal finance. It is allied with www.cnnfn.com, a Web site that adds depth and a stock ticker to the network's television content. CNNsi (CNN/Sports Illustrated) is the newest CNN network; it debuted in December 1996. In addition, CNN Airport Network operates 21 hours a day in several zones in U.S. airports. It carries mostly news, but also coverage of some live sporting events.

FOX News Channel competes directly with CNN. The network launched in 1997, and currently has about half as many U.S. subscribers. The channel is the center of a growing FOX presence in news, which is likely to expand to U.S. FOX broadcast affiliates, and also internationally.

ESPNEWS, a 24-hour sports news network, launched as ESPN's third cable channel in late 1996. The centerpiece is SportsCenter, a popular news series seen on ESPN. ESPN also operates ESPNET SportsZone, a leading Web site for sports information.

NewSport, owned by Rainbow Program Holdings (part of Cablevision), NBC Cable Holdings, and Liberty Sports (part of TCI), is a 24-hour sports news service with nine million subscribers. It debuted in February 1994, but is not yet a factor in national sports coverage.

MSNBC, a joint venture of NBC and Microsoft, was the first network to integrate Internet and cable TV programming. The television programming provides coverage from NBC News and from MSNBC's own staff. The Web site (www.msnbc.com) provides in-depth information about these stories, including analysis, public opinion, and local news, weather, and sports. Many of its prime-time programs are based on clips from NBC News programs, such as *Time and Again,* which features interviews with celebrities who have appeared on various NBC news programs. The network is not, as it turns out, a place where people who are interested in computing get their news (this job is done by ZDTV, c|net and other computer news services), but a full-scale news and public-affairs cable network that happens to operate in parallel with a well-produced Web site.

The Weather Channel, owned by Landmark Communications of Norfolk, Virginia, debuted in May 1982, and now serves nearly 70 million households. Operated as a 24-hour weather news service, every minute of every hour is carefully scheduled. The first seven minutes of every half hour are devoted to *WeatherScope,* a weather highlights report. The *Five-Day Planner* appears at 20 minutes past the hour, *International Weather* appears at 18 minutes before the hour, and so on. Local coverage means cutaways to local cable systems who supply their data, local radar, maps, and forecasts through a standardized system of computers "on the eights": at :08, :18, :28, and so on through each hour. Breaking news changes the schedule, and the occasional documentary about tornadoes or other weather phenomena will also break the sequence.

Local News Programming

I n most markets, ABC, CBS, and NBC affiliates produce at least two daily newscasts, plus cut-ins throughout the day (FOX affiliates typically produce just one newscast per day). In some markets, the UPN and/or WBTV affiliates also produce a daily newscast (either an early- or late-evening broadcast, but rarely both); and in some markets, a PBS station also produces a daily newscast.

PROGRAMMING

For most news departments at major-market stations, the program day usually begins at 6:00 or 6:30 A.M. and, in many large markets, as early as 5:00 or 5:30 A.M. Since the audience is available, programs are produced and advertising support is readily available.

The next task is the preparation of brief local news, weather, sports and commuter information cut-ins for the network morning program (*Good Morning America,* etc.)

A noon newscast has become common. At some stations, this newscast includes not only news, weather, and sports, but an interview or community outreach activities as well.

In most large markets, the evening newscast is at least an hour long. This newscast is the focus of the station's entire news operation, because it reaches the largest number of viewers. The most prestigious anchor appears on the 6:00 news, along with the station's best reporters. Many stations also program a 5:00 P.M. newscast, which often features softer material such as interviews and community outreach.

Almost all network affiliates program an 11:00 P.M. newcast. Stories seen on the 6:00 P.M. newscast are reworked, updated, and usually shortened for the late news. In most large markets, a FOX,

WBTV or UPN affiliate broadcasts a 10:00 P.M. newscast as counter-programming against network prime-time and to capture viewers who retire early.

On some local stations, the news department also produces a weekend news program, newsmagazine, news/talk show, or public-affairs program; though sometimes, these are produced by the station's program department.

OPERATIONS

The success of a local news operation depends largely upon two factors: the quality/appeal of the "front four" (the 6:00 P.M. newscast's two co-anchors, the weather reporter, and the sportscaster) and the creative and managerial abilities of the news director. Certainly, much credit goes to producers, writers, reporters, and other contributors. Still, the solidly crafted newscast, hosted by well-liked, respected on-camera talent, is critical.

The news department is usually the biggest department at a local television station; in the largest markets, such as New York, Los Angeles or Chicago, the staff is likely to total about 200 people. In a mid-sized market, the staff may still be over 100; the average staff size for ABC, CBS, and NBC affiliates in Seattle (market no. 13), for example, is approximately 120 people. Smaller market stations employ as many as thirty or forty full-timers.

The news director—sometimes, the vice president of news—is responsible for almost all aspects of staff selection and supervision. Major decisions, such as changing an anchor or major reporter, are made with the station's general manager. The news director oversees coverage, budget, community relations, and production.

An executive producer is assigned to each program. At a large major-market station, one EP might be assigned to the morning news and noon news, another to the 5:00 P.M., another to the 6:00 P.M., and yet another to the 11:00 P.M. At most stations, however, one or two EPs supervise all news programming. Early-morning and late-night newscasts may be broadcast without the executive producer actually present in the newsroom.

One step down from the executive producer is the producer in charge of preparing the newscast and supervising the broadcast. Consulting with the news director, the producer decides which stories will air, and in what order; which stories will be shortened or dropped because of breaking news or interviews that run longer than anticipated; whether to pass late-breaking information to an on-camera newscaster via newly written pages or by speaking directing into the newscaster's IFB (a clear plastic earphone).

A staff director, typically a full-time employee who also directs some public affairs or local commercials, directs the newscasts.

Most of the news staff is concerned with newsgathering, writing, and preparing stories. The assignment desk—the heart of the newsgathering operation—keeps in close contact with the police and fire departments, the mayor's office, the municipal government, local politicians, and community groups. Some information arrives in a well-organized manner: the mayor's public relations staff arranges a press conference, a publicist furnishes news about a visiting celebrity and arranges a local interview, local activists announce a rally at a specific time and place. But most leads come from telephone tips, aggressive investigative research by the station's reporters, and police radio transmissions. In a sense, the assignment desk is a resource-management system because a limited number of reporters, crews, and vans must cover only the most important stories. Since changes in assignment or location are common, everyone keeps in close touch either by cellular phone or private radio.

Resources at most stations include five to twenty reporters, five to ten crews (usually two people per crew, though one-person crews are becoming more common), and five to ten videotape editors. In a large market, eight or ten editors work the assignment desk. Most stations employ between five and twenty reporters.

In theory, the assignment desk makes objective choices. In practice, pressure from the station's management and from local political leaders may affect coverage.

NEWS COVERAGE

News stories are covered in several different ways. A story coming in from a network or syndicated news feed usually includes a voice-over, sound recorded on location, and all of the necessary visuals. These stories can be aired without further editing, though many stories are edited for time or customized for a local market's creative approach.

Most major stories are covered by a news reporter, working on location with a shooter (a camera operator who also videotapes the news, and monitors the audio as well). The reporter prepares and researches the story in the newsroom and en route to the location (and is likely to be updated by the assignment desk along the way); interviews the key players on camera; does some off-camera interviewing for background; determines the visual and audio elements that will be needed to tell the story; records a "stand-up" (the reporter stands in front of the location at the beginning and/or end of the story); and prepares a basic edit plan on the way back to the station (if time permits, or if the story is a big or tricky one, the reporter may also carefully screen the tapes and revise the edit plan). Typically, the tapes, the rough written edit plan and some notes are passed to an editor. The reporter then writes a script, submits it to the producer for approval, records it as a voice-over or on-camera report, and gives that tape to the editor as well. On a more complicated story, the reporter may supervise the editor. And in very small markets, the reporter may be the editor.

Some stories are not covered by reporters, only by a shooter. In such cases, a newswriter will draft the script. Sometimes, a reporter records a voice-over; otherwise, the anchor narrates the story live.

Most national stories are provided in the network feed. Stations also subscribe to several news wire services, notably AP. Other specialized wires include Bloomberg, Reuters, PR Newswire and SportsWire.

CNN Newsource revolutionized the industry by sending a 24-hour feed of news stories, rather than individual packages a few times per day. Station fees vary depending upon market size, and are negotiable. Competitors include Conus. The individual networks also offer a newsfeed (such as CBS NewsPath) to affiliates.

ANCHORS AND REPORTERS

Most television stations have long-term contracts with anchors who are well suited to the station's community image. Although local traditions vary, a certain amount of typecasting is common. The 6:00 P.M. newscast is anchored by one or two seasoned journalists; the 5:00 P.M. newscast may be hosted by one of these anchors, with a third anchor who is newer to the market or lesser known. That third anchor may do the 11:00 P.M. or the noon newscast. The morning and weekend newscasts are frequently hosted by a reporter gaining anchor experience. In the largest markets, where weekend newscast slots are more meaningful in terms of advertising revenues, regular weekend anchors may be employed.

In a major market, the lead anchor usually earns $500,000 per year, or more (New York City, Los Angeles, and Chicago have some "million dollar anchors"), with the other anchors earning from $200,000 to $400,000 per year. There are local exceptions that are both higher and lower. Weekend anchors generally earn $150,000–$300,000 per year, and their contracts usually call for three days of general-assignment reporting in addition to weekend work.

Reporters may be hired and assigned in several ways. Most stations simply hire general-assignment reporters, and then allot a small number to specific beats (e.g., city government). Some will also hire a few specialty reporters (e.g., health and science), but these stories may also be covered by general-assignment reporters. A top reporter at a major-market station can earn over $200,000 per year (once again, more in New York City and Los Angeles), but most reporters at major-market stations earn between $80,000 and $180,000. Outside of the top-10 markets, the maximum numbers drop below $75,000 or even below $50,000. In a non-union station outside the top-30 or -40 markets, reporter salaries drop below $40,000, even for a reporter with several years of experience.

WEATHER REPORTING

Weather reporting is a self-contained function at just about every television station, supervised by the news director but requiring little ongoing staff or administrative support. Weather is a principal reason why viewers tune to local news programs; women generally make this viewing choice, and the appeal of the weather reporter plays a major role in this decision.

There are essentially two types of television weather reporters: those who are trained meteorologists and those who are not. Some stations insist upon trained scientists, but visual and personality appeal are generally more meaningful than technical knowledge.

The weather reporter is generally supported by a fully equipped weather station. This setup includes not only the typical measurement instrumentation (barometer, hygrometer, thermometer, and so on), but also computer access to one or more national weather services. One service provider, Accu-Weather, feeds not only raw weather data, but full-color video maps that can be used on the air for national, regional, or local forecasts. If the weather reporter is a trained meteorologist, he or she may use this information and construct a custom forecast. Some stations have also invested in sophisticated computer equipment that assists in forecasting, and in computer-graphics equipment to add color and movement to maps and other weather information.

A television station with early-morning, noon, evening, and late-night weather reports typically employs either two or three weather reporters. In a top-10 market, the job pays up to and over $300,000. In a top-20 market, the scale is $75,000 to $150,000; in smaller markets, the job pays less than $50,000. Weather reporters usually earn more than sports reporters (whose appeal is typically male, and who generally appear in the program's final segment).

SPORTS REPORTING

At a major-market station, one sports reporter will appear on the evening and late-night newscasts; a second sports reporter will appear on weekends, filing field reports several days each week. In the largest markets, a third field reporter and a sports producer may complete the team; in medium-sized and small markets, the entire sports department usually consists of two reporters.

Sports reporting is largely dependent upon game footage, which is available from a number of sources. Networks and their affiliates generally provide feeds to one another at no charge, as an accommodation. Major-league baseball and the NFL provide a daily feed during the season, on a contract basis. CBS Newsfeed (see below) also includes sports footage. Its services are provided—for a fee—on an exclusive basis to one station in each market.

A major-market sports anchor typically earns up to $250,000—sometimes more, if the person is especially well-known—or if the contract includes game coverage or a weekend wrap-up show. Even in the top-10 markets, most sports reporters earn under $200,000, and in the top-20, under $75,000.

NEWS CONSULTANTS

Since many local stations share the same needs and challenges, viable ideas are borrowed and adapted from one market to another.

To keep ahead of the competition, many stations employ a consulting firm. In theory, a news consultant represents the viewer's point of view, bringing the station a great deal of knowledge about the audience, and about successes from other markets. McHugh and Hoffman, Frank N. Magid Associates, and ARD (Audience Research & Development) are three of the largest news consulting firms. News consultants work on a confidential, exclusive basis with one station per market; contracts are annual.

Ideally, a news consulting firm analyzes audience response to a station's news programming, and presents information about trends that may be taking shape. The firm does research to demonstrate how viewing habits and lifestyles are changing, and suggests ways to shape the programs, their scheduling, their content, and their presentation around the changes. Typically, a news consulting firm will also work closely with newsroom personnel, offering specific suggestions to improve job performance, efficiency, and on-camera presentation. While this service may be critical, it may also be problematic: since the consultants emphasize presentation over news content, their very presence may be an annoyance to the news staff. Still, their input can be useful, provided that it is taken as useful advice that may improve ratings, and not as gospel truth. The consulting firm usually visits each client station roughly five or six times per year, staying two or three days each time.

LOCAL CABLE NEWS STATIONS

Some of the larger local cable systems operate a news channel. Among the many examples: News 12, which covers Long Island, outside New York City; NY1, which reports to New York City's five boroughs, the Orange County Newschannel in southern California, and New England Cable News. These channels are generally advertiser-supported basic cable services.

CONTENT CONSIDERATIONS

News programming depends, in large part, upon stories about people, and many of these stories involve negative information. While the function of news programming is telling stories *accurately,* fairly, and without bias, there are gray areas. Some news stories involve information of a sensitive nature. And in some situations, sources of information ask to remain private, for fear of damage to personal reputation or injury.

NEWS SOURCES AND SOURCE PROTECTION

As a rule, television news, particularly on a local level, tries to be non-confrontational. Facing the choice of digging deeply into a murky story or introducing the possibility of legal problems, most stations will try to convince the reporter that the legal hassles are not worth the trouble. Still, there are instances in which stations do air controversial stories, and reporters must protect sources. The rule of thumb here is corroboration: if the protected source's information can be verified by a second source, then the station will usually go with the story.

If a news source specifically asks to be protected, then it is generally accepted that the reporter has a moral responsibility to protect the source. Some stations will stand by their reporters' ethical judgment.

On the network level—where stories that have national impact more often require the protection of sources—each news department has guidelines regarding procedures. In general, the reporter must explain the situation to the news director, who generally involves the division's senior vice president or president in the decision to go with the story. Legal counsel is present at the meeting as well. Networks typically stand by their reporters, presenting a formidable united front to any parties that challenge the reporter's information or judgment.

Sports

The business of television sports has been built on the unique ability of sports programs to deliver male viewers to advertisers. Professional football is considered the ideal televised sport because it attracts large numbers of males in every age and economic group. A short schedule allows almost every match-up to be promoted as a major event. Pro basketball has also become popular, but delivers a narrower audience—mainly urban, and somewhat younger than football fans (and with a steadily increasing number of female viewers). Those who watch major-league baseball are generally older, and the same is true of college basketball. Golf and tennis are special cases, reaching specific upscale target groups; tennis is the only sport that consistently attracts large numbers of female viewers. Auto racing is a successful advertising vehicle because it allows automotive companies (car manufacturers, oil and tire companies) to reach car buffs. Although hockey is popular in the North, Midwest, and Northwest, it is not as favored by national advertisers because the sport is not popular in the Sunbelt. Figure skating is the only sport that delivers far more female viewers than male.

While these distinctions between types of sports are broad and somewhat stereotypical, they nonetheless reflect the preconceptions guiding advertising buyers toward one type of event and away from another.

Networks do not always acquire rights and schedule events because of the potential for high advertising dollars. Sporting events attract many viewers to sample the network, which is why so many program promos appear on sporting events. Also, new advertisers are often attracted to the network by first advertising on the sports programming. This strategy worked beautifully for FOX, when it paid a seemingly outrageous amount of money for the rights to the World Series. The same strategy is now helping FX, FOX's fledgling cable network, to gain viewer and advertiser attention. The business decisions behind USA Network's tennis coverage is based on similar tactics.

In the 1990s, the sports television business has become international. FOX and ESPN have emerged as the worldwide leaders, sometimes partnering with, and sometimes competing against, long-established U.S. broadcast networks.

NATIONAL SPORTS COVERAGE IN THE U.S.

Five U.S. networks dominate the national sports business: ABC, CBS, NBC, FOX, and ESPN. Each of these networks regularly schedules large numbers of sporting events. Many other networks have rights to specific sports events, but no longer bid on the largest contracts. USA Network, for example, covers U.S. Open tennis, various golf tournaments, and some boxing. TBS is the home of Atlanta baseball and basketball, plus some motor sports and golf. HBO covers world championship boxing, and the Wimbledon tennis championships.

NETWORK AND CABLE RIGHTS

Networks negotiate with the leagues or other sports organizations for package deals that include multiple events. Each sport has its own traditions, in terms of both organization and pricing policy. As rights become available, and as network priorities change, rights do tend to change hands. This rundown, accurate as of 1997, will certainly look very different just a few years from now. Still, it shows various network strategies.

ABC and ESPN are now part of one large corporation (Disney), and have begun to negotiate together. ABC provides big dollars for high-visibility events. ESPN also gets its share of big-ticket events, but has more airtime to offer. ABC has rights to 17 regular season NFL games and one playoff game; various college football games and championships; the U.S. and world figure skating championships; the Triple Crown horse race series and other races; plus various golf, auto racing, bowling and skiing events. ESPN has nine regular and three pre-season NFL games; 62 college football games and 11 bowl games; 85 regular-season major league baseball games plus six to 12 playoff games; 26 regular season NHL games plus the Stanley Cup playoffs; many PGA, USGA and LPGA golf tournaments; plus a wide range of other rights, from soccer to women's basketball.

CBS has a big investment in football, plus the U.S. Tennis Open (it shares these rights with USA); several college football championship bowl games; the NCAA basketball championship and semifinals; lots of golf; and several high-profile car races.

The FOX broadcast network is more selective: 97 regular-season NFL games plus the Super Bowl XXXI; 72 regular-season baseball games plus some of the World Series and some league championship games. FOX is more than the U.S. broadcast network, however. The combination of FOX, and its cable/satellite networks, FOX Sports Net and FX, covered over 1,000 major league baseball games in 1997. FOX and NBC shared the 1997 World Series, with ESPN handling some of the early playoff games. FOX is also in the cable sports business (see below).

NBC's focus has been the Olympics, tying up rights for years (see below). In addition, the network has acquired the NBA playoffs, finals and all-star games; the baseball All-Star Game and some league championship games; 103 AFC football games, some tennis and golf; and horse racing.

Rights costs are constantly escalating. In 1998, CBS agreed to pay over $500 million for AFC-NFL games, more than twice the amount NBC had paid several years before. The 1995 major-league baseball contract, for example, is worth $1.7 billion over the 1996–2000 period. FOX paid $575 million for even-year World Series games and odd-year All-Star games, plus some playoffs, league championships, and a regional game of the week. NBC paid $400 million for the other World Series and All-Star games, the rest of the league championships, and some playoffs. ESPN paid $435 million for three regular-season games per week, plus playoffs. FOX and partner Liberty, get two weekly regular season games, plus some regional games on a non-exclusive basis (local broadcasters, cable companies and regional networks may cover the same games). Over $100 million more comes from international rights.

CBS paid $90 million for the 1996–2001 rights to the Orange Bowl and Fiesta Bowl.

The NFL's mid-1990s deal with FOX, NBC, ABC, TNT and ESPN was worth a total of $4.4 billion. The next deal, currently in negotiation is likely to be worth over $6 billion.

The current NBA deal works out as follows: NBC pays $1.75 billion for the exclusive broadcast rights to 31 playoff games per season for four years (the previous deal, for 23 games, cost NBC $750 million). In addition, NBC has the rights to 32 regular-season games. Turner Sports (TNT and TBS) gets 80 games per year on a four-year, $890 million contract (up from a $350 million contract for the previous four years).

The cost of the package for each sport is typically based on its mid-term value, with the price of the early games skewed in favor of the sports organization, and the price of the later games balanced in favor of the network. For either a broadcast or cable network, the last year of one contract appears much cheaper than the first year of the next contract—the difference in advertising revenues from one year to the next is never as large. In general, the network either loses money or breaks even during the first two years of the contract, but makes more than enough to compensate during the succeeding two or three years.

THE OLYMPICS

The rights for the 1992 winter Olympics cost $243 million; for the 1996 winter games, it was $300 million. In 1984, ABC spent about $225 million for rights to the summer games; for the 1988 games in Seoul, NBC spent about $310 million for rights; and the same network paid $401 million for the 1992 games in Barcelona.

NBC has committed to all but one season of summer and winter Olympic coverage through 2008. Here are the numbers for rights alone: summer 1996 (Atlanta)—$456 million; summer 2000 (Sydney)—$715 million; winter 2002 (Salt Lake City)—$555 million; summer 2004 (TBA)—$793 million; winter 2006 (TBA)—$613 million; summer 2008 (TBA)—$894 million. CBS's rights for winter 1998 (Nagano, Japan) cost $375 million.

Production costs for locations outside the U.S. can be very high. An extraordinarily large staff for both planning and actual production, the complex logistics of transportation and staff housing, and the need to cover events in multiple locations can add up to $125 million or more for the summer games and about $75 million for the winter games (there are more events in the summer Olympics). The host broadcaster (NBC, for the foreseeable future) provides facilities and feeds for visiting countries for a fee.

THE STRUCTURE OF A NETWORK SPORTS DIVISION

The size of a network sports organization tends to vary over the course of the year, depending upon the number of events and the freelance staff required to supplement the full-time employees. The staff size tends to range from 75 to 150 people, with roughly 100 full-time employees. One chief executive runs the operation, with two vice presidents—one in charge of production, and the other in charge of program acquisition, scheduling, and business affairs. Advertising sales are usually done by the network with the involvement of a liaison working in the sports department; publicity, on-air promotion, and print advertising may be handled by either the network's sports division or the network itself.

REGIONAL AND LOCAL COVERAGE

From the early days of radio until the mid-1980s, local sports were covered primarily by local broadcasters. The New York Yankees, for example, were associated with WPIX (Channel 11) and the New York Mets, with WOR (Channel 9)—television stations that were classic independents—with no network affiliation, so they filled their spring and summer prime-time hours with local baseball action. The stations' alternative was either off-network programming or movies. WOR also covered local basketball (Knicks) and hockey (Rangers).

As cable television reached critical mass, local businesspeople devised regional networks and acquired rights to local sports coverage. Over time, the local affiliates showed fewer and fewer games; the regional sports networks charged viewers a premium subscription fee, and accepted advertising. Viewers perceived an injustice as these regional networks made money by charging for coverage that had previously been provided for free. The bulldozer that is American business continued to plow, and in time, the objections were forgotten. Coincidentally, the formerly independent stations became affiliated with FOX, UPN, and WBTV, so prime-time hours were, by and large, no longer available for local baseball, basketball, hockey, and other sports. Several larger companies pursued the regional sports network, and for about a decade, SportsChannel and Prime Sports were dominant forces. In 1996, FOX Sports Net took shape as the only national brand for regional and local sports coverage. FOX Sports Net is owned by News Corp. (the FOX parent company), Liberty Sports (affiliated with Liberty Media and TCI), and TCI (a large cable MSO). By the mid-1990s, local television broadcasters were no longer a significant factor, and most covered only a small number of local games per year.

FOX SPORTS NET

FOX Sports Net is a national cable sports network made up of four types of regional sports channels. The first type is the owned and operated station (O&O). There are ten O&Os: FOX Sports Arizona, FOX Sports Midwest (St. Louis area), FOX Sports Northwest, FOX Sports Pittsburgh, FOX Sports Rocky Mountain, FOX Sports South (Atlanta area), FOX Sports Southwest (Dallas area and Oklahoma), FOX Sports Detroit, and two FOX Sports West channels (both serving southern California).

The FOX sports network also works with four affiliated regional sports networks (these are owned by other companies, not by FOX Sports Net): Home Team Sports (Washington, DC); Midwest Sports Channel (Minneapolis); NESN (New England Sports Network); and Comcast SportsNet (Philadelphia).

In 1998, the former SportsChannel regional networks (mostly owned by Rainbow Programming Holdings and Liberty Media) started carrying the FOX Sports logo (hence, FOX Sports New England, FOX Sports Chicago, FOX Sports Ohio, FOX Sports Bay Area (San Francisco region), and FOX Sports New York). MSG (Madison Square Garden network) retained its name but became part of the FOX Sports Net family as well. In addition to the obvious benefits of FOX Sports network branding and programming feeds (see below), commercial time on these networks is now sold by FOX Sports Net.

Two additional regional sports networks work with FOX Sports: Sunshine Network (Florida) and Empire Sports Network (upstate New York). These networks carry some FOX Sports programming, but remain independent.

The basic strategy is centered on local and regional coverage. FOX Sports Southwest, for example, covers baseball (Houston Astros, Texas Rangers); basketball (Houston Rockets, Dallas Mavericks, San Antonio Spurs); hockey (Dallas Stars); local news (the weekly press conference of the Dallas Cowboys' coach); and local college teams. The national feed includes an extensive nightly news program (*FOX Sports News Prime Time,* which is produced as a five-hour program, two hours of which are shown live and up-to-the-minute in every time zone); plus *Baseball Thursday* (a major-league baseball game every Thursday night); *Fight Time on FOX;* college basketball coverage; and so on.

Each regional channel negotiates most of its own deals, and the parameters vary widely based on the size of the market, team popularity, and competition for rights.

PAY-PER-VIEW SPORTS

As pay-per-view (see Chapter 7) matures, some national and
regional sports events may be sold on a per-game basis. So far,
ventures by the Los Angeles Dodgers, San Diego Padres and NBC
and Cablevision (the disastrous Olympics Triplecast in 1991),
suggest regional sports networks are the consumer's preferred
means of distribution. Boxing and wrestling, however, have been
consistently successful on pay-per-view.

WRESTLING

One of the most popular sports on cable television, professional
wrestling matches are supplied by WWF (World Wrestling
Foundation) and WCW (World Championship Wrestling). Each
organization maintains a stable of wrestlers, controls and produces
its own programming, and is a well-established brand among
males 12–34. WWF is owned by TitanSports; WCW is a Time Warner
company (it was part of Turner's empire). WCW's showcase is
WCW Monday Nitro on TNT, which competes head-to-head
against *WWF Monday Night Raw* on USA. WCW has been built, in
part, by luring WWF stars Rowdy Roddy Piper, Hulk Hogan, and
Randy Savage. Both WWF and WCW also syndicate events, and
WWF also produces a monthly pay-per-view event.

SPORTS COVERAGE ON LOCAL BROADCAST STATIONS

Local broadcast stations, once so completely associated with local
teams, have been outbid. Most local stations are now affiliated
with networks, typically FOX, UPN and WBTV, and no longer
have the available prime-time slots for game coverage. Networks
discourage their affiliates from prime-time pre-emptions. Still,
some local stations persist with a schedule of several dozen games
per year, and when there is a conflict between local and network
rights, the network typically blacks out local coverage.

SYNDICATED SPORTS

Coverage rights to most sporting events are sold to either broadcast
or cable networks, so syndication plays a relatively minor role in
sports programming. Still, there are some exceptions. The WWF
produces and distributes several series, for example. Some basketball and football games are also syndicated, particularly college
games, as are some golf and racing events. With so many network
sports outlets bidding for rights, syndication plays a relatively minor
role in contemporary sports coverage.

SPORTS BARS

When a sporting event or channel is shown in a commercial establishment, like a bar or a restaurant, the owners must pay a subscription fee. The fee is typically paid to the distributor (FOX Sports Direct, DirecTV, or a local cable company, for example), or to the network directly (as is often the case for "big dish" facilities—those who receive feeds without the intervention of a satellite services provider). Pirated signals are a major problem, and some sports programmers have begun to take legal action to prevent unauthorized use of signals.

AMATEUR SPORTS COVERAGE

Small-scale sporting events can be significant audience draws in their communities. Some cable television systems now regularly cover high school sports. If audience interest is high, sale of commercial time in these programs can more than pay for the cost of covering the game. Since there is rarely competition for rights—and because showing the game generally increases local interest in the team—rights payments are uncommon.

TELEVISION AND SPORTS MARKETING

Television's widespread distribution of sports programming is also the core of the sports marketing business. Team logotypes are valuable merchandise-licensing properties. Corporate sponsorship of events like tennis and racing provides positive exposure above and beyond that afforded by mere advertising. Cigarette advertisers, for example, can gain limited television exposure by sponsoring race cars; these sponsors would otherwise be excluded from the medium. Stadium signage that is seen on television is also an effective type of advertising.

PROGRAMMING OF PREVIOUS SPORTING EVENTS

Sports coverage loses value immediately after it is broadcast. Still, many World Series and Super Bowl games have sold well on videocassette, albeit to a distinct type of fan, who collects sports memories. Two small cable/satellite networks specialize in old material: American Sports Network, from Rainbow (owners of American Movie Classics); and the independent Classic Sports Network. Some sports documentaries have succeeded in home video, and, occasionally, on cable, but audiences generally prefer live coverage.

RIGHTS ISSUES

Each sport has its own management system for historical material. major-league baseball claims ownership of all games—or at least, of the television coverage of all games since there has *been* television coverage. Older baseball footage may be hard to find, and rights are typically cleared by the library providing the footage. The NFL, the NHL, and the NBA operate in a similar fashion, though there may be some dealings with the individual teams as well. Golf and tennis footage is usually owned by either the original production company, the network, or the association that granted the television rights. Use of college sports coverage must be cleared by either the appropriate conference that made the television deal, by the individual school, or sometimes both.

Often, simply finding old sports footage is as difficult as determining who owns the rights, and who can negotiate a deal. Many games were never recorded; if they were, the material may have been destroyed or lost. Most stock-footage houses archive sports footage, but their libraries tend to be spotty.

When the rights are granted, they should include the right to show both the players and the game. As for the fans—and anyone who was in or near the venue before, during, or after the game— releases may be necessary, particularly if the material will be used outside of its purely historical context.

SPORTS OUTSIDE THE U.S.

Although the U.S. has transformed sports into a marketing juggernaut, sports progamming is, and has always been, a significant aspect of television in almost every country. The U.S. game called football doesn't mean much outside the U.S. and a handful of other countries; but the "real" football (called soccer in the U.S.) is the most important franchise in Europe and Latin America. FIFA, which licenses World Cup Soccer, sold the global rights for the 2002 and 2006 matchups for $2.24 billion; the buying consortium included Germany's Kirch Group and Sporis, a holding company based in Switzerland. In 1998, the same rights were sold for $230 million. Throughout Europe, soccer matches are as ubiquitous as baseball is in the U.S., and during the season, on a satellite service, viewers may choose between a half-dozen simultaneous telecasts, or more.

Worldwide networks are also establishing themselves. ESPN International started in 1988, and operates 16 networks outside the U.S., mostly in Asia and Latin America. Eurosport, which reaches nearly 70 million European households, will be a tough competitor as ESPN works its way into that continent. Among many world-wide ventures, FOX Sports International owns Prime Deportiva, currently in 18 countries via a single feed; in time, national feeds will be developed, under a FOX Sports logo.

Sportel, held in Monte Carlo each October, has become a leading international marketplace for the sale of sports rights. Sportel America, recently launched in Miami, focuses on Latin American rights.

Children's Programming and Animation

Ideas for children's programs come from a variety of sources, but much of the development and production is done by production companies and networks that specialize in the form. In the U.S., CBS, ABC, and FOX program mainly half-hour cartoons shown on Saturday mornings. NBC programs live-action sitcoms for teens on Saturday mornings *(Saved by the Bell: The New Class, Hang Time, California Dreams)*. PBS programming includes pre-school live action, a cartoon show, a game show, and other formats. Nickelodeon's schedule of children's programs include a wide range of animated series, sitcoms, variety series, and other types of programs for pre-schoolers, grade-school children, and young teenagers. Cartoon Network fills the schedule with cartoons, from packages, some formerly sold in syndication, and many original series. Several other cable networks also show cartoons.

The U.S. view is somewhat misleading, however. Nearly every children's program seen in the U.S. is also seen in other countries. Children's television, and its related licensing industry, is a global phenomenon. Some program decisions are made, therefore, not only on the basis of U.S. potential, but also on the potential of the program concept in Europe, and, to a far lesser extent, Latin America and Asia.

It's important to consider the business side of the children's equation. In 1997, children's television programs earned over $850 million in advertising revenues, with Nickelodeon responsible for half that amount.

DEVELOPMENT OF ANIMATED SERIES

Animation has become a robust segment of the production business. Nickelodeon has promised a $350 million investment in animation, and other large media companies have countered with large commitments for both television and film projects. There are five primary domestic markets for new animated series: ABC, CBS, FOX, Nickelodeon, and syndication.

Hanna-Barbera, DIC *(Where on Earth Is Carmen Sandiego?)*, and Film Roman *(The Blues Brothers, Felix the Cat, Bobby's World, Garfield and Friends, The Simpsons)* continue to be major suppliers, but success on Nickelodeon has widened the field of animation producers to include relative newcomers like JUMBO Pictures (producers of *DOUG*, and *Disney's DOUG*, now owned by ABC), and Klasky-Csupo (producers of *Rugrats*). Several studios, notably MCA *(Earthworm Jim)*, Warner Brothers *(Animaniacs, Tiny Toons Adventures, Batman)* and DreamWorks, also produce animated projects. Saban produces some cartoon series *(X-Men)* and some live-action children's series *(Sweet Valley High, Mighty Morphin Power Rangers)*.

In network and syndication, development is most often based on a successful license—a comic strip character *(Garfield)*, a line of toys (videogames featuring the Mario Brothers), a spinoff from a successful movie *(Men in Black)*, or a computer game *(Sam & Max)*. On broadcast television, cartoons based on new characters are the exception. On Nickelodeon, most cartoons are based upon new characters. Nickelodeon has also broken the mold of traditional cartoon series with the extreme humor of *Ren & Stimpy,* and the innovative combination of variety show, sitcom, animated action figures, Stone Age documentaries and comic strip characters come to life on *Kablam!*

Successful animated series are largely dependent upon appealing characters and interactions between them. Story does not matter nearly as much as characters and character interaction. Gags and jokes come from relationships between characters—examples include Wile E. Coyote and Road Runner; Ren and Stimpy; Tom and Jerry; Fred Flintstone and Barney Rubble; the group of toddlers on *Rugrats;* the interconnections between and among Homer, Marge, Bart, and Maggie Simpson and the other citizens of Springfield.

The development of a character's personality and relationships is often closely related to the way the character looks. Relative sizes are important: Homer's rotund belly and non-existent hairline, Bart's raggedy hair and Ren's bulging eyes. The rendering style is also key: Matt Groening's Simpsons characters, are line drawings with spot color, essentially comic book characters; the Animaniacs were deliberately designed to look like throw-backs to early Warner Brothers cartoons; Doug uses a very simple line drawing style.

Settling on the way the characters look is often the source of colorful conversations between the creative team and the network or distributor (in theory, this is easier when a new series is based upon existing characters from another medium, but in practice, it is every bit as complicated because the long-term value of a license is at stake).

The choice of voice actors is not as controversial. A limited number of voice actors provide the majority of cartoon voices, and most of these performers carry zillions of different voices in their heads.

Once characters are developed, sample scripts are written, and sample animations are produced and tested. Then, characters are changed, combined, and deleted. New ones are added. Voice actors are changed to better suit the characters' personalities.

Because animation is a highly specialized form, networks tend to depend upon companies that have considerable experience in the field. Film Roman, for example, produces many network and syndicated series. Most animation is produced abroad; the Far East and Ireland are leading manufacturing centers.

LEAD TIME FOR ANIMATED SERIES

Because of the number of steps involved, and the sheer number of hours required to draw and animate a half-hour series, an animated series requires a long lead time. Production of a pilot usually starts a year or more prior to the first airdate. Here's how the timing might work for a typical animated series:

> Month 1: Producer develops general concept and preliminary character sketches.

> Month 2: Producer revises concept and character sketches, pitches first network, which makes suggestions and ultimately turns down the project.

> Month 3: Producer pitches another network, which makes suggestions for changes in characters, style, voices and story-lines, but agrees to finance a pilot. Pilot goes into production immediately.

> Month 4: Contracts are negotiated, but not signed. Designers are hard at work on characters and background concepts. Writers are revising scripts. Arrangements are being made for off-shore production.

Month 5: Contracts are signed. Pilot is in production.

Month 6: Pilot is in post-production.

Month 7: Pilot is tested, evaluated by program executives. In syndication, pilot is shown to station groups.

Month 8: Series begins production.

Month 12: First episode is delivered.

By comparison, a game show or sitcom would require approximately half as much time. (Of course, schedules vary, and many animated series have moved from concept sketch to broadcast series in record time.)

Aside from Nickelodeon and PBS, most children's programming is animation. And while there have been some notable exceptions over the years, such as Captain Kangaroo's long tenure on CBS, Howdy Doody's legendary success on NBC, the retro comedy on *Pee-Wee's Playhouse* and the fast-moving fun science on *Beakman's World*, the vast majority of network and syndication slots have been filled with cartoons.

CHILDREN'S PROGRAMS ON PUBLIC TELEVISION

Public television has generally avoided cartoons, but the success of the *Arthur* series is a notable exception. PBS had previously avoided children's game shows, but the popularity of early Nickelodeon game shows, such as *Double Dare,* encouraged PBS to try games; and the five-year run of *Where in the World of Carmen Sandiego?* (which taught geography), and its replacement series, *Where in Time Is Carmen Sandiego?* (history), showed that game shows could fit the PBS agenda. PBS's long-term strength has been pre-school programming, and for decades, the network had no significant competition against *Sesame Street, Mister Rogers Neighborhood, Reading Rainbow* and more recently, *Barney.* Nickelodeon, with NICK JR., now competes directly with PBS pre-school programming. PBS has also programmed dramatic series for children and teens: *Ghost Writer* (encouraging literacy) and *DeGrassi Junior High* (seen on public television stations, but not distributed by PBS, teaching social values) are two examples. In general, children's series seen on public television stations must have a clear, direct connection to an educational curriculum (such as geography or reading) or agenda item (such as literacy or social skills).

Children's series seen on PBS require a considerable investment of time and resources for creative and educational development as well as audience research to formulate the concept and to evaluate the pilot and each season's episodes. Marketing is often focused on schoolteachers, in the hope that teachers will recommend the program to students.

NICKELODEON

Nickelodeon began as a non-commercial network in 1979, the cable equivalent of PBS's children's schedule. The network grew out of Warner Communications' innovative QUBE venture (the same seedbed that yielded MTV). The network is now a global entertainment brand seen by 66 million households in the U.S., and in more than 70 other countries. Dedicated channels operate in the U.K., Germany, Australia, and Latin America, with plans for a Pan-Asian service. Program blocks are common as well. In 1998, for example, Nickelodeon launched a three-hour daily block with RAI's children's channel in Italy; the block is heavily branded as a Nickelodeon venture, the first step toward a stand-alone channel in the future. A similar setup exists in Turkey and in Scandinavia. Nickelodeon's operation also includes motion pictures, consumer products (with Mattel, Hasbro, American Greetings, and many other licensees), book publishing, CD-ROM publishing, online publishing, live tours, audio and videocassettes, a combination production studio and amusement attraction in Orlando, Florida, and more attractions in the U.S. and the U.K.

Nickelodeon is one network, but it's organized as several brands. On weekdays, NICK JR. runs until 2:00 P.M. (without commercials), then Nickelodeon programming takes over until 8:00 P.M., and from 8:00 P.M. until 5:30 A.M., the network switches to the broad-based family appeal of old TV series on NICK at NITE. On weekends, the schedule includes a Saturday night schedule for pre-teens and teens called SNICK.

NICK JR., the pre-school service, addresses an agenda similar to PBS. Many of the programs involve puppets and live actors (like *Sesame Street* or *Mister Rogers Neighborhood* on PBS), or live action with computer animation, but others are all-puppet or all-animation. *Blue's Clues,* a live-action and animation series, teaches problem-solving skills. *Gullah Gullah Island* is a variety series for pre-schoolers; its developmental core is remarkably like PBS—it features an African-American family living on an island whose culture is based on West African ways. *Allegra's Window* looks at the world through the eyes of a three-year-old; it features puppets and live actors. Schedule slots are also filled with series seen on other networks *(Jim Henson's Muppet Babies)* and in syndication

(The Muppet Show), and in other countries *(Rupert),* but in time most of these will be replaced by original Nickelodeon programs.

Many of the popular series on Nickelodeon are "Nicktoons"— original cartoons produced for Nickelodeon. *Rugrats,* an animated series seen through the eyes of pre-schoolers, has consistently been one of the highest rated series on cable television. *DOUG* was so popular that a new version *(Brand Spanking New Doug)* was picked up by ABC for Saturday mornings and the production company (Jumbo Pictures) was bought by Disney/ABC. *The Ren & Stimpy Show* has been a consistent hit not only with children, but with college students and hipper adults. Newer series, such as *Angry Beavers* and *Hey Arnold,* although successful, have not reached the pop-culture heights of the first three NICKTOON series.

Nickelodeon has programmed sitcoms and dramas since the 1980s, but the 1990s efforts have been especially successful. *Are You Afraid of the Dark?* is an anthology series, a kind of *Twilight Zone* for kids. *The Secret World of Alex Mack* is a drama about a teenage girl with super powers. With the sketch comedy series *All That* (see below), they are the cornerstone of the SNICK service for older children and teens. There have been other sitcoms and dramas, some bizarre *(The Adventures of Pete and Pete),* some downright silly *(Salute Your Shorts).* All of these series feature kids or teens in starring roles, and tell stories from their point of view; they support Nickelodeon's very clear agenda: this is a network for children.

You Can't Do That on Television was an early success with sketch comedy, a tradition continued with the SNICK comedy and variety series *All That.* Green slime was an important part of Nickelodeon's early branding—it fell on the heads of characters on *You Can't Do That . . . ,* and it's memorialized spouting from a fountain in front of Nickelodeon Studios. Slime also played a role in *Double Dare,* one of the many Nick game shows, and easily the most durable. More recent Nick game shows have been more cutting-edge, breaking the bounds of traditional games. *GUTS,* for example, is an arena competition for kids with superior physical skills.

News also plays a minor role in Nickelodeon's schedule.

Nickelodeon's programming and marketing is a brilliant example of media branding in the 1990s. Every program, every series, every on-air promotional announcement, every live show and Nickelodeon paperback book, follows essentially the same creative marketing agenda. Nickelodeon is about fun, but it's also about respecting kids and their world. And no company, not even Disney, has been more successful in developing such a consistently positive image in the minds of children in the U.S.

CARTOON NETWORK

Prior to Turner's merger with Time Warner, the Cartoon Network library consisted of 8,500 titles from the Hanna-Barbera, MGM, Warner Bros., and Paramount libraries (Turner, now Time Warner, owns Hanna-Barbera).

Cartoon Network's primary audience is kids and teens; but 32 percent of the audience is adults 18+. Ratings are generally high; people really do watch this network in large numbers. The U.S. subscriber count is surprisingly low, considering the network's popularity and visibility—just 26 million subs in the U.S. But this is only part of the story. Cartoon Network is seen in 75 countries, and the total subscriber count is over 65 million.

Most of the Cartoon Network's schedule is filled with library product, but there are some original programs. *Big Bag,* a Sunday morning series for pre-schoolers, is produced with CTW. *Space Ghost Coast to Coast* is a talk show hosted by a cartoon character; guests have included the cast of *Gilligan's Island,* The Ramones, Lassie, Adam West, the Jerky Boys, David Byrne, Dr. Timothy Leary and many others. The network's *What a Cartoon Show* is used to try out new concepts, and to air cartoons that don't fit neatly into a series format. So far, three original series have grown out of the *What a Cartoon Show* project—*Dexter's Laboratory, Johnny Bravo,* and *Cow and Chicken.*

THE DISNEY CHANNEL

The Disney Channel, a pay cable service, depends upon the quality of the Disney brand name, rather than its own distinctive identity, to attract subscribers. There is little original programming. Most of the schedule is filled with cartoons. The 1997 weekday schedule, for example, consisted mostly of *Tale Spin, Goof Troop, Chip 'n' Dale Rescue Rangers, Duck Tales, Charlie Brown and Snoopy Show,* and *The Little Mermaid.* Evenings are filled with family movies. Weekend mornings are devoted to animal shows, and weekday afternoons are filled with sitcoms.

The Disney Channel does program some original specials, notably the annual teacher awards.

With new management in 1996, it seems likely that The Disney Channel is due for an overhall, and, perhaps, a rethinking of the pay television strategy.

LICENSING AND CHILDREN'S TELEVISION

Children like to do two things: play and watch cartoons. Television provides the cartoons. Toymakers provide the play experience, frequently with toys that are closely aligned with television (and movie) properties.

Many popular television series earn additional revenues by licensing their characters to toy companies. But toys are only part of the much larger picture, especially when the television series is a long-term success. *Ren & Stimpy* licensees, at the phenomenon's peak in 1994 included: embroidered hats, paper party goods, wall calendars, greeting cards, action figures, boxer shorts, embroidered T-shirts and sweat shirts, animation cels, plush toys, figure mugs, watches and clocks, monthly comic books, boxed valentine cards, books, postcards, computer screen frames, videogames, gum dispensers, trading cards, View-Master slides, posters, and sleep-wear—and this is just the domestic list. *Ren & Stimpy* was not quite a home run in licensing terms, but it was certainly successful; other success stories include *Thomas the Tank Engine* (but not so much the U.S. series, *Shining Time Station*), *Barney, Teenage Mutant Ninja Turtles, Mario Brothers,* and the long-term champ, *Sesame Street.* But not every series is ideally suited to licensing, and not every series of licensing deals pays off as planned. *Beakman's World, Where in the World Is Carmen Sandiego?,* and other series have not fared as well. Possible reasons include timing, lack of coordination between the licensor and the licensees, lack of consumer interest in the title, and so on. (For the regulation of children's television, see Chapter 18.)

There are three components in the licensing business. The licensor, which is the company that holds the master rights to the copyright, is most often a network or large production and distribution company. The licensee may be a toy maker, but is as often a maker of sleepwear or t-shirts. The third component is the licensing agent, the deal maker whose broad-based industry experience helps to link each property with the best possible licensee. Some companies maintain their own licensing departments, but a smaller number actually possess the necessary expertise to identify the best possible licenses, manage and grow the license, and deal with the inevitable decline in the value of the license. This expertise is best acquired either by hiring a licensing director with a real world track record, or by working with an experienced licensing agent for a series of projects before bringing the effort in-house. Smaller production companies are often wise to work with licensing agents—or to organize their company for growth in the licensing sector.

The intimate relationship between larger licensees, notably toy companies, and syndicators has come under some criticism from children's advocacy groups. Toy makers, in exchange for valuable licensing rights, will sometimes pay as much as 30 percent of production costs in a new cartoon or live action series. They may own a part of the property as well.

NEW FCC RULES REGARDING EDUCATIONAL CONTENT ON COMMERCIAL STATIONS

After considerable haggling, the television industry and the FCC agreed to a compromise intended to increase the educational quality of children's television. Beginning in 1997, stations must program at least three hours per week of educational programming for children. This mandate can be fulfilled with network, syndicated, or local programming. In the past, educational programming has virtually assured lower ratings, so local stations have tried every possible strategy to label commercially appealing programs, notably sitcoms and cartoons, as educational. This time, the FCC will be watching more closely. Affiliates of CBS, NBC, and ABC will most likely receive network programs to fill at least some of the mandated hours, but FOX, UPN, and WB affiliates will need syndicated series to fill the slots. Local programming, in general, is not an option— quality children's programs cost serious money, and no single station can afford to produce a competitive program with the limited advertising dollars available in a local market.

The ruling does not affect cable networks. Therefore, the ruling will further benefit the Nickelodeon juggernaut; if the educational hours are uninteresting, kids will leave the commercial stations and watch Nickelodeon (or Cartoon Network) instead.

THE INTERNATIONAL MARKETPLACE

Nickelodeon has established a presence as both a network and a program supplier worldwide. Nickelodeon operates dedicated channels, available via cable and satellite, in Germany, the U.K., Australia, and Latin America. Other dedicated children's channels include Canada's YTV; France's Canal J; the U.K.'s Children's Channel; Germany's Kinderkanal; the Netherlands' Kindernet; and Latin America's Locomotion. Children's programming is also seen more than 20 hours per week (roughly 3 hours per day) on Australia's ABC; Belgium's BRTN; Canada's SRC and TVOntario; Mexico's ZAZ; France 3; Germany's ARD, Pro7 and Super RTL;

The Netherlands' RTL4; Spain's TVE, Antena 3, and Tele5; Japan's MXTV; the U.K.'s BBC and Sky One; and more. Many other networks schedule between 5 and 20 hours per week (in fact, the U.S. commercial broadcast networks schedule considerably less children's programming than their foreign counterparts).

With so many hours to fill, the children's marketplace has been booming. Most of the action is in animation, where new voices can easily be added to customize the episodes for local viewers.

For the producer, the price paid per half hour is the critical issue. For most countries (France, Spain, Italy, Japan, Australia), budgets per half hour are about $5,000 (U.S.), sometimes as high as $10,000, but as often as low as $2,000–$3,000. Some, like Germany's public and private networks, and the U.K.'s ITV, pay two or three times that amount (sometimes, tens of thousands of dollars).

CO-PRODUCTIONS

Co-productions are quite common. For a co-production deal, the appeal of the principal characters must be universal—or they must at least appeal to audiences in the countries of those who are doing the deal. It's best if the character or license has been previously established, most often as a toy, book series, comic book series, or motion picture. This unique selling point, or "hook," is essential to the selling process. A production team with a previous hit series can also be the hook. Rights negotiations are the next step, and they can be complicated, especially if the project is intended for international exploitation, and if the property is well established. Then comes the process of shopping the project around. Most co-producers are very selective, and make their decisions based on highly subjective criteria. Creative control is always an issue; partners who are active in children's television are best suited to co-production, but they're often opinionated, and focused on their own individual business needs (particularly when one partner is involved with an educational or public agenda). Most co-production deals are made between just two companies: one, a producer, and the other, either a distributor/producer or a network/media company. If the deal looks as if it will close, the producer gets to work, investing in character design, storylines, etc. It is not unusual for the attorneys to work for months on finalizing the deal, even though production has already begun. Delivery dates, not contracts, determine production schedules. And yes, there is some risk for the producer in this approach, which is why partners are chosen with the utmost care.

24

Daytime Drama

Daytime serials—also called daytime dramas or, most often, "soap operas" or simply "soaps"—have always been a staple of the network daytime schedule. Research studies show that audience viewing patterns for soap operas are based on astonishing levels of loyal viewing over years, and even decades. Programmers and producers feed this addictive pattern by offering viewers a dose of romance and suspense, but they consciously structure scripts and storylines to leave the viewer wanting more. During the summer, programmers attempt to hook younger viewers on summer vacation. A successful soap commands phenomenal loyalty; even when the scripts or characters are uninspired, audience research shows that viewers will continue to watch, trusting that the situation will improve in time.

Daytime drama is seen almost exclusively on commercial network television. (However, Spanish-language soap operas, called novelas, are extremely popular on Hispanic networks; see Chapter 50.) ABC, CBS, and NBC each program several soaps, generally in the afternoon, with a particular audience in mind. On ABC, for example, *All My Children* has traditionally been issue-oriented; storylines have dealt with AIDS, teenage pregnancy, homosexual relationships, runaways, anorexia, and other topical subjects. On the same network, *General Hospital*, because of its after-school time slot, is produced with storylines and characters that target high-school and college students (the newer *Port Charles* is a spin-off). Several programs on these networks have been popular since radio days, with viewing habits passed from generation to generation; examples include *Guiding Light* and *As the World Turns* on CBS, and *Days of Our Lives* on NBC.

Three soaps—*As the World Turns, Another World,* and *Guiding Light*—are produced by daytime television's largest sponsor, Procter & Gamble. ABC produces its own soaps *(One Life to Live* and *All My Children* in NYC; *General Hospital* and *Port Charles* in LA). Bell-Phillips supplies CBS with *The Young and the Restless* and *The Bold and the Beautiful,* both produced in LA. Spelling is one of the few prime-time producers in history with a daytime soap credit: *Sunset Beach* on NBC. Columbia Pictures also produces *Days of Our Lives* for NBC.

DEVELOPMENT OF A NEW DAYTIME DRAMA

Although ABC, CBS, and NBC constantly develop new daytime dramas, few new ones actually reach the air. Three people developed many of the soaps currently on the air. Agnes Nixon created *One Life to Live, All My Children,* and *Loving,* three of the four soaps currently on ABC. William J. Bell was responsible for *Another World* for NBC, as well as *The Young and the Restless* and its spin-off, *The Bold and the Beautiful,* for CBS. Both Nixon and Bell learned their craft from Irna Phillips, the leading creator and writer of radio soaps; the Phillips legacy includes *As the World Turns,* and substantial creative input into *Guiding Light.* Few new daytime dramas are introduced (perhaps one every five years), and it's rare that a new series succeeds.

General network wisdom dictates that new soaps are best developed by experienced head writers of successful daytime series. Writers without specific experience in the day-to-day head-writing of a successful soap face enormous odds, even with a spectacular idea. Still, given the right cast and the right idea, all of the networks will pay attention to a credible writer or producer.

A writer or producer typically pitches the idea for a daytime drama to the vice president or director of daytime drama development. Decisions are not made quickly. Several months will pass as network executives determine not only whether the idea has merit, but where and when the program could conceivably debut (years may pass before a time slot becomes available). Eventually, the writer may be offered $50,000–$75,000 to write a "bible"—a 150-page document with a description of each character—and a year's supply of storylines. Once the bible is accepted (it is likely to be revised several times along the way), the network will commission a sample week of stories. Then the wait for the time slot begins; the wait could take three to five years.

Pilots for daytime dramas are uncommon. If the network decides to go ahead, the series begins production, typically with six months of lead time prior to air. This period may be extended if the series is launched with a made-for-TV prime-time movie, as is now frequent practice.

PRODUCTION OF DAYTIME DRAMA

The production of a daytime drama is a massive undertaking. On an hour-long series, the equivalent of two motion pictures is produced every week. Daytime dramas employ large numbers of cast members, including a dozen or more regular performers and many more in continuing roles (due to the specialized nature of soap production, special AFTRA, WGA, and DGA rates and work rules apply—see Chapter 45). Storylines are worked out well in advance, but scripts must take budget limitations into account—a new set cannot be constructed for a small number of scenes, location shooting is costly, and complicated scenes are a problem because rehearsal time is precious.

An hour-long soap costs at least $500,000 per week, or about $100,000 per episode. By network standards, this is a bargain (a week of soap episodes costs less than one prime-time hour). But there's a catch. Prime-time dramas produce about 20 episodes per year. In order to maintain the audience's daily interest, a new soap episode airs daily, for a total of 260 episodes per year—and a total investment of about $30,000,000. Approximately half of each budget applies to "above-the-line" expenses, such as a large production staff, multiple writers, and the large cast. The biggest below-the-line items are set construction and decoration (a large number of sets are used), and studio time (long studio days are common). Although these figures are two to three times as high as the costs for game shows, soap operas are disproportionate contributors to each network's profitability. With commercials priced at an average of $22,000 per 30-second spot, and over 20 spots per hour, a day's commercial revenues very nearly pays for a full week's production.

Although the soaps attract over 15 million viewers per week (most of them women), the core audience is older, stay-at-home viewers; as they age out of the significant demographic range, these viewers are not being replaced by younger viewers in sufficiently large numbers. More than 10 percent of soap viewing is done at night; viewers record the daytime dramas and screen them at night. Unfortunately, these viewers typically scan through the commercials, which is, in the advertiser's mind, the same as not watching the shows at all. Some soaps have fallen out of touch with their audiences, others have artlessly emphasized sex and turned off large segments of the audience. Real-life dramas, such as O.J. Simpson's trial, have proven more interesting than the made-up storylines. The (dubious) real-life drama of outrageous talk shows has also cut into viewer attentiveness.

Many cable networks have flirted with soaps, but the production of 260 original episodes per year, the standard for broadcast networks, is daunting. Also, viewers have a habit of "appointment viewing" on broadcast network soaps (they schedule personal time as they would for a lunch date); this behavior is less common among cable network viewers.

25

Game Shows

Once a daytime and syndication staple, game shows now occupy a very small number of hours on local stations' schedules. Most broadcast networks no longer program game shows. Only two are successful in syndication. Most cable networks have graduated to sitcoms and dramas, and no longer program game shows. A cable network devoted to game shows has been slow to grow.

DEVELOPMENT

The development of game shows starts with a basic game concept—like a game based on hangman or a network's desire to base a new game on some aspect of lifestyle, such as shopping. Informal play-testing using game pieces roughed out on index cards and other inexpensive materials, is the second step. The game is played over and over again, first with the office staff and then in more formal run-throughs. The latter are generally staged in a conference room with "civilian" contestants who are paid a nominal fee. This development process lasts at least a month, and sometimes as long as six months, until the game plays smoothly.

The producer pitches the game show concept to networks or syndicators shortly after the informal run-throughs with the office staff. If the network or syndicator feels that the program is worthy of further development, the producer receives up to $10,000 (frequently closer to $20,000) to pay writers, a freelance staff, and run-through contestants. After four to six weeks, the program executive is invited to a run-through. Changes are discussed, and another run-through, incorporating the suggestions, is typically scheduled for the following week. This process is usually repeated several times, and if the program continues to show merit, the program executive invites others from the network or syndication company to watch a run-through. Eventually, either a pilot is ordered or the project is dropped and moves to turnaround (see page 208).

A game-show pilot generally costs $150,000 to $300,000, and requires approximately two months for production. When the pilot is complete, it is tested (by a network), or used as a sales tool (by a syndicator). If the project tests well and fits into a network schedule slot—or if it clears a sufficient number of profitable time slots in large markets for syndication—a season's worth of shows is ordered.

PRODUCTION

Most game shows are developed and produced by a small number of production companies that specialize in the genre. These production companies typically employ one or more development executives responsible for the creation of new properties; a combination of a bonus and an ongoing royalty is paid to those executives responsible for successful shows.

Original game ideas from outsiders may be licensed with the promise of an ongoing royalty, plus a small upfront payment, if necessary, to close the deal. If the outsider is essential to the concept or to the show's success, then he or she may be retained as a consultant or hired as a member of the program's staff. Many of the game shows seen on cable networks are developed and produced in-house. A staff producer takes charge of creating the show and presents the format to network executives. He or she then refines the game, prepares a budget, hires a staff, and goes into production. If the program is especially successful, those associated with the production may receive raises, bonuses, or new opportunities within their companies. Ownership of the show and its concept is almost always retained by the cable network.

Few original game-show concepts succeed. Most game shows are based on successes from other media, or on vintage game shows that were successful in the past. *Where in Time Is Carmen Sandiego?* (PBS) is based on a computer game. *The Price Is Right* (CBS) and *Jeopardy!* (syndication) are based on shows from the 1960s.

The 1990s have been a difficult period for game show producers, and many have left the business. For a while, in the 1980s, inexpensive games filled many of the daytime slots on USA Network and on other cable networks, but in the 1990s, there are almost no network game shows, just a few superhits in syndication, and the occasional game show as a specialty item on MTV *(Singled*

Out), Nickelodeon *(Legends of the Hidden Temple, GUTS)*, or Lifetime *(Supermarket Sweep, Debt)*. The Game Show Network has also been slow to grow; apart from wraparounds and contests, this cable and satellite network shows old game-show reruns whose appeal is far more limited than, say, old sitcoms.

GAME SHOW NETWORK

The Game Show Network debuted in December 1994. The network has not released subscriber numbers, but they're low. The key asset here is a library of 49,000 game show episodes of very popular series of the past: *Password, The Newlywed Game, The Dating Game, Match Game, Family Feud, Joker's Wild, Card Sharks, Beat the Clock,* and so on. In original programming, the emphasis is on wraparounds for old shows, and some interactive programming in which viewers can win prizes. Game shows from around the world are shown on weekends. The network is owned by Sony Pictures.

GAME SHOWS IN OTHER COUNTRIES

In an era when few game shows are on U.S. schedules, the genre is thriving outside the U.S. The programs are inexpensive to produce (it's possible to shoot an entire week's shows in a single day, with only one star salary). Some formats are developed locally, but many are purchased from companies that not only specialize in the sale of format rights, but set up the show with a local company as well.

Pearson All American is one such company; it owns the rights to *Let's Make a Deal,* and all of the Goodson properties, including *Family Feud* and *The Price is Right.* KingWorld works *Wheel of Fortune* and *Jeopardy!* internationally. Australia's Reg Grundy's *Sale of the Century* (which was licensed to the U.S. twice) and the U.K.'s Action Time, which produced more hours of television in 1996 than any other production company, are also leaders.

Pearson All American advertisements clearly state the appeal for a network: a tested and proven format, a team of experienced producers, and back-up and supervision from the show's original production team.

26

Talk Shows

A successful talk show is a result of two key ingredients: a performer that the audience wants to see, and a syndicator with real clout with local station groups.

Most talk shows are syndicated. *The Oprah Winfrey Show* is generally in the top five syndicated programs, the result of superb time slots, clearances in 99 percent of the U.S., and a host with spectacular talent and audience appeal. Talent is also the key ingredient in the success of *The Rosie O'Donnell Show,* a program whose format is based on talk shows from the 1960s. These are the only top twenty talk shows, and neither relies upon troubled relationships or outrageous issues to capture an audience. *Live! with Regis and Kathie Lee* is another successful talker that relies upon personality for ratings.

Talk shows, like other types of programs, tend to run in cycles. Outrageous people and their problems were important to the success of *Geraldo, Sally Jessy Raphael, Montel Williams, Jenny Jones,* and many other talk shows from the late 1980s and early 1990s.

Talk shows have been around since the early days of television. Production is not complicated, given the right host and a steady stream of interesting guests. Until recently, at least one station in each major market produced a daily talk show. In the 1980s and early 1990s, time slots for most local talk shows were taken by syndicated shows—higher ratings and lower production costs were the reasons why.

Syndicated talk shows began in the 1960s with personality-driven properties from Merv Griffin, Mike Douglas, and later, Phil Donahue.

Of the broadcast networks, only NBC has consistently emphasized daytime talk, once with David Letterman, and later with Leeza
Gibbons. FOX programmed an innovative 9:00 A.M. talk show,
FOX after Breakfast, but wasn't widely carried on affiliates, so it
was cancelled.

DEVELOPMENT OF A NEW SYNDICATED TALK SHOW

The process begins with a performer, a personality, preferably one
who is already well known ("pre-sold" in the lingo of syndication).
Rosie O'Donnell is now the classic example. Maury Povich and
Connie Chung are ideal examples.

Step two is the right production company. Multimedia, for
example, established its reputation with Phil Donahue, then made
a star of Sally Jessy Raphael.

Step three is a demo tape or pilot that shows the performer at
work. If the performer is an unknown, he or she would need to be
extraordinary—station groups have seen far too many talk show
demo tapes and pilots to be impressed by anything less than a new
Oprah Winfrey.

Step four is clearing the larger station groups. This is tough; the
best time slots already "belong" to established series. The trick here
is to find a series that is no longer a ratings success, and to offer a
viable replacement. This is where the syndicator's clout makes a
big difference.

Step five is to start production. A new episode must be produced
daily, though for convenience and budget reasons, two shows are
sometimes recorded in a single day. If the performer's schedule
or the budget is tight, a week's worth of programs can be produced
in two days.

TALK SHOWS ON BROADCAST AND CABLE NETWORKS

The term "talk show" somehow doesn't apply to the morning
programs on CBS, ABC, and NBC, but they are, essentially, talk
shows with some news segments. Similarly, "talk show" doesn't
seem to apply to the comedy-driven *LATE SHOW with David
Letterman,* or *The TONIGHT Show with Jay Leno,* but again, these
shows follow a long talk-show tradition. ABC's *Politically Incorrect*
and *Nightline* are also talk shows, but the comedy orientation of
the former and the disciplined news approach of the latter again
rattle the basic formula. The Sunday morning news programs on
ABC, CBS, and NBC are more clearly news talk shows. A talk show's
success is most dependent upon the star or stars of the show.

Donny and Marie Osmond, Roseanne, and Howie Mandel are the latest in a long series of well-known personalities who have hosted talk shows.

Guest are also critical. Booking the best possible guests is never easy, but it becomes more challenging during periods when many talk shows are in production—and compete for the same celebrity guests. According to *Electronic Media,* an industry trade magazine (Feb. 23, 1998), some 4,500 guest slots must be filled annually. The pool of major stars who are actively in promotional mode (and not on location or busy in long production days) does not expand, so competition grows fierce for the best bookings.

Many public television stations have been successful with late night talk shows. Typically produced on a lower budget than the programs seen on the commercial networks, these programs usually emphasize the art of conversation. Charlie Rose, for example, can be a superb conversationalist, and his one-on-one interviews with authors, scientists, performers, politicians, thinkers, and other smart people generally offer more depth than interviews seen on commercial television. But they're watched by a smaller audience.

Some cable networks program talk shows. MTV had one that worked with Jon Stewart for a few years. The Nashville Network and the religious networks have always programmed Mike Douglas—style talk shows. CNBC runs a prime-time talker with Charles Grodin, and CNN's prime-time staple has been *Larry King Live* for years. Once again, these programs are performer-driven, relatively low-budget, and usually feature longer conversations (which means a smaller staff because fewer guests need to be booked for each episode). Most cable networks prefer more elaborate productions, such as sitcoms, dramas, and even documentaries, to conversational television.

INTERNATIONAL MARKETPLACE

To the industry's great surprise, U.S. talk shows have proven popular outside the U.S. *The Oprah Winfrey Show,* for example, has been on the U.K.'s Channel 4 since 1992.

Talk shows are, of course, nothing new. The idea of placing an articulate person beside a guest or two, with or without an audience, has been around since the dawn of TV. The U.S. formula, in which the series is named for the talker, who is surrounded by an active audience, and whose topics are generally heated with social controversy, has allowed syndicators like Multimedia to build relationships with broadcasters in other countries. These two U.S.

firms work with local producers on aspects of the program, in much the same way that game show firms launch successful formats (see page 254).

Germany's RTL has been especially successful with its own talkers, each supplied by a production company: *Barbel Schafer, Ilona Christian* and *Hans Meiser* each have their own weekday afternoon one-hour series on the network. All achieve about a 30 share. On Pro7, there's *Arabella Kiesbauer,* who skews slightly younger than her competitor, *Schafer* at 2:00 P.M. daily.

Like game shows, talk shows are generally inexpensive to produce, and the right one can own a time slot for an extended period of years.

27

Religious Television

Religious broadcasting has always been a world apart from traditional television. It is broadcasting with a mission: generally, to spread the gospel. The support of this mission is frequently the job of the millions of people who watch religious programming, and contribute to its success by sending money to electronic churches. The movement is formidable and growing. Roughly 8 percent of commercially licensed television stations are full-time religious programmers. This number has doubled in the past decade, and does not reflect the even greater growth in domestic cable and in international broadcast and cable operations.

The history of religious broadcasting has its roots in traveling shows, typically held in tents and hosted by evangelists (the tradition of tent shows continues to this day). In 1923, the first "radio church" was formed; there was no physical building, only a microphone and listeners. By 1927, with the formation of the Federal Radio Commission (later, the FCC), it was clear that the U.S. intended to use radio mainly as a commercial medium, and that religious (and educational) broadcasters were not a significant part of the plan. Still, the religious broadcasters saw the medium as a gift from God to spread the Word. And so, an easy alliance came into existence: broadcasters selling airtime to religious organizations. Still, religious programming has managed to reach a huge audience: *The Lutheran Hour,* for example, reached 700 million people worldwide in the 1940s. Host Walter Maier was world-famous—the Billy Graham of his day. There were many others, some locally famous, some nationally known. Some were involved in scandals related to misappropriation of funds, even in those early days.

For most of its history, broadcast networks (first on radio, then on television) sometimes allowed religious broadcasters to buy time, and sometimes prohibited such purchases. Until the 1960s, networks maintained a certain number of hours on their weekly schedules for non-commercial programming; this "sustaining" time was provided free to various organizations, including religious broadcasters. By and large, broadcasters have not provided airtime to religious ventures without cost.

The syndicated radio model became more sophisticated with television: through individual donations, viewers paid for production and airtime, programs were produced and then physically shipped (or, in TV industry lingo of the time, "bicycled") from one station to the next. (Religious programming has not been the exclusive province of tele-evangelists. CBS broadcast *For Our Times* from 1948–88; in later years, only about one in four affiliates carried the program.) Another CBS program, *Lamp Unto My Feet,* was cancelled in 1978. In the 1970s, religious programming had found its stride: Jerry Falwell and Rex Humbard became very well known as television evangelists. Many others followed; hundreds of millions of dollars were collected by the (unregulated) broadcast missions, and, to no one's great surprise, by the 1980s, the news media had found abuses. Jim and Tammy Bakker took the fall; others cleaned up their act, the industry took self-regulatory action, and the flames died down for awhile.

The industry continued to grow. In an increasingly complex society, large numbers of people took comfort in religious programming, and supported the mission with increasingly large donations. The stereotype of an older woman, living alone on a fixed income, looking to Christ and Pat Robertson for solace and friendship, was only part of the story. Through the 1980s, many middle- and upper-class Americans became interested—and religious broadcasting became involved in political change, through the likes of Jerry Falwell's Moral Majority. By the early 1990s, stories about financial abuses periodically flared, but the machine was working. Money was generated from viewers to reach more viewers and to spread the Word, and the networks grew.

CBN

Pat Robertson is credited with changing the system. Along with HBO and Ted Turner, Robertson's *700 Club* was an early purchaser of satellite time. This not only circumvented the awkward system of shipping videocassettes, it dramatically increased the number of television stations that could receive the program. Early in its history, CBN was a traditional network; it owned about a dozen television stations. The promise of satellite technology changed CBN's approach.

The Christian Broadcasting Network, or CBN, is mostly a distribution system for *The 700 Club,* a news, talk and variety show with a Protestant perspective (in religious broadcasting "Christian" and "Protestant" are more or less synonymous; "Catholic" is another matter altogether). For more than two decades, *The 700 Club* has aired daily on The Family Channel, a venture once closely related to CBN (in fact, the network was formerly called CBN Cable). In order to reach viewers who do not subscribe to cable, CBN also purchases airtime on over 200 broadcast television stations to air *The 700 Club* and other CBN programming. The program reaches approximately 700,000 households daily (making it a moderately successful cable program by standards of commercial audience measurement, and quite a bit more so because of the targeted nature of its approach).

A series of animated Bible series, called *Superbook,* has been translated into 33 languages and has aired in over 70 countries. CBN is also a supplier of holiday specials.

CBN is also active outside the U.S. Middle East Television (METV) broadcasts Christian and family programming from south Lebanon; it reaches a potential audience of 11 million households in Israel, Jordan, Lebanon, Egypt, Syria, and Cyprus. CBN International broadcasts and cablecasts programming in the Far East, Canada, South America, Mexico, Africa, and Europe. In addition, CBN produces many special projects; a 1994 "blitz" in Romania and the Philippines was especially successful. In Zaire, in 1996, CBN aired eight consecutive nights of religious programming; nearly six million people watched, and two million prayed as new Christians. The same year, a South American "blitz" brought nearly six million people to the religion. The goal of CBN, simply, is to gain adherents—to spread the gospel and the word of Christ.

TRINITY BROADCASTING NETWORK (TBN)

TBN is the largest Christian network; it's seen on over 500 broadcast stations in the U.S. That fact can be misleading, though. The majority of TBN outlets are LPTV stations and, to a lesser extent, UHF stations. TBN has no outlet in, for example, New York City or Philadelphia. TBN does reach over 40 million U.S. households via broadcast television, and over 30 million via cable television. It is also distributed via DBS satellite (as of this writing, via the DiSH network).

The network is led by founders Paul and Jan Crouch.

TBN features a very broad mix of programming, from Christian music videos to marriage enrichment series, gospel music concerts, health and fitness programs, and so on. The network is also involved in the financing and distribution of Christian motion pictures. Both TBN and CBN attract mainstream stars to their specials and talk/variety programs; TBN's list runs heavily in the country music direction. The heart of TBN's programming is the individual television ministry.

Internationally, TBN Latino is set to launch, as is Brazil's Good News network (broadcasting in Portuguese).

ETERNAL WORD TELEVISION NETWORK (EWTN)

EWTN is a global Catholic network that reaches 55 million households in 38 countries (43 million in the U.S.). Led by Mother Angelica, the network launched an Asian feed in 1996, and, in the same year, switched from an SAP (second audio program) feed to a full-scale Spanish-language network.

Mother Angelica moved to Birmingham, Alabama, in 1962 to build a monastery. She and four other nuns supported themselves by selling fishing lures and peanuts. In the 1970s, she became an author, then a popular public speaker. In response to a local television station's plans to air a movie she considered blasphemous, she transformed a garage into a studio, and through individual, family and group gifts, EWTN has become a major international media concern. In addition to television, EWTN reaches a potential audience of 700 million people via radio, and millions more via the Internet.

EWTN's program schedule includes a considerable amount of teaching, daily prayer services, and the like. In addition, the network features talk shows, Saturday and Sunday morning and weekly afternoon children's programs and some variety specials.

OTHER RELIGIOUS NETWORKS

There are many other religious networks of varying size. Some are program producers who buy time on cable and broadcast stations, others are full-scale international television networks with radio and Web operations.

The Odyssey Channel consists of ACTS (American Christian Television System, the television arm of the Southern Baptist Convention) and VISN (Vision Interfaith Satellite Network, religious and family-oriented entertainment) in a channel-sharing arrangement.

It represents over 50 faiths including Judaism and some Eastern religions. The Odyssey Channel is a 24-hour, 7-day operation that reaches approximately 20 million cable households.

FamilyNet reaches 33 million households as a syndicated package for broadcast stations and via satellite. The network broadcasts 24 hours per day, but only a portion of that schedule is used by affiliates. INSP, or Inspirational Television, reaches over 10 million cable households with an advertiser-supported mix of religious and family programming.

OTHER MINISTRIES

Many of the best-known names in religious television operate ministries that purchase airtime from broadcast and cable networks. Robert Schuller's broadcasts from the Crystal Cathedral, Billy Graham's crusades, Dr. James Kennedy's Coral Ridge Ministries, and other established television entities balance the size of their airtime purchases with a sincere desire to reach as many souls as possible.

Each of these programs has a particular appeal. Schuller's morning worship program, for example, appeals to an upscale, sophisticated, educated constituency. Charles Stanley appeals to a more serious audience with his Bible teachings. Dr. James Kennedy emphasizes variety and music, wears robes, and presents his version of the teachings in a television-friendly format. Graham's congregation is enormous; for decades, he has set the standard in communicating with the average person.

Benny Hinn is one of many newer names. He's seen on TBN (and elsewhere). In Hinn's organization (according to a March 1997 CNN report), 40 people work four shifts to open over 15,000 letters per week, many containing donations, or responding to television offers for coffee mugs, autographed books, and other merchandise. Hinn claimed $33 million in sales in 1995, and $50 million in 1996. Hinn is not a network; he is a program producer and host who says, "It's not the money, it's the miracles that really matter." TBN airs programming from other ministries as well.

PUBLIC INTEREST PROGRAMMING AND NON-PROFIT STATUS

Although its transactional foundation is akin to home shopping—because on-screen personalities ask viewers to send them money—religious programming is often presented as a variation on programming in the public interest. There are two sides to this concept. On the one hand, as reported by CNN, religious broadcasting is "a $3.5 billion unregulated industry." On the other, many people who work in religious broadcasting are truly motivated to do God's will, to spread the gospel by reaching as many people as possible, and, of course, this requires cash.

The Evangelical Council for Financial Accountability is a self-regulatory group that represents organizations with over $5 billion in income (CNN's estimate was, in fact, off by one-third). Any organization with 501(c)(3) (non-profit) status and over $500,000 in either income or expenses is required to submit to an outside audit. The results of that audit are publicly available. There are more standards, all intended to protect the industry from further missteps. For example, the majority of board of directors' seats must be occupied by people who are neither family members nor employees.

28

Music Video

D espite its entertainment industry roots, music video is a form of promotional video—videos are made to sell records. Musical performances have been recorded on tape and film for decades, but it was not until the 1981 debut of MTV, that record companies had a platform for the visual exhibition of individual songs.

Record label executives may consult the artist, but ultimately decide which songs will be produced as music videos. This is a coordinated label effort; the video plays on MTV and elsewhere, the radio promotion staff pushes the song, and the album, hopefully, sells in large numbers.

Most record companies employ a small staff responsible for producing and promoting music videos. The production coordinator selects and modifies idea treatments from independent music-video production companies, determines the schedule and budget, and approves the key hiring and creative decisions. In many cases, the recording artist suggests the concept, and encourages the record company to hire a specific director and production company.

Most music videos cost between $50,000 and $150,000. Some cost as little as $5,000 or $10,000, and others have cost as much as $1.5 million. The artist, or the management company, may add to the production budget to pay for a well-known motion picture director, animation, or exotic location shooting.

Some music videos, notably those produced for artists who are popular locally or regionally, are produced by begging and borrowing, rather than by paying cash for crew, locations, props, performers, and so on (discounted rates and personal favors are commonplace). Many low-budget productions are financed by the artist as a tool for self-promotion. The video may be shown in local clubs, and sent to MTV and other outlets on the outside chance that the video will be programmed and seen by a large audience. The artist's management may also show the video to record companies as an incentive to sign the artist.

Record companies typically finance the production of music videos, with a healthy percentage of production costs charged back to the artist's royalty account and recoupable against CD sales. The advent of music video sales complicates matters, however: should production costs be recoupable against album sales or video sales? The present policy favors album sales, since "long form" videos (such as concert films) rarely break even.

EARNINGS FROM MUSIC VIDEO PRODUCTION

When the record company finances a video, it generally owns the copyright, and the right to exploit the video in all markets. The artist generally performs on the music video without receiving any additional fee; the artist may receive a small royalty from the sale of compilation videos, but only after recoupment of production costs. The production company and other creative contributors do not participate in these royalties, but may participate in royalties generated by the sale of home video compilations.

When a record or home video label releases a compilation of music videos, sales exceeding 200,000 units are common. With suggested list prices at $19.95 or less, royalties for the artists (at $4 per tape) can total up to $1 million for a single release. With ten songs on the tape, and a combined production cost *exceeding* $1 million, the artist may never see any home-video royalty income— since his or her deal with the record company usually allows the label to recoup production dollars *before* paying out royalties.

OUTLETS FOR MUSIC VIDEO

On cable television, MTV, VH1, Black Entertainment Television (BET), THE BOX (Video Jukebox), The Nashville Network, and Country Music Television (CMT) are regarded as the most important showplaces for music video. There are no regularly scheduled broadcast outlets for music videos. THE BOX reaches over 21 million households with a unique interactive pay-per-view music video service.

A few dozen production companies, based mainly in Los Angeles, New York City, and London, produce most of the videos seen nationally (many Latin music videos are produced in Miami and Los Angeles). Proximity to record labels, and to top-notch facilities and crews are the reasons why. Word-of-mouth recommendations, passed from one record company or artist to another, generate work for production companies; it also helps when their videos are seen in clubs and on television.

A music video production company is typically an alliance between a producer and a director. In the best of circumstances, the producer and director collaborate to develop the initial creative concept, later refining it by working directly with the artist, the artist's management, and the record label (each may have a different degree of involvement). Then the producer attends to the usual details—hiring crew, securing locations, and managing the budget. The director works with the performers, the choreographer (if there is to be any dance or specialized movement), the art director, and the wardrobe designer or supervisor. Most music videos are conceived, produced, and edited in about two to four weeks, from start to finish.

Rates and fees are negotiable. Mainstream production companies usually take 15 percent of each production budget for general overhead, plus 5 percent of the budget as the producer's fee, and 10 percent as the director's fee. A small, well-managed mainstream production company can produce between 15 and 20 music videos per year, with budgets in the $50,000–$100,000 range. Many smaller companies supplement their music video work with corporate/industrial videos, commercials, promos, and other assignments; the larger outfits have a virtual army of producers and directors, and turn out dozens of videos each year. For larger companies, short-form music video is rarely the sole source of income—many of them also produce long-form programs, usually concert performances or music video compilations with promotional clips added for home video release.

MTV

MTV debuted in August 1981. The target MTV viewer is 12–34 years old. Music video dominates the schedule, but MTV also programs weekly series and specials that build on the music culture. Recent hit series include *Singled Out,* a dating game show, and *Beavis and Butt-Head,* an animated series. *The State* is a sketch comedy series. The rock-and-roll equivalent of competition is covered by *MTV Sports. House of Style* covers fashion. *Week in Rock* is a weekly news show. Cutting-edge series like

Aeon Flux, with hard-edged animation, and the docu-adventure series *Road Rules* continue MTV's tradition of exciting visuals and road shows. *The Real World* is MTV's reality-based soap opera, now featuring seven people ages 18–24 who share a living space in London. Many programs on the schedule feature music videos within a particular genre, such as rap *(YO!);* new music *(Alternative Nation);* R&B, rap and hip-hop *(MTV JAMS);* and dance *(The Grind);* or special performances *(MTV Unplugged).* Most of the program schedule is filled with mainstream music videos hosted by VJs, but MTV has been schizophrenic in its approach to programming.

In an effort to broaden its base, MTV goes through phases when it emphasizes non-music programming. The network loses viewers who want MTV to show more music. When the network shows more music, viewers become bored and the network supplements music with original programming. The proper formula may not be within MTV's reach because it is reliant upon the music business and its ability to promote stars. In the era when Michael Jackson's *Thriller* was the biggest news in music, MTV was hot stuff. Those were the old days. In 1997, MTV had about 68 million households, just behind The Weather Channel. To put this another way, MTV is no longer a top-10 cable network.

MTV Latino debuted in October 1993. It's a Spanish-language network that features a mix of American and Latin music videos, plus regularly-scheduled series.

M2, another music video channel from MTV, debuted as a digital satellite service in August 1996.

VH1

VH1, an MTV Network, reaches 54 million households and targets ages 25-44. Most of the schedule is filled with mainstream music videos made by artists who appeal to an older audience. There are weekly shows for special genres like R&B *(Soul of VH1).* Programs featuring older music are also popular; these include *8-Track Flashback, VH1's Best of American Bandstand,* and *VH1 Archives.* There's a weekly movie *(VH1's Rock 'n' Roll Picture Show),* news cut-ins through the day (mostly music news), and some fashion programming.

CMT (COUNTRY MUSIC TELEVISION)

Now owned by CBS, CMT debuted in 1983 in the U.S., where its subscriber count is approximately 34 million households. The formula is straightforward: country music videos, all day and all night. The schedule is organized by series, but most of the series are music video showcases: *CMT Top 12 Countdown, The Signature Series* (classic music videos), *CMT Saturday Nite Dance Ranch* (dance videos).

CMT also operates a 24-hour network for Europe and another for Latin America. The network is currently seen in over 50 countries, and fed in three languages. The Spanish-language network incorporates Tejano and other popular music. The Brazilian network, CMT Brazil, is bilingual (Portuguese and English).

THE NASHVILLE NETWORK

Also owned by CBS (both networks were previously owned by Westinghouse and Gaylord; Westinghouse bought CBS and adopted its name, and then bought out Gaylord). The Nashville Network started in March 1983. It reaches about 66 million homes, programming from 9:00 A.M. until 3:00 A.M. Eastern Time. The cornerstone Saturday night show is *Grand Ole Opry Live,* now broadcast from TNN studios near the Opryland theme park. The prime-time series *Club Dance* is country music's version of *American Bandstand.* The highest-rated series is a variety show: *The Statler Bros. Show,* which features Crystal Gayle and Ronna Reeves as regulars. Variety is alive and well at TNN: *Prime Time Country,* produced by dick clark productions, combines music, comedy, and a tried-and-true formula that's rarely seen on other (broadcast or cable) networks. At least a quarter of the program schedule is devoted to music videos. Weekends are largely devoted to sports, like bass fishing and rodeo. Off-network series, such as *The Dukes of Hazzard,* have generated significant numbers of viewers in the desirable 18–34 years-old target.

BET

BET, short for Black Entertainment Television, started in January 1980, and currently reaches 44 million households in the U.S. The daily schedule is mostly music video programs: *Video Vibrations, Video Soul, Rap City, Caribbean Rhythms,* and *Jazz Central.* Some off-network comedies, such as *Sanford & Son* and *Benson,* are also featured. Weekends are a potpourri of music videos, gospel, shopping, and time leased for infomercials.

BET On Jazz started in 1996 and has about 1 million subscribers. Both networks, along with ACTION Pay-Per-View, are owned by BET Holdings, a public company.

OTHER MUSIC CHANNELS

Z Music Television is a Christian music network that debuted in March 1993. It reaches over 27 million homes through cable and broadcast television.

MuchMusic started in Toronto, Canada. The U.S. network is jointly owned by Chum Ltd. (CHUM is the Canadian television station where MuchMusic began) and Rainbow Program Holdings (owners of American Movie Classics and SportsChannel). Like CMT, the formula is entirely music, 24 hours a day, seven days a week.

29

Variety Shows and Specials

VARIETY AND MUSIC PROGRAMS

The development of a variety program is often an outgrowth of discussions between a network or syndicator and a celebrity performer (most often, a comedian or musician) or a producer who has a special vision or experience in a specific genre. If the program or series is to be based on the talents of a performer, he or she will generally work with a producer with a track record on similar programs.

Typically, the producer works with the performer to conceive the program format. The producer then assembles a creative team of writers, a director, and other personnel to develop the program. Often, some of these people have worked with the performer on past projects. The format is usually presented to the network programming executive(s) responsible for the project in a pitch meeting (see page 203) that is also attended by the producer's key creative contributors. At the meeting, the ideas are discussed in detail; the program executive raises issues and concerns, and the producer responds to the best of his or her ability. If the program suits the network's or syndicator's needs, an exclusive option to the property is negotiated, and the producer is paid to develop the program further. This development money usually pays for one or more sample scripts.

The next step is the production of a pilot program, or a limited series (for example, a four-week run). If the program is successful, the network or syndicator orders more episodes. And if, at any step during this process, the network decides to drop the project, the rights eventually revert back to the producer and/or performer (see page 208), who may sell it to another network or syndicator, sometimes after a prescribed period of time (or "hold-back") has elapsed.

Some variety programs do not require extensive development. Awards programs, for example, are frequently expansions of trade or industry banquets. A producer, or a representative from an industry association (such as the Songwriter's Hall of Fame), pitches the network or syndicator. The basic concept may be altered or embellished—adding entertainment segments and interviews with winners—but the process is straightforward. A producer is assigned to the project, and develops a format, a budget, and a list of celebrities who are likely to appear. If the network or syndicator believes the idea will be successful, the program is funded and produced. The network or syndicator typically retains the right to produce the program annually. Usually, the key to the success of an awards show is the underlying organization's ability to book big-name stars as presenters.

Programs featuring stand-up comedians are also developed in a straightforward fashion, and can be quite successful with the right performer. A producer usually works closely with a comedy club or promoter to develop a roster, which is approved by the network or syndicator. A budget is created and approved, the comedians and the staff are hired, and the program is produced and edited. Stand-up comedy series, seen on many cable networks in the 1980s and into the early 1990s, are no longer produced in quantity. There are specials, however.

Music programs generally require little creative development, although some with elaborate concepts call for as much develop-ment as a motion picture. For most music programs, such as concerts, once the act is selected, most of the development and pre-production time goes to choosing locations, lining up equip-ment, building scenery, and arranging travel schedules. Music series are, most often, staged in a single location with different performers each week (*The Grand Ole Opry, MTV Unplugged,* and *Austin City Limits* are three classic examples).

VARIETY SPECIALS

Entertainment specials are based on the talents of a particular celebrity performer, a character license (*Peanuts*), or a special event (Emmy Awards, the Miss America Pageant).

The development of a celebrity special is relatively straightforward. The project may begin with either the celebrity (and his or her management team), a network, or a production company. All three parties meet and agree upon a basic format that will showcase the celebrity's particular appeal. The production company works with the celebrity to develop the format in more detail, submits a budget, receives input from the network, redevelops the concept, reworks the budget, and makes a deal. There is no fixed format for a celebrity special—it can be a concert, a live performance, a magazine show, a variety show, or any other format that suits the performer's unique style.

In some cases, the special may be intended simply to target a specific audience segment. In other cases, the special is used to test the celebrity's appeal—in effect, as a form of market research—and may in fact be a pilot for a series.

Virtually all broadcast and cable networks program celebrity specials. Obviously, the appeal of the celebrity to the network's target audience is the most important part of the sale, but the track record of the creative team, and the creative concept for the special, are also important elements.

SPECIAL EVENTS (AWARDS SHOWS, PAGEANTS, PARADES)

Most awards shows are television staples with histories counted in decades: the Emmy Awards, the Academy Awards, the Tony Awards, the People's Choice Awards, the Golden Globe Awards, and the Grammy Awards. The Oscars are the only consistently excellent performer: ratings generally hover around a 30 (figure 970,000 households × 30 equals 29 million households), with a remarkable 50 share (50 percent of all households currently watching television are tuned to the Oscar telecast). The Emmy and Grammy Awards perform about half as well. The Tonys, which celebrate Broadway, generate only about a quarter of the Oscars' audience—and they've been experiencing a steadily downward trend for a decade.

Launching a new awards program requires three essential elements: (1) a high level of national interest in the subject of the awards ceremony; (2) a promise of major celebrity presenters and award recipients; and (3) a major national institution that does not stand to benefit directly from the airtime. (Most awards shows are presented by academies or associations, not by, for example, magazines.) Few ideas are really new, and many awards ceremonies have been tried at least once—if it's not currently on the air, there's probably a reason why. Budgets are comparatively high for awards specials, and many programmers feel that there are enough awards shows on the air each year. In sum, awards shows are a tough sell.

New pageants are also a tough sell. There are presently two pageant organizations with network exposure for their pageants:

Miss America and Miss USA/Miss Universe. Each show is the pinnacle of a year-long search that begins at the local and state levels, and each one is as much a promotional machine for affiliated products and services as it is a television program.

The difficulty with launching a new pageant is, quite simply, convincing a programmer, a network, or an advertiser of the need for yet another pageant. The present group of network pageants is perceived as satisfactory; efforts at syndicated pageants (Miss Teen USA) missed, mainly because of the inability to get clearances on top stations in good time slots.

Parades suffer from similar problems. Those that have been established for decades remain on the air, such as the Rose Parade (associated with the Rose Bowl) and Macy's Thanksgiving Day Parade—but most programmers consider new ventures risky. Parades seem to play best on holidays, since they run several hours and require substantial breaks with the regular program schedule. Local parades and related events are sometimes covered by local television stations; in Philadelphia, for example, the popular Mummer's parade is covered for many hours by a network affiliate. This type of extensive local coverage becomes less common every year, as stations cut back on operations.

Truly special events, such as the anniversary of the Statue of Liberty's arrival, are judged on their ability to win extremely large numbers of viewers and secure sponsorship. Since they are enormously expensive to produce, big events must deliver extremely high ratings in order to be cost-effective. While every such event is risky, programmers try to limit their risk by working only with producers experienced in the form—and by having large celebrity rosters.

30

Home Shopping

irect-response television is not a new idea. Since the 1950s,
direct marketers have aired television commercials with
telephone numbers for orders taken directly from viewers. The
business changed rather dramatically in the mid-1980s as new
cable television channels were developed as 24-hour retailers.
These channels soon expanded beyond domestic cable television,
and are now seen via direct broadcast satellite, and on local television stations. Program-length commercials, or infomercials, are
now regularly seen on broadcast and cable television channels.
Direct-response television is a worldwide business, a relatively
new industry positioned to benefit from the convergence of
television, the Internet, and telephone development.

SHORT-FORM

Since the start of television, many stations have allotted a percentage
of their unsold commercial time to direct marketers. For decades,
this was a relatively undistinguished retail category dominated by
inexpensive gadgets, but as the television business has matured,
this category has evolved into a serious form of direct marketing.

The cost of media time for a 30- or 60-second spot is, of
course, considerably less than the cost of an entire half hour. The
format is ideal for certain types of products: typically those with
strong brand recognition, a message that is easily understood, and
a price point around $20. Time-Life has mastered the form with
books and book series on home repair and many other topics.
Sports Illustrated and other Time Warner magazines also use this
format very effectively for magazine subscriptions. Some types of

gadgets, particularly those concentrated in specific product categories such as automotive care, also tend to succeed.

Marketers and television stations work together in two ways. The marketer may simply purchase commercial time; in many deals, the marketer purchases a large amount of commercial time at a very low price. The station then schedules the commercials at times when they cannot otherwise sell commercial time at a premium or normal price. Marketers may also share revenues with stations. In some cases, the station takes most of the risk and receives most of the reward (revenues); in others, the station offers a discounted rate in accordance with revenue potential. Stations are sometimes paid on the basis of number of phone calls received by the telemarketer.

PER-INQUIRY

Per-inquiry (P.I.) advertising provides suppliers with a low-cost means of marketing their products, at the same time allowing stations to transform unsold commercial time into revenues.

The deal begins with a supplier, typically a manufacturer or distributor, who identifies a product suitable for this specialized form of direct marketing. The product should be priced in the $20–$50 range or higher, and it should appear special or unique, the sort of product that might not be found in retail stores. The supplier produces a commercial, hiring a broker to place the commercial on cable networks and local broadcast stations. The broker typically receives about 5 percent of the product's selling price.

The cable network or local station does not receive a cash payment in exchange for the airtime. Instead, the commercial is shown, and the network or station receives a percentage of each sale attributable to its activities, usually 25 to 35 percent of the selling price.

When a viewer calls the 800 number on the screen, he or she reaches a telemarketing clearinghouse, a firm hired by the supplier to take orders. This firm charges the supplier one fee for each call for information, a higher fee for each call resulting in a sale, and a still higher fee for each call that can be transformed into an "upsale"—a sale of multiple or additional products. The price per call is typically $1 to $3, though these figures vary depending upon the size of the firm, the time spent per call, the number of orders, and so on.

The supplier receives customer payments and an accounting from the telemarketing firm, then passes the payments and records to the broker. The broker deducts the agreed-upon percentage, then pays the station or cable network. Stations and networks are dependent upon accurate, honest record keeping for their income, so they are likely to require approval of the telemarketing company, or, in some cases, insist upon using a particular company for this purpose. Since the station owns the airtime, it is in a position to force this decision.

P.I. marketing generally requires testing. Several commercials may be produced, for example, before one proves to be successful; several venues may be tried before finding the one or two cable networks most suitable for a particular product. Television stations, whose audiences are broader and less segmented than cable networks, usually start new P.I. spots during the overnight period, then schedule the most profitable ones in late-evening and early-morning time slots. Stations are under no obligation to schedule the spots at all, and may program them in any manner that seems reasonable.

INFOMERCIALS

An infomercial is typically a half-hour program created to sell a product or service directly to consumers. In theory, the concept should become a mainstream format for all types of consumer and business products. With several notable exceptions, the industry has gone for the short-term bucks: consumer products that promise to make viewers rich, thin, or beautiful. This formula works, but it reduces a potentially huge industry to a mass-market format that caters to the lowest common denominator. For those who point to a billion dollars in sales, others point out the larger untapped potential.

Infomercials were made possible in 1984, when the FCC's regulation limiting commercial time to 16 minutes per hour was eliminated. Two other factors contributed to the early development of infomercials. First, consumers were becoming comfortable with the idea of ordering products through 800 numbers, and paying for them with a credit card. Second, there were dozens of new cable television channels. Most lacked the funding needed to acquire or produce compelling programming for fringe times (such as Saturday mornings), so commercial time for those periods was inexpensive.

Producers and distributors of infomercials began buying available time, most often on Saturday and Sunday mornings, and as the system started working, they migrated toward bulk purchases of large amounts of time on many stations and networks. This provided the distribution system, but it also required a considerable upfront cash commitment. Infomercial distributors purchase nearly a half-million dollars in advertising time from local broadcasters annually. Lifetime averages approximately 40 hours per week of paid programming time. Comedy Central, The Discovery Channel, The Family Channel, The Sci-Fi Channel, The Learning Channel, and USA Network are among the many cable networks that sell time to infomercial distributors—most often, on Saturday and Sunday mornings, overnights, and on some weekday mornings. Prices for media time have consistently increased. In 1994, the cost for Saturday 8:00 A.M.–9:00 A.M .on USA Network was $25,000, and by 1995, it was $40,000.

In order to maximize the return on this risk, infomercial companies became sophisticated in their understanding of the marketplace. A single infomercial might be tested in several markets—for example, each with a slightly different offer such as different price points. At $49.95, the beauty system might be perceived as too costly, but at $39.95 with two free refills, the value proposition might be right. The cost of television time is a big expense, but follow-up sales to customers acquired via television are not nearly as expensive. Customers of the same beauty care system might call an 800 number to order refills (this is "inbound telemarketing"). Or, an outbound telemarketing service might call customers who purchased the system with a special offer. Outbound telemarketing to the company's own customer list can be extremely profitable.

Celebrity endorsements can be significant, especially if the celebrity is sincerely committed to the product, as in the case of Victoria Principal, whose Principal Secret cosmetic and skin-care product line has earned $250 million in sales over a six-year period. Revlon's venture with Dolly Parton was more of a straight endorsement deal; Parton was reportedly paid $2 million upfront, and when the product did not succeed, the cost of abandoning the venture was quite high.

HOW THE INFOMERCIAL BUSINESS WORKS

The two key parts of the infomercial business are product and distribution. Finding the right product—and assuring a constant flow of viable products to support the large-scale media purchases— requires considerable outreach to the community of inventors, small-time product shops, and, of course, large companies looking for new ways to market.

In the case of a small-time operator, the pitch is made to the buyer at a large distribution company, such as Guthy-Renker. The decision to work with a product is based on a combination of objective and subjective criteria.

The cost of goods and the potential profit margin are critical. A low cost of goods and a high retail price are, of course, a good combination. But a relatively small margin may be acceptable if the product lends itself to continuity sales (sales to customers acquired through television, who may purchase refills, additional parts, etc.). The product category also affects the decision. Fitness, health, and beauty products have been among the most successful in this retail channel. Self-improvement products related to earning power have also worked; Anthony Robbins' Personal Power audio and video cassettes are among Guthy-Renker's best properties, earning about $250 million since 1990.

The infomercial business is hits-driven. Like the book and movie businesses, the hits more than compensate for the flops. Only one in four infomercial products earns back its investment in media and production. But when a product succeeds, it can make a tremendous amount of money. Some hits are predictable, some are surprises. The Psychic Friends Network, for example, generated some $200 million per year in $4.95-per-minute telephone calls (the average call lasted over fifteen minutes).

A small-time operator can earn a great deal of money, with minimal upfront investment, by selling out to a big infomercial company. The infomercial company takes the risk, but also reaps the rewards. The small-time operator may receive a per-unit royalty, but typically loses the rights to manufacture and market the product (and if a product succeeds, it may also be sold through mail-order catalogs, on the Web, and in retail stores). If the small-time operator takes some risk, then he or she shares in the rewards. Every deal is different.

A big-time operator would be more likely to treat infomercial marketing as a secondary channel, perhaps a way to introduce a new product line, or to expand distribution into a new market. A company that produces products mostly for the retail marketplace might, for example, make a deal with an infomercial company for direct marketing. Guthy-Renker's distribution in China and Japan is relatively strong; a U.S. products company without Asian distribution might test the market by simply selling the product via television.

The two largest companies in the infomercial business are Guthy-Renker and National Media, each with sales exceeding $300 million per year. HSN Direct (part of the Home Shopping Network operation) is also a big player, with a direct (and valuable) link to a 24-hour cable shopping network. There are, however, many smaller companies (many reputable, some not). TV Tye has succeeded by working with large corporations, such as Apple Computer. There are many infomercial producers who have worked for Guthy-Renker and National Media who also handle the whole infomercial package, from product selection and media buying to fulfillment (many of these steps can be sub-contracted). AMI (Alternative Marketing Inc., now merged with First Madison Communications), for example, succeeded with Blue Coral, an automotive care product (the pitchman was Dennis Weaver), and with exercise equipment promoted by Bruce and Kris Jenner. A smaller infomercial firm may handle a project alone, or with partners, or if the project is likely to require a substantial upfront investment, may pitch the project to a larger firm, such as National Media.

In addition to its success in the U.S., National Media has emphasized international growth, broadcasting over 1,500 hours of programming on five continents each week. Programs include *Amazing Discoveries, Ask Mike, Novedades Incredibles,* etc. A joint venture with Japan's Mitsui has helped the company expand into dozens of Asian and Pacific Rim markets with broadcasters who have a keen understanding of local marketing.

TELEVISED SHOPPING SERVICES

Most cable systems offer at least one televised shopping network. These networks are unusual because every minute of airtime is used to sell products. And as the Internet evolves, these already-successful television channels may become significant cyber-merchandisers as well.

HISTORY

Although there are some scattered roots going back to the 1950s, the contemporary home shopping business began in 1982, when the owner of WWQT-AM, a radio station in Clearwater, Florida, accepted merchandise in place of cash to settle an advertiser's debt. The station offered the merchandise for sale, over the air; listeners called in to order, and drove to the station to pick up their purchases. Seeing more than a local radio gimmick, entrepreneurs leased time on a local cable system and discovered that the idea worked in the local Tampa Bay market. After considering expansion to other Florida markets, the venture instead rented satellite time and, in 1985, went national as the Home Shopping Network (HSN).

Within a year or so, there were 30 television shopping services. QVC debuted in November 1986.

In 1987, the Home Shopping Network expanded beyond cable and began purchasing UHF stations. In the same year, QVC made a deal for the exclusive right to represent Sears products. This was followed by JCPenney's entry into the field. JCPenney first bought an existing service called Value Television Network, then re-launched it as the Shop Television Network (STN), which was in turn revamped as JCPenney Shopping Network before ceasing operations. The recent history of HSN involves a conglomeration of the USA Network, The Sci-Fi Channel, Universal Television, Silver-King's station group, and the Home Shopping Network—all under the management of a company called USA Networks.

After a late 1980s shake-out, three networks remained. QVC is the industry leader, with approximately 60 million cable subscribers, followed by HSN, reaching over 70 million households through a combination of cable TV (over 50 million households), satellite, and broadcast television stations.

MERCHANDISING

The reality and the stereotype are quite different. While shopping channels were once dependent upon porcelain figures and costume jewelry, the range of products offered is enormously varied.

QVC's range is the widest in the industry. In home furnishings, the network has sold handmade Oriental rugs, Italian chairs, fine linens, and high-quality down products from the network's own Northern Lights brand. Jewelry has always been a popular cable shopping category; QVC's 1996 sales of $450 million were due, in part, to the network's top position in worldwide gold jewelry retailing. Eighteen-karat gold is a strong seller for two reasons: the network's volume discount permits low prices, and 18-karat gold is not easily found in stores. In fact, jewelry accounts for nearly one-third of all QVC's programming. Fashion, or more accurately, women's clothing and accessories, is also a significant contributor. QVC's many proprietary product lines and joint ventures with well-known apparel and accessory brands include Denim & Co., Urban Wool, Legacy Legwear, etc. There's a parallel in beauty and health products: nationally known brands are sold, and so are celebrity product lines from Susan Lucci, Victoria Principal, and, for men, George Hamilton. In the food and cooking category, there are many stories of cookbooks selling thousands of copies, even tens of thousands of copies, in minutes. In addition, QVC sells steaks, hams, seafood, spices, cakes, gourmet chocolates . . . the list goes on. There's a show dedicated to the Warner Brothers Studio Store. When the Green Bay Packers won the Super Bowl XXXI championship, QVC broadcast live from the studio and the stadium—and sold 30,000 caps in 20 minutes. Consumer electronics products, from digital cameras to VCRs to personal computers to WebTV consoles are among the products positioned mainly for male viewers.

As the network has grown, QVC's audience has become segmented. Its core viewers seem to be women in households earning over $40,000 per year, generally suburban or in fringe cities, but the demographics do tend to change depending on what's being sold. *NFL Team Shop,* for example, is scheduled immediately before ABC's *Monday Night Football.* QVC has focused considerable energy on expanding its reach beyond the core audience: by sponsoring sporting events; touring all 50 states in search of local merchandise (peanut brittle from Virginia); through special events, such as the Presidential Inauguration in 1997 (as the official national retailer, they sold medallions), and The 1996 Olympic Games Showcase; museum tours (Philadelphia Museum of Art); and a holiday shopping spree at Harrod's of London. In July 1995, QVC received over 17,000 orders as it debuted Microsoft's Windows 95 ($1.5 million in sales—plus an enormous boost in credibility from many viewers who had never taken QVC seriously before). In December of the same year, over $8 million in Packard-Bell computers was sold in just two hours. The network's first $10 million day happened on August 17, 1991, less than five years after its debut; the first $20 million day occurred on January 24, 1996. One suggestion of QVC's awesome retailing power: Kellogg's debuted its Cocoa Frosted Flakes on the network, and sold 3,000 boxes of cereal in less than ten minutes.

HSN's approach is more focused. Their market is 85 percent female, and average income is somewhat lower-generally in the $30,000–$60,000 range, with a considerable percentage in the $30,000–$45,000 range. About 40 percent of the network's sales are jewelry, and 10 percent more are cosmetics. Like QVC, HSN sometimes capitalizes on special events, such as The Super Show/97, the enormous sports and fitness trade show (with host Suzanne Somers, Jake Steinfeld of *Body by Jake* fame, and work-out expert Kathy Smith and other celebrities brightening up the presentation); a 1996 White House holiday tour also drew large numbers of viewers. Noted antique and collectibles experts Ralph and Terry Kovel hosted 1996's Collectible Day.

TRUST, CUSTOMER SERVICE AND INFRASTRUCTURE

One key to success in direct-response television marketing (DRTV) is trust. Viewers must trust the people who are selling the products on television. QVC's Kathy Levine, who has been with the service since opening night in 1986, excels in jewelry and fashion presentations; Bob Bowersox, who was also at QVC for the debut, is associated with cooking (his first cookbook—*In the Kitchen with Bob*—sold 155,000 copies in a single day), and also with high-tech gadgets and collectibles. Customers interact directly with the on-camera hosts through telephone conversations, and a relationship is built—not just for the person on the phone, but for other viewers who identify with what's being said. These relationships enhance the trusting relationship between customer and retailer.

Another key to success is customer service. Once the relationship is built, it must be maintained and nurtured by an enormous back-room customer service operation. Many products are carefully tested before they're approved by the network. Customer service representatives are available 24 hours a day to answer consumer questions about products, handle credit issues, and follow up on lost merchandise and returns. A staff of more than 2,000 people is employed in order entry (taking orders by phone) and fulfillment (working in the warehouse or shipping)—and this figure increases during the busy fourth quarter of the year.

The staff required to operate a shopping channel is large in comparison with other television channels, but is consistent with a firm that does national direct marketing. QVC and HSN each employ between 3,000 and 5,000 people.

More than 100 buyers visit trade shows, factories, and other facilities, identify products appropriate for the distribution channel, and make quantity deals. The merchandise is then shipped to the network's warehouse, and programmers schedule segments to sell the merchandise. If the product is an exclusive for a short period, it may go on the air within days. If the product requires the production of a special videotape to explain its unique features or operation, several weeks may pass before it is scheduled. Approximately 10 to 12 products are shown per hour.

Other departments include inventory control, MIS, finance, affiliate relations, merchandising, and broadcasting. Using QVC as a model (HSN is similar), the broadcasting department is headed by an executive vice president who also serves as executive producer. A vice president of talent supervises 18 performers working three- to four-hour shifts each day, three to four days each week. The TV chief engineer performs the traditional function. Several managers take care of specific production tasks— control room operations, post-production (production of promos for QVC, other cable channels, and for affiliates), and backstage operations (displaying products)—and there is also usually a coordinating producer. Including creative, supervisory, and technical staff, the production department consists of roughly 100 people—a small number, due to production efficiencies like robotic cameras.

DOING BUSINESS WITH A HOME SHOPPING NETWORK

With 24 hours a day to fill, the home shopping networks are constantly seeking out new products that solve a problem, lend themselves to presentation on television, and generate audience interest. QVC frequently works with state commerce commissions to set up exhibitions of potential products from smaller operations. TV Direct is one of a growing number of small companies that essentially agent a product for a fee (10 to 15 percent of sales). Networks have become very sophisticated in their product selection process; it is not unusual for a network buyer to ask detailed questions about manufacturing, financing, and other close-to-the-bone issues. There's a reason: the network's reputation is on the line with every product sold.

Since price points and unit sales vary, it's difficult to project a typical scenario for product sales. Most products tend to be priced in the $15 to $100 range, and a successful product sells several thousand units during and after a five-minute program segment. It's no longer unusual to see stories about products priced at $29.95 selling 5,000 units in a single day—a boon for a small supplier, and good sales for a larger one.

The financial relationship between cable operators and the televised shopping networks is unique, and unlike the relationship for any other program service. The cable operator receives approximately 5 percent of the gross collected revenues within the zip codes in their service area. Whereas another cable service might charge its cable operator a fee for each subscriber, the televised shopping network can be a small profit center for the operator.

In 1996, QVC reached approximately 60 million households and averaged $30.67 per household, for a total of nearly $2 billion in sales.

INTERNATIONAL DRTV

Direct response television is not limited to the U.S. Infomercial companies purchase media time and produce commercials throughout Europe, Asia, and Latin America. QVC has a joint venture with BSkyB in the United Kingdom and with Telemercado in Mexico, and operates a network in Germany as well. Quantum, a division of National Media, operates in dozens of countries. (For a discussion of the legal rules governing television retailing, see page 434.)

INTERNET SHOPPING

Internet shopping is still a relatively small business, but it's not difficult to understand its potential. The home shopping networks are uniquely positioned to take advantage of Internet growth— they already have enormous back-room operations, a constant flow of new products, experienced buyers, an understanding of pricing and merchandising for the screen (as opposed to the store), and, perhaps most important, they're already selling products. QVC operates iQVC (www.qvc.com), a general merchandise retailer, and HSN owns ISN, the Internet Shopping Network (www.isn.com), which specializes in computer products. iQVC reports more than a million hits per day, making the site one of the most popular on the Internet.

31

Production Financing and Deal-Making

For most producers, the most challenging aspect of television production is obtaining financing. Even at the most basic level, production costs money. Determining how much money is needed, and where that money will come from, is a skill that every independent producer eventually develops.

PREPARING A PRODUCTION BUDGET ESTIMATE

A production budget is a fairly complicated, often very detailed, estimate of costs. The first column, organized by category (talent, staff, editing, etc.), is further defined in sub-categories (producer, associate producer; off-line editing, tape stock for editing, etc.). The next column lists unit costs ($1,500 per week for a producer; $300 per hour for online editing). The next is a factor (10 weeks of a producer's time; 20 hours of on-line editing), and the next, the product of multiplying unit cost by factor. Then, there are supplemental costs (taxes and benefits on employees; sales tax on tape stock). Finally, each line item is summarized. Summaries are calculated for each main category (talent, staff, editing, etc.), and brought down to a bottom line. Then, contingency and profit (or markup) are added to find the grand total.

A cover sheet summarizes budget categories, followed by individual sheets with detail. Reference numbers on each line item are common; this number is written on every check and on every purchase order, making budget reconciliation less of a challenge.

There are some differences between videotape and film budgets, and for series and one-shot projects, but the basic concepts apply to all budgets.

TALENT

AFTRA or SAG rates should be used to calculate the talent budget; if the production is non-union, then lower rates may apply. For union performers, pension and welfare, plus various employment taxes, must be added. In addition, some productions may involve re-use payments. The initial payment typically buys only one or two plays of the program within a specified period. Performers receive additional compensation for additional plays. These costs are sometimes included in the production budget, and sometimes assumed by the network or distributor as part of the price for deciding to continue to run an old program or series. For more about talent payments, see Chapter 45.

MUSIC

There are several types of costs associated with the use of music. If the music already exists, then there are costs for the rights to the composition and the recording. If the music is original, then there are costs associated with composition, arranging, copying, hiring musicians, and renting a recording studio to record, mix, and edit the music. Deals with musicians inevitably involve complicated payment schemes set forth in the rules and regulations that guide members of the American Federation of Musicians (AFM). For more about the use of music in television production, see Chapter 39.

RIGHTS

Two types of rights are generally included in this part of the budget: rights to a property (such as a book or a life story; see page 204), and rights to include still pictures, video clips, and film clips. This material is licensed from picture and film archives who operate with more or less standard rates (though it's possible to negotiate discounts for large amounts of material).

STAFF

The production staff typically accounts for at least one-quarter and as much as half of the budget. This staff list should include the following people: executive producer, producer, associate producer ("AP"), production assistant ("PA"), writer, researcher, secretary, and director. (Some budgets also include associate director and ("AD") stage manager here; others include these line items in the technical or studio section.) Technical and studio personnel are not, usually, part of the staff. Most rates are negotiable, based on current marketplace conditions. Some staff members, such as the writer and director, may be hired under a union agreement (DGA for director, WGA for writer).

There are two challenges here. The first is to project the actual tasks to be done and the people who will be needed to get the work done. One writer? Two associate producers? Will three PAs be enough? The second challenge is to correctly estimate the amount of time that the entire project will take, and the number of days or weeks to be budgeted for each staff member. A grid showing scheduled days or weeks running along the top or bottom and the staff positions running up and down the side may be useful. A checkmark in each box shows who is working each week. By counting up the checkmarks, it's easy to budget staff needs (this grid is also useful for planning office space and related expenses).

DESIGN AND STAGING

The "design and staging" category is usually more difficult to esti-mate, particularly if the program is not fully developed when the budget is being prepared. The biggest component of design/staging expenses is the cost of building—and, to a lesser extent, renting—set elements. The set designer, usually working for a flat fee, is listed in this category. Set items can include the costs of trucking the set from the shop to the studio, maintaining it over the course of a series, and storing it between seasons. Other elements that may be included in the design/staging section are prop construction and/or purchase, graphic artists and art materials, computer graphics, wardrobe, makeup, lighting design and direction, stagehands, grips, gaffers, carpenters, electricians, and prop specialists.

STUDIO AND LOCATION FACILITIES

A studio is rented by the half-day, day, week, or month, at a negotiated rate. Typically, a studio rental includes a modest com-plement of lights, one or two cameras, some microphones, floor monitors, a working control room and access to two or three tape machines. Other items are rented, either from the facility or from an equipment rental firm. Many studios publish rate cards; typi-cally, these rates are paid by advertising agencies who rent by the day. For television programs, whose needs are often more com-plicated and longer-term, rate cards are often a starting point for negotiations.

Shooting locations are typically rented by the hour or by the day. When a production location is in a public place, a permit from local authorities is required—and this permit also costs money. A state or local film commission can help make the necessary arrangements.

Most remote television shoots involve the use of a truck, a kind of control room on wheels. There are essentially two types of trucks: small and big. Small trucks are usually vans (not mini-vans, but full-sized vans, like an old VW mini-bus). They typically include a small audio console, a switcher for one or two cameras, a tape machine or two, and a camera or two. A big truck, like the one you might see in the parking lot at a major-league baseball game, is a full-scale network-quality control room on wheels that can accommodate a half-dozen cameras, a small room full of tape machines, and so on. Shoots involving a big truck typically involve many additional costs, from special microphones to additional cameras. Non-technical costs must be considered as well, such as security personnel, crowd handlers, trailers for use as offices or dressing rooms, transportation to and from the location, communications equipment (walkie-talkies, cellular phone service, wired phone service), even a power generator if sufficient power is not available nearby.

Technical and staging personnel should be included in the location or studio budget. Every crew member should be listed separately, with the number of hours/days to be worked and an appropriate estimate of overtime. (Union contracts, described in Chapter 45, detail the situations where time-and-a-half, double-time, and the coveted[1] golden-time payments must be made.) Alternately, the supplier of the studio or mobile facility may package the equipment and crew for a single daily price (plus overtime).

PRODUCTION SUPPORT

The production budget should also provide money for catering. On location, if dining facilities are not within minutes of the shooting site, the producer usually saves money by providing meals to cast and crew (since the cost of delays tends to be more than the cost of food). Whether production is on location or in the studio, the budget should include breakfast (rolls, bagels, pastries, coffee, tea)—and lunch and dinner, for production personnel who cannot leave the facility for a proper meal break (an actor in makeup, a writer who must rewrite before afternoon production, a production assistant who must make copies of what the writer has written, etc.). On a complicated production, any pilot, and the start of any new series, money should be budgeted for late dinners and for overnight stays in a hotel near the production office.

---

1 From the crew person's perspective, "coveted" is the appropriate term. From the producer's perspective, "terrifying" might be better.

There are many other items related to shooting that fall under the catch-all category of "production support": miscellaneous equipment rentals, petty cash, on-site office expenses, local transportation, audience/crowd handling, gifts/flowers for cast members, the end-of-shoot or "wrap" party (now quite common), and so on.

PRODUCTION OFFICE

The costs of running an office must be calculated to include not only space rental, but also office equipment, furniture, copying, supplies, shipping, phone usage, local transportation, and related items. Some of these can be difficult to estimate, but past experience and a few phone calls to vendors can help sharpen the estimate.

TRAVEL AND SUBSISTENCE

Most productions involve some travel—tickets (air, train), hotel/lodging, local travel (cabs, rental cars), and per diems (meals, personal incidentals) can mount up. A complicated travel plan might require a separate grid altogether, similar to the one prepared to estimate the number of staff weeks.

BUSINESS EXPENSES

There are four principal types of business expenses. The first is insurance, including Errors and Omissions coverage (see page 365) and general casualty/ loss/ liability coverage. The second business expense is accounting. On a simple project, an outside accountant or auditor can review the invoices and checkbook, and prepare a final accounting. A larger-scale production may require a full-time accountant or bookkeeper. (If the project is produced by a studio, or other large company, the accounting department may be able to cover the task. But the pace of television production is often faster than the pace of accounting offices—many checks, some written on verbal agreements, can drive a standard accounting shop crazy.) The third expense is legal fees, which are best estimated by consulting in advance with an experienced attorney. Legal costs may be related to the financing and distribution deal, or to production issues, such as rights for music and photos, or talent agreements. The fourth business expense is the relatively minor cost of copyright submission (see page 168).

SPECIAL EXPENSES

Many productions require one or more additional categories to cover unique types of expenses—prizes for a game show, satellite uplinking for a live news show, etc. The costs of these items can be high, so careful estimation is essential.

COMPLETING THE BUDGET

The total dollar amount for each category should be tallied and summarized on the cover page. Then, a contingency—typically 5 to 15 percent of some or all budget categories—should be added to the subtotal, to yield the grand total. On a weekly series, the grand total may then be divided into per-episode costs; on a strip series (a program seen five days a week), costs may be indicated both per-episode and per-week.

The producer's initial budget estimate is often much higher than the budget estimate that is ultimately approved, sometimes by as much as 50 percent. This may reflect the producer's desire to deliver the best possible show, to cover every possible eventuality, to keep some "fat" that could subsequently pay for unexpected expenses or (more often) to increase the profits.

The estimated budget should be a defining exercise for both producer and funder. Many projects are greeted with enthusiasm until the budget shows the financial realities. Some budgets are prepared by "backing into a number"—if a project can be delivered for a target figure, then it will be approved. Other budgets are prepared with a "zero-based" approach: the producer draws up a total figure, then attempts to protect the concept while adjusting the costs of line items.

A budget is usually revised several times prior to submission to the financing party, and again after the project has been through development. The grand total matters: producers will sometimes shift money from one category to another to compensate for the difference between the estimate and the actual numbers.

Once work begins on the program, the producer is typically required to submit weekly budget reports to the funder; this report compares the estimated amount in each line item with the likely actual amount. This procedure helps pinpoint problems early. When a production is completed, a final budget accounting is prepared and submitted along with other delivery items (see page 373).

THE CHALLENGE OF PRODUCTION FINANCING

The producer or executive producer's most difficult task is finding the money to make the project. For independent productions, combining sources to build up sufficient capital for the program is an art in itself. Even for programs produced in-house by a television station or corporation, raising money or gaining access to in-house resources can also be challenging.

The style of production financing has changed—particularly in the past ten years—from a single source to a system in which multiple sources participate. Producers of public television and cable programs are especially experienced in multi-source financing (see Chapter 4), but the concept is now familiar to producers who supply programming to the commercial networks as well.

GROWING PROGRAM DEFICITS

Until the early 1980s, ABC, CBS, and NBC bought the right to air a program twice in exchange for a license fee that roughly equaled the production cost. Producers earned their profits from syndication, an area in which the networks did not participate (see page 137). Since then, production costs have increased, but the networks have not raised their license fees sufficiently to cover the difference; instead, the networks have upheld the profitability of their program operations (in the face of shrinking market share) by keeping license fees to a minimum. On most programs, the result is a deficit—the difference between the license fee and the cost of production that must be bankrolled by either the producer (or the producer's affiliated studio or production company), or by a third party. For some properties (especially network series that have run three or more years, making possible a daily strip series), a sale to cable or syndication is the answer. Still, syndication monies don't come in until the sale is made, and this is generally unlikely before the third or fourth year of production.

Today, the network license fee rarely pays for the entire cost of production; at most, it may only cover 80 percent of the total production budget. Given a production budget of $1.2 million (an inexpensive network hour) and a license fee from the network of $800,000, the deficit per program equals $400,000. For 20 programs over the course of a single season, the total deficit is $8 million. With several seasons passing before the program plays either on cable or in syndication, the deficit can easily top $10 million—an unmanageable burden for a small company, and a serious one for a larger company. This is why prime-time network production is classically dominated by large studios. The studios either sell their own product to the networks, or finance, distribute, and co-produce projects from smaller companies—acting, in a sense, like banks for smaller companies. The load may be lightened by the sale of foreign rights, or by a foreign co-producer, however.

When studios or larger production companies absorb the deficit, they view the dollars as an investment against future profits from syndication, cable, and other markets. But as the syndication marketplace has changed, this return has become more and more undependable, so the studios and large production companies have started looking to other financing sources for covering the deficits, leading to complicated multi-source deals. Instead of providing back-end revenues (money generated after the primary release of the program), formerly ancillary markets are now being asked to provide upfront production financing, often in exchange for profit participation and some distribution rights.

In one scenario, the producer of a made-for-TV movie might receive $2 million of a $4 million budget from a basic cable service. An additional $500,000 might come from a home video deal, $1 million from a Canadian producer (provided that the movie is shot in Canada), and $500,000 from assorted sales to foreign broadcasters and home video companies. In addition to the complexity of this kind of arrangement, there is the problem of a disappearing back end: with so many of the ancillary markets pre-sold, the producer is left with little opportunity for profit.

As the number of channels in the world marketplace increases, the number of potential co-production partners and markets for ancillary sales also increases. This is a complicated, fast-moving marketplace where experience, personal relationships, track record, and star power, are more meaningful than a powerful program or movie concept.

It may be no longer enough for the producer to interest one company in a program—he or she must now appeal to several parties, each of which has its own peculiarities of taste and style. Even if the program's initial concept is acceptable to all concerned, each participant is likely to demand approval over key elements as production progresses, and a deadlock among the various parties is always a potential problem. Foreign investors and foreign co-producers can also complicate matters. They need projects that will satisfy local-content rules that can dictate the nationalities of the production staff and talent, as well as the location of production and post-production activities. The program may start looking more and more foreign, which may displease U.S. networks or distributors.

The balance of this chapter will review the types of production financing; sources of funding; the role of the distributor; the key concepts of recoupment and profit participation; and the nuts and bolts of how deals are put together.

TYPES AND SOURCES OF PRODUCTION FINANCING

The world of production financing can be broken down into six general categories: internal working capital, customers and clients, suppliers, inside and outside investors, banks and other lenders, and foreign partners.

INTERNAL WORKING CAPITAL

The early stages of a program's development are usually funded internally. Many production companies—and nearly all television stations and cable networks—budget a certain amount of money per year to develop new projects. Once the program is developed, it will often be "pitched" or "shopped" to other potential participants, and one component part of the deal will be funding for further development of the project.

If the production organization is a distributor or network, then all of the project's development, and some or all of its production, may be financed with internal capital. Sometimes, money is approved only for each incremental step, and additional approval is needed to move the project to the next step. This approval is based on a growing sense that the project will come together as planned, and that it will reach a sufficiently large audience.

In some cases, internal funds are used to produce a demonstration tape or a pilot, which then becomes a selling tool to attract additional investment from other companies.

Internal working capital can also be used to make up for the shortfalls that occur because of the delays in receiving funds from outside sources. Unless advances from customers or distributors are paid on time—and unless all suppliers are patient and understanding of the cash-flow crises that typify the production process—the production schedule is likely to be affected until a certain check arrives and clears. A production company should have ready access to cash or a line of credit in order to smooth out the bumps in cash flow.

Internal capital is also used to close gaps in production funding. For example, if a production company gets a project 95 percent financed from other sources, the company may decide to cover the remaining 5 percent itself from its own reserves in order to begin production. Sometimes, this is preferable to pre-selling rights that might be more valuable once the program is made.

CUSTOMERS AND CLIENTS

Customers and clients are the most common source of production financing, particularly for independent producers. Television is a business in which networks, cable companies, and video distributors pay sizable sums—either in advance, on delivery, or a combination of the two—for the product they need. Customers and clients can take many forms, depending mainly on the type of distribution system. If the law permits, they can also buy rights in the program as part of the deal, or have their license fee treated in whole or in part as an investment.

Many programs are produced for private concerns. A corporation requiring a training video typically pays the entire cost of development and production, for example.

In some cases, a combination of two or more customers furnish funding for a program. For example, a commercial broadcaster could account for partial financing, and a syndicator's advance, the remainder. Or a cable network could provide some financing, with a European broadcaster making up the balance.

SUPPLIERS

Suppliers, like television studios, mobile production facilities, and post-production facilities, may also provide a form of production financing. In exchange for profit participation or partial ownership in a property, these facilities may offer reduced rates, or billing that is deferred until the project earns enough money to pay back both the initial amount and a premium.

Supplier financing is most common for pilots, in which facilities and/or personnel may be traded for the promise of a production contract if the series is commissioned. If that occurs, the supplier will make back its money and then some.

Supplier financing is also common in the home video industry, particularly for independent producers who distribute their own product. In such a case, the tape duplicator may not only manufacture finished product on credit or without charge, but may also supply warehousing, shipping, and inventory control in exchange for profit participation or partial ownership.

INVESTORS

Television and video are glamorous businesses that attract certain types of investors. Investors essentially come in two forms: those who are unaffiliated with the television and/or video industries (outside investors), and those who are in some aspect of the television business and who will buy into a project while acquiring certain distribution or telecasting rights (inside investors).

OUTSIDE INVESTORS

For the pure-equity investor with no other means of benefiting beyond a share of revenues, a television or video project is likely to be a difficult investment. There are at least two potential problem areas. First, television and video programs do not "earn out" in any predictable fashion. This can make any investor nervous, and an inexperienced one, hard to handle. Second, if a producer is relying on outside investment money, he or she may be working outside the established production community, and may lack easy access to production or distribution resources that are essential to a reasonable return and a predictable budget. Nor is it only the investor who may have problems. On a project that is running late and perhaps over budget, with one or more investors anxious to recoup their investments more rapidly than the marketplace will allow, the possibility of all-out panic may cause the producer to question the wisdom of working with outsiders.

That said, there are many isolated instances where outside investment has proven successful, sometimes with enormous returns for both investor and producer.

Wall Street investment firms, major insurance companies, and other traditional sources of investment capital generally invest in television through big production entities like studios, syndicators, and networks. This investment provides the television company with working capital to help with its self-funding efforts. In these situations, the investment in production and distribution is based on an assessment of the overall business of the company.

INSIDE INVESTORS

Distributors and end users of programming often invest in production. Although the distinction between the distributor and purchaser-as-end-user can be blurry, there is an important difference between the two.

The distributor usually pays a production advance. This is deemed an investment (especially if it is not fully covered by pre-sales), since it depends on unpredictable market factors to generate a return. In exchange for taking the risk, the distributor usually gets a share of profits. Of course, by controlling at least some aspect of distribution and revenues, the distributor is able to influence the risk.

A purchaser/end user—for example, a network—is not trading an investment for a return. Instead, it is paying outright for particular rights or territories (in the form of license fees, for a network), and using the program in an active business of its own. Many purchasers, however, want to be treated like investors; they want the recoupment and profit positions traditionally associated with true risk-taking investors.

Because they are in a singularly powerful position, the major networks have exerted this kind of pressure on the producers and distributors that supplied them with programming. This caused the FCC to institute the financial interest and syndication ("fin-syn") rules, which forbade the networks from maintaining a financial interest in the independent productions that they carried on their prime-time schedules. With the increasing role of non-network television of all kinds, and after years of negotiations between the FCC and the networks, the FCC in 1995 abolished these rules (see page 137).

BANKS AND OTHER LENDERS

Banks and other lending institutions play a part in the production financing process, but only if the loan can be secured with property that can be readily valued and turned into cash. Unsold rights to specific program properties are difficult to present as collateral because of their inherently speculative nature. Besides, most lenders do not understand the intricacies of show-business accounting. Therefore, most lending activity is either large-scale—multimillion-dollar loans to studios, networks, syndicators, and technical facilities—or dependent upon the existence of a firm pre-sale.

For the independent producer or production company, a bank will make a loan only if there is a bona fide contract with a creditworthy distributor or end user that provides for set payments on a firm schedule. The bank is essentially covering cash flow—if there is a period in which the producer requires cash, but the distributor or end user will not provide the necessary amount until a later point in production, a bank may provide a bridge loan. The risk of a failure to deliver is offset by a completion bond and other forms of insurance. These are standard practice in film production, and while they apply to made-for-TV movies, they are not often part of series production where incremental adjustments can be made.

Loans for project development, or for independent production without pre-sales, are almost impossible to obtain because of the risk involved.

In some cases, the contribution of an equity investor will take the form of a high-risk, non-recourse loan, generally with a substantial "kicker," such as a large share of net revenues. While this is technically a loan, it is actually treated like an investment.

FOREIGN PARTNERS

With globalization, many companies outside the U.S. have become sources of production capital for U.S. programs. Historically, foreign sales came after the fact, as part of the profit margin. More and more frequently, though, the foreign investment is arranged upfront to minimize production deficits. Sometimes, foreign television companies maintain development offices in Los Angeles and New York City.

Foreign investment in U.S. production is generally linked to a license of rights. In its simplest form, the deal is basically a pre-sale, with the possibility of profit participation and sometimes partial ownership. More often, however, investment from foreign sources is part of a co-production package. In a relationship that resembles a partnership (regardless of its strictly legal structure), the domestic producer and a foreign co-producer each provide certain elements in the production budget. The project may be shot overseas, for example, using facilities provided in whole or in part by the foreign co-producer. Co-production often involves cash from the foreign partner as well, supplementing the cash available to the U.S. producer from licenses to a domestic broad-caster, distributor, cablecaster, or home video company. Partners usually share the distribution rights—each usually retains broad-cast and cable rights in its home country—and split the revenues according to a negotiated formula. These deals are complicated, however, by the domestic-content requirements that commonly apply to foreign broadcasters (see pages 480 and 504), and by fluctuating foreign-exchange rates.

ADVERTISERS

Some advertisers play a signficant role in program development and production. Procter & Gamble, for example, owns a production company that supplies several long-running network soap operas. P&G also co-produces *Sabrina: The Teenage Witch, Clueless,* and the syndicated *Real TV* with Paramount. Buena Vista and Kellogg work together on children's programming; *101 Dalmatians* and *Mighty Ducks* are part of a program block supported by Kellogg advertising dollars. There are other isolated instances and the occasional joint venture, but in general, advertisers do not become involved in the details of program development or production. As a rule, an advertiser simply wants to place commercials in a program environment that delivers the right kind of viewers in sufficient numbers.

THE RELATIONSHIP BETWEEN PRODUCER AND DISTRIBUTOR

As in many industries, the producer manufactures the product, and the distributor takes care of sales and marketing. A successful product combines competent work by the producer with effective sales and marketing clout from the distributor.

Most independent producers license rights to their product to experienced distribution companies. This is especially true in markets that are difficult to sell without a specialized sales force, as in syndication and foreign markets. In some cases, production companies have formed their own syndication companies or home video labels. Ideally, this allows the producer to retain more revenues and pay closer attention to individual product marketing.

THE TYPICAL DISTRIBUTION DEAL

In most instances, the producer licenses a distributor to sell a program or series in a particular territory or group of territories for a specified period of time. The distributor then retains a negotiated percentage of revenues as a fee, frequently 30 to 35 percent (though this figure varies widely, depending upon the product, markets, and advances involved), plus reimbursement for certain distribution expenses (see page 305). The distributor will recoup any advance made to the producer, and may retain a certain amount as profit participation, particularly if the advance was sizable. The distribution deal's definitions and limitations are negotiable, based on bargaining strength, industry tradition, and company policy, and there are many variations on the theme. A checklist for issues in distribution deals appears in Appendix B5; a model distribution agreement is reproduced in Appendix B7.

REVENUE STREAMS: RECOUPMENT

So far, the discussion in this chapter has centered on the spending side of deals. Of equal importance is the revenue side, where— with luck and clear contract language—investments are recouped and profits are earned and shared. When a party finances a commercial venture, it is almost always with the intention of recouping (recovering) the investment and realizing some profit. A television network recoups the investment in its programs by selling time to advertisers, usually earning a profit, too. A home video label recoups by selling videocassettes to dealers and consumers. Even the sponsor of a public television program hopes to recoup its investment, either in cash (from the proceeds of additional sales) or through publicized goodwill.

A true investment is not tied to a sale of particular rights, at least in theory; rather, an investment is recoupable in priority position from all sources of income generated by the property. However, end users may press to be treated as investors, at least for a portion of the fee, so the process of repaying investors can become quite complicated.

RECOUPMENT PRIORITIES

Recoupment usually occurs "in the first position," or from gross revenues received, before any profits or other revenue deductions are allowed. However simple this may sound, there are many layers of activities and entities that are involved in the revenue stream of a television program.

At each layer, deductions are made, and the net at one level is the "gross" at the next layer down: for example, the distributor's net is usually the producer's gross. Where any particular investor's recoupment right "plugs in" may be hotly negotiated. In most cases, distribution costs are recouped at a higher level than production costs.

MULTIPLE PARTIES

With only one party eligible to recoup its investment at any given level, the formula is a relatively simple one. The investment is one of a list of items that are deducted from revenues at that level prior to determining the net. The situation becomes more complicated when several parties are entitled to recoupment, particularly when their investment contributions are not equal to one another. Two related issues must be considered: the relative *size* of each investor's share, and the *order* in which each investor may extract dollars.

The simplest formula is called *pari passu,* a Latin term meaning "by a like step." In pari passu recoupment, each party receives funds at the same time, but in proportion to its percentage investment at a particular point in time. The following example illustrates the pari passu formula: Party A has invested $2 million (50 percent) in a production; party B, $1,200,000 (30 percent); and party C, $800,000 (20 percent). When the first $100 arrives from any and all revenue sources, the parties receive $50, $30, and $20 respectively, at the same time. Pari passu recoupment is a fair means of sharing both risk and reward.

Recoupment by position is the opposite of pari passu recoupment. The party in the first position receives some or all of its investment, then the party in the second position recoups, then the party in the third position, and so on down the line. Take the same $100 income, the same parties A, B, and C above, and an agreement for party A to recoup 100 percent of its $2 million investment in the first position. Party A would then receive the entire $100 and all additional dollars up to $2 million. Parties B and C would receive nothing until party A recouped.

There are several variations on the formulas. In order to provide the other parties with some income, party A might agree to accept less than 100 percent of the income, or to open "windows" for the others at various positions before its own complete recoupment.

In another variation, one or more of the parties might be entitled to recoup more than 100 percent of the original investment. Some deals offer, for example, 200 percent recoupment, but no future involvement in profits (or some lesser involvement in profits). From the perspective of the investor, a formula based on a multiple of the original investment is simple and easily managed. From the perspective of the producer, such a formula limits the long-term distribution of profits, and keeps the project's ultimate profitability unknown to the recoupment partners.

SEPARATING AND COMBINING REVENUE STREAMS

A successful television program or series is likely to generate revenues from a variety of domestic and foreign sources. Sometimes the streams are split apart and treated as different "pots" for recoupment purposes. For example, the producer of a movie-of-the-week may get an advance from one distributor that will cover domestic syndication and cable sales, and another advance from a second distributor that will cover all foreign markets. Frequently, each of these two distributors will recoup its respective advance only from revenues from its own territories and markets. Given the fact that the distributor's efforts will help shape the success of the program in its own area, this is a reasonable arrangement. An outside investor, in contrast, will usually recoup from all revenue sources.

Revenue streams can also be tied together, with the proceeds from one market helping to cover the recoupment of costs or advances in another area. This technique is called "cross-collatera-lization," from a banking term that refers to mortgaging separate properties to support a single loan. Separate programs are some-times cross-collateralized to cover the costs that each one runs up on its own; in that case, the programs would have to break even on an aggregated basis before a net would be earned on any one of them.

WHAT GETS RECOUPED

The definition of what is recoupable is a critical point in negotiations. Since distribution costs, production costs, and advances are all subject to recoupment, these are prime areas for definitional license—here is where "Hollywood accounting" earns its reputation for legitimized theft. Every piece of overhead, interest, or other types of "indirect" costs added to the more truthfully labeled "direct" costs, means a shifting of money from the net participants to the recoupment participants. This issue leads directly to the next topic: net profits and other "back-end" participation.

PROFIT PARTICIPATION AND OTHER BACK-END FORMULAS

"Profits" is both a magical and a cursed word in television. Fortunes have been generated by the sale and resale of specials, series, and motion pictures to network, cable, syndication, home video, and foreign markets. Often, those fortunes are not shared by people who have a "net profit" participation or other formula for *back-end participation.* (The latter refers to money that comes out of revenues, as opposed to a *front-end fee,* which comes out of the production budget.) There are two principal reasons behind this all too frequently accurate statement. The first is the convoluted and blatantly one-sided terms of participation agreements that are presented as take-it-or-leave-it propositions to back-end participants. The second is the "creative accounting" that shifts costs back and forth among various projects, with the most successful ones bearing the greatest burden of items allocated for recoupment. This section will examine both of these problems in detail, as well as several other obstacles to the profitability of any production.

THE PROBLEM OF LABELS

In theory, being a "gross" participant is better than being a "net" one. But in the end, labels mean very little—it is the details in the definition that truly matter.

"Gross revenues" should mean the total amount of money received, prior to any deductions. A network's gross, for example, should equal the total amount of money paid by the sponsors for advertising on the program. Even this simple explanation demands refinement, though: sponsors buy their commercial time through advertising agencies, who retain 15 percent of the sponsor's payment as a commission.

From the producer's perspective, gross might also be defined as the total monies received by the producer from the program's distributors (i.e., the "distributor's net").

A director or writer who negotiates to receive a percentage of the producer's gross is likely to have his own definition. This "gross" might well be offset by agency commissions, legal fees, or a stunning variety of incidentals—from the costs of shipping videocassettes to foreign countries for potential licensing to a full recoupment of basic production costs. The gross is now an "adjusted gross."

Although specific terms may vary, "adjusted gross" often functions as a synonym for what most people would call "net" or "net profits," though the adjusted gross will usually have fewer questionable deductions. The words "net," "profits," and "net profits" should be meaningful terms, but they have become so debased through misuse that they are now scorned, even as labels, by anyone with sufficient negotiating power. Other kinds of back-end payments involve flat fees or bonuses in place of, or in addition to, a percentage in a net or gross formula. "Points" are percentage points, and represent the percentage share of whatever is being divided ("net points," "gross points," and so on). Even the word "revenues" can be misleading. Many agreements only "recognize" revenue after it has come to rest in a particular account in a particular country, even though that may be months or even years after the check was cashed by the foreign subsidiary of the U.S.-based distributor.

In order to get to the root of a typical profit definition, one must ignore the customary meanings of certain terms and focus on the legalese of the profit-participation agreement itself. Hidden there will probably be many of the following issues concerning the recipient of the profit share ("Participant") and the payer of that share ("Company").

REVENUE ADJUSTMENTS

On the revenue side, there are many ways in which the Company can defer acknowledging funds that have actually been deposited into its bank accounts. International companies have particularly wide scope for this action. A common clause in profit definitions says that no funds shall count as being received until paid in dollars into the U.S. accounts of the Company. If the Company has foreign subsidiaries, they can collect foreign revenues in foreign currencies and leave them overseas indefinitely, as a kind of permanent loan from the Participants who are entitled to them. This can be avoided by insisting on a time frame for the repatriation of funds held by the Company or its affiliates.

Some countries, however, have a "blocked currency" problem: restrictions on money leaving the country. This can be circumvented with an agreement allowing the Participant to set up his or her own account in the country and take the appropriate share of blocked funds directly. The Participant may not be able to get the funds out of the country either, but at least they are available to spend over there.

Another method the Company can use for delaying recognition of monies received is the use of reserves and the related concept of "earned." The theory is that advances made are not really "earned" until the product is delivered, since they could conceivably be rescinded if something went wrong with the program. Therefore, the logic goes, all advances must be held in reserve until it is clear that there will be no problems. This line of thinking has been stretched to say that no license fee is earned until the contract has been completely performed. The license may run over several years—and even after the program has run several times with no problems, some or all of the licensing fee may be held in reserve and deemed not yet earned.

These delay tactics can be compounded, quite literally, when they are combined with clauses allowing the Company to earn interest on unrecouped amounts. If income which is actually on hand can be considered non-existent, then the Company will expect interest to be paid on these funds, piling on extra charges to be recouped (even on overhead costs and production fees). Another problem with interest is that the Company charges the prime rate plus some number, whereas it pays lenders several points less. All of these practices can be countered by limiting interest charges to amounts actually paid on amounts actually outstanding on expenses actually incurred.

Company delay can also be used to influence the exchange rate at which foreign receipts are converted into dollars. If the foreign distributor of the program is an affiliate of the Company, it will wait for the moment when the foreign currency is weak to report income, diminishing the dollar total. Similarly, any expenses or deductions will be converted and deducted when the foreign currency is strong. A fair contract will specify average exchange rates or key the rates to specific dates for evaluation.

FEES

Revenues to Participants are also reduced with double charging of fees. The Company collects a fee for selling a program in a particular market, then turns around and sub-licenses it to another organization, which also deducts a percentage fee from its gross. It seems unfair that the Company keeps its full fee when someone else is being paid to do the work—especially when the "someone else" turns out to be an affiliate of the Company, or even a direct subsidiary. This kind of inside licensing for double fees, which is especially common with foreign sales and in other ancillary markets, can be prevented by capping the total amount of fees that can be charged by every party involved in selling into a particular market, and by forbidding the charging of additional fees for work done by an affiliate of the Company.

EXAGGERATED DEDUCTIONS

Having taken steps to delay and minimize the receipt of income, the Company may try to increase the number of deductions that it can take. The first group of deductions consists of "adjustments" to the gross such as collection costs (legal actions for bad debts), agent fees, and applicable taxes. Tax deductions should cover taxes specifically withheld from the project's revenues, not the general income taxes of the Company. If there is a benefit to the Company from an offset or tax credit, the fair share of this should be added back against the taxes deducted or even, if possible, passed along to the Participant.

The next set of deductions is usually the recoupment of distribution and marketing costs. One might think that these expenses are the cost of doing business, and should be covered by the Company out of its distribution fee; this is sometimes the negotiated result. But in the film business, these expenses are sometimes huge, given the prints and advertising necessary for a major release, and so they are recovered separately. The practice has been transferred over to television deals, even though the costs of distribution are actually much smaller.

Most Participants are willing to accept the deduction of direct, out-of-pocket costs of getting the programs on the air: tape stock, dubbing, shipping, customs, and so on. The trouble starts when these and other services are performed in-house and then charged against the program as a hefty fee. The Company may also tack an overhead allowance onto these charges, so that the program's earnings are being in effect charged twice for expenses that the fee should cover. Add an interest factor while these charges remain unrecouped, and the meaning of "Hollywood accounting" becomes clear.

Sales and marketing costs present additional opportunities for Company abuse. Television distribution may not involve massive media campaigns aimed at the general public, but there is quite

extensive marketing targeted to potential end users: printing brochures, dubbing sales tapes, travel, phone, attendance at conventions
and sales markets (see page 311). Armies of television executives
descend on Cannes, New Orleans, and Las Vegas every year to
wheel and deal, trying to outdo one another with expensive display booths and celebrity appearances. Though many Participants
grumble at the lavishness of these efforts, they at least acknowledge that "you have to spend money to make money." The problem
comes when the expenses are allocated among the various
properties that the Company represented at such functions. If the
Company went to Cannes with a list of 20 properties, it may return
with lucrative sales for only five of them. It is useless to allocate
the expenses to the failures (since these properties may never
make enough money to repay them), so the successes are made
to bear the burden of the costs. While the successes probably do
occupy a disproportionate amount of the Company staff's attention, the Participant does not expect its own program to carry
most of the Company's overhead, especially in addition to the fee
that is deducted. Some unscrupulous companies even allocate the
same costs to more than one program, and end up making
money on every expense they incur.

Some of these problems can be thwarted with language in the
agreement between Participant and Company that requires deductions to be "directly related" to the program and to be "actual, out-
of-pocket" expenditures. Another approach is to simply impose a
cap, either as a percentage or (less commonly) as an absolute
amount, which deductions for such items cannot exceed.

Double counting is another deduction tactic. Residuals may
turn up twice as deductibles, as may insurance and other program-
related costs. Sometimes an expenditure is calculated as both a
distribution cost and a production cost; even worse, overhead
and interest expenditures are added to both occurrences, even
though overhead on distribution expenses is relatively rare.

After distribution fees and expenses have been deducted, the
revenue stream—or what is left of it—is applied to recouping the
production costs or the advance. If the Company is recouping the
full production costs, these, too, are defined in a one-sided
manner. For example, most production budgets include a general
overhead factor, sometimes 20 percent or more. In theory, this
factor is supposed to cover all of the small expenses of ongoing
Company overhead that are attributable to the program but that do
not appear in the official budget. In practice, though, many of the

Company's profit calculations *already* account for a wide array of overhead costs, including telephone bills and the cost of parking spaces at the Company's main office. The Participant should keep the overhead factor within reasonable bounds, and should question the addition of interest to overhead and overhead to interest.

The Company's boilerplate definition of "penalties" may allow it to recoup 150 percent of the "normal" production cost if the program is over budget. While the argument goes that this is an incentive to the talent to keep expenses under control, the Company may insist on penalties even when it has final approval on all artistic and business matters relating to the production.

PERCENTAGES OF PERCENTAGES

Once the Company has taken all its deductions, the issue is just what the "points" promised to Participants are percentages of. Are they 10 percent of the "producer's share" of net profits? Because there is a customary 50/50 or 60/40 split between investor and producer, 10 percent of the producer's share will be no more than 5 percent of the "100 percent." In addition, if the promised percentage is 10 percent of the "producer's *retained* share" of net profits, any other grants which the producer has made will be taken off the top before the points are calculated, so the Participant's actual share shrinks even more.

GENERAL DEFENSES AGAINST PROFIT-PARTICIPATION ABUSES

In addition to the specific remedies described above, there are some more general measures to protect a Participant from a Company's creative accounting methods. First, the long, standard-form profit definition in the profit-participation agreement is usually drafted to protect the Company as much as possible; a relatively short statement, with language limiting overhead and other general allocations, can tilt the agreement back in the Participant's favor. Second, the Participant should insist on a "most favored nation" clause. This item is derived from the laws of custom duties, where a "most favored nation" must have the benefit of any concession granted to any other country. In the world of profits, this means that the Participant cannot get a worse deal than anyone else in an agreed-upon class. If the class includes other recipients with some bargaining power, the entire deal may improve some; and if the deal includes the Company or its key executives, the deal might get better still.

ACCOUNTING RIGHTS

One of the most effective means of monitoring a Company's questionable practices is the Participant's right to have an accounting done of the Company's financial books and records on a project. Most clauses will grant the Participant the right to audit the books within a certain time period after receiving the statement, or the right to have a "qualified representative" conduct the audit. The records will be made available at the Company's offices, during regular business hours. The right to audit may be limited to a single audit of any given period; any claims must be made shortly after the inspection. Sometimes the Company will hinder the right to an audit with so many restrictions and such short time intervals that the clauses become almost meaningless.

Auditors do turn up irregularities, even with a relatively honest Company; the problem is that such audits tend to be expensive, although a profit-participation agreement may provide for the Company to pick up the tab if serious shortfalls are discovered.

THE ALTERNATIVE TO PROFIT PARTICIPATION: FIXED PAYMENTS

For those who are skeptical of profit participation and its many blind alleyways, there are alternatives. The easiest way is to structure a bonus or royalty arrangement keyed to reaching easily measurable targets—such as the number of programs actually produced. For example, every time a week of shows is made, the Participant could receive a flat dollar figure as a royalty or bonus: more shows, more money. If these shows air more than once, a further formula can be devised; if these shows air outside the U.S., then each show that airs in a specified list of countries triggers a specific payment. If the series reaches the three- or four-year mark, making syndication possible, then a bigger bonus is triggered.

Some producers receive bonuses when a program reaches, or exceeds, a specific rating point. Some receive bonuses when a pilot triggers a series order, or when a second, third, or fourth year of programs is ordered. Bonuses may be used in combination with revenue-based profit participation. Bonuses may be paid "against" profit participation (that is, deducted from later earnings, if any), or they may be paid in addition to these monies.

In summary, there are no absolute rules regarding profit participation; every situation is different. For those few players with sufficient clout, the terms of profit participation are highly negotiable; for everyone else, "net" is a very flimsy concept.

HOW DEALS GET DONE

How are deals actually made so that a production can be financed? The key to the process is experienced Participants who know how to play the game, who can untangle complications and reconcile contradictions—at least enough to have some type of deal letter signed. (Sometimes the deal letter is all that gets signed; it is not uncommon, with a series several years into production, for the various lawyers to still be wrangling over the terms of the long-form agreement.)

The following section describes some of the essential elements involved in making a deal for production financing.

WHO THE PLAYERS ARE

Certain television executives make programming decisions, and have the power to make financial commitments to a producer. Most networks and distributors have a programming or acquisitions department, which is where much of the initial action takes place. Typically, this department employs creative executives and associates who evaluate and shape the artistic aspects of the program, and business people who judge the program in terms of its cost and revenue potential. The inevitable tensions between creative vision and cost control play out daily between these factions; a successful project satisfies both parties.

On the selling side are the production companies, independent producers, directors, writers, and anyone else with a good idea. The trick is getting the project in front of the right person on the buyer's side. Many projects that are submitted get shunted to low-paid readers (who may not have much experience) for a review, and a bad reader's report can doom a worthy project to obscurity. The project must be seen by someone actually empowered to make a commitment. Personal relationships can be essential here. One of the keys to a successful production career is a Rolodex or Pilot full of senior program executives who will take your call, have lunch with you, or even share a weekend on your boat. For a newcomer, a well-connected agent, manager, or attorney can help open the doors. A powerful agent can operate in the background and make things happen.

Programming decisions are rarely made by one person. Typically, a network or distributor builds staff consensus prior to any commitment. Ultimately, the head of programming must make the final decision, but this decision is rarely made without consultation with others in the program department. Sales and marketing personnel are often part of the process, especially if advertising or rights sales are an important part of the package.

WHERE THE PLAYERS MEET

The players get together in formal meetings scheduled at their offices, in restaurants, or at other business venues. There are also short-notice meetings and impromptu appointments at conferences, sales markets, and conventions, and in informal settings like skiing in Aspen, on the beach in the Hamptons, or sailing off the South of France. Even a haircut can give the barber the chance to make a pitch: hairdressers have risen to some of the most powerful positions in Hollywood.

FORMAL MEETINGS

Although a written submission is often required in advance, and some work can be done over the phone, there is no substitute for a face-to-face meeting in a formal setting. A good part of the art of the deal is the seller infecting the buyer with enthusiasm for a program. Selling projects in any television market—whether local, national, or international—also requires spending time in the city or cities where the principal buyers are located, setting up the necessary round of meetings and cultivating the connections and contacts that will put the person pitching the project into the system. With rare exceptions, this cannot be done effectively if the producer is not a regular part of the local scene.

THE HUBS

The premier deal-making location, both for national and international productions, is still the Los Angeles area; no place rivals LA for the concentration of television business people. The next most important center in the U.S. is New York City; because of the companies located in other cities, some deals are also made in Chicago (Tribune), Washington, DC (PBS), Atlanta (Turner), Miami (Latin entertainment industry), and Nashville (headquarters of the country music business). In Canada, Toronto dominates the television business, although Vancouver and (to a lesser extent) Montreal are also important Canadian centers. Internationally, Tokyo, London, Paris, Munich, and Rome all have concentrations of power, with secondary hubs in São Paolo, Sydney, Mexico City, Madrid and Barcelona.

Before setting out to find fame and fortune in one of these hubs of the television business, an aspiring producer should consider using the resources of his or her local community to acquire basic experience, establish a reputation, and create a demonstration reel.

CONVENTIONS, MARKETS, AND SOCIAL OCCASIONS

There is a series of annual conventions and markets in the U.S., Europe, and now, Asia, where relationships are built and nurtured, programs are bought and sold, and deals are made (or at least discussed). In the U.S., the key meetings are the syndication markets sponsored by the Association of Independent Television Stations (INTV) and the National Association of Television Program Executives (NATPE). INTV and NATPE allow syndicators to show their programs to a wide range of buyers from around the country, and these meetings are central to the syndication sales business (see page 33). These markets are not as important as they once were; syndicators now sell, mostly, to station groups, not to individual stations, and deals are made throughout the year. Still, all kinds of business occurs at these conventions, from finding a new advertising sales company to arranging a corporate merger. Provided the executives can take the time from buying and selling current product, INTV and NATPE are opportunities to pitch, follow up on, and commit to new projects. As the television business becomes more global, international program markets have become more important to U.S. producers and distributors.

Internationally, the most important conventions are held in Cannes: MIP-TV takes place in the spring, and focuses on sales to the traditional broadcast markets; MIPCOM is in the fall, and covers all aspects of the television and video business, including cable and satellite. MIP-Asia, held in Hong Kong, represents a fast-growing cluster of television markets. Other events include the famous Cannes Film Festival (typically held in the late spring) and the lesser festivals held throughout the world. At these gatherings, the production, finance, distribution, and end-user communities from around the world forge alliances, initiate co-productions, and generally discuss deals. While few of these transactions are finalized in the hotel bars by the sea or on the chartered yachts by the pier, many deals are launched before the week of hectic meetings is finished.

Informal contacts in social situations are also a prime starting point for presenting and soliciting television projects. While it is bad form to let discussions centered on business dominate a dinner party, there is plenty of room for mentioning a possible project and setting up a formal meeting to talk further about it. This kind of networking may be difficult for an outsider; in time, as personal relationships are built, it becomes easier.

NEGOTIATING THE DEAL

Television is often a rough-and-tumble world, full of strong cha-racters who have gotten ahead by imposing their wills on others and making deals on their own terms. These people are likely to be adroit at the manipulation, flattery, intimidation, and entice-ment that go into getting one's own way. Nowhere are these skills more evident than at the bargaining table. Countering these per-sonalities is not always easy, especially when you're selling product that will make or break your company, and have little leverage (there are few secrets in the industry; the other party is likely to know precisely who they are dealing with). Nonetheless, there are a few bits of preparation that can guide anyone through the negotiation process.

The first step is examining your own position, weighing its strengths and weaknesses. Identify your minimum requirements; if these are not met, it's best to walk away. The next step is to put yourself in the other side's shoes: what are *their* strengths, weak-nesses, and minimum requirements? This exercise will help you determine just where—and how far—you can push. Do your homework about the deal as well. If you haven't read the fine print or don't know the industry custom on a particular point, you can be pushed around by someone who has and who does. Use your advisers—agents, managers, lawyers—wisely; don't defer all decision-making to them, but borrow their knowledge, experi-ence, and skills in the manipulation game. If the other side insists on yelling and screaming, preserve your dignity by leaving the table or hanging up the phone—if they really want the deal, they will come back to you in a more civilized fashion. And remember: behavior during a negotiation is often a key indicator of behavior during production. (If the negotiation is hell, do you really want these people as partners?)

Once the basic deal is done, a letter agreement may confirm the key points. Since the monied party typically drafts the contract, the wording is likely to favor that party. Negotiation is expected, and several conversations about changes are acceptable. At a certain point, usually the third, fourth, or fifth discussion about changes, this becomes annoying busywork for the other party. So pick your shots—give in on some points, and push hard on others. If the other party becomes weary of your changes, note that this may be a tactic. It may also be a sign that you are driving the other party crazy.

Timing is also a factor. Insisting on the last drop of blood can draw out the deal process by weeks or months. Most deals have their ripe moment, when attentions are focused and the market ready.

Missing that moment can do far more harm than missing the last triumph in the negotiations or subsequent contract changes. In addition, the television community is small enough so that a reputation for gouging at the negotiating table can come back to haunt you. Be firm, but leave something for the other side to take home: there is considerable value in being "a pleasure to do business with." There is also value in being "a tough negotiator." Striking the balance is the key.

Production Companies

Television programs are produced by an enormous variety of entities. Some programs are produced by individuals working with little more than a camcorder and a basement editing rig. Others are produced by huge production facilities with armies of producers and technical personnel.

In general, productions can be classified as either in-house (produced by the network, corporate communications department, etc.) or out-of-house (by freelance producers or production companies). Sometimes, the distinction is blurred; some production companies are owned by networks.

IN-HOUSE PRODUCTIONS

Programs are produced in-house for various reasons. Some types of productions, such as regularly scheduled news programs and network morning shows, are signature properties that help to establish and maintain the network's distinctive programming and marketing profile, its brand. Often, these shows are so complex and so closely linked to the network or station's image that the logistics of approvals that would need to flow between the network and the production company would be intolerable.

Sometimes, an in-house production can cost less than an outside package. This may be the case if the network or distribution organization owns a studio and/or editing facilities. Full-time staff, paid by other departments or by other projects, can be assigned to a new project at minimal cost. (The complexities of inter-departmental billing can make this approach unwieldy.)

Local television stations were once the largest producers of in-house programming, turning out children's programs, talk and public-affairs programs, magazine shows, documentaries, and remote coverage of all sorts. This is no longer the case, most stations produce only local news, though some produce public-service programs.

For some basic cable networks, in-house production simply makes sense. Cable networks that feature continuous news, weather, or sports coverage generally produce their home-base programs in-house; the same is true for music video services whose principal production tasks involve video disc jockeys. Basic networks with a need for original studio-based programming, like the Food Network, may equip a single studio to produce multiple series. As a cable network matures, and advertising revenues support more ambitious projects, the role of outside production companies tends to grow. MTV and Nickelodeon, for example, began with a schedule dominated by in-house productions and acquired programs; in time, each network became a significant market for original programs from production companies.

In-house production is common in most major corporations, where regularly scheduled information programs keep a full-time staff busy. Most companies employ freelancers or outside production companies to supplement the in-house staff; to handle workload overflow; and to work on productions that are beyond the capabilities of the in-house staff, facilities, or other company resources; or just to work around "issues" related to company politics. Some marketing communications pieces, notably commercials, video news releases (VNRs) and product announcements, are typically produced by outside specialists.

In-house productions generally appear to be low-cost ventures, even when the obvious fixed costs of staff and equipment are added. A true evaluation, however, must take into account the project's hidden costs: use of part-time personnel employed by other departments, office space, supplies, equipment, telephone usage, insurance, and other items apparently provided at no charge to in-house production.

OUT-OF-HOUSE PRODUCTIONS

CORPORATE VIDEO

At the simplest level, a corporate manager outlines a project for a producer and director, and they all agree upon a production schedule and budget and determine how the necessary resources will be put together. This approach is appropriate for small-scale video productions (usually single-camera) such as marketing tapes, VNRs, training materials, and speeches (for example, the company chair-man's quarterly address to employees). The producer is usually paid a flat fee, with staggered payments: one-third on the first day of work, one-third on the first shoot day, and one-third on delivery of the finished product. On larger projects, the producer may be paid weekly, biweekly, or monthly for the run of the production schedule. Some producers own the equipment, but most rent what they need.

A larger project—a music video, a sophisticated marketing video, a full-scale training film, a corporate annual report, or a simple series—requires more than one full-time person. Many small pro-duction companies specialize in these types of projects. Some full-service companies offer writing, producing, shooting, editing, and duplication; others concentrate on one or more aspects of production, and work closely with other vendors to complete the package. (These specialists may work directly with the client, or operate as subcontractors.)

Small production companies take many forms: a writer working with a producer/director, an editor working with a videographer, a team of producers or directors, or a collective of people who can do everything from write scripts to compose music to shoot and edit videotape. There is no fixed formula. Some companies consist of nothing more than a producer working in a home office; others employ a half-dozen producers and regularly invest in the latest video equipment. Each of these companies, if successful, finds a niche, develops clients within it, and eventually tries to expand into new industries or segments. One company, for example, specializes in videos for automotive industries; another shoots newsmagazine stories for syndicated television programs. Some companies combine computers and video for video walls, interactive kiosks, and touch-screens for museums, amusement parks, and point-of-purchase retail applications. Each niche has its own business cycle, so specialized companies try to spread the workload over both busy and slow months. Specialty firms may be sensitive to fluctuations in the economy; if the computer business or the auto industry is having a rough year, then production companies in Silicon Valley or Detroit suffer the consequences.

PRODUCTION COMPANIES AND ENTERTAINMENT PROGRAMMING
Entertainment programming is the magnet, the television industry segment associated with fame and fortune. Small and medium-sized production companies find it difficult to compete with their larger-sized counterparts in the entertainment sector, but some of them

succeed with more modest undertakings (and many affiliate with larger companies). They develop special types of projects (such as promotional campaigns), or produce programs with unconventional marketing or financing schemes.

Most network and syndicated programs are produced by large production companies, many of them affiliated with motion picture studios. At the start of the 1997–98 season, the top ten prime-time network suppliers (and their most significant properties) were:

1. Warner Bros. (15 series): *Drew Carey, ER, Family Matters, Friends, Murphy Brown*
2. Columbia Tristar (13 series): *Mad About You, The Nanny, Party of Five*
3. Twentieth Century-Fox (12 series): *Buffy, The Vampire Slayer; King of the Hill; The Simpsons; The X-Files*
4. Paramount (12 series): *Star Trek: Voyager*
5. Disney/Touchstone (9 series): *Ellen, Home Improvement*
6. NBC Studios (9 series): *Homicide: Life on the Street*
7. CBS Productions (7 series): *Caroline in the City; Dr. Quinn, Medicine Woman; Touched by an Angel; Walker: Texas Ranger*
8. Brillstein-Grey (6 series): *NewsRadio*
9. Universal (4 series): *Law & Order*
10. Carsey-Werner (4 series): *Cosby, Cybill, 3rd Rock from the Sun, Men Behaving Badly.*

Many of these larger companies are involved with co-productions and other business deals that skew the count. The number of series may not be as meaningful as the quality of the property. In 1997–98 Castle Rock, for example, produced only one series, *Seinfeld,* but the series' popularity in both network and syndicated runs have made it one of the most valuable properties in domestic television.

Network, local, and cable schedules are filled with programs produced or co-produced by successful suppliers; new companies, particularly new companies that are small and without a serious track record in a very similar genre, need not apply. As a rule, network executives are careful about working with untried production companies. Talented producers, writers, and performers are encouraged to work with an established supplier. The reasons go beyond back-office operations or marketplace clout. Full-scale production companies also provide deficit financing.

A prime-time network license fee rarely pays for the entire cost of production; on the contrary, it may cover only half of the total production budget. A successful prime-time program may play for two or three years before it generates significant profits from foreign markets, and it may take four years for the program to make money from domestic syndication. Only a production company with deep pockets can carry so sizable a deficit (see Chapter 32).

Deficits are not inevitable; some programs, notably many programs made for basic cable networks, are made without them (that is, the network's license fee equals the production budget; and because the network is taking all the risk, it receives all back-end profits). Other programs are produced with foreign partners, or income from a pre-sale is used to cover production expenses. Still, the cash involved in producing any television series requires most smaller companies to secure a joint production agreement with a major production company, like a studio. Banks and other financial institutions do not generally associate themselves with television production companies. Loans against receivables (monies that will be received when production is complete) for example, are extremely uncommon.

Although financial considerations are a significant factor, the television business is dominated by these larger players for other reasons as well. Warner Bros., Paramount, Universal, and similar companies have studio and post-production facilities; wardrobe, set, and casting departments; the marketing power needed to sell the programs; and the financial expertise to assure cash flow in spite of production deficits. They often have exclusive or first-look arrangements with many of the top independent producers and production companies in LA. No wonder the studios are sometimes called program factories.

Each studio employs a team of executives who supervise the production of current programs and the development of new properties. Typically, a development executive will have strong ties to a network program department, often as a former employee. The development executive works closely with individual writers and producers in nurturing a property, and attends most or all of the network pitch meetings. A network will either pass on the concept (most often), or initiate a step development deal (sometimes; see page 208). If there is a deal to be made, it is negotiated by an attorney working in the studio's business affairs department. The writer and/or producer continues to work closely with the studio's development executive through the rough scripts, polished drafts, and, if one is ordered, the pilot. When (and if) the network orders the series, the executive may become even more deeply involved with the project—on the production staff, or as the studio's production executive on the program. Some executives focus only on development; once a series is in production, they move on to another project. (In general, a large number of properties are simultaneously in various stages of development.) This process is described in more detail in Chapter 19.

ANNUAL CYCLES

Although a new project can be pitched, piloted, and premiered at any time of the year, the broadcast and cable networks have historically followed a seasonal cycle focused on September debuts of new series. A new property is pitched during the fall or winter of the year before the debut; by spring, each network announces the programs that will be piloted. These pilots are produced in March and April, then tested with sample audiences. Series commitments are made by early summer, in time for production companies to supply the network with the first completed shows of the new season by early August. A complete season of programs is produced between August and March. There is also a second season of programs that debut in January, February, and March. By and large, these programs follow the normal cycle until March or April of the previous year, but are then placed on hold until time slots become available (by wintertime, the networks know which of the new fall series are not generating an audience). Production on a new second-season series may begin as early as October, or as late as January or February.

Cable, once more flexible, now follows the front buying schedule. As cable has become a viable advertising medium, the networks follow their broadcast counterparts through the upfront buying season (see Chapter 19). Pay networks, which are free from schedules set by ad agencies, debut series when internal strategies deem it appropriate.

In syndication, pitches are made during the spring and summer, with most pilots made in late summer or fall. Syndicators like to have their pilots ready before Thanksgiving, in time for advance screenings to select station groups and advertisers needing to make decisions prior to the Association of Independent Television Stations (INTV) convention in December and the National Association of Television Program Executives (NATPE) convention in January. By NATPE, many key deals are already signed. The next six months are spent clearing stations in as many markets as possible. Production of new series usually begins in July or August, also for a September debut, with the shooting schedule completed sometime during the winter (depending upon the number of shows to be produced).

Public television stations and producers present projects to PBS through the spring and summer, and financing decisions are made in the fall for programs that will air the following fall. Since public television programs almost always involve third-party funding (and, often, interaction between an outside producer and a producing station), the development process actually begins at least a year prior to the PBS pitch. If PBS, and the closely allied CPB, do not provide complete funding, then the producer must continue to seek funding from other sources, and the hunt for financing may even continue for some months into the year in which the production is scheduled to be seen.

BUSINESS AND INSTITUTIONAL VIDEO

Business video might be used to relay quarterly reports from the chairman of the company to employees or stockholders; to provide instruction for operating a new piece of equipment; to train salespeople on a new product line; or to teach proper interviewing techniques. An in-house production group is assigned to the project, and works closely with the department for which the project is being made. In some instances, the project is produced out-of-house. Projects are usually financed by departmental budgets, but may also be subsidized by a corporate video department budget that is available to all departments.

Most companies operate these facilities as audiovisual support services—akin to the company photographer, whose services are available by scheduling a date—and they are often set up as a subdivision of a creative-services unit. The audiovisual facilities are available to any department within the company, with development, production, and duplication costs allocated on a project basis.

The scope and capability of an in-house video group will vary depending upon the company's need and upon budget resources. Some groups employ a bare-bones staff, consisting of a studio manager and a producer or project manager, with freelancers hired as needed for each project. Other video groups employ staff producers, directors, writers, editors, and technical crew. The most common situation is somewhere between the two, with in-house staff responsible for everyday projects—video news releases, point-of-purchase merchandising video, reports from executives to employees, and training tapes—and additional freelancers added for larger projects such as video annual reports, materials for annual sales meetings, and major product introductions. With very few exceptions, these productions have no commercial value beyond internal and external company communications.

Most company executives have the choice of either assigning a project to an in-house video unit or hiring an outside firm. An outside production company may be hired if it specializes in certain types of merchandising video, in interactive presentations that combine videodiscs and personal computers, or in large-scale company meetings. In some companies, the video department serves in an advisory role when outside vendors are hired, offering insights about production personnel and procedures, and occasionally providing facilities as well. In cases where an outside firm is used instead of an in-house group, there may be resentment on the part of the latter: an outside company has been hired to do something exciting and flashy, and the in-house staff has been deprived of the experience.

Every major metropolitan area supports several firms that specialize in video production for corporate clients. Most projects are produced on a work-for-hire basis (see page 166)—the production company is paid a fee for services rendered, and the client owns the master tapes and the copyright. In rare situations where the material may be valuable beyond its use by the company, production companies have arranged for an equity position, outright ownership after a period of exclusive in-company use, or distribution rights to sell the tapes to other companies.

Whenever a video project may have some commercial value, but neither marketing nor distribution plans are clear or well-defined, the production company and the client should each retain a percentage of ownership. The split should be based on the contribution of each party—creative, financial, or entrepreneurial. In situations where marketing and distribution plans are more clearly defined, and the production company will have an active role in the venture, the company may sometimes produce at cost, sacrificing markup for profit participation. Typically, the markup is in the range of 15 to 35 percent of the production budget.

If the client distributes the program, then the production company is often required to do the job on a work-for-hire arrangement, at normal rates, and may negotiate for a royalty. A rate of 5 to 15 percent of distributor's net income, after deductions for marketing and manufacturing, is common.

33

Production Staff

There are two types of staff on every television production. "Above-the-line" staff includes the creative and administrative people: the executives, producers, writers, director, cast, set designer, music composer, and so forth. "Below-the-line" refers to physical facilities, technical people, and people who work in the studio or on location: engineers, construction crew, technical crew, camera operators, makeup artists, editors, mixers, and so forth. The placement of musicians, graphic artists, wardrobe designers, and others who straddle the line is determined by the hiring company for its own convenience. The terms "above-the-line" and "below-the-line" date back to a style of accounting established during the golden age of Hollywood—"below-the-line" apparently refers to crew and facilities maintained as ongoing overhead items versus project-specific items that require special cash payment.

This chapter describes the roles of people who work "above the line." It is organized by titles, but titles can be misleading. Most of the titles described below can apply to several different job functions, depending upon the organization, type of program, distribution channel, industry tradition, and whims of the person doing the hiring.

THE EXECUTIVE PRODUCER

The *executive producer* refers to the business person most responsible for getting the series on the air, or arranging the majority of the production financing. The senior creative person on the project may also get this credit.

On a network series, the executive producer usually supervises all creative aspects of the program. On some projects, where the art of the deal is critical to arranging financing or distribution, the executive producer credit may be taken by the person who arranges for the money—and in extreme cases, this person may not know (or care) much about the small details of making a television program. For this type of executive producer, television is a business, not an art.

The executive producer title is more clearly defined in local television. At a local station, the executive producer in charge of news reports to the news director. For stations that continue to create and produce original programs, the executive producer for "non-news" programming reports to the program director, and supervises original production.

The duties of the executive producer generally include selection of senior staff members; approval of key performers; approval of script (and/or format); approval of technical facility; and approval of the business arrangements for all concerned. Since the executive producer is the senior manager, he or she devotes some percentage of time to people issues, though the day-to-day management of the staff is the responsibility of the producer. Some executive producers become more directly involved in one or more specific areas, such as casting, scripting, or deal-making. In theory, the executive producer's job is supervision and guidance, not execution.

THE PRODUCER

The *producer* of a television program is the person responsible for the creative, logistic, budgetary, and technical aspects of a project or series. He or she reports to the executive producer, who effectively acts as the chairman of the board to the producer's president. The executive producer is concerned with the grand scheme and client/customer contact; the producer, with day-to-day task and staff management. Some producers are concerned only with the creative aspects of production, and others are concerned only with logistics.

For a prime-time network series, the producer may focus almost exclusively on the creative aspects of the production, with other staff members coordinating logistics. Many producers of prime-time programs are also writers who shape the program's characters, story lines, and overall development through close supervision of other writers as well as direct involvement in casting decisions. In fact, a prime-time series may have several producers working at different levels.

The *senior producer* title is a means of elevating a producer to a higher level when the executive producer title is either inappropriate or unavailable.

A *supervising producer* is most often used on a network series, when an entire season's programs require large-scale coordination. A supervising producer is frequently concerned with logistics, schedules, and budgets, though the term may be applied to supervisors with primarily creative functions as well. A supervising producer may also be in charge of the series, while each episode may have its own producer(s). The title *series producer* may be used in this instance as well. What do these titles actually mean? That depends upon the individual situation, and the way the title sounds to those agreeing to its use.

A *line producer* is directly responsible for logistics, schedules, and budgets. Contributions to the creative effort are of secondary importance. It is not, generally, a creative role.

A *segment producer* is responsible for specific segments within a larger production.

Associate producer (AP) is another term that can be defined only within the context of a particular project or series. On a talk, game, or variety show, an associate producer may participate in the writing. On a talk show, an associate producer may be in charge of finding and scheduling ("booking") guests, and may supervise the resulting segments in the studio. On a magazine show, an associate producer may be a field producer—writing, directing, and editing stories. An associate producer on a network series is frequently in charge of post-production, but may also serve as the producer's point person in casting, working with writers, managing the budget and schedules, and so on. These duties are common for associate producers on variety shows, music and comedy specials, and information programs (such as home video how-to programs). In its pure form, the job of associate producer entails assisting the producer, taking care of time-consuming details, and often supervising the other staff members. The associate producer is a liaison between senior and junior staff members, and between different departments (such as public relations and accounting).

The *production assistant* (PA) is a junior staff member. PA may be the first job for a newcomer, but many PAs are more experienced, and may be in line for an associate producer job. A *production coordinator* is an upgraded production assistant, and may do some tasks associated with an associate producer. *Control room PA* is a more specialized job, and may be under the jurisdiction of the

Director's Guild of America (DGA) in some situations. The control room PA logs tapes and time cues, and his or her duties may overlap with those of the associate director (see below).

AGREEMENTS FOR PRODUCERS

There are two key clusters of issues in every agreement for a producer or executive producer. The first is based on rendering services; the second is related to the creation of programs or program elements. Executive producer and producer agreements are typically two to ten pages long (more if a profit definition is involved), and tend to cover many details. Agreements with associate producers are not as long, detailing only the key points related to rights and services. Many production companies hire junior staff people without any written agreement at all, though a short memorandum detailing the key points of the business arrangement, and addressing the transfer of rights, is advisable.

The following items should be covered in all producing agreements. For the sake of convenience, the word "producer" will be used to include executive producer, producer, associate producer, and the other classifications listed above. The checklist and model agreement in Appendixes B10 and B11 should also be consulted.

1. The *business relationship* between the hiring entity and the producer. This must be clearly defined. Is the producer an employee or an independent contractor? This distinction is important for purposes of tax liability, personal injury insurance, unemployment insurance, workman's compensation, vesting in pension plans, and ownership of the proceeds of creative work. In short, an *employee* typically works on premises provided by the employer, under its direct supervision or control. An *independent contractor* works for himself or herself. Although he or she may work at an office or in a facility provided by the hiring company, this is usually a matter of convenience, not a condition of hiring. An independent contractor does not receive the typical employee benefits.

   All of the creative efforts of an employee are considered to be a *work for hire,* whose copyright passes to the employer. In order for the creative work of an independent contractor to be considered a work for hire, it must be specifically described as such in a written work-for-hire agreement between the independent contractor and the hiring company.

   The distinctions between employees and independent contractors are explained in greater detail in Chapter 45.

2. A *description of the services* to be rendered by the producer. Such services may be stated in a general way, as in "the duties and obligations typically required of a producer of a major-market news program." The description can also be a long list of specific responsibilities followed by a catch-all phrase like "and all of the other duties typically required of a producer of a major-market news program." The best agreements provide a detailed list of the prospective employee's day-to-day responsibilities, but allow flexibility for personal growth.

3. The degree of *exclusivity*. May the producer serve in a similar capacity on projects that are unrelated to the employer's programs? And may the producer serve in other capacities—as writer or director, for example—on other programs?

4. *Compensation*—how much, and when it will be paid? Employees are usually paid weekly, bi-weekly, or twice a month; independent contractors are often paid semi-monthly or monthly. One popular alternative is linking partial payments to the project's schedule—an independent contractor might receive one-quarter of the total payment on signing the agreement, one-quarter on the first day of shooting, one-quarter on the start of editing, and one-quarter on delivery of the finished project. The formula varies, but the underlying philosophy is to pay the producer a reasonable wage while insuring his or her involvement through the end of the project. While it is clearly to the producer's advantage to front-load the payments, most agreements reflect a reasonable compromise.

5. A *description of the rights* granted to the hiring company, not only with regard to the current project(s), but also projects in development. For example, if a producer begins development of a new project for a station while an employee of the station, the station will own all rights to the project unless some other arrangement is described in the agreement. Another example: if a segment producer working on a tabloid magazine show develops a story that the employer subsequently sells as a TV movie, the segment producer's involvement in the secondary property must be clear from several perspectives, notably possible employment on the movie project, financial compensation as a member of the movie production's staff, and possibly, additional compensation from the movie's profits. (Whether the segment producer gets any of these benefits is entirely subject to negotiation, though in this instance, tradition

does not favor the segment producer's negotiating position.) Some hiring companies will not make commitments regarding future work, in effect dissuading employees and independent contractors from discussing new concepts with their employers.

6. Who has the *right of "final cut,"* or the right to declare a program complete? In a few cases, a producer will have final artistic control; usually though, the production company or network will retain this right. Related issues include control over marketing, distribution, and other business decisions.

7. The *on-screen credit* to be received by the producer. This should be clearly described: not only the wording of the credit, but also the prominence and the placement of the credit. Will it appear on every episode? In first position? Full-screen or shared? What happens to these promises if additional producers are hired?

8. *Representations, warranties, and indemnities.* In the "Representations and Warranties" section, the producer states that he or she is free to enter the agreement, and that there are no agreements presently in effect that would affect his or her ability to perform the services described in the new agreement. The producer also confirms that any ideas brought to the project will be either original or in the public domain, and that any such ideas will not violate the rights of any other person or institution. The notion of rights here relates to copyrights and property rights as well as personal rights—the right to privacy, and to protection from defamation, slander, and libel (see Chapter 17).

Too many agreements are one-sided: the producer makes representations and warranties, but the hiring company does not. Ideally, both parties should present a comprehensive list of what they represent and warrant to one another. The concept of representations and warranties is discussed in greater detail on page 449.

The "Indemnification" section that usually follows "Representations and Warranties" may include foreboding language; it provides both parties with clear financial remedies should any of the representations, warranties, or any other terms of the agreement be breached or proven untrue. This section is often quite technical and requires a lawyer's reading. In essence, "indemnification" clauses detail who will pay the costs of defending against losses, and who will pay in the case of judgments that require damages. (For more about indemnities, see page 449.)

9. *Credits.* Most agreements require the producer to allow the hiring company, and its licensees, to use the producer's name, biography, photograph, and so forth in the marketing of the program. In some instances, the producer may retain the right to remove his or her name from the program's credits, and from any related advertising or promotional materials—typically to disassociate himself or herself from a product gone bad.

10. The right of the producer for *reimbursal* for travel and entertainment expenses within a reasonable amount of time. Such expenses may be limited by a process of pre-approval, by budget parameters, or by company policies (employees may not be permitted to entertain one another, for example). Some companies will not reimburse items over $25 without a receipt. Reimbursement within 30 days of submission of the expense report is reasonable. It's usually best for individual employees to limit their credit card purchases on behalf of the production; a production account with retail vendors (such as office supply stores and nearby restaurants for late-night meals) has become common practice.

THE DIRECTOR

A television director combines three essential assets: the ability to guide performers to their best work; the taste and discretion to compose and select the optimum visual presentation; and the technical know-how to supervise a crew of engineers and operators.

Although the specific responsibilities of the director's job vary depending upon the type of project, it is fair to say that most directors spend about half their time planning, and the other half either rehearsing, shooting, and/or editing.

The planning phase usually begins with a series of production meetings to determine technical requirements such as set and lighting design. The director will also interact with the cast and the performers.

On a situation comedy, the director typically works a five-day week. A typical week's schedule might run as follows. The first day is devoted to a script reading with cast members in the morning. In the afternoon, the director plans camera angles, frequently with the help of an associate director, and screens the edited version of the previous week's show. He or she spends the second day on the set, working with the performers. The third day is a camera rehearsal where performances and camera angles are integrated (sitcoms are produced on videotape with multiple cameras). The fourth day brings more rehearsal, and the recording of two (sometimes three) takes of the show. At this point, the director spends most of his or her time in the control room, offering performance comments only when necessary. The fifth day is devoted to screening and working with the editor to select the best reading of each line in the script. Some directors are more involved with editing than others.

If a single director handles the entire series, or shares it with perhaps one other director, then a season-long contract is common. Most sitcoms work with several directors who are paid per episode, and may be guaranteed a particular number of episodes per season.

Directors of hour-long dramatic series follow a similar schedule.

A director of soap operas follows a similar routine, though the amounts of time for rehearsal and shooting are compressed in order to produce five shows per week. Several directors may share duties on a single daytime drama series, shooting one or two days per week and prepping on the others. Since soaps run for years, principal directors are typically hired as staff.

On a news program, the director becomes active once tape pieces begin to arrive from the editing rooms, usually a few hours prior to air and during the broadcast itself. The format of a news program is pre-determined, but the director must review the entire script, screen as many of the edited videotape stories as possible (or at least their first and last few seconds), and prepare for any live interview segments. Directors are generally employed as full-time staff working for the station or network.

Talk shows are generally recorded, or broadcast live, one per day, or, in a condensed schedule, perhaps two or even three per day. Rehearsal typically precedes the recording of each episode by an hour or so. A director is typically hired for the entire season, and paid a weekly salary as a freelancer.

Game shows are usually recorded in batches of three to five half hours per day, typically for several weeks. Then, the staff returns to the office for several weeks to prepare more game material (such as questions), book more contestants, etc. The director is paid per week of completed programs on a freelance contract.

ASSOCIATE DIRECTOR

When a production involves more than three cameras and a small number of other cues (such as sound or lighting cues), the director is frequently assisted by an *associate director* (AD). The AD is responsible for all communication with videotape recording and playback facilities, and with departments that do not require the director's explicit creative attention, such as audio or videotape recorders/playback. The AD also times all segments, calls countdowns to time cues, prepares logs of all audiotape and videotape recordings plus playback material, and maintains schedules.

Associate directors work on videotaped and live shows. Sometimes, when there is a great deal of real-time coordination, or when a production's tradition demands, the AD is assisted by a control-room production assistant.

Assistant director is a film term, and applies when a television program is shot on film. A film AD is in charge of the set; he or she issues call times for the cast and crew, prepares production reports (including actual time spent filming each scene, breaks, downtime due to equipment or personnel problems, and so on), and serves as the eyes of the production company on the set.

Freelance directors typically select their own freelance ADs. Staff directors work with the AD assigned to their program. Although ADs are paid considerably less than directors, they are employed on the same basis as directors on most productions.

DIRECTOR'S GUILD OF AMERICA

The Director's Guild of America, or DGA, is a union for directors. The DGA has negotiated collective-bargaining agreements with the commercial networks and with production companies that supply the networks with programming. A network or production company that is a signatory to a DGA agreement agrees to hire only DGA personnel to serve as directors, associate or assistant directors, control-room production assistants, and stage managers. The DGA also has contracts with some suppliers to the syndication and cable markets, but there is no DGA agreement covering syndication in general, or basic cable. Production for these markets is frequently done by directors who are not members of the DGA.

A member of the DGA can only work for DGA signatories; to put it another way, union members can work only in union shops. Since there are many non-union opportunities in cable and home video, younger directors often choose to work there without becoming DGA members. (See page 456 for a general discussion of the role of unions in the television business.)

The following condenses the key points in the DGA Freelance Live and Tape Television Agreement. The DGA Basic Agreement that applies to motion picture production on film is similar in most instances.

- The director contributes to the overall creative effort, and should participate in the selection of key creative personnel. At the very least, the director should be informed of proposed decisions before they are finalized.

- The director must receive minimum compensation as detailed in the agreement. A director of a network prime-time, hour-long dramatic program, for example, would receive a minimum of $26,082 for preparation and shooting. Rates for sitcoms are comparable, but rates for studio series are considerably less. For a dramatic half-hour network prime-time show, the rate is $15,819 for seven days of work, including prep and shooting. For a one-time network variety hour-long special, the rate is $21,322 for up to 18 days of work. For a non-prime network variety series, the rate is considerably lower: $5,076 per week.

- When directing a pilot for a series, the director is entitled to additional compensation if the series is ordered.

- The director receives additional compensation for working on holidays and weekends.

- The director receives additional compensation for development services, for directing talent tests, for shooting underwater or in flight, and for other special situations.

- The director receives residuals for replays. For a network prime-time program, the director receives 100 percent of the base rate. For plays on syndication, the first run pays 50 percent of the network base (or 40 percent of the non-network base if the program was originally produced for cable or syndication); the second run pays 40 percent of the network base (30 percent for non-network); and the scale works its way down to 5 percent for the thirteenth and each subsequent run. These numbers are provided only as rough figures; a detailed explanation of the current rates can be found in the DGA agreement.

- The production is required to pay fringe benefits on behalf of the director to the DGA. The amounts are as follows: $5^1/2$ percent of gross salary for pension, plus 7 percent of gross salary for health and welfare. In addition, the director contributes $2^1/2$ percent of gross compensation to the DGA.

- An insurance policy is required when the director works under dangerous conditions, such as underwater or in flight.

- In theory, the standard DGA agreement should be sufficient as the contract between the hiring company and the director. In reality, a separate or additional agreement, more specific to the individual project and employment situation, is common.

PRODUCER-DIRECTOR HYPHENATES

A producer-director is one person who performs two jobs. From the perspective of the producer-director, the combination provides an unusual amount of control, and the flexibility to pursue the most enticing creative aspects of both jobs. The title, and the premium salary, are also appealing. From the perspective of the hiring company, a producer-director combination is a way to save money on two significant line items. The total paid to one individual is almost always less than the total that would be paid to two; sometimes, the combination can be hired for a premium of only 30 or 40 percent.

The *field producer,* one kind of producer-director hybrid, evolved with the use of portable video equipment. Single-camera production is more like simple filmmaking than traditional multi-camera television production—one person can produce, write, and direct a "field piece." In terms of hierarchy, a field producer is roughly equivalent to a segment producer, who in turn can be equal to or just above associate producer.

DGA rates and rules should be consulted when hiring producer-directors or field producers in guild shops.

WRITER(S)

Most television programs require the services of at least one writer. When several writers are employed, a head writer often supervises the group.

The specific responsibilities of the television writer vary, depending upon the project and its requirements. A newswriter may research a story, assemble and double-check the facts, and produce a work of journalistic substance; a newswriter may also do little more than rewrite stories taken from wire services. Frequently, the job involves a little bit of both. A writer of children's programming takes an active part in developing program segments and character interaction, then scripts the sequences. Writing a soap involves contributions to an ongoing story line. Senior writers and producers determine the story line, and the writing staff then scripts individual episodes based on story outlines. A writer of prime-time comedy or drama usually submits a basic story outline, which is revised by the writer and/or story editor(s) and/or producer(s). This then becomes the basis for a first, second, and polished version of the script, which goes through similar revisions. Scripts are always changed after they've been read by performers; the amount of change depends upon the production schedule, the performer's degree of control, and, often, the degree to which the script "works" as it moves from page to stage.

Some writers function as staff members, or employees; others work on freelance contracts, which may be similar to working on assignment for a specified number of scripts per season. These creative works are acquired by the production company or network, and the writer surrenders all (or most) rights, at least for a period of time (see page 204 for more on transfer of script rights). Most writers also prepare their own original scripts in hopes of getting hired, or selling their own series, and these are owned by the writer.

THE WRITERS GUILD OF AMERICA

In fact, there is no single entity called The Writers Guild of America (WGA). Instead, there are two organizations that work closely together: Writers Guild of America East and Writers Guild of America West. Both negotiate and administer the same collective-bargaining agreements and share a pension and a health benefits plan. Combined, these organizations represent over 10,000 professional writers working in motion pictures, television, and radio, but not commercial advertising. The WGA negotiates agreements with the networks, syndication companies, and other entities involved in hiring writers to create television programming. When a production company or network becomes a signatory to the WGA, it agrees to the terms of the Minimum Basic Agreement (MBA), which requires that all writers hired by the company are members of the WGA (or will become members, as below). When a writer becomes a member of the WGA, he or she cannot write for a company that is not a signatory to the MBA. A production company can hire a writer who is not yet a WGA member; in these instances, the writer must join the WGA within 30 days of employment. Otherwise, the signatory company will be required by the WGA to terminate the writer's employment.

To become a signatory, a company simply contacts the WGA and requests an application. A new company may be required to post a bond prior to employing any writers. When a writer is hired, payments are made directly to the writer, with a pension and health contribution paid to the WGA on the writer's behalf. If a writer earns a sufficient amount per year, he or she can qualify for a year's health coverage at no cost.

To become a member of the WGA, a writer must have an agreement with a signatory for work. (Broadcast companies tend to be signatories; basic cable, home video, and syndication companies may not be signatories. It's best to check with the WGA for specific situations.) Upon signing the agreement, the writer then has 30 days to join the WGA. The initiation fee for freelance writers in WGA East is $1,500, and $2,500 for WGA West, although identical services are provided to writers on both coasts. Members are required to pay $50 per year for dues, plus 1.75 percent of gross compensation related to WGA contracts (0.25 percent is also placed in a strike fund, so members may borrow interest-free in case of a strike).

The following are the key elements of the WGA agreement:

- Minimum rates for the writing of a story, first draft teleplay, and final draft teleplay. These rates are based on the length of the program, and whether it airs in prime-time or on a network. Additional rates are quoted for rewrite and polish; for plot outline, backup script, show format, and narration; and for a show bible (a complete explanation of the history and characters on a series). If the program is produced for pay TV or home video, and if it is in the style that normally airs in network prime-time, then the network prime-time rates apply. Rates are higher for pilots than for series.

- Rerun compensation. Calculating these payments can be complicated, and readers are advised to refer to the WGA Basic Agreement, or the Schedule of Minimums, for a complete explanation and the latest information.

- Compensation for other types of programs are similar in approach, but different in numbers: check the current Basic Agreement for details. Residuals and re-use fees are also paid for replays on basic cable, for home video releases, and for foreign runs.

- Compensation for writers hired on a weekly basis, who work as staff members.

- The minimum rate at which a production company, network, or distributor may purchase an existing work from a WGA member. The minimum for options is 5 percent for the first 180 days, and 10 percent for each period of 180 days thereafter.

- Additional compensation for a writer if a sequel is created based on his or her work—or if a character that first appeared in his or her work becomes the central character in a spin-off series or appears in other episodes.

- Payment rates, and a required number of writers, for variety shows including rates for sketches.

- Payment rates for quiz and audience participation programs on both network and syndication; for daytime serials (soap operas); and for religious programs, documentaries, and news programs.

- The requirement that the hiring company pay 6 percent of the writer's gross compensation to the WGA pension fund, plus 6.5 percent of the writer's gross compensation to the WGA health and welfare fund.

- Rules regarding working hours and conditions, travel, and notice prior to termination.

- Rules regarding appropriate credits. The MBA is very specific about the form and placement of credits: the terms "written by," "teleplay by," and "story by" have particular meanings. These terms may trigger specific residual payments, or lead to a "separation of rights," whereby a writer who originates the project can hold back certain rights for himself or herself.

WRITER HYPHENATES

Since the writer is so critical to the creative development of a television project, many writers follow a natural inclination toward greater involvement in the production. Many writers become producers, or directors. Some become performers (and some writers performed before they became writers).

The *writer-producer* is common in the Los Angeles prime-time community, where capable writers are highly valued, and where they are frequently given the opportunity to stretch their creative muscles. In the best of circumstances, a writer-producer molds a series and its characters with special insight; in the worst, the writer-producer can be a difficult hindrance to efficient production, power placed in the wrong hands. Some writer-producers concentrate on writing (and rewriting the work of others), wielding the producer's power only when needed to win a creative point. Others concentrate on rewrites, or supervise performers or a writing staff without generating original scripts on their own. Every situation is different.

The *writer-director* is doing two discrete jobs. In the office and through the planning stages, he or she concentrates on writing; in the studio or on the soundstage, directing requires total attention, and the writing is either delayed or scheduled for off-hours. As with the producer-director, two fees are paid, based on DGA and WGA agreements; a writer-director hyphenate working on a non-union show is likely to be paid a fee that is less than a full writing fee and a full directing fee combined.

The *writer-performer* is frequently found in comedy. Many successful comedians have worked on the writing staff of comedy programs, or they've been stand-up comedians. The transition from writer or performer to writer-performer often evolves naturally, though the process can be accelerated by an aggressive agent or manager.

34

Performers

Most television performers are members of one or both of AFTRA (the American Federation of Television and Radio Artists) and SAG (the Screen Actors Guild). AFTRA's jurisdiction is essentially videotape and live productions, as well as radio programs and commercials produced on videotape; SAG's jurisdiction is television programs produced on film, film commercials, and theatrical motion pictures. In short, AFTRA is the relevant union if the program is live or on tape, and SAG is the relevant union if the program is shot on film. AFTRA has local chapters in most of the top-30 television markets. SAG works out of about 25 regional offices, including New York, Los Angeles, Chicago, Boston, and Miami. (See page 456 for a general discussion of the role of unions in the television business.)

Nearly all commercial television productions are made with AFTRA or SAG members. The exceptions include productions made in the smallest broadcast markets; some programs on basic cable networks; some corporate video; some made-for-home-video productions; some music video; and most educational video. The vast majority of performers with the skill and talent required for successful on-camera performance are members of AFTRA, SAG, or both. Although producers are loath to admit it, the rules of these unions are not too burdensome. What producers do tend to dispute, however, is how the payment of residuals is becoming more complex and expensive as distribution markets continue to evolve.

AFTRA AGREEMENT BASICS

It is difficult to discuss the provisions of a "basic" AFTRA agreement because there is no single agreement; instead, there are separate agreements between AFTRA and the commercial broadcast networks, public television, local television, and other entities. Copies of these agreements are generally available from AFTRA. There are some differences in work rules, but these separate agreements vary most in terms of minimums, residual schedules, and annual escalations. Each AFTRA agreement is quite complex.

For purposes of broad explanation, this section outlines the key points of the AFTRA network agreement. It should prove useful in understanding the mechanics of all AFTRA agreements.

Each agreement includes wage tables for specific types of performers. Some of the charts simply list a minimum fee for a particular type of program and activity. Sportscasters, for example, receive no less than $938 per event on network television (not including pre- or post-game shows), or $2,382 per week; that payment includes up to seven events in the same sport, or one week's broadcasting of Olympic games. Other wage tables are more complicated. An off-camera announcer speaking more than ten lines, for example, receives fees based on the length of the program. If the program is 15 to 30 minutes long, the fee is $287, and pays for three rehearsal hours during one day, with a two-hour minimum session and a three-hour minimum daily call. Extra time costs $20 per hour. For multiple performances in the same calendar week on the same show, the announcer receives between 1.75 and 3 times the single rate. The numbers for other types of performers vary, but the basic structure is common for most of the wage tables. Rates tend to change year to year; the rates quoted here applied to 1996.

The producing company is required to contribute to AFTRA's pension and welfare fund. Depending upon the type of project, the contribution due is between 11 and 12.65 percent of the performer's gross compensation; the lower rates apply to non-dramatic programs and soaps; a 12 percent rate applies to most network prime-time fiction series; performances in commercials and interactive projects earn the highest contribution amount. ("Gross" includes the amount actually paid to the performer before deductions plus overtime payments, commissions paid to third parties such as agents, fees paid for the use of a performer's own wardrobe, and related subsidies.) There is no ceiling for pension and welfare payments in the AFTRA agreement.

The performer must be given notice of the part to be played, the place of rehearsal, and the number of guaranteed days of performance (if any) not less than 24 hours in advance of the first reading or rehearsal session. Changes in the schedule must be provided 24 hours in advance as well.

When work is completed, payment is due no later than the Thursday following the last working week. Specific rules apply for performers who are working for extended periods of time. Small penalties apply for late payments ($4 per day to a maximum of $120; weekends and holidays are not included).

Residual compensation is due within 10 days of the first network re-broadcast, or within 60 days of a non-network re-broadcast. Compensation for foreign plays must be paid within 90 days of the first broadcast of the program.

Performers receive a 5-minute rest period during each 70-minute rehearsal period. There must be a 12-hour break between the end of work on one day and the start of work on the next (a penalty is charged if the break is less than 12 hours). Meal breaks are 70 minutes long (60 minutes, plus 5-minute breaks at the start and finish). Performers working under hazardous conditions are paid an additional $100 per program.

If a performer is paid over scale, he or she may agree to deduct overtime payments from the over-scale total—but only if this agreement is made at the time of the original contract.

Understudies receive the same minimum scale rate as the performer(s) for whom they are understudying.

Performers are not usually paid for interviews and auditions of reasonable length, but they are entitled to payment for excessive time (e.g., over one hour). If the audition is a more formal affair, then the performer receives half the program rate.

Performers are typically paid a wardrobe allowance when asked to appear in their own clothing. For regular wardrobe, the fee is $10 per outfit, and can go as high as $25 for formal evening wear.

Singers and dancers are entitled to additional monies for "step-outs" (instances in which the performer steps out of the chorus line or group to sing and dance).

Performers who double (play more than one role) may be entitled to additional compensation on certain types of programs.

Performers must be advised of scenes involving nudity, and must approve such appearances in advance.

A performer who warms up an audience is entitled to a percentage of the applicable program fee.

If a performer's photograph is used on a program, but the performer does not appear in the program, he or she is entitled to $25 for each episode in which the photo appears.

A performer who appears in remote telecasts may be entitled to a supplementary payment.

A producer can require a performer's exclusive services only under certain conditions (e.g., a specific level of guaranteed compensation).

For an ongoing series, a specific number of weeks' notice must be given if a program is canceled.

If a program is canceled, the performers are entitled to payment for all hours spent rehearsing prior to the posting of the cancellation notice.

Performers working on daytime serials or other ongoing series are entitled to two weeks of vacation time with pay if employed for less than five years, and three weeks, if employed longer. Performers who work on serials receive a premium for work on holidays.

Performers are entitled to a per diem of $30 per day when working more than 20 miles from the "broadcast center" of New York, Chicago, Los Angeles, or Washington, DC Automobile travel is reimbursed in accordance with company policy; if there is no company policy, then the performer receives 30 cents per mile (at least $3 per day) for using his or her own car. The producer is required to provide a $200,000 accidental death and dismemberment travel-insurance policy for each performer.

Travel time is considered work time—the hours spent traveling to or from a location are counted as rehearsal hours. If the performer's lodgings are more than 30 minutes from the location, then this travel time is also considered to be rehearsal time.

A schedule of residual payments details payments due for reuse of the program in a variety of media. On network replays, for example, performers receive 75 percent of the applicable minimum plus 20 percent of rehearsal and doubling fees. All other replays are paid on a sliding scale (replays 1 and 2, 75 percent; 3, 4, and 5, 50 percent; 6, 10 percent; 7 and each subsequent play, 5 percent). Foreign residuals are based on regions of the world. Area 1, which essentially includes all of the U.K., is the most lucrative, at 25 percent of the original program fee; Area 2 (most of the rest of Europe) is 10 percent; Areas 3, 4, and 5 constitute the rest of the world (except the U.S. and Canada), and plays in these countries pay the performer 5 percent of his or her original fee.

Performers receive 2.5 percent of producer's gross receipts for videocassettes and videodiscs on the first $1 million, and 3 percent thereafter. The monies are distributed pro rata, with a 2-to-1 ratio between principal performers and other players.

AFTRA arbitrates conflicts with producing companies on behalf of its members.

SAG AGREEMENT BASICS

As with AFTRA, there are several types of SAG agreements—for commercials, for network programs, for motion pictures, and so forth. Once again, readers are encouraged to review an up-to-date version of the relevant agreement carefully, since there is a wide range of work rules and rate structures involved.

The most recent SAG network agreement differs from the AFTRA network agreement in several ways:

The pension and health benefit is based on 12.65 to 13.3 percent of gross compensation, including original earnings and residuals, but excluding meal fees and rest-period penalty fees. There is also a ceiling per program on these contributions.

There are detailed provisions for optioning a performer's services.

There is more detail than in the AFTRA agreement on hiring ongoing performers for episodic television, and the contract is arranged so that these details are easy to find. For a series of one-hour programs, with a guarantee of 13 episodes, the work must be accomplished within a period of 18 consecutive weeks (otherwise a penalty must be paid). The rate for this work is no less than $2,334. If the commitment is between 6 and thirteen episodes, then the rate is $2,605. By comparison, for a half-hour program, the rates are $1,942 and $2,220 for similar commitments.

Meal periods run 60 minutes; meals must be scheduled every 6 hours.

The minimum per diem is $53, but the producer may deduct a specified amount for each meal supplied.

When shooting on location, and under certain conditions, the 12-hour rest period may be reduced to 10 hours (but not every night).

Penalties for rest-period violations are one day's salary, with a cap of about $1,000.

In New York City, the area considered "on location" is larger than the 20-mile radius in the AFTRA agreement. The SAG agreement defines "New York" as any area within 30 miles of Columbus Circle.

For nude scenes, prior written consent of the performer is required. Also, the set must be closed, and no still pictures may be taken without the performer's prior written consent.

Of course, there are many other rules. This section should, however, provide a general idea of the ways in which the AFTRA and SAG contracts are structured, and the issues involved in each agreement. Note, also, that the rules regarding FOX, WBTV and UPN series may vary, that there are often different rules and rates for daytime dramas, and that negotiations with AFTRA and SAG are not uncommon. In the entertainment business, special situations frequently turn up.

CASTING

There are several sources of performers for television productions.

TALENT AGENCIES

A talent agency is a company that specializes in representing performers, although many agencies represent producers, writers, directors, and other key creative people as well. Most successful performers working on the national scene are represented by a large agency; William Morris Agency, ICM, and CAA are among the biggest. There are also smaller boutique agencies that either specialize in particular formats (game shows, daytime drama, sports, news) or offer a level of personal service that a larger agency rarely delivers to most of its clients.

Although the business arrangements vary with specific performers, an agency typically collects a 10 percent commission on gross earnings for every job within the entertainment industry—whether the agency arranges for the work or not. The performer's paycheck is sent to the agency, which deducts a commission and issues a new check to its client. If the job is not within the entertainment industry, and was not arranged by the agency—hosting a presentation at an automotive industry trade show, for example—the performer is normally paid directly, without agency involvement.

Contrary to the dreams of many performers, agencies do not usually seek out work for their clients. Instead, agencies are responsive to the needs of the marketplace. When producers, networks, or advertising agencies are casting for a program, they usually call the larger agencies as a matter of course. The smaller agencies do their best to keep up with what's happening, and to stay on the active list of various casting entities.

Some well-known performers work without an agent, instead employing an attorney to negotiate fees on their behalf. In most cases, the attorney earns an hourly rate for services. Some high-powered Los Angeles attorneys take a commission of 5 percent or more in addition to, or in lieu of, an hourly fee. (A more detailed discussion of the roles of agents, lawyers, and business managers appears in Chapter 35.)

PHOTOGRAPHS, RÉSUMÉS, AND VIDEOTAPES

A photograph is a kind of calling card for a performer. The standard format for a performer's photograph is a recent 8 × 10 inch glossy photo, with name printed below the photo. On the back is a printed résumé or list of performance credits, union affiliations, and contact information (address and phone numbers for agency, for home, and for answering service).

Videotapes can be effective résumé tools, if the casting person takes the time to screen them. It is simply faster to scan a pile of photographs; performers whose photos are promising may be evaluated on videotape, but more often, an in-person meeting or audition is the first step. Some types of productions (for example, local news shows) make extensive use of videotapes.

INTERVIEWS AND AUDITIONS

As a prerequisite to getting a job, performers expect to be interviewed and auditioned, sometimes several times.

An interview generally runs under 30 minutes (often, under 15 minutes), and offers the producer or casting director an opportunity to speak informally with the candidate. The session is useful in learning whether the candidate can ad-lib, how the candidate presents himself or herself, how he or she responds to others, and, to a certain extent, the candidate's personal interests and motivations. Under the show business veneer, a casting interview is a job interview, and is subject to the same restrictions and standards that rule all employment proceedings. Questions about age, religious affiliation, marital status, race, and color should not be asked; to do so may bring about a complaint and an investigation of company hiring practices.

An audition may be held in addition to, or in place of, an interview. The audition typically requires the performer to read lines, or to ad-lib within a structured situation. For example, a news reporter may be required to read a news report aloud (in an office, on videotape, or live on the air), or to prepare a sample story; a sportscaster might be recorded doing play-by-play at an event. Some auditions require the candidate to interact with other performers.

Often, the first round of auditions is casual, and does nothing more than eliminate the least likely candidates. It may be conducted by an associate producer, who reports the most promising candidates to the producer, executive producer, and network executive(s). A director may be actively involved in the first round, or may join in as serious contenders are selected; this depends on the type of project and on personal style. A second round of auditions is usually more intensive, and yields between three and five finalists. A third round of auditions, now conducted with great attention to detail, allows the producer and others involved in the process to make a final decision. There may be more rounds, or fewer, depending upon the situation. If a substantial amount of work is required during the auditions, AFTRA or SAG may require that the performer(s) be paid.

NEGOTIATING THE PERFORMANCE AGREEMENT

Producers must balance two key issues when hiring talent: working within budget limitations, and attracting the best possible performers to the project. AFTRA and SAG prescribe minimum fees for performers working in productions within their jurisdictions. In non-union cases, market conditions unofficially dictate rates, subject to minimum wage regulations. Many performers, particularly those with experience, want to be paid more than the minimum fee. In many such cases, the performer sets a day rate for his or her services—this rate is usually negotiable, particularly if employment is for an extended period.

Before the producer tests anyone, or sits down to final auditions, it is important that a *pre-test option* be negotiated. A pre-test option fixes the basic terms of the agreement should the performer be successful in the audition. Without such an option, the network or distributor may "fall in love" with a particular performer, and insist that the producer deliver that performer regardless of price. That situation can place the performer in control, and a savvy agent can drive the price very high. A pre-test option that caps the performer's price is essential protection for the producer.

For well-known performers, or performers with strong agency or legal representation, the producer and the agent may spend hours, days, even weeks negotiating the fine points of daily/weekly/per-show salary, travel arrangements, profit participation, on-screen billing, use and appearance of the performer's name in advertising, and other such details.

A letter agreement is an appropriate form of contract for hiring the performer. This agreement should set forth the dates that the performer will be needed, the fees that will be paid, residuals, and so on. SAG and AFTRA have standard forms for certain kinds of hiring.

A more formal agreement may be prepared for high-paid performers, or for anyone working on a project where lengthy contracts make good business sense. Appendix B11 is a typical short-form agreement for services, adaptable to the performer context.

NON-UNION EMPLOYMENT

Most established television performers are members of AFTRA and SAG, and most major producing organizations are union signatories as well. However, many smaller production companies, home video companies, business video companies, and cable networks are not signatories to agreements with the performance unions. The reason is basically the cost of benefit payments and residuals. Some of these companies are poorly equipped, both financially and administratively, to pay ongoing residuals, while others simply want a more favorable arrangement. A non-union shop can hire anyone it pleases because it is not beholden to an agreement that says otherwise. A union performer, however, is in violation of his or her agreement when working for a non-signatory within the union's jurisdiction, and may be subject to a penalty or, upon repeated offenses, loss of union membership.

In certain situations, both AFTRA and SAG have negotiated "one-shot" short-term agreements covering particular projects, allowing a non-signatory company to hire union performers. AFTRA and SAG have been among the most reasonable unions in television, but even their flexibility has its limits.

The respective jurisdictions of AFTRA and SAG are limited only to American productions, resulting from deals made in the U.S. If the employment is purely foreign, then the producer may hire the performer outside the union agreement. There are gray areas defining the concept of "purely foreign"—if the production company is legitimately based abroad, and the project is produced abroad, then the production is probably foreign. Producers have been known to disguise a production as foreign in order to save on fees, withhold residuals, or avoid certain work rules.

WORKING WITH PERFORMERS

The performer is expected to do his or her job by following the instructions of the producer and director—who represent the production's management and owners—regardless of whether this expectation is explicitly worded in a contract. Most performers recognize this authority, take instructions, add their own creativity, and work hard to please their employers. The ideal situation is a lively give-and-take, with each party respectful of the other's role, but with a certain challenge and spice thrown in so that each does the best possible work. Ultimately, the performer should be comfortable with the words, the style, and the presentation.

Conversely, a strong performer matched with a needy director or production team can head off problems and present a polished product despite poor preparation, less-than-skillful direction, or troublesome production technique. To put this another way, experience counts for much in the television business, and a good performer can save a production.

Some performers, however, display a defiant attitude that can undermine the director's ability to complete the program or the producer's promises to a client. When there are problems, the performer can either (1) do the best he or she can under the circumstances; (2) fight the director and do what he or she believes is right, regardless of consequences; (3) complain to the powers-that-be; or (4) leave. In rare instances, he or she may attempt to have the offending producer or director fired, or try to take over. Both of these actions are predicated on the belief that the audience strongly associates the performer with the program, and that producers, directors, and writers are dispensable. The performer may win these battles, particularly if the producer feels that he or she has no choice—but will, in the process, acquire a reputation for "trouble."

WORKING WITH CELEBRITIES

Celebrities live by special rules—even though being famous and being a capable television performer are not always synonymous, and even though celebrity alone does not guarantee that a given performer is well suited for a particular role or project. Celebrities are typically paid considerably more than minimum union scale and, depending on the project, may receive a profit participation as well. Many celebrities are accustomed to special treatment and perks as part of the deal.

With few exceptions, celebrities are represented by agents, lawyers, or managers, who negotiate on their clients' behalf. The negotiation usually begins with a producer's offer, typically countered by a statement of the performer's going rate. Once the basic price is set, the negotiation moves on to profit participation(s) (if relevant), perks, and working conditions. First-class airfare is required in the union agreements, but many celebrities request additional tickets for family members or other traveling companions. Hotel accommodations and per diems may be subject to the same sorts of requests; these are generally honored if the expense is not too great.

In the best of circumstances, working with a celebrity brings the staff and crew to its professional best. The presence of a celebrity on the set also forces an attentiveness to the schedule, since well-known performers are available only for brief time periods. Sometimes, working with a celebrity is a disappointment, especially when a huge ego is part of the package. In these cases, difficulties can be anticipated and minimized by speaking with other producers and directors who have worked with the performer in the past.

WORKING WITH CHILDREN

There are several key issues that must be considered when hiring young performers. To start with, every state has its own child labor laws; these should be reviewed early in the planning of a production. The following are key provisions common to most child labor laws.

As a general matter, minors cannot be hired for any activity that may be hazardous or detrimental to the minor's moral development. This is an area open to interpretation; the state agency will not issue a work permit if it believes that there may be a problem.

If the work interferes with ongoing school education, then a teacher must be hired, and hours must be allotted to classroom work. This is not a problem for infrequent short-term hires; the parent or guardian simply decides whether to take the child out of school to work.

A parent or guardian must be present while the child is working. For instance, the California code requires that the parent or guardian be present within sight or sound for all minors under 16 years old.

The work permit can be revoked if the commissioner or other supervising authority detects wrongdoing or abuse of rights or privileges.

For each age group, there is usually a maximum amount of time allowed at the workplace, a maximum number of working hours allowed, and a minimum number of rest, recreation, and education hours. Travel time may be considered part of the working day. In California, for instance, children aged two to six are allowed up to six hours at the workplace with up to three hours of working time and not less than three hours of rest, recreation, and education. Children aged nine to 16 can be at the workplace for up to nine hours, and can work up to five hours on school days or seven hours on days off, with three hours minimum of schooling and one hour minimum of rest and recreation.

Unless they are ratified by a court, most ongoing agreements for services are voidable by the minor at any time. In most (but not all) states, a parent or guardian can sign a sample release form on behalf of a minor (see below). Children are paid in amounts equal to what an adult would earn in comparable roles. Payments are made to a parent or guardian, who disburses monies to the benefit of the child. In some states, room and board can be deducted by the parent or guardian as well as professional expenses such as travel, clothing, and legal and accounting fees. Essentially, the parent or guardian becomes the trustee for the child, and is held to standards common for fiduciary relationships.

WORKING WITH UNPAID PERFORMERS

Many of the people who appear on television are unpaid: they are interviewed, they appear in the background in entertainment and news footage, or they are the subjects of news reports.

Most people who appear on television do so of their own volition. The majority of these unpaid performers are willing to cooperate with the television establishment, and will generally agree to sign whatever documents are necessary to assure an appearance.

THE RELEASE FORM

A release form (see Appendix B3) is a type of contract, and it deals with three types of rights, described briefly below, and in detail in Chapter 19.

Any creative expression is usually the property of the creator—in this case, the person signing the release form. In essence, this is a matter of copyright (see Chapter 16). The rights of privacy and publicity are the rights to control the commercial use of a personal likeness or other identifying characteristics (see Chapter 17). If uses beyond the original program are contemplated, these rights should be specifically released.

The right against being libeled or slandered gives redress against someone making assertions that are untrue and harmful to the reputation of another person (see Chapter 17). Under the U.S. Constitution, anyone is allowed to be wrong in such assertions, provided that he or she did not act with negligence with respect to a private person, or with malice or reckless disregard of the truth with respect to a public person.

A typical release form always contains an affirmative grant of rights. It may also contain representations and warranties and a preventative grant.

The *affirmative grant* says that in exchange for good and valuable consideration, the unpaid performer grants the right to record and exploit his or her image, and to exploit his or her name and persona. Typically, the right is granted in perpetuity, for all uses and all media anywhere in the world—not only in the production itself, but also anything connected with advertising and publicity. With such a grant, the producer can exploit programs including the unpaid performer at his/her sole discretion.

The *representation and warranties* section, if present in the form, includes a promise that nothing said by the unpaid performer will be libelous or will otherwise violate the rights of any third party, and that the statements are free of claims.

The *preventative grant* or waiver says that the person who signs the agreement will not make any claims against the producer on issues of copyright, privacy, publicity, defamation, or for any other cause.

Release forms are advisable whenever any unpaid performer speaks on a television production, particularly outside of a news show or other factual context of public interest. For those who appear but do not speak, discretion and circumstances serve as a guide. Members of a studio audience should be ticketed; the use of the ticket is a transaction that shows the intent to participate on the part of every audience member, and a statement to this effect may even be printed on the ticket. People who are part of a crowd observing a public event, or the staging of an event for a television show, may be used in context in cutaway shots. But if anyone will be appearing prominently, it is advisable to secure a signed release form.

35

Agents, Attorneys and Business Management

A substantial industry has been built by agents, lawyers, accountants, and other specialists who advise and act on behalf of people working in television. The governing notion is that many creative people are poor businesspeople, and that the business professional can help generate more money while untangling contractual problems.

AGENTS

By definition, an agent is someone authorized to act on behalf of someone else, the principal. The law of agency is a law of delegation of power. In television, and in the entertainment business at large, an agent is a representative who negotiates deals on behalf of clients, and, under the best of circumstances, finds work for these clients as well.

Agents are extremely common in some areas of the television business, and virtually non-existent in others. They are an important part of the commercial network production system, and agents actively participate in most important talent agreements for network, syndicated, pay cable, and local television productions. Agents are not part of the corporate or business video industries, except when high-priced talent (such as a well-known director, composer, or writer) is involved. The situation in home video and basic cable is similar. Agents tend to specialize, so a performer who appears on daytime drama may have one agent for that activity, and another at the same agency for voice-over work. This is often the case for writers and directors as well.

The largest agencies have offices in Los Angeles and New York, and, frequently, smaller ones in Chicago, London, and several other major cities around the world. The William Morris Agency, ICM, and CAA are among the most powerful agencies, representing performers of every description, as well as writers, directors, producers, scenic designers, and other creative personnel. Their domain is not limited to television—larger agencies maintain literary, motion picture, theatrical, and even corporate departments.

Smaller agencies may devote more attention to individual clients, particularly the lesser-knowns. Some agencies specialize in particular markets, such as news anchors and reporters, juvenile performers, or soap opera performers. Others offer full service, from book publishing to legitimate theater, usually with a concentration of power in one or two areas.

Agencies and creative people can work together for specific periods of time or on a per-project basis. For newcomers, an agreement to work together on a single project can sometimes be arranged; if the project is a success, the agency expects the creative person to sign up as a long-term client. Contracts generally run one to three years, and may be limited to only one type of representation—for performance but not for writing, for example. The agency receives the client's paychecks; deducts a commission of 10 or 15 percent of all income, including fees, royalties, and profit participation; and pays its client. If the client finds his or her own work, the agent is still entitled to the commission, under the terms of most agency agreements.

When an agency works closely with a producer—helping to sell the program to a distributor and supplying many of its own clients to the cast and staff—then the agency is said to be "packaging the project." For such packages, the agency receives 5 percent or more of the total project revenues, but does not deduct commissions from the client's individual income.

An agency typically negotiates all terms and conditions of every agreement, from fees and profit participation to screen credit. After the basic terms have been hammered out by the individual agent, the agency's attorneys attend to the details.

REGULATION OF AGENTS AND OTHER REPRESENTATIVES

Many states regulate the activities of agencies, either as a part of the regulation of employment agencies in general, or under rules specific to the entertainment business. Under such regulation, the agent must register and obtain a license. Failure to do so can lead to civil and even criminal penalties, including the cancellation of the agreements for representation and the refunding of fees previously taken. These laws also generally restrict the fees that the agent can charge to his or her client. Talent agents are not the only ones to whom these regulations apply; a manager or other representative who performs agent-like functions may be under the jurisdiction of the agent rules as well.

In New York, Article II of the General Business Law concerns licensing of all employment agencies, within which are special rules applicable to a "theatrical employment agency." A theatrical employment agency includes any person or company that procures, or attempts to procure, employment or engagements for motion pictures, radio, television, and other categories of the entertainment business. As for the manager-as-agent, the statute specifically excludes from its definition of a theatrical agency "the business of managing such entertainments, exhibitions or performances, or the artists or attractions constituting the same, where such business only incidentally involves the seeking of employment therefor." Although the words "only incidentally involves" are fairly restrictive, this provision at least recognizes that the activities of an agent and those of a manager inevitably overlap.

A New York theatrical agency must register with the state and file a great deal of information about itself, its personnel, and its business premises. It must post a $5,000 bond and file copies of its standard agreements. There is a limitation on the maximum fees that the agency can charge: 10 percent of the compensation payable to the talent (orchestra, concert, and opera fees can go up to 20 percent). Failure to comply is a misdemeanor punishable in some cases by up to a year in jail, and can lead to the return of fees.

In California, under Chapter 4 of the Labor Code, a "talent agent" is one who tries "to procure employment or engagements for an artist or artists." "Artists" include performers, writers, directors, cinematographers, composers, lyricists, arrangers, and other professionals in the entertainment industry, including specifically the television business. The manager problem is addressed in three ways. First of all, the regulations do not cover the activity of procuring recording contracts. Second, a manager can help an agent do his job, at the agent's initiative. Third, there is a one-year limit on bringing claims that a manager has acted as an unlicensed agent.

Other California requirements follow the normal pattern of registration and oversight. The law requires that a fee schedule be filed with the state and conspicuously posted, but there are no set maximums. Form contracts must be filed and approved, and a $10,000 bond is required. Civil penalties are available, but an agency's failure to obtain a license is not subject to criminal punishment.

Even when they do not have problems under the specific talent-agency laws, managers, attorneys, and other artists' representatives generally share fiduciary duties with agencies in their relationships with their clients. Fiduciary duties require that the representative act with strict probity and avoid conflicts of interest. While the representative is allowed to earn an appropriate fee, it may not use its relationship with the client to obtain benefits for itself at the client's expense.

The various talent guilds, and performer unions such as AFTRA and SAG, usually have their own restrictions on the activities of agents, including caps on the fees which can be charged. There is frequently a specific form of agency contract which the union requires to be used.

ATTORNEYS

Attorneys have two principal roles in television: to negotiate and document deals, and to "clean up messes."

Attorneys are usually paid by the hour, and most will be happy to allow the client to set the working parameters. Some clients are competent deal-makers, who consult the attorney as they plan the terms, and remain in contact as problems crop up during the negotiation. The lawyer may then draft the agreement from a basic memorandum of terms written by the client, or the lawyer may draft the entire agreement from information gathered at a meeting or telephone conversation. Alternatively, the lawyer may be asked to review an agreement drafted by the other party in the deal. In each of these situations, the client controls the amount of work done by the lawyer, thereby limiting the number of hours and the resulting legal bill.

Clients may also choose to assign the entire job to the attorney, from structuring the deal through negotiation, drafting, and re-viewing the agreement. The lawyer works on his or her own schedule, contacting the client to review the key points of the deal. This is a more costly technique, but it frees up the client to do what he or she does best. Such work may be done on a flat-fee basis, but only under circumstances which suggest minimal risk for the attorney and the law firm.

The "messes" to which attorneys attend generally involve three areas: contracts, right clearances, and finance. Contracts are not only made, they are sometimes bent and broken—an attorney can offer strategies for dealing with breached promises, and usually works with the other party (or its lawyers) to reach a compromise solution.

Rights matters are best dealt with before the fact. Typical rights problems concern the depiction of people and their stories without a release, or the use of portions of other people's creative work, such as film clips or music excerpts. If an attorney has the chance to review the script or the program in advance, he or she can point out those instances where clearance is necessary. Such an advance review is usually required by the E&O insurer (see Chapter 16). Sometimes the attorney does do the follow-up work. Routine matters can be handled by the production staff or by rights clearance services specializing in particular areas, such as music or film clips. If items are missed before or during production and claims are made, the production company's attorney— together with the insurer—will assess the seriousness of the situation and take the lead in remedying it.

Finance problems are often more serious, and inevitably involve attorneys. Sometimes an agreed-upon payment schedule is not being followed by the financing entity, and the attorney is asked to cajole and threaten to obtain the money; perhaps the production company is at fault because it is running over budget or behind schedule. Asking for this type of legal help is expensive, and the attorney (since he or she is working for a client in financial distress) often asks for his or her fees upfront.

Most large and medium-sized production companies have several attorneys on staff. A general counsel usually attends to corporate affairs, and may become involved in the most important deals; a business affairs department handles the work related to programming and production. Most, if not all, of the deal-makers in the business affairs department are attorneys. A separate legal department drafts contacts and works to prevent and clean up messes.

In this litigious society, attorneys have become an integral part of the production operation. Lawyers should be consulted on any issues related to copyright, insurance, employment practices, government agencies, other producers or production companies, possible instances of libel or slander, music usage, the selection of a program title, and distribution agreements. In sum, almost any agreement signed by a network, station, production company, or individual should be reviewed by an attorney.

BUSINESS MANAGERS AND PERSONAL MANAGERS

A *business manager* helps to oversee the day-to-day financial aspects of a client's business life. The business manager typically receives all incoming checks, keeps the checkbook, makes sure that taxes are paid correctly and on time, deals with the banks, negotiates car leases and other such details, pays the credit card bills, keeps track of receipts for tax preparation, and works with the accountant to prepare taxes. For such services, a business manager may charge a flat monthly fee or, at most, a commission of 5 percent of the client's income.

A personal manager is more difficult to define. In theory, an agent is supposed to get jobs, but a personal manager, who is not legally an agent, is supposed to build a career. In fact, personal-management contracts frequently insist that the manager is not qualified to act as agent, and that he or she will not help the client to find work. Instead, the personal manager offers advice and guidance.

In the real world, successful personal managers sell access to powerful decision-makers and personal attention. Whereas an agent is likely to represent 50 clients, a personal manager handles only five or ten. A personal manager helps the client to make career decisions—about the way he or she looks, the company he or she keeps, the roles that should be accepted and rejected. All the while, the personal manager introduces the client to people who can make a difference.

The fee for a personal manager usually ranges from 15 to 25 percent of the client's entertainment income. Colonel Tom Parker, Elvis Presley's personal manager, reportedly charged 50 percent— and was probably worth every penny.

ACCOUNTANTS

Accountants serve as record-keepers and advisors. The record-keeping function is required for management information and planning, for investors, for tax authorities, and, in the case of public companies, for the SEC. Even a sole practitioner, such as a free-lance associate producer, should have an ongoing relationship with an accountant or accounting firm. Billing is based on hours worked, though flat rates for special projects, such as tax prepa-ration, may be negotiated on a case-by-case basis.

The advising function is equally important. Accountants are excellent sources of information relating to tax rules and government regulations on, for example, unemployment insurance. The financial implications of a new project should be reviewed by an accountant while it is still in the planning stages.

Accountants, bookkeepers, and auditors also play a role in pro-duction, either as full-time or freelance members of a production staff, or as outside contractors. Large productions require careful financial management, and a regular (often, daily) reckoning of expenditures. A production auditor provides detailed cost reports to a centralized production office on a regular basis, highlighting areas of potential difficulty. Some auditors play a broader role, keeping an eye on the entire production, and reporting any problems or potential problems to a production supervisor.

When the project is completed, the production accountant or production auditor works with the production manager to confirm that all invoices have been paid, that all deposits have been returned, and that there are no outstanding bills or expense reports lost in the towering piles of paper and files typically found in a production office. Submission of a final cost report is frequently specified in a production agreement; a final payment to a producer or production company may depend upon it.

The situation is less complex with ongoing production or programming ventures, such as a series. Staff, freelance, or outside accountants prepare and/or review the books regularly—once a week or once a month, depending on the amount of work involved. They may also prepare the payroll, or keep track of royalties. The role of the accountant is an important one; sloppy accounting practices can cause serious problems for independent production companies, and may cause considerable embarrassment for the personnel in charge of expenditure control.

36

Location and Studio Production

Most television programs are produced either on location or in a television studio. Some programs are produced by assembling existing materials such as photographs, film, and videotape. This chapter covers location and studio production; the next chapter discusses post-production and the production of programs that involve assembling existing materials.

LOCATION PRODUCTION

Location production refers to a shoot done anywhere except a studio. Common locations include business offices, homes, sporting venues, city streets, and nightclubs.

For all types of production (with the exception of news coverage), it is necessary to secure permission from the owner of the location prior to setting up to shoot (see Appendix B23). This permission frequently requires negotiating a daily or hourly fee for use of the premises. An insurance policy may also be required; such a policy should cover the property owner for any liability due to personal injury in connection with the production, and should guarantee payment to the property owner in case of physical damage to the property. Failure to secure these arrangements in advance usually results in costly production delays as the producer or production manager negotiates on the spot—or else in rescheduling the shoot.

If the location is outdoors in a public area, or if the project involves any public areas for setup or vehicles, then the municipal or other local government should be contacted well in advance of the shoot. A municipal permit usually carries a fixed daily fee, and must be prominently posted on one of the vehicles during the production.

In larger cities, and for large-scale productions in less populated areas, the city or state film commission can help to make the necessary arrangements. When no such office is available, it is advisable to contact the mayor's office. Fees are generally fixed on the basis of the scale of production; under-the-table payments are uncommon.

If police protection is required, a flat fee is charged per man-hour or per man-day. It is considered poor style (and is also illegal) to tip officers, but it is generally acceptable to treat the officers as if they were members of the production team—to feed them while on location and provide comfortable rest areas during breaks. Friendly relations go a long way toward smooth, problem-free operations. On some productions, similar interaction with the fire department is required as well.

SINGLE-CAMERA LOCATION CREWS

Most major cities support a small community of freelance television technicians, camera people, audio and video engineers, and so forth. Frequently trained in local television news and sports, these versatile crew members work either individually, or in small companies that offer not just engineering capability, but everything from location planning to shooting, editing and duplication of the finished tape.

Crews support themselves by working for a variety of clients. Corporate work (training videos, video news releases, product demonstrations, point-of-purchase merchandising videos) usually accounts for the bulk of the crew's work. Local, syndicated, and network programs may also hire these crews when their own staffs are overextended, or when a situation arises that favors freelancers. An example of the latter is a story breaking in Boise, Idaho: a Seattle-based freelance crew might be able to reach the location faster than a network crew based in San Francisco.

Crews are hired in two different ways. For most projects, the easiest way to hire an entire crew is to contact a production company that specializes in single-camera work. The company quotes a daily or weekly package price, not only for the crew members, but for all of the necessary equipment. Many of these crews offer résumé reels; it is also wise to check references with previous clients. One can also hire each crew member individually, and this may be the better choice if a particular videographer is a must, or if the client company owns equipment. This method, however, is frequently more costly, because individual crew members may not own every piece of equipment needed for the job. The producer also accepts more technical responsibility, especially if the crew members are unaccustomed to working together.

The size of the crew depends upon the job, and is best determined by discussing the job in detail with the crew chief (usually the camera operator). For electronic news gathering (ENG) work, a two-person crew can move quickly and cover most stories: one person lights and operates the camera, the other is in charge of audio and video recording. For most productions, however, using a three- or four-person crew is preferable, and is more likely to result in flawless sound and picture quality. With this setup, the camera operator works with a lighting assistant, one engineer handles audio, and another engineer does video. With lightweight portable gear, one- or two-person crews can handle a remarkable range of jobs.

Most crew-hiring deals are made via telephone, followed up with a letter (or a fax) that confirms the business arrangements: the dates, the number of working days, the rate (per-day or per-week, or the flat rate for the job), a promise to provide transportation and accommodations, confirmation of necessary insurance, and a payment schedule. A typical payment schedule is 50 percent upon hiring and 50 percent upon completion of the shoot. If the job includes editing, then 35 percent on hiring, 35 percent on completion of the shoot, and 30 percent on completion of editing is common. Many crews mark up the cost of tape stock, and for larger shoots, the producer can save money by buying stock ahead of time. If anything goes wrong with producer-supplied stock, the producer pays for the reshoot; if anything goes wrong with crew-supplied stock, then they will often reshoot at no charge, or at a reduced rate.

MULTIPLE-CAMERA CREWS AND TRUCK RENTALS

Single-camera coverage is ideal for news, interviews, magazine stories, and speeches. But additional cameras are necessary for most seminars, meetings, sporting events, and other productions where multiple performers or simultaneous visual images must be captured in real time.

Many small production companies own small vans equipped with modest control-room facilities (up to three cameras, for example). These facilities are frequently modular, so they can be removed from the van and set up anywhere, provided that electrical power and shelter from weather is available.

Mobile facilities range from these minivans to full-scale control rooms on wheels that can handle a dozen or more cameras and seat just as many engineers and members of the production staff. Several "trucks" are available in most major cities, but the nature of the mobile video business is travel. It is not unusual to find a Pittsburgh-based truck accepting assignments throughout the East and Midwest; in fact, a good deal can be struck if the Pittsburgh-based truck is already in St. Louis, and is needed for a shoot in Kansas City or Chicago. Trucks are mainly used for sports coverage, and, to a lesser extent, for concerts and other special events.

A truck is usually rented with all of the necessary equipment and several key engineers and technicians. Additional crew members may be hired by the mobile video company—which is likely to be in contact with experienced personnel all over the country or supplied by the producer. Payment terms for the truck are usually 50 percent on hiring and 50 percent on completion of the shoot; the crew is paid after the shoot. Once again, the deal is made by phone (usually to a distant city) and confirmed in writing.

Specialized mobile facilities, for multiple-track audio recording or for the generation of on-site electrical power, are also available for rental.

STUDIO PRODUCTION

Nearly all television broadcasting stations own and operate at least one studio on the premises, and many operate two or more. These studios are used for daily production of the news and some public-affairs programming. In addition, studios are rented for the production of local commercials and, on occasion, to other clients, such as corporate video producers.

Each of the broadcast networks operates studios in New York, Los Angeles, Washington, DC, and Chicago. In New York, these studios are used principally for news, morning programs (such as *Good Morning America*), sports coverage, and daytime dramas. In Los Angeles, the studios are used mainly for situation comedies, game shows, daytime dramas, and variety shows. Network studios in Washington and Chicago are used for news and public affairs programs and some syndicated talk shows; ABC's *Nightline*, for example, is based in Washington, and so is NBC's *Meet the Press*. When a network and an O&O are housed in the same physical plant, studios, crews, and editing facilities are frequently shared by both organizations.

Many independent programs are not produced in television stations or network facilities, though. Los Angeles, New York, Chicago, and other cities support independently owned and operated television studios that are rented to producers.

Manhattan's Chelsea Piers (large-scale shipping space renovated for TV and film) has been home to *Spin City, Law & Order,* and other series. Kaufman-Astoria studios took years to get off the ground, but ultimately became home to *Where in the World Is Carmen Sandiego?, Sesame Street, The Cosby Show* (the NBC series), *Cosby* (the CBS series), and for many years, it was the headquarters for Lifetime's cable network. Many cable networks operate their own facilities, or work with a studio facility in a long-term arrangement (these include MTV, Food Network, and A&E, among others). Network studios also house syndicated programs: *The Rosie O'Donnell Show* shoots at NBC's Rockefeller Center studios, for example. Production costs for a network prime-time series are about 10 or 15 percent higher in NYC than in LA; the problem of network executives attending readings and rehearsals has been solved through video conferencing and other technologies.

In Los Angeles, many of the old movie soundstages have been converted into television studios. Television studios are available for rental in the Disney/MGM and Universal complexes in Orlando, Florida. In Chicago, Oprah Winfrey's Harpo Studios is home to her own talk show and to outside projects; there are other independent studios in Chicago as well. There are fine studios in some out-of-the-way places such as Nashville's Opryland which includes one of the nation's largest studios, and is the home of the Grand Ole Opry, a huge theater-style studio. Many producers also rent studio space in Canada, where production costs tend to be low; Toronto and Vancouver are production centers for both Canadian and (to a lesser extent) U.S. programming.

In other large cities, such as San Francisco and Philadelphia, some work is done at television stations that have blocks of unbooked time to fill. WHYY-Philadelphia, for example, sometimes rents its studios to producers, (before Nickelodeon opened its Florida studios, *Double Dare* and other series were made in Philadelphia). Some local markets also support a few independent facilities. Outside the top-10 or top-15 markets, though, most studio production is done at television stations.

Studios rent their facilities by the day, usually with a half-day minimum. Since the rental of studio space is a perishable commodity, facilities are happy to package multiple days or weeks at a discount. The goal of every studio owner is to keep the studio busy all of the time. This is best accomplished by signing a long-term cable company (like MTV, which produces studio segments daily), a corporation with ongoing communications needs (such as a teleconferencing center), or any type of series.

Short-term projects—home video productions, television specials, pilots, commercials, corporate video training tapes, and product demonstrations—usually pay higher day rates than long-term clients do.

A television studio is rented as a facility ready for production, complete with a control room, a lighting grid, power, a poured (flat) floor, and cable connections for lights, cameras, monitors, microphones, and other necessary equipment. Use of the control room, dressing rooms, make-up area, and limited office space is always part of the deal. Additional charges, essential to customize the studio for specific production activities, mount up quickly: extra cameras, extra lighting equipment, painting and repainting the floor or walls, purchase of colored gels for the lights, and additional personnel. Some of these costs may be paid directly by the producer, but any costs not covered this way are subject to the studio's markup.

A film soundstage may be larger than a television studio. Many soundstages are used as television studios, with lights and other equipment added as needed. In this instance, the control room is often a mobile production van, or a temporary setup in a nearby office area. These temporary control room facilities are called a carry-in (or, in Los Angeles, a fly pack.)

Studio rentals are always negotiable. The price of the studio should be highest on "full fax" days, or days when the studio and all of its equipment are needed, and far lower—perhaps 75 to 80 percent less—on days when the studio is being used to set up or strike equipment and scenery. There is more flexibility with the costs of the studio, the equipment, and the facility's full-time personnel than there is with items that the studio must purchase on the client's behalf. It may be worth checking into the prices of those items purchased from outside, because the studio may not shop for the best possible prices on items it will buy for the client (since it passes the cost through), and the markup on these items—as well as on phone and copier usage—may be unacceptable.

A studio deal can be complicated, so it is advisable to arrange at least one in-person meeting. This meeting should include the producer or production manager (who actually makes the deal), the director, and if the production is complicated, one or two key members of the technical staff. The facility's sales staff assesses the needs of the production, then submits a bid for the job. After soliciting bids from several studios, the producer or production manager starts negotiating. Upon agreement on key points, a one- or two-page letter agreement confirms the deal and the dates, listing the resources that will be provided by the studio, the price for the entire job (or the price of each day), plus the cost of overtime.

It is wise to leave some room for modification; most television productions change during pre-production, and a deal that it too tightly structured may cost the producer more money than anticipated. Hard negotiating is not recommended, because if there is a breakdown of mutual goodwill, studios can easily add costs for items not included in the original bid. The studio bills some items at its discretion, and if the facility is treated fairly, there are usually fewer surprises when the final bill arrives.

Payment arrangements vary. A common deal is 10 percent to hold the studio dates—refundable if the production is canceled within 48 hours of the shoot—with 45 percent due on the first shooting day and 45 percent on completion. If the client rents the facility regularly, the final payment can be made as late as 30 days after completion.

TECHNICAL AND STAGING UNIONS

In the major U.S. markets, three technical and staging unions dominate the television business: the International Alliance of Theatrical Stage Employees (IATSE), the National Association of Broadcast Employees and Technicians (NABET), and the International Brotherhood of Electrical Workers (IBEW). Each one negotiates rates and rules with employers on behalf of its members, assures fair working conditions, and operates a pension and welfare fund. The terms and conditions vary with each union's agreement, but there are some generally applicable rules. These concern the number of hours in a standard work day; the additional payments due for overtime hours; payments for work on weekends and holidays; notification of call times, changes, and cancellations; rest periods and turnarounds (the number of hours between working days); meal periods and penalties for missed meal periods; hazard pay; travel, food, and lodging; and the need for a payroll bond.

More than half of all television stations are unionized, most often by IATSE, IBEW, and NABET. The Teamsters represent employees at a few dozen stations, and the United Auto Workers at just one, in Flint, Michigan. (For a general discussion of the role of unions in the television business, see page 456.)

IATSE

The International Alliance of Theatrical Stage Employees, often IATSE or just IA, was founded in 1893, when all show business was onstage; electronic media was still decades off. Stage carpenters, propertymen, and electricians built this union; projectionists were added as film exhibition became a business enterprise. IA members are also hairstylists, makeup artists, story analysts, cartoonists, set designers, teachers (of working children), editors, and in some cases, sales or marketing personnel. IA members work in legitimate theater, motion picture production, motion picture exhibition (projectionists), and in network and local television production.

IATSE is represented by local chapters throughout the world, and over 800 local chapters in the U.S. and Canada. The organization of these local chapters, and the areas in which members may exclusively work, are guided by local traditions and by negotiated agreements. In San Francisco, for example, members of IATSE Local 16 are not involved in television production. In Los Angeles, 16 IATSE television and motion picture locals operate in a variety of production crafts and geographic regions. Local 44, Affiliated Property Craftsmen, supplies propmasters in the Los Angeles area. Local 695, International Sound, Cinetechnicians and TV Engineers, supplies audio engineers in the Los Angeles area. Local 706 is the chapter for make-up artists and hairstylists working throughout the U.S., its territories, and Canada (with the exception of 13 eastern states). In New York, IATSE is the union for stagehands.

There are IATSE locals in more than 500 cities throughout the U.S. and Canada. The entire union has 60,000 members, more than one-third of the people working in television.

NABET

The National Association of Broadcast Employees and Technicians succeeded the Association of Technical Employees (ATE), which was organized in 1933 to represent employees of NBC Radio. When the NBC Blue network was spun off to form ABC, jurisdiction expanded to the new network as well. NABET, the broadcasting and cable television workers sector of the Communications Workers of America (CWA), represents most of the technical crew members who work at network facilities, radio stations, and television stations owned by NBC and ABC; at many local radio and television stations not owned by NBC or ABC; and at some production companies. The word "employees" in the union's name is appropriate: half of the union's members are anchors, reporters, producers, directors, desk assistants, talent coordinators, graphic artists, and other non-technical personnel. In addition, NABET represents make-up artists, hairdressers, stagehands, script supervisors, and some film crews.

There are roughly 38 NABET locals in approximately 36 cities, with over 10,000 members working in television. In New York and in Los Angeles, one local serves ABC, one serves NBC, and one serves film workers. In Washington and in Chicago, one local serves all members working for ABC and NBC. San Francisco has one local for ABC and independents. Locals also contract with independent stations and other television production companies.

Until 1974, NABET operated in Canada as well as the U.S. NABET Canada is now autonomous.

NABET covers anyone employed in broadcasting, and competes with AFTRA, DGA, WGA, IATSE, and IBEW to represent employees.

IBEW

The International Brotherhood of Electrical Workers was formed in 1891 to represent telephone company employees. In 1931, IBEW started representing CBS radio engineers and technicians. Today, IBEW (sometimes called IB) represents engineers and technicians at CBS network and local facilities, and at some local stations. IBEW also represents workers in the telephone industry.

INSURANCE

Whether working on location or in a studio, the producer uses several types of insurance to limit the risks involved in creating television productions.

An errors and omissions (E&O) policy—also called a producer's liability policy—insures against claims based on violation of copyright, personal rights, or property rights, including infringement of privacy. Although the range of coverage may vary depending upon the type of production and the risk involved, an E&O policy should protect the producer against suits for libel, slander, and privacy/publicity violations (see Chapter 17). In addition, an E&O policy protects against claims on the creative concepts used in the production: the originality of the concept, the script, the characters, the music, the production design, and so forth. The E&O package for most productions is a routine matter, but it may take on special importance when the risk is higher. For example, with a tabloid-type magazine program, a celebrity might claim libel, slander, or defamation of character. Another example is a basic story line with a history of copyright problems and lawsuits.

There are several companies that supply E&O coverage. The so-called production package typically protects the producer against losses due to property damage or personal injury. It contains some or all of the following coverages, depending, again, upon the producer's level of risk and the costs involved.

- Faulty Stock, Camera, and Processing Insurance pays for re-shooting and other losses due to problems with the set's physical equipment, the raw materials used, or the editing facility.

- Negative Film Insurance covers physical damage to the master videotape(s) or film negative.

- Weather Insurance covers delays due to inclement or unusual weather.

- Aviation Accident Insurance, Marine Accident Insurance, and Animal Mortality Coverage are examples of special coverages, and are self-explanatory.

- Extra Expense Insurance reimburses the producer for the costs of any delays due to failure or loss of any equipment, wardrobe, and so on.

- Third Party Property Damage covers property that is donated, loaned, or rented to the producer.

- Cast Insurance pays the producer for any costs from delays re-lated to key cast members who become ill during the course of shooting and editing. If a cast member dies, and material must be reshot or re-edited with a new performer, cast insurance covers this situation as well.

- Comprehensive General Liability covers damage to vehicles loaned to, rented, or donated to the production. Coverage is available for props, sets, and wardrobe, as well as for lighting, camera, and sound equipment.

- Worker's Compensation and Employer's Liability is not exclu-sively a production insurance; it provides coverage against claims for workers who are injured or disabled on the job. The cost and coverage varies on a state-by-state basis—high in California, lower in New York. There are some surprises in some states, so research is necessary.

As can be expected, there are limitations on coverage. Faulty Stock, Camera, and Processing Insurance, for example, does not cover errors in judgment made by the camera operator, such as the use of the wrong film, improper loading, or incorrect or inappropriate use of the camera. Similar limitations apply to most of the types of insurance listed above.

Insurance can be expensive, so coverage should be selected with a thorough understanding of the risks involved, the costs of correcting problems without insurance coverage, and the likelihood of mishaps. E&O and a basic production package are required in almost every contract for financing or distributing a program. Because the costs of coverage do vary, it is advisable to request bids from several companies that specialize in production insurance. Special cast insurance may be required if a key cast member is especially old or in poor health. Other types of specialty insurance may be required by contract if production conditions are unusual— for example, if dangerous animals will be used, or if shooting will take place in a rough inner-city neighborhood.

One further note: deductibles are often high, so the producer should make some allowances for loss, damage, and theft in order to insure items valued in the hundreds or low thousands of dollars. This will cover the producer for small problems that do not warrant, or qualify for, a claim.

An accurate estimation of costs can be made only by an insurance agent. For budgeting purposes, it is normally safe to gauge insurance costs at roughly 3 to 5 percent of the below-the-line portion of the total production budget. However, if there are above-the-line elements subject to risk, then these should factor into the estimate. Factors may include risky shooting situations (underwater photography, scenes involving explosives), dicey rights issues, situations that may adversely affect property owned by others, and so on. If the project is relatively small, then the 3 to 5 percent should be increased. The cost of insuring a pilot will be, proportionately, far higher than the cost of insuring an entire series. Part of the reason may be minimum fees that are due regardless of the size and budget of the production. A blanket policy, held by a larger company, may help reduce costs; an independent producer or small production company will usually pay more than a larger company would for insurance.

37

Post-Production

Post-Production is an umbrella term that covers editing, the addition of special effects, sound mixing and preparation of the completed master tape. There are several phases in the post-production process, and the complexity of each step is defined by the needs of the project.

First, the videotapes recorded on location or in the studio are logged: a list is made of each scene, and each acceptable take. The tapes are then screened by the person in charge of the edit (a producer or director, for example), who makes further notes and begins to visualize the completed production. Notes, logs, and ideas are used to prepare an editing plan, sometimes with additional written material to be recorded as a voice-over.

The second step occurs in an editing room. If the project is re-latively simple—a news story or a corporate speech that must be illustrated with footage, for example—the videotapes are edited into their final form in one step. If the project is more complicated—a situation comedy or a documentary, for example—then a rough cut is made from dubs of the master tapes as a basis for further discussion and criticism. A project may be rough-cut several times. Then the master tapes are edited to generate the final cut. Film editing proceeds in a similar fashion, sometimes rough cutting on video and then fine cutting on film.

The third step is audio post-production. On a small-scale project, sound work is done in the editing room by adding voice, music, and sound effects. On larger projects, the soundtrack is dubbed onto 16- or 32-track tape (or, in a digital facility, onto a computer system whose hard disk drives replace tape); sound effects, music, and voices are recorded or re-recorded on individual tracks and mixed, in much the same way a record is made. Finally, the tracks are "laid back" onto the master videotape or film negative, in synchronization with the video images.

A standardized time code system called SMPTE (pronounced "sim-tee," and named for the Society of Motion Picture and Television Engineers) is used on all audio and video tapes so that the work can be organized and accessed by a computerized editing system. SMPTE code is also used in digital video.

EDITING FACILITIES

Compared with a fully equipped television studio, an editing facility costs less to build and to maintain, so there are more of them. Networks and local stations typically build editing facilities for individual departments, such as news and on-air promotion. Programs that depend heavily upon editing, like magazines, frequently build editing suites in their production offices. Independent post-production houses are common in most cities—even a small independent facility may operate two or three editing suites.

The equipment, and the ability to maintain it, may vary from one editing facility to another—but the greatest difference lies in the skill and craftsmanship of the editor. For a creative endeavor in which a fraction of a second can make the difference between an effective presentation and a tedious one, in which unusual cutting can transform a mundane project into something that sparkles, the editor can be a significant contributor.

Networks do not normally rent out their editing facilities, usually because they lack excess capacity. Local stations do, when time is available. Independent editing houses handle most of the outside program and commercial work.

Editing facilities charge by the hour. Hourly charges depend upon the type of editing system used; a rough-cut (or off-line) system used for news stories and for rough-cutting high-budget projects costs about one-third as much as an on-line system used for fine cutting. Rates also depend upon the number of playback machines and the use of additional equipment, such as a title camera, animation stand, or digital special-effects devices. Dubs and window dubs—which show time code on the screen and make edit-planning easier— cost extra, as do materials like blank tape stock.

Rate cards are published mainly for corporate clients and for agencies who pass costs on to clients. Most program production clients, receive a 10 to 15 percent discount off the rate card. Clients with full-length programs, who buy large numbers of hours, may negotiate a deeper discount, typically up to 25 to 35 percent off.

If editing is tied to a studio rental deal, as is often the case at larger facilities, then a package deal is common.

Every deal should be based on an hourly charge; even flat rates should reflect a maximum number of hours. This is because editing often takes longer than anticipated—it is often difficult to estimate the job accurately (especially if the project is new), and clients and distributors may request unexpected changes.

Since post-production is the final step in the overall production process, editing facilities are often the last to get paid. For new clients, and clients who have not established a reputation for paying bills on time, most editing houses have strict rules regarding the removal of tapes from their premises prior to payment of invoices. The best way to minimize problems is to estimate the cost of the job, pay a portion as a down payment (20 percent is common), and cut a check for the estimated balance, to be held in reserve until it is due. If the final total is more or less, adjustments can be made. And if the project is likely to exceed the budget estimate, incremental payments are frequently requested by the editing facility. Unpaid bills, or unpaid portions of bills, are an unfortunate fact of life in the post-production business.

A lab letter (see Appendix B25) is an agreement between the "lab" (a film term carried over to TV) or post-production facility, producer, and a financier or distributor. It says that the lab has tapes and/or films, and will not release the materials without permission of the authorized party (distributor or producer); that the distributor or producer may use the materials within the lab for duplication or further editing; and, finally, that the lab will not put a lien on the materials or hold them unavailable if the party has unpaid debts to the lab. Each party is allowed access, provided that they have paid their own bills to the facility.

USE OF EXISTING MATERIALS

Some television projects are put together in whole or in part by assembling existing materials, including photographs, illustrations, film, and videotape footage.

Strictly speaking, every piece of existing material that is protected by copyright should be cleared by the copyright holder for use—regardless of the amount of time that the sound or image is heard or seen, regardless of the size or character of the intended audience. This means that a producer must identify and contact the copyright holder for each item, then describe the production, how the material will be used within it, and where the program will be distributed. In many cases, the copyright holder will have already sold properties for use on television, so past experience may be the basis for either a fixed rate or negotiation. An agreement should be signed before the material is edited into the production. This agreement should detail the name of the program, its intended market and audience, the item to be used, limitations on its use, and the payments due.

In the real world, clearances are important, but in some cases, a producer does not obtain them. If, for example, a production is to be seen internally by a small number of company employees, or if the production is a rough demo made to secure future funding, a producer sometimes takes a chance and proceeds without the necessary clearances—but this action is never without an element of risk. If the material is seen for only a very short time, or if it is distorted or manipulated to a point where recognition may be difficult, then once again the producer may choose to risk using the material without a clearance. The copyright holder is under no obligation to sell or license the material, of course, and many copyright holders routinely turn down requests for usage (for certain types of productions, or for any production at all).

If the copyright holder is difficult to reach, and the producer has made a conscientious effort to contact the party, then the producer can take the risk of using the material—with the understanding that the copyright holder may see the production. Once the copyright holder is aware that the material is being used, the producer may negotiate a reasonable fee. But the copyright holder may have little motivation to negotiate in a reasonable fashion, and he or she may quote very high rates, demand that the material be removed from the program, or insist that the program be pulled from distribution as long as it contains the material. If the program has already aired with the material included, the copyright holder can stop the program from being shown or distributed until the material is removed, or can charge a very high licensing fee.

Items that are in the public domain—material on which the copyright has not been renewed, for example—may be used without clearances. Sometimes, it is difficult to determine or to verify ownership; in these cases, the producer must make an honest, earnest effort to determine whether or not the item in question is in the public domain. Clearing music is especially tricky; a song or composition may be in the public domain, but the specific recorded performance may be protected by copyright, thus requiring clearance. Short excerpts, particularly on news or information programs, may fall into the category of "fair use," which does not require permission in some cases (see page 170). This is a limited exception, however, and should not be stretched beyond its proper bounds.

If a program is produced for distribution, the distributor must document all clearances. If something is not cleared, it is advisable for the producer to keep a history of contact (or attempted contact) with the copyright holder and advise the distributor of the potential for difficulties later on. (See Chapter 16 for more on copyright and the protection of creative properties.)

SCREEN CREDITS

The completion of a television program frequently involves on-screen credits for people who worked on the production. The form and style of these credits largely depends upon tradition, negotiated agreements with individual staff and crew members, and rules set forth in union and guild agreements. On a network drama or situation comedy, for example, an individual full-frame credit (a credit that is the only one on-screen at a particular time) is shown at the start of the program for the producer(s), writer, and director, usually in that order; the other names appear at the end of the program. On most other programs, such as game, talk, news, magazine, and variety shows, all of the credits are shown at the end. These end credits begin with the producer(s), director, writer(s), production staff, and technical crew, then move on to music, design, business, and other departments. There is a trend against full-screen credits, or against long credits; viewers don't find credits interesting, so they're more likely to change channels.

The exact running order of credits, and the job titles, are usually determined by the producer, who is guided by contractual requirements, union requirements, and personal judgment. Sometimes, for example, the executive producers appear first on the credits, sometimes they appear last. Networks frequently have their own conventions and policies on what credits are allowed.

The name of the program, or its logo, does not need to appear on the credits. Some producers prefer to see it; others do not.

A television program may be produced without including credits of any kind. A copyright notice, however, must be included at some point in the program. It is most often shown either just before or just after the end credits. A proper form for the copyright notice is as follows:

Copyright © 1999, Blumenthal and Goodenough's Mega-Global Production Company

The name of the show need not be included in the copyright notice. Some producers include the words "all rights reserved" in addition to the copyright notice, but this is redundant. The notice should be large enough to be read clearly on any television set. For more on copyright notice and protection. For instructions on the submission of a program to the copyright office, consult their Website, http://lcweb.loc.gov/copyright/.

"DELIVERABLES"

When a program is complete, one of the staff members should arrange all of the important documents, neatly typed, in a production file or production book. Such materials are routinely required by distribution agreements in a section or schedule called Delivery Requirements, but they should be assembled upon completion of every television production, regardless of its intended market, and kept in a file that is cross-referenced to the master videotape. The following "deliverables" are likely to be required—along with the master tape (and sometimes work tapes)—before an independent producer or production company can receive final payment:

- Agreements. All cast, staff, crew, music, set design, and other agreements. If the program is likely to have a commercial life beyond its initial showing, a memo outlining residuals should be included here as well.

- Credit List. The list of screen credits, as it appears on the final version of the program.

- Release Forms. Each form should be labeled to identify it with the person appearing in the program.

- Final Budget Accounting. On a larger production, a final accounting may not be possible until 60 or 90 days after completion because invoices may arrive late; still, the most accurate and up-to-date accounting possible should be included, sometimes accompanied by copies of all paid invoices.

- Final Script. A final script, if available, is especially useful if the production may be edited in the future. A show rundown, listing each program element and its duration in minutes and seconds, should be included as well.

- Music Cue Sheet. This details every piece of music, its composer, publishing, running time, and, preferably, time-code position in the program.

- Insurance Forms. A copy of the producer's E&O policy should be included in the file; for many productions, such as those done by a local TV station, coverage will be part of a larger policy, and need not be included.

38

Design

Television is a visual medium in which scenic and graphic design can contribute in a significant way to a project's success. Fortunately, the business side of creating television stage settings, graphics, animation, and digital art is relatively straightforward and uncomplicated.

SCENIC DESIGN

Several titles are used to describe the person who designs the scenery. *Production designer* is a term borrowed from the motion picture industry; when used in television, the title suggests the design of the set and props, plus active supervision of all graphic elements. The role of the *art director* may include only set design, only graphics, certain aspects of animation, or the entire production-design package. *Scenic* or *set designer* is the most common term in television; a designer is hired to visualize a concept for the scenery and to supervise its construction. Some producers and directors have very specific ideas, and the designer is asked mainly to execute these ideas in a stylish fashion; other producers and directors meet with the designer with only a vague sense of how a project will look, which may allow the designer more creative latitude.

The process typically begins with several scenic designers attending creative meetings with the project's producer, director, or other production staff members. Each designer is told about the concept of the program, its style, and the functions that the set must fulfill. These may include, for example, a performance area for a band, a talk area to accommodate up to six guests, or a seating area for an on-camera audience of 150. Each designer is expected to contribute creative ideas to the discussion.

Promising candidates are then asked to submit a pencil sketch, or several sketches, showing ideas. These sketches may be prepared "on spec" (with the designer speculating time against the promise of future work) or for a small fee, perhaps a few hundred dollars. The schedule for submissions varies, but one week from first meeting to delivery is common. The sketches remain the property of the designer, but it is not unusual for a producer to incorporate some of the submitted ideas in the final design, even if another designer is hired. This is neither moral nor legal, particularly if the designer has been a principal contributor to the concept. In practice, however, such concepts are often developed as a result of group meetings, so that attribution of specific concepts may be difficult.

The sketches are a kind of audition: the designer with the best ideas is most likely to be awarded the work, although reputation and a history of on-time, on-budget delivery may also be determining factors. The sketches do not usually come with construction bids, but designers are expected to provide a rough, non-binding estimate of construction costs.

The winning designer meets with the producer and production staff several times to revise the design. Throughout this process, large-sized pencil sketches are common. A color sketch is sometimes necessary, with paint and material swatches often used instead of, or in addition to, the color sketch. A white cardboard scale model is useful because it presents the set in a three-dimensional plan. A full-color scale model is uncommon because of the expense and the time involved in making one; still, for certain types of projects, a color model is essential for proper production planning. Color models usually require the designer to hire a model maker, for an additional fee. In some cases, a computer simulation may be used in place of a physical model, allowing the director to consider possible camera angles.

Once the sketch or model has been approved, the designer prepares construction drawings—blueprints for the construction of each scenic element. The designer also requests bids from one or more scenic construction shops, recommends the best one for the job, and supervises the shop through construction, painting, and finishing. In theory, the designer must also be concerned with loading the set onto the trucks, and out to the studio; in practice, most designers try to leave these headaches to the shop and the studio stagehands.

When the set arrives in the studio, the designer works closely with the stagehands, who place the pieces in the correct position in the studio and dress the set with props and small graphics.

After the set is seen on camera, some repainting or resurfacing is usually required. The designer assumes that minor changes will be necessary, and does not normally charge any additional design fees for fix-ups or alterations. It is also common for a small number of set pieces to be redesigned or modified as a result of changes in the production—as the director starts blocking and rehearsing, unanticipated problems become evident and adjustments have to be made to the set. Major changes usually involve overtime payments to the carpenters, electricians, prop people, painters, stagehands, and other specialists who must physically transform the set, often on a tight schedule.

A designer may have an ongoing relationship with a program whose scenic needs keep changing: late-night talk shows and daytime dramas keep staff designers busy. Once the basic set is completed, most programs require only maintenance of existing set pieces, or the occasional extra piece of scenery. At the networks, staff designers are typically assigned to this follow-through.

DESIGN AGREEMENTS

Most designers routinely negotiate on their own behalf. Increasingly though, top designers are working with agents or, in some cases, with attorneys.

Design agreements are sometimes verbal rather than written. This is because the entire job may take only a month, while the written agreement may take longer to draft, revise, redraft, and sign. Sometimes, the producer or designer requires a brief written agreement stating basic terms. Any agreement—written or verbal—with a scenic designer should cover the following elements:

- A list of responsibilities, including the conceptualization and rendering of a scenic design acceptable to the producer, with necessary revisions; supervision of construction and painting; on-site supervision of load-in and strike(s) (a strike is the disassembling and removal of scenery); availability for revisions and new scenic elements.

- A payment schedule. The designer is typically paid half of the fee on acceptance of preliminary designs, and the rest when the set is physically in the studio (or when the program first airs). There may also be incremental payments pegged to acceptance of the completed design, but the short time that the designer works and the number of weeks from invoice to payment often makes incremental payments unwieldy.

- A negotiable weekly fee, if the designer is working on a series in network or syndicated television. This fee may also involve a promise to maintain ("babysit") the production.

- A credit for the designer, usually Production Designer, Art Director, or Scenic Designer. The use of this credit is largely negotiable.

- Ownership of the designs. Sometimes, all rights in the designs are transferred to the production company; increasingly, however, designers are seeking to keep the copyright themselves, subject to limits on re-use, and only to license rights for the specific production to the producer.

THE SCENIC ARTISTS UNION

One union for scenic artists is United Scenic Artists, Local 829. Local 829, is part of the International Brotherhood of Painters and Allied Trades (IBPAT). It's an AFL-CIO affiliate, and represents over 130,000 people, mostly paperhangers, decorators, scenic artists, and professionals in related fields (many outside the entertainment fields). Technically, Local 829 has jurisdiction nationwide through three business offices in New York, Chicago, and Los Angeles; in practice, though, its jurisdiction over the television industry is primarily in New York. Los Angeles art directors and related personnel usually work under the jurisdiction of the Art Directors' Guild, Local 876, an IATSE affiliate. If a union designer wants to work for a company that is not a union signatory, a project-specific agreement can usually be arranged.

The locals set minimum rates for television productions, commercials, and motion pictures, and require a pension and welfare payment of 10.5 percent of gross earnings, with a cap. As with other unions, there are rules regarding minimum call, meal periods, rest periods, penalties, and notification of calls and changes. Many designers do not strictly adhere to these rules, since they are trying to get the job done within limited studio hours, and before rehearsals begin, but the spirit of the rules is certainly respected on most productions.

SCENIC CONSTRUCTION, TRUCKING, LOAD-IN, STRIKES AND RESETS

Television scenery is usually built to the designer's specifications by shops that specialize in scenic construction. (Other types of construction shops can do the work, but the results are generally better with a shop that specializes in television.) Work is done on a contract basis between the shop and the producing company. The shop submits a bid, with payment terms, and once the bid has been negotiated, and is acceptable to both parties, work begins in accordance with a delivery schedule. The shop is supervised by the designer—who visits several times during the construction and painting—but the shop actually contracts with, and is paid by, the producing company.

The scenery seen on network television, and on much of syndication and pay TV, is built in union shops, where union workers stamp each piece of scenery with a union symbol (called a "bug"). If the program is to be produced in a studio with union stagehands, it is important to coordinate the activities of the unions whose members construct, truck, and load the set into the studio. If all of these are workers are members of IATSE, as is often the case in New York and Los Angeles, then the coordination is routine. If a variety of unions are involved—or if one of the links in this chain is to be non-union—then arrangements must be made (and sometimes, negotiated) in advance.

Television scenery is fragile, and should be moved only by companies and stagehands experienced in the trucking of scenery. The scenic construction shop usually makes arrangements for trucking.

Load-in is the process of removing scenery from the truck and assembling it in the studio. The trucking crew unloads, and stagehands hired for work in the studio set up. The crew chief follows the designer's floor plan for instructions as to placement, but the designer is available to answer questions. In some studios, under union rules, the designer is allowed to touch, but not move, scenery. (Some crews are more lenient than others, and some designers assume more responsibility than others do.)

Striking a set is the process of removing it from the studio, or, in some cases, taking it apart and setting it aside to make room for another show. The potential for damage is increased when the set is struck and reset often; in such cases, a long-term maintenance deal with the designer may be wise. Several stagehands who work on the show generally earn extra pay for working on strikes and resets; since these activities often take place before or after regular production hours, overtime pay scales are frequently involved.

GRAPHICS, COMPUTER ART, AND ANIMATION

Television graphics now encompass two-dimensional and three-dimensional still graphics, as well as animation. Aside from some hand props, most TV graphics are made with a computer.

The business of television graphics is handled in one of three ways. The first is setting up one or more staff members to operate as an in-house art department, taking care of the graphics (and sometimes, the scenic requirements) for programs, on-air promotion, and other activities. The second is hiring freelancers to work on a project basis; an example would be graphics for an awards show. More common, however, is work on a contract basis with an established graphics firm, either on a long-term contract or per-project basis.

Regardless of the arrangement, the hiring process is similar to the one described above with regard to scenic design. The producer establishes a need for specific graphics, and meets with one or more graphic artists or firms to discuss style, approach, schedule, and budget. The artist(s) work out some ideas and, within a few days, present(s) sketches to the producer (and/or the producer's staff). The sketches are revised and approved, with the finished work delivered in accordance with a schedule.

LOGO DESIGN

A logo is a graphic representation of the program's title. It may be straightforward—little more than a type treatment—or more complicated, involving illustrations, graphic work, and motion.

The design of logos for television is best handled by a graphic artist with experience in logo design. This may be a staff member or a freelancer, or even a producer working with a paint-box artist who is paid by the hour. Logos are considered just one of many television graphics, so logo design should not necessarily command a supplementary fee. But in today's marketing-savvy world, a logo design may have real commercial value, and this should be considered while negotiating.

LEGAL CONSIDERATIONS IN GRAPHIC DESIGN

A graphic design is subject to the same legal considerations as any other creative element in a production. Under copyright law, the use of a particular image requires the permission of the owner of that image. In addition, the work may not infringe on the rights of any third parties (see Chapter 16); any photographs or graphic works that are owned by third parties must be cleared for use within the context of the program. Companies that sell old photographs and other vintage graphics set rates based on the type of production, its distribution, and the number of times the program will be seen. These rates are flexible if the material will be seen by a very limited audience, or if the production leases multiple images. The producer should confirm that the rights fee covers all types of possible uses—otherwise, he or she will be held accountable for infringements. If a graphic element is owned by a third party who is not in the business of selling images, then the rate should be based on a fair-market price. Signed agreements must be completed prior to inclusion of the image in the production.

There is a gray area in the use of public images. The trade "dress" and trademarks of commercial products, such as packaged goods and their labels, are owned by their producers, and normally should not be used without permission. If the material itself is the subject of a legitimate public-interest program, however, the First Amendment will generally permit its use, provided that no false designation of origin is implied. Photos and video images of public figures can also be used in a news or public-affairs context; otherwise, the trademark, privacy, and publicity rules can prevent use without permission (see Chapter 16). Images may, under certain circumstances, be used for satire or parody without permission of the rights holder. Art in museum collections can be especially troublesome; because the museum may hold the only copy (or one of a limited number of copies) of a particular work, the institution's permission may be required in order to use a particular work of art, or a particular representation of that art, regardless of its age or origin.

DIGITAL IMAGE TRANSFORMATION

There are no clear rules regarding the line of demarcation between truly original images and existing images that have been transformed to create new originals. The legal question is whether the new work is close enough to the old one to constitute a "derivative work." This is determined by a highly subjective test of "substantial similarity" (see page 164). As a practical matter, if the artist or the rights holder who owns the original image is likely to recognize the connection and demand money, deny permission to use the original image, or insist that the new work infringes on the work's copyright, then the new work is probably too similar to the original image to be used without permission. New images that satirize older ones are subject to greater latitude; satire is a recognized exception to usual copyright protections.

ANIMATION

There are several forms of animation currently in use. The first is traditional cel animation, involving the painting and photographing of a gradually changing series of animation cels (hand-painted images on acetate sheets). The second is a computerized system whereby images are drawn and manipulated without the use of any physical materials outside the computer's domain. Some limited animation is possible via digital post-production still-store and character-generator devices.

The animation process begins with the development of a basic story line and the preparation of a storyboard that shows key frames in sketch form, usually with corresponding dialogue printed below the frame.

The designer is responsible for the visual development of the concept, and for revisions based on the client's suggestions and requests.

The client approves several key stages of the production process: the storyboards, a rough version of the animation, and then the finished work. Since animation projects proceed over the course of weeks, incremental reviews by the client are common, especially on larger or more complicated projects. This process is essentially the same for both traditional film-animation and for the newer computer-animation techniques. Normally, fees are paid in installments, in percentage payments keyed to the production schedule.

THE ARTIST AND RIGHTS OF OWNERSHIP

Most artists work either as employees or as independent contractors on a work-for-hire basis (see Chapter 45). The proceeds of their work, therefore, belong to the employer or client who becomes the copyright holder. There are, however, two subtleties to be considered.

First, most artists—and most creative people, for that matter—are especially competent in certain styles and types of work. It is not unusual for an artist to rework an idea previously submitted to, or prepared for, another client. Since ideas are not subject to copyright protection (see Chapter 16), the new work need not infringe on the rights of the former client, unless a great level of restriction was specified in the first contract.

Second, a situation may arise in which the work of the artist is exploited beyond the parties' original intent. For example, an artist is hired to create an animated character for use in an industrial film, and that character proves to have value beyond its original use. The continuing ownership of the character (as opposed to its first appearance in the industrial film) may belong to the artist, or to the company that owns the industrial film, or to both parties. In the case of a true freelance arrangement, if the producing company intended to purchase rights to the character beyond its original use in the industrial film, the rights should have been clearly specified, or included in a grant of all character uses in all markets in perpetuity. If the work was made for hire, then the producing company, as a matter of law, owns the rights. Ideally, the contract should provide for continuing financial participation for the artist, even if the artist does not own part of the copyright. Even better (for the artist), the original contract should allocate only those rights that the producing company will actually exploit, reserving all other rights for the artist. Since situations like these are rarely simple, the reader may wish to consult an attorney who specializes in such matters.

39

Music

The music business is a highly evolved one in its own right. Music on television is a complicated subject, involving issues that range from ownership of compositions and recordings to the creation of original music. Readers wishing additional detail should consult *This Business of Music,* by Sidney Shemel and M. William Krasilovsky.

MUSIC AND COPYRIGHT LAW

Two aspects of copyright law apply specifically to the use of music on television: synchronization rights and performance rights.

SYNCHRONIZATION RIGHTS

The copyright holder of a musical composition controls its reproduction in fixed, or recorded, form. The right to reproduce music on a record, tape, or compact disc is called a mechanical license (the term is left over from the days of player pianos and music boxes). A record company must acquire a mechanical license if a copyrighted composition is fixed or recorded in a way that can be read or replayed by a mechanical, electrical, electronic, or computer device.

A synchronization right, or sync right, is, in effect, a kind of mechanical license. The sync right permits the music to be fixed to an audiovisual recording. The grant of the sync right permits the producer and/or distributor of a film or television program to affix a particular piece of music to the film, tape, videodisc, or other audiovisual embodiment. This license has traditionally been obtained by the television producer, either through direct negotiation with the composer or via the music publisher.

A synchronization license is not needed for a live show because the element of recording is absent; only a performance right is needed. If the live production is taped or filmed for later use, however, then a sync right is needed to cover the incorporation of the music in this physical form.

PERFORMANCE RIGHTS

The second aspect of copyright law that applies to television music comes into play when the program is shown to the public—the right to control public performances of the composition. When a television program, commercial, or other visual form is broadcast or cablecast, this constitutes a public performance of the music that the program contains. The performance right must be licensed from the copyright holder; this license has traditionally been secured on a blanket basis (see below) by the local station or cable network, usually from a performing rights society.

If the music is only incidental to the dramatic content of live action—for example, a radio is playing a particular song in the background of a television program—then the right is called a "small performing right." If the music is an integral part of the program, as with a film musical or a televised opera, then the right is called a grand performing right. The "grand" and "small" rights are generally administered in a very different fashion, as separate aspects of music publishing.

A private viewing of a videotape at home will generally not constitute a public performance requiring a license. However, if money is charged for the viewing, or if the viewing takes place in a commercial establishment (a bar, for example), then the viewing may be considered a public performance, and may require the acquisition of a performance license. (Typically, bars pay a special public performance fee to a satellite distributor for the use of ESPN and other channels; part of this fee pays for musical performance rights.)

MUSIC PUBLISHING

The administration of both the synchronization and performance rights falls under the general activity of music publishing. A composer and a music publisher enter into a business arrangement in which the publisher agrees to administer these and other rights on behalf of the composer, acting as a clearing house and collecting agent for producers and others seeking to license the musical compositions. Music publishers vary greatly in their size, their clout, and their ability to make money for their client composers. Even composers of considerable stature license their songs to music publishing companies, though some artists own their publishing companies, in whole or in part. Grand performing rights are sometimes withheld by the composer and licensed through a different publishing company or agent.

A music publisher—like any other publisher—is responsible for the marketing of the property, the negotiation of licensing agreements, the collection of revenues, the issuing of royalty statements, and the payment of royalties.

The traditional split of performance and synchronization revenues between publisher and composer is 50/50. Sometimes, a publisher may yield to negotiating pressure and grant some of its usual share to the composer in what is called a co-publishing arrangement. The publisher, in turn, may deduct an administrative fee and/or charge for out-of-pocket expenses before revenues are distributed. In some cases, the publisher has pressured the composer to grant a portion of his or her 50 percent, but few publishers are successful in this effort (see discussion of performing rights organizations below).

OBTAINING A SYNCHRONIZATION LICENSE

The television producer typically negotiates for the synchronization license prior to including the music in the production; if the rights are too costly, he or she can then move on to another composition. These rights can be obtained either directly from the composer (and lyricist, if there is one); by arrangement with the music publisher; or through an intermediary such as the Harry Fox Agency, which specializes in this activity. The cost of the sync license can be substantial for a well-known work.

In most modern television productions, the producer commissions the music, keeping the cost of the sync license low as part of the overall deal for the composer's work. This is possible because the performance license fees for a commissioned work—which the producer typically does not pay—can be extremely lucrative for the composer and for whomever is serving as the music publisher. Many producers own music-publishing companies specifically to cash in on a share of the music revenues. In an extreme case— such as a show with daily, weekly, or national exposure—the composer and publisher may absorb all of the recording costs just for the opportunity to collect their share of the performance license fees. These are collected from television stations on an annualized basis; complicated formulas determine how much stations pay, and how much publishers and composers receive.

PERFORMANCE LICENSES AND PERFORMING RIGHTS ORGANIZATIONS

Music publishers normally do not collect small-performance revenues directly. Instead, monies are collected by performing rights organizations: ASCAP (American Society of Composers, Authors and Publishers), BMI (Broadcast Music Inc.), and—for European works, some religious, and gospel music—SESAC (Society of European Stage Authors and Composers).

Performance fees can also be negotiated and paid directly to the composer or publisher. This is called "source licensing," and it is a relatively uncommon practice.

ASCAP and BMI grew out of a need for composers to band together to monitor the performance of music onstage, in live concerts, on radio, and later, on television. Neither the artist nor the publisher can possibly monitor every usage—a live band in North Dakota, a music video played on a local cable system in Oregon, a radio station in Florida, and so on. The performing rights organizations were formed to track usage, collect the appropriate license fees, and divide the income fairly among rights holders.

After the deduction of overhead, income from these sources is divided between the composer (and lyricist, if there are lyrics) and the publisher on a 50/50 basis. If no publishing company is listed on the cue sheet (see below), and the performing rights organization is unable to find the proper publisher, then the publisher's share goes uncollected. If there is no individual composer associated with the work, his or her share goes uncollected.

BLANKET LICENSES

Most performance rights licensing takes place at the level of the broadcast station or cable network. Rather than negotiating deals for each individual use, stations and networks use *blanket licenses.* A blanket license allows the licensee to use any item in the performing rights organization's catalog for a specified period of time, without the need to negotiate for the performance right of each individual composition. Cue sheets provide the basis of allocating blanket license fees to ASCAP/BMI members. Some cable networks work only with original or library music, and do not routinely work with ASCAP or BMI material.

TRACKING USAGE

In theory, ASCAP and BMI attempt to track the use of every piece of music used on every television program airing on every national, regional/local broadcast, cable, and satellite system. Indeed, when the stakes are high and the audiences are large—as on network television—tracking is extremely accurate. On local and other forms of television, the tracking may be somewhat less rigorous. The key to tracking is the music cue sheet.

A music cue sheet is a list of every piece of music used in a particular television program or film. The cue sheet lists the title and running time of each piece of music, as well as its composer, lyricist (if any), publisher, copyright owner, and performing arts institution (ASCAP, BMI). This list is generally delivered to the network or distributor along with the master videotape; copies should be provided to the exhibitor and, in turn, to the appropriate performing rights society, every time the videotape is publicly shown.

Whenever the program airs, ASCAP or BMI must be contacted and furnished with the information from the cue sheet. The performing arts organization feeds all of this information into its computers, and works out a formula which is used to determine the performance license fees due to the composer and publisher.

In those special cases where a grand license is required, ASCAP and BMI are not involved; instead, the license is sought directly from the publisher, or from the composer and lyricist.

AMERICAN FEDERATION OF MUSICIANS (AFM)

The American Federation of Musicians (AFM) is a performance union with hundreds of chapters throughout the U.S. and Canada. In these cities, the majority of working musicians are members of the union, and most television work is controlled by negotiated agreements between the AFM and producers, stations, networks, or distributors. The relevant agreements are the AFM Television Film Agreement which covers movies made for television, and the AFM Videotape Agreement, which covers other programs made for syndication and network television, regardless of whether the program is produced on film or videotape.

To understand the basic format of an AFM agreement, it is first necessary to understand the types of musicians covered by the agreement. A *recording musician* actually performs; his or her work is heard on the production. A *production musician* performs only during rehearsal. A *sideline musician* does not actually play an instrument, but pretends to do so on camera; if the sideline musician has a speaking part, then he or she is entitled to an additional fee for that type of performance. A *contractor* is required if more than seven musicians are hired to play (under the Videotape Agreement); he or she hires the musicians, and takes care of billing, collection, adherence to AFM work rules, and other paperwork. The *arranger* or *orchestrator* reworks the basic composition and assigns parts to individual musicians. A *copyist* provides final versions of arrangements and orchestrations, ready for duplication. A *librarian* provides a copy of the score to each musician. For larger projects, a *proof-reader* is hired to check the score and the copies, and a *librarian* maintains the library of sheet music.

There are different minimum fees, and some variations in work rules, for each type of musician. In addition, the fees and rules vary depending upon the type of production and its intended market.

The rules in the basic Television Film Agreement are typical of most union agreements, but the many variations mentioned above make accurate computation tricky.

The current agreement lists scale payments per "sideman," a term that covers recording/performing and sideline musicians. These payments are based on hourly rates with a three-hour minimum, and overtime is broken down into 15-minute increments. For a single session, lasting up to four hours, the scale payment is roughly $220 for a three-hour base; an additional hour costs about $75. If the work is performed on a holiday, the rates double. The basic rates are subject to night and holiday premiums of 110 to 200 percent.

When budgeting with an AFM agreement, it's important to read very carefully, for there are many conditions and special situations. For example, if a musician serves as a leader, or as the sole performer, then he or she is paid twice the straight-time rate (if the work is done at night, or involves overtime, these calculations can become quite complicated). If a musician plays a second instrument (this is called "doubling"), he or she is entitled to a 50 percent premium for the first double, and 20 percent for each additional double. Doubling is different from a "double session," which is a pair of two three-hour work sessions that must be completed within eight hours, with a one hour break. Work done after the eighth hour is paid at 120 percent of straight time, billable in 15-minute units. Musicians are also entitled to a fee for carting, the cost of transporting some of the larger instruments to and from the studio. Travel fees for work outside of designated geographic areas are, of course, reimbursed within a reasonable period. Musicians who appear on camera are also paid for time spent on wardrobe and make-up; rest periods, meal breaks, and notification of calls are all detailed in the Agreement as well.

The Television Videotape Agreement is similar, but some rates and rules differ slightly. There are specific limitations on the use of music in news and magazine programs. When music is heard in the background at a live event (such as a parade or a sporting event), no payments are made.

The most severe limitation in the Videotape Agreement is in the use of excerpts from other, usually older, programs. If a clip involving a full-scale production number with music is used, every musician on the original production is entitled to receive between one and two hours' payment at the current Variety Show rate.

Theme music—music composed as the opening and/or closing theme (up to three minutes total), as opposed to music used in the body of the program—is also subject to special rules. Theme rates do not apply to a series, for example, unless musicians are employed for every episode within the series. Different rules apply for theme music to news, commentary, public-affairs, religious, and sports programs. Most AFM agreements are quite complex; when in doubt, the producer should request a written interpretation of any confusing clauses from the national AFM office.

Different rate scales apply for variety programs, including both specials and regularly scheduled weekly programs, and for strip shows.

The Videotape Agreement also contains terms for basic cable and pay TV. These rates are somewhat lower than network and syndication rates, and offer the added advantage of easy accommodation for multiple plays.

A third AFM agreement, for Documentary and Industrial Films, differs mainly in the minimum pay scales and the absence of reuse fees from the other two.

The pension rate for AFM is 10 percent of all payments. The contribution to the health and welfare fund is $7.50 per session per musician (the rate for copyists, arrangers, and orchestrators differs).

USE OF LIVE MUSIC

Earlier in the history of television, live music was an important part of variety shows and a surprising number of other types of programs, including talk and game shows.

Today, the use of live musicians on television is generally limited to concert and performance programs, late-night talk/variety shows employing relatively small bands, large-scale variety specials, and the occasional musical game show.

The process of working with live musicians should begin with the selection of a music director, who supervises composition, arrangement, and copying, as well as the hiring of musicians. Each of these areas includes personnel who are guided by AFM rules, and paid according to AFM minimums. Some of these people are frequently paid over scale, notably the composer.

Rehearsals must be carefully scheduled to maximize the number of usable hours; this can be difficult when other elements of the production must be rehearsed as well. If the live show is scheduled at night, then additional payments may be due, and if the program is recorded and replayed, then reuse rates apply. Cartage, doubling, and leader rates must be considered as well.

The rates and rules regarding the use of star performers are similar, though over-scale fees are common.

USE OF RECORDED MUSIC

Most of the music heard on television is pre-recorded by companies that specialize in creating and producing television music. Opens and closes for local news programs, show themes, music for promos and commercials—the list of customized music types is a long one.

COMMISSIONED MUSIC

Several music production companies generally compete for a commission to produce a project's music (or, as is often the case, a producer develops an allegiance to one composer or firm). Music producers are asked to bring samples of previous work. Some companies take the initiative and prepare a demo specific to the project's unique requirements, at their own expense, on spec, but the more successful ones produce demos only at the client's expense. The job is described in broad terms; the producer selects a company based on its previous experience and on the producer's instinct. Terms are negotiated, and the job is awarded.

In a typical arrangement, the music production company is paid 50 percent to start work. Music is composed and presented to the client, who offers comments and criticism. After a few revisions, arrangements are written, players are hired (or, often, one or two musicians get to work on digital instruments), and the music is recorded. An additional 25 percent is usually due on the first day of recording. The music is mixed and edited, with the final 25 percent payable on delivery.

The music publishing rights in commissioned music are usually divided 50/50, as per the traditional split between publisher and composer. Larger television production companies frequently own an affiliated music publishing company which administers publishing rights in its productions. Other arrangements may be negotiated, of course.

Rates may change over the years, but one leading music house suggests five pricing levels for the production of music for television. The low end is represented by a hungry newcomer using several synthesizers and recording all of the necessary work for a flat fee of roughly $1,500. One step up—$3,500–$5,000—pays for a demo from a successful house, or a small-scale job (a "bed" for a series of on-air promos, a theme for a low-budget show). Generally, $6,000–$8,000 will pay for a small to medium-sized job, like a news theme for a station in a small market or the score for a basic cable, low-budget syndication, or medium-priced industrial project. Most of the well-known syndication and pay TV programs are in the next echelon: $15,000–$20,000. In the music production business, the best jobs pay over $25,000.

Sync license fees are included in these prices, and so are recording costs. Performance royalties may be handled via a traditional ASCAP or BMI license, with the proceeds split between composer and publisher. Sometimes, a source licensing deal is negotiated, particularly for projects that the performing rights organization might not count when calculating license fees.

Lower-budget jobs are often done by non-AFM musicians, or sometimes by union members working secretly or under assumed names (see page 458).

If all rights are not transferred as part of the deal, music composed for one client may also be resold to another, non-competitive client. This is common practice, for example, when selling music to local television news programs. A theme may be sold to no more than one station in each market, of course—but there is no reason why a station in Chicago cannot use the same music as a station in Denver, presuming both stations' creative needs can be satisfied.

LICENSING PRE-RECORDED MUSIC

The use of existing recordings for television music requires several layers of rights and payments. First, there is the synchronization license for the use of the composition. Second, there is the payment to the musicians whose work is included in the recording. Third, there is a payment to a producer and/or record company, or to the artist who holds the rights to television use of the recording. The latter payment is often called a "needle-drop" right.

The synchronization license has already been discussed (see page 383).

The payment to the artist and musicians can be costly, and if the recording is an old one, some research may be necessary to find not only the names, but the addresses of the people involved (or their estates). Many older recordings were made on a flat-rate buyout contract, in which musicians exchanged their right to future earnings for a flat fee. This greatly simplifies matters. Also, prior to February 15, 1972, the recorded *performance* of music could not be copyrighted under federal law in the U.S., although the music itself might be. This is another advantage to using older recordings.

Most well-known recordings feature artists who are not only famous, but protected by lawyers and others who guard their interests. Securing permission to use a recording by Michael Jackson is likely to be difficult and costly, while the rights to a work by the World Saxophone Quartet or Ravi Shankar might be a more reasonable undertaking. Popular recording stars are likely to be unimpressed by typical television music fees, and, viewing the usage as a possible dilution of the music's value, they often refuse such offers.

The music publisher must also grant permission for the music's use and, if it is not handled by a performing rights society, a performance license. Determining who owns this right—and who may traffic in it—usually requires some patience. When negotiations do begin, the seller has the advantage of knowing the producer's specific interest. However, since this is found money, the seller is also motivated to accept any reasonable figure.

In the real world, many smaller television productions incorporate well-known music without permission. This is especially true of programs produced for private use (an in-company training video, for example), and on local TV in the smallest markets, where the likelihood of any knowledgeable viewer questioning use is small. Still, this practice is technically a violation of copyright, and the consequences for the guilty can be severe. In larger markets, and on all forms of national television, producers are far more careful in securing the necessary permissions.

MUSIC LIBRARIES

Many television productions do not require original music or the use of well-known recordings. A handful of companies specialize in the production and distribution of pre-cleared music that requires no additional sync or performance licenses and no permissions from performers or record companies. The library is paid a fee for its music plus an annual renewal fee. A producer, production company, recording studio, television station, or other entity is then permitted unlimited use of the music.

PUBLIC-DOMAIN RECORDINGS

The use of recordings in the public domain can be a tricky business. Thorough research is required in order to determine that the recording, and all of its underlying rights, are in the public domain. Simply identifying the copyright of the recording itself is not sufficient to establish public-domain status.

If the musical composition is under copyright, then a sync license is required. This, too, can be complicated, particularly for an older song. Published sheet music, for example, may have a different copyright date from the copyright date of the composition itself.

Although, in the U.S., performances could not be copyrighted until 1972, arrangements have been copyrighted since early this century.

AFM payments and residuals may also be due via contract to musicians who played on the recording of a public-domain composition. The original record company, which may no longer be in operation, probably sold its master recordings—and the rights to use them—to a successor, and this entity should be tracked down as well.

The work involved in researching the history of particular recordings can be daunting. Many producers have found out about this unique world's complexities the hard way—by assigning a production assistant to a task that really should be done by a professional music researcher and/or rights-clearance service.

PART 5

Audience Measurement and Advertising

40

Television Marketing

When there were just three commercial networks, marketing was uncomplicated. Each network had its logo, and its general identity. CBS had its eye. NBC developed the peacock as an introduction to its color programs, but did not adopt the peacock as an official corporate logo until the mid-1980s. ABC's circular logo was developed in the 1960s. Identities were derived from programming choices, and emphasized in promotional announcements. ABC was youthful and hip, and a sports innovator; NBC was serious about its news, the leader in sports, and venturesome in its comedy; CBS was solidly mid-American, also serious about its news, the network of the stars. Each network had its personality, and the average American could describe them with the accuracy of a senior corporate marketer.

Then cable happened.

At first, cable was not perceived as a threat. The three networks enjoyed an enormous audience share, and even the initial special-interest incursions, from MTV, for instance, were not taken seriously. MTV was unique; the network was packaged as if it was a product. There was a company logo, and a playful one at that—a giant M that might be made of clay or bricks or watercolors, that might be filled with goldfish. Once an hour, an astronaut planted an MTV flag on the moon. Between programs, promos encouraged viewers to think about MTV as a cross between a consumer network and a consumer product. The network was advertised as a consumer product—"I want my MTV" was the campaign's slogan. A television network had never been sold as a consumer product before. To attract viewers, MTV ran catchy promos for contests with outrageous prizes. As part of MTV's "Little Pink House Weekend," for example, MTV presented 22-year-old Washington State college student Susan Miles, with the deed to a pink house in Bloomington, Indiana. The prize also included round trip Seattle-Indiana airfare for Miles and 19 of her friends to travel, plus an outdoor barbecue, a pink Jeep, a widescreen TV and 500 cases of Hawaiian Punch (prizes totaling over $15,000). In addition, John Cougar Mellencamp (whose song "Pink Houses" provided the contest's foundation) played a living room concert for Miles and her friends. MTV sold tour jackets, sweatshirts, t-shirts, anything that would get its logo into the lives of its viewers.

Nickelodeon played the same game, eventually with more flair and greater impact than MTV. Nick's logo was no logo at all. Instead, it was the word "Nickelodeon," in simple white letters, played against a vivid orange background. The background could take any shape: a dinosaur, an airship, a fish. It could be two- or three-dimensional. Bright orange became Nickelodeon's color (actually, slime green became associated with Nick as well).

BRAND DEVELOPMENT

Today's marketing students are taught about the importance of developing and managing brands. There is equity in brands, real long-term value in a logo and an identity that paint a clear picture in the minds of customers.

But how does that brand come to be?

The development of a brand comes about with the blending of three processes.

- The first is a complete understanding of the target customer— an understanding that begins with demographics (age, income, etc.) but extends deeply into "psychographics" (why people behave as they do, who they think they are, groups with whom they identify). *WIRED* magazine is a successful print brand; people who read *WIRED* are generally 18–45 years old, mostly male, earn more money (and have less time) than most other people; they're also technically inclined, interested in the future, and plugged into the Internet.

- The second, which is closely related, is the development and production of a product that is consistent with the brand identity. MTV, for example, is mostly a music video channel, but the network does program news, game, comedy, animation, and drama programs that support and expand the brand. Examples include *MTV's Real World* and *Beavis and Butthead.*

- The third process is marketing and promotion. MTV tour jackets support the MTV brand. Touring shows, event sponsorships, motion pictures, merchandise, compact discs, and a Web site all extend the brand beyond the television medium.

Some television networks lend themselves to exploitation as major consumer brands. These include MTV, Nickelodeon, ESPN, and The Discovery Channel; NBC has also succeeded in developing a distinctive brand (ABC and CBS have not focused as much energy on brand development). Other brands are simply not as powerful— The Weather Channel, for example, lacks the kind of rabid fan support enjoyed by MTV or Nickelodeon. Other networks, such as A&E, Lifetime, and USA Network, offer products that are too diffuse to focus consumers on the simplicity of a single branded identity.

BRAND MANAGEMENT

The importance of brand management and product management has migrated from packaged consumer goods to the entertainment business with varying degrees of success. Once a brand name is developed, it must be carefully managed so that the initial value of the brand is protected. At the same time, television operates in a dynamic marketplace, so media brands typically require periodic updating and sometimes-risky expansion.

This updating is readily apparent in local television. For decades, each local station emphasized its own identity—promoting the station call letters first and the network affiliation second. NBC, in a move to establish its brand, changed that strategy. NBC stations are encouraged to identify themselves as, for example, "NBC10" and not as "Channel 10—WCAU-TV, Philadelphia." This approach is supported by a clean logo treatment with a peacock on one side and a number on the other—and no call letters at all.

Consistent presentation of the brand's logo and identity is essential. NBC's peacock is the brand's most prominent graphic identity. It is used everywhere—in print advertisements, on billboards, on the scenery used for local news, on jackets and t-shirts and other apparel. And everywhere it appears, the peacock looks the same. Colors never vary, lines and shapes never vary. And so, there is never any confusion. The peacock is NBC, and NBC is the peacock.

The story of the peacock is worth telling. NBC's first logo, a microphone and lightning bolt, was introduced in 1943. The three-note chimes (the notes G-E-C, short for General Electric Company) were visualized on a small xylophone and used as an NBC logo from 1954 until 1956. In 1956, NBC introduced its first peacock, with 11 colored feathers, to precede programs broadcast "in living color on NBC"; this bird was used as a kind of mascot until 1975 (when it was retired in a company-wide attempt at modernization). "The snake" outlined the three network letters in a simple line pattern and identified the brand from 1959 until 1975. A red-and-blue trapezoid representing a large letter N was introduced in 1975,[1] again a part of the new and updated NBC. By 1980, the peacock was back, still with 11 feathers, but this time the feather tips were rounded and it had no feet. The peacock was made part of the NBC logo and there was some marketing mumbo-jumbo about pride. In 1986, the trapezoidal N was gone, replaced by a six-feathered peacock that has become a well-known logotype in the U.S. and in the many other countries where NBC is seen.

When an affiliate shows the network logo on its air and in its advertising, the viewer makes an important connection that should, at least in theory, generate loyalty to the network and its programs. NBC's peacock is the most recognized logo, CBS's eye is second, and MTV's logo is third, according to a WBTV survey. (WBTV was testing the effectiveness of Michigan J. Frog as part of its network logo.)

There is more to brand identity than the logo, of course. There is the challenge of maintaining a consistent, refined image in the minds of consumers. Here, NBC's branding is not as sharp as, for example, MTV's. NBC's identity encompasses sitcoms for people in their teens and twenties, but also for older viewers, sports, news, *Saturday Night Live, Today,* Jay Leno, *Seinfeld,* daytime drama; the same logo is used to identify NBC outside the U.S. Still, NBC has skillfully pulled all of these disparate ideas together under one company—and manages to maintain a strong connection in the minds of consumers between the network and its many products. In some ways, this is a strategy similar to the one employed by CBS in its heyday—when Red Skeleton, Danny Kaye, and other variety stars populated prime-time. At the time, "everyone" knew these performers could be found only on CBS.

With so many networks on cable, an identifying mark on the lower right corner of the screen has become common. This small "CBS eye" or ABC circle logo, subtly encourages the viewer to identify

1   This move was something of a corporate nightmare. The logo was unveiled with considerable hoopla, costing either $500,000 or $750,000—sources vary—a great deal of money at the time. A remarkably similar logo was already in use by Nebraska's public television operation, and it was apparently designed for less than $100. In order to use the new company logo, NBC paid the organization $25,000, and contributed a half-million dollars's worth of equipment.

the network's brand with the individual program, and, in theory, encourages the viewer to watch more programs on that network.

The ways in which a brand can be expanded and exploited really depends upon the individual brand's image, product, and customer. Nickelodeon, for example, is a brand that easily moves from television to toys and theme park attractions. The Weather Channel has lent its name to CD-ROM products and a Web site, but there aren't as many opportunities, nor is the profile of the target consumer as evident, for a channel based on weather information and forecasts.

ON-AIR LOOK, ON-AIR PROMOTION

The "look" of a channel can be as important as its programming. This was certainly proven in the repackaging of programs seen time and again in syndication on Nick at Nite, and took a different, but equally significant form, on Cartoon Network. On-air look contributes mightily to brand identity. One look at The Weather Channel, for example, is all most people need in order to identify the network. MTV can also be identified quickly and easily; Bloomberg Information Television's multimedia, multi-segment screen helps to set it apart from other news networks.

Given a disparate range of programs, the development of a consistent on-air look can be especially challenging. Singular marketing strategies can be hard to sell internally. Still, there is good reason to fight the good fight—NBC's "Must See TV" campaign provided a central theme for the network's on-air marketing. Sometimes, an individual program series can help to establish branding. This has been true for A&E's *Biography* and to a lesser extent, Comedy Central's *South Park*. Lifetime's on-air look emphasizes programs for women, but the product (the program schedule) includes programs of interest to women and in some cases, to both men and women. Nickelodeon's on-air promotions are fun to watch, but Nick is clear on strategy: contribute to brand identity by making the promo fun, but tell the kids the name of the show, and what time it's on the air.

THE GROWING IMPORTANCE OF WEB SITES

Apart from the channel itself, the company's Web site is the most direct way of communicating with customers/viewers. Most Web sites are promotional—they promote the network, the individual programs, the schedule, and if relevant, the celebrities associated with the network. Some Web sites have become very popular: the

Sci-Fi Channel's site, consistently scores high numbers when Web audiences are measured. As the Web continues to grow, and the technology matures, some networks may broadcast programs, or portions of programs, directly on their Web sites.

A typical Web site also includes e-mail access to the network. This updated version of viewer mail can become very powerful as names and e-mail addresses are collected and used for direct online marketing.

LICENSING AND MERCHANDISING

For decades, the broadcast networks were reluctant to license manufacturers to create products based on their television series (the exceptions were children's programs and some sitcoms, thus permitting school lunch boxes with characters from *The Beverly Hillbillies*). This changed in the 1980s for two important reasons: the licensing business was growing, and the networks were searching for new revenue streams.

A license is a right granted to a manufacturer (or a publisher, etc.) to develop and sell a limited line of products based upon a particular program (or, in the case of MTV or Nickelodeon, based upon a particular network). The license typically runs for several years, and the manufacturer bears the entire risk, and reaps all but a percentage of the reward. The network typically receives a guarantee, often paid annually, from which royalties are deducted. Contract renewals are typically based on success in the marketplace, and upon the payment of escalating guarantees for subsequent years.

In the licensing world, some products "work" better than others. *Cheers,* for example, has been a success, and so has *Star Trek.* In both cases, the licenses were controlled by Paramount, a studio with unusual skill in the licensing area. Most television series (apart from children's shows) are not at all suitable for licensing, and few result in anything like the range of *Star Trek* products. Licensing rights to older programs are also valuable; there are many *Twilight Zone* products in the marketplace, for example.

For more about licensing in the children's marketplace, see Chapter 23.

41

Audience Measurement, Research and Ratings

I n the U.S. and in many other countries, broadcasting and advertising share a symbiotic relationship. Broadcasters provide the
distribution of programs that include commercials; advertisers
subsidize program production, acquisition, and other operations
by paying for access to the broadcaster's (or cablecaster's) audience.

THE BASICS OF AUDIENCE MEASUREMENT

Effective advertising is a business of numbers. In both print and
electronic media, the effectiveness of an advertisement is based
upon the estimated number of people who saw the advertisement. To be more precise, it's not the total number of people that
matters. Instead, it's the total number of people within the advertiser's target demographic that matters. Counting these people is
nearly impossible, so the media has devised systems to estimate
these numbers. In the print world, the system is based upon the
actual number of copies sold and an estimated number of readers
who handled each copy. Advertisers then pay a specific amount for
each 1,000 readers (this is called a cost per thousand, or "CPM").

Since electronic media are not distributed as physical units, the
process of estimating audience size has traditionally been based
upon statistical units known as samples. In theory, these carefully-
chosen groups of representative households speak for the whole
of the U.S. To count any other way, at least in the era preceding
the convergence of telephones and computers, would have been
prohibitively expensive, and, according to market research experts,
unnecessary.

DATA COLLECTION

Nielsen Media Research selects a few hundred metered households to represent a population of several million for immediate local ratings, plus a few hundred more diary households (explained below) in the same cities. For national ratings, 5,000 households represent nearly 100 million.

In a large market, Nielsen may contact up to 5,000 households for participation in a single week's survey. Roughly two-thirds of the households contacted agree to make regular written entries in diaries—notations in a small schedule booklet each time any set in the house is turned on or off, and each time the channel is changed, always noting who is doing the viewing. (Approximately half the households do the job properly, and half do not.) Nielsen collects four weeks' worth of diaries, tabulates the data, and enters the information into a database. Their findings are presented as a series of reports to advertising agencies, sponsors, networks, media buyers, rep firms, producers, distributors, and local stations, all of which pay a subscription fee for access to the information.

For national ratings, and for measurement in many local markets, electronic metering systems have replaced the older diary format.

A BRIEF HISTORY OF AUDIENCE MEASUREMENT

The need for measurement of radio audiences became clear by the late 1920s, as an experimental medium was changing into a viable advertising medium. Crossley ratings were first taken in 1930, via telephone polling: listeners were asked to recall what they had heard during the preceding hours. Hooperatings, introduced in 1935, improved upon the formula by collecting coincidental information—asking listeners not to recall what they had heard (which was likely to be inaccurate), but only what they were currently hearing. Trendex was among the early audience-measurement services; once again, polling was done via phone calls to viewers.

In the 1950s, Nielsen began inserting a record-keeping mechanism in television sets; it was called an Audimeter. By 1960, the American Research Bureau had introduced the Arbitron rating; the name came from an electronic box, installed in sample homes, that delivered viewership data every 90 seconds to a central computer. Although this method was a dramatic improvement over telephone polling, the same company's ARB ratings—which were based on telephone polling—remained dominant throughout the 1960s. Videodex, a diary-based ratings service, also appeared in the 1960s. In time, Nielsen and Arbitron became the only significant audience measurement services. In the mid-1990s, Arbitron left the television business, but continues in radio and in other market research businesses.

Since the 1930s, two principal trends have guided the evolution of audience measurement. First, the information has become more and more accurate, as technology, data collection methodology, and sophistication in dealing with statistics have improved. Second, the information has become available more quickly—where two weeks were once required for collecting and formatting diary data, the same information (and more) is now available overnight from electronic metering systems. Both trends are likely to continue, and to become more sophisticated in terms of tie-ins with other marketing measurement systems. For example, in the future, a single household's viewing patterns might be correlated with their super-market buying patterns to determine the true effectiveness of commercial advertising.

MEASUREMENT OF NATIONAL AUDIENCES

The Nielsen Television Index (NTI) is Nielsen's national system for measuring broadcast network audiences. Five thousand households have their viewing habits monitored by electronic PeopleMeters. Households are paid $50 for the installation, remain in the sample for two years, and receive token gifts for their participation from a merchandise catalog (most of the items are worth less than $20). Households are selected in accordance with statistical rules of sampling; according to Nielsen, the size and composition of the sample is representative of national viewership.

NTI data is reported in more than a dozen standard formats; it is reported daily, weekly and monthly in print and electronic form (via a PC connection to Nielsen). The best-known report, called Pocketpiece (because the booklet is small enough to fit into the pocket of a suit jacket), is published weekly. Pocketpiece includes estimates of program viewership presented in three ways: alphabetically, by name of the program; in a color-network schedule grid; and chronologically, by time period. The alphabetical listing shows the number of stations carrying the show, the percentage of the country that can see the show, the rating and share for the total audience, and viewers per thousand households, broken down by demographic groups. The schedule grid shows the HUT (Homes Using Television) level, or the number of households watching TV at that time; average audience size in gross numbers and in rating percentages; the share; and each quarter hour's rating. The time period estimates show ratings by demographic groups. (See below for definitions of these terms.)

30 PROGRAM AUDIENCE ESTIMATES (Alpha)   **OCT.27-NOV.2,1997**

PROGRAM NAME				HOUSEHOLD AUDIENCE				TOTAL PERS	WORKING WOMEN		LOH	WOMEN						MEN						TEENS		CHILDREN	
			K E Y	AVG. AUD. %	VCR CNTRB %	SH %	AVG. AUD. 000		18+	18-49	18-49	TOTAL	18-34	18-49	25-54	35-64	55+	TOTAL	18-34	18-49	25-54	35-64	55+	TOT. 12-17	FEM. 12-17	TOT. 2-11	TOT. 6-11
DAY TIME DUR NET NO.OF #STNS CVG% TYPE T/C								2+			W/CH <3																
EVENING CONT'D																											
PUBLIC EYE-BRYANT GUMBEL-CONT'D 9.30 - 10.00			A	8.8	.1	14	860	1308	301	177	36	792	91	286	340	403	437	455	60	180	216	247	226	32^	18^	29^	16^
SABRINA-TEENAGE WITCH FRI 8.00P 30 ABC 221 99 CS			A B C	7.9 8.2 8.2	.2 .2 .2	15 16 16	772 799 799	1411 1502 1502	303 251 251	230 203 203	45 62 62	700 605 605	204 197 197	416 392 392	423 367 367	359 302 302	204 166 166	420 339 339	113 101 101	250 224 224	230 216 216	222 181 181	139 87 87	120 207 207	65 124 124	171 351 351	133 255 255
SEINFELD THU 9.00P 30 NBC 219 99 CS			A B C	20.3 21.5 21.5	.9 1.2 1.2	31 33 33	1991 2106 2106	1519 1525 1525	405 420 420	331 351 351	82 87 87	742 752 752	252 285 285	542 561 561	558 549 549	414 391 391	131 129 129	608 579 579	242 227 227	477 440 440	460 433 433	313 302 302	86 93 93	89 98 98	42 49 49	80 96 96	47 57 57
SENTINEL, THE WED 8.00P 60 UPN 164 88 GD 8.00 - 8.30 8.30 - 9.00			A B C A A	3.6 3.4 3.4 3.5 3.7	.1 .2 .1 .1 .2	6 6 6 6 6	353 335 334 344 362	1490 1457 1457 1493 1486	291 264 264 294 288	211 173 171 212 211	40^ 49 50 36^ 43^	648 632 635 645 651	178 142 144 171 185	354 311 311 348 361	355 326 333 352 357	335 360 362 331 338	215 250 248 219 211	616 574 579 600 631	195 140 143 189 200	330 316 325 306 353	377 351 355 356 397	300 333 337 287 312	198 184 182 201 196	95 99 96 111 81^	26^ 24^ 28^ 35^ 17^	130 152 146 35 124	90 98 95 93 86
7TH HEAVEN - WB(R) MON 8.00P 60 WB 87 88 GD			A B C	3.6 3.7 3.6	.0 .0 .0	5 6 6	350 362 351	1556 1453 1470	258 269 275	186 208 215	67^ 64 64	560 575 587	186 198 202	391 383 389	413 378 380	321 297 298	103 142 149	317 270 275	124 112 111	244 210 212	237 200 199	188 139 142	47^ 40 44	303 300 298	196 202 202	376 309 310	274 222 222

8.00 - 8.30 8.30 - 9.00			A A	3.2 3.9	.0 .0	5 6	318 382	1578 1537	258 258	187 185	68^ 66^	567 555	196 177	395 387	420 407	313 327	103 102	324 312	129 120	243 245	235 238	190 186	54^ 41^	294 310	187 203	393 361	288 263
SIMPSONS SUN 8.00P 30 FOX 198 98 EA			A B C	10.5 9.8 10.0	.4 .4 .4	15 15 15	1028 957 975	1753 1692 1685	298 285 283	278 263 261	86 70 69	518 513 511	268 273 271	447 446 446	375 374 376	225 219 218	37 37 38	728 665 656	399 375 362	634 589 583	553 498 493	311 272 276	50 45 43	239 244 250	52 71 77	269 270 269	185 191 190
SISTER, SISTER - WB WED 8.00P 30 WB 86 86 CS			A B C	3.7 3.4 3.3	.0 .0 .0	6 6 6	358 334 321	1467 1457 1466	193 217 225	159 187 190	94 60 64	504 498 510	215 223 216	401 400 404	306 311 323	236 243 259	89 81 85	250 267 268	88 109 107	172 200 200	125 159 166	125 137 141	65^ 52 51	346 315 316	210 176 173	368 377 373	253 272 270
60 MINUTES SUN 7.00P 60 CBS 211 99 DN 7.00 - 7.30 7.30 - 8.00			A B C A A	12.7 12.7 12.8 12.1 13.3	.2 .2 .2 .1 .2	19 21 22 19 20	1244 1241 1257 1187 1301	1492 1431 1429 1496 1489	249 254 253 254 245	134 144 144 141 129	14^ 21 22 13^ 15^	774 788 789 769 779	59 64 66 63 56	204 220 224 208 200	265 279 282 269 262	354 367 364 355 354	496 494 492 484 507	667 597 595 670 664	89 70 71 95 83	241 205 204 245 239	272 244 244 278 265	323 296 294 321 325	372 338 337 368 376	20^ 19 19 22^ 19^	14^ 9^ 10 13^ 14^	31 27 26 35 27	19^ 17 16 24^ 15^
SLEEPWALKERS SAT 9.00P 60 NBC 217 99 GD 9.00 - 9.30 9.30 - 10.00			A B C A A	5.9 5.9 5.9 6.0 5.8	.6 .6 .6 .6 .6	10 10 10 10 10	577 577 577 590 564	1491 1491 1491 1496 1486	411 411 411 406 416	312 312 312 305 320	46^ 46^ 46^ 43^ 50^	806 806 806 811 801	202 202 202 199 206	495 495 495 484 507	525 525 525 514 535	495 495 495 494 496	227 227 227 214 214	570 570 570 567 573	197 197 197 196 198	374 374 374 367 382	361 361 361 354 369	312 312 312 306 318	150 150 150 154 145	44^ 44^ 44^ 46^ 42^	21^ 21^ 21^ 20^ 23^	71 71 71 70 70	49^ 49^ 49^ 47^ 47^
SMART GUY - WB WED 8.30P 30 WB 86 86 CS			A B C	3.7 3.6 3.5	.0 .0 .0	6 6 6	362 355 340	1502 1497 1502	190 214 225	162 181 187	79^ 59 63	488 475 487	190 197 193	392 376 380	304 303 315	252 251 263	84 79 81	255 267 266	93 118 114	187 205 204	127 158 164	128 131 136	60^ 48 46	348 331 332	198 175 172	410 423 418	304 318 317

A=CURRENT REPORT   B=QUARTER-TO-DATE AVERAGE   C=PREMIERE-TO-DATE AVERAGE   FOR EXPLANATION OF SYMBOLS SEE PAGE B

31

Sample pages, THE POCKETPIECE: NIELSEN TV NATIONAL TELEVISION RATINGS for all of the U.S. during the week of October 27 to November 2, 1997. This handy sized research tool shows national viewership of programs on the commercial broadcast networks, broken down by demographic category. (Copyright 1998, Nielsen Media Research)

The PeopleMeter collects minute-by-minute viewing information. It also reports when the set is turned on or off, what channel is being watched, and how long the set has been tuned to that channel. The PeopleMeter also allows viewer identification by pressing a button on a special remote control (in some instances, it's a number, and in some, it's a symbol representing, for example, a young child or a teenager). National overnight ratings for prime-time programs as determined by PeopleMeter households are available by 3:15 P.M. on the following day.

Nielsen's other NTI publications include more detailed reports on total U.S. household television usage, demographic breakdowns, and reports specifically written for advertisers, such as the Household & Cost Per Thousand Report.

Nielsen also provides overnight ratings information from more than 40 major markets. This local information is collected by an electronic meter (not the PeopleMeter); the information is limited to whether the set is on or off, and the channel being viewed. The information can be retrieved from Nielsen's computers by 6:00 A.M. on the following day.

MEASUREMENT IN LOCAL MARKETS

All markets continue to use the diary format; in addition, several dozen markets also supply data through meters. The diaries go to one sample and the meters go to another in the same market. PeopleMeters are not used in local-market measurement.

Stations pay about 80 percent of the cost of Nielsen's audience measurement services. In Memphis, Tennessee, for example, the 42nd largest TV market, stations paid a total of $75,000 per year for ratings information. Advertisers and media-buying services add approximately $20,000, for an annual total of nearly $100,000. These figures do not include meters—whose annual cost is approximately $350,000 per year. In theory, more accurate results justify the additional cost.

More than forty markets are now metered markets—that is, their ratings information is collected primarily through meters attached to the television sets—and are no longer reliant upon diaries.

When a market makes the changeover, there are some predictable results. Diaries tend to skew toward more popular programs—those are the ones that people remember to write down. A diary keeper, for example, may remember watching *Spin City* but forget the few minutes spent at CNN before watching *Spin City*. The diary keeper may also not recall that a teenager watched MTV. The meters change the dynamics because the meters remember everything. Meters tend to hurt the ratings of the bigger stations, and help the ratings of cable networks, particularly those based on short-form programming (MTV, The Weather Channel, CNN).

Programs that appeal to younger audiences tend to report higher ratings. When it comes to filling out Nielsen's diaries, older viewers tend to be more diligent than younger ones; since meters record the channel to which the set is tuned, shows that skewed younger tended to experience a ratings increase in metered households. Ratings for children's programs also tend to increase. Broadcast networks also tend to lose some audience in metered households as the loyalty reflected in the diaries may not match the actual viewing patterns measured by the meters. Similarly, some people "vote" for favorite shows by listing them in the diaries. This is not possible with a meter. These trends tend to level off over time, as results are measured from one metered period to another, but

they are indicative of the differences in reported information resulting from the changeover from manual to automated systems.

THE "RATINGS BOOK"

Nielsen publishes viewership statistics in several formats. The most
common is the market ratings book, which Nielsen calls Viewers in
Profile ("VIP"). The Nielsen book begins with a profile of the market
and the research sample: the total number of households; the
number of television households; the percentage of households
with multiple sets, with UHF, and with cable; the relative sizes of
the counties within the market; and the demographic breakdown
of households in the sample. In addition, there is statistical data
about the sample (the standard errors, the measurement schedule)
as well as information about the stations (pre-emptions of network
schedules, operating hours).

The Daypart Summary provides share information, and detailed
rating information, by times of day: 7:00–9:00 P.M., 9:00 A.M.–12:00 P.M.,
12:00–4:00 P.M., 4:00–6:00 P.M., 6:00–8:00 P.M., 8:00–11:00 P.M.,
11:00–11:30 P.M., and 11:30 P.M.–1:00 A.M. There are other configu-
rations shown as well, such as 3:00–5:00 P.M., and 4:00–7:30 P.M.
This information is useful for sponsors who purchase rotation
schedules, rather than spots on individual programs. It also shows
trends that are difficult to detect on more detailed reports. For each
station, in each daypart, these charts show the ratings and shares in
the central metropolitan area (Metro) and in the DMA (Designated
Market Area; see below). The charts show share history over the
past four rating periods, with the DMA ratings broken down by
demographic group (women, for example, are classified as 18+,
12–24, 18–34, 18–49, 21–49, 25–49, 25–54, and working). The Daypart
Summary also shows distribution of viewers over adjacent DMAs,
the gross numbers of viewers (in thousands), and other information
relating to the percentage of Metro and DMA households who
sampled the station during the daypart.

The Program Averages section of Nielsen's VIP provides information about the performance of entire individual programs. Each
program is listed with its rating and its share, for each of the four
weeks of the measurement period. The share trend shows the
program's share during the past four measurement periods (16
weeks). A HUT figure represents the total number of homes using
television during the time period. As in the dayparts summary, the
ratings statistics for each program are broken down by demographic
group (there are some additional breakdowns in this section), plus
gross viewership numbers, again broken down by group.

The longest section in the book, Time Period, shows viewership by time period (typically, half hours). This section provides many of the same statistics as the Program Averages section, but the presentation makes it easier to see program performance within individual time periods.

MINNEAPOLIS-ST. PAUL, MN

WK1 10/30-11/05 WK2 11/06-11/12 WK3 11/13-11/19 WK4 11/20-11/26

[A large, dense Nielsen TV Station Index ratings table spanning the page. Column group headers read: METRO HH; MONDAY-FRIDAY 4:00PM - 6:00PM; DMA HOUSEHOLD (RATINGS WEEKS 1 2 3 4, MULTI-WEEK AVG, SHARE, TREND); DMA RATINGS (PERSONS, WOMEN, MEN, TNS, CHILD). Rows are organized by time period (4:00PM, 4:30PM, 5:00PM, 5:30PM) with STATION/PROGRAM entries including KARE, KLGT, KMSP, KSTP, KTCA, KTCI, WCCO, WFTC and programs such as AVG. ALL WKS, AMERCN JOURNAL, PINKY-MF-WB, BRKR HI-MF-UPN, ROSIE ODONNELL, MAGIC SCHL BUS, RADAR WEATHER, OPRAH WINFREY, HARD COPY, OPRAH WINFREY, JUDGE JUDY, BOY MEETS WRLD, EW NWS 5P M-F, ARTHUR-PTV, 4 NEWS-5PM, SIMPSONS B, NBC NITELY NWS, LIVING SINGLE, WORLD B, ABC-WORLD NWS, NITE BSNSS RPT, CBS EVE NWS, and HUT/PUT/TOTALS.]

Sample pages, NIELSEN TV STATION INDEX: VIEWERS IN PROFILE for Minneapolis-St.Paul, Minnesota (Metered Market Service), for the month of November 1997. These pages, taken from a 245-page research report, estimate viewership by program and by demographic group. (Copyright 1998, Nielsen Media Research)

The Person's Shares section shows the viewing habits of individual demographic groups (e.g., Men 18–49, Children 6–11, Persons 12–24). As the complex organization of the ratings book suggests, viewer-related data can be processed in a variety of meaningful ways. Most large clients use the books for reference, but access

NSI AVERAGE WEEK ESTIMATES — MINNEAPOLIS-ST. PAUL, MN

STATION TOTALS (000) — PERSONS / WOMEN / MEN / TEENS / CHILD (left block)

Column key: HH (58) | 2+ (59) | 18+ (60) | 12-34 (62) | 21-49 (63) | WMN 18+ (65) | 18-34 (67) | 18-49 (68) | 25-49 (69) | 25-54 (70) | WKG (73) | MEN 18+ (74) | 18-34 (75) | 18-49 (76) | 21-49 (77) | 25-49 (78) | 25-54 (79) | TEEN 12-17 (81) | GIRLS (82) | CHILD 2-11 (83) | 6-11 (84)

HH	2+	18+	12-34	21-49	W18+	W18-34	W18-49	W25-49	W25-54	WKG	M18+	M18-34	M18-49	M21-49	M25-49	M25-54	T12-17	GIRLS	C2-11	C6-11
7	14	11	12	12	7	9	8	7	7	6	8	11	9	8	8	8	8	7	15	12
2	4	3	3	3	2	2	2	2	2	1	2	3	2	2	2	2	2	2	4	3

4:00PM

HH	2+	18+	12-34	21-49	W18+	W18-34	W18-49	W25-49	W25-54	WKG	M18+	M18-34	M18-49	M21-49	M25-49	M25-54	T12-17	GIRLS	C2-11	C6-11
66	73	68	9	16	41	3	9	8	10	9	27	4	7	7	6	9	2	1	2	2
66	79	79	5	13	38			1	1	1	40	5	12	12	8	8				
66	71	65	11	17	42	4	11	10	13	12	23	3	6	6	6	9	3	1	3	3
21	30	6	7	2	2	2	2				4	2	4	2	2	6			21	12
24	32	6	9	6							6		2	6	6	6	9		18	14
20	29	6	7	1							3	3	3				1		22	11
36	43	8	23	4	3	5	2	4	2	2	3	3	3	2	1	1	19	16	16	16
75	101	84	37	51	69	24	42	39	44	22	15	7	10	10	9	10	6	5	11	5
87	105	87	37	52	71	24	43	40	45	25	16	7	10	10	9	10	6	5	11	5
30	54	10	12	9	7	5	6	5	5	3	3	3	3	3	3	3	6	5	39	17
26	47	4	1	4							4	4	4	4	4	1			43	24
31	57	12	15	11	9	7	8	7	7	5	3	2	2	2	2	2	6	2	38	15
2																				
100	128	116	41	58	90	25	48	39	46	27	25	8	14	14	13	15	8	4	5	4
120	144	131	43	60	99	26	50	41	48	29	31	8	15	15	14	16	9	5	5	4
15	6	2	1		1	1	1	1	1		1	1	1				1		14	8
376	465	313	134	145	227	64	115	98	112	70	86	25	42	38	35	40	45	30	108	63

4:30PM

HH	2+	18+	12-34	21-49	W18+	W18-34	W18-49	W25-49	W25-54	WKG	M18+	M18-34	M18-49	M21-49	M25-49	M25-54	T12-17	GIRLS	C2-11	C6-11
85	95	90	11	22	52	5	11	11	14	13	38	4	11	11	10	13	2	1	3	2
87	101	99	6	22	44			1	1	3	55	6	21	20	16	17			2	
85	93	87	12	22	55	6	15	14	18	16	32	4	8	8	8	12	2	1	4	3
19	25	7	8	4	1		1	1	1	1	6		6	6	6	6	1		15	9
26	35	16	17	6							16	16	16	6	6	6	4		17	9
17	22	4	5	3	2		2	1	1	1	2	1	2	2	2	2	4		14	10
47	64	14	33	7	9	6	8	4	4	4	5	3	5	2	2	2	24	20	25	25
89	116	96	42	57	79	27	48	44	51	26	17	7	11	11	10	12	8	6	13	6
100	122	102	43	60	84	29	51	47	53	30	18	7	11	11	10	12	8	6	13	6
28	49	8	6	6	3	1	2	2	2	1	4		3	3	3	3	8	8	39	25
3																				
116	145	133	45	62	103	28	51	42	50	32	30	9	16	14	14	16	4	4	4	4
137	164	151	49	67	114	31	55	45	54	35	37	9	17	16	15	17	9	5	4	4
20	29	3	3	3	1			1	1	1	2		2	2	2	2	9	1	23	15
22	42	3		1							4		3	3	3	3			35	20
440	549	374	153	169	264	72	131	112	130	84	110	29	54	48	45	52	52	34	123	87

5:00PM

HH	2+	18+	12-34	21-49	W18+	W18-34	W18-49	W25-49	W25-54	WKG	M18+	M18-34	M18-49	M21-49	M25-49	M25-54	T12-17	GIRLS	C2-11	C6-11
158	206	199	49	95	111	28	59	56	67	48	87	19	39	36	36	48	3	1	5	4
162	221	218	52	89	111	27	51	49	56	40	106	26	42	40	40	51			3	2
156	202	192	48	97	111	28	62	58	71	50	81	17	38	35	35	47	4	2	5	4
12	14	10	9	6	6	4	5	4	4	1	5	4	5	3	3	3	1		4	1
14	15	18	16	9	10	8	10	7	7	2	8	6	8	5	5	2	1		2	3
10	3	2			2						2		2	2	2	2				
10	2	2	1		2	1	1	1	2	1										
64	98	38	48	27	24	13	20	14	15	13	14	5	13	11	9	10	30	20	31	26
64	87	34	48	25	36	21	30	21	25	14	12	6	9	9	8	8	23	16	12	
65	102	34	48	24	20	10	16	12	12	9	15	6	15	11	11	11	32	20	35	30
98	131	124	21	45	71	11	27	23	30	22	53	7	21	20	20	24	2		3	2
107	143	136	22	47	77	11	27	24	31	25	59	7	22	21	20	25	4	3	3	2
30	61	14	10	12	11	7	10	6	6	4	2	1	1	1	1	1	4	1	46	17
3																				
138	170	163	23	49	103	11	31	28	35	32	59	9	21	19	18	22	3	2	5	3
164	205	196	27	54	124	13	34	30	39	36	72	10	23	22	20	25	3	2	5	5
71	121	49	64	40	21	13	20	16	16	13	28	18	27	20	22	33	33	9	38	31
610	848	643	229	285	374	89	176	150	178	140	268	64	131	119	112	135	75	35	130	85

5:30PM

HH	2+	18+	12-34	21-49	W18+	W18-34	W18-49	W25-49	W25-54	WKG	M18+	M18-34	M18-49	M21-49	M25-49	M25-54	T12-17	GIRLS	C2-11	C6-11
172	229	221	55	112	122	31	65	64	76	55	99	23	49	47	47	59	2	1	6	4
13	14	11	9	10	7	6	7	5	5	1	4	2	5	3	3	3			4	2
15	24	20	15	17	13	11	12	8	8	2	7	5	6	5	5	6			4	1
10	1																1			
11	5	4	4	4	4	2	4	2	2									1		
75	118	51	57	37	32	17	27	18	20	16	19	9	18	16	13	14	31	18	36	30
73	111	68	61	49	51	24	40	26	31	28	17	13	17	16	9	9	24		19	16
75	121	46	56	33	26	14	22	16	16	12	20	8	19	16	14	15	34	19	42	35
102	135	129	14	44	72	8	25	22	30	23	57	5	21	20	21	25	2	1	4	2
116	151	144	15	47	80	8	26	23	31	27	64	5	21	21	21	25	2	2	4	2
15	14	11	1	2	4	1	1	1	1	2	8			1					4	1
161	193	187	17	48	113	6	27	26	36	36	74	8	22	21	20	27	3	2	6	4
188	233	224	20	54	136	8	32	29	40	41	88	8	26	24	22	29	4	2	6	4
97	166	74	88	64	33	21	32	24	25	22	41	26	39	34	32	33	41	12	51	37
678	924	737	246	325	415	92	190	164	199	163	322	74	157	146	138	166	80	35	107	79

HH STATION TOTALS (000) — right block

Column key: DMA RTG (7) | HH (58) | WM 18+ (65) | MEN 18+ (74) | CHILD 2-11 (83)

TIME-BREAK STATION	DMA RTG	HH	WM 18+	MEN 18+	CHILD 2-11
	LT	7	7	8	15
	LT	2	2	2	4
4:00PM					
KARE	4	61	38	20	2
KLGT	1	21	3	3	18
KMSP	2	29	3		20
KSTP	3	52	46	13	8
KSTP+	4	63	48	14	8
KTCA	2	25	7	4	31
KTCI	**	2			
WCCO	6	87	73	22	5
WCCO+	3	52	27		5
WFTC	1	14	2		10
H/P/T.*	30	320	181	71	93
4:30PM					
KARE	5	73	45	31	3
KLGT	1	21	2	5	18
KMSP	3	42	7	4	21
KSTP	5	81	73	16	12
KSTP+	6	93	77	17	12
KTCA	2	29	5	4	40
KTCI	**	3			
WCCO	8	129	107	35	5
WCCO+	1	18	1	2	20
WFTC					
H/P/T.*	35	407	244	96	117
5:00PM					
KARE	8	122	82	62	4
KLGT	1	15	3	5	8
KMSP	3	54	16	9	27
KSTP	6	94	75	35	8
KSTP+	7	104	81	38	8
KTCA	2	28	6	3	41
KTCI	**	3			
WCCO	10	126	104	44	4
WCCO+	3	43	10	14	28
WFTC	8	38	31		
H/P/T.*	41	521	318	186	122
5:30PM					
KARE	11	168	119	95	6
KLGT	1	12	6	4	2
KMSP	5	72	29	17	35
KSTP	6	102	73	56	4
KSTP+	7	114	80	62	4
KTCA	2	25	9	5	27
KTCI	**	2			
WCCO	10	151	108	66	4
WCCO+	11	176	130	79	6
WFTC	6	86	27	36	46
H/P/T.*	49	656	400	299	125

TIME PERIOD

For explanation of symbols, see page 3.
For RSE explanations, see page 2.

83

the database via desktop computer, a setup that allows subscribers to request and compare specific pieces of information. For example, in considering an anchor candidate, a station in Baltimore might review the ratings history of his news show in Milwaukee. A station in Boston might determine whether to move a popular syndicated prime access (7:00–8:00 P.M.) series into early fringe (3:00/3:30–5:00/5:30 P.M.) by examining the history of similar strategies in Albany, Columbus, and Providence. These sophisticated computations are now commonplace in local television, and although they can be done by hand using printed ratings books from each of the markets, the database provides a far more flexible system for research. Syndicators, for example, use this information to show stations how specific properties can attract larger audiences within specific time slots.

DEFINITION OF MARKET SIZES

The terms "city" or "metropolitan area" are often vague. The New York City metropolitan area, for example, includes the cities of Newark, New Jersey, and Stamford, Connecticut. The even more loosely defined Bay Area may include not only San Francisco and Oakland, California, but also the entire Silicon Valley to the south, as well as San Jose. The shapes of cities are also based on a relatively old paradigm based on distinct city centers and outlying suburbs. Some suburbs have become their own cities.

Nielsen defines television market areas not by city, but by DMA (Designated Market Area). Every U.S. county is assigned to a DMA, typically the one that receives a nearby city's broadcast signals. In general, counties are assigned to just one DMA, though Nielsen sometimes splits a county into two DMAs if viewing patterns within the county are split between markets due to unusual terrain or the reception of peripheral signals. For many years, Arbitron defined market size by ADI (Area of Dominant Influence), a similar concept whose market definitions did not always match Nielsen's DMAs. As a result, some markets were considered larger on Nielsen's list and smaller on Arbitron's (and vice versa). The term ADI is still sometimes used by research veterans, but it is no longer relevant to the television audience measurement business (although it is still used by Arbitron for radio).

SWEEPS

In February, May, July, and November, Nielsen measures viewership in 211 markets. Because these surveys sweep the country, these four-week periods are called *sweeps*. If there is client demand for additional surveys, as is often the case in the larger markets, then additional surveys are conducted, typically in January, March, and October. Individual households participate for only one week during the sweep.

The resulting ratings are used mainly by local stations (network affiliates and independents) to set advertising rates. Although past performance cannot forecast future viewership, these ratings are, at least, a basis for negotiation.

Sweeps have been widely criticized. Networks, syndicated programs and local stations abuse the concept so that it is not particularly representative of long-term viewership trends. Networks put on their high-profile motion pictures, and pack sitcoms and dramas with unusually exciting story lines. News programs, both network and local, tend toward the scandalous stories. Syndicated programs add guests who might not otherwise appear, and add special features to lure audiences, even for short-term viewership. Local stations also run "watch-and-win" contests, effectively "buying" viewers who might not otherwise be watching. All this is for sound business reasons—advertising rates are set on the basis of sweeps performance.

RATINGS AND SHARES

Local stations and other subscribers receive three basic types of information from Nielsen: a program's rating, its share, and the gross number of viewers watching a station each quarter hour. A program's *rating* is the percentage of *total television households* in the sample area whose sets were tuned to that program; a program's *share* is the percentage of *total viewing households* whose sets were tuned to that program. The difference between these definitions is significant. Ratings indicate the absolute number of possible viewers, regardless of the time period. Shares, however, are based on the number of households whose television sets are actually turned on. The figure for these viewing households with sets actually turned on is often called the HUT (Homes Using Television). Share and rating information is provided for each station by quarter hour, as are gross numbers of viewers watching that station every quarter hour.

The different numbers vary in their significance among advertisers, programmers, and producers. For a local advertiser, the total number of households that saw the program—and its commercials—can be the most important figure. The ratings information is also useful because it shows the relative strength, or value, of each station and program as an advertising medium. To a network programmer or producer, the program's share—its drawing power against competitors in the time slot—may be critical. Programmers and producers are also extremely interested in ratings; after all, a local program with a low rating may not be able to attract or sustain sponsorship, regardless of its share relative to other programs in the time slot. A syndicated program with poor ratings will either be rescheduled to another time slot where it may perform better (or do less damage to the schedule), or it may be canceled.

SYNDICATION RATINGS

Nielsen also uses its NTI data from PeopleMeters to prepare the NSS Pocketpiece, a weekly report of the Nielsen Syndication Service. The format follows that of the NTI Pocketpiece (see example on page 405). All three sections list the programs alphabetically, but there is no information provided about the time that programs air, because in syndication programming, a program's time slot varies from one market to the next. Program audience estimates are presented in three series of charts. The first lists each syndicated program, the number of stations carrying the program, the percentage of television households that can receive the program, and ratings broken down by demographic segment. The second chart shows viewership in thousands for a program, again by demographic group; the third chart shows viewers per thousand households. Coverage-area ratings measure the audience in markets where the program can actually be seen, and are particularly useful for syndicated shows, which may not be seen in 100 percent of the country. The national rating for a program not seen in all markets will be lower than its coverage-area rating.

Cassandra, an analysis system acquired by Nielsen in 1980, provides data on individual syndicated programs. In addition to household and demographic data, Cassandra reports comparative information regarding lead-ins, as well as competitive history. (A lead-in is a program that precedes another program, and that presumably brings some of its viewers to the subsequent show.) Cassandra statistics are developed on a market-by-market basis, but their cumulative (nationwide) results are frequently used to compare the relative ratings success of syndicated programs. At the end of every sweep period, Cassandra provides rankings of syndicated shows.

CABLE RATINGS

Nielsen also collects data relating to cable television viewership. Diary households are encouraged to write down the cable channel number and the name of the program; with electronically measured households, cable viewership is automatically reported, and PeopleMeters are also used. Nielsen provides detailed viewership information about cable viewing in their regular reports, and also offers special cable television reports on a regular basis, in print and via a computer-accessible database.

On an average weekday night, the share of audience earned by *all* cable networks is generally equal to the shares earned by ABC, CBS, NBC, PBS and FOX combined.

Cable ratings have been steadily increasing. In the November 1995, sweeps, ABC, CBS and NBC averaged a 33.2 rating and a 53 share, while basic cable scored a 16.3 average rating and a 26 share. The next year (November 1996), the broadcast network numbers were 31.6 and 50, down several points on both rating and share, while the cable numbers were up to a 17.9 rating and a 29 share. Viewed from a season-long perspective, the networks controlled 62.1 percent of prime-time viewing in the 1996–97 season, compared with 65.2 percent in the 1995–96 season. Cable increased from 29.5 percent to 32.4 percent in the same period. Since the 1993–94 season, the networks have lost about 10 rating points to cable. This is fairly representative of a trend: network viewership is declining slightly each year, as more households tune into cable programming (this is a cycle: higher cable ratings mean more cable advertising revenues, which leads to more cable programming dollars and more cable viewership).

In time, increased ratings generally result in increased advertising revenues. The key is not raw viewer numbers, but the numbers within desirable demographic groups. For example, Nickelodeon has dramatically increased its advertising revenues because ratings prove the network to be an extremely effective medium to reach children.

SNAPSHOTS VERSUS TRENDS

There are a lot of ways of taking a snapshot of a television audience. One day's worth of data makes interesting newspaper copy and *USA Today* charts, but researchers tend not to look at data that way. It's far more important to analyze audience trends over time. This would tell a network, for example, not how a particular program performed on a particular night, but how a program is performing, within a particular demographic, within a number of weeks or months. This information is then used to renew or cancel programs, and to make advertising buying decisions.

NEW AUDIENCE MEASUREMENT TECHNOLOGIES

In the real world, audience measurement services (and the market research industry in general) live by statistically reliable samples that are, in fact, only a small percentage of viewers. Networks and advertisers often question the reliability of these samples, and the ways in which data is collected, but they continue to rely upon available information for lack of a better system.

SMART is a $40 million venture being developed for ABC, CBS and NBC (as well as several cable networks, major advertisers and advertising agencies) by Statistical Research Inc. (SRI is a company well known for measurement of radio audiences). The SMART acronym translates as Systems for Measuring and Reporting Television. It's a broad-based attempt to improve the accuracy of audience measurement. SMART uses the household's existing wiring, eliminating most of the fuss involved with installation of a PeopleMeter. The SMART system's button console is designed to be easy for every family member to use—but the system still requires individual family members to identify themselves (which is essential for the accurate demographic information so vital to advertisers). In theory, SMART makes it easy for children to enter their viewing habits as well (in practice, children should not be expected to participate in a commercial venture and are probably unreliable in any case). Since SMART is designed with broadcasters in the funding role (and may therefore be beholden to the networks), they've reached out to a wider funding base that includes advertisers. SMART is addressing the need for a competitive national ratings service. As of 1998, SMART was testing in Philadelphia for a national launch early in the next century.

The Active/Passive Meter System is Nielsen's product for the future. The A/P Meter employs one sensor located near each TV set in the household. Each sensor reads codes embedded in the audio and video signals. To make this work, every program or commercial (and even every videogame) must be tagged with a unique code. If there is no code, the A/P Meter records part of the audio and video track, then sends this digital sample back to Nielsen for matching against a catalog. The A/P Meter System is being tested with a small sample of Florida households in 1998.

CHALLENGES CREATED BY CHANGING MEDIA

The popularity of cable television and home video has complicated the audience measurement process. Many viewers armed with remote controls bounce back and forth between numerous broadcast and cable channels within limited periods. In just one minute, a viewer armed with a remote control can easily sample a dozen or more channels. Were this easily measured and reported, the value of the information would be dubious at best. For example, a viewer who is more or less simultaneously viewing three or four programs would be difficult to count for advertising purposes; indeed, it is often the ads that are skipped.

Home video presents a special challenge for audience measurement. Normally, broadcast and cable data is collected by noting the channel number—and this is done either by having the viewer fill out a diary or by connecting a meter to the television's tuner. As for time-shifting (recording broadcast or cable programs for viewing at a later date), PeopleMeter systems can measure the program as it is being recorded, but cannot determine whether is actually seen, or how many times it has been seen. In order to collect data on other aspects of home video, it is necessary to know the name of the software being played—be it a videogame, a videocassette, or DVD software—and how it is being used. Manual identification of video is relatively simple—a viewer need only write down a title—but this information cannot be verified. More reliable electronic identification would require an encoded signal on every piece of software, and a reading mechanism connected to the videogame, or VCR. Identification is only part of the issue, though. If a videocassette contains a commercial, a sponsor needs to know if the commercial was viewed, whether it was viewed at standard speed, and how many times the tape, and the commercial, were viewed.

As television changes, audience measurement must change as well. Dozens of channels are becoming hundreds. VCRs make time-shift viewing and scanning through commercials possible. Digital communications will enable more viewership options, not only in terms of the program watched, but the format (widescreen, high-definition, standard resolution, and so forth). Convergence with computers and telephones will allow interactive television. Audience measurement in this rapidly changing environment where even the definition of the term "program" is questionable, will change all of the rules. This is not a wild-eyed future; in some form, it is a future that is emerging today.

42

Advertising

A dvertising provides nearly all of the financing for commercial domestic broadcast television, and approximately half of the financing for domestic cable television (the other half is provided by subscriber revenues). This chapter explains how television advertising works.

Television accounts for approximately one-fifth of all U.S. advertising expenditures (by comparison, roughly the same amount is spent on magazines). Of the dollars spent on TV advertising, broadcast networks take just over one-third; cable networks, just under one-third, and spot TV about one-fourth. The remainder is spread over syndication and local broadcast TV, with a very small percentage to local cable TV.

ADVERTISING AGENCIES

A full-service advertising agency provides its clients with consumer and market research, as well as the development, implementation, and evaluation of advertising strategies and campaigns. Specifically, the agency works with the client to determine the target customer(s), identify one or more marketing objectives, and recommend a message and a style of presentation. The agency produces the physical materials—such as print advertisements and television commercials—then selects and purchases the space (print media) and time (electronic media) for these advertisements.

The largest agencies are huge corporations offering not only advertising, but also related services, including public relations, direct marketing, and sales promotion. Some agencies will even produce specialized programming for a client. According to *Advertising Age,* the top ten advertising agencies in 1996, in terms of U.S. network television billings, were D'Arcy Masius Benton & Bowles ($1.15 billion); McCann-Erickson Worldwide ($1.05 billion), Y&R Advertising ($0.97 billion); J. Walter Thompson ($0.97 billion); BBDO Worldwide ($0.94 billion); Ogilvy & Mather Worldwide ($0.91 billion); Saatchi & Saatchi Advertising ($0.89 billion); Leo Burnett Company ($0.84 billion); Foote, Cone & Belding ($0.80 billion); and Grey Advertising ($0.75 billion). Medium-sized agencies that have established distinguished reputations for television advertising include TBWA Chiat/Day and Hal Riney & Partners; Wieden & Kennedy are also well-known for their Nike advertisements. Among advertisers, those that spend the most on network television annually include, in order, from *Competing Media Reporting*, General Motors ($614 million); Procter & Gamble ($590 million); Johnson & Johnson ($505 million); PepsiCo ($423 million); Philip Morris Companies ($403 million); McDonald's Corp. ($372 million); Ford Motor Company ($320 million); Grand Metropolitan ($294 million); Chrysler Corp. ($280 million); and Walt Disney ($267 million).

ORGANIZATION

An advertising agency is typically organized in three basic groups. *Creative Services* develops the advertising concepts, refines them as required by the account team and the client, then produces the commercials and other materials. A creative director is the senior person on the creative team; one creative director may be responsible for several accounts. *Media Services* negotiates for airtime and other media buys on the client's behalf. Finally, *Account Services* is responsible for client relations. This group works with Creative Services to assure that the client's needs are met; that the storyboards and commercials are consistent with the marketing strategy, and that production is proceeding in accordance with the client's requirements and budget limitations. The account executive is the senior person on the account team; one account supervisor usually manages several accounts.

AGENCY BILLING

The advertising agency makes money in three ways:

First, the agency receives a commission on every media buy, sometimes as much as 15 percent. In today's world, most large clients negotiate long-term deals with their agencies, based, at least loosely, on the 15 percent figure (or less). If, for example, a 30-second spot costs $1,000, the agency actually buys the spot for $850, bills the client for $1,000, and retains $150 as a commission. If client billings total $1 million for a year, the agency retains $150,000 in commissions. The agency's commission or fee structure can be negotiated as part of the client-agency agreement.

Second, the agency may receive a fee for its services, often a monthly retainer that the client will pay over and above, in lieu of, or in combination with, the agency's commissions. The monthly retainer generally reflects the number of hours spent by members of the account and creative teams working on the assignment. For example, an art director earning $1,000 per week might spend half of his or her time on a certain account, or 20 hours per week. This time is billed at approximately three times the labor cost (which covers taxes, benefits, office, overhead, supervisory management, and other related expenses, plus a profit). The client is billed $1,500 for the artist's 20 hours of work per week. Unlike legal charges, these billings are based not on the time logged by any one or two people, but on a reasonable estimate of the hours spent by the team assembled for, or assigned to, a given project.

Third, the agency receives a reimbursement for production costs. When the agency arranges for the production of a commercial or series of commercials, the agency bills the client for the cost of production. In addition, the agency usually (but not always) receives a markup on production costs, typically in the range of 10 percent.

MEDIA DECISIONS

Television is only one of many media available to the media buyer. Television's combination of sound and moving images, and its ability to reach large numbers of attentive viewers in their own homes in real time makes the medium ideal for certain types of product and image advertising.

Television advertising has its drawbacks as well. The cost of producing a television commercial is almost always higher than the cost of producing advertising materials for radio, print, billboards, or other media. Although the CPM can be lower than with other media, the larger number of viewers can drive the gross cost far higher than it would be with other media. This is especially true of network television; local television and cable, however, can be surprisingly affordable.

Network television is a true mass medium, in the sense that it reaches all kinds of demographic groups. Regional networks, local syndication, and cable channels can be better choices if the goal is to reach more specific demographic or psychographic groups, such as country music lovers or young teens.

Through the late 1960s, television advertisements were 60 seconds long; now, they are mostly 30 seconds and, more and more often, 15 seconds long. As a result, commercials with complicated messages may not be effective. Clutter is a growing problem as well—too many messages barraging the viewer. Unlike print advertisements, which may only interrupt the reader every few minutes, television commercials work in a dynamic environment where messages can speed by too quickly to register an impact on first, second, or even third viewing. Zapping via remote control further aggravates the situation.

ADVERTISING ON NETWORK TELEVISION

There are several methods by which advertisers buy time on network programs: sponsorship, spot buying, and upfront buying.

SPONSORSHIP

The most involved form of television advertising is sponsorship of an individual program. Two types of sponsorship are available on network television.

The first is *full-program sponsorship* (a classic example is *Hallmark Hall of Fame*). In this format, a single sponsor buys most or all of the commercial time within a program. Full sponsorship can provide enhanced visibility amidst a cluttered programming and commercial environment. If there is a synergy between the program and the advertiser or its message, a full sponsorship can provide viewers with the image of corporate importance. The advertiser's involvement frequently goes beyond buying commercial time; the production may be promoted by a public-relations and print-advertising campaign. Full sponsorship was more prevalent in the 1950s than it is today; examples from that period include *Armstrong Circle Theater, General Electric Theater, Camel News Caravan, U.S. Steel Hour, The Lux Show with Rosemary Clooney,* and *GE College Bowl*. Full-program sponsorship is uncommon on commercial television, since skyrocketing productions costs have made many advertisers wary of putting all their eggs in one basket. This advertising format is relatively uncommon today; however, Ford's sponsorship of *Schindler's List* is a contemporary example of this practice. Still, a form of exclusive participation is evident on public television. Several large corporations have successfully identified themselves with high-visibility public television programs—Mobil with *Masterpiece Theatre*, for example.

With a *participating sponsorship,* several sponsors share a form of exclusive sponsorship within a program or series. For a premium fee, and a commitment to an ongoing position within the program or series, each participating sponsor is assured exclusivity within its product category. If, for example, Bud Lite helps sponsor the World Series, then no other light-beer brand can advertise (a non-light beer may be allowed, depending upon the arrangement). The participating sponsor may also receive a "billboard," or an on-screen logo with a voice-over advertising slogan, such as "Brought to you by . . . . "; the billboard usually appears at the beginning of a program. Participating sponsorships may be sold either for entire programs or events, or for parts of events, such as the first and second halves of a football game.

Advertising categories worth $1 billion or more to network television include automotive (mostly automobile manufacturers), proprietary medicines (aspirins, cold and flu remedies, etc.), food and food products, toiletries and toilet goods, restaurants (mostly fast food), and consumer services (mostly telephone, some online).

SPOT BUYING

Most network advertising is not sold on the basis of a sponsor affiliation with program content. Instead, commercial time is sold on a *spot* or *scatter* basis. In a relatively recent development, advertisers buy time in groups of programs whose *cumulative* viewership offers the desired demographics, psychographics, and geographic skew.

In the 1950s and 1960s, a company that wanted to advertise on network television would select a program that seemed compatible with its advertising message, and buy one 60-second commercial in the program each week. At that time, there were 39 weeks of original shows, with 13 weeks of reruns; now, there are 20 to 22 weeks of original shows. By the mid-1970s, the networks changed their scheduling practices, largely as a result of intramural competition. They began to drift away from programming the same shows in the same time slots week after week. Instead, they started debuting new shows at times other than September (and other than January, which once marked the "second season"), canceling programs in mid-season and moving shows around on the schedules. The old buying practices were no longer viable, so each advertiser had its agency's media department buy television time as a package (of commercials) whose cumulative impact would, hopefully, equal the impact of the old system. The immediate benefit to the networks was the ability to place advertisers in less desirable shows. Given the possibility of a less desirable audience, or a smaller one, the networks began to guarantee a specific number of viewers (within specific demographic and geographic groups)— but on the basis of the entire package, not on the performance of any particular program.

Makers of automotive products are, by a large margin, the largest buyers of spot TV. The next two categories are about a third as large (foods, and consumer services such as telephone companies).

UPFRONT BUYING

This "package guarantee" method of selling advertising time on network shows evolved into the tradition known as *upfront buying*. In upfront buying, the networks offer advertisers "avails" (time slots) at a discount months before the season begins.

UPFRONT BUYING: NETWORK PRIME-TIME

Immediately after each network's program department announces the prime-time schedule for the fall season (usually in May), the network sales departments start selling commercial time on those programs. They offer advertisers approximately 65 to 75 percent of prime-time avails at a 15 percent discount. The prime-time upfront buying season generally begins in May and goes through early July (the upfront buying season begins as early as March for Saturday morning children's programming and for other dayparts).

During the upfront buying season, advertising agencies register each client's budget with the network, along with a request for a package of shows that reach the client's target audience. The network sales department responds with a proposal detailing the number of spots, the programs, and their air dates. After negotiation, agreement is reached on the CPM (which may actually be cost per thousand *households,* if only one viewer in each household is in the proper demographic category). The network and advertiser also work out the list of shows, the dates on which the spots will appear, and the probable rating. The advertiser commits to the time, but the degree of commitment can vary. If the client commits to 52 weeks, the deal is likely to be more flexible than a deal for a smaller commitment. A deal might include the option to cancel up to 25 percent of the order for first quarter, for example. Rates are likely to be lower if the advertiser buys more time overall, or more time in less desirable shows.

For a client with $10 million to spend in prime-time, the advertising agency's media planning department devises a plan. The media planners work closely with the client, in conjunction with the account group and media buyers, and eventually make recommendations as to the best way to reach the target audience. Based on estimates of how the package will perform, the network and the agency negotiate a CPM. Working from estimated ratings, the network guarantees to deliver a certain number of viewers in each demographic group. If the ratings turn out to be lower than the network promised, the advertiser is entitled to *make-goods,* or additional commercials in prime-time programs. The new shows and dates, however, may not be desirable ones, or may not meet the client's needs. The agency, therefore, tries to avoid make-goods by buying time in programs for which the anticipated ratings and the actual ratings are most likely to be similar.

Negotiations are staged on several fronts. First, the agency may want more units within specific programs—"Can you give me one more *Buffy, the Vampire Slayer* and take out a *Law & Order*"—or may require a lower CPM to compensate for potentially low ratings (which translate into a missed opportunity to reach some viewers). A provisional deal is made: the time is reserved, and the network will not sell that inventory within a specified number of days. In the interim, the agency presents the package to the client for approval. The client usually approves, but only after discussing problems with the deal: the cost is higher than it should be, the program mix is not right. As a rule, a hold on network time is a commitment, and is rarely released.

A client with a $10-million network prime-time budget might assign $3–$4 million to each network. The average cost of a spot works out to about $125,000, so the client's budget would probably buy 80 prime-time spots. A spot on a top-rated show costs roughly $300,000–$400,000; a spot on a lower-rated show with comparatively weak performance, about $50,000. The most expensive prime-time series in the 1996–97 season included *Seinfeld, ER, Home Improvement, Friends,* and *Monday Night Football,* all in the $400,000–$550,000 range per 30-second spot.

For the networks, the benefit of the upfront buy is that the money is on the books; the downsides are the 15 percent discount offered, and the need to make good on programs that did not perform as hoped or planned. For the agency and client, the upfront buy assures the best possible commercial positions, and saves money, but the prospect of make-goods can put the client in the position of having commercials run on the wrong shows.

In recent seasons, there has been a great deal of brinkmanship on the upfront market. With the shrinking network audience share and a general slump in advertising spending, many advertisers have balked at the networks' high prices. The spot market has been weak, and some major advertisers—unimpressed by the so-called "discount" being offered for an upfront buy—have been holding out for better rates. The risk to the network is that with fewer upfront sales, already low spot prices will drop even further; the risk to advertisers is that if spot buying increases, the market will tighten up so that spot rates end up higher than upfront rates. Basically, upfront buying works well only so long as the market for commercial time slots is predictable.

UPFRONT BUYING: NETWORK DAYTIME

There is an upfront buying season for daytime programs as well, typically during the early summer. Daytime revenue has been stagnating recently. As the population of women outside the home increases, and more household chores are handled by teenagers, husbands, and other family members, the traditional daytime audience—adult, female—is changing.

Compared with the cost of prime-time, advertising on daytime is inexpensive. The CPM for women under 50 during daytime (about $5, on average) is roughly 25 percent of the CPM for the same group during prime-time ($20, on average). Daytime television still delivers a relatively "pure" audience of women under 50. While maintaining traditional ties with household, food, and other longtime daytime advertisers, networks have been wooing new types of sponsors (e.g., automotive companies) into daytime, with only limited success.

UPFRONT BUYING: NETWORK NEWS

The upfront buying season for network news also takes place during the summer. Most advertisers buy time on the news because it is the best way to reach the 25–54 group, and 55+ men and women.

ADVERTISING ON NETWORK SPORTS PROGRAMS

From the perspective of large national advertisers, the key concept for sports programs is exclusivity. Spots in major national events are sold on an exclusive basis within product categories. In automotive, one of the larger categories for sports advertising, the general rule is one domestic and one foreign automotive sponsor. Beer, soft drinks, and fast food may also be subject to exclusive buys. Many exclusivity agreements are negotiated well in advance, and run for more than one year. Because of the pervasiveness of exclusivity, the idea of an upfront buying season is not as strict here as in other parts of network television. The sales department gets to work selling time shortly after rights to sports events are purchased. Many sports programs are sold on a series basis: some or all of the baseball or football season, for example. A sponsor with one or more spots in each game is called a strip sponsor; a spot participant buys time in individual events.

Of network events, the weekly NFL broadcasts are the best performers; the cost of a spot on a regular telecast is over $500,000 per 30-second spot (a 30-second spot on the Super Bowl costs over a million dollars—though most spots are not sold individually, but instead as part of a package). The cost of an average prime-time spot, by comparison, is approximately $170,000. An event with somewhat less appeal, such as a weekend bowling match, would cost about $20,000 per spot. All of this is dependent upon the competitive market environment; in a very soft market, these rates drop by as much as 50 percent.

LOCAL TELEVISION ADVERTISING

Two types of advertising buys are available on local stations: (1) time slots that the network leaves open for affiliates during and between its own programs and (2) slots that are available on non-network shows, mainly during non-prime-time hours.

The process of putting national advertising onto local stations begins with a media plan, a strategic breakout for the entire year. The advertiser determines the plan's broad requirements; the agency refines the strategy, produces the commercials, and buys the time.

Once the list of target markets is determined by agency and client, the agency contacts some or all of the stations in each market (often through a "rep firm"; see page 28) and makes an avail request. Specifically, this might be a buy for first quarter, favoring men 18–49, based on a specific number of 700 gross rating points (GRPs) per week, distributed 30 percent in prime-time, 15 percent in early fringe (before evening news), 15 percent in late fringe (after late news), and 40 percent in daytime. The avail request also specifies the amount of money that the advertiser is willing to pay: $200 per rating point in early fringe and $350 in prime-time, for example.

In trying to reach all of the viewers in a given market, the agency purchases time on most or all of the stations. Each station responds to the avail request, and then the negotiations begin, often with the involvement of a national rep firm. Stations agree to sell some spots, but hold back others in anticipation of higher rates from other advertisers. For example, an advertiser who needs to reach teens may be willing to pay a premium for a spot in *The Simpsons*. An advertiser with more general needs might also buy *The Simpsons,* but not at a premium price. The station's sales manager makes decisions not only on price, however. Advertising time is perishable, so it may be wiser to sell for 75 percent of the desired rate than to wait and have the time unsold. There is no highest or lowest available rate; rates are based entirely on supply and demand.

Although some stations publish rate cards, the consensus is that rates are generally negotiable. Many agencies refer to rates published in the *Media Market Guide* or a similar seasonal directory. Rates in these directories are based on polls of media buyers nationwide; they can be a useful starting point for negotiations. This marketplace changes rapidly, however, so rates are likely to be out of date soon after publication.

Stations are expected to "post" (report) results. If the station sold commercial time based on an average 4 rating, and the program gets only a 2 rating, then the station arranges a make-good for the advertiser in the form of additional advertising time. Stations do not refund money paid for advertising, and a good sales manager insures important clients' success on his or her station by filling open commercial slots with additional client spots, at no charge. This is generally preferable to using the commercial time for per-inquiry advertising (see Chapter 30) or for direct-response advertising.

Restaurants (specifically, fast-food restaurants) are by far the largest purchasers of local TV time (they outbuy each of the next three largest buyers—auto dealers, furniture stores and movie companies—by a factor of 3 to 1).

Direct-response advertising, used mainly for the sale of magazine subscriptions, books, and records, allows stations to fill unsold time. Direct-response advertisers pay reduced rates for standby positions within a "wide rotator"—a large chunk of the schedule. If the station is sold out, the spots don't run.

Many stations do not run direct-response or per-inquiry advertising. Instead, they fill open time with promos, to encourage viewers to watch other shows on the schedule, or with public-service announcements that fulfill FCC public-service mandates.

In many markets, the concept of value-added selling is becoming popular. Stations sell not only airtime, but involvement in station promotions as well. This technique is common in local radio.

The mix of local versus national advertising varies with each station. Some stations prefer the relative stability of national advertisers, whose large advertising budgets do not change as often as local advertisers' budgets. Large national clients can be faceless, though—and when times get rough, local advertisers are more likely to support broadcasters with whom they have worked successfully during the good times.

NEWER ADVERTISING MEDIA

Cable television has changed the television advertising marketplace in several significant ways. Cable has spread the television audience over 30 or more channels, more than five times the number of broadcast channels available in most markets. Although many of these channels are watched by relatively small numbers of viewers, or watched for only limited periods of time by larger numbers of viewers, they have contributed to a steady decline in viewership of ABC, CBS, and NBC. Home video has also contributed to this decline. Households with VCRs rent, on average, three to five tapes per month, which means less time spent watching broadcast television. Videogame use also cuts into broadcast television viewing. Household viewing activity as measured by Nielsen—which does not include VCR playback or videogames—peaked in the mid-1980s at 7 hours 10 minutes per day, but dropped by the 1989–1990 season to 6 hours 55 minutes. As of winter 1997–98, women 18+ watched an average of 5 hours and 12 minutes per day; men 18+ watched 4 hours and 29 minutes and children 2–11 watched 3 hours and 34 minutes. The average total home use was 7 hours and 48 minutes per day.

CABLE NETWORKS

As the cable networks have matured, they have become more like the commercial broadcast networks in their style of doing business. The cable networks announce their fall schedules in the spring, and an upfront buying season follows. Audience research techniques for cable have been steadily improving, so advertising agencies are now confident that a system based on ratings guarantees will provide the appropriate level of coverage for their clients. Cable buys on the largest networks, such as CNN and USA, are considered to be very solid investments; the smaller networks are not regarded quite as highly.

Since there is a substantial percentage of TV households that do not subscribe, cable buys are evaluated against other cable buys. And unlike network-audience research, cable-audience research is not provided by day, but only by month. Any given daily rating is not as meaningful as the average daily performance over the course of a week or more.

Cable television has increased the supply side of the economic equation for television sports. With cable, sports programming is now available all day, every day. Since sports programs appeal to a particular audience segment—mainly males 18–49 (though most events are viewed by other audience segments as well)—advertisers tend to reach the same audience with commercials on cable sports programs as they do with commercials on network programs. In general, CPMs are in the $4–$7 range, but if the market is soft, the rates are lower.

South Park, a Comedy Central program, provides an interesting case study in the cost of commercial time on a midline cable network. For Comedy Central, a single rating point represents 460,000 viewers (it's seen in 46 million homes, and 1 percent of 46 million is 460,000). The network's typical program rating is about half a rating point, representing perhaps a quarter-million viewers. The network's commercials typically cost up to $7,500 per 30-second spot, and many are sold for less than $5,000. *South Park,* an unorthodox animated series, found its audience shortly after a much-publicized debut, and soon, its ratings were the highest on the network. With a rating nearing four points, the cost of a 30-second spot set a network record at over $30,000. The program's language and themes are a problem for some advertisers (it's quite nasty, and frequently deserving of its TV-MA content rating; see Chapter 18). For America Online, MCI, Volkswagen, Snapple, and other advertisers, it's the right vehicle to reach the right viewers. The program costs about $250,000 per episode to produce and more than recoups costs in a single play; episodes are played many times through the year, making the series very profitable. This phenomenon is often accompanied by some degree of success for other series—and the likelihood of carriage on more cable systems.

PRODUCING TELEVISION COMMERCIALS

The advertising agency starts development on a commercial by meeting with the client and identifying the client's marketing objective: increased market share, new product launch, or product differentiation, for example. The creative department works closely with the account department to define and shape an advertising strategy that supports the client's marketing goals. This strategy includes developing creative concepts for print and television advertising, including an overall style and look for the campaign; choosing a slogan, or a spokesperson (if appropriate); preparing scripts and storyboards; suggesting casting ideas; and considering other creative elements such as computer animation and special effects.

These sketches, scripts, and storyboards are presented to the client—or, more specifically, to a team consisting of the advertising manager, the product manager, and the marketing manager. This team reviews everything to be sure that the commercial's message and style are consistent with the marketing objective and strategy, and that the commercials do not conflict with company policy.

The approved storyboard is shown to several (usually three) independent production companies, who submit cost estimates for production and post-production of the spot(s). At the same time, these companies offer suggestions to improve the commercials. Some commercials are bid to a single entity—for example, a director who has worked successfully with the client in the past, or one who has a special style that is the basis for the storyboard. The choice of director is almost always based on reputation—and on the quality/style of the commercials on the director's sample "reel" (a cassette filled with the director's work). Many directors are associated with production companies, working as a principal or partner.

The director works with the agency on casting, scripting, and the choice of crew and locations. A national spot generally requires several weeks of pre-production: designing and building sets, choosing locations, composing/arranging/recording music, and attending to the many small details that are part of any television shoot. The shoot itself usually lasts between one and three days for one or more commercials, though some spots take longer. Budgets vary depending upon the campaign and the client's needs; the average is in the low $200,000 range.

The production is completed in the editing room (where scenes are assembled and graphics are added) and in the sound-editing room (where the voice-over, sound effects, and music are added, and where the soundtrack is mixed and equalized). Most national commercials are shot on 35mm film; many local spots are produced on videotape.

For most campaigns, several different commercials are produced and tested. The commercials are shown to various groups of people who buy similar products. Commercials are analyzed on the basis of their appeal to specific demographic, psychographic, and geographic groups. While a network spot must appeal to the widest possible audience within a specific target category (such as children), many spots are produced with narrower national audiences in mind—urban black viewers, for example. Other spots are produced for specific regions where certain product preferences are already strong, or need strengthening. A commercial should test successfully before it is placed on the air. While remakes can be quite expensive, the long-term cost of the commercial time—and the potential effect of a successful campaign on a product's market penetration and market share—can more than justify the additional expenditure.

43

Regulation of Advertising

Television advertising is subject to rules and regulations at a number of different levels. Content can be scrutinized and controlled, principally by the Federal Trade Commission at the federal level and by a variety of governmental authorities at the state and local levels. There are also some rules, enforced by the FCC, on the amounts and types of advertising carried on broadcast stations, cable, and the other FCC-regulated media. Finally, there is regulation by the industry itself: stations, networks, and cable companies all have their own standards on what they will accept. In addition, there are industry groups, made up of advertising agencies and their clients, that suggest codes of practices.

THE FTC AND THE CONTROL OF ADVERTISING

The Federal Trade Commission (FTC) is the government's principal overseer of the content and methods of advertising; in fact, it regulates advertising across all fields of publication, not just television. The FTC is an independent agency, like the FCC, with five Commissioners nominated by the President and confirmed by Congress (see page 119 for further discussion of agencies). When the FTC was set up in 1912, its principal intended purpose was to regulate in the area of antitrust law. The legislation that established the FTC, however, included the power to regulate unfair business practices, and from the beginning, this jurisdiction was held to cover false advertising. The FTC's power to control false advertising has been confirmed and expanded by congressional action in the years since, most importantly by the Wheeler-Lea Act in 1938. Section 5(a)(1) of the Federal Trade Commission Act now prohibits both "unfair methods of competition in commerce" and "unfair or deceptive acts or practices in commerce," and the Act gives the FTC the power to intervene and prevent them. These phrases have been interpreted to include false, misleading, or deceptive advertising. The "commerce" referred to in the Act is interstate commerce or international commerce; a finding of interstate commerce will generally be made in the case of an advertisement on a television station or a cable or satellite service.

The Federal Trade Commission Improvement Act of 1975 gave the FTC authorization to establish industry-wide trade rules over and above the prevention of deceptive advertising. One consequence of the 1975 Act was the FTC's proposing extensive restrictions on children's advertising on television. The proposal was not only controversial at the time, but also became an oft-cited example of burdensome over-regulation. Continuing concern about children's television led Congress to enact, in 1990, a set of laws governing many aspects of children's television (see page 195).

The backlash against regulation that characterized the 1980s and 1990s affected the FTC, and the Commission's power to set industry-wide trade rules on advertising fairness was restricted. The FTC is still empowered, however, to investigate and resolve individual cases of advertising deception. Complaints can be filed with the FTC by a consumer, a competitor, Congress, or any local, state, or federal agency.

"DECEPTIVE": THE STANDARD

"Deceptive" advertising was defined in 1983 by a three-member majority of the Commission as occurring if there is a "representation, omission or practice that is likely to mislead the consumer acting reasonably in the circumstances to the consumer's detriment." The more traditional formulation, reaffirmed by the other members of the Commission, states that an act is deceptive if it has a tendency or capacity to mislead a substantial number of consumers in a material way. Is there a difference between these definitions? Some interpretations say yes: the first approach might require proof of actual injury, while the second requires only that the advertising have the *capacity* to mislead. In practice, it has been held that regardless of which standard is applied, no actual injury need have taken place.

In determining whether or not an advertisement is deceptive, the FTC asks whether the *average* purchaser—not necessarily the least sophisticated or least intelligent possible buyer—would be deceived. Specially targeted ads, however, are examined in light of the target audiences. Advertising directed at children, for instance, may be judged by a standard reflecting the lessened sophistication of the younger audience. The context of the entire ad is considered in deciding whether or not the advertisement is deceptive. Thus, the "Joe Isuzu" ads, which combined blatant lies about Isuzu cars with the statement that lies are being told, would not be deemed deceptive.

The false information can be visual as well as verbal or written. A depiction of a product can be touched up in such a way as to make the picture itself a misleading item. In one commercial which caused difficulty, a knife was shown cutting through a nail, which it could indeed do. When the cutting edge was shown later in the commercial, however, a different knife was substituted, which looked fresh and perfect. This was a deceptive practice. Similarly, in one demonstration comparing shaving creams, the advertiser added foreign substances to the creams to make its own cream look superior. Time-compression photographs can be deceptive, in that they present a distorted picture of a product's characteristics; the use of an actor in a white doctor's coat can give the false impression that the product is endorsed by doctors. As much care should be taken in avoiding misrepresentation through images as through words.

Whether written, verbal, or visual, the misrepresentation need not be an affirmative one. Leaving *out* important details can be as much a source of deception as putting in affirmative lies.

For advertisers seeking to avoid false or misleading ads, the first line of defense should be common sense: be truthful in fact and in spirit. In making statements about a product, the advertiser and the creative people at the advertising agency should stick closely to substantiated facts. From the FTC standpoint, the key element is to have adequate backup—gathered in advance—for product claims. If the advertiser does not have proof that the product will do what he says it will do, the statement simply should not be made.

As any observer of American advertising will surely understand, however, advertising statements are not limited to dry facts. A certain level of exaggeration and hyperbole is par for the course in the advertising world, and is permitted as "puffing." Generalizations like "it's great," "amazing," or "wonderful" make no specific claim which can deceive or mislead, and the average buyer will know to discount them. Claims that a toothpaste will "beautify the smile" or that a sewing machine is "almost human" have been permitted under this standard. Unfortunately, the line between permitted puffing and punishable deception is not always clear.

Most large advertising agencies have in-house legal counsel who review all advertising copy with an eye toward avoiding deceptive claims; smaller firms frequently retain outside counsel to examine the material. It is strongly recommended that any advertising involving claims of performance or superiority over other brands should be vetted by an attorney.

FTC GUIDES

The FTC has issued a series of guides concerning particular products and practices. They are available in loose, individually bound form from the FTC, and are also reprinted in standard reference works on the FTC.

Some of the guides focus on specific methods of advertising, including bait advertising, debt collection, endorsements and testimonials, the use of the word "free," guarantees, and statements about prices. Others guides are directed at specific products, claims or industries: automobile fuel economy, beauty schools, pet foods, film and film processing, vocational schools.

CONSUMER PROTECTION TRADE RULES

In addition to the guides that concern deceptive advertising, the FTC has issued rules on a variety of commercial practices. Most of these rules focus on consumer protection issues that do not affect the television industry (for example, used car sales and funeral industry practices). One rule, though, concerns advertising about the size of television picture tubes. There are also rules on advertising consumer-credit and leasing arrangements. The most important of the FTC's consumer protection rules related to television—those governing advertising aimed at children—were never adopted. In 1980 Congress, bowing to industry concerns, intervened to suspend consideration of the rules. In 1990, Congress took steps to rectify its prior FTC interference through an FCC mandate (see page 434).

THE FTC AND COMPLAINTS AGAINST ADVERTISERS

Complaints against advertisers can come from competitors, consumers, or the FTC's own internal monitoring staff. After investigating, the FTC takes one of several courses of action. Most often, it simply requests that the advertiser change the offending commercial or remove it from the air, and the advertiser complies or works out a compromise with the FTC. If that doesn't work, a cease-and-desist order from the FTC will insist that the offending ad be removed; in the case of knowing violations, the FTC can impose a fine of $10,000 per violation, increasing to $10,000 per day for failure to obey an FTC order. The advertiser may also agree to sign a consent decree in which the company does not admit guilt, but agrees to stop running the commercials and to refrain from similar practices in future advertisements. In severe situations involving food, drugs, medical devices, and cosmetics—where the FTC has broader authority—the FTC may ask the Department of Justice to try the advertiser on a misdemeanor charge.

Advertisers are given up to 30 days to respond to FTC requests, and may contest any decision to the full Commission. They can eventually appeal FTC decisions in the federal court system.

THE FCC AND ADVERTISING CONTENT

The FCC has largely given up its role as a regulator of the content of advertising. The 1934 Communications Act does allow the FCC to suspend the license of any broadcaster transmitting false or deceptive signals or communications. Nonetheless, as early as the 1970s, the FCC recognized the greater expertise of the FTC on these matters, and by 1985, the FCC had dropped most of its specific policies on false and misleading advertising. However, the FCC still makes broadcasters generally responsible for controlling any false, misleading, or deceptive matter over the air, by virtue of the public-interest standard.

FCC PROHIBITIONS ON TELEVISION ADVERTISING

The FCC prohibits subliminal advertising (messages that are so brief or so inconspicuous that they work only at a subconscious level), holding this technique to be against the public interest. Specific federal legislation also bars advertising cigarettes and small cigars on the electronic media under the jurisdiction of the FCC, including cable television and satellite transmissions. The mention of a cigarette producer that sponsors a sports contest or other reported event is acceptable, however, provided that the references are not so exaggerated that they become, in effect, commercial messages.

There are also long-standing statutory and FCC prohibitions against television advertising of certain kinds of lotteries and gambling activities. In a commercial context, a prohibited lottery has (1) a prize which is (2) awarded by chance, and (3) involves entrants who have paid money or supplied some other valuable consideration (which can include the purchase of a product). A "contest" that lacks one of these elements is exempt, and can be advertised on television. For instance, if "no purchase is necessary to enter and win," the element of consideration is missing. If the prizes are awarded on the basis of some bona fide measure of skill, the element of chance is not there. However, since the interpretation of these rules can get quite technical, consulting with legal counsel is advisable before advertising a lottery on television.

In the past, these rules prohibited the advertisement of gambling activities in general. With the spread of state lotteries and other legal gambling activities, in 1990 Congress amended the law to permit the advertising via broadcast of all legitimate lottery and gambling activities that are legal in the state in which they are conducted. Because of the skill involved in picking a winner and because you can attend without betting, the advertising of horse racing did not come under the old bans.

Telemarketing-from infomercials to cable shopping channels—is regulated under a mix of FCC and FTC rules. The FTC requires that infomercial-style programming make periodic disclosure that the program is a paid-for commercial and not a regular consumer program. Both the FTC and the FCC have targeted telemarketers who charge for phone conversations, such as psychics and adult oriented services. The 1992 Telephone Disclosure and Dispute Resolution Act mandated a series of protections, including clear disclosure of costs in all ads (including television commercials), avoiding ads targeted at children, and avoiding using "800" or other usually toll-free numbers to initiate the call. These restrictions have been imposed on the telemarketers by FTC rules and on the phone companies by FCC rules.

The FCC has dropped many of its old rules banning particular kinds of advertising. These discarded prohibitions include rules on ads for alcoholic beverages and astrology. Minor limitations on beer ads (for example, advertisers cannot list the alcohol content of beers in most states) and states' control over liquor commercials have persisted, but been thrown into question by a 1996 Supreme Court ruling.

CHILDREN'S TELEVISION

After many false starts at the regulatory level, Congress enacted the Children's Television Act of 1990. This law mandated the FCC to impose limits on the amount of advertising that can be included in children's programs. It also directed the FCC to review compliance with these restrictions in connection with license renewals, as well as to evaluate the licensee's attention to the educational and informational needs of children in its programming. Finally, the Act calls on the FCC to tackle the issues of program-length commercials and the general commercialization of children's television. As described on page 195, FCC rules limit advertising time during children's programs to no more than 10.5 minutes per hour on weekends and 12 minutes on weekdays. The FCC has also defined program-length commercials as programs linked to a product in which commercials for that product are aired.

AMOUNTS OF ADVERTISING

As a general matter, television stations and cable operators are not obligated to accept commercials at all. Those that do accept commercials may turn down particular ones they do not wish to run, provided the reason doesn't invoke some other general principle of the law. Stations and cable operators are not "common carriers" in this respect, and there are no minimums. The main exceptions to this principle are the equal opportunity and reasonable-access rules for political advertising (see page 134).

The broadcast networks, most cable companies, and most individual broadcast stations do set limits on the number of ads that they carry on their programs. These amounts vary, depending on the time period and the particular medium involved. For instance, the major networks generally restrict advertising on prime-time programs to 8 to 10 minutes per hour; for their daytime programming, the maximum is typically 12 to 15 minutes. Ad time on cable and local stations may run in the range of 12 to 15 minutes per hour. Special events like the Olympics can attract more than the usual number of ads.

Until 1984, the FCC set its own limits on the total amount of commercial time that could be included in television programming. As a general matter, ad time was restricted to 16 commercial minutes per programming hour. In June 1984, however, these rules were repealed, as part of a general deregulation of television broadcasting. The new policy was to allow the balance between ads and programming to be set by the marketplace and factors of public acceptance. The private sector used to have its own rules on the maximum number of commercials, and the National Association of Broadcasters suggested time limits in its Television Code. The Code and its limits, however, were effectively abolished in 1982 in connection with the settlement of antitrust litigation. As described above, the FCC has proposed limits on the amount of advertising on children's television.

Public broadcast stations are supposedly prohibited from airing advertisements to promote any for-profit product or service, and from carrying ads for or against any political candidates. Public broadcasters may include limited mentions of program funders (see page 58)—a practice that has become quite ad-like over time.

UNFAIR COMPETITION AND THE LANHAM ACT

Certain federal and state laws permit companies and individuals to take private legal action to prevent certain kinds of false advertising, under the theory that it constitutes unfair competition to misdescribe one's own product or to lie about a competitor's. The most important of these laws is Section 43(a) of the Federal Lanham Act § 1125, available through the FTC Website, http://www.ftc.gov/.

In the context of advertising, Section 43(a) allows damaged parties to sue over misrepresentations about the nature, characteristics, qualities or geographic origin of goods, services or commercial activities. The Lanham Act applies to direct trademark violations—for example, the use of the words "Coca-Cola" on a product not manufactured by the Coca-Cola company. It also forbids advertising a product as made by a certain company or as endorsed by an individual when that simply is not the case. Nor need the claims be made explicitly: false involvement or endorsement can also be implied. The Lanham Act can affect certain kinds of comparative ads, if there is the implication that the manufacturer of the other product is in some way endorsing the advertisement or the statements in it.

The Lanham Act does not provide for private action against all false advertising, however. Most courts have held that false claims which have nothing to do with the origin or quality of the goods are simply not covered; a few courts and certain commentators have construed the Lanham Act a bit more broadly. In addition, the right to sue is limited to competitors or to the person or company whose involvement is being impermissibly suggested. The Lanham Act does not give the general public a right to sue for these misrepresentations.

STATE LAWS

Many states have adopted unfair competition laws which provide protections similar to those given under the Lanham Act. As a general matter, it must be proved that the advertising is confusing the buying public as to the origin of the goods and services being advertised. Some states allow claims for other kinds of deceptions, not necessarily limited to those about origin.

The states frequently have their own laws prohibiting false advertising in general. One form of these is generically called "Printer's Ink" laws; another, less common model is the Uniform Deceptive Trade Practice Act. Whatever the approach, enforcement will vary widely, depending on the priority that the state regulatory and prosecuting authorities give deceptive advertising. The Association of Attorneys General has from time to time encouraged its members to actively pursue false advertising claims. There are even some local rules, administered by bodies such as a municipal consumer-protection commission or bureau, that concern local advertisers.

CONSUMER CLAIMS

It is possible for consumers to bring claims against false advertising, either singly or as part of a class action. The legal theories for such actions include fraud, misrepresentation, breach of contract, and breach of warranties, express and implied. Since, in many cases of misleading advertising, the harm to any one individual is likely to be small in comparison to the legal costs, almost every such suit is brought on a class-action basis, and even here, the rules on class actions can be fairly restrictive. Although they have been successfully maintained in some instances, and have produced significant recoveries, consumer suits for false advertising are uncommon.

INDUSTRY REVIEW OF ADVERTISING CONTENT

The first step in checking the content of a commercial occurs between the client and the advertising agency. As the ad is scripted and story-boarded, it is often reviewed by the ad agency's counsel and, in many instances, the client's counsel as well; advertising that makes affirmative claims will be subject to particular scrutiny. Substantiating backup is assembled for any claims made, and general attention is given to the legal issues—not only pertaining to advertising itself, but also to matters of copyright clearance, privacy and publicity, and those content restrictions that apply to all television programs.

The broadcast networks are quite active in reviewing the content of the advertisements that they run, insisting that they have some input at the storyboard level. The networks' review involves not only the substantive questions of legal compliance, but also the advertising's adherence to network standards and practices. Areas of particular sensitivity to the networks include beer and wine, toys, over-the-counter drugs, contraceptives, and astrology. The networks have also declined to run advertising for distilled alcoholic beverages. All in all, such standards are fairly predictable for mass-market distributors concerned with their image and accustomed to avoiding controversy.

Cable is, by and large, much more permissive about advertising than broadcast is (with the exception of The Family Channel and other consciously wholesome companies), and local stations vary greatly. As a result, cable companies are more lenient in their review of commercials.

Various trade groups of advertising agencies and their clients have issued guidelines for their members to follow in making ads. These relatively platitudinous and commonsensical codes have helped shape the attitudes of the industry for the better, in turn influencing the types of ads that appear on television. One such guide covers children's advertising. Some groups have even set up review committees with the power to review potentially offensive ads and recommend (but not force) their change or withdrawal. The American Association of Advertising Agencies has been active both in promoting a creative code (adopted in 1962) and in setting up a review system. In 1971, the AAAA joined with the Council of Better Business Bureaus, the Association of National Advertisers, and the American Advertising Federation to establish the National Advertising Division, which reviews ads for misleading or deceptive content, and the National Advertising Review Board, which hears appeals.

Compliance with NAD and NARB rulings is voluntary, but re-markably uniform. Non-compliance would bring adverse publicity to an advertiser, and non-compliance can be reported to the appropriate governmental agency for action.

PART 6

Legal and
Business Affairs

44

Contracts

Contract law is one of the great developments of Western mercantile culture. Under contract law, courts will grant the force of law to an arrangement agreed upon by private parties. But courts will not enforce every statement or promise, for instance, a gratuitous or frivolous offer. What courts enforce is a serious transaction between two or more parties in exchange for value on all sides. This value is sometimes called "consideration," and it is a necessity for a binding agreement. In some instances, however, consideration can be supplied by the known reliance of one party on the promise of the other, even if nothing of material value is being exchanged.

VERBAL AND WRITTEN AGREEMENTS

Notwithstanding the old truism that "an oral agreement isn't worth the paper it's written on," verbal deals were generally enforceable under common law until 1677. The change came with the adoption in England of the "statute of frauds," a measure intended to prevent the frauds that may occur whenever there is no signed, written agreement. Although England has since dropped its statute of frauds, most U.S. states have adopted some form of it. Typically, sales agreements for goods over $500, contracts requiring performance over a significant amount of time (commonly a year), the sale or transfer of real estate, contracts for marriage, and contracts of guaranty and surety must all be in writing, and signed, to be enforced. In television, verbal agreements are often used for short-term employment, particularly if there are no rights in intellectual property or privacy being transferred. Whenever rights are being transferred, or whenever any future service or right is contemplated, a written agreement should be used.

The signed agreement need not be a single piece of paper. If a distributor writes a signed letter offering to license a program to a station and the station sends back a signed letter saying it accepts the deal, the requirements of the statute of frauds will be met. Informal documents such as job orders, booking sheets, and deal memos (see page 443) can also constitute a sufficient writing.

In most states, it is also necessary for one party to deliver the contract to the other party, or to the other party's representatives, for a contract to be formed. If you sign the deal but keep the signed copy to yourself, delivery has not occurred.

As discussed on page 173, federal copyright law requires that an *exclusive* assignment or license take the form of a signed document in order to be effective. Similarly, some privacy-law statutes require that any waiver of privacy rights be done in writing.

In the television business, sometimes a *deal memo* is sent that confirms a deal without any provision for signature. In other cases, correspondence and contract drafts may go back and forth for months without a final agreement getting signed. In some cases, the money may be paid, the services may be provided, the program may be broadcast on national television—and still no signatures.

In cases in which a contract is not signed but performance has gone forward, the courts are at least aware that some kind of agreement existed between the parties: they have "performed" the agreement. The courts will seek to determine that the deal was governing the performance and enforce it even though the technical requirements of the statute of frauds have not been met. Then there is the concept of reliance. If one party makes a verbal promise to another party, and this other party relies on it with the knowledge of the party that made the promise, then the promise can often be enforced even in the absence of any signed contract.

Since the television industry is somewhat casual about signing agreements before work begins on projects, term sheets, confirming letters, or deal memos—even if unsigned by the other side—are sometimes used to guide a court once performance has begun, particularly if these items go uncontroverted. The ultimate weapon, short of a signed contract, is the reliance letter. It gives notice to the other side that actual reliance is being put on the submitted terms, even though there is nothing yet signed. Of course, the other side can send back a "don't rely" letter, or even a "don't rely but we are relying" letter. If performance continues and a dispute breaks out, the courts may have a hard time untangling the record.

CONTRACT FORMATS

The signed document embodying a contract need not be in any particular form, but it must include adequate evidence of the necessary terms of the agreement, and must indicate the intent of the persons signing it to be bound by it.

In effect, anything that says "this is a contract, these are the parties, and these are the terms" should do the job. Over time, a series of generally accepted forms have evolved. The oldest and most formal is the *indenture form*. The wording is derived from the forms used for contracts in the late Middle Ages. The indenture form looks something like this:

AGREEMENT

This agreement made as of this 1st day of January, 1999 by and between the Smith Corporation, a Delaware corporation, and John Doe, an individual,

WITNESSETH

WHEREAS, the Smith Corporation wishes to undertake a transaction with Doe and Doe wishes to undertake a transaction with the Smith Corporation;

NOW, THEREFORE, the parties hereto agree as follows:

Buried within the arcane language of this form is a simple statement: The document is a contract between Smith Corporation and Doe, the reasons for the contract are that Doe and Smith Corporation want to do a deal, the deal is as follows. Such a contract might close:

IN WITNESS WHEREOF, the parties hereto have executed this Agreement as of the date first above written.

SMITH CORPORATION

_____   By: _____

John Doe   Lisa Smith, President

A more modern but equally enforceable form of contract is the *letter agreement*. The letter agreement begins by stating who the parties are, and that the letter is a contract. A typical starting clause might read:

John Doe
[address]

January 1, 1999

Smith Corporation
[address]

Dear Ms. Smith:

When the enclosed copy of this letter is signed on behalf of the Smith Corporation and returned to me, this letter will set forth the terms of our agreement concerning the deal to be done between us on the following terms:

Such a contract might close with:

Please confirm that the foregoing accurately represents the agreement between us by executing the enclosed copy on the indicated line and returning it to me.

Yours sincerely,

John Doe

ACCEPTED AND AGREED:
SMITH CORPORATION

By: _____
    Lisa Smith, President

Similarly, a memorandum form may be used to set forth an agreement:

From: Smith Corporation
To: Doe
Re: Deal
Date: January 1, 1999

This memorandum will set forth the terms of our deal and, when signed on the indicated lines below, will constitute our binding agreement.

The memorandum form usually closes with some type of signature lines.

None of these forms has any special advantage as a matter of law, although particular industry segments may have their preferences or traditions. They are all equally binding as contracts. By and large, the indenture form is considered more formal than the letter agreement, and the letter more formal than the memo. As a matter of style, the formality of the agreement should match the complexity of the transaction. For instance, the memo form is fine for a deal that can be adequately described within a page or two. If the agreement requires several pages, the letter agreement is better; if dozens of pages are necessary, the indenture form may be the most appropriate format.

FORM AGREEMENTS

People in the television business frequently use pre-printed form agreements, which can be real time-savers—with two provisos. First, the contract must fit the deal and vice versa. Although using a form agreement helps save on legal costs, this can be a false economy if the form simply isn't the right one, or if the deal has a complication not covered by a standard form. Second, the forms must be fair enough to both sides to actually get signed. Although there is always the temptation, when using a form agreement, to make it as favorable as possible to the drafter, the contract cannot be so one-sided that no one will sign it.

STYLE

As a matter of law, a contract does not require any particular style of writing; it need only state, in language that is specific and clear, the principal terms of the deal. A certain style of writing known as "legalese" has developed over the years, but to the extent that it confuses the untrained reader, legalese is not recommended. In certain instances, time-honored legal formulas may save space or provide a shorthand for complicated concepts. In general, though, if the use of legalese might lead to a misunderstanding, the contract should be worded in plain language.

NECESSARY TERMS

To be enforceable, a contract must contain certain critical, basic terms. If the price, dates, or items to be sold or licensed are left out or are left to future negotiations, the entire contract will probably not be considered binding by a court. In such cases, there just isn't enough actually agreed upon to constitute a real deal. The common television-industry practice of leaving terms for later good-faith negotiation runs the danger of rendering at least the provision—and perhaps even the entire agreement—unenforceable. To prevent this possibility, negotiation clauses should never be for basic terms, and when they are used, they should outline a detailed procedure, with specific dates, parameters, and other objective criteria on how negotiations are to proceed.

ORDER OF TERMS

The order in which terms of an agreement are set forth does not effect its binding nature; as a practical matter, however, a good agreement should read easily and logically. Thus, it is customary to begin with the terms of greatest importance and proceed to the more minor details as the contract progresses. In drafting a contract, one should begin as if telling an uninitiated person about the contents of the deal. A program license agreement, for instance, might well start by saying that a license is being granted and move on to describe the programs and the term or territories involved. The next topic might be the compensation for the license; further topics would include representations and warranties of the parties (see below); and the final provisions might cover choice of law (see below) and other technical matters.

SIGNATURES

Any signature that identifies the signing party and its intent to be bound is adequate for a contract. Thus, the use of a first name or initials, if effective on these points, can constitute a signature. Although it is the custom in this country that signatures should appear at the end of a document, there is no requirement for this in most states, provided the signatures appear at a place in the document where they demonstrate the necessary intent to be bound. The agreement is generally signed at an indicated space, frequently on a line over the printed or typed name of the person signing. In order to make clear whether the person is signing individually, as an officer of a corporation, or as a partner, agent, or trustee, the signature line should specify the capacity in which this person is signing. Also, if the person is signing on behalf of another entity, the signature line should be proceeded by the word "by." This designates that the person is signing on behalf of the entity, such as a corporation or partnership, and not on his or her own behalf.

WITNESSES, NOTARIES AND SEALS

Corporate and personal seals are generally not a necessity for agreements. In most instances, the signatures on a contract do not have to be authenticated by witnesses, and the contract does not have to be signed in front of a Notary Public (although these steps can be useful as evidentiary matters should the signature ever be disputed). For land transactions and other circumstances in which the contract is to be filed as a matter of public record, witnesses or notarial authentication may be required, but this is seldom the case for a television contract. In some instances, a corporate seal may be used as an additional piece of formal evidence to authenticate that a corporate action was properly taken. An emerging area of the law concerns purely electronic communications. For instance, how does one sign an e-mail? While the law settles this out, it is best to be cautious. On the one hand don't rely on an e-mail—get a *signed* original; on the other hand, don't presume that an e-mail isn't binding—it may well be.

ORIGINALS

Original signed copies are clearly preferred by a court called upon to enforce an agreement. If an original signed copy is not available, however, the best available copy will have to be presented to the court. A conformed copy, a photocopy, or even a telefaxed copy of the signed original is usually considered acceptable-as long as there is sufficient evidence establishing that the signed original existed and that the offered copy is a true copy of it.

INITIALING

Initials next to a change in the contract indicate that the parties were aware of it at the time of the signing and that it was not inserted after the fact by one of the parties. In the case of changes added, whether by hand or in print, to an otherwise clean agreement, it is advisable to initial the changes to minimize the potential for future disagreements. Likewise, initials at the bottom of a contract page indicate that it is one of the original pages and that substitute pages have not been inserted. Unless a conflict between the parties is likely, the level of trust is exceedingly low, or a high degree of formality is desired, the individual pages of an agreement do not have to be initialed— particularly if each side will have a fully signed copy.

SIGNING AUTHORITY AND POWERS OF ATTORNEY

Real people can sign for themselves; business entities, being artificial creations, cannot. Therefore, people must sign on behalf of business entities. The ability to sign on behalf of an entity hinges on the person's having either general or specific authorization to do so. In the case of a corporation, one can generally presume that the chairman, president, or a senior vice president can execute most customary business contracts for a company. For a contract involving large amounts of money, however, specific board approval may be required to grant the authority. The other party to such a deal may request to see a certified copy of this board action, together with certified specimens of the signatures of the officers who are signing. In the case of a partnership, any general partner can usually sign on behalf of the partnership and bind it. Limited-liability company contracts should be signed by a manager, or, if no managers are designated, by a member.

A person acting under a power of attorney can also bind a business entity—or an individual—within the scope of the granted power. Talent agents will sometimes sign on behalf of their clients and, if properly authorized as agents, will have the power of an attorney-in-fact for entering contracts within the scope of the agent's authority. If this is not so, it may be grounds for the agent's client to disown the contract, particularly if it was not reasonable to think that the agent had the power to sign.

In the final analysis, the ability of a party to bind another entity is usually evaluated on the basis of apparent authority. If the entity in question has apparently authorized the agent to sign—and this authority is relied upon by a person who could not have possibly known that the agent actually had no such power—then the entity will be bound by the signature. For better or worse, in most television deals, the parties rely on the apparent authority of an appropriate corporate officer to bind the corporation to the contract, without requiring the inspection of the corporate resolution granting the power.

DATES

Every contract should have a date to indicate when it was signed, when it is to be effective, or both. Certain widely understood codes apply in giving a date. For instance, if an agreement is to be effective on a date that is specified, but which is not necessarily the date of signature, this date should be expressed with the words "as of." A contract that reads, "This agreement, dated *as of* the 1st day of January, 1999" could have actually been signed weeks before or after January 1, 1999. By contrast, if the contract date is to indicate the date of actual signing, then "as of" should not be used. The words "This contract, made this 1st day of January, 1999" imply that the signatures were affixed on the date given. Sometimes a date is put next to the signature line to indicate the date of signature.

This practice can be used in conjunction with an "as of" date for the entire contract, showing both the effective date for the agreement and the actual dates of execution.

STATIONERY AND LETTERHEAD

There is no magic to the use of stationery or letterhead in connection with an agreement, although in some situations there may be some evidentiary value in the use of original letterhead. If the letter agreement form is to be used, it is logical that it appear on the customary letterhead of the party that is writing the letter.

CHOICE OF LAW

Contract law is basically state law, and there are the inevitable variations between the states on specific points. The choice of which state's law will apply to the contract is too frequently neglected by contracting parties. Sometimes, the variations in contract law between different states can have significant implications.

Parties cannot simply choose any law, however, to govern their agreements. There must be some relation of a logical and substantial nature between the law which is chosen to govern the agreement and the subject matter of the agreement, the location of the parties in general, or the location of the parties at the time of signing. In the absence of an affirmative choice of law, the applicable state law will be chosen by the court seeking to enforce the contract. As a starting point, most courts will prefer their own local law. A court may consider other factors as well, such as the respective domiciles of the parties, the state in which performance is to take place, and the state in which the contract was signed.

MINORS

Minors—children under the age at which they become independently responsible adults (in most states, at 18)—receive many protections under traditional common-law principles. At common law, most contracts with a minor can be voided by the minor at any time until he or she becomes an adult, and for a reasonable time thereafter. Some states, recognizing that such a blanket rule would not be appropriate for a contract with a minor that was not abusive, have made provision for a court to review such a contract; if the court approves it, the contract would be binding and not voidable. In California, for instance, the court has discretion to

approve a wide range of agreements with minors, including contracts for acting services, management and agency agreements,
and grants of rights in creative properties and life stories. No time
limit is set on the duration of service contracts, beyond the seven-
year limit generally applicable in California.

New York law is more stringent about the scope of agreements
with minors that the court can approve. Although the court can
permit service contracts, management agreements, and agency
agreements, these documents cannot have terms of greater than
three years (certain negative covenants [see page 454] and participation agreements may extend beyond the three-year limit). In
addition, New York law does not empower courts to approve
grants of rights in intellectual property, although the "work for hire"
doctrine may take care of much of this at the copyright level. By
contrast, a parent is specifically authorized to waive privacy rights
under the New York statute without a court proceeding.

REPRESENTATIONS AND WARRANTIES

Many contracts contain items which are called *representations and
warranties*—fancy words for promises about statements of fact.
Thus, if a party represents and warrants that the contract was
signed on Tuesday, he is stating that it is a fact: Tuesday is the date
when the contract was signed. If this fact turns out to be wrong
and damages result, this is grounds for a suit by the other party for
a breach of the contract. Representations and warranties are frequently linked in the television world to statements about rights
clearances and the authority to enter into agreements. As a general matter, parties only make representations and warranties
about matters with which they are personally acquainted, or over
which they have personal control. In some instances, a representation and warranty can be softened by the insertion of "to the best
of the party's knowledge" or similar words. In this case, a breach
will not occur if the statement proves wrong—but it will occur if
the representing and warranting party *knew* before signing that the
statement was wrong. Claims under a "to the best of knowledge"
representation and warranty can bog down in arguments over
what constitutes knowledge.

INDEMNITIES

An *indemnity,* frequently paired with representations and warranties,
is a promise by one party to pay specified costs and losses of another

party. In the contract context, an indemnity clause generally says that if Party A suffers a loss because of Party B—for example, because one of the reps and warranties proves to be untrue—then Party B will make Party A's losses good, and will cover any expenses. An indemnity should be given only for matters which the giver agreed to do, as to which the giver has provided a representation and warranty, or which are otherwise within the indemnifying party's knowledge, control, and legitimate risk.

Indemnities can have important wrinkles. One is whether the indemnity covers only breaches (actual defaults) or whether it also covers "alleged breaches," or defaults which someone else asserts. With an alleged breach, if someone wrongfully sues Party B, claiming that certain rights were not cleared, and if that claim is then defeated in court, Party A, as the indemnifier, would still have to reimburse Party B for the costs of the lawsuit. If it were an indemnity limited to actual breaches, the indemnifying party (Party A) would not be called upon to pay the costs of Party B. Unless specifically mentioned, indemnities may not include legal fees, and so a provision for reasonable attorney's fees is frequently inserted. Indemnities sometimes give the indemnifying party a right to be involved in directing any litigation for which he or she is financially responsible. Likewise, the indemnifying party sometimes has the right to approve any settlements for which it will have to reimburse the other party.

LENGTH OF YEARS

Although in most instances the term, or duration, of an agreement is up to the parties to decide between themselves, there are some general limitations which can apply. Most courts will impose some time limit on service contracts, if only as a matter of public policy to prevent endless employment commitments. In New York, factors such as the level of compensation and the customs of the industry are considered. In California, the legislature has set a statutory limit of seven years for any contract for personal services.

There are also limitations on the duration of certain grants of rights. Under the Copyright Act, there are reversions permitted of copyright transfers and licenses (see page 171). Options, including those for turnaround (see page 208), may be subject to the arcane "rule against perpetuities." This rule prohibits property (including creative works) from being tied up with contingent rights for endless periods. As a rule of thumb, options that are open for more than 21 years may be subject to cancellation.

TERMS CONTRARY TO LAW OR PUBLIC POLICY

A court will refuse to enforce individual terms—or, indeed, whole contracts—which it deems to be contrary to public policy. For instance, contracts for murder or theft will not be enforced. Also, laws on certain points may take precedence over the agreement of the parties. The California limit of seven years for employment agreements is one example of this.

FORCE MAJEURE

Force majeure describes a circumstance where performance of the contract is rendered impossible or unreasonably difficult by the intervention of a force beyond the control of the affected party. In television productions, this might include earthquakes, labor disputes, fires, wars, or other natural and manmade disasters. In such a case, the contract can be suspended, or even terminated, with consequences less than for full breach of contract. Television contracts frequently describe in detail those events that constitute force majeure, and also the consequences—including the suspension and termination of the contract.

INCAPACITY

Television contracts, particularly those for talent services, frequently have clauses dealing with the incapacity of the talent. In most cases, after a short waiting period, the producer can choose to either suspend the contract and start it up again when the talent recovers, or terminate the contract without further obligation.

BREACHES

What happens when one or both parties to a contract fail to live up to the deal they have made? This failure, often called a breach or a default, can occur in several ways. One party can fail to carry out an *affirmative obligation* (making a payment or delivering a finished program), or can breach a *negative obligation* (by failing to adhere to an exclusivity provision). If a representation and warranty turns out to be false, this can also cause a default.

A default or breach may be grounds for action if it is "material." Technical lapses which have no real consequences for the aggrieved party are generally shrugged off as being non-material by a court brought in to settle the dispute. If seemingly trivial points are indeed of importance, a party can strengthen his or her hand by providing

that full performance of them is "of the essence" (see page 453—
"time is of the essence"). Even then, if the default is truly trivial, a
court may still disregard it.

Contracts will sometimes provide time periods for remedying
certain kinds of lapses, generally running from when the failing party
gets notice of its default. This allows accidental failures to be fixed
without the whole contract going into default.

Sometimes a party declares that he or she is not going to be bound
by the contract. Even though there may not yet be any actual failure
to perform, such a statement can constitute an anticipatory breach,
particularly if it is not disclaimed after a request for confirmation
by the other side.

REMEDIES

If a contract is in material breach, the injured party has a number of
possible responses. As a starting point, there are certain measures
of "self-help." For instance, the aggrieved party can suspend his or
her own performance under the contract. If a producer has failed
to make payments required by the contract, an actor may stop
showing up at the set. If there is a dispute over who is in breach,
however, suspension of performance can be a dangerous step. If
money is due for a print, for a soundtrack, or for other production
elements, the lab or sound mixer may be able to hold onto the
material under a "mechanic's lien" until the debt is paid.

While the dispute is pending, the aggrieved party should seek to
mitigate his or her damages, taking whatever steps are reasonably
available to minimize the losses coming from the breach. Thus, if
contracts with suppliers can be canceled, this should be done; if
another purchaser for the project is waiting in the wings, he or she
should be considered. A failure to mitigate can be held against the
aggrieved party when it comes time for a court to make good his or
her losses.

Beyond the self-help steps, the aggrieved party may have to go
to court—or, if the contract so provides, to arbitration—to get
satisfaction for the breach. If there has been a breach, a court or
arbitration panel normally awards damages, that is, payments that
will rectify the losses incurred. In deciding how much to award, the
first consideration is restitution, or reimbursing the aggrieved party
for any out-of-pocket losses that the failure of the contract has
caused. An additional consideration will be lost profits, some or
all of which a court may force the breaching party to pay. If the
defaulting party made profits through breaking the deal ("unjust

enrichment"), a court can force some or all of these profits to be turned over to the aggrieved party. There is also the possibility of an award of punitive damages, although this is unlikely in a contract case, absent some elements of especially willful misbehavior. If the case involves a copyright claim, the statutory damages provided by the Copyright Act may apply (see page 174).

In addition to damages, a court may grant equitable remedies (the term refers to the old-fashioned "courts of equity" in which these remedies evolved). Equitable remedies are given only when money damages are inadequate in some fashion. These remedies include "specific performance," that is, the ordering by the court that the contract be carried out. Specific performance is appropriate if the contract is for the sale of some existing tangible item, such as a motion picture negative; it is untenable in the case of a contract to perform some kind of skilled service, such as writing, acting, or directing. Recision, or the undoing of the entire contract, may be appropriate if there has been a sale of rights in a program for which no payment has ever been made. A third equitable remedy is injunction, a court order that forbids some act—for example, the telecast of a show for which the rights were improperly cleared.

Equitable remedies tend to be more powerful contractual medicine than simple damages; therefore, courts tend to use them only if it is shown that damages will not do the job. In addition, the parties themselves may have agreed in the contract to waive equitable remedies. Producers and distributors particularly dread the possibility of an injunction on the entire program because of a payment dispute on a talent contract. This waiver often occurs when rights are being transferred or credits being given.

"LAWYERS' TERMS" IN EVERYDAY LANGUAGE

Contracts frequently use terms and expressions that have very specific legal meanings. However, these meanings may not be obvious to the layperson who reads them in a contract, or, even worse, who includes them without consulting a lawyer. This section will address some of these words and phrases, and explain the perils and pitfalls they involve.

Time is of the essence: This phrase means that the actions specified in the contract *must* be taken on or by a particular date. There is no extension, no grace period, no time to remedy. If the event does not happen on the date specified, there is potentially a serious breach of the agreement.

Best efforts: More than just a good try. Some states will interpret this phrase to mean the very best effort of which the person is capable—including, if necessary, making a significant financial sacrifice or employing the utmost effort. A better formulation for giving something a good try is "endeavor in good faith."

Consultation vs. approval: Consultation on a matter means just that: the other party must consult you. It does not mean that they have to agree with you. After fair consultation, they may tell you, "I appreciate your ideas, but I don't want to use any of them." A right of "review" is similarly limited. A right of *approval,* by contrast, permits the party to say no and make it stick. A requirement for *written* approval is essentially an evidentiary matter, to avoid swearing matches between parties over what was said verbally.

Reasonable and sole discretion: There is an implied duty to act reasonably and in good faith under a contract. Nonetheless, it is frequently written in television contracts that certain actions can be taken only if they are "reasonable," or if there is a "reasonable basis," or if they are taken "reasonably." Such a provision is often linked to a circumstance in which one of the parties is empowered to take a discretionary action, such as exercise approval. If approval is "not to be unreasonably withheld," or "is to be given on a reasonable basis," this puts some limit on the discretion of the approving party. Should the approving party fail to approve something, the other party can claim that this failure is unreasonable and then proceed anyway, with some possibility of not being found in breach of the contract. By contrast, a phrase like "in her sole discretion," when linked to an approval right, makes it probable that a whim of the approving party will be enforceable—and that any action taken by the other party in disregard of that whim is risky.

Covenants: "Covenant" is a fancy word for an agreement or promise. Covenants are sometimes divided between "affirmative covenants" and "negative covenants." Affirmative covenants are promises to actually do things; negative covenants are promises to refrain from doing things. A contract will usually be binding without ever mentioning the word "covenant."

Work Relationships, Unions, Legal Entities and Tax Issues

Several types of working relationships and business entities are commonplace in television program development and production, station and network ownership, and distribution. These forms are also common to other industries.

EMPLOYEES AND INDEPENDENT CONTRACTORS

An *employee* is an individual who works directly for a business entity. Typically, an employee works under the direction and supervision of an employer, usually in accordance with a fixed schedule, in facilities provided by the employer. The employer pays the employee a salary, with deductions taken for federal, state, and local taxes, and makes contributions to a worker's compensation fund and social security in the name of the employee. The employer may also provide health insurance and benefits such as a pension fund, profit sharing, and a company car. An employee does not hire other employees, except as a representative of the employer.

An *independent contractor* (IC) is an individual who is self-employed; an independent contractor may also be a company, partnership, or corporation. Unlike an employee, an individual who is an IC works without direct supervision of the employer, sets his or her own hours, and frequently works at his or her own location rather than at company facilities. An IC is normally paid a gross fee for services rendered, and is responsible for the payment of all taxes, insurance, and other monies due to government agencies.

An IC costs the hiring company less to maintain than an employee; with an IC, the employer does not have responsibility for all of the related costs discussed above. An employer may, in effect, hire an employee, but seek to save money (illegally) by calling the employee an IC. In this scenario, the employer may, in the short term, avoid some liability in taxation, social security, unemployment insurance, and workman's compensation. But the penalties can be severe—the employer may be liable for taxes not paid by the employee, and for additional penalties. Rules regarding deductions for home-office and other business expenses are generally in favor of the IC (see page 466); employees have a tougher time justifying the use of a home when a traditional office is provided.

The employee/contractor distinction can be of considerable importance under copyright law when determining the owner of a work for hire. Unless alternate contractual arrangements are made, the courts will usually judge the proceeds of employment as a work for hire, whereas the ownership of an independent contractor's creations must be specifically transferred by written agreement (see page 167).

An independent contractor may hire other independent contractors or even employees on his or her own account.

UNIONS

Most productions made for the mainstream television marketplace involve unions that represent on- or off-screen talent or crew. (Several of these unions are discussed in Part 4.) Unions and employers are now regulated by federal law, particularly the National Labor Relations Act (NLRA); state law, once very active in this area, has been largely preempted by the federal rules.

VOLUNTARY UNION PRODUCTION

Because the television unions have attracted a substantial number of high-quality professionals, many broadcasters and production companies voluntarily choose to use union labor. In effect, using union labor is like buying brand-name goods: although they cost more than no-name products, by and large, one knows the quality one is getting. The union choice may also reflect a desire to avoid the difficulties that can plague a production if there should be a dispute over representation or jurisdiction.

If a company has decided to use union labor in one or more job categories, it can either hire members directly by becoming a union signatory, or in most cases, it can arrange for a service company that is already a signatory to provide the workers. If the company will be the direct employer, then it contacts the appropriate union about signing a union agreement. This agreement establishes the minimum terms and conditions for employing union members. For small independent companies, bonds or personal guarantees by the owners may be required, to ensure payment of wages and benefits in the case of a budget shortfall or other financial problems.

The union agreement typically requires the employer to use only union labor in the agreed-upon category, either on the project in question or in all the company's activities. The NLRA imposes limits on this kind of hiring agreement, however. The most a union contract can legally require is that any employee hired in a unionized job pay initiation fees and dues; the employee need not agree to other union membership provisions, such as exclusivity (that is, the rule that he or she can work only for a union signatory). In "right to work" states, even this provision is dropped, and the union signatory can hire non-union workers, who must nonetheless be treated the same as union employees.

Even outside the right-to-work states, organizations can often use both union and non-union employees. The affiliation agreement with a union typically has effect moving down a chain of corporate subsidiaries, not upward. Therefore, the company should investigate having a subsidiary company become the union signatory. That way, while one branch of the corporate tree will be union-only in the specified job categories, other branches can operate union-free. In addition, becoming a union signatory in one job area does not necessarily mean across-the-board affiliation; many companies are signatories with some of the television unions and not with others.

A union can sometimes compel an employer to recognize its role in bargaining. If enough employees (30 percent) in an appropriate bargaining unit—usually a particular job category—get together and request a union election, the employer must comply. If the election is in favor of the union, it will then have the right to nego-tiate a contract with management; if the union loses, it is barred from trying again for 12 months. Should any company find itself facing a union-organizing campaign, it should seek advice from professionals experienced in labor relations.

While most of the talent unions do not have overlapping juris-dictions (for example, the film/videotape split of SAG and AFTRA), some of the craft and technical areas are potentially represented by different unions. This is sometimes an accident of history: who organized what union when. If a company without an established union tie is contemplating using union labor where there are alternative choices, it is somewhat possible to pick the more attractive union in advance, based on rates, skills, work rules, and so on.

NON-UNION PRODUCTION

If the budget permits, union production is usually the easiest choice. Non-union personnel may be hired when the budget is tight; when some aspect of the union work rules or residual structures would be a burden on the production; or when the production is being done for a company whose tradition is non-union in certain categories. Sometimes the unions will cooperate with a producer, cutting special deals to reflect unusual circumstances. Some of the unions even have special codes for low-budget or non-commercial productions. It can be worth talking to the union if the hardship is real, and the concessions sought are not too major. In other cases, the employer may have the money, but may still opt for non-union personnel to avoid irksome restrictions, or simply to help the bottom line.

Using non-union labor can be a plus, particularly where there is a reservoir of solid independent talent from which to draw. Often, young people starting in the television business are not yet signed to a union, and will be willing to work for less money to get the experience and a credit. Even experienced workers may choose to remain non-union, enjoying the freedom to seek jobs on their own terms. However, especially when undercapitalized and independent operators are involved, the old problems of exploitation and non-payment which led to the founding of unions in the first place may recur; employees should approach these jobs with their eyes open.

Having unionized labor working for a company that is not a union signatory can be risky for all concerned, especially if it lasts for any significant length of time. Assumed names are often used, which renders the credit largely useless for résumé purposes. If the union finds out, it can fine or even expel the offending members. On the other hand, the union members can also turn around, once hired, and seek union representation for the entire production (particularly if they have been found out by the union). This can put the producer in a box, because it is illegal under the NLRA to fire an employee for union activity. The last thing most producers need is a representation battle in the middle of production.

FOREIGN PRODUCTIONS AND UNIONS

The jurisdiction of U.S. unions over foreign employment is limited. If the employer is U.S.-based, then union jurisdiction may apply, even to shooting abroad. Even if the employer is truly foreign-based, and the employment (typically shooting and post-production) takes place abroad, the unions sometimes try to assert authority if the deal was made in the U.S., or if the union member leaves the U.S. specifically to negotiate the agreement. The validity of this "location of the deal" approach is questionable, but some prospective employees—particularly those with savvy agents—have been known to "just happen to run into" a foreign producer while "coincidentally" traveling to Canada, Mexico, or St. Barts.

SOLE PROPRIETORSHIP

The sole proprietorship is an individual doing business on his or her own behalf. In most states, a sole proprietor using a fictitious business name must be identified and registered by filing a "doing business as" (DBA) certificate, with a designated authority (e.g., a county clerk). A sole proprietorship may hire employees, and the individual in charge must personally comply with tax, social security, insurance, and other employee-related government requirements. A sole proprietor is also subject to unlimited personal liability for all debts, claims, and obligations of the business. A sole proprietor pays personal income tax on the profits from the business; for larger businesses, this can become rather complicated, and retaining the services of a good accountant throughout the year is recommended.

Outsiders can make investments in the form of a loan, or by contractual arrangements that set a rate of return. If profits and losses are shared, however, the law may deem the entity to be a partnership.

PARTNERSHIP

Until quite recently, there have been just two types of partnerships: general and limited. A general partnership is an association of two or more persons who jointly own and operate a business, typically sharing profits and losses. A limited partnership has two kinds of partners: general partner and limited partner. The general partner is responsible for the operation of the business and is liable for its financial obligations; the limited partners, who are not involved in the operation of the business, are passive investors liable only up to their stated capital contributions.

Partnerships do not pay federal taxes on their income. Instead, profits and losses are passed on to the partners, who pay taxes as individuals. Profits and losses from the partnership can be offset by the performance of other ventures, but limited partners and other passive investors face restrictions, which often limit the offset to other so-called passive investments. The partnership must file an information return with the IRS and with applicable state and city agencies. It may also be subject to sales, property, and other non-income taxes.

GENERAL PARTNERSHIPS

A general partnership is usually formed by negotiating and signing a partnership agreement which defines the duties and rights of the partners. In most states, the partners can be any recognizable independent entity: individuals, agencies, limited liability companies, corporations, trusts, even other partnerships. The agreement normally specifies the amount of capital or the kinds of services that each partner is to contribute to the partnership, and it specifies how profits and losses are to be allocated to the partners (profits may be treated differently than losses). The agreement may also detail how the partnership is to be operated: who is to work full-time, and in what capacity; whether unanimous agreement is needed to admit new partners; how partnership decisions are to be made; and how and when the partnership is to be dissolved. If particular conditions are not specified, or no formal agreement has been signed, the relevant state law will apply and will usually provide answers to these and other questions. As to third parties, each general partner is individually liable for all of the debts, claims, and other obligations of the partnership.

In most states, a partnership using an assumed name must file an assumed-name certificate with the county clerk or some other designated official. It must also comply with employment rules and other laws applicable to any business structure.

JOINT VENTURES

A joint venture is a general partnership formed for a specific, limited purpose, such as the production of a particular television program or series. Joint ventures are governed by the agreements founding them and by normal partnership rules.

LIMITED PARTNERSHIPS

A limited partnership is similar to a general partnership except that it has two kinds of partners: general and limited. A limited partner is akin to a shareholder in a corporation—a passive investor who is not individually liable for the debts of the company. In fact, a limited partner may not, by law, participate in the day-to-day management of a limited partnership without risking the loss of limited partner status. Because it resembles both a partnership and a corporation, the limited partnership is appealing to a partner who wants to supply capital but not be involved in management.

Limited partnerships are frequently governed by the rules made for general partnerships, with some key differences. For instance, statutes authorizing limited partnerships go to considerable length to insure that third parties are not led to believe that the full credit of limited partners is standing behind the debts of the limited partnership.

In order to form a limited partnership, the general partner(s) must file a certificate of limited partnership in the office of the appropriate state official (e.g., secretary of state, county clerk). This certificate generally states the name, address, and class of business of the partnership, as well as the name of each partner, his or her address, and his or her status as a general or limited partner. In some states, the certificate also details each limited partner's contribution to the partnership (in cash or property), to what extent any additional contribution may be required, and the right of each limited partner to compensation (a share of income, for example). The certificate must be amended whenever the information changes. A general or limited partner may be an individual, a general partnership, a limited partnership, or a corporation. Many states also require the publication of this information in a local newspaper.

If a limited partner's name is used in the name of the limited partnership, or if he or she takes part in the management of the business, then he or she is likely to be considered a general partner, no matter what the agreements say. Still, a limited partner usually has the right to give general advice concerning the operation of the business, to inspect the books periodically, to receive a formal accounting on a regular basis, and to seek dissolution of the business by court order. A limited partner may also do business with the limited partnership; for example, a limited partner may loan money to the limited partnership.

The partnership agreement may authorize or restrict the admission of additional limited partners. The agreement may provide an order of priority among the limited partners with respect to profits or return of their contribution. In the absence of such an agreement, all limited partners are equal, usually on a *pari passu* basis (see page 300).

Typically, a limited partner may not withdraw his, her, or its money unless (1) the other partners consent; (2) the certificate is canceled or amended to reflect the reduced capital of the partnership; or (3) the assets of the partnership exceed its liabilities (excluding the liabilities of the partnership to the general and limited partners for their respective contributions). If the partnership is being dissolved, then procedures are detailed by either state guidelines or the partnership agreement. If a limited partner withdraws, that partner still remains liable for the amount of money withdrawn (plus interest) if that money is needed to pay debts incurred before the withdrawal.

In the past, there were many tax advantages to investing through limited partnerships, and they were frequently used for tax shelters.

As with other partnerships, losses could be passed through directly to partners, including the limited partners, but profits were not subject to double taxation. Tax reform has severely limited the benefits by making limited partnership income and loss "passive." Passive losses can only be offset against passive income, which does not include wages and fees. This has put an end to most limited-partnership investments motivated by tax savings.

HYBRID FORMS: LLC AND LLP

Since the early 1990s, the world of business organizations has been significantly altered by the addition of new hybrid forms such as the "Limited Liability Company" (an "LLC") and the "Limited Liability Partnership" (an "LLP"). Until these arrived, business owners who wanted to limit their personal liability for the debts of the business either had to use a corporation, which was not always as flexible as might be desired and which had significant tax complications (see below), or had to use a limited partnership, which gave limited liability only to non-active participants. Starting in North Dakota, and now in every state, however, a new form, the LLC, was adopted. It is a hybrid—with much of the flexibility of a partnership and yet with the limited liability of a corporation.

In order to form an LLC, it is necessary to file "articles of organization," typically with the state's secretary of state. These articles usually set forth the name of the LLC (which requires including the words "limited liability company," the abbreviation "LLC," or some other permitted variant), its registered address, its agent for service of process, the name and address of each organizer (who need not be one of the business principals), and any personal liability which the owners are assuming. It must also describe whether the LLC is to be managed by its members (i.e., owners) as a whole or by some designated group of "managers" who may or may not be members as well. Certain other principles of management may also be put in the articles, although these usually are part of the basic agreement between the members, called the operating agreement. Although the LLC statutes of most states provide backup "default rules" by which the LLC can be run, in most cases these rules can be superseded by the provisions of the operating agreement. This gives the LLC tremendous flexibility in the hands of a skilled attorney.

From a tax standpoint, the LLC is a major beneficiary of the current "check the box" approach to classifying non-corporate business forms. The organizers of an LLC get to "check the box" on an election form to tell the IRS whether they want the LLC taxed as a partnership or as a corporation. This further flexibility has helped to make the LLC very popular as a form for organizing new businesses in the U.S., and one that just about anyone setting up a new business should at least consider.

In some states, even the LLC is no longer the last word in hybrids; the LLP is the new form of interest. This innovation initially came about to allow a limited liability to be applied to law firms and accounting firms which could not, for certain licensing reasons, be LLCs. They have taken on a life of their own for some small businesses as well, particularly with the possibility of "check the box" tax treatment. It may be worth asking your attorney about the availability and advisability of using an LLP for a new business.

CORPORATIONS

In Latin, the root word "corpus" means "body." As this suggests, the corporation is viewed by law as a separate legal entity, a body distinct from any other entities which may own interests in it. Most U.S. corporations are established under state laws. A corporation is formed by filing a certificate of incorporation, sometimes called "articles of incorporation," with the appropriate state official (usually the secretary of state). This certificate first states the name of the corporation, which must usually include the words "Incorporated," "Corporation," or "Limited" (or an abbreviation of any of these terms) to indicate corporate status—specific terms vary from state to state. The certificate also indicates the business location; its purpose; the number, type, and stated value of shares, along with a description of the rights or restrictions applicable to any type of stock; and the duration of the corporation (usually it is perpetual). Amending the corporate certificate normally requires special majority approval of the stockholders, and there may be other requirements in addition. Further rules regarding the operation of the corporation (usually called the "bylaws") may be written and used, but they do not need to be filed. The bylaws provide specifics on how the company is to be operated; if neither they nor the certificate covers a particular matter, then standard rules under the governing state law apply.

Those who have invested in the corporation become stockholders, but the class of their shares, and the rights that go along with them, may vary. "Common shares" normally carry some form of unlimited profit participation and some form of voting power. "Preferred shares" normally carry a first right to profits (though frequently with a limit) and may entitle the shareholder to limited voting rights.

Various hybrid types of shares may be created for specific purposes. Shares of stock are normally transferable; they can be bought or sold at any time, subject to certain state, SEC, and in-company restrictions. Profits are paid as dividends in accordance with the rules regarding types of shares, or are held for corporate expansion. Shareholders may inspect the books and records of the corporation, and if they believe that the directors or officers are behaving improperly, they may take legal action to stop the wrongdoing and seek damages.

The business of a corporation is overseen by a board of directors, which often consists of three members or more, elected yearly by the shareholders. If there are fewer than three shareholders, then there usually can be fewer than three seats on the board of directors. The board is responsible for setting corporate policy, for approving significant corporate actions (like large expenditures), and for electing the principal corporate officers.

In a small corporation, only a president and a secretary are required in most states, although treasurer and vice president are other common officers. Further creativity with titles is possible, within the limits of the bylaws and the cleverness of the board of directors.

Since corporations are treated as separate legal entities, they file income tax returns and pay taxes on income. They do not have the "check the box" options enjoyed by LLCs and LLPs. Profits are taxed at the corporate level, and dividends to shareholders are taxed as individual income. The exception is the S corporation, described below.

S CORPORATIONS

The S corporation, formed in accordance with Sub-Chapter S of the IRS Code, is a special type of corporation for tax purposes. (The regular corporation is called a C corporation, a term rarely used.) An S corporation has the same basic organizational structure as a regular corporation, but has some of the tax advantages of a partnership. S corporation status is obtained by filing an election within two-and-a-half months of formation, or, with respect to succeeding years for established companies, within two-and-a-half months of the start of the year that precedes the year that the election is to take place.

An S corporation must file an information return with the IRS, but it pays no federal income tax. Instead, profits and losses are passed on to shareholders, and monies are treated as personal income. This helps to avoid double taxation on profits and allows losses to be deducted (up to the shareholder's investment in the S corporation). Excess losses may be carried over from previous years on personal returns—subject to limitations that are best described by an accountant familiar with current IRS regulations.

An S corporation may have up to 75 stockholders, none of whom can be foreign or corporate entities. In addition, an S corporation cannot be a subsidiary of another corporation. Other rules are equally stringent. Some states do not recognize S corporations as distinct from regular corporations for purposes of state income tax.

LOAN-OUT CORPORATIONS

Individuals active in the entertainment business have often used "loan-out corporations" as a vehicle for providing their services. The theory of the loan-out corporation is simple enough. The individual forms a corporation which he or she controls. This corporation hires the individual who formed it, with the salary to be set from time to time to reflect the activity of the corporation and its other financial needs. Then the individual gets a job—either short-term (a writing, directing, or acting assignment) or long-term (becoming executive producer on a series). Instead of the individual being hired directly, the deal is made with the loan-out company, which in turn lends the services of its employee. In order to give the hiring company legal comfort that the individual will be committed to doing the work, the individual invariably signs an "inducement letter," which confirms that he or she will do the work and will look only to the loan-out corporation for compensation.

The original reason why many people in the television business set up loan-out companies was to take advantage of favorable tax breaks that were available to corporations but not to self-employed individuals. In particular, there were considerable advantages in the amount of pension monies that could be saved on a pre-tax basis. Over the years, most of the benefits have been eroded by reforms to the tax laws; furthermore, the IRS has taken a dim view of loan-out arrangements, and has challenged their use in some cases. Nonetheless, many people who have loan-out corporations have kept them in place, in part to preserve old benefits (such as existing pension and/or profit-sharing plans, or health-insurance relationships), in part because they provide some centralization to a fragmented set of employment relationships, and in part because certain kinds of deductions—such as those for a business car or a personal assistant—may be less scrutinized by the IRS if taken by a corporation rather than an individual.

Setting up and maintaining a loan-out corporation does involve some trouble and expense, so anyone who is considering forming one should consult with a tax advisor over the potential costs and benefits.

FOREIGN ENTITIES

With the increased globalization of television, video, and other media, many foreign entities are now doing business in the U.S. These entities will have their own names, rules and forms, governed by the laws of the country in which they are established. Any entity (a corporation or an individual) not resident in the U.S. that is judged to be "doing business" in the U.S. may be liable for U.S. income taxation, and subject to state corporate qualification. If U.S. taxes apply, then the company must fill out a tax return covering all worldwide income allocable to the U.S., and must pay at the applicable standard rate (for example, personal or corporate). Cross-border co-production deals can be deemed to be partnerships doing business in the U.S., and potential foreign-production partners should structure the arrangement to avoid U.S. tax involvement. A non-resident foreign entity which is not judged to be doing business in the U.S. may receive income earned from business dealings with U.S. companies or from passive investments in the U.S. without filing a U.S. return—although a withholding tax of up to 30 percent will often be deducted at the source of payment. This approach can be varied by tax treaties, which frequently exist between the countries in question.

TAX ISSUES

BUSINESS DEDUCTIONS

Many people in the television business are self-employed, or work freelance, without a permanent business affiliation. For tax purposes, these people will need to deduct a variety of expenses related to their work. Unfortunately, the IRS has made the deduction of many of these expenses more and more difficult. For instance, freelancers often work out of their homes, and would like to deduct the expense of a home office. This is now possible only if the home office is fully dedicated (100 percent) to work purposes: a desk in the corner of what is otherwise a bedroom, living room, or family study will not qualify. In addition, home-office expenses can only be deducted from the income which the business conducted from that office actually produces.

Home workers are often writers or artists. The IRS has required writers to hold off on deducting some kinds of writing expenses on projects until the project is completed. The IRS also generally forces a writer to treat advances as taxable income when the advances are actually received, as opposed to delaying until delivery of the finished work.

PRODUCTION ADVANCES, EXPENSES, AND COSTS

The tax treatment of production advances, expenses, and costs can be a source of potential problems to a production company. On the expense side, a television project is a capital asset, and the expenses associated with its development and production should be capitalized by the producing entity until such time as the project is put into distribution, sold off, or abandoned. If it is sold or abandoned, all of the costs then become deductible. If the project is put into distribution, or the producer otherwise retains an ongoing participation, the costs are deductible over a period of time. This period is usually the anticipated economic life of the program as calculated using the "income forecast method," which ties the deductibility to the rate at which the anticipated revenues are received.

In most instances, however, the producer will have received advances over the course of the production to help finance the program. In a worst-case scenario, the IRS could characterize these advances as income that is taxable when received—yet not allow any deduction of the related expenses until the program is delivered or shown. If these two events—the receipt of the advance, and the showing or delivery of the project—fall in different tax years, it is conceivable that there could be a distorted amount of income recognized. Most production companies avoid this by claiming that they are not in receipt of the advance until the program is delivered, and that until that point, the advance is really just a non-taxable loan. They also point out that if the advance is income, then the show has in effect gone into service already, so that they should deduct its expenses. Unfortunately, the theoretical underpinnings of these arguments may be open to question. Any production company that is likely to be receiving substantial production advances should consult with tax advisors to help structure ways to avoid unrealistic bulges in taxable income.

PART 7

International Television

46

An Introduction to Global Television

In the U.S., television programming is largely a domestic affair: aside from occasional British programs shown on U.S. public television stations, the vast majority of programs seen on U.S. television are produced in the U.S. In most other countries, however, domestic productions share the schedule with imports.

In the past decade, two major forces have conspired to change television in almost every country. One is a move toward the addition of terrestrial television stations and networks. The other is the popularity of new national and international networks delivered via satellite.

FOREIGN DISTRIBUTION OF U.S. PROGRAMS

Network shows are usually distributed by the international distribution arm of the producing studio, or, if the program was independently produced, through the international arm of a domestic syndication company.

Programs produced for pay or basic cable TV may be handled by the international sales arm of the network, or may be licensed to another distributor.

Shows produced for first-run domestic syndication are sold by the syndicator's own international department. Larger syndication companies operate offices in key television markets worldwide, and serve smaller markets through commissioned sales representatives. The sale of *format rights* is common for game shows and some other non-fiction programs. *Family Feud, Wheel of Fortune, Jeopardy!,* and *Sesame Street* are among the U.S. series whose formats have been adapted for production in other countries.

Joint ventures are common, but they are not limited to individual programs or series; many networks are also created as joint ventures between a large U.S. or European television company and a local media company in, for example, an Asian country. These combinations come about for several reasons, including shared production requirements, investment, and a desire to deepen business relationships for future projects.

FOREIGN DISTRIBUTION OF U.S. NETWORKS

Many U.S. cable networks are international. The approach to international distribution varies. Many are partnerships, joint ventures, and related collaborations with media companies in their home companies. Generally, the U.S. program schedule forms the basis for the local schedule, with programs of local interest substituted as necessary. Each channel works the delicate balance between significant local presence and U.S. exports (attitudes toward the U.S. and its programming, and the degree to which U.S. ideas are permitted to become a part of another country's culture, tend to vary). Programs are often dubbed in the local language. This works to the advantage of Cartoon Network, whose animated programs tend to be entertaining in any language.

Nickelodeon, although clearly centered in the U.S., operates in over 90 countries. The network's creative executives meet regularly to share development and production ideas.

The various MTV operations in Europe, Asia, and Latin America take a different approach. The format is generally exported, but the programming is not. Music tends to be culturally specific, and stars in one country may be unknown in another. Then again, CMT (Country Music Television) is often taken as representative of a distinctive U.S. musical genre. It travels surprisingly well.

Some networks, like Hallmark Entertainment and National Geographic, are not currently available in the U.S.

A few other countries export their networks. In the English-speaking world, the BBC is seen almost everywhere. In the Spanish-language world, Spain's TVE International is also ubiquitous. Many networks created in one European country are seen in several. This is largely a result of cable and satellite channel capacity; the programming is not tailored to other cultures.

OVERVIEW OF WORLD TELEVISION MARKETS

Many U.S. companies see the world in two discrete halves: our country and the other countries. Since the individual markets outside the U.S. can be difficult to comprehend, the natural—and invalid—assumption is that each country's system is in some way based upon a U.S. model. Indeed, some systems were originally based upon a U.S. model, but they have since evolved. In some countries, the government or an agency owns and operates the television networks. Some countries permit private networks, but only in partnership with the government. And although it may be convenient to refer to "Japanese television" as if all of Japan's networks function as a single entity, NHK and Fuji are very different companies.

Canada is the largest market for programs produced in the U.S.; programs from the U.K. and Australia are seen about as often in Canada as they are in the U.S. Most French-language programs seen on Canadian television are produced domestically. In order to protect Canada's national identity, a quota system for domestic programs is in effect.

Germany, the U.K., France, Spain, and Italy are the most active buyers and sellers of television programming in Western Europe. The Scandinavian and Benelux countries are medium-sized markets. The importance of television in Eastern Europe is growing, and as the business climate stabilizes, investment is increasing and audiences are growing. Pan-European networks, generally specializing in a particular type of programming, are seen throughout the western part of the continent via DBS and cable systems.

Japan and Australia are only slightly smaller than the largest European markets. Japanese companies occasionally co-produce with European broadcasters, and own, either jointly or wholly, worldwide entertainment companies. Australia supplies some English-language programming seen in the U.S., the U.K., and elsewhere. Taiwan, Hong Kong, the Philippines, Thailand, India, China, and South Korea are all considered to be smaller markets for Western-style programming. Language and cultural issues are beginning to melt away, as television exerts its considerable power on older cultures.

In Latin America, Mexico and Brazil are medium-sized markets dominated by large, powerful networks. Mexico is a leading supplier of Spanish-language programs seen in the U.S. and throughout Latin America; Venezuela is also a vital player in South America. The smaller countries, and the islands, buy programming, but their populations are generally small, so license fees are low.

The Middle Eastern countries are minor markets, often with tough censorship rules. African nations are not considered vital television markets, but South Africa and Egypt are emerging as significant regional players. Slow growth of terrestrial television is no longer a major issue; stations are easily received by any household with a TV and a satellite dish. As Africa slowly becomes more westernized, cultural differences become less significant. Still, a general lack of involvement in the global business marketplace makes most African and Arab countries marginal players in terms of television.

Rapid changes in technology, politics, and economics are certain to alter the pecking order overseas. The importance of Asian countries is likely to grow, and some countries in Latin America, and Africa are likely to mature into robust markets as new media develop and systems of distribution become more sophisticated, and as international television companies seek new markets to compensate for mature growth in their primary territories.

TELEVISION STANDARDS

Three different systems are used throughout the world to record, play back, transmit, and receive television signals. NTSC is a system that transmits the television image at 525 lines per second. This system is the standard used in the U.S., Canada and Asia. It was developed in the U.S. and became the standard in 1954. A new form of digital television will slowly replace NTSC in the early years of the next century. This system is described in detail in Chapter 10.

PAL, a 625-line system, was developed in Germany. PAL is used in the U.K., Western Europe (except France), and much of South America.

SECAM, developed by the French, is the standard for France; like PAL, it uses 625 lines. SECAM is also the system predominant in Africa, because of French political involvement on that continent during the period when television standards were being adopted. SECAM is the system used throughout the Middle East; a modified version is the standard in Eastern Europe and the former Soviet Union.

Digital television and HDTV are beginning to change the adherence to old standards (see Chapter 10 for details). Because both PAL and SECAM were first adopted in 1967, more than 15 years after the NTSC standard was adopted, both systems are superior to NTSC, offering greater image clarity.

Tapes recorded in one system cannot be played on a video player from another—an NTSC tape, for example, cannot be played on a PAL or SECAM videotape machine. Multi-standard VCRs and TV sets are becoming available, though, at reasonable prices for consumers. It is also possible to hire a facility to convert tapes from one standard to another, with generally acceptable results.

A LOOK AT WORLD TV VIEWERS

The number of TV households does not always equate with strong programming markets. Some countries, such as India, program primarily in local languages and buy a limited number of programs from U.S., European, and Asian program suppliers. And although the Netherlands has a relatively small population, the country's networks are a solid market for European and U.S. programming. Although China may represent a large number of TV households, an accurate count is difficult to find. China is not a major buyer of programming from outside sources. (Sources include *BiB World Guide to Television* and other industry trade publications.)

	(APPROXIMATE TV HOUSEHOLDS IN MILLIONS)
UNITED STATES	97
RUSSIA	56
INDIA	50
JAPAN	44
BRAZIL	35
GERMANY	34
UNITED KINGDOM	24
FRANCE	22
ITALY	19
INDONESIA	18
MEXICO	18
TURKEY	14
THAILAND	13
SPAIN	12
POLAND	12
SOUTH KOREA	12
CANADA	11
ARGENTINA	10
PHILIPPINES	9
NIGERIA	9
COLOMBIA	7
ROMANIA	7
AUSTRALIA	6
PAKISTAN	6
NETHERLANDS	6
VIETNAM	6
TAIWAN	5
SOUTH AFRICA	5

47

Canada

Since its inception in the 1930s, broadcasting in Canada has been a mix of public and private endeavors. Adopting the most appealing aspects of the U.S. and the U.K. systems, Canada developed its own model, with one additional twist. Because Canada is home to two different cultures—each with its own language—there are both English-language and French-language broadcasters.

For nearly half a century, Canadian broadcasters offered a mix of U.S. programs and their own original productions. Critics complained because U.S. television programs did not promote, or even recognize, Canadian identity. Rules regarding Canadian content, the employment of Canadian creative and technical talent, production and post-production done in Canada—all of these were attempts to nurture a Canadian identity through television. By the mid-1990s, new cable networks were set up as primarily Canadian companies, often with strict requirements regarding Canadian content ("CanCon"). And in 1997, the Canadian Broadcasting Corporation began broadcasting 100 percent Canadian programming in its prime-time schedule.

Approximately 28.5 million people live in Canada. There are 17 million TV sets, more than one per home.

THE CANADIAN BROADCASTING CORPORATION (CBC)

Founded in 1936 as Canada's version of the BBC, the government-owned Canadian Broadcasting Corporation (CBC) operates radio and television networks and other services in English and in French. The television operations are supported by tax revenues (about $900 million Canadian) and by commercial revenues (about $300

million), such as advertising and foreign sales of CBC productions. The CBC owns and operates television stations (English and
French) in the provincial capitals and other large cities. In smaller
cities and outlying regions, CBC programming is carried by privately owned affiliates. The network employs over 8,000 people.
The CBC operates a pair of domestic radio networks plus Radio
Canada International, an international radio service. The CBC's main
headquarters are in Ottawa; the English-speaking networks are
based in Toronto, and the French-speaking networks, in Montreal.

ENGLISH-LANGUAGE NETWORKS AND STATIONS

CBC ENGLISH TELEVISION NETWORK

The CBC English Television Network offers a wide range of entertainment, sports, children's, news, and other types of programming.

Prime-time schedules tend to be the same on every CBC station.
Daytime schedules vary, but the program types and sources are
essentially similar. CBC provides regular coverage of hockey and
baseball, the two most popular sports in Canada.

Local CBC stations provide additional news, public-affairs, and
children's programming. Private CBC affiliates buy their own programming to supplement the CBC schedule.

The 1996 changeover to Canadian prime-time content came about
as a result of several factors: increasing competition from strong
commercial networks who simply outbid the CBC for the best properties, the need for change in a much-criticized network, and an
honest belief that Canada's public broadcast network should strongly
emphasize Canadian life. The formula has worked, in part because
of long-established comedy hits such as *This Hour Has 22 Minutes,*
produced by Salter Films of Halifax, Nova Scotia. (The network's
top program, it reaches about 1.5 million viewers on its first airing
each week, and about a million more on a repeat during the same
week, and on CBC's Newsworld cable service.)

The daily CBC schedule begins with two hours of *The CBC
Morning News* (7:00 A.M.–9:00 A.M.), followed by children's pro-
gramming, notably the pre-school hit *Fred Penner's Place,* and
Sesame Park (the Canadian version of *Sesame Street,* staged in a
Canadian park setting with Canadian Muppets). Children's pro-
gramming continues until 11:30 A.M.; a sitcom makes the transition
to a noon news/service hour, followed by some soaps *(Coronation
Street, All My Children)*. After a late-afternoon mix of cooking,
games, and sitcoms (including, in 1997, *Family Matters, The
Simpsons,* and *The Fresh Prince of Bel-Air)*, then it's off to a local

news hour at 6:00 P.M., magazine shows from 7:00 P.M. until 8:00 P.M., and a mix of documentary, comedies, movies, until the 10:00 P.M. news, a longtime staple known as *The National*. Local news follows at 11:00 P.M.; some comedy and a movie closes out the day. Weekend schedules differ, often with more family programming and sports.

CTV TELEVISION NETWORK

The English-speaking CTV network was formed in the early 1960s by privately owned commercial stations operating in several large Canadian cities. Sixteen stations own the network; in addition, a handful of supplemental affiliates, mainly in smaller cities, carry its shows (for a total of 25 stations in the network). The network supplies national news and most prime-time entertainment. Stations produce some local programs, then fill in the rest of the schedule with acquisitions, largely from the U.S. CTV supports itself through advertising revenues. For its 1994–99 license, CTV agreed to broadcast approximately 3 hours per week of Canadian drama, 48 hours per year of Canadian mini-series, movies, and the like, and 18 hours of Canadian specials, plus one hour per week of children's programming.

CTV's schedule is intended to attract large audiences; this is accomplished, mostly, through licensed prime-time series and syndicated talk shows from the U.S.

Baton Broadcasting, a Toronto-based firm, owns 24 stations in Ontario, Saskatchewan, and Alberta. Baton is CTV's largest shareholder, and controls three specialty channels: Outdoor Life, Talk TV, and The Comedy Network. Baton's BBS Productions is also a leading program supplier.

CANWEST GLOBAL SYSTEM

CanWest Global covers about three-quarters of English-speaking Canada. This story begins in 1974, when an early version of the company was licensed to operate a Winnipeg station. The station became dependent upon Global Television for its programming, but Global did not do well during its early years, and the Winnipeg station led a coalition of stations—MITV (Maritime Provinces), CKND (Winnipeg), STV (Saskatchewan), UTV (Vancouver), and Global Television (Toronto)—into what became CanWest Global, Canada's most profitable network. CanWest Global reaches about three-quarters of Canada. Over half of its overall schedule is Canadian content, nearly all of which is acquired from Canada's thriving production community. U.S. series also do well, notably *Seinfeld, The X-Files, Friends, NYPD Blue,* and so on. Hockey is also a major attraction. CanWest Global has also invested in New Zealand's TV3 and Australia's Network Ten. The approach there, as in Canada, is strictly business—advertisers want 18–49, and that's what they get throughout the CanWest Global system.

WIC (WESTERN INTERNATIONAL COMMUNICATIONS)

Vancouver-based WIC operates in television, radio, pay TV and satellite services; the company owns eight television stations. On the pay TV side, it operates Superchannel (a pay movie channel in western Canada), MovieMax (another pay service), and Home Theater (a pay-per-view network). With Astral (another Canadian media company), WIC owns The Family Channel, a pay service for children's and family programming. ExpressVu, a DBS service, is also partially owned by WIC.

INDEPENDENT ENGLISH-LANGUAGE STATIONS

Early in the 1970s, the Canadian Radio-Television Commission licensed independent stations for the first time. Toronto's CityTV is a unique alternative to traditional broadcasting. Operating on a "small is beautiful" principle, CityTV started with a young staff, portable video equipment, and innovative, inexpensive, and highly localized programming. In time, CityTV has evolved into a hip urban station with three specialties: news, music, and movies. CityTV programs on fashion and lifestyle are regularly exported to other countries, including the U.S.

REGIONAL ENGLISH-LANGUAGE NETWORKS AND STATIONS

The CRTC has licensed numerous regional broadcasters, often with an educational or public-service charter. These include ACCESS (Alberta), CFCF12 (Montreal), SCN (Saskatchewan), and TVOntario.

TVOntario (TVO), operated by the Ontario Educational Communications Authority, started in 1970 with a mission: to educate Ontarians of all ages. TVO provides English-language programming throughout the province (it also operates a parallel French service called TFO). Some 70 percent of TVO's content (and 60 percent of TFO's content) is Canadian; still, the networks have long participated in the international children's marketplace. TVO also operates OLA, which covers the Ontario Legislature.

TVO is particularly notable for its children's programming. Every morning, TVO programs four and a half hours of *Get Ready to*

Learn, for pre-schoolers. *TVO Kids* occupies three and a half hours every weekday afternoon. These programs respect diverse learning styles, and address gender, bias, and other issues. TVOntario produces approximately 200 hours of original children's programming each year.

FRENCH-LANGUAGE NETWORKS AND STATIONS

French-language television is parallel in structure to the English-language system. The CBC's French network is Société de Radio-Canada (SRC). Headquartered in Montreal, SRC owns and operates eight stations in Quebec City and in other French-speaking city centers, and completes its national network with five private affiliates. Canadian content fills 80 percent of SRC's prime-time schedule.

Television Quatre Saisons (TQS) is another network of privately owned stations throughout Quebec. Approximately half of its schedule must be Canadian content. Both networks offer a commercial program schedule of children's, news, comedy, drama, and variety shows.

Télé-Québec, primarily funded by Quebec's provincial government, is an educational station. Secondary funding is received via sale of commercial time during specific dayparts. The daytime schedule is educational. In prime-time, Télé-Québec competes with a select group of dramas, some original productions, some shows produced in France, and some independent productions. Canadian content accounts for 80 percent of total broadcast hours.

As a rule, French-language broadcasters show a far higher percentage of Canadian-made programming than their English-language counterparts. Little is imported from France because the cultural differences are too pronounced; tolerance for dubbed or subtitled programming is also low. As a result, a vibrant French-language production community has grown up in and around Montreal.

CANADIAN RADIO-TELEVISION AND TELECOMMUNICATIONS COMMISSION (CRTC)

Canada's regulatory body for all forms of television, radio, telephone and satellite communications is the Canadian Radio-Television and Telecommunications Commission (CRTC). The CRTC works as an independent agency with administrative and quasi-judicial authority. It is responsible to Parliament through the Minister of Canadian Heritage. It's based in Ottawa, and maintains offices throughout Canada. From the CRTC's mission statement: "We aim to help Canadians better understand how their values and diversities shape Canada's unique personality in the world. We do so by regulating our broadcasting and telecommunications industries in open, flexible ways to foster creative freedom and strengthen the prosperity of all our citizens."

The CRTC is staffed by a chairman plus thirteen full-time and six part-time commissioners. The part-time commissioners from different regions add regional balance to the commission. All commissioners participate in public hearings and decision-making regarding broadcasting; only full-time commissioners are involved in telecommunications issues.

The day-to-day operations of the CRTC are supervised by four executives. The Secretary General is in charge of broadcast planning, analysis, distribution and technology, as well as licensing, finance, human resources, and several other areas. In addition, the CRTC senior staff includes an Executive Director for Telecommunications, a Senior General Counsel, and a Director of Public Affairs (for a detailed description of the CRTC's organization, and for additional information about the commission, visit www.crtc.ga.ca).

The commission takes a more active role in controlling Canadian broadcast programming than, for example, the FCC does in the U.S.

In order to keep Canadian culture distinct from U.S. culture, the CRTC requires that a certain percentage of programming seen on Canadian networks and stations support a Canadian-content agenda. The degree to which a particular program satisfies the Canadian-content requirement is determined by a formula that considers such factors as cast, story line, setting, casting, production personnel, and production and post-production facilities. Private television licensees must maintain an average of not less than 60 percent Canadian content through their daily schedules, and 50 percent in their prime-time schedules, for example.

The CRTC imposes many restrictions and limitations on the use of the public airwaves. Hard liquor is one of several product categories that cannot be advertised on Canadian television (this type of restriction exists in most countries). In addition, scripts for food products are subject to approval. Abusive language is not permitted, on the grounds that society must be protected.

The commission licenses stations, renews licenses, and issues sanctions when a problem exists. Occasionally, it will attach conditions to a station's broadcast license or license renewal. For example, if better work in children's programming is desired (or demanded) by the public, this will be stipulated in the license grant. If complaints have come to the attention of the CRTC regarding cultural stereotyping, violence, or other objections, the CRTC may act on these matters as well. The CRTC's highest priority, though, is ensuring that broadcasters provide a substantial quantity of high-quality Canadian programming. If a broadcaster has been financially successful, the CRTC may increase the quota of Canadian content required, or the amount of money spent on Canadian productions. This is quite different from the way that the FCC, and most other regulatory bodies, operate. Much of the reason for this unusual relationship between regulators and broadcasters is Canada's population distribution (the population is concentrated in a small number of cities, with vast open spaces and a large gap between the east and west coasts) as well as the view that Canadian broadcasters must be protected from the vast influence of the U.S. At the core of the CRTC philosophy is what is often called "the old Canadian schizophrenia"—a belief that unfettered free enterprise alone will not allow success without some government involvement.

Still, the CRTC does not act as a censor. In fact, the CRTC does not intervene with regard to specific programs, only to general programming direction.

A new Broadcasting Act was passed in 1991, granting the CRTC jurisdiction over cable television, satellite delivery, fiber optics, and other new technologies. The CRTC does not regulate home video.

CABLE TELEVISION

The CRTC has awarded licenses for exclusive service to approximately 2,000 cable systems; three in four Canadian households subscribe. In smaller communities, one cable company serves the entire population; in larger communities, the CRTC divides the city into zones, and several companies provide exclusive service. Three multiple-system owners (MSOs) dominate: Rogers Cable TV, with 51 systems, has 2.6 million subscribers; Shaw Cablevision, based in Calgary, is second with 101 systems and 1.6 million subscribers; Montreal-based Vidéotron is in third place with 1.2 million subs in 45 systems. Rogers has 32 percent of the market; Shaw, 20 percent; and Vidéotron, 15 percent. Two more Quebec-based cable companies, OF Cable TV and Cogeco Cable, each have 5 percent. The remaining quarter of the country is served by smaller systems, most with fewer than 100,000 subscribers.

In Canadian cable's early years, access to U.S. channels was a primary selling point; in some areas, reception was also primary. Most high-profile U.S. programs are currently available on Canadian networks—either through commercial broadcasters or through Canada's many specialty channels.

In order to protect Canadian broadcasters, who depend upon Canadian advertisers for income, the rule of *simultaneous substitution* applies to cable systems. If the CBC and CBS both carry *Dallas*, for example, the cable operator must substitute the CBC signal (with CBC commercials intact) in place of the CBS signal. The reasoning is that since the CBS affiliate in Buffalo, New York (for example), is not licensed to operate in Toronto, it should not profit from Toronto's viewership.

The CRTC also regulates cable rates. When the cable system is first set up, the CRTC approves fees and small increases; from that point on, the CRTC must also approve large fee increases. The costs for basic cable service and for pay channels are roughly comparable to the rates charged in the U.S.

CABLE NETWORKS (SPECIALTY SERVICES)

Canada's basic cable services—called specialty services—earn revenue via both commercials and per-subscriber fees. They are licensed by the CRTC, and are required to satisfy Canadian-content requirements. Unless otherwise noted, these networks are based in Toronto.

YTV broadcasts a 22-hour schedule of programming for children and families. It's the Canadian home of *Goosebumps, ReBoot, Are You Afraid of the Dark?*, and Canadian series like *What-a-Mess TV*. It's owned by Shaw Cable.

Bravo! is a performing arts channel with a somewhat flexible scheduling strategy that accommodates both short and long works, and allows commercials only during program breaks. The programming encompasses not only the usual music and dance, but also cinema, discussion, and experimental arts.

CMT (Country Music Television) plays both American and Canadian country music videos. Part of the objective in creating this network was the promotion of Canadian artists. If a Canadian video satisfies some fairly rigid rules (regarding the artist's and the production team's Canadian heritage), it will be played at least 30 times, and the producer will receive $150 per play (if the video is played more than 30 times, the producer can collect a maximum of $15,000).

TCN (The Comedy Network) is owned by Baton Broadcasting (with lesser percentages owned by Shaw Cable, Astral, and Les Films Rozon). The programming consists of comedy series, standups, etc.

Life Network is a general-interest channel that emphasizes health, home and garden, and outdoors programming.

H&E (The History & Entertainment Network) is a partnership between CTV and a leading Canadian/international producer, Alliance Communications. Programming is mostly documentaries with an emphasis on Canadian history. Canadian content requirements are keyed to subscriber growth: 40 percent up to 4 million subscribers, 50 percent up to 5 million. A minimum of 180 hours of Canadian history programs must be produced each year.

WTN (Women's Television Network), based in Winnipeg, broadcasts 70 percent information and service programming. For entertainment and dramatic programs, women are generally in the key decision-making roles. The network produces and funds a wide range of programming, from music to comedies.

CTV N1 is a 24-hour news channel from the CTV Television Network. It's 100 percent Canadian content.

Vision TV is a non-profit network that leases its schedule to bona fide religious groups. The network also produces discussion and documentary programs, and some dramas.

CLT (Canadian Learning Television) is owned by CHUM, another independent Toronto station (with some partners including the BBC). It's a 24-hour adult-education channel offering credit course-work. The network is one of several recent licensees; it is set to debut in 1999.

MuchMoreMusic is also owned by CHUM. Its intended audience is adult, and its mix encompasses not only pop, but blues, reggae, New Age, and country. At least 30 percent of each week's music videos must be Canadian, and at least 60 percent of the overall program schedule must be Canadian as well. It's coming in 1999.

Also set for 1999 are the following: Prime TV, based outside Toronto in Don Mills, will serve a 50-plus audience; it's owned by Global and CanWest. ROBTV (Report on Business TV) will be a 24-hour business news channel. Space: The Imagination Station will be a science fiction and fact network from CHUM. Sportscope Plus will be a sports news and feature service. Star-TV, also from CHUM, will provide entertainment news. S3 Regional Sports Service will combine four regional feeds to provide wide-ranging sports coverage; owners are CTV, Molson, Rogers, and LMC International. Talk TV will feature roughly 70 percent Canadian content; it's owned by a Baton subsidary. Teletoon—owned by The Family Channel (a Canadian operation unrelated to the U.S. network), YTV, and by Cinar and Nelvana, two leading animation firms—will feature animated programs. The network will include a French-speaking feed. Treehouse TV, from YTV, will feature pre-school programming from 6:00 A.M.–9:00 P.M., then programs for parents and caregivers at night.

U.S. cable networks generally participate in the Canadian specialty channel marketplace with Canadian partners. Discovery Channel, based in Willowdale, Ontario, is positioned as an international channel with documentaries, and scientific and technical programs. HGTV Canada, set for 1999 availability, is only 20 percent owned by Scripps Howard (which owns the U.S.-based HGTV, or Home & Garden Television Network). Content is gardening/landscaping, building/remodeling, home decorating/interior design, hobbies/ crafts, and special interests. Outdoor Life is a joint venture between Baton, Ralph Ellis Corporation, and the U.S.-based Outdoor Life Network (seen mainly via DBS in the U.S.). It's coming in 1999, and must program at least 30 percent Canadian content. It's managed by Baton, along with their other networks: Talk TV and TCN.

There are other regional specialty channels as well.

PAY SERVICES

The Family Channel, owned by WIC and Astral, fills 60 percent of its schedule with Disney programming. Still, it must adhere to a 30 percent CanCon requirement in prime-time. In addition, 11 hours per day must be children's programming.

TMN (The Movie Network) is a 24-hour premium movie service serving eastern Canada. In order to support its requirement for 30 percent CanCon in prime-time, TMN has become a major force in the production of new Canadian motion pictures (spending over $240 million from 1983 until the end of its first license period in 2001). It's owned by Astral. The same owner operates MoviePix, a second pay service that shows films from the 1960s–1980s with a schedule of at least 20 percent CanCon. MoviePix is also involved with film restoration.

Superchannel is western Canada's pay movie network. It's operated out of Edmonton, Alberta, and subject to 25–30 percent CanCon requirements. It's considerably smaller than TMN, with just 250,000 subs.

PAY-PER-VIEW

Viewer's Choice is the brand name for Canada's pay-per-view services. Viewer's Choice Canada (VCC) operates 19 channels for 550,000 subscribers in eastern Canada. TMN, Rogers, and NetStar own the business. Home Theatre/Viewer's Choice West is the smaller service for western Canada.

CTV also operates Sports/Specials PPV. Partners are Molson and LMC. The CanCon requirement is 20 percent.

FRENCH SPECIALTY CHANNELS

Most specialty channels are English-language. Some have French equivalents. They're generally based in Montreal. RDI (Le Réseau de l'Information) is a 24-hour all-news channel. Le Canal View is very specific in its target demographic: ages 35–64. Programming focuses on quality-of-life issues, health, and the outdoors and takes the format of talk, documentary, service and movies. Canadian content fills half the day. Musimax serves the same demographic with a 24-hour music video schedule; it's owned by Montreal's Radiomutuel and Toronto's CHUM. Its license requires 60 percent Canadian content.

48

Europe

In almost every Western European nation, the number of viewing choices has increased at least tenfold in the 1990s. Until the 1980s, most nations licensed one or two public and one or two private broadcast networks. The number of broadcast licenses generally increased, allowing all viewers (or, all viewers in a country's most populous regions) access to additional programming. With cable, new channels were developed, imported from other countries (in some cases), and, (in some other cases), organized based upon U.S. models, often with U.S. partners. Every country's situation is different, but most require some degree of domestic ownership and control over their networks.

Europe leads the world in the purchase of U.S. programming. In general, properties are licensed before the programs are actually produced. The reason: a very competitive marketplace.

PAN-EUROPEAN SERVICES

Pan-European networks now serve viewers in multiple countries. With digital satellites, increased channel capacity has dramatically increased the number of available networks, and the degree to which one nation's television networks are shared with another country.

The prime example is Eurosport, owned in thirds by ESPN, France's TF1, and Canal Plus. The network presents soccer, tennis, motor sports, athletics, boxing, and skiing, each with local-language commentary. Approximately 20 million households watch Eurosport daily. Two-thirds of its viewers are male. It's supported by fees paid by cable and satellite operators, and by advertisers.

THE UNITED KINGDOM

The U.K. is the second largest English-language market in the world, and the second largest television market in Europe (Germany is first). There are 24 million TV households, roughly one-fourth as many as in the U.S. British viewers tend to be keen on their BBC, ITV, and perhaps, Channel 4. Cable and satellite penetration is under 25 percent.

Broadcasting began in the United Kingdom in 1922 as a private collaboration of radio manufacturers operating their own stations. Five years later, the British Broadcasting Corporation (BBC) was established by royal charter. In 1954, Parliament passed a bill authorizing a second government-owned broadcasting corporation, the Independent Television Authority, later renamed the Independent Broadcasting Authority (IBA). In 1991, the IBA was succeeded by the Independent Television Commission (ITC). The ITC regulates privately operated broadcast and cable companies.

BBC

The BBC operates two television networks seen throughout the U.K.: BBC 1 and BBC 2. (In fact, there are four sub-networks within each network, covering England, Scotland, Northern Ireland, and Wales.) Each employs its own program staff, which acquires, produces, finances, and co-produces large numbers of programs. The BBC started television broadcasts before World War II, hit a high point as 20 million people watched Queen Elizabeth's coronation in 1953, and has since been one of the world's leading broadcast organizations. BBC 2 was launched in 1964.

BBC 1, the more popular of the two networks, is generally considered to be the mainstream service. There are six program categories, each supervised by a head of programming. Light Entertainment includes variety shows and situation comedy (Wallace and Gromit's animated adventures, *Men Behaving Badly*). Drama comprises long- and short-term series *(EastEnders, Pride & Prejudice)*. U.S. drama series seen on BBC 1 include *Chicago Hope* and *The X-Files. Neighbours,* from Australia, has been very successful. Sports Programming features tennis, soccer, cricket, golf, snooker, horse racing, and other sports. General Interest offers programs such as *Antiques Roadshow* (the highest-rated general-interest program in the U.K.). News and Current Affairs is responsible for the *Six O'Clock News, Nine O'Clock News, Breakfast Time* (which resembles *The Today Show* or *Good Morning America)*, and some documentary/magazine shows. Programmes for Children and Family covers a wide range of shows. *The National Lottery Live,* seen on Saturday nights, is especially popular, and the longtime favorite *Top of the Pops* is still seen on weekends.

In theory, BBC 2 features programs for narrower audiences, and although its ratings are often half the size of BBC 1's, the second network has developed many hits. BBC 2 is responsible for some of the popular dramatic shows seen in the U.S. and worldwide, as well as specialties such as the Chelsea Flower Show, *The Nature of Australia*, and the World Snooker Final. It also programs cutting edge comedies such as *The Thin Blue Line* (a Rowan Atkinson venture poking fun at the police), and an anarchic celebrity quiz called *Shooting Stars*. BBC 2 allots time for programming of interest to specific ethnic groups. Acquisitions include *Seinfeld,* and *The Larry Sanders Show.* BBC 2 also offers adult-education programming, for credit. BBC 1 generally averages a market share in the low 30s; BBC 2's is about one-third that size.

BBC 1 spends a good deal more money on its programs than BBC 2: an average of about 120,000 pounds per hour compared with about 90,000 pounds per hour on BBC 2. The biggest per-program investment is in drama, with an average of about $750,000 per hour. Documentaries cost about a third as much. Children's programs cost an eighth as much. (These numbers are reasonably consistent for worldwide production, but the BBC routinely offers a great deal of quality per production dollar.) BBC 1 produces about 1,000 hours of feature films and documentaries per year, compared with about 900 from BBC 2. Both networks produce in excess of 600 hours of sports coverage. The big differences are in children's programs (400 vs. 200 hours), music programs (about 10 vs. about 50), dramas (375 vs. 80), and light entertainment (550 vs. 350). BBC 1 produces over 3,000 hours of news per year, compared with about 2,500 on BBC 2, but BBC 2 adds a few hundred hours of parliamentary coverage, which is only sampled on BBC 1. Both networks acquire about 2,000 hours of feature films and television series annually. Approximately half of the 20,000 hours of television produced annually by the BBC is made by the BBC's London office. Midlands, North and South each contribute roughly 1,500 hours per year, with the remainder supplied by Northern Ireland, Scotland, and Wales.

BBC's television operations are funded by a mandatory license fee, essentially a user tax on television sets ($135 per year per household), plus a government subsidy. In the mid-1980s, the BBC employed over 25,000 people; the number has come down since that time.

In the 1990s, the BBC was reorganized into six divisions: BBC Broadcast, BBC Production, BBC News, BBC Worldwide, BBC Resources, and the BBC Corporate Center. Radio and television are jointly managed within these divisions. This reorganization was done, in part, to take advantage of digital television and international opportunities.

BBC World, which launched in 1991 as BBC World Service Television, was relaunched as BBC Europe in 1995, and subsequently renamed. This news and information service is currently available to 45 million households in 114 countries. BBC World programs are also seen on many airlines. BBC Prime is a 24-hour entertainment channel seen in Europe; it reaches just over 4 million subscribers with programs from BBC 1 and BBC 2 (75 percent of the schedule), and from Thames Television (25 percent). Both channels are managed by a joint venture between Pearson (a large media company), Cox Communications (a U.S.-based cable and TV operator), and the BBC. After years of on-again, off-again discussions, the BBC is seriously planning to enter the U.S. market, initially with the help of Discovery Networks, and subsequently, as its own entity.

An all-news channel called BBC News 24 debuted in 1997. It competes directly with CNN International (which covers world news but a relatively small percentage of U.K. news), and with Sky News (a U.K. service from News Corp.)

In addition, for the digital satellite systems, there are eight more BBC channels, all available via subscription. They are: BBC Showcase (entertainment), BBC Horizon (documentaries and nature), BBC Style (lifestyles), BBC Learning Arena (arts), BBC Sport, BBC Catch-up (reruns of popular series shown a few days after their BBC airings), and BBC One (music).

The BBC also operates five domestic radio networks: BBC Radio 1 (pop music), BBC Radio 2 (middle-of-the-road/easy listening), BBC Radio 3 (classical), BBC Radio 4 (news, drama, general-interest), and BBC Radio 5 (sports, news, talk, some music). In addition, the BBC operates local radio stations throughout the U.K. BBC External Services broadcasts in 35 languages to nations throughout the world; BBC World Service broadcasts worldwide in English via short-wave.

COMMERCIAL BROADCASTING: ITV

Despite a substantial faction of lawmakers who were originally opposed to the idea of commercially supported broadcasting (Lord Reith of the House of Lords likened it to the bubonic plague), advertiser-supported programming began in 1955 with the licensing of ITV. Regional commercial television stations now operate throughout the U.K. In the early 1990s, many of these licenses changed hands. Thames Television, for example, lost its weekday license for London broadcasting to Carlton; London Weekend

Television (LWT) maintained its license to work weekends on the same channel (this is an unusual arrangement; most licenses are granted to single broadcasters).

The commercial independents remain squarely in the entertainment business, producing and purchasing programs that are likely to garner the largest possible audiences for their advertisers. In real terms, this means game shows, situation comedies, popular motion pictures, soap operas, sports, news, and other mass-audience formats. The regional independents, as a whole, receive 90 percent of their income from advertising.

Carlton's daily schedule provides some insight. The day begins with 3¹/₂ hours of news and service programs, followed by a half-hour game show (Supermarket Sweep, in the 1996 schedule). Then, some local talk and magazine shows precede a lunchtime news program. The afternoon is soaps, then children's programs (a combination of live action, animated material like Scooby Doo, and science fiction for kids). Dinnertime is for news, but it's followed by Bruce Forsyth (longtime British entertainer) hosting The Price is Right (the format is licensed by a U.S. firm). Prime-time is about movies, sitcoms, and dramatic series, with a 10:00 P.M. newscast, followed by a movie. For years, Coronation Street has been one of the most popular ITV series; it is also a hit in Canada. Other ITV hit series include Emmerdale, Touching Evil, and an Australian import, Home & Away. ITV programs through the night with a mosiac that might consist of programs about the Internet, crime, late-night recipes, and music videos. This schedule is, by and large, carried by other ITV outlets in other cities through England.

With a market share in the mid-30s (slightly higher than BBC 1), ITV is the U.K.'s most popular network.

CHANNEL 4

In 1982, when Channel 4 was launched, founder Sir Jeremy Isaacs promised programs "for everybody some of the time." With grand intentions of offering a true programming alternative and a nursery for new forms and new methods of presenting ideas, Channel 4 has delivered distinctive programming, often for small audiences. Channel 4 does not create its own programming; instead, it finances (or co-finances) productions and purchases completed work. Its market share is approximately 10 percent.

In 1993, Channel 4 became a state corporation—not quite owned by the government, but closer to that concept than not. The network is entirely advertiser-supported. Channel 4 considers itself a "publisher-broadcaster"—all of its programs are acquired or commissioned from independent producers. The network does not produce any of its own programs. Roughly half of the schedule is programming from the U.S. It's also known as a source of film financing. Channel 4 completely financed *Trainspotting,* and was also involved with *Four Weddings and a Funeral, The Madness of King George,* and others.

The day's schedule begins with *The Big Breakfast,* a morning news and service show, followed by several hours of programs for use in schools. The afternoon is a mix of *Sesame Street,* racing, political coverage, game shows, and, in 1996, *Ricki Lake* from the U.S. at 5:00 P.M., followed by an old standby, *The Avengers* (with Patrick McNee and Diana Rigg). Prime-time programming is very much a mixed bag. *Bombay Blue* is an original police series shot in India; the lead, from Glasgow, deals with feelings of displacement as he tracks down drugs in thriller plot lines. *Brookside* is a long-running dramatic serial. *Cutting Edge* is a newsmagazine. *Drop the Dead Donkey* has been a very popular newsroom comedy series. *Leaving Home* was a seven-part series hosted by Sir Simon Rattle about twentieth century orchestral music. Channel 4 often programs limited series— and not just dramatic mini-series. *Equinox* is a prime-time science magazine series. One prime-time favorite is a witty comedy game, *Whose Line Is It Anyway?* Some U.S. imports, like *Ellen, Friends, Homicide: Life on the Street, Party of Five, E.R.,* and *NYPD Blue* fill out the prime-time schedule. *Right to Reply,* one of five shows that have been on for the entire life of the network, encourages outspoken viewers to challenge the network's programmers. On Sunday nights, *Art House* highlights all forms of visual and performing arts, and it's often edgy. *The Music School* covers a very wide range of music stories, from Ken Russell's search for English folk songs to 1960s girl singers like Marianne Faithfull. Travel programming include *The Lonely Planet* and *Routes Around the World.*

C5 (CHANNEL 5)

C5 was supposed to launch in 1994, but did not launch until the spring of 1997. The target audience for this commercial service is younger mainstream viewers, roughly 14–35 years old (this audience has been successfully served by Germany's Pro Sieben, France's M6, and FOX in the U.S.). A nightly movie, scheduled for 9:00 P.M., is intended to be a centerpiece. U.K. channels are typically programmed with different schedules each day and night; C5 is programmed more like a U.S. network, with the same programs "stripped" across the weekday schedule to build loyal viewership. A soap opera, *Family Affairs,* scheduled at 6:30 P.M., is the prime example of this strategy. Top performers in the first year have included *Xena: Warrior Princess, Hercules: The Legendary Journeys, La Femme Nikita,* and *Poltergeist: The Legacy.*

The start-up period has been shaky, with lower ratings than expected (3 percent, not 5 percent of the audience, as planned, though the network has been building steadily). This has been due, in part, to lackluster movies in the 9:00 P.M. slot, and to technical problems that prevented some 40 percent of British households from seeing the service early on. (By late 1997, C5's transmitters reached 80 percent of the viewing public.) Other stations are well entrenched, and the establishment of this fifth network probably requires larger investments in programming and technology in order to gain widespread acceptance.

C5 is owned by a trio of big media companies: Pearson, CLT and United News and Media.

Because of technical limitations, about 15 percent of the U.K. will not be able to receive Channel Five; some population centers in the south and east will not be able to receive the signal, nor will those in the northern reaches of Scotland.

CABLE TELEVISION

High costs of physical installation, strong broadcast-signal quality, and a scarcity of programming until the late 1980s discouraged the growth of British cable TV. In addition, the ITC restricted operation of foreign companies in the U.K. media, and did not permit the granting of cable franchises to companies that owned television, radio, or newspaper operations within the franchise area; local authorities, religious groups, and political organizations were also prohibited from owning a franchise. While these rules discouraged cable growth, they tended to encourage the growth of the direct-to-home (DHT, or in U.S. terms, DBS) satellite businesses. (In fact, an inspection force drives through neighborhoods to check on what people are watching.)

In the 1990s, many new channels emerged, some with foreign partners. Although some are available exclusively on satellite or via cable, most can be received through either subscription system.

New local television stations, available only on cable, are also emerging. The two London players are L!ve TV, from the Mirror Newspaper Group, and Channel One, from Associated Newspapers (owners of the *Daily Mail,* etc.). Both formats are local journalism, often served up with style.

The principal local system operators in England include Telewest, NTL, General Cable, and Diamond Cable.

SATELLITE BROADCASTING

In the early 1990s, two DBS companies competed for a foothold in a small but potentially lucrative market. Within two years, British Satellite Broadcasting (BSB) was absorbed by Rupert Murdoch's News International. The new company, called British Sky Broadcasting, operates two sets of services, each on a separate satellite.

To satisfy viewers in the U.K. who invested in the original BSB, five channels are offered on the high-powered Marco Polo satellite: British Sky News, British Sky Galaxy (both described above), a sports channel, British Sky Movie Channel 1, and British Sky Movie Channel 2. The movie channels require a decoder.

In 1998, four leading British cable operators (Telewest, NTL, General Cable, and Diamond Cable) announced plans for a new pay-per-view satellite movie service, in association with Time Warner.

On the ASTRA satellite, DBS subscribers can receive a different set of services (based on the original Murdoch offering): Sky One, a general interest network; Sky News, which is similar to CNN, and offers newscasts from ABC and NBC News; Sky Movies; and the Movie Channel. The latter two are encoded pay TV services.

Digital broadcasting is currently in the planning stages, and is likely to launch in late 1998 or early 1999.

CABLE AND SATELLITE CHANNELS

Rupert Murdoch's cluster of channels established its presence via satellite, but they're also seen via cable. Sky One offers U.S. comedy and drama, as well as British game shows, sitcoms, dramas, talk shows, documentaries, and so on, plus some programming from other countries. Sky Soaps broadcasts a schedule of soap operas, including many from the U.S. Sky News is a 24-hour news service. Sky Travel offers not only travel programming, but also many special travel offers. There are three sports channels, and two movie channels (one new, one classic) as well.

Other British cable and satellite channels include TCC (The Children's Channel). The Parliamentary Channel, UK Living, and The Family Channel. TCC's schedule is largely U.S. reruns: *Casper and Friends, Dennis the Menace, Earthworm Jim, Sweet Valley High,* mixed with other material from the U.K. and other English-speaking countries. UK Living is a mix of gardening, cooking and service shows interspersed with U.S. talk shows, some movies and games. The Family Channel is games, off-network reruns, and the like.

In addition, several pan-European channels are available to U.K. viewers, such as EBN (European Business News), and Eurosport.

Many U.S. channels operate with British partners (typically, large British media companies). These include A&E, The Cartoon

Network, The Discovery Channel (owned by United Cable and United Artists), The Disney Channel, The History Channel, Nickelodeon, QVC, Quantum TV (infomercial and home shopping), The Playboy Channel, The Sci-Fi Channel, Turner Network Television (TNT), Discovery Home and Leisure (formerly called The Learning Channel), and VH1. In addition, U.K. subscribers have access to MTV Europe, CNN International, and NBC Superchannel. Approximately one-third of British cable and satellite networks are rooted in the U.S. Paramount has its own channel, showing TV series *(Entertainment Tonight)*, and some movies.

The digital satellite business in the U.K. has grown more slowly than in other parts of Europe. The market is likely to be built by the fast-growing Flextech (which is half-owned by the U.S.'s TCI), whose joint venture with the BBC currently offers four channels, with three more in the works for late 1998. The first four channels are UK Gold (TV comedy and drama), UK Arena (arts and fine entertainment), UK Horizons (history, travel, science, adventure), and UK Style (cooking, leisure, hobbies).

GERMANY

For program sellers, Germany is the key market in Europe. Prices are highest, co-productions are the most flexible, and business is conducted in a way that makes sense throughout the world.

Germany is the world's second largest advertising market (the U.S. is first), with billings of over $4 billion annually. The German marketplace has exploded with new channels, and the landscape has been somewhat rocky for many of the new ventures. In a pitched battle for viewers and market share, the commercial networks have invested enormous sums, and are finding it difficult to earn back their risk capital.

Two of the biggest players in the German television marketplace are the oldest: ARD, and ZDF. Each of these networks maintains roughly a 15 percent market share. Other commercial networks have come along recently, some quite successfully, via cable and satellite. Private TV began in the mid-1980s, and there are now more than 20 broadcast channels available in Germany, more via cable and DHT (direct-to-home) satellites.

Programming on Germany's radio and television channels is funded, in large part, by license fees payable by owners of radio and TV receivers: nearly DM 30 per month, with about one-third of the fee financing programs on ARD, ZDF, and their related channels. DM 30 is roughly $17 U.S.

There are 34 million TV households in Germany. Roughly half subscribe to cable TV, out of a possible maximum cable penetration of 24.5 million households. About 9 million own satellite dishes (DHT—small dishes), and only 19 million own VCRs. Viewership averages three hours per day (well under half the U.S. average), with viewers over age 50 watching about four hours per day, and children watching less than two hours per day.

Germany will be one of a handful of countries that will lead Europe into the digital era. By 2000, roughly 20 percent of German households are likely to own a digital receiver.

ARD

In an effort to limit the power of a centralized German government after World War II, the Allies placed the development of cultural matters (broadcasting included) in the hands of the states, or *länder*. Broadcasting stations developed in the länder, and in several cases, länder combined resources; the result was a total of nine regional broadcasters in eleven states (comprising the former West Germany), plus two more owned by the federal government. Each of the regional broadcasters is owned by its regional government. All of these are part of a network cooperative known as ARD, short for Arbeitsgemeinschaft der Offentlich-rechtlichen Rundfunkstalten der Bundesrepublik Deutschland (rough translation: the Federation of Public Broadcasting Corporations of the Federal Republic of Germany). ARD is also called Das Erste (Channel One).

ARD broadcasts from early morning until late night, with a mix of sports, news, drama, and cultural programming with highbrow appeal. Regional member WDR (Westdeutscher Rundfunk), located in Cologne, serves the west; NDR (Norddeutscher Rundfunk), in Hamburg, serves the north; and BR (Bayerischer Rundfunk), in Munich, serves the southeast. Together, these three entities provide approximately 60 percent of ARD's network programming.

ARD programs most of the day; the regional stations program from the early evening onward. All ARD members are active locally, and all contribute at least some programming to the network. ARD members work with independent production companies, acquire completed programs, and produce some of their own programming (such as sports). Popular ARD programs include the nightly newscast called *Tageschau,* and a detective series called *Tatort.*

Co-production deals are made at the member level, not by the national headquarters (which moves each year to a different regional broadcast facility). WDR International is very active in co-producing internationally. Studio Hamburg and NDR International are both international program operations within NDR; NDR International is charged with reviewing proposals for new projects. BR is smaller, but an ambitious co-producer, particularly in the motion picture area. WDR and NDR also distribute programs outside the network, and other regional members have followed suit. The commercial arm of ARD, Degeto Films, buys and sells programming for the national network and for regional stations.

ARD is a non-profit commercial service, with advertising limited to 20 minutes per day (none on Sunday), shown in four 5-minute blocks. Restrictions are being lifted, however, so that more time can be sold at higher unit prices.

ZDF

Zweites Deutsches Fersehen (ZDF), or Second German Television, was launched in 1961 as a national public network, but not without a fight from the länder, which believed that they alone had the right to establish broadcast stations. ZDF is owned by the eleven länder, but decision-making is centralized in the head offices in Mainz. As with ARD, the programming is sophisticated; but unlike ARD, ZDF is a national service without local affiliates or local producing entities. Of the two, ZDF is more aggressive, both in ratings competition at home and in international ventures.

Among the most popular ZDF series: *Derrick*, a detective series, and a very popular export; *Aktenzeichen XY . . . ungeloest*, a reality series that focuses on crime stories; *Geld oder Leibe*, a game show; *Lindenstraße*, a soap opera; and soccer coverage.

LOCAL INDEPENDENT CHANNELS

In addition to ARD and ZDF, the broadcast organizations in the länder operate independent channels. WDR3 and BR3, two of the biggest of these independents, are available on cable throughout most of Germany (and seen via cable and satellite throughout Europe). Private regional broadcasters include Berlin's 1A and FAB, Hamburg 1, and TV München (in Munich).

RTL

RTL—previously known as Radio-Television Luxembourg, and as RTL-Plus—is owned by CLT (Compagnie Luxembourgeoise de Télé-diffusion and Bertelsmann. The network, based in Cologne, is seen throughout Germany on terrestrial, cable, and satellite TV. It's Germany's number-one network, with nearly 20 percent of the market share.

When it began in 1984, RTL programmed low-cost studio-based productions. By 1987, it was building strength by acquiring U.S. series and by featuring programming with wide audience appeal, like big variety shows on Saturday nights. Some soft-core pornography and aggressive sports-rights acquisitions helped build the network.

RTL2 launched in 1993. Its programming schedule was built, in part, by the sheer availability of large numbers of movies. A typical program day might include cartoons from various markets, a low-cost syndicated series like *Flipper,* old reruns of *Knight Rider,* a film like *Psycho III,* and an attention-getting U.S. series like *Beverly Hills 90210.* RTL's films and sports coverage are also very popular. It's owned by Bertelsmann, ABC, Telemünchen, and Heinrich Bauer.

Super RTL launched in 1994 as a family channel owned 50 percent by Disney and 50 percent by CLT. The schedule's highlights, at least in these early years, have been Disney cartoons, with the remainder of the schedule filled with the likes of *Owen Marshall, Nancy Drew, Hardy Boys,* and *Harry and the Hendersons*—all U.S. series.

SAT.1

Sat.1 is owned in large part by Germany's Springer-Verlag publishing group, APF (a combination of 140 publishers), and PKS (a joint venture between the German Co-operative Bank and Germany's Kirch Group). Working from a general-interest entertainment base, Sat.1 has roughly a 15 percent market share with game shows, televised shopping, morning talk, and soft-core erotica. In addition, there's the inevitable *Cagney & Lacey, LA Law,* and *Remington Steele* (these types of series have been very popular on all German networks).

PROSEIBEN (PRO7)

After an ill-fated launch as a service called Eureka, this channel changed its name and its programming in 1989. It's popular among the target 18–40 market, and its feature films (largely from the Kirch library, spiced with *Jurassic Park, Schindler's List,* and other hits), have gained a substantial following. U.S. programs like *ER, NYPD Blue,* and *The X-Files* have also helped to build audience and brand loyalty. The network also produces its own cartoons *(The Neverending Story)* and sitcoms, all with a promise of non-violence. PRO7's market share is about 10 percent. Over 80 percent of PRO7 viewers are under age 50.

ProSeiben also owns about half of Kabel1 (also known as Kabelkanal), a new channel that debuted in 1992. Kabel1 has been active in cutting-edge technology. It produced *Hugo,* an interactive program from a virtual studio, for example.

ProSeiben is part of a techno-savvy media group that produces CD-ROMs, sells media time for Nickelodeon, NBC and CNBC, and leads in Internet advertising ventures. In short, ProSeiben is uniquely positioned as the network of the future, the hotbed of development for digital TV and new technologies, and convergence. Leo Kirch's son Thomas and REWE, a German retail operation, own ProSeiben.

RTL and ProSeiben have been spectacularly successful for advertisers; together, they reach about one-fourth of the German audience, but collect about half of Germany's broadcast advertising revenues.

OTHER CHANNELS

Kinderkanal launched in 1997; it's a non-commercial satellite and cable channel for children. Phoenix is also non-commercial; it's entirely news, public affairs, and current events. Both are owned by ARD and ZDF, and financed by receiver license fees. Home Order Television (HOT) launched in 1995 as a satellite network. It's owned by Thomas Kirch, catalog retailer Quelle Schikedanz, and ProSeiben president George Kofler.

Nickelodeon's German version is owned by Viacom Deutschland, and Beteilingungen, with minority participation from Ravensburger. It reaches 13 million households, making it the largest of Nickelodeon's non-U.S. operations. VIVA, a music video channel owned by the world's five largest record labels, competes with MTV Europe. Onyx, owned by the London-based Capital Media Group, programs music for older, more affluent viewers who watch via cable. There's also VH1 and VIVA 2.

Premier is a pay-TV movie service owned by Kirch, Bertelsmann, and several other companies. It's similar to HBO.

VOX is yet another programmer that fills its schedule mostly with old series *(Starsky & Hutch, Matt Houston, Highlander).*

3SAT

3Sat is a three-way venture between three country's public broadcasters: Germany's ZDF and ARD, Austria's ORF, and Switzerland's SRG. 3Sat is seen throughout Europe via several satellites. Half of the program's schedule is ballet, opera, classical and other types of music, but there are also documentaries, satire, news and cultural magazines, and even a cultural game show. During prime-time, each of the national networks provides their best program from their own schedules. ZDF and ARD provide approximately one-third of the programming.

ARTE

ARTE is a joint venture between French and German broadcasters. ARD and ZDF hold half the shares. The French partner is La Sept (see below). In addition, RTBF also contributes programming.

CABLE TELEVISION

Just under 60 percent of German households subscribe to cable. Homegrown cable services are few; instead, the cable networks are conduits for broadcasters from Germany and from neighboring countries, including Austria, France, the U.K., and Switzerland. German viewers receive Sky Channel and pan-European services like MTV Europe, NBC Superchannel, and EuroSport. Channel capacity is a big issue, limiting the growth of several smaller networks.

SATELLITE SERVICES

German viewers can subscribe to satellite services offering several dozen channels. These were developed in the pre-digital era. DF-1, from Kirch, and Premier, from Bertelsmann, are likely to emerge as the two major suppliers. Canal Plus, which is building similar systems in other European countries, may also play a role.

REGULATION OF GERMAN TELEVISION

Each of the sixteen (post-reunification) länder has its own rules and regulations for broadcasting and cablecasting, and its own media authority; these are based upon a national standard. The Federal Office of Post and Communications (Deutsche Bundespost) controls the technical side of television broadcasting and cablecasting for all of Germany.

Neither ARD nor ZDF is permitted to run advertisements after 8:00 P.M.; a small percentage of other airtime may be devoted to commercials.

FRANCE

The organization of French television is complicated. Originally, radio broadcasting in France was private, but because some French broadcasters sided with the German occupation forces following World War II, the system was nationalized. A series of political changes have further altered the system. The result is a group of state-owned organizations, an unrelated group of privately owned companies, and one large network that was once public and is now private. With many new companies and combinations of older players in a new format, plus public subsidies and quotas, the mix of old and new can be confounding for outsiders.

STATE-OWNED SERVICES

TDF, Télédiffusion de France, is responsible for the transmission facilities used by all government-owned French broadcasters.

Société Française de Production et de Creation Audiovisuelles (SFP) is an enormous production operation. It employs several thousand people, and operates studios throughout the country (including over a dozen in Paris) plus mobile units. SFP sells programs to all of the French networks (including the private ones), co-produces with companies outside France, and commissions work from companies inside and outside France. SFP is not, itself, a network or broadcaster.

FRANCE TÉLÉVISION

The two public networks in France, formerly called Antenna-2 (A2) and France Régions 3 (FR3), are now part of a single organization called France Télévision. France Télévision also includes France Espace, which sells advertising time, and France Télévision Distribution is responsible for international sales of the organization's programming.

France 2 (previously A2) emphasizes world-class news and documentary programs, and popular programming with a quality veneer. There are game shows, news, variety programs, films, children's programs, and imports such as the popular German series *Derrick*. France 3's mission is more youth-oriented, and more likely to broadcast programs that appeal to a more limited audience. France 2 is the country's second most popular network with a market share in the mid-20s. France 3's share is usually in the high teens.

Revenues for both of these channels are generated roughly 50 percent by advertising sales and 50 percent by fees levied on television set owners.

LA SEPT

La Sept, which debuted in 1989, is a cultural service available mainly on cable during the week (mid-afternoon until late night) and over the air, via national broadcasting facilities, on Saturdays (early afternoon through late night). The plan is for La Sept to become a pan-European service; it is presently seen in Germany, Switzerland, Luxembourg, and Denmark. La Sept is a relatively small network with limited financial resources.

The French government also operates Radio France (three radio networks) and RFO (Radio Télévision Française d'Outre-Mer), which broadcasts French programming overseas.

LA CINQUIÈME (LA 5IÈME)

A learning channel whose majority owner (83 percent) is the French government, this public television venture broadcasts programming to about 85 percent of France via terrestrial, cable, and satellite systems. It's primarily funded by license fees, though some advertising is accepted (roughly five percent of revenues). The majority of programming is, by definition, educational, though the concept is expanded to include various types of children's and documentary programs as well. The network launched in 1994.

COMMERCIAL SERVICES

The majority of commercial services are available only on cable and satellite systems, but TF1 is one of several major commercial broadcasters.

TF1 (TÉLÉVISION FRANCAIS I)

The top-rated Télévision Français 1 was a government-owned network until it was sold to Bouygues, a large French construction concern, and Maxwell, a British communications conglomerate. Current ownership is 51 percent public stockholders (with a high percentage in U.K. hands), 39 percent Bouygues, 6 percent by Société Genere, and smaller percentages scattered among several entities. Within the TF1 group, there are many other entities, including one-third ownership in Eurosport,[1] complete ownership of La Chaine Info, a 24-hour news channel, and a documentary channel called Odyssée. Like most large networks, the company has a division for sale of program rights, another for advertising sales, and some studio and production company ownership. In addition, TF1 Enterprises is involved with online services (Minitel), CD-ROMs,

---

1   In France, Eurosport is known as TV Sport. It's owned by TF1, Canal Plus, Générale d'Images, with ESPN as a minority partner.

videogames, home videos, and a music publisher that co-produces music with major labels.

TF1 produces a great deal of original programming, including game shows, news, sports, and cultural shows. Sitcoms and dramas are produced both in-house and by outside production companies, such as AB Productions, Elma, Gaumont TV, DEMD, Carrère TV, and Marathon. The company is restricted in feature film production, and must work with partners on such ventures. Movement toward children's programming, and deeper involvement in animation, was on the late 1990s agenda.

A typical day's schedule begins with cartoons, then some talk and game shows, and some televised shopping. Then, there's a block of U.S. programs, followed by a few French sitcoms. News runs at 8:00 P.M., thus delivering a prime-time audience for movies, magazine shows, sitcoms and dramas. No movies appear on Wednesday or Saturday nights—new films debut in the theaters on Wednesdays, and people are encouraged to patronize theaters on Saturday nights.

TF1's market share is less than 35 percent, but the network has struggled to maintain younger viewership (under, say, age 50), which is essential for advertisers. Their classic example was a French version of *Wheel of Fortune;* as demographics steadily skewed older, the network moved the show from its decade-old slot in the early evening to noon, and then cancelled the series. A younger game-show called *L'Or à l'appel* has achieved better ratings with the desired demographic. With a 35 percent market share, TF1 attracts more than 50 percent of the total advertising revenues for French television, and 92 percent of its revenues come from advertising. There is a limit on how much time can be allotted to advertising—12 minutes per hour.

METROPOLE 6 (M6)

Metropole 6 (M6), seen in about 85 percent of French households, is an ambitious smaller service that broadcasts 8 hours of music programs daily, and although it must broadcast 70 percent European content, M6 has become known as the place to see U.S. sitcoms. M6 is owned by CLT, Lyonnaise des Eaux Dumez, Union D'Études et D'Investissements (Crédit Agricole), and several other investors. Its market share is typically 10 to 12 percent.

OTHER CHANNELS

Many more channels are seen on cable and via satellite. La Chaine Météo is a weather channel. MCM Euromusique is a French music video network. RTL9 shows movies, magazines shows, and documentaries; it's owned by the CLT group. MTV Europe is seen throughout France (with French VJs and some programs produced exclusively for French viewers). Ellipse produces several channels, including Canal Jimmy (music and movies for teenagers), Canal J (kids), and Planète (similar to The Discovery Channel). Movie channels include Ciné Cinéma (new movies via pay TV), and Cinéphile (classic films via pay TV). CNN International, LCI (news produced by TF1), Euronews, and Eurosport France are widely available. Newer digital channels, available mainly via satellite packages like Canal Satellite Numérique (see below), include Voyages (a travel channel), Animaux (cartoons), Histoire (history programs), and many others.

CANAL PLUS (CANAL+)

Canal Plus began as a broadcast pay channel in 1984; it currently serves approximately 4 million subscribers. Its scheme differs from the U.S. model. Customers pay Canal+ directly; there is no cable operator between the pay network and its subscribers. Much of the programming follows the standard pay TV formula: recent movies, sports, and major entertainment events. Canal+ is a major player in French and European media with revenues in excess of 11 billion francs. The French media company Havas owns 34 percent of Canal+ and public shareholders own 44 percent; the remainder is owned mostly by Richemont and CDC, two large stockholders of Nethold, a Dutch company folded into Canal+ in 1997.

Canal Plus also operates as a commercial network, offering its service at no charge until mid-evening. A talk show, *Nulle Par Ailleurs,* is among several popular programs.

Canal Plus has also launched pay TV operations, frequently with local partners, in Spain, Belgium, French-speaking Africa, Germany (in a venture called Premier) and Poland.

In 1996, Canal Plus introduced Canal Satellite Numérique (Numérique = Digital). Already established as a leader in direct-to-home satellites, with more than a decade's experience in a realm that's essentially new for most organizations, Canal Plus is likely to succeed not only in France, but in Germany and elsewhere as well.

The package includes dozens of channels including Canal+, and Canal+ 16:9 (showing only wide-screen movies), plus C:Direct, which is devoted entirely to computer software downloads (the computer gets connected to the system). The system's Kiosque channels are pay-per-view.

The plan includes interactivity. France Courses, for example, offers horse races with interactive betting.

REGULATION OF FRENCH TELEVISION

The Conseil supérieur de l'audiovisuel (CSA), or National Audiovisual Communications Council is charged with the allocation of radio and television frequencies, as well as the assignment of transponders and the awarding of cable franchises. The CSA supervises program practices (limits on sex and violence, and the quota system described below). It also appoints the heads of French public television companies.

CSA regulations prohibit commercial interruptions on the public channels, France 2 and France 3. The private networks, notably TF1, are restricted to 12 minutes of advertising per hour; TF1 is allowed one 6-minute break during movie presentations (for La Cinq and La Sept, the breaks may be slightly longer).

French broadcasters are held to a quota of 60 percent European programming, of which 40 percent must be French. This naturally limits the amount of U.S. programming seen, but no major U.S. series has not found its way to this large market.

Original French programming has its difficulties in the international marketplace, where English-language soundtracks are essential. These soundtracks add an average of 20 percent to the cost of the production. Still, international monies are often needed to complete a large production, and so the extra costs can be worthwhile.

ITALY

Over 58 million people live in Italy, but there are only about 19 million TV viewing households, and about 10 million VCRs.

Two organizations dominate Italian television: Radiotelevisione Italiana (RAI), owned by a corporation that is in turn owned by the government, and Fininvest, a large private media concern owned by Silvio Berlusconi. Italian television is frequently called a "duopoly."

RAI television began in 1954 (the organization began in the 1920s with Eiar radio). It has long been linked with Italian politics, and this has been the cause of many problems—for example, Italy did not receive color TV until 1977, long after the rest of Europe. The RAI monopoly began losing ground in 1971, when a small, privately operated cable system started up in a northern Italian town. After three years of fighting, Tele Biella won the legal right to serve a region, paving the way for other local cable companies and local broadcasters. The courts continue to uphold the RAI monopoly for national broadcasting, but unofficial networks—called "soft" networks or para-networks—evolved as independent local stations throughout Italy. There are, in fact, 21 regional networks, most of which rely upon studios in Rome for most of their programming, adding only local news. Eight of these networks are owned by Berlusconi.

RAI

RAI operates three networks: RAI-1, RAI-2, and RAI-3. Each network is managed independently, but all three share the same chairman. RAI-1 is Italy's highest-rated network; light entertainment (situation comedies, big-name variety shows, major series from the U.S. and elsewhere) is the strong suit. RAI-2 does not compete as aggressively, either as a counter-programmer to the commercial networks, or within the international programming marketplace. RAI-3, emphasizing news and culture, is the more traditional public channel; it relies heavily on non-fiction and factual programs, presents serious music, and has a distinctly Italian flavor. RAI-1's market share is in the low twenties, RAI-2 is in the mid-teens, and RAI-3 is about ten percent.

Traditionally, news programming on the RAI networks has been party-controlled: RAI-1, by the Christian Democrats, RAI-2, by the Socialists, and RAI-3, by the Communists. These factions are involved in the details of news operations—including selecting the staff and talent. Political change is a way of life in Italy, so the status of these affiliations does change from time to time.

RAI has a significant advantage over the Reteitalia networks (see below) because it has a legal monopoly on the right to show live programming without paying a special license fee. This means that viewers turn to RAI for news and for sports coverage. RAI is Italy's leader in sports broadcasting. Approximately 75 percent of RAI's programming is live—a tradition that differs from most of the world's public networks.

RAI is supported by a combination of license fees and advertising; advertising is limited to 4 minutes per hour. Tobacco and alcohol cannot be advertised on RAI.

RAI also operates RAI Canale Sportivo, a live channel that specializes in soccer, cycling, and tennis.

SACIS is a commercial RAI subsidiary that buys and sells programming for all three networks in the international marketplace, and also controls advertising for these networks. SIPRA sells advertising time for the RAI channels.

MEDIASET/RETEITALIA

The Mediaset networks operate under an international broadcasting company called Reteitalia. All of the Reteitalia networks began in 1986. Based in Milan, they are almost entirely devoted to light entertainment (movies fill almost half of their schedules). The Reteitalia channels were built by scheduling U.S. imports, such as game shows *(Routa della Fortuna,* known here as *Wheel of Fortune,* was one hit series). Some of Reteitalia's decisions were dubious: in daytime and late-night, in the years when the networks were weak during those dayparts, Reteitalia "dumped" programs of lesser appeal in order to meet quota requirements.

Reteitalia's Canale-5 (also called La Cinque) is its highest-rated service (with a market share in the low-20s), competitive with RAI-1. The other two Reteitalia networks are Italia 1 (just over 10 percent market share) and Rete 4 (just under 10 percent).

OTHER NETWORKS AND STATIONS

Odeon TV, owned by Pathé and other investors, is a private television network that reaches two-thirds of Italian households. Other networks include RETE A and TeleMonteCarlo, one of several channels owned by Cecchi Gori.

Hundreds of regional stations are also in operation, many of them unlicensed. Telepiù 1 and 2 are pay TV services specializing in sports and movies. Telepiu is also involved in digital satellite television with DSTV, and with Telepiùcalcio, a package of desirable soccer matches for subscription.

Cable television has never materialized in Italy. This is mostly due to the widespread dominance of Berlusconi and RAI. Stream, a new venture from Stet, one of the world's top ten telecommunications companies, has attempted to cable Italy's cities with digital technology. The success of this venture, and its potential to transform the entire Italian TV industry, depend upon politics. Developments in satellite distribution are also likely to alter the landscape.

REGULATION OF ITALIAN TELEVISION

Italy's Ministry of Post and Telecommunications provides RAI with its operating authority, but the Ministry of Finance controls and regulates RAI's expenditures, collecting the license fees that fund a large percentage of its operation (the equivalent of about $100 U.S.—among Europe's lowest set fees). Regulation of commercial television in Italy is limited.

SPAIN

The reach of Spanish broadcasting extends throughout Europe and Latin America. The size of the country itself is misleading (40 million people, 12 million TV households); when considering Spain, one must consider Spanish speakers worldwide.

RTVE

Spanish television has historically been dominated by a government broadcaster, the RTVE (Radio Televisión Española), which replaced SNR in 1973. According to *Variety* (September 22, 1996), RTVE "rivals the Mexican media group Televisa, the largest Spanish-language consortium in the world, which had revenues of $1.2 billion in 1995."

There is no set license fee or tax in Spain; the RTVE networks support themselves through advertising and, to a far lesser extent, through exploiting ancillary rights. Essentially, RTVE operates like a private company, but it is owned by the government. Advertising is restricted to no more than eight minutes per hour (and an average of no more than six minutes per hour).

TVE-1, which debuted in 1955, is the light-entertainment network. TVE-2 began in 1964, and emphasizes news, information and cultural shows, as well as programs of regional interest. TVE Internacional reaches 10 million subscribers in Europe and an additional 7 million in Latin America.

TVE-1 and TVE-2 networks follow a long tradition of in-house production, though about one-third of their programming is currently acquired or jointly produced. They've historically been very aggressive regarding rights, mainly because they are so powerful. In recent years, as the new private stations have wrecked their revenue pictures, and as the international marketplace has flourished (more buyers, but also more sellers), RTVE's approach to rights has become more modern, and more flexible. The networks' audience share had historically been enormous (they were the only large networks in Spain). As new channels settled in, however, their market share settled into a range that's common for national public broadcasters: around 30 percent.

U.S. series are part of the story, but they're not as popular in Spain as they are elsewhere. When a series on RTVE succeeds—as in the case of *Hostal Royal Manzanares,* starring a popular actress named Lina Morgan—8 million viewers may tune in regularly. That's one-fifth of the country's entire population. Generally, TVE-1 gets about 25 percent of market share. It battles for viewers with Antena 3 and Tele 5, which viewers watch only slightly less frequently.

REGIONAL NETWORKS

Spain's regional channels, called *autonomas,* are publicly owned, and funded largely by local governments. Advertising is proving to be a productive form of financing as well; Televisio de Catalunya (TV3), the largest *autonoma,* is funded exclusively through advertising revenues. Based in Barcelona, TV3 reaches roughly one-sixth of the Spanish population. TV 33 is a sister station owned by the same company, and shares TV3's programming department. Euskal Telebisa in the Basque region operates two channels, one in the Basque language and one in Castilian. Televisia de Galaicia (TVG), Televisión de Andalucia (Tele-Sur), Televisión de Valencia, and Televisión Autonoma de Madrid (Telemadrid) are regional channels that reach small portions of the overall population. Telemadrid serves a young, affluent, urban audience, and because of its sophisticated programming needs, it is becoming an increasingly significant player in the world marketplace. Many *autonomas* went on the air in the mid-1980s or later; all of them are affiliated as members of the Federation of Autonomous Channels, and they may eventually form a network. These channels do work together in some acquisitions and co-productions with companies outside Spain, but the process requires patience on the part of the producer.

PRIVATE CHANNELS

Private channels did not appear on the Spanish television scene until the early 1990s. Socialist Premier Felipe Gonzalez took the better part of a decade to pass a private television bill and to assign network franchises. The apparent reason: 80 percent of the Spanish public depends upon television as its primary source of information, so Gonzalez was reluctant to weaken the government's power to control information.

Each of the new private networks is headquartered in or near Madrid. Antena 3-TV, owned by Zeta publishing, began in 1990 with a mix of prime-time sports, situation comedies, and game shows, with "balanced" (i.e. not government-controlled) news and current-affairs programming. The network's share is approximately 25 percent (Spain's second most popular network), and a hit series, *Farmacia de guardia (All-Night Drugstore)* was regularly watched by over 60 percent of Spanish households. Another 1990 launch, Telecinco (Tele 5), is owned by Berlusconi and a wealthy charity for the blind called ONCE. It features entertainment, sports, and a minimum of news, and garners a consistent share of about 20 percent, making it Spain's third most popular network.

Canal Plus España is a Spanish version of the popular French service, owned with the French by Prisa, a Spanish media group.

Limited in its access to Spanish films because the majority of them are owned by RTVE, the Canal Plus network programs imports, while fighting for rights to Spanish-language features. Canal Plus España has been a major success with well over 1 million subscribers.

SOGECABLE AND THE FUTURE

Formed in 1996, Sogecable is a film and television company involved in a great many ventures. It's owned by managing partner Prisa (25 percent), Canal Plus (of France; also 25 percent), and several other investors. CanalSatelite Digital (CSD) is a 25-channel digital satellite venture, similar to Canal Satellite Numérique in France, that's managed by Sogecable and owned by some of Sogecable's owners and a few other companies. Sogecable, with Antena 3-TV and TV3, a regional station, have tied up lucrative soccer rights for the next decade.

As of this writing, CSD was off to a very promising start. One reason: Spanish viewers have access to only a handful of television channels. CSD does have competition though: Via Digital, a government-backed channel jointly owned with the national telephone company, Telefonica. (The plot thickens as Telefonica announces plans to buy Antena 3-TV.) Stay tuned *(Variety* is probably the best source of updated information).

REGULATION OF SPANISH TELEVISION

Spain's private networks are generally owned by multiple partners. Government regulations stipulate that only 25 percent of a broadcasting company can have non-Spanish ownership. Also, no single entity can own a percentage of more than one channel.

Spanish content regulations are also restrictive: nearly half of the programs seen on Spanish television must be of Spanish origin. Also, 15 percent of programming must be original, produced by the license-holder.

OTHER EUROPEAN COUNTRIES

The following European countries are medium-sized television markets.

THE NETHERLANDS

There are 6 million television households in the Netherlands.

Broadcasting in the Netherlands is quite complicated; for example, individual networks, owned by the government, are each programmed by multiple companies, with each company representing a special-interest group. The special-interest organizations include many dues-paying members, who pay for subscription magazines with program listings. Each company has a social, political, or religious outlook that is, at least in theory, reflected in its programming.

NOS (Nederlandse Omroep Stichting), the public broadcast network service, offers three channels. Netherlands 1 carries shows from a variety of religious and social groups, including Catholic KRO, Protestant NCRV, AVRO, IKON (an ecumenical group), and Humanistisch Verbond (humanists). Netherlands 2's airtime is programmed by EO, TROS, and the sports program department of NOS. Netherlands 3 is carried by RVU, VARA, and a new company called NPS (which was part of NOS, and supplies cultural programming). Programs from each of these groups are scattered throughout each network schedule; this helps to explain why each of the eight major broadcasters publishes a weekly program guide.

Other commercial stations include SBS6 (promoted as a reality-based programmer); TV10 (U.S. series with sub-titles, owned mostly by Saban, so there are many children's cartoons, bolstered by some old U.S. series and some original game shows); and Music Factory (music videos). Another new niche channel, launched in 1996 by several large Dutch media companies, is Sport 7, whose schedule is 25 percent soccer (it's owned by Endemol, Philips, the Dutch phone company, and other partners). KinderNet is a non-violent children's network with a good amount of U.S. product dubbed into Dutch. There's also a pay TV network called Filmnet.

RTL4, formerly called Véronique, is a popular commercial television channel broadcasting to the Dutch from Luxembourg. It is majority-owned by CLT (Compagnie Luxembourgeoise de Télédiffusion); 38 percent of the company belongs to VNU, and just over 1 percent, to Philips. RTL4 built its base with children's programming, then moved into family fare with the slow start of TV10, which was originally intended to be a family service. The channel dominates the top ten with *Good Times Bad Times*, *The Andre van Duin Show*, *Baanntjer*, and *Star Playback Show*. RTL4 with its hold on FOX product is also a leader in children's programming.

Canal Plus is setting up operations in the Netherlands, and a private news channel is also in development.

BELGIUM

Most Belgians speak either Flemish (Dutch) or French, so there are two distinct television industries. (In fact, a third language, German, is spoken by a minority; a Belgian public television channel, RTBD, serves this group.)

RTBF Belgian Television operates two channels for French-speaking viewers: RTBF 1 and RTBF 2 (called La 1 and La 2). La 1 is a general program service, while La 2 is a cultural and special-interest channel with concerts, documentaries, and so on. A third channel, Eurosport 21, is owned by RTBF and Eurosport. RTBF has accepted commercial advertising since 1989, though it is a government-owned broadcaster. Due to its small budget, RTBF makes an honest effort in developing newsmagazine programs to emphasize Belgian issues and culture. The network also programs interesting films from throughout Europe, often with family appeal. In addition, RTBF fills in its schedule with lower-priced programming, or with programs bulk-purchased from suppliers. RTBF generally dubs its programming into French.

Canal Plus Belgique, part owned by RTBF, was launched in 1989. After a difficult start-up (and the addition of essential soccer coverage), the network has thrived.

There are no private advertiser-supported stations in Belgium's French community. However, RTL-TV1, based in nearby Luxembourg, serves the area. This commercial French-language station is so well entrenched that it raised objections when the RTBF began to accept advertising. Club RTL, also from Luxembourg, and a local Eurosport affiliate are also available.

Flemish viewers are served by both public and private channels. Belgium's BRTN TV1 is a general-entertainment and news service for Flemish-speaking viewers; Canvas, formerly called TV2 focuses on news, documentaries, and programming for children and teens. Both are government-owned, and are operated by Belgishe Radio en Televisia. BRTN TV1 and BRTN TV2 feature mostly local programming, and neither service accepts advertising. Most of the programming is presented in original languages with Dutch sub-titles (the situation is the same for the Dutch commercial stations).

Vlaamse TV Maatschappi (VTM) is a private service in operation since 1989. It's very successful, with roughly a 40 percent market share (among Flemish, not among the whole of Belgium). About half of VTM's programming is imported (*Raad van Fortuin*, a local *Wheel of Fortune* production, has been especially popular; most VTM programs are not original productions, however, but dubbed versions of an original show from another culture). VTM is advertiser-supported, and has been granted a monopoly for commercial broadcasting in Belgium. Canal 1 and Canal 2 are operated as pay TV networks by Canal Plus.

VT4 has been very successful with youthful audiences, and in attracting some of VTM's advertising revenues. VT4 generally builds its program schedule based on acquisitions. A pair of pay TV channels from Canal Plus, and the Hallmark Entertainment network complete the Belgian/Dutch channel listing.

Belgium leads the world in cable penetration (more than 9 out of 10 households subscribe to cable). Most channel offerings are broadcast imports from other countries, or cable services originating abroad.

SWEDEN

Swedish public television is financed entirely by receiver taxes; television advertising is not permitted in Sweden. This is the practice in Norway and Denmark as well.

State-run Sveriges Television operates two channels. Stockholm-based SVT1 has a national emphasis, while SVT2 has more of a regional focus. Programming is general-interest, with the Swedish Educational Broadcasting Company supplying much of the daytime schedule. These two networks account for roughly half of Sweden's viewership.

ScanSat's TV3 is a satellite channel seen throughout Scandinavia. Its schedule is built mostly from acquisitions, though some lower-priced productions, like game shows and news programs, are made by or for the network. TV4 is a commercial terrestrial channel, and a popular one at that (nearly one-third of the market)—it's home to the top-rated contemporary drama, *Three Crowns*. Commercials are permitted, but only between programs, and nothing related to tobacco, liquor, or products aimed at children may be advertised. In fact, a percentage of advertising profits must be assigned to children's programming.

Commercial services operating outside Scandinavia are also beamed into Sweden from the U.K. and from Norway. TV Norge (from Norway) offers predominantly British programming.

49

Asia and the Pacific

Although Asia's total television program buying power pales by comparison with Europe's, the marketplace is taking shape quickly. Japan is the powerhouse, but Indonesia, and many smaller countries are also becoming stable markets for U.S. and European programming. Pan-Asian networks are emerging too. They are also producing product for the international marketplace.

In this era of globalization, the rules are changing. MIP ASIA has become the hot international television convention, and Asia, the hot new marketplace. NBC Asia, with a provocative local programming strategy, serves 8 million Asian households, and MIP serves about 5 million. The younger generation is breaking down barriers. MTV operates throughout Asia, often with country-specific feeds (the MTV India feed, for example, concentrates on music from the popular "Bollywood" Hindi film industry). Thailand launched its first private TV station, Independent Television (ITV), a news channel, in 1995. One ITV venture is a cooperative program with six other Asian countries, a youth-oriented talk and magazine series called *Super Asia*. The Philippines and several other Asian countries have become major centers for animation production; *X-Men* is one of many series made in the Philippines.

JAPAN

Through acquisitions, Japan has become a major player on the international scene. SONY owns not only Columbia Pictures, but also Merv Griffin Productions *(Wheel of Fortune, Jeopardy!)*. At home, more than 42 million Japanese households are served by seven networks. NHK General Network and NHK Educational Network are both government-owned; Fuji TV, Tokyo Broadcasting

System (TBS), Nippon Television (NTV), TV Asahi, and TV Twelve are commercial networks.

Programming is, by and large, original. Japanese people tend to prefer their own programming to Western-style productions. When representatives of Japan's networks attend international program marketplaces, they go mainly to sell, not to buy. Japanese series consistently perform better in Japan than U.S. or European programs, regardless of the success of these properties elsewhere.

Japan's regulatory agency is the Ministry of Post and Telecommunications. Japan is one of the few large countries in which tobacco and alcohol can be advertised on television. However, there is a list of businesses that cannot buy commercial time on Japanese television: companies that arrange marriages; funeral parlors; hostess bars; and Pachinko parlors.

NON-COMMERCIAL NETWORKS

NHK (Nippon Hoso Kyokai, or Japanese Broadcasting Corporation) was originally based on the BBC model. It was set up in the radio era as a public-service system financed by license fees. These voluntary payments come from thousands of fee collectors who appeal to the Japanese sense of honor and civic duty as they go door-to-door throughout Japan. NHK sets its own fees, subject to government approval; presently, the fee is U.S. $95 per household for one or more color sets. Based in Tokyo, with seven additional regional headquarters, NHK operates several Japanese networks. Nearly all of NHK's revenue comes from either government subsidies or set license fees.

NHK General's program mix is dominated by news, commentary, cultural shows, and educational programming. For many years, NHK was Japan's ratings leader, but because of competition from the commercial stations, NHK has dropped from first to last place in the ratings. A typical day's schedule would begin with a two-hour morning program, *Good Morning Nippon,* with much of the day filled with 30-minute dramas (the equivalent of soap operas), cooking and lifestyle shows, and some sports and music. In prime-time, a few U.S. series also make it onto the schedule, notably *Dr. Quinn, Medicine Woman* and *Beverly Hills 90210.*

NHK Education is a second channel distributed via broadcast television. True to its mission, NHK Education provides lessons in conversational English, Spanish, French, and German every day, and provides programming for Japan's youth, from pre-school through high school. These programs fill most of the hours. The other slots are filled with the occasional arts or sports program.

NHK also operates a nationwide news and sports channel via satellite (Channel 7), and NHK Hi-Vision, a schedule of HDTV programming for households equipped with the new TVs (NHK has been broadcasting in high-definition for several years on Channel 9). NHK also operates an entertainment channel via satellite (Channel 11). NHK Channels 7 and 11 are free; no decoder is needed for reception.

MICO, a consortium of Japanese banks and trading companies, was formed by NHK to extend its enterprises beyond regulations that would otherwise encumber NHK's activities. Officially, NHK is a large client of MICO; in effect, MICO is the international co-production arm of NHK.

COMMERCIAL NETWORKS

Japan's five commercial networks grew from local stations operating in the Tokyo area. In theory, commercial networks are not permitted to operate in Japan. In practice, the more powerful Tokyo stations began transmitting their programs to affiliated stations elsewhere in Japan; because the Tokyo stations were owned by newspapers with nationwide advertising capabilities, it wasn't long before the newspapers were selling national advertising for their television operations as well.

Nippon Television (NTV), the largest private network, went on the air in 1953. It currently has 30 affiliated stations. The network is supported by advertising. NTV's programming strengths include sports (especially Yomiuri Giants baseball coverage), talk shows, and the popular period dramas depicting old Japan. The three top-rated series are: *Magical Brain Power* (quiz), *The Yoru Mo Hippare* (musical variety), and *Touko Tokuhou Oukoku* (an amusing documentary-quiz).

The Tokyo Broadcasting System's TBS, which started in 1955, is a light-entertainment network. The network's top-rated programs include *Tokyo Friendly Park 2* (quiz/variety), *Kyoosookyoku Concerto* (drama), *Doobutsu Kisootengai* (Amazing Animals; a quiz), and *Hitori Kurashi* (Living Alone). The popular U.S. series *America's Funniest Home Videos* was based on TBS's *Kato-chan Ken-chan.*

TBS's affiliate network of 28 stations receives about 60 percent of its programming from the Tokyo-based network, and generally produce 40 percent on their own. Most local programs are news and talk; only the major city affiliates in Osaka and Nagoya attempt larger-scale projects. Only 7 percent of the network's programming is made outside Japan, and many of these slots are filled with co-productions in which TBS is a partner.

On a typical day, TBS begins with a morning news program from 6:00 A.M. until 8:30 A.M., then follows with a morning service program for housewives. Most of the afternoon is filled with half-hour dramas, the Japanese equivalent of soap operas: *Kaoo Love Theater, The Eldest Son's Wife, I Want Love,* etc. These run until the 6:00 P.M. evening news, which is followed by various game or variety shows, depending on the night, from 7:00 P.M. until 8:00 P.M. These include *Tokyo Friendly Park 2, Wedding Bells,* and *Famous Inventions Show.* In prime-time, there's a teen-idol entertainment show, *Jungle TV,* starring a well-known comedian, and on some nights, a two-hour drama. A news and interview show is scheduled for 11:00 P.M. until midnight. Then, the schedule is mostly comedy series, with some TV shopping, *CBS Evening News,* and a few U.S. series (such as *Quantum Leap*) filling the after-midnight slots.

The Fuji Telecasting Company's Fuji TV is a general-interest network that features game shows, sitcoms, and variety shows. In terms of income, Fuji has long been Japan's top broadcaster. Fuji TV has 28 domestic affiliates. Programming tends to skew young, with strong appeal to female viewers. Variety and comedy series with hot Japanese performers have contributed to the network's buzz. The network has also established a leadership position as a program supplier for the Asian television market; the success of series like *Tokyo Love Story* indicate the degree of interest in Tokyo among Asian youth (rather like NYC or LA for Americans). The related Fujisankei Communications Group, is becoming involved in Hollywood film projects, and in videogames.

The Asahi National Broadcasting Company's TV Asahi also began in 1959. The TV Asahi network has been especially successful with its news and talk shows.

TV Tokyo—also known as Twelve TV—is a comparatively small network. It's owned by Japan's Nikkei Newspaper Group.

DIRECT-TO-HOME SATELLITE

In late 1996, PerfecTV launched. True to Japanese form, the majority of its 65 television channels are Japanese, but there were some from the U.S. and elsewhere: Bloomberg Information TV, BBC World, Sports-i (an ESPN venture), The Golf Network, Koreavision, KNTV (Korea New Television). In addition, there's a channel of Brazilian and another of Spanish programming. Japanese channels that come as part of the basic package include DigiCube (downloadable software, for teens), Shop Channel, Mall of TV, 24 Hour Shopping Channel. Premium services include Fighting TV Samurai! (wrestling and martial arts), Gaora (baseball, wrestling, and American football), several educational channels, Space Shower TV (music videos), Weather Shower 24, Kids Station, Oki-Doki (international programming), Channel WE (more international programming), and a choice of two karaoke channels, plus lots of PPV movies.

PerfecTV is owned by several Japanese trading houses, with some minority ownership from SONY and Toyota. It's one of three competitors in the multi-channel race. The others are from the U.S. company DirecTV, which debuted a year later, and JSkyB, a joint venture from News Corp., SONY, Fuji TV, and Softbank, whose 150 channels will be available in 1998.

A leading Japanese trading company Sumitomo, along with the U.S.'s TCI, announced plans for Japan Entertainment Television, a pan-Asian service for DTH and cable services whose reach would extend to Australia and New Zealand. Several Japanese networks own part of the venture as well.

REGULATION OF JAPANESE TELEVISION

Japanese television is regulated by the Ministry of Posts and Telecommunications in Tokyo. The National Association of Commercial Broadcasters also has a regulatory code, but compliance with it is voluntary.

It may come as a surprise to Western viewers that Japanese television permits nudity on late-night television—and that soft-core pornography is a regular feature of several late-night programs.

CABLE TELEVISION AND DIRECT BROADCAST SATELLITE

Crowded Japanese cities, and old construction, make cable installation difficult, so DTH satellites became the popular system for receiving additional channels. NHK and Japan Satellite Broadcasting (JSB) compete with analog dishes. JSB's WOWOW pay movie channel is well established, offering some home shopping and other programming in addition to films.

In many areas outside the large cities, cable has taken hold. Most systems are small and these smaller systems support some local TV stations not available over the air.

OTHER ASIAN NATIONS

In India, there is a substantial English-speaking population. The combination of a strong local entertainment industry and significant cultural differences have kept India outside the international marketplace. Still, there are 50 million TV viewers in India. The big change is likely to occur as digital satellites reach the majority of households by early in the next century. Indian households currently watch an average of four hours of television per day. India's broadcast television offerings have been limited. The dominant force, Doordarshan, is a public channel broadcasting primarily in Hindi and English. Doordarshan's programming is almost entirely Indian, with the occasional U.S. or German program. It was founded in 1965.

India's satellite-delivered Zee TV is one of several related channels; the others are Zee Cinema and EL TV. Zee TV was India's first private television venture in 1992, and it has been enormously successful, reaching over 16 million households. Half of Zee TV is owned by News Corp., through a Hong Kong company called Asia Today, Ltd. Zee TV has also launched a music channel called Music Asia. Zee TV's top series include mostly soap operas *(Banegi Apni Baat, Tar, Parampara)*, films, and a game show *(Close-up Antakshari)*. Roughly 50 percent of the schedule is news, talk, current-affairs and magazine shows, and 20 percent more is films. Zee TV's programming is seen in Europe, the U.S., and elsewhere. Zee TV's competitors include Sony Entertainment Television and Home TV (owned by TVB in Hong Kong, two large U.K. entertainment firms, Carlton and Pearson, the *Hindustan Times* and a bank, Schoders).

Approximately fifty DTH channels are available to Indian viewers. This is an enormous change for viewers who had only government channels less than ten years ago.

In Malaysia, where modernization has been a priority, there are two government channels, RTM 1 and RTM 2 and two private channels, TV 3, and Metrovision, which is seen only in Kuala Lumpur. Channels from Thailand, Singapore, and Indonesia are also seen on Malaysia's cable and satellite systems. TV 3 is the most popular, and its program mix is mostly an original slate of talk, news, drama, game shows, and documentaries. Approximately one in four hours is acquired. TV 3 is supported entirely by commercials; revenues in 1995 were approximately U.S. $120 million. Government channels are also commercial: the profit goes to the nation's treasury. Malaysian citizens pay the equivalent of about $10 per year to the Ministry of Information, which operates RTM 1 and RTM 2. With regard to foreign product, Malaysia has its language issues: over half of the population speaks Bahasa Malyasia; Chinese is the second language at 30 percent, and various Indian languages make up the rest. English is widely understood. In general, programming tends toward the tame and family oriented. Programs involving sex or violence are not well received.

New channels are available via a 20-channel digital service called Astro. The Ministry of Information offers a locally produced sports channel whose offerings point at the uniqueness of individual Asian countries. In addition to football (soccer), motor racing, hockey, tennis and golf, the most popular sports are badminton (huge in Malaysia), sepak takraw (similar to volleyball, played with the feet), and table tennis.

The situation in Singapore roughly parallels that of Malaysia. There are two government channels, two private channels, and a mix of languages: English, Chinese, various Indian languages, and Bahasa Malaysia.

Thailand supports four commercial television stations (called, simply, Channels 3, 5, 7, and 9), whose entertainment fare is highlighted by very successful soap operas. There is a small but thriving pay TV market as well, from services like Universal Cable TV Network (UTV), whose programming is mostly imported. On the DTH front, Universal Cable, Thai Sky Cable, and International Broadcasting (also a cablecaster) are competing. UTV's specialty is movies; IBC is known for sports.

In the Philippines, a country with 65 million people, roughly half the households own television sets. In Manila, with its population of 5 million, TV penetration is over 90 percent.

The key name in the Philippines is ABC-CBN. The company owns not only the leading cable firm (SkyCable), but is also active in international co-productions, including action adventure motion pictures in the $3–$10 million range. Other ventures include the ABS-CBN network, a UHF channel, and many local affiliates. Among SkyCable's channels: Kid Central, Knowledge Channel, and imports such as The Discovery Channel.

The second largest network in the Philippines is GMA-7, owned by Worldwide Philippines, whose promise for the future is the development of a DTH business (the Philippines is made up of 7,000 islands, so satellite distribution makes good sense). Still, cable has become very popular in the big cities.

Over 200 million people live in Indonesia; only China, India, and the U.S. have more people. About 85 percent live in TV households. TVRI, the public station, started in 1962, and continues to air primarily Indonesian programming. Four private stations—RCTI (the ratings champ), SCTV, Anteve and Indosiar—compete with entertainment product, much of it imported. Anteve's big hit series is a local version of *Family Feud*. MTV Asia also airs on Anteve for about one-third of each day's schedule. Indovision, a DTH service, offers several dozen channels.

Indonesia has become a kind of manufacturing center for Asian dramatic series, known here as "sinetrons." Over 3,000 sinetrons are produced annually. This activity keeps over 200 production companies active, the most prominent being PT Multivision Plus (which produces hundreds of hours of programming per year) and PT Parkit Films, both ventures controlled by Raam Punjabi. Fremantle, Grundy, and other international companies are also active in Indonesia.

Nusantara TV is a cooperative venture involving Malaysia, Indonesia, and Thailand. The programming, just about all original product, is broadcast in Bahasa, Indonesia's national language.

Hong Kong is the world's third largest film producer, and it's a major center for Asian television activities. Many international television firms have their Asian headquarters in Hong Kong. Locally, ATV operates two channels: Home, which broadcasts in Chinese, and World, which broadcasts in English. ATV is also one of the largest Cantonese program suppliers in the world. TVB is the other terrestrial broadcaster, and it also operates a Cantonese channel (Jade) and a principally English channel (Pearl). TVB produces more Chinese-language programming than any other company. On both ATV and TVB, programming is mostly original, with some acquisitions from the U.K., U.S., Australia, Europe, and Asia. RTHK is a public broadcaster that exhibits its programming on these commercial stations. RHTK programming is curriculum-based, and cultural, but some programs have become popular.

AUSTRALIA

As in the U.K., the Australian television system is a combination of public and private networks. It's a country with about 18 million people, and about 6 million TV households, but almost no cable television. Satellite ventures are thriving.

PUBLIC NETWORKS

The Australian Broadcasting Corporation (ABC) began in 1932 as a public radio service. With nearly 100 broadcast stations (600 transmitters), the ABC television network covers nearly all of Australia. Its programming is generally upscale, with a strong news and information focus. ABC boasts the largest newsgathering organization in Australia—over 300 journalists on the continent and elsewhere. *The 7:30 Report* is a prime-time news and current-affairs analysis program that appears nightly. *Four Corners* is another respected current-affairs program. *Foreign Correspondent,* another prime-time series, features ABC's worldwide newsgathering force in a nightly magazine. *Landline* provides rural news. Approximately two new dramatic hours are produced each year; the emphasis is on quality. ABC is also Australia's principal buyer of independent documentaries;

series include *Media Watch, Quantum* (science), and *Defining Moments* (history of Australia). In addition, there are about two new hours a week of classical, opera, and arts programming, and also some popular sitcoms. Children's programming is a primary focus, and many ABC programs are seen throughout the world, including *Bananas in Pyjamas, Blinky Bill,* and *Johnson and Friends.* Sports coverage completes the ABC package.

Special Broadcasting Service (SBS), established as a public broadcaster in the early 1980s on UHF stations, serves Australia's ethnic minorities with a unique agenda. The program schedule is filled with high-quality programs from around the world, typically with sub-titles so they can be enjoyed by any Australian viewer. Programs include *Toyota World Sports, ICAM* (Indigenous Aboriginal Cultural Affairs Magazine), and many prime-time movies from a wide range of countries—much of it very appealing.

In addition, ABC's affiliated Australia Television transmits to 28 countries in Asia and the Pacific.

COMMERCIAL NETWORKS

By assembling key local stations in Australia's large cities—Sydney, Melbourne, Brisbane, Adelaide, and Perth—Australia's commercial networks were consolidated in the 1960s, and began aggressive national competition in the 1980s. In the 1980s, these networks made a financial mess of themselves by competing too aggressively, and "nearly destroyed the industry in the process," said Australian media consultant Peter Cox in the November/December, 1989 issue of *TV World,* an industry trade magazine. Since then, the situation has largely sorted itself out.

Nine Network began with the licensing of Sir Frank Packer's first TV license; TCN-9 debuted in 1956. In 1957, GTV-9 launched in Melbourne. By 1960, there were stations in Brisbane and Adelaide, and the group began operating as a network. After an ill-fated late-1980s period as part of Bond Media, Nine is now part of Publishing and Broadcasting Limited (PBL). PBL also owns ACP (Australian Consolidated Press), the country's largest magazine publisher, and interests in Sky Channel (sports), Sky News, various Optus Vision ventures (pay TV), and interactive theme parks.

Nine Network is the top-rated Australian network. Here's the structure of their evening programming. At 6:00 P.M., there's a half hour of news, followed by (the original version of) *A Current Affair,* then *Sale of the Century,* and *Australia's Funniest Home Video Show.* This leads into an 8:00 P.M. *Weddings,* 8:30 P.M.'s *Mad Mad World of Sports,* 9:00 P.M.'s *Real TV,* and a U.S. import at 9:30 P.M., *Spin City.* The evening continues with *Pearl* at 10:00 P.M., *Nightline* at

10:30 P.M., and at 11:00 P.M., an hour of *Star Trek: Deep Space Nine*. The network's long-term strengths have kept it on top: news and current-affairs, sports, variety and information-based entertainment programs such as *Animal Hospital,* and *RPA* (human hospital series). The weakness has been dramatic series, though some recent acquisitions have helped, notably *Halifax f.p.,* from one of Australia's top suppliers, Beyond, and *Water Rats,* from another top production house, Southern Star. Network Nine does not generally run sitcoms.

Network Ten, owned by CanWest, has the rights to *The Simpsons, M*A*S*H*, Party of Five, The Single Guy, Neighbours* (a popular U.K. series), *The X-Files,* and other imported series, and uses them as the basis for an evening and prime-time schedule. Original non-fiction programs, news, and sports coverage further distinguish the network's strategy. Seven Network tends more toward drama in prime-time with *FX: The Series, The Practice, Homicide: Life on the Street,* and various news programs in the evening hours.

REGULATION OF AUSTRALIAN TELEVISION

The Australian Broadcasting Authority (ABA) was created by the Broadcasting Services Act of 1992. The new agency took over the licensing, programming ownership and control functions previously performed by the Australian Broadcasting Tribunal (ABT). In addition, the new ABA assumed responsibilities for planning the broadcasting spectrum (previously done by the Federal Minister for Transport and Communications and the Minister's Department which is now re-organized under the Minister for Communications, the Information Economy and the Arts).

The ABA is empowered to grant, renew and cancel station licenses (as in other countries, licenses are cancelled very infrequently). Commercial television broadcasting licenses are subject to renewal every five years. The license is an agreement to honor restrictions regarding content, behavior of owners, and responsibilities to children.

Cable services are licensed by the ABA as well.

As of 1996, ABA's Australian content standard (ACS) required commercial broadcasters to include 50 percent Australian programming (from 6:00 A.M. until midnight). In 1998, the percentage increased to 55 percent. In addition, commercial broadcasters must schedule minimum amounts of original Australian drama, documentary and children's programs. Pre-school programming must be Australian-made.

On pay TV movie services, at least 10 percent of the program budget must be spent on Australian dramas.

To satisfy these requirements, an Australian program must be produced under the creative control of Australians who ensure an Australian perspective. The ACS specifies key creative roles that must be performed by Australians to satisfy this criterion. The roles include producer, either writer or director, at least 50 percent of the lead actors or on-screen presenters, and in the case of a drama program, at least 75 percent of the major supporting cast. The rules for co-productions are slightly different. A specific point system is used to encourage original Australian drama.

CABLE TELEVISION

There is no cable television in Australia, for two reasons. First, there are no reception problems with the existing television system—everyone in the cities receives strong, clean signals. Second, the outback regions are too sparsely settled for cable to be economically viable. DBS systems, which are in the planning stages for a mid-1990s start-up, may include pay-per-view service.

DTH SATELLITE

The DHT phenomenon is relatively new in Australia, launched in the mid-1990s. The two principal players are Optus Vision and Foxtel.

Optus Vision is owned by a mobile phone company, Optus Communications, Continental Cablevision (the third largest MSO in the U.S.), and two broadcasters, Nine Network and Seven Network. The Optus Vision channel lineup includes Cartoon Network, Disney Channel, ESPN, Horizon (cooking, computers, parenting, documentaries, etc.), a localized MTV, Odyssey (similar to Discovery), and some movie channels.

FOXTEL, from Murdoch's News Corp. and telecommunications partner Telstra, acquired an Australian DHT pioneer, Galaxy, from Australis Media, making this a two-company race. More than half of FOXTEL's channels are local in origin, and the venture buys a good deal of original programming from Australian producers. FOXTEL's channel lineup includes Arena (general entertainment), BBC World, Cartoon Network, CNN, Discovery, Encore (a movie channel), the FOX network (*The Simpsons, NYPD Blue, E! Uncut,* and other programs, some from the U.S. network, some acquired). FOX Soap Talk (talk shows and soap operas), FX: THE SERIES, FOX Sports, an original comedy channel, Hallmark, Lifestyle, The National Geographic Channel, Nickelodeon, Showtime, Sky, TNT, UKTV (an accumulation of programs from the U.K.), and TVSN (TV shopping network) make FOXTEL one of the most appealing DHT packages in the English-speaking world.

50

Mexico and South America

L atin America is one of television's more promising emerging markets. The region is generally defined as including Mexico, Central America, and South America, but not Cuba or any of the other Caribbean islands. Brazil is the largest market with 35 million households, and roughly 95 percent television penetration. Mexico is the second largest, with 18 million television households and just under 90 percent penetration. Argentina has about 10 million TV homes, and Colombia, about 6.5 million. Venezuela has only 4 million TV households, but it has become a major production center.

CABLE AND SATELLITE CHANNELS

In the mid- and late 1990s, Latin America was invaded by new cable and satellite channels. Many of these new channels were developed by U.S. media companies, and two came from Spain.

Entertainment channels include Canal FOX (6 million subscribers) and Hallmark Entertainment (about 1 million). HBO runs two channels: HBO Ole and HBO Ole 2, with partners Sony and Disney, and Olé Communications. Cinecanal, another pay movie service, competes with HBO Ole, and has under 4 million subscribers. Sony has its own channel, Sony Entertainment TV. USA Network and WBTV are also in the marketplace.

Much of the action is in children's channels. Cartoon Network feeds most of Latin America in Spanish, and feeds Brazil in Portuguese, for a total of nearly 8 million subscribers. FOX has a kids' channel. Nickelodeon has 2 million. Hearst and Cisneros TV Group are partnered in Locomotion.

Among the many music channels, CBS's CMT (Country Music Television) is seen in both Spanish and Portuguese. MTV Latino has 7 million Latin American subscribers.

Discovery operates Discovery Kids, and Discovery Latin America. The Travel Channel has 5 million subscribers, and TNT has 6 million. NBC has a joint venture with National Geographic for a Latin American channel as well.

CNN en Español, and MSNBC/CNBC each broadcast in Spanish to about 4 million Latin viewers. CBS Telenoticias is a broadcaster and cablecaster with 10 million viewers. E! Entertainment Television runs an English and a Spanish feed. ESPN has almost 9 million subscribers in Latin America, and it competes with FOX Sports Americas. The Weather Channel has begun operations in Spanish and Portuguese.

The two Spanish networks are Antena 3 Internacional and TVE (Televisión Española).

Other international networks broadcast in English. These include Bloomberg, BBC World, and CNN International.

This list covers roughly one-fourth of the entire rundown. There are many more movie channels, religious broadcasters, educational and shopping ventures, plus channels from countries within Latin America who are anxious to grow, and channels from Italy (RAI America), and elsewhere.

DTH

The distribution system for most of these channels is direct-to-home satellite. Under the ownership of DirecTV International (60 percent), the Cisneros Group (20 percent), Multivision (10 percent) and TVA (10 percent), DirecTV Latin America is in the process of launching local ventures in each country. Local deals are then made with 60 percent local ownership, with 20 percent held by Hughes (DirecTV is owned by Hughes), and 20 percent owned by Cisneros.

MEXICO

Mexican television consists of one group of broadcast channels that is operated by the government, and a second group that is operated under government concession by Televisa, a large private company. TV Azteca, a newer company, has drawn viewers and advertisers from Televisa's longtime hold on commercial television. TV Azteca's market share has grown from the low teens in 1994 to twice that amount just two and three years later. Mass-market successes like tabloid news programs and novelas (soaps), plus U.S.

sitcoms like *The Simpsons* and *The Nanny,* have stolen viewers from Televisa.

PUBLIC NETWORKS

Instituto Mexicana de Televisión (also known as Imevisión) operates three government networks. Channel 7 is a national network, and Channel 13 covers most of Mexico's populated regions. Channel 11 is operated by the Instituto Politécnico Nacional and shows movies and cultural programs, more than half of them imported; Canal 22 is also cultural. All of these channels offer entertainment, information, and a wide variety of program formats. There are some regional public (and private) channels as well.

PRIVATE NETWORKS

Televisa operates four commercial networks, all of which are headquartered in Mexico City. Of the 298 local affiliates that carry Televisa's signals, 240 are owned by the network, and 19 more are majority owned by Televisa. In addition, Grupo Televisa owns 17 radio stations, three record companies, and the largest cable system in Mexico, Cablevision. In addition, Televisa owns part of Univision, has 30 percent of Sky Entertainment Latin America, and part of the PanAmSat, which provides satellite space for rent. Televisa is an enormous operation—certainly the largest in the Spanish-speaking world, with over 20,000 employees (after a 12 percent staff reduction). It produces over 50,000 hours of new programming each year. This library has proven quite valuable; in 1995, 50,000 hours of programs were sold to networks all around the world.

Channel 2, known as The Channel of the Stars, was the first network to serve all of Mexico; programming is nearly all Mexican, consisting of both film product and shows produced in Televisa's large studio complex. These highly rated programs include telenovelas, game shows, sports, news, and children's programs. Channel 2 has 164 affiliates, and reaches 98 percent of the audience. Its market share is nearly 40 percent, accounting for about half of Televisa's viewership. Channel 4, reaches 4 million Mexico City households, but covers over half the country through 50 affiliates. While news and sports are supplied by Televisa, the majority of Channel 4's programs are imports and movies. Channel 5 is larger, reaching 90 percent of Mexican television households but scoring somewhat lower ratings than Channel 2 with children's programs and lots of cartoons, plus sitcoms and movies from the U.S. and elsewhere. Channel 9 is the newest network; it started in 1994 and reaches about two-thirds of Mexican TV households. On weekday mornings, it broadcasts educational programming, but variety shows, sitcoms, talk shows, and lots of movies fill out the schedule. In addition, Televisa's two stations on the Texas border broadcast FPX programming and telenovelas.

Program producer TV Azteca operates two national networks, Canal 7 and Canal 13. Canal 7's strong suit is movies and U.S. children's programs, dubbed into Spanish. Canal 13's calling card is telenovelas, many produced in Brazil, Colombia, Venezuela, and Argentina, and seen in many Spanish-speaking countries.

REGULATION OF MEXICAN TELEVISION

The Mexican government maintains close control over broadcasting through the Communication and Transportation Ministry, which handles frequency allocations and other technical matters, and the Interior Ministry, which supervises program and operational practices. Even private stations must provide the government with 30 minutes per day for "social advertising"—promoting good health, for example. Network facilities must be made available to the President on his request, and emergencies must be broadcast. Then there is the concept of *fiscal time*. Private stations almost had to surrender 49 percent ownership in their companies to the government, or pay a 25 percent tax on revenues. Instead, fiscal time became the form of payment—the government uses 12.5 percent of each private network's daily schedule for its own cultural and educational programming.

CABLE TELEVISION AND HOME VIDEO

Mexico's 145 cable operators serve approximately 1 million subscribers. The country's two largest cable operators are Cablevision (owned by Televisa), and Multivision. The latter has 300,000 subscribers in four cities, making it Mexico's largest operator. On most cable systems, programming includes both Mexican and U.S. channels.

BRAZIL

Roughly 160 million people live in Brazil: about 10 million in São Paolo, another 5.5 million in Rio de Janiero, about 2 million in the medium-sized cities of Salvador, Belo Horizonte, and Fortaleza. Many Brazilians live in smaller cities, towns, and rural areas. The country has fewer than 50 million TVs (less than one per household), and less than 20 million VCRs.

On the public side, there are two dominant channels, São Paolo's TV Cultura and Rio de Janiero's TV Educativa. On the private side, the dominant force has always been Rede Globo, but SBT, and several other channels are also popular. TV Cultura has been the bright light, with award-winning programs, and high ratings (generally, it's number three after Globo and SBT). Government funding has been the traditional source of TV Cultura's funding, but with São Paolo nearly $50 billion in debt, the network has begun accepting a limited form of advertising in order to stay alive.

The Brazilian government operates regional stations, but does not run a network as such. Funteve is the controlling body for many, but not all, of these stations. The private networks operate as government concessions, and are extremely careful about breaching their relationship by airing politically or morally sensitive programming.

Globo, part of the Brazilian media conglomerate Rede Globo, is the country's most successful private network—and one of the world's largest broadcast entities. It began in 1965 with a Rio de Janiero license, then acquired TV Paulista to expand into São Paolo, continuing this path until it covered 99.84 percent of Brazil's 5,043 municipal districts with 108 affiliates. Rede Globo takes in 75 percent of Brazil's television advertising dollars with astonishing audience shares: 74 in prime-time, 59 in the afternoon, and almost never less than 50. Telenovelas are one reason why: *O Rei do Gado* gets a 50 share; some score even higher. These soap operas appear in prime-time, generally three different series running each night, with stories told over the course of 200 episodes. A sitcom called *Sai de Baixo* is one of Globo's most popular series. All of Brazil's top ten series are Globo series, generally with audience shares in the high 30s. Virtually every hour seen on Globo is produced by the company, in its own studios. The network employs 8,000 full-timers, plus another 4,000 regular freelancers (typically, studio personnel). Globo is the world's largest television producer, responsible for over 4,000 original hours annually.

An aggressive player in the international television marketplace, the network has achieved roughly 65 percent audience share with original productions, but selected U.S. series have also done well, notably *Lois & Clark* and *ER*. Globo also supplies Globo News (24 hours on cable), Canal Rural (agricultural news and information), and Telecine 2, a multi-channel pay movie service. In addition, Globo is involved in a music channel, a 50/50 venture with FOX Sports, and other ventures.

SBT is Brazil's second biggest private network; it started up in 1981, and is led by a popular TV host and politician, Silvio Santos (he hosts one of the network's highest-rated series, a Sunday night variety show). SBT buys more U.S. series than Globo; their range of purchases includes sitcoms, dramas, and movies. SBT also imports telenovelas from Mexico's Televisa.

Beating Globo is nearly impossible, so the smaller networks program against SBT instead. Bandeirantes and Manchete, which debuted in 1967 and 1983, respectively, vie for third place and get 5–10 percent of the audience. Bandeirantes is known as a solid sports network; Manchete's hit has been *Xica da Silva,* a novela. Other broadcast networks in Brazil include TV Gazeta and TV Record (a commercial network owned by a wealthy Protestant church called Igreja Universal).

Specialty broadcast channels have begun to emerge in Brazil, often with some or all of their schedules filled with original Portuguese content or, at least, live Portuguese hosts introducing cartoons and other programs with Portuguese soundtracks. Abril TV has had some success with MTV Brasil on its UHF station in São Paulo; four stations are now affiliated with the service. TV Jovem Pan, another UHF station in São Paulo, programs hard news. FOX Sports and FOX Kids have launched (carried on the two largest cable operations), with many more networks coming in the next few years. CBS Telenoticias also supplies 14 hours a day of Portuguese-language news, including several U.S. series with Portuguese sub-titles *(CBS Evening News, 48 Hours,* etc.) The Weather Channel serves Brazilian viewers with a staff of Portuguese meteorologists in the network's Atlanta studios.

In pay TV, it's a battle of media titans: Globo from the TV industry vs. the giant publisher Grupo Abril. TVA is an MSO owned by Abril; it's a partner in the DirecTV Latin America venture expected to blanket Spanish- and Portuguese-speaking viewers with a 50-channel digital satellite system. Globo's NET Brasil is currently the largest cable MSO with nearly 1 million subscribers in about 50 systems. Also on Globo's side are Mexico's Grupo Televisa, and the U.S.'s TCI. Soccer is a primary driver of pay TV viewership; the Club of 13 (13 of Brazil's 16 most popular teams) negotiates as a block; the current deal, involving both free and pay TV, is worth $250 million over three years (1997–99).

One technical note: Brazil's television standard, a variation on PAL called PAL-M, is a 525-line system that is compatible with NTSC but not with traditional PAL.

Private networks and television stations in Brazil must be owned by Brazilian nationals, so international involvement in Brazilian television is limited to co-productions. Also, all foreign films must be dubbed into Portuguese before they are shown on the air.

VENEZUELA

As the Latin American television business has evolved, Venezuela's major player has become The Cisneros Group, or, more formally, Organización Diego Cisneros (ODC). The company owns Venevisión (see below), and owns 25 percent of Univision, the U.S.-based Latino network. Cisneros is also a partner in Galaxy Latin America, a DTH venture with DirecTV and Mexico's Multivisión. It's also partnered with Hearst on Locomotion, a Spanish-language children's network.

The two primary commercial networks are RCTV (Radio Caracas TV) and Venevisión. RCTV's success has come, in part, as a result of telenovelas—but unlike U.S. soaps, the story cycle on a telenovela is finite. And when *Por Estas Calles,* a big mid-1990s hit, drew to a close, RCTV did not find a replacement to garner similar ratings. Still, RCTV averages roughly a 28 percent market share. Venevisión is the market leader with over 50—and on some series, over 60 percent. Venevisión recently increased telenovela capacity from three to five simultaneous productions.

Venezuela's public channels are Canal 5, and CVTV.

APPENDIX A

Legal Documents and Forms

USER'S GUIDE

This appendix, which appears only on the disc, contains excerpted provisions of the principal statutes and regulatory sections applicable to the television industry. These include excerpts from the Communications Act of 1934 (Appendix A1), the regulations of the FCC (Appendix A2), and the Copyright Act of 1976 (Appendix A3). They are in a form supplied by the United States Government on the World Wide Web in early 1998. It is presented in a format that should be accessible with most word processing software programs. In order to search these items, the "go to" function designating a particular word, phrase or section number should be used. The omitted materials often relate to technical and operating standards and procedural matters. Those wishing more complete and/or updated versions of this information should try the following websites:

WEB ADDRESSES

CODE OF FEDERAL REGULATIONS
http://www.access.gpo.gov/nara/cfr/cfr-table-search.html

FEDERAL COMMUNICATIONS COMMISSION (site includes the Telecommunications Act of 1996, and the Communications Act of 1934)
http://www.fcc.gov

FEDERAL COPYRIGHT OFFICE (site includes 1976 Copyright Act and copyright forms)
http://lcweb.loc.gov/copyright/

GOVERNMENT PRINTING OFFICE (source of many statutes and regulations)
http://www.access.gpo.gov/su_docs/dbsearch.html

APPENDIX B

Contracts

USER'S GUIDE TO THE CONTRACT FORMS

Appendix B is devoted to contract forms and related materials. These forms cover many of the kinds of deals that an independent producer, actor, director, writer, or other television professional will have to make. For the most part, we have not included contracts relating to station or cable system operations, on the theory that such entities are more likely to have the benefit of regular legal counsel to help educate them and initiate any drafting. We have also left out most long-form or otherwise complicated contracts, for similar reasons. Standard-form Union and Guild contracts can generally be obtained directly from the organization in question—contact information is set out in Appendix C.

To highlight the important issues and customary terms of the deals, each section begins with an issue checklist, to be used as a reminder when negotiating or drafting. These include issues that may not have been addressed in the short-form agreements that we have included. The contracts themselves are meant more as educational tools than as specific models to be copied verbatim.

Should you wish to use the contract forms as the basis for actual agreements, we urge you to proceed with caution. The match between the form on the diskette and your actual circumstance may be less than perfect. For instance, most of the agreements we have included are relatively short and somewhat simplified. While this makes them more accessible, there are, by necessity, possible concerns that have not been addressed. Variations in applicable law may also require changes to the basic form. We recommend that you consult with an attorney about any specific application.

APPENDIX B1
Rights Acquisition: Issue Checklist

1. What rights are being granted?
   - Rights in a pre-existing property?
   - Rights in a life story?
   - Rights in a newly created work, like a script?
   - Rights of privacy and publicity?
   - Rights to use name, likeness and biography in advertising?
   - Rights in a title?
   - Rights to change, alter and edit?
   - Rights in any successor work?
   - Is the grant exclusive?
   - Is the grant irrevocable?
   - Is there any obligation to use the material?

2. Are there any reserved rights?
   - Live stage rights?
   - Publication rights?
   - Any holdbacks?

3. What markets and media are covered?
   - All television, film and related rights?
   - Broadcast television?
   - Standard cable?
   - Pay cable?
   - Multipoint service?
   - Open video system and video dial tone?
   - Home video?
   - Business and educational video?
   - Direct broadcast satellite?
   - Multimedia?
   - Other new technologies?
   - Theatrical film?
   - Book publishing?
   - Merchandising?

4. What territories are covered?
   - The whole universe?
   - The U.S., its territories and possessions?
   - North America?

- English-speaking countries?
- Europe?
- Japan?
- Other specific territories?

5. Is the deal an option?
   - How long is the option?
   - Can it be extended?
   - Will force majeure extend it?
   - Are there successive dependent options?
   - How is the option exercised?

6. Is it a firm deal?
   - Are there any preconditions?
   - Is it pay-or-play?

7. What payments must be made for the rights?
   - Is there an option payment?
   - Is there an option extension payment?
   - Do the option payment(s) apply against the purchase price?
   - What is the purchase price?
   - When is it paid?
   - What uses does the purchase price cover?
   - Are there additional payments due for additional uses or subsequent productions?
   - Is there a profit share or other back-end participation being granted?
   - Are there any expenses to reimburse?

8. What representations and warranties should be given?
   - Is the work either original or in the public domain?
   - Does the grantor own the rights and have the rights to grant them?
   - Does the work contain any libelous or slanderous material?
   - Does the work violate any rights of privacy or publicity?
   - Does either the work or its intended use violate any rights of any third parties?

9. Is either party giving an indemnity?
   - Does the indemnity cover alleged breaches, or only actual breaches?
   - Does the indemnity cover attorney's fees and costs?
   - Who controls the defense and settlement of any claim?

10. Are the agreement and the rights granted assignable?
    - If so, does the original purchaser remain liable?

11. Does the grantor get a credit?
    - Is it in the lead or tail credits?
    - Is it on a single card or is it shared?
    - Is it a verbal credit?
    - Is there any credit obligation in advertising and promotion?
    - Are the consequences of a failure to give credit limited in the customary way?

12. Are there limitations on the grantor's remedies?
    - Are injunctions prohibited?
    - Is recision prohibited?

13. Is there any union or guild involved?
    - If so, what impact does it have?

APPENDIX B2
Submission Release Letter

[Producer Letterhead]

[Date]

[Name and Address]

Dear _____ :

As you know, _____ ("Producer") is engaged in the production of television programs for exploitation in any and all entertainment media. In this context, Producer reviews various source ideas, stories and suggestions. Such material may relate to format, theme, characters, treatments and/or means of exploiting a production once completed. In order to avoid misunderstandings, Producer will not review or discuss ideas, scripts, treatments, formats or the like submitted to it on an unsolicited basis by persons not in its employ without first obtaining the agreement of the person submitting the material to the provisions of this letter.

By signing the enclosed copy of this letter and returning it to us, you hereby acknowledge and agree as follows:

1. You are submitting to Producer the following material for its review: _____

_____

2. You warrant that you are the sole owner and author of the above described material and that you have the full right and authorization to submit it to Producer, free of any obligation to any third party.

3. You agree that any part of the submitted material, which is not novel or original and not legally protected, may be used by Producer without any liability on its part to you and that nothing herein shall place Producer in any different position with respect to such non-novel or original material by reason hereof.

4. Producer shall not be under any obligation to you with respect to the submitted material except as may later be set forth in a fully executed written agreement between you and Producer.

5. You realize that Producer has had and will have access to and/or may independently create or have created ideas, identical to the theme, plot, idea, format or other element of the material now being submitted by you and you agree that you will not be entitled to any compensation by reason of the use by Producer of such similar or identical material.

Very truly yours,
[Producer]

By: _____

AGREED TO AND ACCEPTED:

By: _____

Date: _____

APPENDIX B3
Personal Release

1. BASIC INFORMATION

Program: _____

Production Company: _____

Its Address: _____

Individual Giving Release: _____

His/Her Address: _____

His/Her Age (check one): Over 18 ___ Under 18 ___

2. RELEASE

The undersigned individual hereby grants to the above named Production Company, and its successors, licensees and assigns, the perpetual and irrevocable right to use the undersigned's name, likeness, voice, biography and history, factually or otherwise, and under a real or a fictitious name, in connection with the production, distribution and exploitation of the Program, and of any elements of the Program and any remakes or sequels based on the Program. Such grant includes use in advertising in connection with the foregoing, and use in any and all media, whether now existing or hereafter devised, throughout the universe. It also includes the right to make such changes, fictionalizations and creative choices as the Production Company may decide in its sole discretion.

The undersigned individual: (i) agrees not to bring any action or claim against the Production Company, or its successors, licensees and assigns, or to allow others to bring such an action or claim, based on the Program or the depiction of the undersigned in the Program or the use of material relating to the undersigned in the Program or as otherwise described above, and (ii) releases the Production Company, its successors, licensees and assigns, from any and all such actions or claims that the undersigned may have now or in the future.

The undersigned acknowledges the receipt of good and valuable consideration for the release and other grants and agreements made herein, and understands that the Production Company is relying on them in proceeding with the production and exploitation of the Program and elements thereof as authorized above. The undersigned warrants that the use of the rights granted hereunder and of any material supplied by the undersigned will not violate the rights of any third party.

3. SIGNATURE AND DATE.

Signature: _____

Date: _____

APPENDIX B4
Short-Form Rights Option Agreement

Dear _____ [Author]:

This letter, when signed by you, will confirm our agreement for an option for us to acquire the exclusive television, film and allied rights in the work written by you (the 'Work'), and described in the attached Exhibit A, on the following terms:

1. In return for $_____, you are giving us the exclusive option for ___ months from the date of this letter to acquire the exclusive television, video, film, multimedia and allied rights for the Work, in perpetuity, for exploitation worldwide in all media.

2. Should we exercise our option, we will give you notice and pay you a fee of $____, less the amount described in Paragraph 1 above.

3. If we exercise our option, we will have the right to produce or co-produce one or more projects based on the Work, adapted as we feel necessary, or to license the production to any other producer, broadcaster, etc. We will have the right to use your name and likeness in publicizing any such production.

4. You do not grant us any literary publishing rights in the Work, other than the right to use customary excerpts and synopses in connection with productions. You warrant that the grant of rights you are making, and our exploitation of those rights as provided herein, will not infringe on the rights of any third party.

5. It is our intention to enter into a longer agreement containing these and other terms customary in the entertainment industry, but unless and until such a longer agreement is fully signed by both you and us, this letter will be the complete agreement between us.

Yours sincerely,
[Production Company]

By: _____
[Producer]

AGREED TO AND ACCEPTED:

_____
[Author]

[Note: Attach Exhibit A describing the Work]

APPENDIX B5

Development, Distribution and Finance Agreements: Issue Checklist

1. What media are covered?
   - All television, film and related rights?
   - Broadcast television?
   - Standard cable?
   - Pay cable?
   - Multipoint services?
   - Open video and video dial-tone?
   - Home video?
   - Business and educational video?
   - Direct broadcast satellite?
   - Multimedia?
   - Other new technologies?
   - Theatrical film?
   - Book publishing?
   - Merchandising?

2. What territories are covered?
   - The whole universe?
   - The U.S., its territories and possessions?
   - North America?
   - English-speaking countries?
   - Europe?
   - Japan?
   - Other specific territories?

3. Are there any holdbacks or restrictions on rights or territories not granted?

4. What is the term of the distribution contract?
   - Is it for a term of years?
   - Is it for the life of the copyright?
   - Can it be canceled if the distributor defaults?

5. Is the distributor providing production finance?
   - If so, what is the schedule of funding?
   - Will the distributor have a financial representative on the set?

- Will the distributor take a security interest in the program and all related rights?
- Will the distributor require a completion bond?
- Will the distributor have the right to take over the production if the producer goes over budget?
- How will the investment be recouped?
- What share of profits or other back-end participation will be paid for this finance?
- Is a bankable pick-up guaranty being provided instead of cash advances?

6. What input will the distributor have into the production process? (In general, the more finance being provided, the more the input.)
   - What production elements (writer, script, director, cast, designers, director of photography, music) are subject to distributor approval?
   - What business elements (locations, facilities, labs) are subject to approval?
   - Is the budget subject to approval?
   - Are any individual agreements subject to approval?
   - Are the producer's fees and overheads subject to approval?
   - Is there a distributor overhead factor or production fee?
   - Will the distributor bring the production in-house?

7. What are the required delivery items?
   - What are the technical items, tape masters, etc.?
   - Is a lab letter needed?
   - What are the non-technical items, such as script, publicity materials, cue sheets, cast lists, credit lists, residual schedules, E&O insurance certificate?

8. What input does the producer have into the distribution process?
   - Will there be consultation or approval over publicity?
   - Does the producer approve the deals?
   - Are there minimum targets?
   - Does the producer approve any sub-distributors?
   - Is there any obligation to distribute, or termination for inactivity?

9. When does revenue start to be counted?
   - On actual receipt in the U.S.?
   - On receipt by a subsidiary or affiliate?
   - How are blocked funds in foreign countries handled?
   - Are there any deductions for taxes or other charges off the top?

10. What is the distributor's fee?
   • Is it the customary percentage of gross revenues?
   • Does it vary by territory and medium?
   • Is it inclusive of the fees of any sub-distributors, particularly affiliates?

11. What expenses can the distributor deduct?
   • Are there any caps?
   • Are the costs of physical distribution covered (tapes, satellite time, etc.)?
   • Are the costs of publicity and marketing covered?
   • Are there any limits on conference, sales-market and other travel and entertainment costs?
   • Can the distributor deduct for interest, taxes and a distribution overhead?
   • Does the distributor pay and recover residuals, reuse fees and music performance license costs?
   • Who pays for initial and ongoing E&O insurance coverage?
   • Who pays any litigation and collection costs?

12. How does the distributor recoup any advances and share in profits?
   • Does the distributor recoup in the first position, or does it share, pari passu or by some other formula, with other financing sources?
   • Is any interest charged on outstanding amounts?
   • How are profits determined?
   • Does the distributor, producer or any other party share in revenues on a different basis (gross, adjusted gross, etc.)?

13. What kinds of reports and accountings are given?
   • How frequently?
   • How detailed?
   • What are the rights to audit these statements and the distributor's books and records?
   • When do statements become unchallengeable?

14. What representations and warranties should be given?
   • Is the program original and protected by copyright?
   • Have all the necessary rights and clearances, including music rights, been obtained?
   • Does the producer own the rights that are being granted free and clear, and does he/she have the right to grant them?

- Does the program contain any defamatory material?
- Does the program violate any rights of privacy or publicity?
- Does the program or its intended distribution violate any other rights of any third parties?

15. Is either party giving an indemnity?
    - Does the indemnity cover alleged breaches, or only actual breaches?
    - Does the indemnity cover attorney's fees and costs?
    - Who controls the defense and settlement of any claim?

16. Are the agreement and the rights granted assignable?
    - If so, does the original distributor remain liable?
    - Are sub-distributors permitted?

17. Are there limitations on the producer's remedies?
    - Are injunctions prohibited?
    - Can the rights revert on termination, or is recision prohibited?

18. Are there any rights with respect to further projects, such as sequels, remakes, series, spin-offs, etc.?

APPENDIX B6

Short-Form Development Deal

This agreement between _____ ("Purchaser") and _____ ("Producer") sets forth the terms of the agreement between them concerning the development and production of the television project tentatively entitled _____ (the "Program"):

1. *The Program:* The Program as currently envisioned consists of:

_____

2. *Development Steps:* Upon the authorization of Purchaser as indicated for each successive step, Producer will take the following development steps:

(a) *Step 1:*

Action: [indicate step or steps to be taken, e.g., treatment, budget, script, re-write, etc.]

Completion Dates:

Approval Dates: [date for Purchaser to approve and commission next step, require a re-write (if applicable), or cancel; date typically tied to completion date of step.]

Personnel: [i.e., a named writer or production person or person to be designated by one or both parties at the time.]

Fees and Expenses Paid by Purchaser: [can be a fixed amount, all approved costs, a mixture of the two, or some other approach; list payment schedule.]

Other Agreed Points:

(b) *Step 2:*
[Same list. Repeat as necessary for additional steps.]

3. *Production Commitment:* Upon the completion and approval of the final step set forth above, or at any other time during the development process mutually agreed between Purchaser and Producer, Purchaser shall have the exclusive right to commission the production of the Program by Producer, in accordance with the terms and conditions set out in the Agreement attached as Exhibit A. All major business and creative elements, including, without limitation, the budget, production schedule, facilities and locations, cast, production manager, director, writer and heads of technical departments, will be subject to the mutual approval of Purchaser

and Producer. Such approvals may be given at any time in the development process. Should Purchaser and Producer fail to agree on any such points within a reasonable time after good-faith negotiation, then such failure to agree shall constitute a cancellation of development.

4. *Cancellation and Turn-Around:* Should development be canceled, either by a failure by Purchaser to approve and commit to the next step under Paragraph 2 within the required time or by a failure by Purchaser to agree on a major business or creative element under Paragraph 3, then all rights in the program will revert to Producer, subject only to the right of the Purchaser to receive the following amounts should there be a production of the Program or of any other project substantially based on, or directly derived from, the Program:

(a)   from the production budget, upon the first day of taping, shooting or principal photography, Purchaser shall be reimbursed for all fees and expenses paid by Purchaser to Producer under this agreement, together with interest at the rate of ___ % per year on the balance of such fees and expenses outstanding from time to time (such interest not to exceed, in the aggregate, 100% of such fees and expenses); and

(b)   the following interest in the net profits, adjusted gross or other 'back-end' formula from the revenues of the project, calculated and paid on a favored-nations basis with all other recipients of such a revenue interest, including the Producer and financing entity of the project, expressed as a percent of one-hundred percent of such revenue interest:

if Step 1 is completed, ___ %;
if Step 2 is completed, ___ %;
[etc.].

5. *Development Process:* During the development process (i.e., for so long as Purchaser has continuing rights under Paragraph 2), Purchaser may approach any third parties concerning finance, transmission or any other aspect of distribution of the Program. If any of such approach leads to a "pitch" or other formal presentation of the Program, Purchaser will involve Producer directly, and Producer will provide all reasonable assistance. Purchaser will pay the reasonable expenses of a representative of Producer attending a formal pres-entation, which occurs outside of the _____ metropolitan area. During the development process, neither party will make any third-party commitment on any matter relating to the Program requiring mutual approval without the agreement of the other.

6. *Representations and Warranties:* Producer represents and warrants that (i) it is free to enter into and to perform this agreement; and (ii) the Program and any material to be included in the Program (other than material provided by Purchaser) is and will be either owned by Producer, or in the public domain, or fully cleared with respect to all applicable rights, and their use and exploitation as contemplated hereunder will not violate the rights of any third party. Purchaser represents and warrants that (i) it is free to enter into and to perform this agreement; and (ii) any material provided by it to be included in the Program is and will be either owned by Purchaser, in the public domain, or fully cleared with respect to all applicable rights, and their use and exploitation as contemplated hereunder will not violate the rights of any third party.

7. *Miscellaneous:*

   (a)   The addresses, including phone and fax, of each of the parties are as follows:

             Purchaser: _____

             Producer: _____

   (b)   Notices and other communications hereunder may be sent by certified mail, personal delivery, courier service or fax, to the address specified above or such other address as may be specified by notice and will be effective upon delivery at such address or upon return, if undeliverable at such address.

   (c)   This agreement will be subject to the laws of the State of _____ applicable to contracts signed and to be performed solely within such state. It sets forth the full and complete agreement of the parties relating to the Program. It may not be modified except by a writing signed by the party against which the change is asserted.

   (d)   All payment to Producer hereunder will be sent to:

IN WITNESS WHEREOF, the parties have executed this agreement as of the date set forth below.

DATE: _____

[Purchaser]   [Producer]
By: _____   By: _____
Title: _____   Title: _____

[Note: Exhibit A should consist of the applicable form of production finance/distribution agreement or license. The form in Appendix B7, which follows and is part of this agreement, may be used.]

APPENDIX B7
Television Distribution/Finance Agreement

TERM SHEET

1. PARTIES:

Distributor: _____

(hereinafter "Distributor")

Producer: _____

(hereinafter "Producer")

2. ADDRESSES (with phone and fax):

Distributor: _____

_____

_____

Producer: _____

_____

_____

3. PROGRAM(S):

_____

_____

(hereinafter the "Program(s)").

4. MEDIA (strike out anything non-applicable):
   (a) all television (including video);
   (b) theatrical;
   (c) multimedia;
   (d) book publishing;
   (e) and all other media, now existing or hereafter invented;
   (f) licensing and merchandising; and
   (g) except for: _____

5. TERRITORY:

The whole universe except for: _____

6. TERM:

_____

_____ , thereafter terrainable per the Standard Terms.

7. PRODUCTION FINANCE/ADVANCE (if any):

_____

8. PRODUCTION PROCEDURES (attach additional sheet(s), if necessary):
Distributor Approvals: _____
Approved Elements: _____
Credits: _____
Schedule: _____
Budget: _____
Overheads: _____
Music Rights: _____
Production Insurance: _____
Completion Bond: _____
Other Requirements: _____

9. REPORTING PERIODS:

_____

10. DELIVERY ITEMS AND DATES (attach additional sheet(s), if necessary): _____

11. STANDARD TERMS:
    The attached Standard Terms are hereby incorporated by reference into this Agreement, subject only to any express modifications or additions set forth in this Term Sheet, including the following (attach additional sheet(s) if necessary): _____

_____

12. COMPLETE AGREEMENT:
    This Term Sheet, together with the attached Standard Terms and any Exhibits, constitutes the sole and complete agreement between the parties concerning the Program(s).

13. APPLICABLE LAW:
    This agreement shall be construed according to the laws of the following State applicable to contracts made and wholly to be performed therein: _____

14. SIGNATURES:
    Distributor: Producer:
    By: _____   By: _____
    Name: _____   Name: _____
    Title: _____   Title: _____

STANDARD TERMS

1. *GRANT OF RIGHTS*

Producer hereby grants to Distributor the exclusive right to distribute, license, market and exploit the Programs and all elements thereof in the Media and in the Territory. These rights include the rights to dub the Programs into foreign languages, and to make cuts and edits to meet standards and practices, censorship and time segment requirements, provided that Distributor shall not delete the credits or copyright notice as they may appear in the Programs.

2. *MEDIA*

The licensed media (the "Media") shall be those set forth in the Term Sheet. The grant of television rights shall permit Distributor to exploit the Programs and all elements thereof in all forms of television now or hereafter known, including but not limited to free television, cable television, pay cable television, pay-per-view television, subscription television, over-the-air pay television, open video system television, television via telephone and/or the internet, video-dial tone, closed circuit television, master antenna television, multipoint service television, direct broadcast satellite television, armed forces, in-flight use, video cassettes and video discs for home use, and non-theatrical educational sales (collectively "Television Rights").

3. *LICENSED TERRITORY*

The territory described in paragraph 5 of the Term Sheet shall constitute the "Licensed Territory."

4. *TERM*

The initial term of this Agreement is as set forth in paragraph 6 of the Term Sheet. The Agreement shall thereafter renew itself automatically for further periods of one (1) year, which renewal periods shall be subject to the right of termination by either party, at the end thereof, by the giving at least of ninety (90) days written notice to the other party.

5. *DISTRIBUTION*

Distributor shall seek in good faith, subject to Distributor's reasonable business judgment, to maximize the exploitation of the rights granted hereunder. Notwithstanding the foregoing, Distributor shall have the sole control over all distribution activities, and may at any time suspend or resume active distribution of the Programs, as it deems fit, without any penalty.

6. *DELIVERY*

Producer shall deliver to Distributor the delivery items described in paragraph 10 or in the Term Sheet and any other elements of each of the Programs that may be reasonably necessary for Distributor to perform Distributor's services hereunder. Except as pre-approved in the Term Sheet, the Programs as delivered shall be subject to Distributor's sole approval for acceptance.

7. *DISTRIBUTION FEES*

(a) In consideration for the services Distributor is rendering to Producer hereunder, Distributor shall retain as its sole and exclusive property from all exploitation of the Programs the distribution fees described on Exhibit A attached hereto.

(b) In calculating such fees, "gross sales" shall be defined to mean all revenue (without any deductions), generated by the exploitation of the Programs by Distributor, including the gross amounts received by any of its subsidiaries or affiliates acting as sub-distributors, sub-licensees and agents. The commissions indicated above are maximum commissions for Distributor and any such subsidiaries or affiliates. If Distributor uses unaffiliated sub-distributors, sub-licensees, agents, etc., however, the fees of such entities shall not be subject to any limitation, but shall be deducted prior to calculating gross sales. Distributor and its subsidiaries and affiliates may take fees for additional services undertaken by them connected with the distribution of the Program, including fees for placing advertising in connection with syndication, provided that such fees shall not exceed those customary in the industry and shall not be subject to the limitations set forth above and shall be deducted before calculating gross sales.

(c) To the extent that Distributor may grant licenses longer than the term of this Agreement or, if this Agreement shall be terminated early for any reason, Distributor shall be entitled to receive commissions due to it in respect of all agreements, and extensions and renewals thereof, for exploitation of the Program in the Licensed Territory, and made by or on behalf of the Producer between the dates of the commencement and termination of the rights granted to Distributor hereunder.

8. *DISTRIBUTION COSTS AND EXPENSES*

After deduction of the fees described in paragraph 7 above, Distributor shall recoup from gross sales of the Programs all distribution costs and expenses that have been advanced or incurred by Distributor in connection with the distribution of the Programs hereunder.

The foregoing distribution costs and expenses shall include, without limitation, a pro-rata share of festival and market expenses, costs incurred in connection with promotional cassettes, sales and withholding taxes, shipping of promotional material, the manufacture of prints and videotapes, music and effects tracks, script duplication, publicity material, bank transfer charges, dubbing and production of foreign language tracks, advertising expenses and legal and agent fees.

Producer shall bear the cost of all rerun, reuse, residual and other similar payments required by any applicable union or guild agreement relative to persons performing services in the production of the Programs. Producer shall supply distributor with an accurate list of all recipients and rates of residuals and other similar payments. Distributor shall supply Producer with all necessary reports and information required to calculate and make such payments.

9. *RECOUPMENT OF ADVANCES*

After the deduction of the amounts set forth in paragraphs 7 and 8 above, Distributor shall recoup from the remaining proceeds to it from the Programs the Production Advance, together with interest thereon, as specified in paragraph 13 hereof.

10. *REPORTS, PAYMENTS AND ACCOUNTINGS*

(a) Distributor shall report and account to Producer in writing within forty-five (45) days after the end of each reporting period as set forth in the Term Sheet. A separate report will be issued for each of the Programs, although a series may be reported as a single unit. The reports shall contain reasonable detail and shall conform with customary industry practice.

(b) After retaining Distributor's fees and recouping the distribution costs and production finance as provided in paragraphs 7, 8, 9 and 13 hereof, Distributor shall attach to the report(s) a check payable to Producer in the appropriate amount for the balance of gross sales received during the period covered by the report(s). With respect to blocked or restricted funds, Distributor will report such funds to Producer and, to the extent permitted by applicable law, Producer will have the right to require Distributor to deposit Producer's share of such funds in a bank account established by Producer in the country where such funds are blocked or restricted.

(c) Distributor shall keep true, complete and accurate books of account and records pertaining to all financial transactions in connection with the performance of Distributor's obligations under this Agreement. Such books and records shall be available for inspection by Producers or its representatives at Distributor's place of business during normal business hours at a time or times mutually acceptable. No more than one such inspection shall occur within any twelve (12) month period, no statement shall be open to challenge later than two years after its receipt by the Producer, and no inspection shall be made as to any given statement more than once. Producer or its representatives shall have the right to make copies of the pertinent parts of all such books and records that directly relate to such financial transactions.

11. *COPYRIGHT AND COPIES*

(a) Producer shall ensure that its copyright in each of the Programs is properly protected and registered, if required, in any market in which the Programs are distributed.

(b) Distributor will not duplicate or otherwise reproduce the Programs in any manner, nor permit any of its sublicensees to do so, except specifically in connection with the distribution of the Programs as permitted hereunder. Distributor will provide in all license agreements that its licensees will return any prints or tapes distributed by Distributor, or submit an affidavit of erasure or destruction, promptly after the expiration of the period of use permitted to any of such licensees. Distributor will use its reasonable efforts to obtain the return of such items or the submission of such affidavit.

12. *WARRANTY AND INSURANCE*

(a) Producer warrants that it has the right to enter into this agreement and that it has the right to grant Distributor the rights granted herein and that Distributor's exercise of those rights will not infringe or violate the rights of any third party.

(b) Producer warrants that it has obtained the necessary music synchronization and performance licenses for the exploitation of the Programs as contemplated herein other than those customarily licensed through a performing rights society; and that all musical compositions in the Programs are controlled by ASCAP, BMI or another performing rights society having jurisdiction, or are in the public domain, or are controlled by Producer (in which case performance licenses therefor are hereby granted at no cost to Distributor).

(c) Producer will maintain a standard Errors and Omissions insurance policy for the Programs during the term hereof having limits of not less than One Million Dollars ($1,000,000) for any single occurrence and of not less than Three Million Dollars ($3,000,000) for all occurrences taking place in any one year. Such insurance shall provide for coverage of Distributor, its affiliated companies and the officers, directors, agents and employees of the same.

(d) Distributor warrants that it has the right to enter into this Agreement.

13. *PRODUCTION FINANCE*

(a) As used herein, "Production Advance" shall refer to all sums advanced or paid by Distributor in connection with the production of the Programs, including (but not limited to) all amounts advanced to Producer under the Term Sheet and any residuals, royalties and/or clearance costs, insurance premiums, attorneys' fees and/or any other production related costs paid or advanced by Distributor in its sole discretion.

(b) Interest shall accrue on the Production Advance from time to time outstanding until repaid or recouped at a rate equal to the Prime Rate declared by Distributor's principal bank from time to time plus two percent (2%).

(c) Producer shall deliver the Programs as set forth in the Term Sheet. Producer shall be solely responsible for any costs relating to the Programs that exceed the amount of the Production Advance agreed to in the Term Sheet for the Programs.

(d) In the event Producer fails to deliver any of the Programs as provided in this agreement or is otherwise in material breach of this Agreement, then without limiting any other right or remedy of Distributor, Distributor shall be entitled to demand, and Producer shall immediately thereupon pay to Distributor, the then outstanding amount of the Production Advance on any Program not yet delivered at the time of such demand, together with interest thereon as set forth above.

(e) To secure Producer's full and complete performance hereunder and any and all amounts owing to Distributor hereunder, Producer hereby grants Distributor a first priority lien and security interest in all right, title and interest in and to the Programs and each Program, and all elements, properties and proceeds thereof, whether now in existence or hereafter coming into being, and wherever located, including (but not limited to):

(i) the copyright in and to each Program;

(ii) all film, sound and/or videotape copies and/or elements of or relating to the Programs whether now or hereafter in existence and wherever located;

(iii) all literary property rights and ancillary rights as specified herein in relation to the Programs including, without limitation, all right, title and interest of Producer in the teleplays of the Programs;

(iv) all right, title and interest of Producer in the music used in the Programs to the extent of Producer's rights therein;

(v) all contract rights of Producer relating to the Programs in any and all media throughout the world as set forth herein;

(vi) all proceeds of the Programs and of any of the elements of the Programs referred to in (i) through (v) above, including without limitation all income and receipts derived and to be derived from the marketing, distribution, exhibition, exploitation and sale of the Programs and of said elements thereof, and all proceeds of insurance relating to the Programs and said elements thereof.

Producer agrees to execute such financing statements and/or other instruments as Distributor deems necessary or appropriate to perfect such security interest, and irrevocably appoints Distributor its attorney-in-fact to execute any such instruments in Producer's name should Producer fail or refuse to do so promptly on Producer's request.

(f) In the event Producer is in material default of this Agreement or materially breaches any of its obligations hereunder, then without limiting any other right or remedy of Distributor, Distributor shall have the right, but not the obligation, to take over and manage production of any or all of the Programs, without any obligation to Distributor as to the results of its efforts.

14. *INDEMNIFICATION*

(a) Producer shall indemnify and hold Distributor harmless from and against any demand, claim, action, liability and expense (including reasonable attorneys' fees) arising out of Producer's breach of any of the representations, warranties or provisions contained in this Agreement; provided that Distributor shall promptly notify Producer of any such demand, claim, etc., and that Producer shall have the right to control the defense and to approve any settlement thereof.

(b) Distributor shall defend, indemnify and hold Producer harmless from and against any demand, claim, action, liability and expense (including reasonable attorneys' fees) arising out of Distributor's breach of any of the representations, warranties or provisions contained in this Agreement; provided that Producer shall promptly notify Distributor of any such demand, claim, etc., defense and to approve any settlement thereof.

15. *PRODUCER REMEDIES*

The rights granted to Distributor hereunder are irrevocable, and the sole remedy of Producer in the case of a default by Distributor shall be an action for monetary damages.

16. *NOTICES*

Any notice required to be given hereunder shall be given by receipted telefax or by prepaid telegram or certified mail to the parties at their respective addresses set forth in the Term Sheet or at such other address as either party may hereafter notify the other. Any notice sent by telegram or by fax shall be deemed given on the day such notice is faxed or given to the telegraph office. Any notice sent by certified mail shall be deemed given three business days after such notice is mailed.

17. *NO PARTNERSHIP*

This agreement shall not be construed so as to constitute a partnership or a joint venture between the parties hereto, and no party is deemed to be the representative or the agent of the other except as herein otherwise provided.

18. *LAB LETTER*

Producer shall supply Distributor with a lab access letter covering all material relating to the Program. Such letter shall be in form acceptable to Distributor in its reasonable discretion.

EXHIBIT A: SCHEDULE OF DISTRIBUTION FEES

1. All Television Rights Except 2 and 3 Below:
   (a) for sales in the United States:
      (i) ___ % of gross sales for a national sale.
      (ii) ___ % of gross sales for a syndicated sale.
   (b) for sales in Australia, Canada and/or the United Kingdom:
      (i) ___ % gross sales for a national sale.
      (ii) ___ % of gross sales for a syndicated sale.
   (c) for sales in all other countries:
      ___ % of gross sales.

2. For armed forces, in-flight and any other ancillary television use:
   ___ % of gross sales.

3. For videocassettes and videodiscs and other devices for home use and non-theatrical educational uses:
   ___ % of gross sales, provided that if Distributor or its subsidiary or affiliate actually manufactures and distributes the cassettes and/or discs, gross sales shall be deemed to equal 20% of actual retail sales, subject to Distributor's customary adjustments.

4. For theatrical release:
   ___ % of gross sales.

5. For licensing and merchandising:
   ___ % of gross sales.

APPENDIX B8
Short-Form Home Video License

This agreement, when executed by the parties identified below as the Licensor and the Licensee, will set forth the terms of the agreement between them concerning the license of home video rights in the Program(s) described below.

1. *Licensor Name, Address, Phone and Fax:*

2. *Licensee Name, Address, Phone and Fax:*

3. *Title and Description of the Program(s):*

4. *Distribution, Licensed Media; Territory; Term:* The Licensor hereby grants to the Licensee the exclusive right to distribute the Program(s) in all aspects of home video, including tape, disc, chip and any other similar tangible medium capable of being played by an individual consumer on a home viewing device without transmission from a remote point:

    (a) in the following territories:
    (b) and for the following term:
    (c) subject to the following exclusions (if any):

Except as expressly provided in paragraph 9, Licensee will have sole control over the exercise of its home video rights hereunder, provided, however, that if Licensee ceases to actively distribute the Program(s) hereunder, and fails to recommence active distribution within three months of a written request to do so from the Licensor, then the rights granted hereunder to Licensee shall terminate and revert to Licensor.

5. *Advance and Royalties:* The Licensee will pay to the Licensor the following consideration for the license granted hereunder:

    (a) An advance in the amount of $____, payable upon delivery of the items specified in Exhibit A hereto.

    (b) A royalty at the rate of ___ %, to be calculated and paid in accordance with the procedures specified in Exhibit B hereto.

6. *Publicity and Advertising:* During the term hereof, Licensee will have the right to use the names, likeness and other attributes of personality of the performers appearing in the Program(s) and of the producer, director, writer and other principal off-screen contributors to the program in connection with advertising and publicity for the distribution of the Program(s) hereunder. Licensee agrees not to alter the titles and credits contained in the Program(s) (other than to add its own credit as video distributor at the very beginning and/or end of the Program(s)), and will abide by (and will require, as a matter of contract, all sub-distributors and other entities in the chain of distribution to abide by) all of the credit requirements specified in Item 2 of Exhibit A. No inadvertent or third-party failure to abide by such credit requirements will be a breach of this agreement provided that Licensee takes all reasonable steps to correct any such failure upon learning of it.

7. *Warranties:* The Licensor warrants that (i) it is free to enter into and to perform this agreement; and (ii) the Program(s) and any material contained in the Program(s) is either owned by Licensor, or in the public domain, or fully cleared with respect to all applicable rights, and their use and exploitation as contemplated hereunder will not violate the rights of any third party. In this regard, the Licensor agrees to pay any and all residuals, reuse, music or other similar rights fees or costs related to the exploitation and distribution of the Program(s) hereunder, except as may be expressly provided in Paragraph 9.

The Licensee warrants that it is free to enter into and to perform this agreement.

8. *Limits on Remedies:* Except as otherwise expressly provided in this agreement, all grants of rights hereunder are irrevocable during the Term, and Licensor waives all rights to any equitable relief in connection with any breach or termination of this agreement. The foregoing shall not apply in the case of a breach of this agreement by the Licensee, not subject to unresolved litigation or dispute in good faith, which continues uncured for a period of one month following written notice of such breach to Licensee from Licensor.

9. *Additional Provisions:* The following additional provisions shall apply (include any agreements on approvals of the distribution process, designs, rights payments, and any other further agreements (if none, write "none"):

10. *Miscellaneous:* This agreement will be subject to the laws of the State of _____ applicable to contracts signed and to be performed solely within such state. It sets forth the full and complete agreement of the parties relating to the license described herein. It may not be modified except by a writing signed by the party against which the change is asserted.

Dated: _____

LICENSOR   LICENSEE

By: _____   By: _____

Title: _____   Title: _____

EXHIBIT A

[Insert delivery requirements here]

EXHIBIT B

ROYALTIES:

Royalties will be calculated and paid in accordance with the following provisions:

1. *Retail Price and Sale Date.* Subject to the adjustments set forth below, the royalty will be calculated based on the suggested retail price of the Program(s) sold. In the case of a direct retail sale by Licensee or its affiliates, the retail price will be that actually received. A sale will be deemed to have occurred and a royalty will be payable, upon receipt by the Licensee or an affiliate of the purchase price for the item sold (or upon the accrual of any offset or other non-cash consideration), but reasonable amounts may be held in a good faith reserve for returns, if permitted, for a period not to exceed 6 months.

2. *Adjustments.* The retail price will be adjusted in the case of sales made at discount, remainder or other bona fide exceptions to Licensee's normal practices. In such a case, the retail price will be deemed to be twice the amounts actually received by Licensee or its affiliates from such a sale at wholesale, or, if Licensee or an affiliate makes the retail sale in such a circumstance, the retail price will be the amount actually received.

3. *Payments and Reports.* Licensee will provide written reports of sales, income and the royalty payable at the following intervals:

All accrued royalties will first be applied to the recoupment of any advance paid on the Program(s), and then will be paid by check included with the applicable statement.

4. *Accountings*. Licensee will keep complete and accurate records of the financial transactions relating to the Program(s), and shall not destroy such records for at least five years. Licensor will have the right to conduct an inspection of such books and records of the Licensee to verify the accuracy of the reports at Licensee's normal business premises during normal business hours, once within any twelve-month period. No report can be challenged any later than two years after it has been received by Licensor.

APPENDIX B9
Sales Representative Letter Agreement

[Producer Letterhead]

[Name and Address]

Dear _____ :

This letter, when signed by you, will set forth the agreement between us concerning your acting as a sales representative for us in connection with the Programs described below, on the following terms:

1. *Programs Covered.* This agreement covers the following programs (the "Programs"): _____

_____

2. *Markets and Media Covered.* This agreement covers sales and licenses of the Programs in the following markets (the "Markets") and media (the "Media") (describe the degree of exclusivity, if any, for each): _____

3. *Term.* The term of this agreement is as follows: _____

_____

4. *Sales Duties.* You agree to use your best efforts to seek potential buyers and licensees (collectively "Buyers") for the Programs in the Markets and Media. Once you have identified a prospective Buyer, you will inform us of its identity and degree of interest. Although you will assist us in pursuing the possible sale or license, you will have no authority to finalize or enter into any agreement with the Buyer on our behalf, except as we may expressly grant by a separate written authorization.

5. *Compensation.* If we close a sale or license, either during the Term or within ___ months of the end of the Term, of any of the Programs with a Buyer introduced to us by you hereunder for any of the Media and Markets, we will pay you a fee of ___ % of the amounts actually received by us during the Term and any time thereafter from such sale or license. We will pay you this fee within ___ days of our receipt of good funds on the payment to which it relates. Such fee shall be calculated and paid net of (describe any

deductions which come off the top or from the sales representative's share):

6. *Limits on Sales Representative.* Nothing in this agreement will constitute you our agent or attorney in fact. You will not hold yourself out as having any greater authority with respect to the Programs and our business generally than has been expressly granted to you by us in this agreement.

7. *Further Provisions.* This agreement is subject to the following additional provisions [include any further agreements on such topics as expenses, excluded contracts or other matters]:

8. *Miscellaneous.* This agreement will be subject to the laws of the State of _____ applicable to contracts signed and to be performed solely within such state. It sets forth the complete understanding of the parties relating to the sales representation described above. It may not be modified except by a writing signed by the party against which the change is asserted.

Please confirm that the foregoing accurately reflects our understanding on this matter by signing the enclosed copy of this letter and returning it to me.

Yours sincerely,

[Producer]

Accepted and Agreed:

_____

[Sales Representative]

APPENDIX B10

Talent and Service Agreements: Issue Checklist

1. What services are to be performed?
   - Is the contract for acting, writing, directing, or some other creative service?
   - Is it for producing, finance-raising, or some other business service?
   - Is it for a mixture of services?
   - Is the service being provided as an employee or as an independent contractor (see #2)?
   - Are the services exclusive to the producer or the production?

2. How are the services to be performed?
   - Are they subject to the producer's direction and control?
   - Are they at locations designated by producer?
   - Does the service provider retain any approvals or controls over the project as a whole, over his/her work process, or over the product?
   - Are there special facilities, accommodations, transport, or other amenities being provided?

3. What are the dates for the services?
   - Are there dates for the delivery of certain items?
   - Are the dates tied to the production process?
   - Are they set to particular calendar dates?
   - Can they be extended or altered?
   - Will a talent provider be available for post-production services, such as dubbing or looping?
   - What is the effect of force majeure or the disability of the service provider?
   - What are the arrangements for rehearsals, wardrobe, travel, post-production publicity and other additional services?

4. What rights are being granted?
   - Rights in newly-created product, like a script, direction, acting, etc.?
   - Rights to use name, likeness and biography in exploitation of the project, including advertising?

- Rights to change, alter and edit?
- Is the work product a work for hire?
- Is the grant exclusive?
- Is the grant irrevocable?

5. Are there any reserved rights?

6. What markets and media are covered?
   - All television, multimedia, film and related rights?
   - Are there any restrictions?
   - Is merchandising and print publishing included?

7. What territories are covered?
   - The whole universe?
   - Any specific territories included or excluded?

8. Is the deal contingent or pay-or-play?
   - What are the contingencies or option aspects?
   - How long is the option?
   - Can it be extended?
   - Will force majeure extend the option?
   - Are there successive dependent options?
   - How is the option exercised?
   - Is it a firm, pay-or-play deal?
   - Are there any preconditions?
   - Is the pay-or-play commitment for the full amount?
   - Is there any obligation to use the services?

9. What is the compensation for the services?
   - Is there an option payment or holding fee?
   - Is there an option extension payment?
   - What is the basic fee?
   - Is it set to any union or guild rate?
   - When is it paid?
   - What is the fee for any overtime or work beyond the basic dates? (The producer should set this in advance.)
   - Are there additional payments, such as residuals or other agreed-upon amounts due for additional uses or subsequent productions?
   - Are there any expenses to reimburse?
   - Is there a profit or other back-end participation?
   - What is the definition of such a participation?
   - Is there most-favored-nation protection on the definition?

10. What representations and warranties should be given?
    - Is any creative work either original and subject to copyright, or in the public domain?
    - Does the service provider have the right to enter into the contract?
    - Does the work product of the service provider contain any libelous or slanderous material?
    - Does the work product violate any rights of privacy or publicity?
    - Does either the work product or its intended use violate any other rights of any third parties?

11. Is either party giving an indemnity?
    - Does the indemnity cover alleged breaches, or only actual breaches?
    - Does the indemnity cover attorney's fees and costs?
    - Who controls the defense and settlement of any claim?

12. Are the agreement and the rights granted assignable?
    - If so, does the original producer remain liable?

13. Does the service provider get a credit?
    - Is it in the lead or tail credits?
    - Is it on a single card or is it shared?
    - Is it a verbal credit?
    - Is there any credit obligation in advertising and promotion?
    - Are the consequences of a failure to give credit limited in the customary way?
    - Are there any union or guild requirements?

14. Are there limitations on the service provider's remedies?
    - Are injunctions prohibited?
    - Is recision prohibited?

15. Is there any union or guild involved?
    - If so, what impact does it have?
    - Have its minimums been met?
    - Does the producer retain the maximum benefits available to it?

APPENDIX B11
Short-Form Services Agreement

This agreement, when executed by the parties identified below as the Employer and the Employee, will set forth the terms of the employment agreement between them.

1. *Employer Name, Address and Tax Identification Number:*

2. *Employee Name, Address and Social Security Number:*

3. *Duties and Services of Employee; Term:* The Employee will have the following duties and will perform the following services:

All of the Employee's services and duties will be performed subject to the direction and control of the Employer and at such times and places as the Employer may designate. The regular term of the employment will be as follows [can be day-to-day or for a set period]:

_____

Employee will also perform any required services outside the regular term at mutually convenient times.

The Employer will not be obliged to actually use any of Employee's services or work product, but the failure to use such services or work product will not in itself relieve Employer of the obligation to pay the compensation set forth herein.

4. *Compensation:* The Employer will pay the Employee the following compensation [include any bonus, overtime, benefits, or other agreed provisions]: _____

_____

The Employer will also reimburse the out-of-pocket expenses of the Employee relating to his/her employment, provided they are approved in advance by the Employer and customary documentation is presented.

5. *Warranties:* The Employee warrants that (i) she/he is free to enter into and to perform this agreement; and (ii) any material that she/he creates or adds to any project or production during the course of her/his employment will be either original or in the public domain and its use and exploitation will not violate the rights of any third party. The Employer warrants that it is free to enter into and to perform this agreement.

6. *Legal Requirements:* The Employee will abide by all applicable laws and regulations, including those under Section 507 of the Communications Act of 1934 prohibiting the undisclosed acceptance of consideration for the inclusion of material in a television program.

7. *Grant of Rights; No Equitable Relief for Employee:* The Employee grants all rights of every kind in the fruits and proceeds of his/her employment hereunder to the Employer and its licensees, successors and assigns. Any copyrightable material created by Employee hereunder will be treated as a work for hire, and the Employer will be the author thereof. The Employee also grants to Employer and its licensees, successors and assigns, the right to use his/her name, likeness, voice and biography in connection with the exploitation of any project or program with which the Employee has been involved through his/her services hereunder. All grants of rights hereunder are irrevocable and perpetual, and Employee waives all rights to any equitable relief in connection with any breach or termination of this agreement.

8. *Additional Provisions:* The following additional provisions shall apply [include any agreements on credits, any applicable unions and guilds, any locally-required provisions and any other further agreements; if none, write 'none']:

9. *Miscellaneous:* This agreement will be subject to the laws of the State of _____ applicable to contracts signed and to be performed solely within such state. It sets forth the full and complete agreement of the parties relating to the employment described herein. It may not be modified except by a writing signed by the party against which the change is asserted.

Dated: _____

EMPLOYER   EMPLOYEE
By: _____   Signature: _____

Title: _____   Name: _____

APPENDIX B12
Service Description Clauses

The following clauses describe typical services required of a variety of production employees, and may be used in conjunction with the agreement in Appendix B11. Other service descriptions may be drafted following the same general model.

Producer:
Employee will provide all of the services customarily provided by the producer of a television program, including, without limitation, overseeing the business aspects such as budgets, finance and banking, the production aspects such as facilities, equipment and creative and technical staff, the rights acquisitions and the creative aspects such as scripts, director and casting. Employee recognizes that all such matters will be subject to the ultimate approval of the Employer.

Director:
Employee will provide all of the services customarily provided by the director of a television program, including, and without limitation, involvement in the pre-production aspects such as script development casting, rehearsals and the selection of designers and music; directing the filming, taping or other production steps; and overseeing the editing and other post-production steps. Employee recognizes that except to the extent expressly otherwise agreed hereunder or as may be provided by applicable union agreement, all such matters will be subject to the ultimate approval of the Employer.

Writer:
Employee will provide the following services customarily provided by a writer in the television industry: [specify what is to be written, what editing, re-write or other general services are to be provided, and any applicable deadlines]. Employee recognizes that all such matters will be subject to the ultimate approval of the Employer.

Actor:
Employee will provide all of the services customarily provided by an actor in a television production, including rehearsals, make-up, wardrobe, and on-camera appearance, and at mutually convenient times and places subsequent to production, dubbing, looping, retakes and publicity support. Employee will play the role of _____.

APPENDIX B13
Performer Contract: Deal Memo

TO: [Performer]
            [Agent]

FROM: [Producer]

DATE:

The following has been agreed between the parties listed above for the services of the Performer to perform as an actor in production company's television production entitled "_____". Performer grants Producer all rights in his performance for exploitation throughout the universe in all media in perpetuity.

Role: _____

Start Date: _____

Compensation: _____
            [Total]

            _____
            [Pro-rata per week]

Guaranteed Term: _____

Other matters (if not applicable put "NA"): _____

Expenses: _____

Travel: _____

Lodging: _____

Union/Guild: _____

Other Arrangements: _____

Billing: _____

Location: _____

Estimated Schedule: _____

Personal Information:

    Address: _____

    Telephone: _____

    SS #: _____

Agent Information:

    Address: _____

    Telephone: _____

    SS #: _____

Producer Information:

    Address: _____

    Telephone: _____

    SS #: _____

Signatures:

Performer _____   Producer _____

APPENDIX B14

Performer Contract: Pre-Test Option and Series Option Clauses

These clauses may be inserted at the appropriate place in an otherwise usual performer service agreement.

[Pre-test option clause]

This letter will confirm that _____ ("Artist") has agreed to test for the role of _____ (the "Role") in _____ (the "Series"), a one-hour dramatic weekly series to be produced in _____ and such other locations as Producer may designate, by _____ (the "Producer"). The time and place for the test will be determined by mutual agreement. On the basis of this test, the Producer shall have the exclusive and irrevocable option to cast Artist in the Role by giving written notice to that effect to Artist's or Artists' agent on or before _____, 20__. Should Producer exercise this option, Artist agrees to render his/her acting services to the Series, and the following terms shall govern Artist's employment in the Series.

[Series option clause]

Dates/Options. If Producer exercises the initial option granted to it herein, Producer shall have five further consecutive, exclusive and irrevocable options, in each case exercisable no later than _____, to obtain Artist's acting services hereunder in episodes to be produced in the immediately following production year. The base commitment to Artist for each production year for which any option is exercised is for ___ (__) episodes. In each production year, including the initial year, Producer shall have the further option, exercisable no later than [December 1] in such year, to employ Artist's services in connection with no fewer than ___ (__) or more than ___ (__) additional episodes for such production year, the number to be designated by Producer at time of exercise. Each production year hereunder will run from [June 15 to June 14], with the initial production year beginning June 15, 20__.

APPENDIX B15

Music: Issue Checklist

[See the issue checklists for Rights Acquisitions and for Talent and Service Agreements for general considerations applicable to music-related rights and services.]

1. What compositions and recordings are covered?
   - Pre-existing music?
   - Pre-recorded music?
   - Specially commissioned music?
   - Specially recorded music?

2. What rights are being granted?
   - Synchronization rights?
   - Small or grand performance rights?
   - Master use rights in the recording?
   - Rights to use name, likeness and biography in advertising?
   - Rights in a title?
   - Rights to change, alter and edit?
   - Do the rights include the right to use the music in advertising and publicity?
   - Are publishing rights being granted?
   - Is the composition a work for hire?
   - Is the grant exclusive?
   - Is the grant irrevocable?

3. What media are covered?
   - All television, multimedia, film and related rights?
   - Are there any specifically included or excluded media?

4. What territories are covered?
   - The whole universe?
   - Are there any specifically included or excluded territories?

5. Does the producer participate in the music publishing?
   - Who is the publisher?
   - What is the split—traditional 50/50, or some form of co-publishing?
   - Are there any administrative, overhead, or expense deductions?

- How are decisions on other uses and administrative matters made?

6. Are composing services being supplied?
   - What music is to be supplied?
   - What is the approval process?
   - What are the delivery dates?
   - Is parts copying and arranging included?

7. Are recording services being supplied?
   - What music is being recorded?
   - Who handles and pays for booking the facilities and hiring the musicians?
   - Are union players being used?
   - Are real players or a synthesizer being used?
   - What kind of finished product is being delivered and in what technical format?

8. Are mixing and post-production services being supplied?

9. What payments must be made for the rights and services?
   - What is the composing fee?
   - What is the recording fee and expense payment?
   - When are they paid?
   - What uses do these prices cover?
   - Are there additional payments due for additional uses in subsequent productions or a series?
   - Are there any expenses to reimburse?

10. What representations, warranties and indemnities should be given?

11. What credit does the composer get?

12. Are there limitations on the composer's remedies?

13. Is there any union or guild involved? If so, what impact does it have?

APPENDIX B16
Composer Deal Letter

[Producer's Letterhead]

[Date]

[Composer Name and Address]

Re: [Name of Program]

Dear _____ :

This letter, when executed by you (the "Composer"), will set forth the agreement between the Composer and _____ (the "Producer") relating to the original music and recordings thereof _____ (the "Music") for Producer's television series currently entitled _____ (the "Series") and a pilot for the Series (the "Pilot").

1. *Ownership of Copyright.* Producer and Composer will own jointly the copyright in the Music composed by Composer and all rights, title and interest therein (the "Rights") throughout the universe in perpetuity. In particular, producer will own fifty percent (50%) of the copyright in the Music and Rights and Composer will own fifty percent (50%) of the copyright in the Music and Rights.

2. *Use of Music.* Producer will use the Music in the Series unless the network or other primary licensee objects to the use thereof. Composer will provide the copy of appropriate masters of the Music to Producer. Composer will provide additional masters to Producer on a cost basis if and when required by Producer. Producer and Composer hereby irrevocably license such use.

3. *Compensation.* For all rights to use the Music in the Pilot and, if produced, the Series, Producer will pay the following compensation to Composer:

(a)   The sum of $_____ payable upon the signing of the agreement for the direct, out-of-pocket recording costs of the master tape for the Pilot.

(b)   The sum of $_____ if the Series is produced and the Music is used therein.

(c)   The sum of $_____ if the Series is produced and the Music is not used therein pursuant to Paragraph 2 hereof. Composer shall be solely liable for any third party talent payments due at any time with respect to any use of the Music or the Rights hereunder.

4. *Small Performance Rights*. Customary small performance royalties will be shared as and when received through performance rights organizations. Producer, or a company designated by Producer, will act as publisher for this purpose and Producer and Composer will each take fifty percent (50%) respectively of the Publisher's share and the Composer will receive one hundred percent (100%) of the writer's share.

5. *Credit*. Composer will receive on-screen credit in the closing titles of each program of the Series in substantially the following form:

Music By _____

No inadvertent or accidental failure to provide such credit shall constitute a breach.

6. *Decisions*. Administrative decisions, licensing arrangements and other business decisions relating to the Music and the Rights and not otherwise discussed herein will be resolved by the mutual consent of Composer and Producer.

7. *Representations and Warranties*. Composer hereby represents and warrants that:

(a)   Composer is free to enter into this Agreement and is able to comply with the obligations and agreements hereunder. Composer has not made, and will not make, any commitment or agreement which could or might materially interfere with the full and complete performance of Composer's obligations and agreements hereunder or which could or might in any way diminish the value of Producer's full enjoyment of the rights or privileges of Producer hereunder.

(b)   All material which Composer may write, prepare, compose and/or submit in connection with the Music (except any such material in the public domain) shall be wholly original with Composer, and no such material shall be copied in whole or in part from any other work or shall infringe upon or violate any right of privacy of, constitute a libel against or violate any right of any entity.

Please indicate your acceptance of these terms by signing the enclosed counterpart copy on the indicated lines below and returning it to the undersigned. While we will, in all likelihood, enter into a more detailed agreement containing additional provisions customary in the entertainment industry, unless and until such agreement is executed by us, this letter shall constitute the binding agreement between us relating to the Music in the Series and Pilot.

Yours sincerely,
[Producer]

By: _____

Title: _____

AGREED TO AND ACCEPTED:

_____

[Composer]

APPENDIX B17

Performer Release

[Producer Letterhead]

The undersigned Performer hereby releases the above specified Producer and its successors, licensees and assigns from any and all claims, actions and damages relating to or arising out of the use in any context and in any form by Producer, its successors, licensees and assigns, of the musical compositions described below and any recorded performances thereof in which Performer may have participated.

Performer irrevocably assigns to Producer any and all rights which he/she may have to such compositions and performances, and agrees that any matter subject to copyright which he/she may have created in connection therewith will be a work for hire, with Producer deemed to be the author. Producer, and its successors, licensees and assigns, may change or edit any aspect of such compositions and performances as it sees fit, and may exploit them throughout the universe in any medium now known or hereafter discovered in perpetuity.

Performer acknowledges that she/he has received good and valuable consideration for the agreements set out above, and that Producer is relying on these agreements in connection with its exploitation of the compositions and performances.

Signed: _____

Performer's Name, Address,
and Social Security Number:

_____

_____

Dated: _____

Compositions: _____

APPENDIX B18

Video Synchronization and Distribution License

THIS AGREEMENT made and entered into this _____ day of _____ by and between _____ ("Publisher") and _____ ("Licensee").

WHEREAS Publisher owns or controls the musical composition ("Composition") entitled _____, written by _____; and

WHEREAS Licensee desires to utilize the Composition in that certain production entitled _____ ("Production"), and to reproduce the Production and Composition in videocassettes and videodiscs (both devices being referred to herein as "Videograms");

NOW THEREFORE the parties hereto do hereby mutually agree as follows:

1. In consideration of the royalties to be paid hereunder by Licensee to Publisher and the other covenants herein on the part of the Licensee, the Publisher hereby grants to Licensee the nonexclusive right and license to reproduce and make copies of the Composition in Videogram copies of the Production and to distribute the Videograms to the public by sale or other transfer of ownership.*

2. No right to rent Videograms is hereby granted. If Licensee wishes to utilize Videograms via rental, Licensee shall advise Publisher in writing and the parties hereto shall negotiate in good faith the compensation or other participation to be paid to Publisher in respect of rental receipts.

---

* If there is a one-time payment for the Videogram license, then the foregoing license should be modified as follows: the first line of Paragraph 1 should be changed to read, "In consideration of the sum of $_____ to be paid by Licensee to Publisher upon execution hereof and the"; paragraphs 5, 6 and 7 are to be deleted; and paragraphs 8, 9 and 10 are to be renumbered 5, 6 and 7, respectively.

3.   This license and grant is for a term of _____ years only, commencing on the date of this agreement. At the expiration or earlier termination of such period, all rights and licenses granted hereunder shall cease and terminate.

4.   The rights granted hereunder are limited solely to the territory of _____ (the "licensed territory").

5.   As compensation to the Publisher, Licensor agrees to pay to the Publisher the following royalties:

   a) As to each copy of a videodisc sold in the licensed territory and paid for and not returned _____, and

   b) As to each copy of a videocassette sold in the licensed territory and paid for and not returned _____.

6.   Accountings shall be rendered by Licensee to Publisher within sixty (60) days after the close of each calendar quarter, showing in detail the royalties earned, and any deductions taken in computing royalties. Publisher shall be responsible for paying royalties to writers and any third party by reason of the grant and license hereunder. No statement shall be due for a period in which Videograms are not sold. All royalty statements shall be binding upon Publisher and is subject to any objection by publisher for any reason unless specific objection in writing, stating the basis thereof, is given to Licensee within one (1) year from the date rendered.

7.   Publisher shall have the right to inspect and make abstracts of the books and records of Licensee, insofar as said books and records pertain to the performance of Licensee's obligations hereunder; such inspection to be made on at least ten (10) days written notice, during normal business hours of normal business days but not more frequently than once annually in each year.

8.   The rights and license granted hereunder may not be assigned or transferred, either affirmatively or by operation of law, without Publisher's written consent.

9.   Publisher warrants and represents that it has full right, power and authority to enter into and to perform this agreement.

10. This agreement shall be deemed made in and shall be construed in accordance with the laws of the State of New York. The agreement may not be modified orally and shall not be binding or effective unless and until it is signed by both parties hereto.

IN WITNESS WHEREOF the parties have entered into this agreement the day and year first above written.

Publisher

By: _____

Licensee

By: _____

APPENDIX B19

Television Film Synchronization License

To: _____ TV Lic. # _____ Date _____

Composition: _____

1. In consideration of the sum of _____ payable upon the execution hereof, we grant you the non-exclusive right to record on film or video tape the above identified musical composition(s) in synchronization or timed relation with a single episode or individual program entitled _____ for television use only, subject to all of the terms and conditions herein provided.

2.   (a) The type of use is to be _____

        (b) On or before the first telecast of the said film, you or your assigns agree to furnish to us a copy of the Cue Sheet prepared and distributed in connection therewith.

3. The territory covered by this license is the world.

4.   (a) This license is for a period of _____ from the date hereof.

        (b) Upon the expiration of this license all rights herein granted shall cease and terminate and the right to make or authorize any further use or distribution of any recordings made hereunder shall also cease and terminate.

5. This is a license to record only and does not authorize any use of the aforesaid musical composition(s) not expressly set forth herein. By way of illustration but not limitation, this license does not include the right to change or adapt the words or to alter the fundamental character of the music of said musical composition(s) or to use the title(s) thereof as the title or sub-title of said film.

6. Performance of the said musical composition(s) in the exhibition of said film is subject to the condition that each television station over which the aforesaid musical composition(s) is (are) to be so performed shall have a performance license issued by us or

from a person, firm, corporation, society, association or other entity having the legal right to issue such performance license.

7.   No sound records produced pursuant to this license are to be manufactured, sold and/or used separately or independently of said film.

8.   The film shall be for television use only and may not be televised into theatres or other places where admission is charged.

9.   All rights not herein specifically granted are reserved by us.

10. We warrant only that we have the legal right to grant this license and this license is given and accepted without other warranty or recourse. If said warranty shall be breached in whole or in part with respect to (any of) said musical composition(s), our total liability shall be limited either to repaying to you the consideration theretofore paid under this license with respect to such musical composition to the extent of such breach or to holding you harmless to the extent of the consideration theretofore paid under this license with respect to such musical composition to the extent of said breach.

11. This license shall run to you, your successors and assigns, provided you shall remain liable for the performance of all of the terms and conditions of this license on your part to be performed and provided further that any disposition of said film or any prints thereof shall be subject to all the terms hereof, and you agree that all persons, firms or corporations acquiring from you any right, title, interest in or possession of said film or any prints thereof shall be notified of the terms and conditions of this license and shall agree to be bound thereby.

_____

(Licensor)

By _____

Reprinted from *This Business of Music,* by permission.

APPENDIX B20
Performance License

1. *BASIC INFORMATION.*

Program: _____

Producer: _____

Composition: _____

Type of Use: _____

Duration of Use: _____

Composer: _____

Lyricist: _____

Publisher: _____

Medium of Use: _____

Territory of Use: _____

Dates of Use: _____

Number of Repeats: _____

Consideration: _____

License Grantor: _____

2. *GRANT OF LICENSE.*

All capitalized terms used in this license refer to those items specified in the Basic Information set forth above. Provided that the Consideration is paid in full upon signing hereof, the undersigned License Grantor hereby grants Producer, and its licensees and assigns, the right to perform the Composition publicly through television in connection with the exhibition of the Program through the Medium of Use and throughout the Territory of Use. This license shall only cover the Type of Use and Duration of Use specified above, and shall only apply during the Dates of Use and only for the specified Number of Repeats. Producer represents and warrants that it has received a valid synchronization licensee for this use. The License Grantor represents and warrants that the License Grantor has the power to grant this performance license, and that the performance of the Composition in accordance with this license will not violate the rights of any third party. This license is subject to the receipt by the License Grantor from the Producer, on or about the first performance authorized hereunder, of a copy of the complete musical cue sheet for the Program.

3. *SIGNATURES AND DATE.*

License Grantor: _____

Signature: _____

Name and Title: _____

Date: _____

Producer: _____

Signature: _____

Name and Title: _____

Date: _____

APPENDIX B21

Sample Motion Picture or Television Film Cue Sheet

[Production Company Name]
[Program Title]
[Date]

No.	Selection	Composer	Publisher	Extent	How Used	Time
REELS 1 & 2						
1.	Medley consisting of:					
	(a) Signature	Jane Doe	XYZ	Entire	Bkg. Inst.	0.07
	(b) Juniper	Jane Doe	XYZ	Entire	Vis. Voc.	5.37
2.	Cowboys	Mike Roe	ABC	Partial	Bkg. Inst.	0.34
3.	Medley consisting of:					
	(a) Juniper	Jane Doe	XYZ	Partial	Bkg. Inst.	0.09
	(b) Cowboys	Mike Roe	ABC	Entire	Bkg. Inst.	0.45
	(c) Juniper	Jane Doe	FGH	Partial	Bkg. Inst.	0.38
	(d) The Boys	Irv Grow	XYZ	Partial	Bkg. Inst.	0.47
4.	The Girls	May Joe	ABC	Entire	Byg. Inst.	0.05
5.	The Birds	May Joe	ABC	Entire	Vis. Voc.	2.45
REELS 3 & 4						
6.	Kermits	May Loe	ABC	Entire	Vis. Voc.	2.09
7.	Kermits	May Loe	XYZ	Partial	Bkg. Inst.	0.23
8.	Medley consisting of:					
	(a) Juniper	Jane Doe	XYZ	Partial	Bkg. Inst.	1.40
	(b) Cleo	Bob Smith	ABC	Entire	Vis. Voc.	1.50
	(c) Kermac	May Loe	ABC	Entire	Bkg. Inst.	1.30
9.	Kermac	May Loe	ABC	Entire	Vis. Voc.	1.25
10.	Medley consisting of:					
	(a) Juniper	Jane Doe	ABC	Partial	Bkg. Inst.	0.24
	(b) Cowboys	Mike Roe	ABC	Partial	Bkg. Inst.	0.24
	(c) Juniper	Jane Doe	XYZ	Partial	Bkg. Inst.	0.12
	(d) Cowboys	Mike Roe	ABC	Partial	Bkg. Inst.	0.14
	(e) Juniper	Jane Doe	XYZ	Partial	Bkg. Inst.	0.30
	(f) Cowboys	Mike Roe	ABC	Entire	Bkg. Inst.	0.45

Adapted from *This Business of Music*, by permission.

APPENDIX B22
Design/Location: Issue Checklist

[Note: See the checklists for Rights Acquisition and for Talent and Service Agreements for general considerations applicable to design and location agreements.]

1. How are the design services being handled?
   - What is to be designed?
   - What is the approval process?
   - Who arranges for, and oversees, construction and fabrication?
   - What are the delivery dates?
   - What are the ongoing responsibilities of the designer?
   - What is the initial compensation of the designer?
   - What is the ongoing compensation of the designer?
   - Are there residuals or reuse fees?
   - Who owns the designs?
   - Is there an applicable union or guild?

2. How is the location being arranged?
   - Is a location manager or outside location service being used?
   - Are you dealing with an owner or leaser who has the power to grant both the right of access and any necessary media rights?
   - What are the times of access?
   - Who is responsible for damages?
   - Who is responsible for carrying insurance; what types and how much?
   - Are changes and construction permitted?
   - What maintenance staff is required, and who pays for it?
   - What compensation is payable for the location use and any media rights?

APPENDIX B23
Location Release

Owner/Tenant: _____

Producer: _____

Premises: _____

Program: _____

The undersigned Owner/Tenant hereby agrees to permit the Producer to use the Premises, both exterior and interior, for the purpose of filming, photographing and/or otherwise recording scenes for the Program. Producer and its licensees and assigns shall have the right to use the film, photographs and/or other recording made on and showing the Premises in any manner throughout the world in perpetuity without any limitations or restrictions.

Producer will have the right to film, photograph and/or otherwise record in and around the Premises for _____ days, commencing _____ (subject to change due to adverse weather conditions).

Producer will leave the Premises in the same condition as existed prior to use, and Producer will indemnify and hold the Owner/Tenant harmless from all claims for damages occurring during its use of the Premises, which arose out of its activities.

Owner/Tenant acknowledges that it has received good and valuable consideration for this grant and warrants that it has the authority to grant the rights granted herein with respect to the Premises.

PRODUCER

By: _____

Title: _____

OWNER/TENANT

By: _____

Title: _____

APPENDIX B24
Production: Issue Checklist

1. What production facilities will be used?
   - Which studio?
   - Which location(s)?
   - Which mobile unit (truck)?
   - Does the facility offer sufficient technical and staging resources for the production?
   - Can rentals fill in the gaps?

2. Does the facility provide adequate non-technical support?
   - Are dressing rooms, make-up and hair, and wardrobe provided, or must facilities be rented?
   - Is an audience holding area needed? Is it available on the premises, or must other rental arrangements be made?
   - Is office space available for the production staff, or must it be rented? What is the cost of renting it from the facility? Is this a fair price?
   - Is parking available, or must arrangements be made?
   - Are dining facilities available nearby, or must catering be arranged?

3. On what basis will the facilities be rented?
   - Hourly?
   - Daily?
   - Weekly?
   - Monthly?
   - On a bulk rate, based on multiple uses?

4. What equipment and other facilities will be included in the studio or soundstage rental package?
   - Will lighting equipment be provided? How many instruments? What types? What are the capabilities of the lighting board?
   - Does the facility have adequate power and air conditioning to service the production?
   - How many cameras will be provided? How many hand-helds, how many pedestal cameras, how many with special mounts (such as cranes)?
   - Will audio be handled by the house, or by an outside contractor?

- How many microphones will be provided? What types? Any special mountings? Are there any special charges, or special technical issues, related to the use of RF wireless microphones? What are the limitations of the house PA system?
- What type of equipment will be used to record and to mix the program?
- What audio playback facilities come with the package?
- How many videotape machines will be provided? What are the formats? What is the cost of additional machines?
- What is the make and model of the video switcher? Does it offer the flexibility needed for the production?
- What type of computer graphics devices (including character generator, DVE, still-store) are available?
- What are the capabilities and limitations of the communications system?
- Is the facility available after hours for the scenic crew?
- What is the overall quality of the technical facility? Is the equipment relatively new and properly maintained? Does the facility offer the flexibility needed for the production?

5. Technical Crew:
   - Who will hire the crew?
   - Will the crew work under union rules? Which union?
   - What are the hourly or daily rates for each individual crew member? What are the overtime charges?
   - Are there any special work rules for crew members, such as guaranteed meal breaks or rest periods? Are there penalties associated with breaking these rules?
   - Who will the key crew members be? Can the director approve these crew members? Can the director replace them?

6. Stage Crew:
   - Who will hire the stagehands?
   - Do they belong to a union?
   - What are the rates and work rules?
   - How many people will be needed to set up, run and strike the production?

7. Financial Arrangements:
   - Is a payment required to reserve the facility? Is it refundable? Under what circumstances?
   - On what basis will the facility be billed?
   - How often will the studio bill (for a series)?

- Will outside rentals and free-lance personnel be billed through the facility (at a mark-up), or hired directly by the producer?
- Does the facility carry adequate insurance?
- What is the cost of using the facility's phones, copier and fax machine? For a big project, can the production install its own phone system?
- If the program is a pilot, is there any further responsibility to the facility regarding the series?

APPENDIX B25
Lab Letter

[Date]

[Name and Address of Laboratory]

Gentlemen:

The undersigned, _____ ("Producer") has entered into an agreement (the "Agreement") with _____ ("Distributor") under which Agreement Distributor has been granted certain distribution rights in and to the television programs entitled _____ (the "Programs").

For good and valuable consideration, receipt of which is hereby acknowledged, it is hereby agreed, for the express benefit of Distributor, as follows:

1. You now have in your possession in the name of Producer the materials ("Materials") listed in Exhibit A attached hereto for said Programs; you certify that all materials are ready and suitable for the making of commercially acceptable release copies and duplicating material, including visual elements and soundtracks.

2. You will retain possession of all Materials at your laboratory located at _____ and you will not deliver any of said Materials to anyone without the written consent of Producer and Distributor.

3. Distributor and its designees shall at all times have access to said Materials.

4. You will at all times perform all laboratory services requested by Distributor or its designers relating to the Programs, which laboratory services will be performed by you at prevailing rates at Distributor's sole expense.

5. Neither Distributor nor Producer shall have any liability for any indebtedness to you incurred by the other.

6. You presently have no claim or lien against the Programs or the Materials, nor, insofar as Distributor is concerned, will you assert any claim or lien against the Programs or the Materials except for your charges for services rendered for and materials furnished to Distributor.

7. This Agreement is irrevocable and may not be altered or modified except by a written instrument executed by Distributor and Producer.

Please signify your agreement to the foregoing by signing where indicated below.

Very truly yours,
[Producer]

By: _____

AGREED TO:
[Name of Laboratory]

By: _____

CONSENTED TO:
[Distributor]

By: _____

EXHIBIT A

[For Videotape Productions]

(a) the fully edited, titled and assembled electronic master of each Program on SMPTE 1-inch Type C format videotape with fully synchronized sound;

(b) all videotape footage shot or created in connection with each Program including all title and credit sequences;

(c) all separate dialog tracks, sound effects tracks and music tracks recorded on magnetic media; and

(d) any scripts, notes and logs relating to the editing of the Programs.

APPENDIX B26
Business Entities and Tax: Issue Checklist

1. What kind of business entity is appropriate?
   - Is the economy and simplicity of a sole proprietorship important?
   - Will there be more than one owner, requiring a partnership or a limited liability company or corporation?
   - Is the flexibility of a partnership or a limited liability company important?
   - If the business is for a limited purpose, would a joint-venture form of partnership or a specific purpose limited liability company be appropriate?
   - Is the limited liability of a corporation, a limited liability partnership, or a limited liability company important?
   - Would a limited partnership, if available, provide enough limited liability?
   - Are the tax benefits of a partnership or a limited liability company important?
   - Would a Sub-Chapter S corporation provide enough tax benefits?
   - Is Sub-Chapter S treatment available?
   - Is the corporate form or a limited liability company too expensive to set up and maintain?

2. What is the most advantageous state in which to establish the business?
   - The state where the headquarters of the business will be located?
   - Some other state where there will be a significant business presence?
   - A state with flexible and attractive corporate, limited liability company or partnership laws and taxes, such as Delaware or Nevada?

3. If a sole proprietorship, partnership, or joint venture, have the usual filings been made?
   - The 'doing business as' or 'fictitious name' certificate?

- The federal taxpayer identification number?
- The employment-related filings at the state and federal level?
- If a limited partnership, has the limited partnership certificate been filed and any publishing requirement been met?

4. If a corporation, have the usual filings been made?
   - The certificate or articles of incorporation?
   - The federal tax identification number?
   - The employment-related filings at the state and federal level?
   - The federal and any state Sub-Chapter S filing, if applicable?

5. If a limited liability company, have the usual filings been made?
   - The certificate or articles of organization?
   - The election of federal tax treatment as a partnership or corporation?
   - The federal tax identification number?
   - The employment related filings at the state and federal level?

6. Have matters of governance and management been decided?
   - Who are the officers, managers or managing partners?
   - Who are the directors?
   - How are officers, directors, managers and managing partners elected?
   - How are day-to-day and major decisions made?
   - Who has banking authority?
   - Who decides to admit new partners or new members or sell more stock?
   - Who approves mergers, sales of the business, major loans, other significant business events?
   - Who designates the lawyers, accountants and other major service providers?

7. Have matters of finance been determined?
   - Who is contributing to capital?
   - In cash?
   - In kind?
   - Who is loaning money or other property?
   - What is the return on these investments?
   - Is there a priority return through contract recoupment, debt, or preferred stock?
   - Has a budget estimate showing working capital needs been prepared?

8. How have management and financial matters been established?
   - By default, as a matter of applicable law?
   - If a joint venture, partnership or limited liability company, in a written agreement?
   - If a corporation, in the certificate of incorporation, in the By-Laws, or in a shareholders agreement?
   - Through a loan agreement and notes?

9. Have a lawyer and an accountant been consulted?

Resources

APPENDIX C 1

Selected Bibliography

Battersby, Gregory J., and Charles W. Grimes. *The Law of Merchandise and Character Licensing*. New York: Clark Boardman, 1992.

Boorstyn, Neil. *Boorstyn on Copyright*. 2d ed. Cleveland: West Group, 1998.

Brenner, Daniel L., Monroe E. Price, and Michael I. Meyerson. *Cable Television and Other Non Broadcast Video, Law and Policy*. New York: Clark Boardman, 1990.

Brinson, J. Dianne, and Mark F. Radcliffe. *Multimedia Law and Business Handbook*. Bodega, California: Interactive Multimedia Assoc., 1996.

Castleman, Harry, and Walter J. Podrazik. *The TV Schedule Book: Four Decades of Network Programming from Sign-On to Sign-Off*. New York: McGraw-Hill, 1984.

Castleman, Harry, and Walter J. Podrazik. *Watching TV: Four Decades of American Television*. New York: McGraw-Hill, 1982.

Crandall, Robert W., and Harold Furchgott-Roth. *Cable TV: Regulation or Competition?* Washington, DC: The Brookings Institution, 1996.

Creech, Kenneth C. *Electronic Media Law and Regulation*. Woburn, Massachusetts: Focal Press, 1996.

Epstein, Michael A. *Modern Intellectual Property*, 3d ed. Gaithersburg, Maryland: Aspen, 1998.

Goldstein, Paul. *Copyright*. Gaithersburg, Maryland: Aspen, 1998.

Goodale, James C. *All About Cable, Legal and Business Aspects of Cable and Pay Television*. New York: Law Journal Seminars Press, 1997.

Holmes, William C. *Intellectual Property and Antitrust Law*. Cleveland: West Group, 1998.

Kitwak, Mark. *Dealmaking in the Film and Television Industry*. Los Angeles: Silman-Jones/DGA, 1994.

Knauer, Leon T., et al., *Telecommunications Act Handbook*. Rockville, Maryland: Government Institutes, Inc., 1996.

Krattenmaker, Thomas G. *Telecommunications Law and Policy.* Durham, North Carolina: Carolina Academic Press, 1994.

Lindey, Alexander. *Lindey on Entertainment, Publishing and the Arts: Agreements and the Law.* New York: Clark Boardman, 1990.

London, Mel. *Getting into Video: A Career Guide.* New York: Ballantine Books, 1990.

McCarthy, J. Thomas. *McCarthy on Trademarks and Unfair Competition,* 4th ed. Cleveland: West Group, 1998.

McCarthy, J. Thomas. *The Rights of Publicity and Privacy.* New York: Clark Boardman, 1994.

Miller, Philip. *Media law for Producers,* 2d ed. Woburn, Massachusetts: Focal Press, 1996.

Minow, Newton N., and Craig L. LaMay. *Abandoned in the Wasteland: Children, Television, and the First Amendment.* New York: Hill and Wang, 1995.

Nimmer, Melville B., and David Nimmer. *Nimmer on Copyright.* New York: Matthew Bender, 1997.

Resnik, Gail, and Scott Trost. *All You Need to Know about the Movie and TV Business.* New York: Fireside, 1996.

Roman, James W. *Cablemania: The Cable Television Sourcebook.* Englewood Cliffs, New Jersey: Prentice-Hall, 1983.

Rosini, Neil J. *The Practical Guide to Libel Law.* Westport, Connecticut: Praeger, 1991.

Sableman, Mark, *More Speech, Not Less: Communications Law in the Information Age.* Carbondale, Illinois: Southern Illinois University Press, 1997.

Sanford, Bruce W. *Libel and Privacy: The Prevention of Defense of Litigation.* Englewood, Cliffs, New Jersey: Prentice Hall Law and Business, 1987.

Selz, Thomas D., Melvin Simensky, and Patricia Acton. *Entertainment Law: Legal Concepts and Business Practices.* Colorado Springs, Colorado: Shepards/McGraw-Hill, Inc., 1990.

Shemel, Sidney, and M. William Krasilovsky. *This Business of Music,* Sixth Edition. New York: Billboard Books, 1997.

Smolla, Rodney A. *Smolla and Nimmer on Freedom of Speech.* New York: Clark Boardman Callaghan, 1997.

Streeter, Thomas. *Selling the Air*. Chicago: University of Chicago Press, 1996.

Vogel, Harold L. *Entertainment Industry Economics, A Guide for Financial Analysis*, 3rd ed. Cambridge: Cambridge University Press 1994.

Williams, Huntington. *Beyond Control: ABC and the Fate of the Networks*. New York: Atheneum, 1989.

Winship, Michael. *Television*. New York: Random House, 1988.

APPENDIX C2

Source Directories for Further Information

Motion Picture, TV, and Theatre Directory
Motion Picture Enterprises Publications, Inc.
P.O. Box 276
Tarrytown, New York 10591
212-245-0969 Fax: 212-245-0974
Annual directory of services and products used in industry.

The Producers Masterguide
60 E. 8th Street, 34th Floor
New York, New York 10003
212-777-4002 Fax: 212-777-4101
Annual international production manual for motion picture, television, commercial, cable and videotape industry including current labor contract wage scales, information on major awards, guidelines and bidding procedures for commercial production and directory of suppliers.

APPENDIX C3
Guilds and Unions

NATIONAL OFFICES

American Federation of Musicians (AFM)
1501 Broadway, Suite 600
New York, New York 10036
212-869-1330 Fax: 212-764-6134
http://www.afm.org
info@afm.org
Union headquarters for all local AFM musician unions. Representation for local musician unions in the interpretation of agreements, negotiations and settlements.

American Federation of Television and Radio Artists
(AFTRA)
260 Madison Avenue
New York, New York 10016
212-532-0800 Fax: 212-545-1238
http://www.aftra.org
Union representing performers and news people in the fields of videotape, television, radio, commercials and phonograph recordings. Local offices have web sites off the main site.

American Guild of Musical Artists (AGMA)
1727 Broadway
New York, New York 10019-5284
212-265-3687 Fax: 212-262-9088
Representing ballet dancers, opera singers and other concert performers.

Alliance of Canadian Cinema, Television and Radio Artists
(ACTRA)
2239 Yonge Street
Toronto, Ontario, M4S 2B5
416-489-1311, 800-387-3516 Fax: 416-489-8076
http://www.actra.com/
apg@actra.com

Directors Guild of America (DGA)
7920 Sunset Boulevard
Los Angeles, California 90046
(310) 289-2000 Fax: 310-289-2029
http://www.dga.org
dga@dga.org
The work of DGA members is represented in theatrical motion pictures; television (filmed, live, or taped); radio, industrial, educational and government films; and commercials.

International Alliance of Theatrical Stage Employees
(IATSE)
1515 Broadway, Suite 601
New York, New York 10036
212 730-1770 Fax: 212-921-7699
http://www.iatse.lm.com
newsgroup: alt.union.iatse
Represents pre-production, production and post-production; technical and artistic (behind the camera) workers in the motion picture and television industries.

National Association of Broadcast Employees and Technicians
(NABET)
501 3rd Street, N.W.
Washington, DC 20001
202-434-1254 Fax: 202 434-1426
Represents pre-production, production and post-production; technical and artistic (behind the camera) workers in the motion picture and television industries.

Screen Actors Guild (SAG)
5757 Wilshire
Los Angeles, California 90036
213-954-1600 Fax: call for specific fax number
http://www.sag.com/
Trade union that negotiates minimum wages and working conditions for professional screen actors who perform in theatrical motion picture, prime-time television, commercial, industrials films and music videos.

Writers Guild of America (WGA)
555 West 57th Street
New York, New York 10019
212-245-6180 Fax: 212-582-1909
http://www.wgaeast.org/
info@wgaeast.org

(West Coast Office)
7000 West Third Street
Los Angeles, California 90049
213-951-4000 Fax: 213-782-4800
http://www.wga.org/
wga@wga.org
Union representing screen, television, and radio writers for the purpose of collective bargaining. The WGA's service also covers the enforcement and administration of agreements made from collective bargaining negotiations.

CALIFORNIA

Affiliated Property Craftspersons (IATSE), Local 44
11500 Burbank Boulevard
North Hollywood, California 91601
818-769-2500 Fax: 818-769-1739
Members consist of prop makers, coordinators, property masters, set decorators and special effects personnel.

American Federation of Musicians (AFM)
7080 Hollywood Boulevard
Suite 1020
Hollywood, California 90028
213-461-3441 Fax: 213-462-8340
http://www.afm.org
info@afm.org
California headquarters for all local AFM musicians. Representation for local musicians in the interpretation of agreements, negotiations and settlements.

American Federation of Television and Radio Artists (AFTRA)
5757 Wilshire Boulevard, 9th Floor
Los Angeles, California 90036
213-634-8100 Fax: 213-634-8246
http://www.aftra.org

American Guild of Variety Artists
4741 Laurel Canyon Boulevard, Suite 208
North Hollywood, California 91607
818-508-9984 Fax: 818-508-3029
Represents singers, dancers, ice skaters, circus acts and other variety performers.

Broadcast TV Recording Engineers & Communication Technicians (IBEW) Local 45
6255 Sunset Boulevard, Suite 721
Los Angeles, California 90028
213-851-5515 Fax: 213-466-1793
Represents broadcast recording engineers and technicians

Costume Designers Guild (IATSE) Local 892
13949 Ventura Boulevard, Suite 309
Sherman Oaks, California 91423
818-905-1557 Fax: 818-905-1560

Directors Guild of America (DGA)
7920 Sunset Boulevard,
Los Angeles, California 90046
310 289-2000 Fax: 310 289-2029
http://www.dga.org
dga@dga.org
The work of DGA members is represented in theatrical motion pictures; television (filmed, live, or taped); radio, industrial, educational and government films; and commercials.

IATSE & MPMO International (AFL-CIO)
13949 Ventura Boulevard, Suite 300
Sherman Oaks, California 91423
818-905-8999 Fax: 818-905-6297
http://www.iatse.lm.com
kayp22@earthlink.net

Illustrators & Matte Artists (IATSE) Local 790
13949 Ventura Boulevard, Suite 301
Sherman Oaks, California 91423
818-784-6555 Fax: 818-784-2004
Representing illustrators and matte artists who create scenes using photographic prints together with live action footage.

International Brotherhood of Electrical Workers Local 40
5643 Vineland Avenue
North Hollywood, California 91601
213-877-1171 Fax: 818-762-4379
Studio responsibilities: electrical construction and maintenance, power distribution, handling generators for power supply, house panel hook-ups, repairs of electronic equipment and air conditioning.

International Photographers (Cameramen) (IATSE) Local 659
7715 Sunset Boulevard, Suite 300
Hollywood, California 90046
213-876-0160 Fax: 213-876-6383
Representing people who direct photography and operate camera/photographic equipment.

International Sound Technicians, Cinema Technicians, Studio Projectionists & Video Projection Technicians (IATSE) Local 695
5439 Cahuenga Boulevard
North Hollywood, California 91601
818-985-9204 Fax: 818-760-4681
Labor union representing people who operate sound, transparency process and projection equipment, and who maintain and rebuild camera and other equipment used for picture projection. These people do not operate the movieolas used for editing and/or cutting.

Laboratory Film-Video Technicians, Local 683
2600 West Victory Boulevard, P.O. Box 7429
Burbank, California 91505
818-955-9720 Fax: 818-955-5834
Representing people who handle all phases of film processing for motion pictures and television.

Make Up Artists and Hair Stylists (IATSE) Local 706
11519 Chandler Boulevard
North Hollywood, California 91601
818-984-1700 Fax: 818-980-8561
Representing people who apply make-up and style hair.

Motion Picture & Television Editors Guild (Film Editors) (IATSE) Local 776
7715 Sunset Boulevard, Suite 200
Hollywood, California 90046
213-876-4770 Fax: 213-876-0861
web: http://www.editorsguild.com
email: mail@editorsguild.com

Representing the people who edit and/or cut positive prints for motion pictures, serials, short films and trailers. This includes people who assemble and synchronize sound or sound effects on film tracks.

Motion Picture Costumers (IATSE) Local 705
1427 North LaBrea Avenue
Los Angeles, California 90028
213-851-0220 Fax: 213-851-9062
Representing people who supervise and operate the wardrobe department, test shooting, script breakdown and research (in regards to costume), requisition, fitting, handling, manufacturing and wardrobe storage.

Motion Picture Craft Service (IATSE) Local 727
13949 Ventura Boulevard,
Sherman Oaks, California 91423
818-385-1950 Fax: 818-385-1057
Representing on-location personnel, production-oriented unskilled labor. Responsibilities include assisting members of other crafts, supplying, moving and/or maintaining benches/tables and opening/closing stage doors.

Motion Picture First Aid Employees (IATSE) Local 767
14530 Denker Avenue
Gardena, California 90247
310-352-4485 (818-760-5341-personnel)
Representing people who give medical treatment to crews, instruct and/or train in first-aid techniques and assist or advise on medical-related set decoration and/or procedures.

Motion Picture Screen Cartoonists (IATSE) Local 839
4729 Lankershim Boulevard
North Hollywood, California 91602
818-766-7151 Fax: 818-506-4805
Has jurisdiction over the entire animation process: animation writing, storyboard, layout, background, animation, checking and ink-and-pen.

Motion Picture Set Painters & Sign Writers (IATSE) Local 729
11365 Ventura Boulevard, Suite 202
Studio City, California 91604
818-984-3000 No Fax
Representing people who paint, decorate and make signs for sets.

Motion Picture Studio Grips (IATSE) Local 80
2520 West Olive Avenue
Burbank, California 91505
213-931-1419 Fax: 818-526-0719
Representing people who build, handle, maintain, load, unload and store grip equipment, including camera perching and installation. Also represent people who rig, strike, build and move equipment on sets and backlots.

Musicians Union (AFM) Local 47
817 North Vine Street
Hollywood, California 90038
213-462-2161 Fax: 213-461-3090

National Association of Broadcast Employees & Technicians (NABET) Local 53
1918 West Burbank Boulevard
Burbank, California 91506
818-846-0490 Fax: 818-846-2306

Office & Professional Employees (OPEIU) Local 174
120 S. Victory Boulevard, Suit 201
Burbank, California 91502
818-842-5572 Fax: 818-842-7813
Representing office, clerical and professional employees.

Ornamental Plasterers & Sculptors Local 755
13949 Ventura Boulevard, Suite 305
Sherman Oaks, California 92401
818-379-9711
Representing modelers, sculptors and plasterers for the entertainment industry.

Production Office Coordinators & Accountants Guild (IATSE)
Local 717
14724 Ventura Boulevard, Penthouse Suite
Sherman Oaks, California 91423
818-906-9986 Fax: 818-990-8287
Production office coordinators set up and run the production offices, working in conjunction with the unit production manager to coordinate all aspects of the production from shooting schedule through rental of equipment to daily production reports. Production accountants set up and maintain a full set of general ledger books, handling all aspects of accounting for the production.

Publicists Guild (IATSE) Local 818
13949 Ventura Boulevard, Suite 302
Sherman Oaks, California 91423
818-905-1541 Fax: 818-905-6944

Scenic & Title & Graphic Artists (IATSE) Local 816
13949 Ventura Boulevard, Penthouse 5
Sherman Oaks, California 91423
818-906-7822 Fax: 818-906-0481
Representing scenic artists, set painters, graphic designers, title designers, courtroom illustrators, portrait artists, electronic graphic artists and video illustrators.

Screen Actors Guild (SAG)
5757 Wilshire Boulevard
Los Angeles, California 90036
213-954-1600 Fax: call for specific number
http://www.sag.com

Screen Story Analysts (IATSE) Local 854
13949 Ventura Boulevard, Suite 301
Sherman Oaks, California 91423
818-784-6555 Fax: 818-784-2004
Representing people who read, synopsize and/or comment on literary and dramatic properties. This includes critique, editorial, analytical breakdown, legal comparison, foreign translation and synopsis.

Script Supervisors (IATSE) Local 871
13111 Ventura Boulevard
Studio City, California 91614
818-995-6195
Representing people who break down scripts for motion pictures, television and commercials. This includes recording timings, verification of actor's lines and assistance with scene blocking and continuity.

Set Designers & Model Makers (IATSE) Local 847
13949 Ventura Boulevard, Suite 301
Sherman Oaks, California 91423
818-784-6555 Fax: 818-784-2004
Representing people who prepare layouts, set models, working drawings, miniatures and backgrounds.

Studio Electrical Lighting Technicians (IATSE) Local 728
14629 Nordhoff Boulevard
Panorama City, California 91402
213-851-3300 Fax: 818-851-5288
Representing people who handle all on-set electrical equipment and apparatus.

Studio Transportation Drivers (Teamsters) Local 399
4747 Vineland Avenue, Suite E
North Hollywood, California 91602
818-985-7374 Fax: 818-985-0097
Representing chauffeurs and truck drivers of all rolling stock, automotive service (other than mechanical repair), dispatchers, wranglers (men employed in connection with the handling and feeding of livestock) and animal trainers.

Studio Utility Employees Local 724
6700 Melrose Avenue
Hollywood, California 90038
213-938-6277 Fax: 213-938-4046
Representing labor used in construction of new sets, and for the sweeping and cleaning around sets where active construction is taking place. This includes maintenance of streets, landscapes and lawns; washing windows; hauling refuse from construction area.

Theatre Authority West Inc. (Charity Clearing House)
6464 Sunset Boulevard, Suite 640
Hollywood, California 90028
213-462-5761 Fax: 213-462-1930
Administers and regulates the free appearances of performers and provides assistance to members of the theatrical community.

Theatrical & Television Stage Employees (IATSE) Local 33
1720 West Magnolia Boulevard
Burbank, California 91506
818-841-9233 Fax: 818-567-1138
Representing people who handle props, electrical, and grip for television, cable and video productions.

Theatrical Wardrobe Union (IATSE) Local 763
13949 Ventura Boulevard, Suite 307
Sherman Oaks, California 91423
818-789-8735 Fax: 818-905-6297

Writers Guild of America West (WGA)
7000 West 3rd Street
Los Angeles, California 90049
213-951-4000 Fax: 213-782-4800
http://www.wga.org
wga@wga.org

CHICAGO

American Federation of Musicians (AFM)
175 West Washington Street
Chicago, Illinois 60602
312-782-0063 Fax: 213-782-7880

American Federation of Television & Radio Artists (AFTRA)
1 East Erie, Suite 650
Chicago, Illinois 60611
312-573-8081 Fax: 312-573-0318

Directors Guild of America (DGA)
4000 North Michigan Avenue, Suite 307
Chicago, Illinois 60611
312-644-5050 Fax: 312-644-5776

Screen Actors Guild
1 East Erie, Suite 650
Chicago, Illinois 60611
312-573-8081 Fax: 312-573-0318

NEW YORK

American Federation of Musicians (AFM)
1501 Broadway, Suite 600
New York, New York 10036
212-869-1330 Fax: 212-764-6134

American Federation of Television and Radio Artists (AFTRA)
260 Madison Avenue
New York, New York 10016
212-532-0800 Fax: 212-532-2242

American Guild of Musical Artists (AGMA)
1727 Broadway
New York, New York 10019-5284
212-265-3687 Fax: 212-262-9088

Directors Guild of America, Inc. (DGA)
110 West 57th Street, 2nd Floor
New York, New York 10019
212-581-0370 Fax: 212-581-1441

International Brotherhood of Electrical Workers Local 1212
230 West 41st Street, Room 1102
New York, New York 10036
212-354-6770 Fax: 212-819-9517
Represents radio and television broadcast engineers.

Make Up Artists Local 798
152 West 24th Street
New York, New York 10011
212-627-0660 Fax: 212-627-0664
Represents people who style hair and apply make-up.

Screen Actors Guild (SAG)
1515 Broadway, 44th Floor
New York, New York 10036
212-944-1030 Fax: 212-944-6774

Screen Cartoonists, Local 841
80 8th Avenue, 14th Floor
New York, New York 10011
212-647-7300 Fax: 212-647-7317

Studio Mechanics Local 52
326 West 48th Street
New York, New York 10036
212-399-0980 Fax: 212-245-5230
*Representing people such as sound monitors, recordists, boom men,
recording engineers, video technicians, electricians, grips and shop
craftsmen; property, drapery, and generator men; and special effects
workers.*

Theatrical State Employees (IATSE) Local 1
320 West 46th Street, 3rd Floor
New York, New York 10036
212-333-2500 Fax: 212-586-2437
Representing stagehands in television production studios.

Theatrical Teamsters Local 817
1 Hollow Lane
Lake Success, New York 11042
516-365-3470 Fax: 516-365-609
Representing chauffeurs and truck drivers of all rolling stock, automotive services (other than mechanical repairs), and dispatchers. This includes all pick-up, delivery, or hauling of any description performed by or for the company in a vehicle.

United Scenic Artists Local 829
16 West 61st Street, 11th Floor
New York, New York 10023
212-736-4498 Fax: 212-977-2011
Representing art directors responsible for the design and production of all illustrations and sketches, scenery and sets, props and set dressing. Scenic artists prepare and apply all texturing and/or painting or coloration on sets, scenery and props. They also do all lettering and sign work, sculpturing, portraits, or special artwork.

Wardrobe Attendants Local 764
151 West 46th Street, 8th Floor
New York, New York 10036
212-221-1717 Fax: 212-302-2324
Representing people who supervise the general operation of the wardrobe department, including the maintenance, fittings, manufacturing, remodeling, alterations of all costumes/wardrobe and accessories used in production.

Writers Guild of America East (WGA)
555 West 57th Street
New York, New York 10019
212-245-6180 Fax: 212-582-1909
http://www.wgaeast.org

CANADA

Alliance of Canadian Cinema, Television and Radio Artists
2239 Yonge St.
Toronto, ON M4S 2B5
416-489-1311 Fax: 416-489-8076
http://www.actra.com

American Federation of Musicians (AFM)
75 The Donway West, Suite 1010
Don Mills, ON Canada M3C 2E9
416-391-5161 Fax: 416-391-5165

International Alliance of Theatrical Stage Employees (IATSE)
258 Adelaide Street East, Suite 403
Toronto, Ontario M5A 1N1
416-362-3569 Fax: 416-362-3483

ALBERTA

Alliance of Canadian Cinema, Television and Radio Artists
Mount Royal Place
1414 8th Street S.W.
Calgary, Alberta T2R 1J6
403-228-3123 Fax: 403-228-3299

Alliance of Canadian Cinema, Television and Radio Artists
201-10816A 82nd Avenue
Edmonton, Alberta T5J 2W9
403-433-4090 Fax: 403-433-3099

BRITISH COLUMBIA

Alliance of Canadian Cinema, Television and Radio Artists
200-856 Homer Street
Vancouver, British Columbia V6B 2W5
604-689-0727 Fax: 604-689-1145

International Alliance of Theatrical Stage Employees (IATSE),
Local 891
1640 Boundary Road
Burnaby, British Columbia V5K 4V4
604 664-8910 Fax: 604-298-3456
http://www.iatse.org
elenak@891.iatse.com

MANITOBA

Alliance of Canadian Cinema, Television and Radio Artists
Phoenix Building
110-388 Donald Street
Winnipeg, Manitoba
204-943-1307 Fax: 204-947-5664

MARITIMES

Alliance of Canadian Cinema, Television and Radio Artists
210 Water Street
P.O. Box 575
St. Johns, Newfoundland A1C 5K8
709-722-0430 Fax: 709-722-2113

Alliance of Canadian Cinema, Television and Radio Artists
1660 Hollis Street, Suite 103
Halifax, Nova Scotia B3J 1V7
902-420-1404 Fax: 902-422-0589

ONTARIO

Alliance of Canadian Cinema, Television and Radio Artists
130 Slatter Street, Suite 808
Ottawa, Ontario K1P 6E2
613-230-0327 Fax: 613-230-2473

Alliance of Canadian Cinema, Television and Radio Artists
2239 Yonge Street
Toronto, Ontario M4S 2B5
416-489-1311 Fax: 416-489-1435

QUEBEC

Alliance of Canadian Cinema, Television and Radio Artists
530-1450 City Councilors Street
Montreal, Quebec H3A 2E6
514-844-3318 Fax: 514-844-2068

SASKATCHEWAN

Alliance of Canadian Cinema, Television and Radio Artists
1808 Smith Street, Studio. 212
Regina, Saskatchewan S4P 2N2
306-757-0885 Fax: 306-359-6758

APPENDIX C4
Music Organizations

MUSIC PERFORMANCE RIGHTS ORGANIZATIONS

American Society of Composers, Authors and Publishers (ASCAP)
1 Lincoln Plaza
New York, New York 10023
212-595-3050 Fax: 212-724-9064
http://www.ascap.com
info@ascap.com, ascapmail@trinet.com

Broadcast Music, Inc. (BMI)
320 West 57th Street
New York, New York 10019
212-586-2000 Fax: 212-956-2059
http://www.bmi.com

Broadcast Music, Inc. (BMI) — West Coast
8730 Sunset Boulevard, 3rd Floor
Los Angeles, California 90069-2211
310-659-9109 Fax: 310-657-6947

SESAC
421 W. 54th Street, 4th Floor
New York, New York 10019
212-586-345- Fax: 212-489-5699
http://www.sesac.com

Music Synchronization Licensing Agency
National Music Publishers Agency/Harry Fox Agency
711 3rd Avenue, 8th Floor
New York, New York 10017
212-370-5330 Fax: 212-953-2384
http://www.nmpa.org
*Currently representing more than 600 American music publishers,
NMPA works to interpret copyright law, educate the public about
licensing and safeguard the interests of its members. The Harry Fox
Agency provides an information source, clearing house and monitoring service for licensing musical copyrights. The agency also
licenses music on a worldwide basis for use in films, commercials,
television programs and all other types of audiovisual media.*

APPENDIX C5
Producers Organizations

Alliance of Motion Picture & Television Producers (AMPTP)
15503 Ventura Boulevard
Encino, California 91436
818-995-3600 Fax: 818-789-7431
A service organization that handles labor negotiations and monitors legislation for television and film producers.

Association of Independent Commercial Producers
(National Office)
100 East 42nd Street
New York, New York 10017
212-867-5720 Fax: 212-986-8851
http://www.aicp.com
Serving commercial producers for the purpose of exchanging information and ideas, as well as strengthening the relationships between clients and suppliers.

Association of Independent Commercial Producers
(West Coast Office)
5300 Melrose Avenue, Suite 226E
Hollywood, California 90038
213-960-4763 Fax: 213-960-4766

Producers Guild of America
400 South Beverly Drive, Suite 211
Beverly Hills, California 90212
310-557-0807 Fax: 310-557-0436
Represents executive producers, associate producers and producers for motion pictures and television.

APPENDIX C6
Trade Organizations

Academy of Motion Picture Arts & Sciences (AMPAS)
8949 Wilshire Boulevard
Beverly Hills, California 90211
310-247-3000 Fax: 310-859-9619

Academy of Television Arts & Sciences
5220 Lankershim Boulevard
North Hollywood, California 91601
818-754-2800 Fax: 818-761-2827

American National Academy of Performing Arts
10944 Ventura Boulevard
Studio City, California 91604
818-763-4431 Fax:

American Association of Advertising Agencies (AAAA)

East Coast
405 Lexington Avenue, 18th Floor
New York, New York 10174
212-682-2500 Fax: 212-682-8391
http://www.commercepark.com/aaaa

West Coast
130 Battery Street, Suite 330
San Francisco, California 94111
415-291-4999 Fax: 415-291-4995

American Film Institute
2021 North Western Avenue
Los Angeles, California 90027
213-856-7600 Fax: 213-467-4578

American Film Marketing Association (AFMA)
10850 Wilshire Boulevard, 9th Floor
Los Angeles, California 90024
310-446-1000 Fax: 310-446-1600

American Guild of Variety Artists (AGVA)
4741 Laurel Canyon Boulevard, Suite 208
North Hollywood, California 91607
818-508-9984 Fax: 818-508-3029

American Society of Cinematographers (ASC)
1782 North Orange Drive
Hollywood, California 90028
213-876-5080 Fax: 213-882-6391

Association of Local Television Stations (ALTV)
1320 19th Street N.W., Suite 300
Washington, DC 20036
202-887-1970 Fax: 202-887-0950
http://www.altv.com

Association of Talent Agents
9255 Sunset Boulevard, Suite 318
Los Angeles, California 90069
310-274-0628 Fax: 310-274-5063

Cable Advertising Bureau (CAB)/Multi Channel Adv. Int.
830 3rd Avenue, 2nd Floor
New York, New York 10022
212-508-1200 Fax: 212-832-3268
http://www.cabletvadbureau.com

Cable Television Administration & Marketing Society (CTAM)
401 North Union Street, Suite 440
Alexandria, Virginia 22314
703-549-4200 Fax: 703-684-1167
http://www.ctam.com

Casting Society of America (CSA)
6565 Sunset Boulevard, Suite 306
Los Angeles, California 90028
213-463-1925

Electronic Industries Association
2500 Wilson Boulevard
Arlington, Virginia 22201
703-907-7500 Fax: 703-907-7501
http://www.eia.org

Hollywood Foreign Press Association
292 South La Cienga Boulevard, Suite 316
Beverly Hills, California 90211
310-657-1731 Fax: 310-657-5576

Hollywood Press Club
P.O. Box 3381
Hollywood, California 90028
213-466-1212 Fax: 213-663-2820

Independent Feature Project/West (IFR)
1969 Westwood Boulevard, Suite 205
Los Angeles, California 90025
310-475-4379 Fax: 310-441-5676
http://www.ifpwest.org

International Documentary Association (IDA)
1551 South Robertson Boulevard, Suite 201
Los Angeles, California 90035
310-284-8422 Fax: 310-785-9334

Interactive Services Association
(formerly Videotex Industry Association)
8403 Cloesville Road, Suite 865
Silver Springs, Maryland 20910
301-495-4955 Fax: 301-495-4959

Motion Picture Association of America (MPAA)
15503 Ventura Boulevard, Suite 210
Encino, California 91436
818-995-3600 Fax: 818-382-1799

Motion Picture & Television Credit Association
1653 Beverly Boulevard
Los Angeles, California 90026
310-556-0759

Musicians Contact Service
P.O. Box 788
Woodland Hills, California 91365
818-347-8888 Fax: 818-227-5919

National Academy of Cable Programming
1724 Massachusetts Avenue, N.W.
Washington, DC 20036
202-775-3611 Fax: 202-775-3689

National Association of Broadcasters (NAB)
1771 N Street, N.W.
Washington, DC 20036
202-429-5300 Fax: 202-429-5410
http://www.nab.org

National Association of College Broadcasters
71 George Street
Providence, Rhode Island 02912-1824
401-863-2225 Fax: 401-863-2221
http://www.hofstra.edu/nacb
nacb@brown.edu

National Cable Forum
1724 Massachusetts Avenue, N.W.
Washington, DC 20036
202-775-3550 Fax: 202-775-3675

National Cable Television Association (NCTA)
1724 Massachusetts Avenue, N.W.
Washington, DC 20036
202-775-3629 Fax: 202-775-3675

National Cable Television Institute
801 West Mineral Avenue
Littleton, Colorado 80120-4501
303-797-9393 Fax: 303-797-9394
http://www.ncti.com

National Conference of Personal Managers
10231 Riverside Drive, Suite 303
Toluca Lake, California 91602
818-762-NCPM Fax: 818-980-8212

(East Coast Office)
964 2nd Avenue
New York, New York 10022
212-421-2670 Fax: 212-838-51-2

Pro Max International/Broadcast Promotion and Marketing
Executives
2029 Century Park East, Suite 555
Los Angeles, California 90067
213-465-3777 Fax: 310-788-7616

Radio and Television News Directors Association (RTNDA)
1000 Connecticut Avenue, N.W., Suite 615
Washington, DC 20036
202-659-6510 Fax: 202-223-4007
http://www.rtnda.org

Satellite Broadcasting & Communications Association (SBCA)
225 Rienekers Lane, Suite 600
Alexandria, Virginia 22314
703-549-6990 Fax: 703-549-7640

Screen Composers of America
2451 Nichols Canyon Road
Los Angeles, California 90046-1798
213-876-6040 Fax: 213-876-6041

Society of Cable Telecommunications Engineers
140 Philips Road
Exton, Pennsylvania 19341
610-363-6888 Fax: 610-363-7133

Society of Motion Picture & Television Engineers (SMPTE)
595 West Hartsdale Avenue
White Plains, New York 10607
914-761-1100 Fax: 914-761-3115

Stuntmen's Association of Motion Pictures, Inc.
4810 Whitsett Avenue, 2nd Floor
North Hollywood, California 91607
818-766-4334 Fax: 818-766-5943

Stuntwomen's Association of Motion Pictures, Inc.
12457 Ventura Boulevard, Suite 208
Studio City, California 91604
818-762-0907 Fax: 818-762-9534

Television Movie Awards
415 Route 10 P.O. Box 1000
Mount Freedom, New Jersey 07970
201-366-6691 Fax: 201-361-1391

Theatre Equipment Association
244 West 49th Street, Suite 200
New York, New York 10019
212-246-6460 Fax: 212-265-6428

United Stuntwomen's Association of America
3518 Cahuenga Boulevard West, Suite 206B
Hollywood, California 90068
213-874-3584 Fax: 213-874-8439

Wireless Cable Association
1140 Connecticut Avenue, N.W., Suite 810
Washington, DC 20036
202-452-7823 Fax: 202-452-0041

Western States Advertising Association (WSAA)
6404 Wilshire Boulevard, Suite 1111
Los Angeles, California 90048
213-655-1951 Fax: 213-655-8627
http://www.adswest.org

Women in Cable
230 West Monroe, Suite 730
Chicago, Illinois 60606
312-634-2330 Fax: 312-634-2345

Women in Film (WIF)
6464 Sunset Boulevard, Suite 550
Los Angeles, California 90028
213-463-6040 Fax: 213-463-0963

APPENDIX C7
Federal Government Agencies and Legislative Committees

Corporation for Public Broadcasting
901 E Street, N.W.
Washington, DC 20004
202-879-9600 Fax: 202-783-1019
http://www.cpb.org

Department of Justice
10th & Constitution Avenue, N.W.
Washington, DC 20530
202-514-2000

Department of Labor
200 Constitution Avenue, N.W.
Washington, DC 20210
202-219-6666

Equal Employment Opportunity Commission
1400 L Street, N.W.
Washington, DC 20507
202-663-4900

Federal Communications Commission
1919 M Street, N.W.
Washington, DC 20554
202-418-0200

Federal Trade Commission
Pennsylvania Avenue at 6th Street, N.W.
Washington, DC 20580
202-326-2222

Food and Drug Administration
5600 Fishers Lane
Rockville, Maryland 20857
301-443-1544

House of Representatives Subcommittee on Telecommunications
and Finance
316 Ford House Office Building
Washington, DC 20515
202-226-2424 Fax: 202-225-2447

National Telecommunications and Information Administration
U.S. Department of Commerce
14th and Pennsylvania, N.W., Room 4898
Washington, DC 20230
202-482-1551 Fax: 202-482-1635

Senate Subcommittee on Communications
Hart Senate Office Building, Room 227
Washington, DC 20510
202-224-5184 Fax: 202-224-9334

U.S. Copyright Office
Library of Congress
1st and Independence Avenue, S.E.
Washington, DC 20540
202-707-3000

U.S. Trademark Office
2900 Crystal Drive
Arlington, Virginia 22202-3513
800-786-9199

Voice of America
330 Independence Avenue, S.W.
Washington, DC 20547
202-619-4700

APPENDIX C8

Broadcast Networks, Public Broadcasters and Cable Networks

BROADCAST NETWORKS

American Broadcasting Companies, Inc. (ABC)
77 West 66th Street
New York, New York 10023
212-456-7777
http://www.abc.com

(West Coast Office)
2040 Avenue of Stars
Los Angeles, California 90027
310-557-7777

Columbia Broadcasting System, Inc. (CBS)
51 West 52nd Street
New York, New York 10019
212-975-4321
http://www.cbs.com

(West Coast Office)
7800 Beverly Boulevard
Los Angeles, California 90036
213-852-2345

FOX, Inc.
40 West 57th Street
New York, New York 10021
212-452-5555
http://www.fox.com

(West Coast Office)
P.O. Box 900
Beverly Hills, California 90213
310-369-1000

National Broadcasting Company (NBC)
30 Rockefeller Plaza
New York, New York 10112
212-664-4444
http://www.nbc.com

West Cost Office
3000 West Alameda Avenue
Burbank, California 91505
818-840-4444

PUBLIC BROADCASTERS

Corporation for Public Broadcasting
901 E Street, N.W.
Washington, DC 20004
202-879-9600 Fax: 202-783-1019
http://www.cpb.org

Public Broadcasting Service (PBS)
(Executive Headquarters)
1320 Broddock Place
Alexandria, Virginia 22314
703-739-5000 Fax: 703-739-0775
http://www.pbs.org

(New York Headquarters)
1790 Broadway, 16th Floor
New York, New York 10019-1412
212-708-3000 Fax: 212-708-3018

CABLE NETWORKS

American Independent Network (AIN)
6125 Airport Freeway, Suite 200
Halton City, Texas 76117
817-222-1234 Fax: 817-222-9809
ain@interserv.com
http://www.aini.com/

American Movie Classics (AMC)
150 Crossways Park W.
Woodbury, New York 11797
516/364-2222 Fax: 516-364-8924
http://www.amctv.com/

ANA Television
500 North Capitol Street, N.W., Suite 801
Washington, DC 20001
202-637-8889 Fax: 202-637-3561
70712.1645@compuserve.com

The Arts & Antiques Network (AAN)
The National Press Building, Suite 2003
Washington, DC 20045
703-553-0472 Fax: 202-347-1342
ep@thatnet.com (executive producer)
http://www.thatnet.com/arts&antiques/

Arts and Entertainment Network (A&E)
235 East 45th Street
New York, New York 10017
212-661-4500 Fax: 212-697-0753

Black Entertainment Television (BET)
1899 9th Street, N.E.
Washington, DC 20018
202-636-2403 Fax: 202-529-4009
info@betnetworks.com
http://www.betnetworks.com/

Bravo Cable Network
150 Crossways Park West
Woodbury, New York 11797
516-364-2222 Fax: 516-364-7638

Cable News Network (CNN)
One CNN Plaza
Atlanta, Georgia 30348
404-827-1500

Cable Satellite Public Affairs Network (C-SPAN)
400 North Capital Street, N.W., Suite 650
Washington, DC 20001
202-737-3220 Fax: 202-737-3323
http://www.c-span.org

Cable Video Store
536 Broadway, Seventh Floor
New York, New York 10012
212-941-1434 Fax: 212/226-9075

Cartoon Network
1050 Techwood Drive, N.W.
Atlanta, Georgia 30315
404-827-1500

Christian Broadcasting Network
977 Centerville Turnpike
Virginia Beach, Virginia 23463
804-579-7000
http://www.cbn.org/

Cinemax Cable Pay Television
1100 Avenue of the Americas
New York, New York 10036
212-512-1000

Comedy Central
1775 Broadway
New York, New York 10019
212-767-8600

Consumer News & Business Channel (CNBC)
2200 Fletcher Avenue
Fort Lee, New Jersey 07024
203-965-6000 Fax: 203-965-6315
http://www.cnbc.com/

Consumer Resource Network (CRN)
P.O. Box 989
Equinox Junior Building
Manchester, Vermont 05254
802-362-0505 Fax: 802-362-5401
http://www.crninfo.com/

Country Music Television (CMT)
2806 Opryland Drive
Nashville, Tennessee 37213
212-916-1000

Court TV
600 Third Avenue
New York, New York 10016
800-COURT-56, 212-973-3383
http://www.courttv.com/

The Discovery Channel
7700 Wisconsin Avenue
Bethesda, Maryland 20814-3522
301-986-0444
http://www.discovery.com/

The Disney Channel
3800 West Alameda Avenue
Burbank, California 91505
818-569-7711 Fax: 818-845-3742
http://www.disneychannel.com/

E! Entertainment Television
10 Columbus Boulevard
Hartford, Connecticut 06106
203-249-3700
http://www.eonline.com/

ESPN, ESPN2, ESPNEWS
ESPN Plaza
935 Middle Street
Bristol, Connecticut 06010
203-585-2236 Fax: 203-584-5890
espnet.sportszone@starwave.com
http://www.espn.com/

Encore
5445 DTC Parkway
Suite 600
Englewood, Colorado 80111
303-267-4000

The Family Channel
2877 Guardian Lane
Virginia Beach, Virginia 23450
804-459-6000
http://www.famfun.com/

fX
212 Fifth Avenue, 2nd Floor
New York, New York 10010
212-802-4000
fxmgr@delphi.com
http://www.fxnetworks.com/

The History Channel
235 E. 45th Street
New York, New York 10017
212-661-4500 Fax: 212-210-9755
http://www.historychannel.com/

Home Box Office, Inc. (HBO)
1100 Avenue of the Americas
New York, New York 10036
212-512-1000 Fax: 212-512-8700
http://www.hbo.com

(West Coast Office)
2049 Century Park East
Los Angeles, California 90067
213-201-9200

The Independent Film Channel
150 Crossways Park West
Woodbury, New York 11797
516-364-2222 Fax: 516-364-7638
http://www.ifctv.com

The Inspirational Network
9700 Southern Pine Boulevard
Charlotte, North Carolina 28173
704-525-9800
http://www.insp.org

Jewish Television
9021 Melrose Avenue, Suite 309
Los Angeles, California 90069
310-273-6841 Fax: 310-273-6844

The Learning Channel
7700 Wisconsin Avenue
Bethesda, Maryland 20814
800-813-7409, 301-986-1999

Lifetime
Worldwide Plaza
309 W. 49th. Street
New York, New York 10019
212-424-7000
http://www.lifetimetv.com/

Music Television (MTV)
1515 Broadway, 23rd Floor
New York, New York 10036
212-258-8000 Fax: 212-258-8560
http://www.mtv.com/

The Movie Channel (TMC)
1633 Broadway
New York, New York 10019
212-708-1600

The Nashville Network (TNN)
2806 Opryland Drive
Nashville, Tennessee 37214
615-883-7000

Nickelodeon
1515 Broadway
New York, New York 10036
212-713-7010
nickmail00@aol.com
http://www.nick.com/
http://nick-at-nite.com/
http://www.nickatnitestvland.com/

The Outdoor Channel
43445 Business Park Drive #103
Temecula, California 92590
909-699-6991 Fax: 909-699-6313
outdoorch@aol.com
http://www.outdoorchannel.com/

Prevue Channel
3801 S. Sheridan Road
Tulsa, Oklahoma 74145
918-664-5566
http://www.prevue.com/

QVC Shopping Channel
1365 Enterprise Drive
West Chester, Pennsylvania 19380
215-430-1051
http://www.qvc.com/

Sci-Fi Channel
Rockefeller Center
P.O. Box 331
New York, New York 10185
212-408-9100
feedback@usanetworks.com
http://www.scifi.com/

Showtime
1633 Broadway
New York, New York 10019
212-708-1600
http://showtimeonline.com/

Superstation TBS
(WTBS, WTBS-17 Atlanta, Turner Broadcasting System)
1050 Techwood Drive, N.W.
Atlanta, Georgia 30318
404-885-4488
tbs.superstation@turner.com
http://www.turner.com/

TV Food Network
1177 Avenue of the Americas, 31st Floor
New York, New York 10036
212-398-8836 Fax: 212/736-7716
foodtv@www.sw-expo.com
http://www.foodtv.com/

USA Network
1230 Avenue of the Americas
New York, New York 10020
212-408-9100
http://www.usanetwork.com/

Video Hits One (VH1)
1515 Broadway
New York, New York 10036
212-258-7800
vh1@here.viacom.com
http://www.vh1.com/

The Weather Channel
2600 Cumberland Parkway
Atlanta, Georgia 30339
404-434-6800
feedback@landmark.net
http://www.weather.com/

APPENDIX C9

Television Syndicators, Television Distributors and Video Distributors

TELEVISION SYNDICATORS AND DISTRIBUTORS

ABC Distribution Company
77 West 66th Street
New York, New York
212-456-7777

(West Coast Office)
2040 Avenue of the Stars
Century City, California 90067
310-557-6600 Fax: 310-557-7925

Carolco Films International Limited
260 5th Avenue
New York, New York 10001
212-683-1660 Fax: 212-683-1662

CBS Broadcast International
51 West 52nd Street
New York, New York 10019
212-975-8585 Fax: 212-975-7452

(West Coast Office)
7800 Beverly Boulevard
Los Angeles, California 90036
213-852-2345 Fax: 213-651-5900

Columbia TriStar International Television
10202 West Washington Boulevard
Culver City, California 90232
310-280-3080

D.L. Taffner, Ltd.
31 West 56th Street
New York, New York 10019
212-245-4680 Fax: 212-315-1132

EyeMark
10877 Wilshire Boulevard
Los Angeles, California 90024
310-446-6000 Fax: 310-446-6066

Films Around the World, Inc.
342 Madison Avenue, Suite 812
New York, New York 10173
212-752-5050 Fax: 212-599-6090

Fox/Lorber Associates and Gaga Communications, Inc.
419 Park Avenue South
New York, New York 10016
212-686-6777 Fax: 212-685-2625

Fremantle Corporation
660 Madison Avenue
New York, New York 10021
212-421-4530 Fax: 212-207-8357

Fries Distribution Company
6922 Hollywood Boulevard
Hollywood, California 90028
213-466-2266 Fax: 213-464-6082

Hearst/King Features Entertainment
235 East 45th Street
New York, New York 10017
212-455-4000 Fax: 212-983-6379

King World Productions, Inc.
1700 Broadway, 33rd Floor
New York, New York 10019
212-315-4000 Fax: 212-582-9255

Lorimar Telepictures
300 Television Plaza
Burbank, California 91505
818-972-0777

MCA TV
100 Universal City Plaza
Universal City, California 91608
818-777-1000 Fax: 818-777-6276

MGM/UA Telecommunications
2500 Broadway Street
Santa Monica, California 90404-3061
310-449-3000

MTM TV
12700 Ventura Boulevard
Studio City, California 91604
818-755-2400

NBC International
30 Rockefeller Plaza
New York, New York 10019
212-644-4444 Fax: 212-333-7546

Orbis Communications
405 Lexington Avenue
New York, New York 10174
212-661-9722

Orion Pictures
1888 Century Park East
Los Angeles, California 90067
310-282-0550

Paramount Pictures Corporation
5555 Melrose Avenue
Los Angeles, California 90038
213-956-5000

Public Television International
4802 5th Avenue
Pittsburgh, Pennsylvania 15213
412-622-1410 Fax: 412-622-6413

Republic Pictures Corporation
12636 Beatrice Street
Los Angeles, California 90066
213-965-6900

Television Program Enterprises
1 Dag Hammarskjold Plaza
New York, New York 10017
212-759-8787

Tribune Entertainment Company
435 North Michigan Avenue, Suite 1800
Chicago, Illinois 60611
312-222-4441

Turner International
1050 Techwood Drive
Atlanta, Georgia 30318
404-827-4380 Fax: 404-827-3224

Twentieth Century-Fox Television
10201 Pico Boulevard
Los Angeles, California 90213
310-369-1000

Viacom International
1515 Broadway
New York, New York 10036
212-258-6000 Fax: 212-258-6391

The Walt Disney Company/Buena Vista International
500 South Buena Vista Street
Burbank, California 91521
818-560-5000

Warner Brothers International Television Distribution
4000 Warner Boulevard, Towers Building, Suite 449
Burbank, California 91525
818-954-5491 Fax: 818-954-4040

Video Distributors
CBS/Fox Video
1330 Avenue of the Americas, 6th Floor
New York, New York 10019
212-373-4800 Fax: 212-373-4803

Time Life Video
2000 Duke Street
Alexandria, Virginia 22314
703-838-7003 Fax: 703-838-7192

APPENDIX C10
International Broadcast and Cable Networks

AUSTRALIA

Australian Broadcasting Corporation
ABC Ultimo Centre
700 Harris Street, Ultimo 2007
GPO Box 9994, Sydney NSW 2001
02-333-1500 Fax: 02-333-5305
http://www.abc.net.au
comments@your.abc.net.au

Community Access TV Broadcasters, Ltd.
1 The Boulevard
Cnr City Walk and Akuna Street
First Level (Cracca Gallery)
Canberra 2601

Mailing Address:
P.O. Box 944
Civic Square ACT 2608
61-6-248-0744 Fax: same

Community Broadcasting Association of Australia
Level 3, 44-54 Botany Road
Alexandria NSW 2015
02-310-2999 Fax: 02-319-4545
cbaa@peg.apc.org
www.scu.edu.au/cbaa

FOXTEL
http://www.foxtel.com.au

Imparja Television
14 Leichhardt Terrace
Alice Springs
NT 0870
AUSTRALIA
http://www.imparja.com.au

Optus Network
http://www.optusvision.com.au/

Seven Network
Mobbs Lane
Epping NSW 2121
http://www.seven.com.au/

Special Broadcasting Service
14 Herbert Street
Artarmon NSW 2064
61-2-430-3791 Fax: 61-2-430-3700
http://www.sofcom.com.au/SBS/

Ten Network
Aspinal Street
Watson
ACT, 2602
06 2422400 Fax: 06 241 6511
http://www.ten.com.au/

BELGIUM

BRTN
Reyerslaan 52
B-1043 Brussel
32 (0)2 741 31 11 Fax: 32 (0)2 736 57 86
info@brtn.be
http://www.brtn.be/ (official)

Euro TV
Avenue d'Overhem, 34
1180 Brussels
Belgium
32 2 374 33 35 Fax: 32 2 375 03 32
voxbox@eurotv.com
http://www.eurotv.com

BELARUS

TBN Television Broadcast Network
15-a F.Skariny Street, Minsk, Belarus
Tel/fax:375 172 394171 172 394536
mmc@glas.apc.org
http://unibel.by./HomePages/mass-media/tbnmaine.html

BRAZIL

Gazeta Brazilian Regional Television
http://www.gazeta-paulista.com.br/

Globosat
http://www.globosat.com.br/

Rede Globo de Televisao
Rua Lopes Quintas, 303
Jardim Botanico, 22460-010
Rio de Janeiro, Brasil
55-021-529-2000 Fax: 55-021-294-2042
Telefax: 55-021-31616
webmaster@redeglobo.com.br
http://www.redeglobo.com.br/

Sistema Brasileiro de Televis„o
http://www.sbt.com.br/

TVA
http://www.tva.com.br

CANADA

Atlantic Television (ATV)
http://www.atv.ca/

Baton Broadcasting Incorporated
9 Channel Nine Court
Agincourt, Ontario M1S 4B5
415-299-2000
programming@baton.com
http://www.baton.com/

Canadian Broadcasting Corporation
P.O. Box 500, Station A
Toronto, Ontario M5W 1E6
416-205-3700
cbcinput@toronto.cbc.ca
http://www.cbc.ca/
http://www.halifax.cbc.ca/

Knowledge Network
4355 Mathissi Place
Burnaby, British Columbia
Canada, V5G 4S8
604-431-3000 Fax: 604-431-3333
KNonline@ola.bc.ca
http://www.ola.bc.ca/knowledge/

Newfoundland Television (NTV)
P.O. Box 2020
446 Logy Bay Road
St. John's, Newfoundland A1C 5S2
ntvnews@ntv.ca
http://www.ntv.ca

Société Radio-Canada (SRC)
C.P. 6000, succ. centre-ville
Montreal, Quebec H3C 3A8
auditoire@montreal.src.ca
http://www.src-mtl.com/src-tv/intro.htm

Tele-Quebec
1000, rue Fullum
Montreal, Quebec
Canada H2K 3L7
514-790-0141
http://www.telequebec.qc.ca
info@telequebec.qc.ca

TV5
1755 Rene-Lovesque Blvd. E. Suite 101
Montreal, Quebec H2K 4F6
514-522-5322 Fax: 514-522-6572
tv5@tv5.ca
http://www.tv5.ca/tv5info.html

TVOntario
Box 200, Station Q
Toronto, Ontario
Canada, M4T 2T1
800-613-0513
online@tvo.org
http://www.tvo.org/

CHILE

Santiago de Chile, Canal 13
Universidad Catolica de Chile
Inis Matte Urrejola 0840
Bellavista
Santiago de Chile
562-251-4000, 562-777-7133
http://huelen.reuna.cl/teletrece/

Teletrece Chilean TV
http://www.teletrece.cl/teletrece
TVN 7
Bellavista 0990
Providencia, Santiago
56-2-7077 600 Fax: 56-2-7077 761
http://iusanet.cl/tvn/tvn.htm

HONG KONG, TAIWAN

Asia Television Limited (ATV)
852-2992-8888 Fax: 852-2338-0438
atv03@hkatv.com
http://www.hkstar.com/atv

Chinese Television Network
10th floor, Block A,
Ming Pao Industrial Centre,
18 Ka Yip Street
Chai Wan, Hong Kong
852-2515 6333 Fax: 852-2515 6520
mktprom@ctn.net
http://www.ctn.net

Chinese Television System
100 Kuang Fu South Road
Taipei, Taiwan, R.O.C.
886-2-751-0321
webmaster@mail.cts.com.tw
http://www.cts.com.tw

Radio Television Hong Kong
Programme Development
Radio Television Hong Kong
1A Broadcast Drive, Television House
Hong Kong
852-2339-7774 Fax: 852-2338-4151
http://www.cuhk.hk/rthk/index.html

Taiwan Television Enterprise
10 PA TE Road
Sec. 3
Taipei, Taiwan, R.O.C.
886-2-5781515
886-2-5773211 (News)
Fax: 886-2-5799617, 886-2-5799618, 886-2-579-99619

COLOMBIA

Canal 'A'
Ave. Suba 106A-28 (Of. 405)
Bogota, Colombia
Fax: 57-1-617-9525
http://www.rcn.com.co/rcntv/indice.htm

CROATIA

HRT
http://www.hrt.hr

CZECH REPUBLIC

Czech Television
Kavci Hory
140 70 Prague 4
Czech Republic
420 2-61131111
http://www.czech-tv.cz/
info@czech-tv.cz

Czech Television, Brno
Behounska 18
658 88 Brno
Czech Republic
420 5-42132111

Czech Television, Ostrava
Dvorakova 18
729 20 Ostrava
Czech Republic
420 69-6201111

Nova TV
Czech Independent TV Company, Ltd.
Vladislavova 20
113 13 Praha 1
Czech Republic
42.2-211 00 111 Fax: 42.2-211 00 378

DENMARK

Denmark's Radio / Danish Broadcasting
http://www.dr.dk/

TV2
http://www.dknet.dk/tv/tv2/

ECUADOR

Gamavision
gamavisi@telconet.net
http://www.gamavision.com/

ESTONIA

Riigi Elekterside Inspektsioon
Republic of Estonia Inspection of Telecommunications
Adala 4d
Tallinn EE0006
372-639-9054 Fax: 372-639-9055

FRANCE

Eutelsat
Tour Main
Montparnasse
33 Avenue du Maine
F-75755 Paris

France Telecom
6 Place d'Allenery
F-75740 Paris
http://www.francetelecom.com

France Television
42 Avenue d'Iena
75116 Paris
44 31 60 00 Fax: 47 23 56 48

France 2
22, Avenue Montaigne
75387 Paris Cedex 08
44 21 42 42 Fax: 44 21 42 53
http://www.france2.fr/

France 3
116, Avenue du President Kennedy
75790 Paris Cedex 16
44 30 22 22 Fax: 46 47 92 94
tvtel3@vtcom.fr
http://www.france3.fr/

La Cinquieme
10/12, Rue Horace Vernet
92 136 Issy les Moulineaux Cedex
41 46 55 55 Fax: 41 08 02 22
info@lacinquieme.fr
http://www.lacinquieme.fr

GERMANY

ARD Das Erste
http://www.ard.de/

DF1
http://www.df1.de

HR2 & HR3
http://hr-online.de

Pro Sieben
http://www.pro-sieben.de/

ZDF
http://www.zdf.de

IRELAND

Ireland Film & Television Network
http://www.iftn.ie

RTE 1
http://www.rte.ie

ISRAEL

Israel Broadcasting Authority
97 Jaffa Road
Jerusalem 91280
972-2-6291888 Fax: 972-2-6242944
http://israel.org/gov/brdcast.html

ISRAEL TV
Romema
Jerusalem 91071
972-2-5301333 Fax: 972-2-5301345

ISRAEL TV
6 Makleff Street
Tel Aviv 61070
972-3-9366444 Fax: 972-3-6918334

ITALY

Canale 5
Palazzo dei Cigni - Milano 2
20090 Segrate (MI)
39.2.21021
http://www.c5.mediaset.it/

EuroTel s.r.l.
Via della Birona, 30/32
20052 Monza (MI)
39-39-230.2645 Fax: 39-39-230-2650
http://www.eurotel.it/

Telepiù 1/2/3
Via Piranesi 44/46
20137 Milano
0039 2 700271 Fax: 0039 70027201
infopiu@telepiu.it
http://www.telepiu.it

JAPAN

Asahi Broadcasting Corporation
http://www.tv-asahi.co.jp

Kansai Telecasting Corporation
http://www.hankyu.co.jp/ktv

Nagoya Broadcasting Network
http://www.nbn.co.jp/nbn_home/nbn.htm

Nippon Hoso Kyokai (NHK)
http://www.nhk.co.jp

Nippon Television Network Corporation
http://www.ntv.co.jp

Tokyo Broadcasting System, Inc. (TBS)
http://www.tbs.co.jp

KOREA

Korean Broadcasting System
Yodio Dong 18
Youngdeungpo-ku
Seoul, Republic of Korea
82-2-781-1470 Fax: 82-2-781-1497
pr@www.kbs.co.kr
http://www.kbs.co.kr/

Munhwa Broadcasting Corporation
http://www.mbc.co.kr/

Seoul Broadcasting System
http://www.sbs.co.kr/

MEXICO

Super 6 TV
http://www.super6.com.mx

Televisión Azteca
http://www.dataflux.com.mx/publimax

XEW 2
http://www.televisa.com/television/canal2/

XHGC 5
http://www.televisa.com/television/canal5/

NETHERLANDS

Netherlands 1
http://www.omroep.nl/cgi-bin/tt/nos/page/201

Netherlands 2
http://www.omroep.nl/cgi-bin/tt/nos/page/202

Nederland 3
(0)35-623.7968 Fax: (0)35-623.0474
nps@omroep.nl
http://www.omroep.nl/cgi-bin/tt/nos/page/203

NEW ZEALAND

GTV
31-33 White Street
P.O. Box 583
Rotorua
New Zealand

SkyNZ
Sky Network Television Ltd.
10 Panorama Road
Mt. Wellington, Auckland
64 9 579-9999 Fax: 64 9 579-0910
sky@skytv.co.nz

Television New Zealand
http://www.tvnz.co.nz/

NORWAY

Norwegian National TV and Radio (NRK)
http://www.nrk.no/

PANAMA

Corporacion Panamena de Radiodifusion (RPC) 4
P.O. Box 1795
Panama 1
507-225-0160
tv@rpctv.com

SINGAPORE

Chinese Television Network
200 Victoria Street, br.
#03-30 Parco Bugis Junction
Singapore 188021
65 338 8088
http://www.channelktv.com/ktvhome.html
info@channelktv.com

Television Corporation of Singapore Pte Ltd.
Caldecott Broadcast Centre
Andrew Road
Singapore 299939
Fax: 2538119
http://tcs.com.sg/

Television Twelve (TV12)
12 Prince Edward Rd.   .
#05-00 Bestway Bldg.
Singapore 07912
255-8133 Fax: 223-0966
http://tv12.com.sg/

SLOVENIA

POP TV
Kranjèeva 26
1113 Ljubljana
061-189-32-00 Fax: 061-189-32-08
info@pop-tv.si
http://www.pop-tv.si/

SOUTH AFRICA

South African Broadcasting Corp.
Private Bag X1
Auckland Park 2006
27 11 714-9111
tvnews@sabc.co.za
http://www.sabc.co.za/

SPAIN

Antena 3 Television
Avda. Isla Graciosa s/n
28700 San Sebastion de los Reyes
Madrid, Spain
34-1-623 05 00 Fax: 34-1-654 85 17

SWEDEN

Sveriges Television SVT1, SVT2
http://www.svt.se/

TV 4
Storangskroken 10
Stockholm
46-8-459 40 00 Fax: 46-8-459 44 44
http://www.tv4.se

SWITZERLAND

Swiss Broadcasting
Giacomettistrasse 3
Postfach 610, CH-3000
Bern 15
41 31-350 91 11 Fax: 41 31-350 92 56
http://www.srg-ssr.ch./

UNITED KINGDOM

BBC Corporate Headquarters
BBC Broadcasting House
London W1A 1AA
0171 580 4468
Cables: Broadcasts, London
Telex: 265781 BBC HQ G
http://www.bbc.co.uk/

BBC TELEVISION
BBC Television Centre
Wood Lane
London W12 7RJ
0181 743 8000
Cables: Telecasts, London
Telex: 265781 BBC HQ G

BBC WORLD SERVICE
PO Box 76
Bush House
Strand
London WC2B 4PH
0171 240 3456
Cables: Broadbrit, London
Telex: 265781 BBC HQ G

Channel 4
124 Horseferry Road
London SW1P 2TX
dot4@channel4.com
http://www.channel4.com/

APPENDIX C11
Internet Sources for Further Information

INTERNET SEARCH ENGINES

Aliweb
http://www.nexor.co.uk/public/aliweb/search/doc/form.html

Alta Vista
http://www.altavista.digital.com

Dejanews
http://www.dejanews.com

Excite
http://www.excite.com

Hotbot
http://www.hotbot.com

Infoseek
http://www2.infoseek.com/

Lycos
http://www.lycos.com

Open Text
http://www.opentext.com

Webcrawler
http://www.webcrawler.com

World Wide Arts Resources
http://wwar.com/

Yahoo!
http://www.yahoo.com

SPECIALIZED DIRECTORIES

Animation World Network
http://www.awn.com/

The Association of America's Public Television Stations
http://www.universe.digex.net/%7Eapts/index.html
Provides information on Public Television and includes links to
public television resources.

Cable TV Advertising
http://www.cabletvad.com/
Resource for information on Cable Television advertising.

Cable Television Connect
http://www.cableconnect.com/
Information about the cable television industry.

Cinemetography.com
http://www.cinematography.com/
A site for professional motion picture camera people and resources.

The Collaborator Lounge
http://www.collaborator.com/
A commercial site for writing aid; it provides some useful infor-
mation for screenwriters.

Directors Net
http://www.directorsnet.com/
http://www.directorsnet.com/links/index.html
Provides useful information to directors and has a comprehensive set
of industry links.

Directory of Radio and TV News Awards, Grants and Fellowships
http://www.rtnda.org/rtnda/awards.html
A comprehensive listing of major electronic journalism awards, grants
and fellowships.

European Audiovisual Observatory's links to television channels in
Europe
http://www.obs.c-strasbourg.fr/eurtv.htm
This page has been designed to give professionals access to European
television channels via the Internet.

EuroTV
http://www.eurotv.com/

Entertainment Directory
http://www.edweb.com/

Entertainment Recruiting Network
http://www.showbizjobs.com/

FilmFolks
http://www.filmfolks.com/
International directory of technicians and artisans for the motion picture and television industry.

Filmvision
http://www.filmvision.com/
One-stop Internet resource for the independent film community.

Garrick Film and TV Resource
http://www.filmtv.com/

Gist TV Listings Guide
http://www.tv1.com/

Hollywood Creative Directory
http://www.hollyvision.com/
Database of television and film executives. Updated weekly.

Hollywood Reporter
http://www.hollywoodreporter.com/
A daily trade paper.

How to Start Your Own Cable TV Network
http://www.cablemaven.com/

The Independent Film and Video Makers Internet Resource Guide
http://www.echonyc.com/%7Emvidal/Indi-Film+Video.html
A hypertext reference to resources on the Internet for the independent film and video community.

In the Background
http://www.myna.com/~chridean/index.html
A Canadian actors resource.

International Internet TV Resources
http://www.rogers.com/miss/tv_int.htm
This listing of international sites feature cable and public access stations and commercial stations.

Mandy's International Film & TV Production Directory
http://www.mandy.com/index.html
One of the better resources for information on international television. Includes detailed information about technicians, facilities and producers worldwide.

Media Line
http://www.medialine.com/
Job listings and other resources.

The Music Industry Contact List
http://www.prozac.org/CME/MIC/mic.html

New York City Mayor's Office of Film, Theatre & Broadcasting
http://www.ci.nyc.ny.us/html/filmcom/home.html

New York Film and Video Web
http://www.nyfilm-video.com/
Comprehensive listing of New York production information.

Production Weekly
http://members.aol.com/prodweek/index.html
A weekly breakdown of projects in pre-production, preparation and development for film, television, music videos, commercials, etc., covering all of the major markets from Los Angeles to New York and all points in between, including Canada.

Showdata
http://www.showdata.org.za/
Information on film and TV production in southern Africa.

Television Pointers
http://www.cs.cmu.edu/afs/cs.cmu.edu/user/clamen/misc/tv/REA DME.html
Has links to information/data about television.

TV2Nite
http://www.tvtonight.com/
This site has program listings and rates the quality of each program.

TV Rundown
http://www.tvrundown.com/
For 17 years, the Rundown has reported weekly on local television news, programming and community service projects.

TV Week Network
http://transdigital.com/
Online news concerning the television industry.

Ultimate TV
http://www.ultimatetv.com
One of the best resources for television information on the net.

The World Wide Web Virtual Library: Broadcasters
http://gruffle.comlab.ox.ac.uk/archive/publishers/broadcast.html
This page contains a list of national and international TV and radio broadcasters, together with other relevant links.

WORST — World Resource for Student Television
http://www.af.lu.se/af/steve/worst.html
Has links to existing student stations from around the world.

Index